Rhodes
& the Dodecanese
plus the East Aegean

THE ROUGH GUIDE

Rough Guide credits

Text Editor:	Vivienne Heller
Series Editor:	Mark Ellingham
Editorial:	Martin Dunford, Jonathan Buckley, Samantha Cook, Jo Mead, Alison Cowan, Annie Shaw, Amanda Tomlin, Catherine McHale, Lemisse al-Hafidh, Paul Gray, Al Spicer (UK), Andrew Rosenberg (US)
Production:	Susanne Hillen, Andy Hilliard, Judy Pang, Link Hall, Nicola Williamson, Helen Ostick
Cartography:	Melissa Flack, David Callier
Finance:	John Fisher, Celia Crowley, Catherine Gillespie
Marketing & Publicity:	Richard Trillo, Simon Carloss (UK); Jean-Marie Kelly, Jeff Kaye (US)
Administration:	Tania Hummel

Acknowledgements

While this book is a natural outgrowth of the author's decade-long participation in the *Rough Guide to Greece*, and an equally lengthy residence on Sámos, it would not have been nearly as complete without the **support** of the following individuals. In Athens, Maria Throumouli at the Ministry of Culture, Christina and Ritsa for the good company, John Chapple for repeated moped rides, and Thanos and Monica for years of support; on Rhodes, Sotiris and Marianne Nikolis (since 1991), and Jonathan Abery for thorough fact-checking and extra listings; Baz Ward and Peter Plumley of FOTA for inside scoops on Tílos; Stephanie Ferguson for the straight dope on Psérimos and Alimniá, and a running start on Hálki; Katerina Tsakiri on Sími; Alexis Zikas, Koan patriot and inverterate taverna-crawler; Louise Edeleanu, for setting the record straight on Astipálea, Andrew and Tricia for tolerating my taste in Lerian tavernas; to my sister Gail for accompaniment to Agathoníssi and Pátmos; on Sámos, to Claire Sharp and Jack Holland, who survived my best efforts to do them in by various methods; to Khryssoula Kritikou for extra GTPs; to Ippokratis Pandelis for lightning repairs and fine music; to Michael and Avra Ward for the most thorough errata in the history of Rough Guides, plus safaris to incredibly remote beaches; to Jonathan and Myriam Peat for gourmet suppers; on Híos, to Markos Kostalas, Theodhoros Spordhilis and Stella Tsakiri for hospitality and bags of information; and on Lésvos, to Detlef Siebert-Bartling for the lowdown on Mólivos.

At **Rough Guides**, thanks to Mark and Martin for suggesting that an island-group guide might be a good idea, to Vivienne Heller for editing under pressure and putting up with my wobblies and panicky phone calls, to Andy Hilliard for enduring the Greek-script tables, and to Susannah Walker for proof-reading, and Stratigraphics for the maps.

Special thanks to Pete Raine, whose previous account formed the basis for the "Wildlife" article; Lance Chilton, for the rapid fine-tooth combing of same; Alison Walsh for the advice to disabled travellers in *Basics*.

This first edition published June 1996 by Rough Guides Ltd, 1 Mercer Street, London WC2H 9QJ.

Distributed by the Penguin Group:
Penguin Books Ltd, 27 Wrights Lane, London W8 5TZ.
Penguin Books USA Inc., 375 Hudson Street, New York 10014, USA.
Penguin Books Australia Ltd, 487 Maroondah Highway, PO Box 257, Ringwood, Victoria 3134, Australia.
Penguin Books Canada Ltd, 10 Alcorn Avenue, Toronto, Ontario, Canada M4V 1E4.
Penguin Books (NZ) Ltd, 182–190 Wairau Road, Auckland 10, New Zealand.

Printed in the United Kingdom by Cox and Wyman Ltd (Reading).
Typography and original design by Jonathan Dear and The Crowd Roars.
Illustrations throughout by Edward Briant.

416pp. Includes index.

A catalogue record for this book is available from the British Library.

ISBN 1-85828-120-2

Rhodes
& the Dodecanese
plus the East Aegean

THE ROUGH GUIDE

Written and researched by
Marc Dubin

THE ROUGH GUIDES

List of maps

MAP SYMBOLS

Road
Minor road
Steps
Path
Railway
Ferry route
National border
Chapter division boundary
River
Airport
Campsite
Castle
Archeological site
Viewpoint
Church
Mosque
Monastery
Cliffs
Waterfall
Marsh land
Mountain peak
Tourist office
Post office
Telephone
Taxi rank
Wall
Building
Church
Cemetery
Park
National park
Beach

Contents

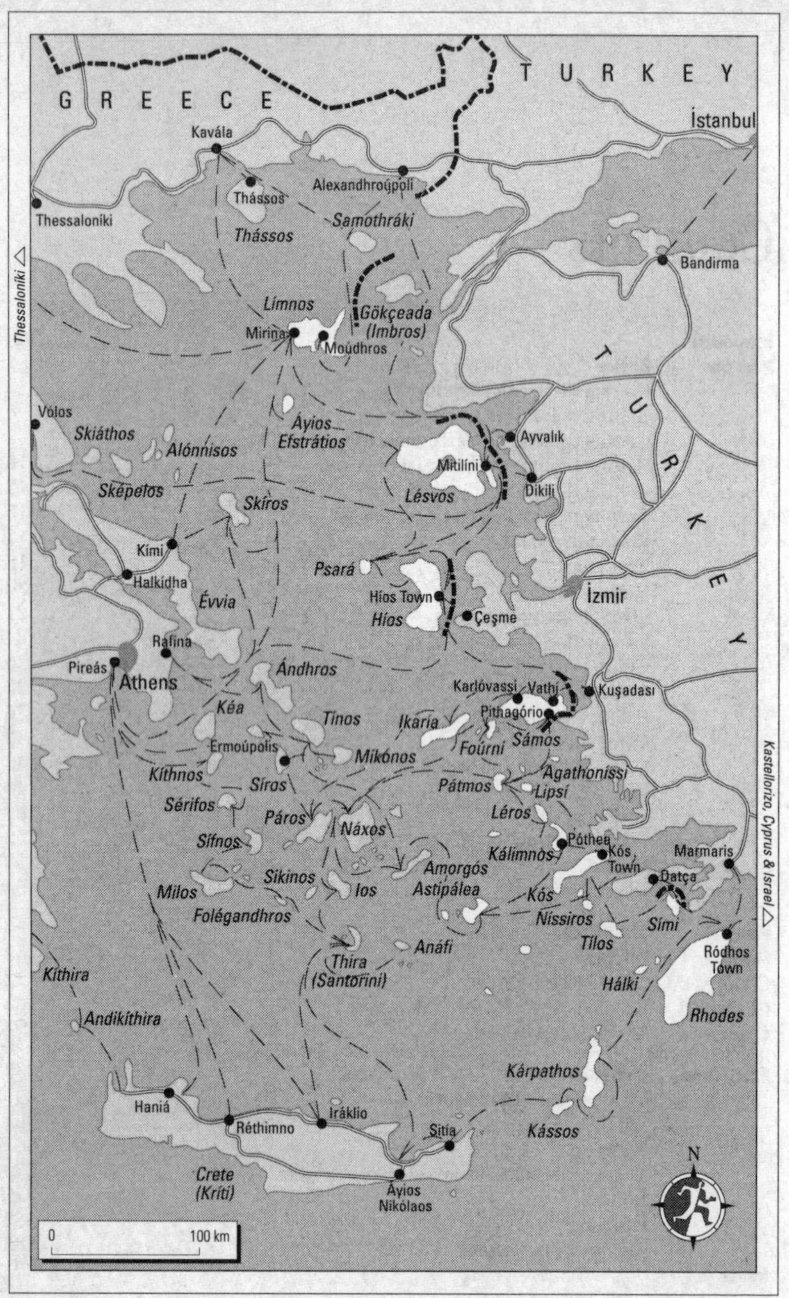

GREECE
TURKEY
İstanbul
Kavála
Alexandhroúpoli
Thássos
Thessaloníki
Samothráki
Thássos
Bandirma
Thessaloníki
Límnos
Gökçeada (Imbros)
Mirina
Moúdhros
TURKEY
Vólos
Skiáthos
Alónnisos
Áyios Efstrátios
Ayvalık
Mitilíni
Dikili
Skópelos
Skíros
Lésvos
Kími
Psará
Halkídha
Híos Town
İzmir
Évvia
Híos
Çeşme
Rafína
Pireás
Athens
Ándhros
Karlóvassi
Vathí
Kuşadası
Kéa
Tínos
Ikaría
Pithagório
Sámos
Foúrni
Ermoúpolis
Míkonos
Kíthnos
Agathoníssi
Síros
Pátmos
Lipsí
Sérifos
Léros
Páros
Náxos
Sífnos
Póthea
Kálimnos
Kós Town
Marmaris
Amorgós
Sikinos
Datça
Mílos
Íos
Astipálea
Kós
Folégandhros
Níssiros
Sími
Anáfi
Tílos
Thíra (Santoríni)
Ródhos Town
Kíthira
Hálki
Andikíthira
Rhodes
Kárpathos
Haniá
Iráklio
Réthimno
Sitía
Kássos
Crete (Kríti)
Áyios Nikólaos
N
0
100 km
Kastellorizo, Cyprus & Israel

Introduction

Rhodes and the other **Dodecanese islands** form the remotest territory of the modern Greek state, up to 250 nautical miles from Athens. All of them are closer to Turkey than mainland Greece, a fact not lost on the two states concerned; indeed these scattered islands have only been part of Greece since 1913 and 1948 respectively, representing the last successful phase of the *Megáli Idhéa*, a century-long campaign to reclaim historically Greek territories. Even now the threat (real or imagined) of invasion from Turkey is very much in evidence. When you ask about the heavy military presence, locals talk in terms of "*when* the Turks come", rarely "*if . . .*" . Greek nationalists began referring to the islands as the Dhodhekánisos (or "Twelve Islands") after 1908, though in actual fact there are 14 major and 4 minor inhabited isles in the group, plus 9 more, large and small, which make up the more northerly **east Aegean archipelago**.

Unlike the poor, remote Cyclades in the central Aegean, these stepping stones en route to the Middle East or Anatolia have always been fated for invasion and occupation: too rich and strategic to be ignored, but never powerful enough to rule in their own right. Romans, Byzantines, crusading Knights of Saint John, Genoese, Venetians, Ottomans and Italians have for varying periods controlled these islands since the time of Alexander the Great. Whatever the rigours of these occupations, their legacy includes a wonderful blend of architectural styles and of eastern and western cultures: frescoed Byzantine churches and fortified monasteries, castles of the Genoese and Knights of Saint John, Ottoman mosques and grandiose Italian Art Deco buildings. These are often juxtaposed with (or even rest upon) ancient Greek cities and temples that provide the foundation for claims of an enduring Hellenic cultural identity down the centuries. Museums, particularly on Sámos, Rhodes and Límnos, amply document the archeological evidence; and, although much has vanished in recent decades, intrinsically Greek songs and dances, costumes and vernacular architecture survive to this day. Indeed only on two islands – Rhodes and Kós – has local character come to be principally determined by tourism, and even there pockets of traditional life persist.

Most visitors are here, however, primarily for hedonistic pursuits: going lightly dressed even on a moped, swimming at dusk without succumbing to hypothermia, talking and drinking under the stars until 3am – pleasures that easily compensate for the often simple standard of much of the food and accommodation on the islands. What may impress most is that despite the strenuous efforts of property developers, arsonists and rubbish-dumpers, the environment has not yet been utterly destroyed. Seen at the right time of day or year, the islands very nearly conform to their fantastic travel-poster image: views of purple-shaded islands and promontories, floating on a cobalt-and-rose horizon; island beaches that vary from discreet crescents framed by tree-fringed cliffs to deserted, mile-long strands backed by wild dunes; burgeoning resorts as cosmopolitan as any in the Mediterranean. And if you're used to the murky waters of the Mediterranean, the Aegean will come as a revelation, with thirty-to-forty-foot visibility the norm in calm conditions; in many coves starfish or octopi curl up to avoid you, and sole or rays skitter off across the bottom. The sea here is also perfect for watersports: the joys of snorkelling and kayaking are always on offer to the untrained, and there are some of the best windsurfing areas in the world. Yacht charter, whether bare-boat or skippered, is now big business, particularly out of Rhodes and Kálimnos. For the months when the sea is too cold to enjoy, many islands offer superb hiking on still-surviving trails between hill villages, or up the highest summits.

The islanders

To attempt an understanding of the **islanders**, it's useful to realize how recent and traumatic were the events that created the modern Greek state. The east Aegean and the Dodecanese islands remained in Ottoman or Italian hands until well into this century. Meanwhile, many people from these "unredeemed" territories lived in Asia Minor, Egypt, western Europe, mainland Greece or elsewhere in the Balkans. The Balkan Wars of 1912–13, the Greco-Turkish war of 1919–22, and the organized population exchanges – essentially regulated ethnic cleansing – which followed each of these conflicts had profound effects. Orthodox refugees from Turkey suddenly made up a noticeable proportion of the east Aegean's population, and with the forced or voluntary departure of their Levantine merchant class, Jews and Muslims, both these islands and the Dodecanese gradually lost their multicultural traits. Even before the experience of World War II, the Italian occupation of the Dodecanese was characterized by progressively stricter suppression of Greek Orthodox identity, but in general the war years were not quite so dire as on the mainland. After the war, benign neglect was about the best most of the islands could expect until the late 1960s, when many entrepreneurial islanders emigrated to Australia, Canada or Africa, continuing a trend of depopulation that was only reversed in the 1970s, as worldwide recession and the advent of retirement age for the original migrants started to spur a return home. There are now a number of islanders who were born Ottoman subjects before 1912, educated in Italian between 1920 and 1926, lived through fierce battles in 1943 and 1944, emigrated to Australia or Canada after 1948, and who have returned as pensioners to live out their days in the modern Greek state. Get talking to any of them and you'll have a first-hand idea of how this century has affected the Dodecanese and east Aegean.

The advent of tourism in the 1960s arguably saved a number of the islands from complete desolation, though attitudes towards this deliverance have been decidedly ambivalent. It galls local pride to have become a class of seasonal service personnel, and the encounter between outsiders and villagers has often been corrosive to a deeply conservative, essentially rural society. Though younger Greeks are adaptable as they rake in the proceeds at resort areas, tourists still need to be sensitive in their behaviour towards the older generations, in a country where the Orthodox church remains an all but established faith and the guardian of national identity. In the presence of Italian-style expresso bars and streetcorner autotellers, it's easy to be lulled into thinking that Greece at one stroke became thoroughly European when it joined the EU – until a flock of sheep is paraded along the main street at high noon, or the noon ferry shows up at 2pm, if at all.

Where to go

There is no such thing as a typical east Aegean or Dodecanese island; each has its distinctive personality, history, architecture, flora – and tourist clientele. Disregarding the scars from a few of the more unfortunate man-made developments, it would be difficult to single out an irredeemably ugly island, and aesthetically there will be something for everyone across the spectrum of insular traits. Landscapes vary from lush swathes of cypress, pine and olive, to volcanic crags, wind-tormented bare ridges, salt marshes or even year-round streams.

Indeed, the east Aegean islands seem to alternate in character: harsh, masculine **Límnos**, **Híos** and **Ikaría**, with their dry climates and stark scenery, bracketing lusher, damper and greener **Sámos** and **Lésvos**, the most important of these islands in antiquity. This trend is continued in the Dodecanese, which display equally marked topographic and economic contrasts. The dry limestone outcrops of **Kastellórizo**, **Sími**, **Hálki**, **Kássos** and **Kálimnos** have always relied on the sea for their livelihoods, and the wealth generated by this maritime culture – especially in the nineteenth century – fostered the growth of attractive port towns. The sprawling, relatively fertile giants, **Rhodes** (Ródhos) and **Kós**, have had their traditional agricultural economies almost totally displaced by a tourist industry attracted by good beaches and nightlife, as well as the Aegean's most exciting ensembles of historical monuments. **Kárpathos** lies somewhere in between, with a (formerly) forested north grafted on to a rocky limestone south; **Tílos**, despite its relative lack of trees, has ample water, though the green volcano-island of **Níssiros** does not. Shaggy **Léros** shelters softer contours and more amenable terrain than its map outline would suggest, while **Pátmos** and **Astipálea** at the fringes of the archipelago boast architecture and landscapes more appropriate to the Cyclades.

When to Go

The islands and their inhabitants are far more agreeable, and more resolutely Greek, outside the busiest period of **early July to late August**, when crowds of foreigners, soaring temperatures and the effects of the infamous **meltémi** wind can detract considerably from enjoyment. The *meltémi* is a cool, fair-weather wind which originates in high-pressure systems over the far north Aegean, gathering steam as it travels south and assuming near-gale magnitude by the time it reaches Rhodes. North-facing coasts from there up to Sámos bear the full brunt of the *meltémi*'s howling. It is less pronounced in the northeast Aegean, where Turkey provides some shelter.

You won't miss out on warm weather if you come between **late May and mid-June** or in **September**, when the sea is warmest for swimming. During **October** you are likely to hit a week's stormy spell, but for most of that month the so-called "little summer of Áyios Dhimítrios", the Greek equivalent of Indian summer, often prevails. While choice of restaurant and shop-bought food in early autumn can be limited – Greece still eats by season, and as yet imports little – the light is softer, and going out at midday becomes a pleasure rather than an ordeal. The first migratory fish from the Dardanelles also arrive in mid-October, with various species caught until May. If you're a fish enthusiast, you can take advantage of the main netting season while on a winter break in Rhodes.

December to March are the coldest and least comfortable months, though even then you have unpredictable stretches of fine days, and the glorious wildflowers begin to bloom very early: January in the Dodecanese, February in the east Aegean for the same species. The more northerly islands endure the coldest and wettest conditions, with the higher peaks of Sámos, Híos and Lésvos wearing a brief mantle of snow around the turn of the year. The most reliable venues for winter breaks are Rhodes and the islets immediately around, where swimming at noon in November is not unheard of. The south Dodecanesian sea also warms up comfortably again by early May.

Average Temperatures (°C) and Rainfall (cm)

	Jan	March	May	July	Sept	Nov
Rhodes	11/14	13/10	20/2	27/0	25/1	16/12
Kós	11/17	13/11	19/2	25/0	23/1	16/12
Lésvos	9/12	12/8	20/3	26/1	24/1	14/11

As the year progresses, you simply shift focus further north, keeping in mind that a distance of several islands or fifty nautical miles may mean the difference between open or still-shut tourist facilities as well as blossoms gone or yet to bloom. **April** weather is notoriously unreliable, though the air is crystal-clear, the landscape green and all colours true – a photographer's dream. **May** conditions are more settled, with an added bonus of the last wintertime fish and spring vegetables, though the sea is still a bit cool for prolonged dips around the more northerly islands.

As a rule, the further south you go, the longer the **tourist season**: Lésvos and Sámos, for instance, are pretty well shut down by mid-October, even though the last charters leave at the end of the month, while Rhodes and its surrounding islets see trade well into November. In high season everywhere service standards, particularly in tavernas, inevitably slip. Room rates are at their highest from July to September, and rental cars and bikes are booked days ahead. The food is often the dreariest representation of Greek cuisine possible: a monotonously endless sequence of tomato salads, frozen pork chops and frozen squid, and no fish to speak of. If you can only visit during mid-summer, reserve a package well in advance, or plan an itinerary off the beaten track.

Between November and April, you have to contend with pared-back ferry schedules (not to mention almost nonexistent hydrofoil departures), and skeletal facilities when you arrive, except on Rhodes, which is beginning to emphasize "winter sun" tourism. You will, however, find fairly adequate services to the most populated islands, and at least one hotel and taverna open in their main town.

Place names: a warning!

The art of rendering Greek words in Roman letters is in a state of chaos. It's a major source of confusion with **place names**, for which seemingly each local authority, and each map-maker, uses a different system. The word for "saint", for instance, one of the most common prefixes, can be spelt Áyios, Ágios, or Ághios. And, to make matters worse, there are often two forms of a name in Greek – the popularly used *dhimotikí*, and the old "classicizing" *katharévoussa*, with different spelling and accentuation. Thus you will see the island of Inoússes written also as Inoússai; or Póthia, capital of Kálimnos, as Póthea (or even Pothiá). Throw in the complexities of Greek grammar – with different case-endings for names – and the fact that there exist long-established English versions of Classical place names, which bear little relation to the Greek sounds, and you have a real mare's nest.

In this book, we've used a modern and largely phonetic system, with *Y* rather than *G* for the Greek gamma, and *DH* rather than *D* for delta, in the spelling of all modern Greek place names. We have, however, retained the accepted "English" spellings for the **ancient sites**, and for familiar places like Athens (Athiná, in modern Greek). We have also accented (with an acute or sometimes an umlaut) the stressed letter of each word: getting this right in pronunciation is vital in order to be understood.

Help us update

We've gone to a lot of effort to ensure that this edition of The Rough Guide to Rhodes and the Dodecanese is up-to-date and accurate. However, prices, addresses and opening hours are all liable to change, while hotels, restaurants and bars, and above all ferry routes and schedules, are notoriously fickle. Any suggestions, comments, corrections or updates towards the next edition would be much appreciated.

We'll credit all contributions, and send a copy of the next edition (or any other Rough Guide, if you prefer) for the best letters. Please mark letters "Rough Guide Rhodes Update", and send to:

Rough Guides, 1 Mercer Street, London WC2H 9QJ, or

Rough Guides, 375 Hudson Street, 9th Floor, New York NY10014

E-mail: rhodes@roughtravl.co.uk

Part 1

The Basics

Getting there from Britain

It's close on 2300 miles from London to virtually any of the Dodecanese or east Aegean islands, so for most visitors flying is the only viable option. By plane, the trip takes around three and a half hours, compared to three to four days by train or bus, and prices are less. There are seasonal direct flights to the largest of these islands from several major British airports, and the cost of charter flights is reasonable, though in many cases the scheduled, semi-direct services on *Olympic Airways* is no more expensive and has an edge in terms of flexibility. Sample summer return fares to Rhodes or Kos, gateways to the Dodecanese, start at around £160 from London, but there are often bargains to be had, and outside of high season (which includes Easter), flights can be snapped up for as little as £110 return. Costs can often be highly competitive if you buy a flight as part of an all-inclusive package: see pp.5–6 for details of holiday operators.

Most of the cheaper flights from Britain to Greece are **charters**, which are sold either with a package holiday or as a flight-only deal. The flights have fixed and unchangeable outward and return dates, and often a maximum stay of four weeks.

For longer stays or more flexibility, or if you're travelling out of season (when few charters are available), you'll need a **scheduled** flight. As with charters, these are offered under a wide variety of fares, and are again often sold off at discount by agents. Useful sources for discounted flights are the classified ads in the weekend travel sections of newspapers like the *Independent*, *Guardian*, *Observer* and *Sunday Times*. *Teletext* – and, if you're on line, *Compuserve* – is also worth checking, while your local travel agent shouldn't be overlooked.

You can fly **direct** to the islands of Rhodes, Lésvos, Límnos, Sámos and Kós, though you'll find that the cheapest tickets available tend to be to Athens, or sometimes Thessaloníki. With any flight to Athens, you can buy – at considerable discount – a domestic connecting flight (on the national carrier, *Olympic*) to all of the islands that have airports; see below for more details.

Charter flights

Travel agents throughout Britain sell **charter flights** to Greece. These usually operate from May to October, often with late-night departures and early-morning arrivals. Even the high street chains frequently promote flight-only deals, or discount all-inclusive holidays, when tour operators need to off-load their seat allocations. In any case, phone around for a range of offers. Charter airlines include *Air 2000*, *Britannia*, *Caledonian*, *Excalibur* and *Monarch*, but you can only book tickets on these through travel agents.

The greatest variety of **flights** tends to be from London Gatwick and Manchester. In summer, if you book in advance, you should have a choice of most Greek regional airports. Flying from elsewhere in Britain (Birmingham, Cardiff, Glasgow or Newcastle), or looking for last-minute discounts, you'll find options will be limited, most commonly to Athens, Kós and Rhodes.

It's worth noting that **non-EU nationals** who buy charter tickets to Greece must buy a return ticket, valid for no fewer than three days and no more than four weeks, and must accompany it with an accommodation voucher for at least the first few nights of their stay – check that the ticket satisfies these conditions or you could be refused entry. In practice, the "accommodation voucher" has become a formality; it has to name

Scheduled Airlines

Balkan Airlines ☎0171/637 7637

British Airways ☎0345/222111

ČSA Czechoslovak Airlines ☎0171/255 1898

LOT Polish Airlines ☎0171/580 5037

Malev Hungarian Airlines ☎0171/439 0577

Olympic Airways ☎0171/409 3400

Virgin Atlantic Airways ☎01293/747747

Flight Agents

Alecos Tours, 3a Camden Rd, London NW1 ☎0171/267 2092. Regular *Olympic Airways* consolidator

Argo Holidays, 100 Wigmore St, London W1H 9DR ☎0171/331 7000. Designated consolidator for *Olympic*, *BA*, *Virgin Atlantic*

Avro, 1 Weir Rd, London SW19 8UX ☎0181/715 0000. Specialist agent for all charter flights, including to Rhodes and Kós

Campus Travel, 52 Grosvenor Gardens, London SW1 OAG ☎0171/730 3402; 541 Bristol Rd, Selly Oak, Birmingham B29 6AU ☎0121/414 1848; 61 Ditchling Rd, Brighton BN1 4SD ☎01273/570 0226; 39 Queens Rd, Clifton, Bristol BS8 1QE ☎0117/929 2494; 5 Emmanuel St, Cambridge CB1 1NE ☎01223/324283; 53 Forest Rd, Edinburgh EH1 2QP ☎0131/668 3303; 166 Deansgate, Manchester M3 3FE ☎0161/833 2046; 105–106 St Aldates, Oxford OX1 1DD ☎01865/242067. Student/youth travel specialists, with branches also in YHA shops and on university campuses all over Britain, and its own student/youth charter flights to Athens during the summer

Council Travel, 28a Poland St, London W1V 3DB ☎0171/437 7767. Flights and student discounts

Flyaway Travel, Unit 4, Perronet House, St George's Rd, London SE1 ☎0171/620 3333. Budget flights to Athens

Springways Travel, 28 Vauxhall Bridge Rd, London SW1 ☎0171/976 5833. Reliable discount flight agent

STA Travel, 86 Old Brompton Rd, London SW7 3LH, 117 Euston Rd, London NW1 2SX , 38 Store St, London WC1 ☎0171/ 361 6161; 25 Queens Rd, Bristol BS8 1QE ☎0117/929 4399; 38 Sidney St, Cambridge CB2 3HX ☎01223/ 366966; 75 Deansgate, Manchester M3 2BW ☎0161/834 0668; 88 Vicar Lane, Leeds LS1 7JH ☎0113/244 9212; 36 George St, Oxford OX1 2OJ ☎01865/792800; and branches in Birmingham, Canterbury, Cardiff, Coventry, Durham, Glasgow, Loughborough, Nottingham, Warwick and Sheffield. Worldwide specialists in low cost flights and tours for students and under-26s

Sunset Air Fares, Sunset Business Centre, Manchester Rd, Bolton BL4 8RT ☎01204/ 701111. Flight-only and fly-drive deals to Rhodes and Kós on charter airlines

Trailfinders, 42–50 Earls Court Rd, London W8 6FT ☎0171/937 5400; 194 Kensington High St, London W8 7RG ☎0171/938 3939; 58 Deansgate, Manchester M3 2FF ☎0161/839 6969; 254–284 Sauchiehall St, Glasgow G2 3EH ☎0141/353 2224; 22–24 The Priory, Queensway, Birmingham B4 6BS ☎0121/236 1234; 48 Corn St, Bristol BS1 1HQ ☎0117/929 9000. One of the best informed and most efficient agents

Travel Bug, 125A Gloucester Rd, London SW7 ☎0171/835 2000; 597 Cheetham Hill Rd, Manchester ☎0161/721 4000. Large range of discounted tickets on scheduled airlines only

an existing hotel but you're not expected to use it (and probably won't be able to if you try).

The other important condition regards **travel to Turkey** (or any other neighbouring country). If you travel to Greece on a charter flight, you may visit another country only as a daytrip; if you stay overnight, you will invalidate your ticket. This rule is justified by the Greek authorities because they subsidize charter airline landing fees and are reluctant to see tourists spending their money elsewhere. Whether you buy that excuse or not, there is no way around it, since the Turkish authorities clearly stamp all passports, and the Greeks usually check them. The package industry on the east Aegean and Dodecanese islands bordering Turkey, however, does sometimes prevail upon Turkish customs officials to back-date re-entry stamps when bad weather strands their tour groups overnight in Anatolia.

Student/youth charters are sold as one-way flights only. By combining two one-way charters you can, therefore, stay for over a month. Student/youth charter tickets are available to anyone under 26, and to all card-carrying full-time students under 32.

Finally, remember that **reconfirmation** of all return charter flights is vital and should be done at least 72 hours before departure; if you're travelling with a package company, this service will usually be included, but you should not assume that it has been done. Personal visits to the airline representative office are best, as phone numbers provided on ticket wallets are often engaged.

Scheduled flights

The advantages of **scheduled flights** are that they can be booked well in advance, have longer ticket validities (90 or even 180 days), involve none of the above restrictions on charters, and tend to leave at more sociable hours. However, many of the cheaper PEX, APEX and Super APEX fares do have advance-purchase and/or minimum-stay requirements, and have severe restrictions on date changes and refunds. Scheduled flights have an additional advantage in that they are often daytime flights. As with charters, discount fares on scheduled flights are available from most high-street travel **agents**, as well as from a number of specialist flight and student/youth agencies. Like charters, they must be reconfirmed within 72 hours of the return leg.

The biggest choice of scheduled flights is with the Greek national carrier **Olympic Airways**, and **British Airways**, who both fly direct from London Heathrow to Athens (3–4 times daily for each airline) and also to Thessaloníki (daily on *BA*, 2–4 weekly on *Olympic*). Each of these airlines offers

Specialist UK package operators

Argo Holidays, 100 Wigmore St, London W1H 9DR ☎0171/331 7070. Packages to luxury hotels on Híos, Lésvos, Límnos, Sámos and Sími. Even wider choice on Kós and Rhodes (Ródhos Town and Faliráki); also "Winter sun" specialists to Rhodes

Best of Greece, 23–24 Margaret St, London W1N 8LE ☎0171/677 1721. Exclusive, upmarket villa and hotel arrangements from a long-established, very discriminating operator

Direct Greece, Oxford House, 182 Upper Richmond Rd, Putney, London SW15 2SH ☎0181/785 4000. Villas, apartments and restored houses on Rhodes (Líndhos and Péfkos), Hálki and Lésvos (Sígri)

Elysian Holidays, 14 Tower St, Rye, East Sussex, TN31 7AT ☎01791/225482. Emphasis on restored old houses at Volissós, Híos and Hóra, Pátmos; also Kámbos, mastic-village and beachside accommodation on Híos

Grecofile/Filoxenia, Sourdock Hill, Barkisland, Halifax, West Yorkshire HX4 0AG ☎01422/375999. Tailor-made itineraries and specialist packages to unspoiled areas on many islands

Greek Sun Holidays, 1 Bank St, Sevenoaks, Kent TN13 1UW ☎01732/740317. Good-value package holidays, including some fly-drive options, on Kárpathos, Pátmos, Foúrni, Ikaría, Sámos and Límnos

Island Wandering, 51a London Rd, Hurst Green, East Sussex TN19 7QP ☎01580/860733. Booking agency for hotels and studios, as well as inter-island transport, on Pátmos, Lipsí, Léros, Kálimnos, Astipálea, Kós, Níssiros, Kárpathos, Ikaría and Sámos. Flights arranged separately

Kosmar Villa Holidays, 358 Bowes Rd, Arnos Grove, London N11 1AN ☎0181/368 6833. Self-catering apartments on Sími, Kós and Rhodes

Laskarina Holidays, St Marys Gate, Wirksworth, Derbyshire DE4 4DQ ☎01629/824881. This upmarket company features villas, quality hotels and restored houses on Hálki, Sími, Tílos, Kálimnos, Léros and Lipsí

Manos Holidays, 168–172 Old St, London EC1V 9BP ☎0171/216 8070. Budget packages to most of the major island resorts

Sunvil Holidays, Sunvil House, 7–8 Upper Square, Old Isleworth, Middlesex TW7 7BJ ☎0181/568 4499. Upmarket hotels and apartments on Híos and Límnos

WALKING HOLIDAYS

Athenogenes, Platía Kolonáki 18, 106 73 Athens ☎30/01/36 14 829, fax ☎36 18 849; or (Nov–March) Ste Quitterie, Route de Barran, 32000 Auch, Franch (fax) ☎33/62.05.89.21. Spring and autumn walking tours on Sámos, Lésvos and Ikaría, lead by an Anglo-Greek/French couple. Flights arranged separately

Ramblers Holidays, Longcroft House, Fretherne Rd, Welwyn Garden City, Herts AL8 6PQ ☎01707/331133. Easy walking tours on Sámos, Pátmos and Híos

Waymark Holidays, 44 Windsor Rd, Slough SL1 2EJ ☎01753/516477. Spring and autumn walking holidays on Sámos and Híos

SAILING HOLIDAYS

Sunsail, The Port House, Port Solent, Portsmouth, Hampshire, PO6 4TH ☎01705/210345. Tuition in dinghy sailing, yachting and windsurfing on Kós.

The Moorings, 188 Northdown Rd, Cliftonville, Kent CT9 2QN ☎01843/227140. Operates charters out of Rhodes and Kós

a range of special fares, and even in July and August, specialist flight agents can come up with deals as low as £200 return; more realistically, though, you'll pay around £250–325 return during high season. In the spring or autumn, return fares to Athens run at about £180 including taxes, and in winter dip to about £140. You'll also be able to book onward connections simultaneously to domestic Greek airports, though discounts will apply only if using *Olympic* on all legs of the journey.

Virgin Atlantic Airways also has a daily service from Heathrow to Athens, though it usually arrives in the small hours and fares work out pricier than *BA* or *Olympic* – £250–400 during most of the year, even more at peak season. Its flights from British regional airports route through Heathrow in the first instance, with a supplement applicable.

Tickets on **central European airways** such as *CSA, Balkan, Malev* and *LOT* are no longer the money-savers they once were, especially out of season when airlines offering direct services to Greece undercut them; count on £120 one-way, £240 return to Athens for much of the year. Bear in mind, though, that these flights nearly always involve delays, with connections in (respectively) Prague, Sofia, Budapest and Warsaw, plus a change of planes and airports in Athens – in addition, in-flight service is typically minimal. It is also not always possible to book discount fares direct from these airlines, but you'll often pay no more by going through an agent (see box opposite).

Packages and tours

Virtually every British **tour operator** includes Greece in its programme, though with many of the larger, more mainstream groups you'll find choices limited to the established resorts on Rhodes, Kós, and to a lesser extent Lésvos or Sámos.

If you buy one of these at a last-minute discount, you may find it costs little more than a flight – and you can use the accommodation offered as much or as little as you want. For a more low-key and genuinely "Greek" resort, however, it's better to book your holiday through one of the **specialist agencies** listed below and overleaf. Most of these are fairly small-scale operations, offering competitively priced packages with flights (unless otherwise stated) and often more traditional village accommodation. They also make an effort to offer islands without over-developed tourist resorts.

The **walking** holiday operators listed below run trekking groups of 10 to 15 people plus an experienced guide. Walks tend to be day-long hikes from one or more bases, or point-to-point treks staying in village accommodation en route. Camping out is not usually involved.

Sailing holidays usually involve small flotillas of four- to six-berth yachts, and can be based on shore or at sea. All levels of experience are catered for. Prices start at around £350 per person per week off-season. Alternatively, confident sailors can simply arrange to charter a yacht from a broker; the Greek National Tourist Organization has lists of companies.

Getting there from Ireland

Summer charters operate from Dublin and Belfast to Athens and Rhodes. A high-season charter from Dublin to Athens costs upwards of IR£200 return, while a week's package on one of the islands costs from IR£440 per person for a fortnight.

Year-round **scheduled services** with *Aer Lingus* and *British Airways* operate from both Dublin and Belfast via Heathrow to Athens, but you'll find them pricey compared to charters. Youth and student fares are offered by *USIT* (see below for address).

Travelling **via London** is an alternative if flights are in short supply, and may sometimes save you a little money, but on the whole it's rarely worth the time and effort. For the record, budget flights to London are offered by *British Midland*, *Aer Lingus* and *Ryan Air*.

Airlines in Ireland

Aer Lingus (Belfast) ☎01232/314844; (Cork) ☎021/327155; (Dublin) ☎01/844 4777

British Airways (Belfast) ☎0345/222111; (Dublin) ☎1800/626747

British Midland (Belfast) ☎0345/676676; (Dublin) ☎01/283 8833

Olympic Airways (Dublin) ☎01/677 4555

Ryanair (Dublin) ☎01/677 4422

Travel Agents in Ireland

Balkan Tours, 37 Ann St, Belfast BT1 4EB ☎01232/246795. Direct charter flights

Joe Walsh Tours, 8–11 Baggot St, Dublin ☎01/676 3053. General budget fares agent.

Thomas Cook, 11 Donegall Place, Belfast ☎01232/240833; 118 Grafton St, Dublin ☎01/677 1721. Package holiday and flight agent, with occasional discount offers

USIT, Fountain Centre, Belfast BT1 6ET ☎01232/324073; 10–11 Market Parade, Patrick St, Cork ☎021/270900; 33 Ferryquay St, Derry ☎01504/371888; Aston Quay, Dublin 2 ☎01/679 8833); Victoria Place, Eyre Square, Galway ☎091/565177; Central Buildings, O'Connell St, Limerick ☎061/415064; 36–37 Georges St, Waterford ☎051/72601. Student and youth specialists for flights and trains

Getting there from North America

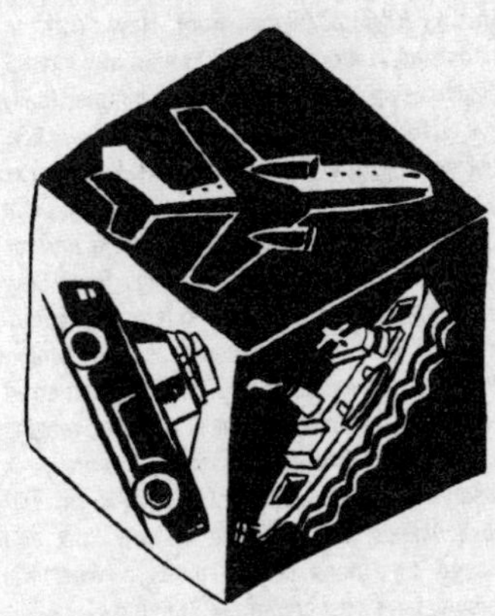

Only a few carriers fly directly to Greece from North America, and nobody offers direct flights to any of the Greek islands. Most North Americans choose to travel to a gateway European city, and pick up a connecting flight on from there with an associated airline. If you have time, you may well discover that it's cheaper to arrange the final Greece-bound leg of the journey in Europe, in which case your only criterion will be finding a suitable North America–Europe flight. For details of onward flights from the UK, see "Getting There from Britain".

In general there just isn't enough traffic on the North America–Athens routes to make for very cheap fares. The Greek national airline, *Olympic Airways*, only flies out of New York (JFK), Boston, Montreal and Toronto, but always offers reasonably priced add-on flights within Greece, especially useful if you want to head straight on to the Dodecanese and east Aegean islands, since they leave from the same Athens terminal at which you will arrive.

Shopping for tickets

Barring special offers, the cheapest of the airlines' published fares is usually an **APEX** (Advance Purchase Excursion) ticket, though this will carry certain restrictions: you have to book – and pay – at least 21 days before departure, spend at least seven days abroad (maximum stay three months), and you tend to get penalized if you change your schedule. On transatlantic routes, there are also winter **Super APEX** tickets, sometimes known as "Eurosavers" – slightly cheaper than an ordinary

Airlines in North America

Air Canada (Canada) ☎ 1-800/555-1212; (US) ☎ 1-800/776-3000

Air France (US) ☎ 1-800/237-2747; (Canada) ☎ 1-800/667-2747

Alitalia (US) ☎ 1-800/223 5730 or ☎ 1-800/442 5860; (Canada) ☎ 1-800/361-8336

British Airways (US) ☎ 1-800/247-9297; (Canada) ☎ 1-800/668-1055

Canadian Airlines (Canada) ☎ 403/569-4180; (US) ☎ 1-800/426-7000

Czechoslovak Airlines (US) ☎ 1-800/223-2365

Delta Airlines (US) ☎ 1-800/221-1212

Iberia (US) ☎ 1-800/772-4642; (Canada) ☎ 1-800/221-6002

KLM (US) ☎ 1-800/374-7747; (Canada) ☎ 1-800/361-5330

LOT Polish Airlines (US) ☎ 1-800/223-0593; (Canada) ☎ 1-800/361-1017

Lufthansa (US) ☎ 1-800/645-3880; (Canada) ☎ 1-800/563-5954

Olympic Airways (US) ☎ 1-800/223-1226

TWA (US) ☎ 1-800/892-4141

Apex, but limiting your stay to between 7 and 21 days. Some airlines also issue **Special APEX** tickets to people younger than 24, often extending the maximum stay to a year. Under-25s can benefit from the youth and student fares offered by many airlines – a passport or driving licence are sufficient proof of age – though these tickets are subject to availability and can have eccentric booking conditions. It's worth remembering that most cheap return fares involve spending at least one Saturday night away and that many will only give a percentage refund if you need to cancel or alter your journey, so make sure you check the restrictions carefully before buying a ticket.

You can normally cut costs further by going through a **specialist flight agent** – either a **consolidator**, who buys up blocks of tickets from the airlines and sells them at a discount, or a **discount agent**, who in addition to dealing with discounted flights may also offer special student and youth fares and a range of other travel-related services such as travel insurance, rail passes, car rental and tours. Bear in mind, though, that changing your plans can incur stiff penalties. Some agents specialize in **charter flights** (almost non-existent to Athens, incidentally), which may be cheaper than anything available on a scheduled flight, but again departure dates are fixed and withdrawal penalties are high (check the refund policy). If you travel a lot, **discount travel clubs** are another option – the annual membership fee may be worth it for benefits such as cut-price air tickets and car rental.

Don't automatically assume that tickets purchased through a travel specialist will be cheapest – once you get a quote, check with the airlines and you may turn up an even better deal. Be advised also that the pool of travel companies is swimming with sharks – exercise caution and *never* deal with a company that demands cash up front or refuses to accept payment by credit card.

Regardless of where you buy your ticket, fares will depend on the **season**, and are highest from around June to September; they drop either side of this, and you'll get the best prices during the low season, November to February (excluding Christmas and New Year). Note also that flying on weekends ordinarily adds around $50 to the round-trip fare. **Price ranges quoted below assume midweek travel.**

From the USA

Non-stop *Olympic* flights **from New York** to Athens start at around US$720 return in winter (5 weekly), rising to around $980 in summer (daily service) for a maximum thirty-day stay; tickets must be bought at least seven days in advance. For about the same price, *Olympic* also flies out of **Boston** once a week in winter, twice a week in summer. *Delta* has daily services from New York to Athens via Frankfurt, with fares and conditions that are much the same as on *Olympic*. *TWA* offers direct, daily flights from the east coast to Athens which are marginally cheaper, ranging from $700 in low season to $1060 in peak season. One particularly good deal is on *LOT Polish Airlines*, which fly out of New York and **Chicago** to Athens several times a week via Warsaw; fares cost around $700 return.

Since all scheduled flights to Athens from the **west coast** go via New York or another eastern city, you basically end up paying for a transcontinental flight on top of the transatlantic fare: round-trip APEX tickets from Seattle, San Francisco or Los Angeles on *TWA* or *Delta* start at $960 in winter, rising to about $1200 in summer. Most European airlines (including *Air France, British Airways, Iberia, KLM* and *Lufthansa*) also connect selected American cities with Greece via their gateway

Travel Agents in North America

USA

Air Brokers International, 323 Geary St, Suite 411, San Francisco, CA 94102 ☎1-800/883-3273. Consolidator

Air Courier Association, 191 University Boulevard, Suite 300, Denver, CO 80206 ☎303/278-8810. Courier flight broker

Airhitch, 2472 Broadway, Suite 200, New York, NY 10025 ☎212/864-2000. Standby-seat broker. For a set price, they guarantee to get you on a flight as close to your preferred destination as possible, within a week

Council Travel, Head Office: 205 E 42nd St, New York, NY 10017 ☎1-800/743-1823. Student travel organization with branches in many US cities. A sister company, *Council Charter* (☎1-800/223-7402), specializes in charter flights

Educational Travel Center, 438 N Frances St, Madison, WI 53703 ☎1-800/747-5551. Student/youth discount agent.

Encore Travel Club, 4501 Forbes Blvd, Lanham, MD 20706 ☎1-800/444-9800. Discount travel club

Interworld Travel, 800 Douglass Rd, Miami, FL 33134 ☎305/443-4929. Consolidator

Last Minute Travel Club, 132 Brookline Ave, Boston, MA 02215 ☎1-800/LAST MIN. Travel club specializing in standby deals

Moment's Notice, 7301 New Utrecht Ave, Brooklyn, NY 11204 ☎718/234-6295

New Frontiers/Nouvelles Frontières, Head offices: 12 E 33rd St, New York, NY 10016 ☎1-800/366-6387 or ☎212/779-0600. French discount travel firm. Other branches in LA and San Francisco

Now Voyager, 74 Varick St, Suite 307, New York, NY 10013 ☎212/431-1616. Courier flight broker

STA Travel, Head office: 10 Downing St, New York NY 10014 ☎212/627-3111; nationwide ☎1-800/777-0112. Worldwide specialist in independent travel with branches in the Los Angeles, San Francisco and Boston areas

TFI Tours International, Head office: 34 W 32nd St, New York, NY 10001 ☎1-800/745-8000. Consolidator; other offices in Las Vegas, San Francisco, Los Angeles

Travac, Head office: 989 6th Ave, New York NY 10018 ☎1-800/872-8800. Consolidator and charter broker; another branch in Orlando

Travel Avenue, 10 S Riverside, Suite 1404, Chicago, IL 60606 ☎1-800/333-3335. Discount travel agent

Traveler's Advantage, 3033 S Parker Rd, Suite 900, Aurora, CO 80014 ☎1-800/548-1116. Discount travel club

UniTravel, 1177 N Warson Rd, St Louis, MO 63132 ☎1-800/325-2222 or 314/569-2501. Consolidator

Worldtrek Travel, 111 Water St, New Haven, CT 06511 ☎1-800/243-1723 or 203/772-0470. Discount travel agency

Worldwide Discount Travel Club, 1674 Meridian Ave, Miami Beach, FL 33139 ☎305/534-2082. Discount travel club

CANADA

New Frontiers/Nouvelles Frontières, 1001 Sherbrook E, Suite 720, Montréal, Quebec H2L 1L3 ☎514/526-8444. French discount travel firm. Another branch in Québec City

Travel Cuts, Head office: 187 College St, Toronto, Ontario M5T 1P7 ☎416/979-2406. Canadian student travel organization with branches all over the country

cities in Europe, but these stopovers often mean a wait of a few hours, sometimes even an overnight stop – be sure to ask your ticket agent.

From Canada

As with the US, air fares **from Canada** to Athens vary tremendously depending upon where you start your journey. The best-value scheduled fare is on *Olympic*, which flies non-stop out of Montréal and Toronto once a week in winter for CDN$1190 round-trip, and twice a week in summer for CDN$1390.

KLM operates several flights a week to Athens via Amsterdam from Toronto, Montréal, Calgary, Halifax and Vancouver – from Toronto, expect to pay around CDN$1190 in winter, CDN$1390 in high season. Travellers from Montréal can also try the European carriers *Air France, Alitalia, British Airways, Iberia, Lufthansa* and *Swissair*, all of which fly several times a week to Athens via major European cities. One unlikely source for good deals is *Czechoslovak Airlines* (*CSA*), which flies from Montréal to Athens via Prague for around CDN$1190 (low season); summer fares are less good value at CDN$1630. Finally, *Air Canada* flies to Frankfurt only, with the onward connection on *Delta*; from Vancouver, flights cost CDN$1650 in winter, CDN$1850 in summer.

Specialist tour operators in North America

USA

Astro Tours, 2359 E Main St, Columbus, OH 43209 ☎1-800/543-7717; cruise packages to Greek islands, including Rhodes, Kós and Pátmos

Avenir Adventures, 1790 Bonanza Dr, Suite 207, PO Box 2730, Park City, UT 84060 ☎1-800/367-3230; excellent, small-group expeditions on foot and by boat, taking in Rhodes, Sími, Lésvos, Sámos, Kós, Pátmos and Lipsí, as well as Turkey

Brendan Tours, 15137 Califa St, Van Nuys, CA 91411 ☎1-800/421-8446; independent itineraries and packages to islands, including Rhodes

Epirotiki Lines/Royal Olympic Cruises, 1 Rockefeller Plaza, New York, NY 10020 ☎1-800/872-6400; Greek cruise specialist, calling regularly at Rhodes and Pátmos

Grecian Travel Inc, 29–11 Ditmard Blvd, Astoria, NY 11105 ☎1-800/368-6262; customized tours including most of the major islands

Guaranteed Travel, 83 South St, Box 269, Morristown, NJ 07963 ☎201/540-1770; specializes in "Greece-Your-Way" independent travel.

Homeric Tours, 55 E 59th St, 17th Floor, New York, NY 10022 ☎1-800/223-5570; charter flights and custom itineraries

Kompas Holidays International, 2826 E Commercial Blvd, Fort Lauderdale, FL 33308 ☎1-800/233-6422. Personalized itineraries to and between Rhodes, Sími, Kós, Pátmos, Sámos

Odyssey Travel Center, 7735 Old Georgetown Rd, Bethesda, MD 20814 ☎301/657-4647. Independent package tours to selected islands.

Travel Dimensions, 350 Park St, Suite 204, North Reading, MA 01864 ☎1-800/752-5055. Customized packages to selected islands

Triaena Tours, 850 Seventh Ave, New York, NY 10019 ☎1-800/223-1273. Island-hopping itineraries, packages, cruises, apartments and villas

Unique Tours, 2020 Pioneer Court #14, San Mateo, CA 94403 ☎1-800/5-HELLAS. Customized tours; specialists for honeymoon tours and weddings

Zeus Tours and Yacht Cruises, 566 7th Ave, New York, NY 10018 ☎1-800/447-5667 or ☎212/221-0006. General cruise agent that also does hotel packages and private yacht charter

CANADA

Trianena Poseidon Tours International, 72 Hutchison St, Montréal, Quebec H3N 1ZL ☎1-800/361-0374. Affiliate of Triana USA, with similar program

Worldwide Quest, 36 Finch Ave West, North York, Ontario M2N2G9 ☎1-800/387-1483. General tour operator whose offerings include a cruise which stops at Pátmos and Rhodes

Getting there from Australasia

It's fairly easy to track down flights from Australia to Athens, less so from New Zealand, but given the prices and most people's travel plans, you'll probably be better off looking for some kind of round-the-world ticket that includes Greece. If London is your first destination in Europe, and you've picked up a reasonably good deal on a flight there, it's probably best to wait until you reach the UK before arranging your onward travel to Greece; see "Getting There from Britain" for details.

Note that **fares** given below are for published high-season (May–Aug) return fares; they drop by as much as A/NZ$600 at other times of the year, and travel agents (see box opposite) should be able to get at least ten percent off these figures year-round. **Students** and anyone **under 26** should in the first instance try *STA Travel*, which has a wide range of discounted fares on offer.

You can also get better value with "**Global Explorer**" round-the-world tickets on airlines such as *BA*, *Qantas*, *Cathay Pacific* and *United*. For around A$2900-3100/NZ$3000-3500, these allow up to six free stopovers, including Athens. Greek airport taxes, sometimes added to the ticket at the time of purchase, are A$31/NZ$44

Airlines in Australasia

Aeroflot, (Sydney) ☎02/9233 7911; no NZ office

Alitalia (Sydney) ☎02/9247 1308; (Auckland) ☎09/379 4457

Britannia Airways (Sydney) ☎02/9251 1299; no NZ office.

British Airways (Sydney) ☎02/9258 3300; (Auckland) ☎09/356 8690

Cathay Pacific (Sydney) ☎02/931 5500; (Auckland) ☎09/379 0861

Garuda (Sydney) ☎02/334 9900; (Auckland) ☎09/366 1855

Gulf Air (Sydney) ☎02/9321 9199; no NZ office

KLM (Sydney) ☎02/9231 6333; toll-free 1800/505 747; no NZ office

Lufthansa/Lauda Air (Sydney) ☎02/367 3888; (Auckland) ☎09/303 1529

Olympic Airways (Sydney) ☎02/9251 2044; no NZ office.

Philippine Airlines (Sydney) ☎02/9262 3333; no NZ office

Qantas (Sydney) ☎02/957 0111; (Auckland) ☎09/357 8900

Singapore Airlines (Sydney) ☎02/9236 0144; local-call rate 13 1011; (Auckland) ☎09/379 3209

Thai Airways (Sydney) ☎02/844 0999; toll-free 1800/422 020; (Auckland) ☎09/377 3886

United Airlines (Sydney) ☎02/237 8888; (Auckland) ☎09/307 9500

Travel agents in Australasia

AUSTRALIA

Accent on Travel, 545 Queen St, Brisbane ☎07/3832 1777

Adventure World, 73 Walker St, North Sydney ☎02/956 7766; 8 Victoria Ave, Perth ☎09/9221 2300

Anywhere Travel, 345 Anzac Parade, Kingsford, Sydney ☎02/663 0411

Brisbane Discount Travel, 360 Queen St, Brisbane ☎07/3229 9211

Thomas Cook, 330 Collins St, Melbourne ☎03/9602 3811; branches in Sydney and other state capitals

Flight Centres, Circular Quay, Sydney ☎02/9241 2422; Bourke St, Melbourne ☎03/650 2899; plus other branches nationwide

Grecian Holidays, 115 Pitt St, Sydney ☎02/9231 1277; 71 Grey St, Brisbane ☎07/9846 4006

Grecian Mediterranean Holidays, 49 Ventnor Ave, West Perth ☎09/9321 3930

Grecian Tours and Travel, 237a Lonsdale St, Melbourn; ☎03/9663 3711

Greek Tours, Floor 2, 243 Edward St, Brisbane ☎07/9221 9700

House of Holidays, 298 Clayton Rd, Clayton, Victoria ☎03/9543 5800

Harvey World Travel, Princess Highway, Kogarah, Sydney; ☎02/567 6099; branches nationwide

Northern Gateway, 22 Cavenagh St, Darwin; ☎08/8941 1394

Passport Travel, 320b Glenferrie Rd, Malvern, Melbourne; ☎03/9824 7183

STA Travel, Australia: 732 Harris St, Ultimo, Sydney ☎02/9212 1255, toll-free 1800/637 444; 256 Flinders St, Melbourne (☎03/9654 7266); other offices in Townsville, state capitals and major universities

Thomas Cook, 330 Collins St, Melbourne ☎03/9602 3811; branches in sydney and other state capitals

Topdeck Travel, 45 Glenfell St, Adelaide ☎08/8232 7222

Tymtro Travel, 428 George St, Sydney ☎02/9223 2211

UTAG Travel, 122 Walker St, North Sydney ☎02/956 8399; branches throughout Australia

NEW ZEALAND

Budget Travel, 16 Fort St, Auckland; other branches around the city ☎09/366 0061, toll-free 0800/ 808 040

Destinations Unlimited, 3 Milford Rd, Milford, Auckland ☎09/373 4033

Flight Centres, National Bank Towers, 205–225 Queen St, Auckland ☎09/209 6171; Shop 1M, National Mutual Arcade, 152 Hereford St, Christchurch ☎03/379 7145; 50–52 Willis St, Wellington ☎04/472 8101; other branches countrywide

Thomas Cook, Shop 250a St Luke's Square, Auckland ☎09/849 2071

Traveller's Centre, 10 High St, Auckland ☎09/309 9995); 233 Cuba St, Wellington ☎04/385 0561; 223 High St, Christchurch ☎03/379 9098; other offices in Dunedin, Palmerston North and Hamilton

for the international leg, A$18/NZ$24 for the Greek domestic sector.

From Australia

The cheapest fares to Athens **from Australia** are with *Aeroflot* (A$2120), flying weekly from Sydney via Moscow; *KLM* (A$2410), thrice weekly out of Sydney via Amsterdam; and *Gulf Air* (A$2270) thrice weekly out of Sydney via Bahrain. *Olympic* flights, which leave from Melbourne and Sydney, work out slightly pricier at A$2480, but have the advantage of discounted add-on fares for the final leg of your journey.

From the eastern cities, for A$2900, *Thai Airways* flies thrice weekly from Sydney, Melbourne and Brisbane; *Singapore Airlines*, twice weekly from these, plus four weekly from Perth (A$2700); *Quantas*, twice weekly from all major airports via Singapore; and *British Airways*, daily from all major cities via London.

Some savings may be realized by flying **to London** instead; both *Garuda* and *Philippine Air Lines* make the trip several times weekly from Sydney, Melbourne and Brisbane for A$2000, and *Britannia* for A$1800 during their Nov–March charter season.

From New Zealand

From New Zealand, the best deals from Auckland to Athens, all with several departures a week, are on *Alitalia* (NZ$2850 to Rome, but add-on to Athens often included free), *Thai* (NZ$2899 via Bangkok) or *Singapore Airways* (NZ$2899 via Singapore). For about the same amount, *Quantas, Air New Zealand, KLM* and *Lufthansa* provide equally frequent services, with the added advantage of possible stopovers in their hub cities.

As with flights out of Australia, travellers may find it to their advantage to get as cheaply as possible to **London**, rather than Athens, and arrange onward travel there; currently the best deals are on *Garuda* (NZ$2420) and *Britannia* during their Nov–March charter season (NZ$1800). For Christchurch departures, add NZ$350 to the fare figures cited above.

Getting there from the mainland

Given the limitations of direct flights to Rhodes, the Dodecanese and the east Aegean, many travellers – of necessity those from North America and Australasia – will touch down first at Athen's Ellinikó airport, with a few Brits flying into Thessaloníki or Kavála as well. From the first two cities you have a choice of making your way to the island of your choice by plane or ferry. Rhodes, Kastellórizo, Kárpathos, Kássos, Kós, Léros, Sámos, Híos, Lésvos and Límnos all have airports served by *Olympic Airways'* domestic flights, with Rhodes additionally served by *Air Greece*.

Ferries

For those islands without airports, or Athens travellers who prefer to island-hop, the first order of business will be getting to Pireás and onto a ferry bound for the island group of your choice (for routes, see "Getting Around", p.26). Boats heading for the east Aegean usually depart in the early evening, while those bound for the Dodecanese leave in the afternoon. There are few morning sailings, so if you arrive on a charter in the small hours, you could face a wait of up to twelve hours. Thessaloníki or Kavála arrivals will have to contend with sparse ferry connections to the east Aegean – at most two or three weekly even in summer.

Flights

Flying out as soon as possible will probably be the most attractive option, especially if you've arrived jet-lagged from another continent. *Olympic Airways* offers a great incentive for using them for the international leg of your trip: a hefty discount on the internal return flight from Athens or

Athens: Transport Information

Many of the phone numbers below may be constantly engaged during business hours; you will often have to go in person to the address listed or (more easily) to an authorized agent on the Pireás quay.

Athens Airport Information

Olympic Airways ☎01/93 63 363

Air Greece ☎01/96 00 646

all other companies ☎01/96 99 466

Midtown Airline Offices

Olympic, 96 Singroú, Makriyánni ☎01/92 67 251

Air Greece, Níkis 20, Síndagma ☎01/32 55 011

Ferry Companies

DANE, Aktí Miaoúli 33, Pireás ☎01/42 93 240

Agapitos Lines, Kolokotróni 99, Pireás ☎01/41 36 246

Arkadhia Lines, Aktí Posidhónos 42, Pireás ☎01/42 22 127

G&A Ferries, Etolikoú 2 corner Aktí Kondhíli, Pireás ☎01/42 25 100

Ilio Lines Hydrofoils, Goúnari 2, Pireás ☎01/42 24 772

NEL, Pávlou Koundouriótou 47, Mitilíni, Lésvos ☎0251/23 097

Nomicos Lines, Karaïskou 120, Pireás ☎01/42 96 740

Ventouris Lines, Kapodhistríou 2, corner Aktí Posidhónos, Pireás ☎01/41 14 911

Thessaloníki to the selected island. As an example, Athens to Sámos costs the equivalent of £70 return if purchased within Greece, but as little as £40 if purchased as part of an all-*Olympic* itinerary originating overseas – little more than the price of a cabin ticket on an overnight ferry. Making your **onward connection** involves nothing more strenuous than strolling 100m from international arrivals to domestic departures at *Olympic*'s designated west terminal, with waits often as short as two hours. Additionally, you're entitled to the full international 23-kilo **baggage allowance**, not just the puny 15-kilo Greek domestic one.

Olympic flight frequencies (see "Travel Details" for each island) from Athens are adequate – three to six daily for the biggest islands – though seats are in heavy demand during peak season. Fully booked or not, it can be worth trying for a **standby** ticket, especially if you land in the middle of the night and can be first in the queue when the sales office opens at dawn. You have to purchase a ticket (credit cards accepted) in order to get on the standby list; if in the end you don't manage to fly, you can get a refund – if not cash, then a flight voucher. Once you're on the list, just make sure to be at the departure gate when they call out the names of the lucky few – experience has shown that there are almost always three or four unclaimed seats on any flight.

If you've arrived at Ellinikó's east terminal on another airline, you might want to investigate *Air Greece*'s flights out of this terminal to Rhodes, which are rather cheaper than *Olympic*'s non-discounted offerings.

Travelling via Athens and Pireás

If you opt for a cheap flight **to Athens**, you may find yourself with some time on your hands in the Greek capital before the island leg of your journey. This is not necessarily a hardship; the city is, admittedly, no holiday resort, with its concrete architecture and air pollution, but it has modern excitements of its own, as well as some superlative ancient sites. A couple of nights' stopover will allow you to take in the Acropolis, the ancient Agora and some major museums, wander around the old quarter of Pláka and the bazaar area, and sample some of the country's best restaurants and clubs.

Otherwise, a very early morning flight into Athens would allow you just enough time to take a look at the Acropolis and Pláka, before heading down to the port of **Pireás** (Piraeus) to catch one of the overnight ferries to the east Aegean or the Dodecanese.

What follows is a brief guide to getting in and out of the city, and some pointers on what to do while you're there. For a full treatment of the city, see *The Rough Guide to Greece*.

ARRIVING

Athens airport – Ellinikón – has two separate terminals: **West** (Dhitikó) which is used by *Olympic Airways* (both national and international), and **East** (Anatolkó) which is used by all the other airlines, including charter companies.

continues over

Travelling via Athens and Pireás cont.

The terminals are on opposite sides of the runway, so you have to drive halfway round the perimeter fence to get from one to the other. Blue-and-white express buses #090 or #091 connect the two regularly from around 6am to midnight (160–200dr); taxis are available, too, and should cost no more than 800dr.

Both terminals have **money exchange** facilities, open 24 hours at the east terminal, 7am to 11pm at the west one; the west terminal also has automatic teller machines that accept *Visa*, *Mastercard*, *Cirrus* and *Plus* cards. Insist on some small-denomination notes for paying for your bus ticket or taxi ride.

It's about 9km **to central Athens** or to the ferry port of Pireás (Piraeus). The easiest way to travel is by **taxi**, which should cost around 1300–1600dr, depending on traffic. Make sure that the meter is switched on, as new arrivals are often charged over the odds. You may find that you have fellow passengers in the cab: this is permitted, and each drop-off will pay the full fare.

If you're happy to carry your bags around, you could also travel in by **bus**. The blue-and-white #090 and #091 buses connect both terminals with the centre of Athens (Omónia and Síndagma squares). They run every half-hour 6am–9pm, every 40 minutes 9pm–12.20am, and every hour (on the half hour) 1.30–5.30am. Tickets cost 160dr, except between 1.30 and 5.30am when they rise to 200dr.

If you wish to get straight to the ferries, express bus #19 runs from both airport terminals **to Pireás** 12 times a day between 6am and 9.20pm, with tickets again costing 160dr. Take the bus to the end of the route, Platía Karaïskáki on the main harbour, where you'll find a line of ferry agencies.

If you intend to spend only a day in Athens, you can either check your **baggage** onto your connecting flight, or store it for 200dr per piece at *Pacific Ltd*, Nikis 26 – just off Síndagma (Mon–Sat 7am–8pm, Sun 7am–2pm). Longer-term storage can also be arranged if you wish to take the minimum to the islands.

ACCOMMODATION

Finding **accommodation** in Athens poses little problem except at the very height of summer – though it's best to phone ahead. A small selection of places is listed below, or you can book more upmarket rooms through the hotel reservations desk inside the National Bank of Greece on Síndagma square. There is also a **Tourist Office** inside the National Bank, which can supply you with maps of the city.

Though it is possible to stay in the port of **Pireás**, you should make the most of your time in Athens. The best place for a short stay is **Pláka**, the oldest quarter of the city, which spreads south of Síndagma square; it's within easy walking range of the Acropolis, and has many outdoor restaurants and cafés.

All the listings below are in the Pláka; prices are for a double room in high season (see p.341 for price categories).

Acropolis House, Kódhrou 6 ☎01/32 22 344 ④–⑤

Adonis, Kódhrou 3 ☎01/32 49 737 ④–⑤

Dioskouri, Pittákou 6 ☎01/32 48 165 ③

George's Guest House, Níkis 46 ☎01/32 26 474 ②

John's Place, Patróou 5 ☎01/32 29 719 ②

Kouros, Kódhrou 11 ☎01/32 27 431 ③

Myrto, Níkis 40 ☎01/32 27 237 ④–⑤

Nefeli, Iperídhou 16 ☎01/32 28 044 ④–⑤

Phaedra, Herefóndos 16 ☎01/32 27 795 ③

Solonion, Spírou Tsangári 11 ☎01/32 20 008 ②

EATING AND DRINKING

Pláka is bursting with touristy restaurants, most very pleasantly situated but serving poor-value fare. Three with both good locations and food are *Kouklis* (Tripíodhon 14), *O Platanos* (Dhioyénous 4) and *Iy Klimataria* (Klepsídhras 5). *Eden* (Liossíou 12) is a decent vegetarian restaurant, pricier than the preceding three.

THE CITY AND SIGHTS

Central Athens is a compact, easily walkable area. Its hub is **Síndagma Square** (Platía Sindágmatos), flanked by the Parliament, banks and airline offices, and, as mentioned, the National Bank with the Tourist Office. Pretty much everything you'll want to see in a fleeting visit – the Acropolis, Pláka, the major museums – lies within 20–30 minutes' walk of here. Just east of the square, too, are the **National Gardens** – the most pleasant spot in town for a siesta.

Pláka and the Bazaar

Walk south from Síndagma, along Níkis or Filellínon streets, and you'll find yourself in **Pláka**, the surviving area of the nineteenth-century, pre-Independence village. Largely pedestrianized, it's a delightful area just to wander around – and it straddles most approaches to the Acropolis.

For a little focus to your walk, take in the fourth-century BC **Monument of Lysikrates**, used as a study by Byron, to the east, and the Roman-era **Tower of the Winds** (Aéridhes), to the west. The latter adjoins the **Roman Forum**. Climb north from the Tower of the Winds and you reach **Anafiótika**, with its whitewashed Cycladic-style cottages (built by workers from the island of Anáfi) and the eclectic **Kanellópoulos Museum** (Tues–Sun 8.30am–2.45pm; 600dr).

Head north from the Roman Forum, along Athinás or Eólou streets, and you come to the equally colourful **bazaar** area. **Monastiráki square** is worth a look, too, with its Turkish mosque that now serves as a museum of ceramic art (daily except Tues 9am–2.30pm; 400dr). On Sundays a genuine **Flea Market** sprawls to its west, out beyond the tourist shops promoted as the "Athens Flea Market".

The Acropolis and ancient Agora

Even with only a few hours to spare between flight and ferry, you can take in a visit to the **Acropolis** (Mon–Fri 8am–6.45pm/5pm summer/winter, Sat & Sun 8.30am–2.45pm; 1500dr/students 800dr). The complex of temples, rebuilt by Pericles during the Classical "Golden Age" of the fifth century BC, is focused on the famed Parthenon. This, and the smaller Athena Nike and Erechtheion temples, are placed in context by a small museum housing some of the original statuary left behind by Lord Elgin.

If you have more time, make your way down to the **Theatre of Dionysos**, on the south slope (Mon–Sat 9am–2.45pm, Sun 9am–1.45pm; 600dr), and the **ancient** (Classical Greek-era) **Agora**, northwest of the Acropolis hill (Tues–Sun 8.30am–2.45pm; 800dr), presided over by the Doric **Thiseion**, or Temple of Hephaestus.

Museums

Athens' major museum is the **National Archeological Museum** (Patissíon 28; Mon 12.30–6.45pm, Tues–Fri 8am–6.45pm; Sat & Sun 8.30am–12.45pm; 1500dr/students 750dr). Its highlights include the Mycenaean (Odyssey-era) treasures, Classical sculpture, and, upstairs, the brilliant Minoan frescoes from Thíra (Santoríni).

Two other superb museums are the **Benáki** (Koumbári 1; daily except Tues 8.30am–2pm), a fascinating personal collection of ancient and folk treasures, and the **Museum of Cycladic and Ancient Greek Art** (Neofítou Dhouká 4; Mon & Wed–Fri 10am–4pm, Sat 10am–3pm; 250dr), with its wonderful display of figurines from the Cycladic island civilization of the third millennium BC.

ON TO THE ISLANDS: PIREÁS

Pireás (Piraeus), the port of Athens, is the last stop on the single-line **metro**, which you can board at Omónia or Monastiráki squares. The journey takes about 25 minutes – trains run from 5.30am to midnight – and there's a flat fare of 75dr. **Taxis** cost around 1500dr from the city centre or the airport.

Ferry ticket agencies can be found at the harbour in Pireás, or in central Athens along Letóros Amalías, which runs south of Síndagma square. Try to get a ferry that makes a reasonably direct run to your destination. There may be little choice to obscure islands such as Astipálea or Foúrni, but ferries to the larger Dodecanese or East Aegean islands can take very different routes.

Travellers with disabilities

It is all too easy to wax lyrical over the attractions of the Greek islands: the stepped, narrow alleys, the ease of island-hopping by ferry, the thrill of clambering around the archeological sites. However, these attractions can be potential hazards for anyone who has some difficulty in walking, is wheelchair-bound, or has some other disability.

Don't be discouraged: it is possible to enjoy an inexpensive and trauma-free holiday in Greece if some time is devoted to gathering **information** before arrival. Addresses of contact organizations are published below and overleaf, and the Greek National Tourist Office is a good first step as long as you have specific questions to put to them; they publish a useful questionnaire which you could send to hotels or owners of apartment/villa accommodation. Where possible, double check all information, as too often it's all outdated.

Useful contacts

National Tourist Organization of Greece (see p.24 for addresses). Offers general advice on terrain and climate. They have nothing specific for disabled visitors except a brief list of hotels which may be suitable

AUSTRALIA

ACROD (Australian Council for Rehabilitation of the Disabled), PO Box 60, Curtin ACT 2605 ☎06/682 4333; 55 Charles St, Ryde ☎02/9809 4488

CANADA

Jewish Rehabilitation Hospital, 3205 Place Alton Goldbloom, Montréal, PQ H7V 1R2 ☎514/688-9550. Guidebooks and travel information

Twin Peaks Press, Box 129, Vancouver, WA 98666 ☎206/694-2462 or 1-800/637-2256. Publisher of the *Directory of Travel Agencies for the Disabled* ($19.95), listing more than 370 agencies worldwide; *Travel for the Disabled* ($14.95); the *Directory of Accessible Van Rentals* and *Wheelchair Vagabond* ($9.95), loaded with personal tips

GREECE

Association Hermes, Patriarchou 13, Grigouiou E, 16542 Argyroupolis ☎01/99 61 887. Can advise disabled visitors to Greece

Evyenia Stravropoulou, Lavinia Tours: Egnatía 101, 541 10 Thessaloníki ☎031/240 041. Will advise disabled visitors and has tested many parts of Greece in her wheelchair. She also organizes tours within Greece

IRELAND

Disability Action Group, 2 Annadale Ave, Belfast BT7 3JH ☎01232/91011

Irish Wheelchair Association, Blackheath Drive, Clontarf, Dublin 3 ☎01/833 8241. A national voluntary organization working with people with disabilities, with related services for holidaymakers

NEW ZEALAND

Disabled Persons Assembly, PO Box 10, 138 The Terrace, Wellington ☎04/472 2626

UK

Holiday Care Service, 2nd floor, Imperial Building, Victoria Rd, Horley, Surrey RH6 9HW ☎01293/774535. Information on all aspects of travel

RADAR, 12 City Forum, 250 City Rd, London EC1V 8AS ☎0171/250 3222; Minicom ☎0171/250 4119. A good source of advice on holidays and travel abroad

Opus 23, Sourdock Hill, Barkisland, Halifax, W Yorks HX4 0AG ☎01422/375999. Part of *Grecofile*; will advise on and arrange independent holidays, or for those with carers

Tripscope, The Courtyard, Evelyn Rd, London W4 5JL ☎0181/994 9294. A national telephone information service offering free transport and travel advice

USA

Directions Unlimited, 720 N Bedford Rd, Bedford Hills, NY 10507 ☎1-800/533-5343. Tour operator specializing in custom tours for people with disabilities

Mobility International USA, PO Box 10767, Eugene, OR 97440; voice and TDD ☎503/343 1284. Information and referral services, access guides, tours and exchange programs. Annual membership $20 (includes quarterly newsletter)

Society for the Advancement of Travel for the Handicapped (SATH), 347 5th Ave, New York, NY 10016. ☎212/447 7284. Non-profit travel-industry referral service that passes queries on to its members as appropriate; allow plenty of time for a response

Travel Information Service, Moss Rehabilitation Hospital, 1200 W Tabor Rd, Philadelphia, PA 19141; ☎215/456 9600. Telephone information and referral service

Planning a holiday

There are **organized tours and holidays** specifically for people with disabilities – both *Thomsons* and *Horizon* in Britain will advise on the suitability of holidays in their brochures. Travelling more independently is also perfectly possible, provided you are completely confident that you can manage alone. For example, to get between the terminals at Athens airport, you will have to fight for a taxi; it is not the duty of the airline staff to find you one.

Read your travel **insurance** small print carefully to make sure that people with a pre-existing medical condition are not excluded. And use your travel agent to make your journey simpler: airlines or bus companies can usually provide wheelchairs at airports and prime staff to help. A medical certificate of your fitness to travel, provided by your doctor, is also extremely useful; some airlines or insurance companies may insist on it.

If you do need to take a wheelchair with you, have it serviced before the trip, and carry a repair kit. You should also make a **list of facilities** that will ease your way: a ground-floor room or access to a large elevator, special dietary requirements, and level ground to enable you to reach shops, beaches, bars and places of interest. Keep track of other special needs, making sure, for example, that you have extra supplies of prescription drugs –carried with you if you fly – and a prescription that includes the generic name in case of emergency. Carry spares of any kind of drug, clothing or equipment that might be hard to find in Greece; if there's an **association** representing people with your disability, contact them early on in the planning process.

Visas and red tape

UK and all other EU nationals need only a valid passport for entry to Greece; you are no longer stamped in on arrival or out upon departure, and in theory enjoy the same civil rights as Greek citizens (see "Work", p.53). US, Australian, New Zealand, Canadian and most non-EU Europeans receive entry and exit stamps in their passports and can stay, as tourists, for ninety days.

Visa extensions

If you wish to remain in Greece for longer than three months, you should officially apply for an **extension**. This can be done in Ródhos Town at the *Ipiresía Allodhapón* (Aliens' Bureau); brace yourself for concerted bureaucracy. In other locations you visit the local police station, where staff are usually more cooperative.

Unless of Greek descent, visitors from **non-EU countries** are currently allowed only a three-month extension to the basic tourist visa, and this costs 11,000dr. In theory, **EU nationals** can stay indefinitely, but for a non-employment resident visa you will still have to present yourself every six months to the relevant authorities; only the first extension is free. In all cases, the procedure should be set in motion a couple of weeks before your time runs out. If you don't have a work permit, you will be required to present pink, personalized **bank exchange receipts** (see "Costs, Money and Banks: Currency Regulations", p.21) totalling at least 450,000d for the preceding three months, as proof that you have sufficient funds to support yourself without working. Possession of unexpired credit cards, a Greek savings account passbook or travellers' cheques can to some extent substitute for this requirement.

Some non-EU resident individuals get around the law by leaving Greece every three months and re-entering a few days later for a new,

Greek Embassies abroad

Australia 9 Turrana St, Yarralumla, Canberra, ACT 260; ☎062/273 3011

Britain 1a Holland Park, London W11 ☎0171/221 6467

Canada 80 Maclaren St, Ottawa, ON K2P 0K6 ☎613/238-6271

Ireland 1 Upper Pembroke St, Dublin 2 ☎01/767254

New Zealand Cumberland House, 237 Willis St, PO Box 27157, Wellington ☎04/847-556

USA 2221 Massachusetts Ave NW, Washington DC 20008 ☎202/667-3168

ninety-day **tourist stamp**. However, with the recent flood of refugees from Albania and former Yugoslavia, plus a smaller influx of east Europeans looking for work, immigration personnel don't always look very kindly on this practice.

If you **overstay** your time and then leave under your own steam – ie are not detected and deported – you'll be given a 22,000dr spot fine upon departure, effectively a double-priced retroactive visa extension; no excuses will be entertained except perhaps a doctor's certificate stating that you were immobilized in hospital. It cannot be overemphasized just how exigent Greek immigration officials often are on these issues.

Customs regulations

For EU citizens travelling between EU countries, the limits on goods already taxed have been relaxed enormously. However, **duty-free allowances** are as follows: 200 cigarettes or 50 cigars, two litres of still table wine, one litre of spirits and 60ml of perfume. Exporting **antiquities** without a permit is a serious offence; **drug smuggling**, not surprisingly, incurs severe penalties.

Insurance

UK and other EU nationals are officially entitled to free medical care in Greece (see "Health Matters", p.20) upon presentation of an E111 form, available from most post offices. "Free", however, means just admittance to the lowest grade of state hospital (known as a *yenikó nosokomío*), and does not include nursing care or the cost of medication. In practice, hospital staff tend to greet E111s with uncomprehending looks, and you may have to pay and request reimbursment by the NHS upon return home. In any case, if you need prolonged medical care, you're better off using private treatment, which is expensive – 8000dr minimum for a brief clinic consultation.

Some form of **travel insurance** is therefore advisable – indeed essential for **North Americans** and **Australasians**, whose countries have no formal health care agreements with Greece (other than allowing for free emergency treatment). For **medical claims**, keep receipts, including those from pharmacies. You will have to pay for all private medical care on the spot (insurance claims can be processed if you have hospital treatment), but it can all be claimed back eventually. Travel insurance usually provides cover for the **loss of baggage, money and tickets**, too. If you're thinking of **renting a moped** or motorbike on the islands (most people do), make sure the policy covers motorbike accidents.

European cover

In **Britain and Ireland**, travel insurance schemes (from around £23 a month) are sold by almost every travel agent or bank, as well as by specialist insurance companies. Policies issued through the companies listed in the box below are all good value. *Columbus* also does an annual multi-trip policy which offers twelve months' cover for £125.

Most **banks** and **credit-card** issuers also offer some sort of vacation insurance, often automatic if you pay for the holiday with a card. Travel agents and tour operators are also likely to recommend insurance when you book, indeed some will insist you take it. These policies are

Travel insurance companies

UK AND IRELAND

Campus Travel ☎ 0171/730 3402

Columbus Travel Insurance ☎ 0171/375 0011

Endsleigh Insurance ☎ 0171/436 4451

Frizzell Insurance ☎ 01202/292 333

STA Travel ☎ 0171/ 361 6161

USIT (Belfast) ☎ 01232/324073

NORTH AMERICA

Access America ☎ 1-800/284 8300

Carefree Travel Insurance ☎ 1-800/323 3149

Desjardins Travel Insurance (Canada only) ☎ 1-800/463 7830

International Student Insurance Service (ISIS) – sold by *STA Travel* ☎ 1-800/777 0112

Travel Assistance International ☎ 1-800/821 2828

Travel Guard ☎ 1-800/826 1300

Travel Insurance Services ☎ 1-800/937 1387

AUSTRALASIA

UTAG (Sydney) ☎ 02/9819 6855; toll-free 1800/ 809 462

AFTA (Sydney) ☎ 02/9956 4800

Cover More (Sydney) ☎ 02/9968 1333; toll-free 1800/251 881

Ready Plan (Victoria) toll-free ☎ 1800/337 462; (Auckland) ☎ 09/379 3399

usually reasonable value, though as ever, you should check the small print. If you have a good "all risks" home insurance policy it may well cover your possessions against loss or theft even when overseas, and many private medical schemes also cover you when abroad – make sure you know the procedure and the helpline number.

North American cover

Before buying an insurance policy, check that you're not already covered. **Canadians** are usually covered for medical mishaps overseas by their provincial health plans. Holders of official **student/teacher/youth cards** are entitled to accident coverage and hospital in-patient benefits. Students will often find that their student health coverage extends during the vacations and for one term beyond the date of last enrollment. **Bank and credit cards** (particularly *American Express*) often have certain levels of medical or other insurance included, and you may automatically get travel insurance if you use a major credit or charge card to pay for your trip. **Homeowners' or renters' insurance** often covers theft or loss of documents, money and valuables while overseas, though conditions and maximum amounts vary from company to company.

After exhausting the possibilities above, you might want to contact a specialist **travel insurance company**; your travel agent can usually recommend one, though most can arrange the insurance themselves at no extra charge (see box above). Policies are comprehensive (accidents, illnesses, delayed or lost luggage, cancelled flights, etc), but maximum payouts tend to be meagre. Premiums vary, so shop around. The best deals are usually to be had through student travel agencies – *ISIS* policies, for example, cost $80–105 for a month. If you're passing through Britain in transit, you may prefer to buy a British policy (see above), which is usually cheaper and wider in scope, though some British insurers may require a permanent UK address.

Most North American travel policies apply only to items lost, stolen or damaged while in the custody of an identifiable, responsible third party such as a hotel porter, an airline or a luggage consignment. In all cases of theft or loss of goods, you must contact the local police – often within a certain time limit – to have a complete report made out so that your insurer can process the claim. This can occasionally prove tricky in Greece, since many officials simply won't accept that anything could be stolen on their turf, or at least don't want to take responsibility for it. Be persistent, and if necessary enlist the support of the local tourist police or tourist office. Note that very few insurers will arrange on-the-spot payments in the event of a major expense or loss; you will usually be reimbursed once you're home.

Australasian cover

Travel insurance is put together by the airlines and travel agent groups (see box above) in conjunction with insurance companies. They are all comparable in premium and coverage – a typical insurance policy will cost A$190/NZ$220 for one month, A$270/NZ$320 for two months and A$330/NZ$400 for three months. Most adventure sports are covered, but check your policy first.

Health matters

There are no required inoculations for Greece, though it's wise to ensure that you are up to date on tetanus and polio. Don't forget to take out travel insurance (see "Insurance", above), so that you're covered in case of serious illness or accidents.

The water is safe pretty much everywhere, though you will come across shortages or brackish supplies on some of the drier and more remote islands. Bottled water is widely available if you're feeling cautious, though see the box on Eco-Friendly Travel, p.35.

Specific hazards

The main health problems experienced by visitors have to do with **overexposure to the sun**, and the odd nasty from the sea. To combat the former, don't spend to long in the sun, cover up and wear a hat, and drink plenty of fluids in the hot months to avoid any danger of sunstroke; remember that even a hazy sun can burn. For sea wear, goggles or a dive mask are useful, as well as footwear for walking over slippery rocks.

Hazards of the deep

In the sea, you may have the bad luck to meet an armada of **jellyfish** (*tsoúkhtres*), especially in late summer; they come in various colours and sizes including transparent and minute. Various over-the-counter remedies are sold in resort pharmacies; baking soda or diluted ammonia also help to lessen the sting. The welts and burning usually subside of their own accord within a few hours; there are no deadly man-of-war species in Greek waters.

Less venomous but more common are black, spiky **sea urchins** (*ehíni*), which infest rocky shorelines year-round; if you step on or graze one, a sewing needle (you can crudely sterilize it by heat from a cigarette lighter) and olive oil are effective for removing spines from your anatomy; if you don't extract them they'll fester. You can take your revenge by eating the reddish-purple ones (see "Eating and drinking", p.36).

The worst maritime danger – fortunately very rare – is the **weever fish** (*dhrakéna*), which buries itself in tidal zone sand with just its poisonous dorsal and gill spines protruding. If you tread on one, the sudden pain is excruciating, and the exceptionally potent venom can cause permanent paralysis of the affected area. The imperative first aid is to immerse your foot in water as hot as you can stand, which degrades the toxin and relieves the swelling of joints and attendant pain, but you should still seek medical attention as soon as possible.

Somewhat more common are **sting rays** (Greek names include *platí, seláhi, vátos* or *trígona*), who mainly frequent bays with sandy bottoms, against which they can camouflage themselves. Though shy, they can give you a nasty lash with their tail if trodden on, so shuffle your feet a bit on entering the water.

Sandflies, mosquitoes, snakes, scorpions

If you are sleeping on or near a beach, a wise precaution is to use insect repellent, either lotion or wrist/ankle bands, and/or a tent with a screen to guard against **sandflies**. Their bites are potentially dangerous, as the flies spread visceral leishmaniasis, a rare parasitic infection characterized by chronic fever, listlessness and weight loss.

Mosquitoes (*kounóupia*) in Greece carry nothing worse than a vicious bite, but they can be infuriating. The best solution is to burn pyrethrum incense coils (*spíres* or *fidhákia*), which are widely and cheaply available. Better, if you can get them, are the small electrical devices (trade name *Vape-Net*) that vaporize an odourless insecticide tablet; many "rooms" proprietors supply them routinely. Insect repellents, such as *Autan*, are available from most general stores and kiosks.

Adders (*ohiés*) and **scorpions** (*skorpii*) are found throughout the Dodecanese and East Aegean; both species are shy, but take care when climbing over dry-stone walls where snakes like to sun themselves, and don't put hands or feet in places (eg shoes) where you haven't looked first.

Pharmacies and drugs

For **minor complaints** it's easiest to go to the local **farmakío**. Greek pharmacists are highly trained and dispense a number of medicines that elsewhere could only be prescribed by a doctor. In the larger towns and resorts there'll usually be one who speaks good English. Pharmacies are usually closed evenings and Saturday mornings, but are supposed to have a sign on their door referring you to the nearest one that's open. **Homeopathic and herbal remedies** are quite widely available, too, and the larger island towns such as Kós and Ródhos have dedicated homeopathic pharmacies, delineated by the green cross sign.

If you regularly use any form of **prescription drug**, you should bring along a copy of the prescription together with the generic name of the drug – this will help should you need to replace it and also avoid possible problems with customs officials. In this regard, it's worth pointing out that codeine is banned in Greece. If you import any you might find yourself in serious trouble, so check labels carefully; it's the core ingredient of *Panadeine*, *Veganin*, *Solpadeine*, *Codis* and *Empirin-Codeine*, to name just a few compounds.

Contraceptive pills are more readily available every year, but don't count on getting them outside of a few large island towns; Greek women tend not to use any sort of birth control systematically, and have an average of four abortions during their adult life. **Condoms**, however, are inexpensive and ubiquitous – just ask for *profilaktiká* (the slangy *lastiká* or slightly vulgar *kapótes* are even better understood) at any pharmacy or corner *períptero* (kiosk); the pill, too, can be obtained from a *farmakío*.

Lastly, **hay fever** sufferers should be prepared for the early Greek pollen season, at its height from April to June. If you are taken by surprise, pharmacists stock tablets and creams.

Doctors and hospitals

For **serious medical attention**, phone ☎166 – you'll find English-speaking doctors in any of the bigger towns or resorts; the tourist police or your consulate on Rhodes should be able to come up with some names if you have any difficulty.

In **emergencies** – for cuts, broken bones, etc – treatment is given free in **state hospitals**, though you will only get the most basic level of nursing care. Greek families routinely take in food and bedding for relatives, so as a tourist you'll be at a severe disadvantage. Somewhat better are the ordinary state-run **out-patient clinics** (*yatría*) attached to most public hospitals and also found in rural locales; these operate on a first-come, first-served basis, so go early – hours are usually 8am to noon.

Don't forget to obtain **receipts** for the cost of all drugs and medical treatment; without them you won't be able to claim back the money on your travel insurance.

Costs, money and banks

The cost of living in Greece has spiralled during the years of EU membership: the days of renting an island house for a pittance are gone forever, and food prices at corner shops now differ little from those of other member countries. However, outside the established resorts, travel between and around the islands remains reasonably priced, with the cost of restaurant meals, short-term accommodation and public transport still cheaper than anywhere in northern or western Europe except Portugal.

Prices depend on where and when you go. The larger tourist resorts and trendier islands (like

Rhodes, Kós, Sími and Pátmos) are more expensive, and costs everywhere increase sharply in July, August and at Easter. **Students** with an *International Student Identity Card* (*ISIC*) can get free – or discounted – admission fees at many archeological sites and museums, though these, and other occasional discounts, are sometimes limited to EU students.

Some basic costs

On most islands a **daily budget** of £18–22/US$27–33 will get you basic accommodation, breakfast, picnic lunch and a simple evening meal, if you're one of a couple. Camping would cut costs marginally. On £25–30/$38–45 a day you could be living quite well, plus treating yourself and a companion to motorbike rental.

Inter-island **ferries**, one of the main expenses, are reasonably priced, subsidized by the government in an effort to preserve island communities. A deck-class ticket for the four-hour trip from Rhodes to Kos costs about £7/US$10.50, while Sámos to Híos, another four- or five-hour journey, runs to just £6/US$9. For even less you can catch a ferry to the numerous small islands that lie closer to Rhodes, Kós and Sámos, the most likely touchdown points if you're flying in on a direct charter.

The simplest double **room** generally costs around £11–16/$16.50–24 a night, depending on the location and the plumbing arrangements. Organized **campsites** are little more than £2.50/US$3.75 per person, with similar charges per tent and perhaps 25 percent more for a camper van. With discretion you can camp for free in the more remote, rural areas.

A basic taverna **meal** with local wine can be had for around £7/US$10.50 a head. Add a better bottle of wine, seafood, or more careful cooking, and it could be up to £10/US$15 a head – but you'll rarely pay more than that except in Ródhos Town. Sharing seafood, Greek salads and dips is a good way to keep costs down in the better restaurants, and even in the most developed of resorts, with inflated "international" menus, you'll often be able to find a more earthy but decent taverna where the locals eat.

Much has been made in some publications of the supposed **duty-free** status of the Dodecanese, making those islands attractive for the purchase of luxury goods and alcohol. Alas, this quirk became a casualty of EU convergence in 1993, its only legacy a slightly lower local rate of VAT than the rest of Greece – which is normally cancelled out by simply raising the basic price of items.

Currency

Greek currency is the **drachma** (*dhrahmí*), and the exchange rate is currently around 370dr to the pound sterling, 240dr to the US dollar. The most common **notes** in circulation are those of 100, 500, 1000, 5000 and 10,000 drachmae (*dhrahmés*), while coins come in denominations of 5, 10, 20, 50 and 100dr; you might come across 1-drachma and 2-drachma coins and 50-drachma bills too, though they're rarely used these days. Shopkeepers rarely bother with differences of less than 10dr.

Banks and exchange

Greek **banks** are normally open Monday–Thursday 8.30am–2pm, Friday 8.30am–1.30pm. Certain branches in larger island towns or tourist centres are open extra hours in the evenings and on Saturday mornings for **exchanging money**. Outside these times, the larger hotels and travel agencies can often provide this service – though with hefty commissions. Always take your passport with you as proof of identity, and be prepared for at least one long line; sometimes you have to line up once to have the transaction approved, and again to pick up the cash.

The safest way to carry money is in **travellers' cheques**. These can be obtained from banks (even if you don't have an account) or from offices of *Thomas Cook* and *American Express*; you'll pay a commission of between one and two percent. You can cash the cheques at most banks and post offices, and (often at poorer rates) at quite a number of hotels, agencies and tourist shops. Each transaction in Greece will incur a **commission** charge of 400–800dr, so you won't want to change too many small amounts.

Small-denomination **foreign bank notes** are also extremely useful, and relatively unlikely to be stolen in Greece (see "Police and Trouble", below). Since the freeing up of all remaining currency controls for Greek residents in early 1994, a number of authorized brokers for exchanging foreign cash have emerged in Athens and major tourist centres. Choose those that charge a flat percentage commission (usually one percent) rather than a high minimum when you're changing small amounts.

Most British banks can issue current account holders with a **Eurocheque** card and cheque-book; these are accepted in some shops, and, if you know your PIN number, they can also be used for withdrawing drachmae from cash machines or Greek banks. An annual card fee is payable for this service, plus a two percent processing charge on the debit facility subject to a minimum of about £1.75, but there's no on-the-spot commission levied on straightforward transactions. The current limit is 45,000dr per cheque, and the bank or merchant does not need to know the prevailing exchange rate – useful if bank computers have gone down.

Exchanging money at the **post office** has considerable advantages in Greece. Those small islands that have no bank – Lipsí, Kássos, Kastellórizo for example – almost all have a post office, giving you access to exchange almost anywhere you go. In addition, commissions levied for exchanging cheques or cash tend, at a flat rate of about 300dr per transaction, to be much lower than at banks or travel agencies. If you have a UK-based *Girobank* account, you can also use your cheque book to get money at remote post offices.

Finally, there is no need to purchase drachmes **before arrival** unless you're coming in at some ungodly hour at one of the remoter land or sea frontier posts, or on a Sunday. Airport arrival lounges will always have an exchange booth open for passengers on incoming international flights.

Credit cards and ATMs

Major **credit cards** are not usually accepted by cheaper tavernas or hotels, but are useful – indeed almost essential – for renting cars, for example. If you run short of money, you can get a **cash advance** on a credit card, but be warned that the minimum amount is 15,000dr. The *Emborikí Trápeza* (*Commercial Bank*) handles *Visa*, and the *Ethnikí Trápeza* (*National Bank*) services *Access/Mastercard* customers. However, there is usually a two percent credit-card charge, often unfavourable rates and always interminable delays while transaction approval is sought by telex.

It is far simpler to use the growing network of Greek **cashpoint machines (ATMs)** that are now found in most towns of any size, though not yet on any of the smaller islands apart from Pátmos. The most useful and well distributed are those of the *National Bank/Ethnikí Trápeza*, which take *Cirrus* and *Mastercard/Access* cards, and those of the *Commercial Bank/Emborikí Trápeza*, which handles *Plus System* and *Visa* cards; *Visa* is also compatible with ATMs at the *Trápeza Písteos/Credit Bank* and the *Ionian Bank/Ioniki Trapeza*.

Emergency cash

All told, learning and using the **PIN** numbers for any debit or credit cards you have will be the quickest and least expensive way of securing moderate amounts of emergency funds from abroad. In an emergency, however, you can arrange to have **money sent** from home to a bank in Greece. Receiving funds via telex takes a minimum of three days and often up to six days, so be prepared for delays. **From the UK**, a bank charge of three percent, or minimum £17, maximum £35, is levied. Bank drafts can also be sent, with higher commission rates. You can retrieve the amount in foreign currency, or even as travellers' cheques, but heavy commissions apply.

From the USA and Canada, funds can be sent via *Western Union* (☎1-800/325-6000) or *American Express MoneyGram* (☎1-800/543-4080). Both companies' fees depend on the destination and amount being transferred, but as an example, wiring $1000 to Europe will cost around $75. The funds should be available for collection at *Amex*'s or *Western Union*'s local office within minutes of being sent.

Currency regulations

Since 1994, Greek **currency restrictions** no longer apply to Greek nationals and other EU member citizens, and the drachmae is freely convertible. Arcane rules may still apply to arrivals from North America, Australia or non-EU nations, but you would have to be extremely unlucky to run foul of them.

If you have any reason to believe that you'll be acquiring large quantities of drachmae – from work or sale of goods (the latter illegal, incidentally) – declare everything on arrival, then request (and save) pink, personalized receipts for all **exchange transactions**. Otherwise you may find that you can only re-exchange a limited sum of drachmae on departure; even at the best of times many banks stock a limited range of foreign notes, though you can usually strike lucky at airport exchange booths. These pink receipts are also essential for obtaining a non-employment resident visa (see p.17).

Information and maps

The National Tourist Organisation of Greece (Ellinikós Organismós Tourismoú, or EOT; GNTO abroad) maintains offices in most European capitals, and major cities in Australia and North America (see box below for details). It publishes an impressive array of free, glossy, regional pamphlets that are good for getting an idea of where you want to go, even if the actual text should sometimes be taken with an pinch of salt. Also available from the EOT are a reasonable fold-out map of the country and a large number of brochures on special interests and festivals.

Greek national tourist offices abroad

Australia 51 Pitt St, Sydney, NSW 2000 ☎02/9241 1663

Britain 4 Conduit St, London W1R 0DJ ☎0171/734 5997

Canada 1300 Bay St, Upper Level, Toronto, ON M5R 3K8 (☎416/968-2220); 1233 rue de la Montagne, H3G 1Z2, Montréal, Quebec ☎514/871-1535

Denmark Copenhagen Vester Farimagsgade 1,2 DK 1606-Kobenhavn V ☎325-332

Netherlands Leidsestraat 13, NS 1017 Amsterdam ☎20/254-212

Norway Ovre Stottsgate 15B, 0157 Oslo 1 ☎2/426-501

Sweden Grev Turigatan 2, PO Box 5298, 10246 Stockholm ☎8/679 6480

USA 645 Fifth Ave, New York, NY 10022 ☎212/421-5777; 168 North Michigan Ave, Chicago, IL ☎312/782-1084; 611 West 6th St, Suite #2198 Los Angeles, CA ☎213/626-6696

NB If your home country isn't listed here, apply to the embassy. Note that there are no Greek tourist offices in Ireland or New Zealand.

Tourist offices

In the Dodecanese and East Aegean you'll find offical **EOT offices** only in Ródhos Town and Mitilíni Town; elsewhere, specifically on Kós, Sámos, Híos, Pátmos, Kálimnos, Mólivos and again Ródhos Town, **municipal tourist offices** can be as good or better. Staff at either breed of office are happy to provide advice and photocopied sheets on ferry and bus departures, the opening hours for museums and sites, plus occasionally assistance with **accommodation**.

Maps

Maps are an endless source of confusion and sometimes outright disinformation in Greece. Each cartographic company seems to have its own peculiar system of transcribing Greek letters into English – and these, as often as not, do not match the semi-official transliterations on the road signs.

The most reliable **general map** of the Dodecanese and East Aegean is the *GeoCenter* map *"Greek Islands/Aegean Sea"*, which covers all points described in this book at a scale of 1:300,000. It's not perfect, and like all double-sided maps can be cumbersome to use; the single-sided *Freytag-Berndt* (1:650,000, with index booklet) is a possible alternative, while *Michelin #980* (scale 1:700,000) ranks a distant third despite recent revisions. All of these are widely available in Britain and North America, less easily in Greece (see box opposite). *Freytag-Berndt* also publishes a series of more detailed **regional island maps**, including *"Kos – Samos – Ikaria"* (1:150,000), *"Rhodos"* (1:100,000) and

Map outlets

AUSTRALIA

The Map Shop, 16a Peel St , Adelaide ☎08/8231 2033

Bowyangs, 372 Little Burke St, Melbourne ☎03/9670 4383

Perth Map Centre, 891 Hay St, Perth ☎09/322 5733

Travel Bookshop, 20 Bridge St, Sydney ☎02/9241 3554

CANADA

Open Air Books and Maps, 25 Toronto St, Toronto, ON M5R 2C1 ☎416/363-0719

Ulysses Travel Bookshop, 4176 St-Denis, Montréal ☎514/289-0993

World Wide Books and Maps, 1247 Granville St, Vancouver, BC V6Z 1E4 ☎604/687-3320

IRELAND

Easons Bookshop, 40 O'Connell St, Dublin 1 ☎01/873 3811

Fred Hanna's Bookshop, 27–29 Nassau St, Dublin 2 ☎01/677 1255

Hodges Figgis Bookshop, 56–58 Dawson St, Dublin 2 ☎01/677 4754

Waterstone's, Queens Building, 8 Royal Ave, Belfast BT1 1DA ☎01232/247355

NEW ZEALAND

Specialty Maps, 58 Albert St, Aukland ☎09/307 2217

UK

Daunt Books, 83 Marylebone High St, London W1 ☎0171/224 2295

National Map Centre, 22–24 Caxton St, SW1 ☎0171/222 4945

Stanfords, 12–14 Long Acre, London WC2 ☎0171/836 1321; 52 Grosvenor Gardens, London SW1W 0AG; 156 Regent St, London W1R 5TA. Maps available by mail or phone order.

The Travel Bookshop, 13–15 Blenheim Crescent, London W11 2EE ☎0171/229 5260

The Travellers Bookshop, 25 Cecil Court, WC2 ☎0171/836 9132

John Smith and Sons, 57–61 St Vincent St, Glasgow G2 5TB ☎0141/221 7472

USA

The Complete Traveler Bookstore, 199 Madison Ave, New York, NY 10016 ☎212/685 -9007; 3207 Fillmore St, San Francisco, CA 92123 ☎415/923-1511

Forsyth Travel Library, 9154 W 57th St, Shawnee Mission, KS 66201 ☎1-800/367-7984

Map Link Inc, 25 E Mason St, Santa Barbara, CA 93101 ☎805/965-4402

Phileas Fogg's Books & Maps, #87 Stanford Shopping Center, Palo Alto, CA 94304 ☎1-800/233-FOGG in California; ☎1-800/533-FOGG elsewhere in the US

Rand McNally, 444 N Michigan Ave, Chicago, IL 60611 ☎312/321-1751; 150 E 52nd St, New York, NY 10022 ☎212/758-7488; 595 Market St, San Francisco, CA 94105 ☎415/777-3131; 1201 Connecticut Ave NW, Washington, DC 20003 ☎202/223-6751. For maps by mail order, call ☎1-800/333-0136 (ext 2111)

Sierra Club Bookstore, 730 Polk St, San Francisco, CA 94109 ☎415/923-5500

Travel Books & Language Center, 4931 Cordell Ave, Bethesda, MD 20814 ☎1-800/220-2665

Traveler's Bookstore, 22 W 52nd St, New York, NY 10019 ☎212/664-0995

"*Hios – Lesvos – Lemnos*" (1:150,000); these are best bought overseas from specialist outlets, though *Efstathiadis* rejackets and sells them at roughly the same price in Athens.

Maps of **individual islands** are more easily available on the spot, and while some are wildly inaccurate or obsolete, with strange hieroglyphic symbols, others are reliable and up to date; we've indicated in the guide where particular maps are worth buying or not. *Toubi*'s series of maps, often available overseas, are the most comprehensive and cover most islands of any size, but they're also the the poorest quality and worth avoiding if you have a choice.

Hiking/topographical maps

Hiking/topographical maps of the East Aegean and Dodecanese islands, including Rhodes, are virtually impossible to obtain in Greece. The Greek government's equivalent of Ordnance Survey or USGS topographic maps are unavailable indefinitely for "security reasons" due to continuing tension with Turkey and other Balkan neighbours. Should the rules change, you can try your luck at the Army Geographical Service (*Yeografikí Ipiresía Stratoú*) in Athens at Evelpídhon 4, north of Aréos Park (Mon–Wed & Fri 8am–noon).

At present, the best hiking maps are those prepared before and during World War II by foreign powers. For the east Aegean islands you want those prepared by the British War Office at a scale of 1:50,000, with twenty- or forty-metre contour intervals; while they don't show paths, they depict roads more accurately than many contemporary Greek tourist maps. For Rhodes and the Dodecanese, under Italian occupation from 1913 to 1943, the map set published by the *Instituto Geografico Militare* in Florence from 1927 onwards is your best choice. Sheets for each island have been published at a 1:25,000 scale, with ten-metre contour intervals. Despite their antiquarian appearance, they are eminently reliable for natural features, village positions and trails. The main problem lies in the Italianization of all Greek place names, eg Terrarossa for Kokinokhóma.

These two series are not commercially available overseas, let alone in Greece, and you'll have to make do with photocopies of originals kept by certain large institutions. In the US or Canada, try the map room of a major university library; most will have at least the Italian set, and charge nothing or a nominal fee for copying. In the UK, the only source of both the British and Italian cartography is the map library of the Royal Geographical Society, Kensington Gore, London SW7 2AR (☎0171/589 5466). Recently, however, restrictions on public access have been threatened owing to funding crises, so you should phone ahead to check. Even if you are allowed to make copies (approx. £2 per large sheet), you first have to petition the British Military Survey authorities by letter or fax for permission; staff at the *RGS* library will furnish you with current contact addresses and phone numbers.

Getting around

Island-hopping is one of the best features of a holiday in the Dodecanese or East Aegean, as much a pursuit in itself as a means of transport. The local ferry and hydrofoil network is extensive, and few of the 27 inhabited isles featured in this book are difficult to reach. Inter-island flights are expensive, costing up to four times as much as a deck-class ferry ticket and twice as much as a first-class cabin, but useful if you need to save time. Especially in the north Dodecanese, planes are being replaced by more competitively priced hydrofoils.

For getting around the islands themselves, there are basic bus services, which most tourists choose to supplement at some stage with moped, motorbike or car rental.

Sea transport

There are three types of boats carrying passengers around the islands: **regular car ferries** (which connect the Dodecanese and East Aegean with each other, the mainland, the Cyclades and Crete), **hydrofoils** (confined to relatively sheltered waters between neighbouring islands and the lee of Asia Minor), and local **kaïkia** (small passenger-only boats which in season undertake short hops and excursions). Costs are very reasonable on the longer journeys, though proportionately more expensive for shorter, inter-island connections.

We've detailed **ferry connections** on the general and chapter maps as well as in the "Travel Details" at the end of each island account. Be warned, however, that schedules are notoriously erratic, and that the departure details we have given are essentially for the May-to-September period – always check timings on the spot. **Out-of-season** services are severely reduced, with many islands served only once or twice a week. However, in spring or autumn those ferries that do operate are often compelled by the transport ministry to call at extra islands, making possible some interesting connections.

The most reliable, up-to-date information is available from the local **port police** (*limenarhío*), who can be found on or near the harbour at every substantial island; smaller places may have only a *limenikós stathmós* (marine post), no more than a single room with a VHF radio. Their officers rarely speak much English, but they keep complete schedules posted and are the final arbiters of whether or not a ship will sail in stormy weather. *Apagorevtikó*, or obligatory grounding of all seaborne traffic, applies for conditions in excess of Force 7 on the Beaufort scale.

Another excellent resource is *The Thomas Cook Guide to Greek Island Hopping*, which features a comprehensive overview of ferry services. Although updated yearly, this is again no substitute for on-the-spot intelligence.

Regular Ferries

On most **ferry** routes, your only consideration will be getting a boat that leaves on the day, and for the island, that you want. However, when sailing from Rhodes to the other Dodecanese islands, you should have a choice of two, possibly three, sailings, and may want to bear in mind a few of the factors below.

Most importantly, remember that **routes** taken and the speed of the boats can vary considerably. The journey from Rhodes to Pátmos, for instance, can take anything from eight to ten and a half hours. Before buying a ticket it's a good idea to establish how many stops there'll be before your island, and the estimated time of arrival. Many agents act only for one specific boat (they'll blithely tell you that theirs is the only available service), so you may have to ask around to uncover alternatives. Especially in high season, early arrival is critical in getting what may be a very limited stock of accommodation.

The boats themselves have improved somewhat recently, with a fair number of the older tubs consigned to the scrap heap or dumped overseas – just about the only ferry you might want to avoid if you have the choice is the odoriferous *Ayios Rafael*, run by *NEL* in the East Aegean. You will more often than not be surprised to encounter a former English Channel or Scandinavian fjord ferry, rechristened and enjoying a new lease of life in the Aegean.

Buying **ferry tickets** in advance will tie you down to a particular vessel at a particular time –

Mainline ferry companies: principal routes

Agapitos Lines (home port: Pireás)
Sámos–Foúrni–Ikaría (Évdhilos)–Páros–Pireás

DANE (home port: Ródhos Town)
Rhodes–Kós–Kálimnos–Léros–Pátmos–Pireás
Rhodes–Kós–Pátmos–Thessaloníki

G&A Ferries (home port: Pireás)
Sámos–Foúrni–Ikaría–Náxos–Páros–Míkonos–Síros–Pireás
Rhodes–Kós–Kálimnos–Léros–Lipsí–Pátmos–Náxos–Síros–Pireás
Rhodes–Kárpathos–Kássos–Crete–central Cyclades–Pireás
Rhodes–Tílos–Níssiros–Kós–Astipálea–Páros–Síros–Pireás
Rhodes–Kastellórizo

Miniotis Lines (home port: Híos)
Hios–Sámos–Ikaría–Foúrni–Pátmos
Hios–Sámos–Agathoníssi–Lipsí–Pátmos
Hios–Psará

NEL (home port: Mitilíni)
Mitilini–Límnos–Kavála
Mitilini–Híos–Pireás
Mitilini–Híos–Sámos–Pátmos
Kavála–Límnos–Áyios Efstrátios–Sígri–Rafína

Nissos Kalymnos (home port: Kálimnos)
Kálimnos–Kós–Níssiros–Tílos–Sími–Rhodes–Kastellórizo
Kálimnos–Léros–Lipsí–Pátmos–Arkí–Agathoníssi–Sámos
Kálimnos–Astipálea

Nomicos Lines (home port: Kavála)
Kími (Évvia)–Límnos–Kavála
Rafína (Attica)–Skíros–Áyios Efstrátios–Límnos–Kavála

Ventouris Lines (home port: Pireás)
Rhodes–Hálki–Kárpathos–Kássos–Crete–west Cyclades–Pireás

NB Reverse itineraries are valid in all cases. Contact addresses and phone numbers for ferry lines are given in the island accounts and the "Athens: transport information" box on p.13.

and innumerable factors can make you regret that. Most obviously there's bad weather, which can play havoc with the schedules (although the shipping company should refund your ticket for cancelled departures). However, it might be a wise precaution around March 23–25, the weeks before and after Easter, and in mid-August, or if you need to reserve a cabin berth or space for a car. Otherwise, you can always buy regular ferry tickets on board with no penalty, despite what travel agents may tell you. **Fares** for each route are currently set by the transport ministry and should not differ between ships or agencies, though curiously, tickets for journeys towards Athens are marginally more expensive than those in the opposite direction.

The cheapest class of ticket, which you'll probably automatically be sold, is **deck class**, variously called *tríti* or *gámma* (third or C-class). Class consciousness has increased of late, so deck-class passengers will find themselves firmly locked out of second-class facilities to prevent them from crashing on the plush sofas. On the shorter, summer journeys the deck is the best place to be in any case, and your first priority on board will be to stake out some space. However, the newer boats, with their glaring overhead lights and moulded-plastic seats, seem expressly designed to frustrate sleeping on deck, so for long overnight trips it's worth paying the extra drachmae for a **cabin bunk**. First-class cabin facilities usually cost as much as a flight, and often the only difference between first and second is a bathroom in the cabin. Most cabins, incidentally, are overheated or overchilled, and pretty airless; ask for an *exoterikí* (outer) cabin if you want a porthole (though these are always bolted shut).

Motorbikes and **cars** get issued extra tickets, in the latter case up to four times the passenger fare. Technically, written permission is required to take rental motorbikes and cars on ferries, though in practice few people bother – in any case, it's almost always cheaper to rent another vehicle at your destination.

Most ferries sell a limited range of **food on board**, though it tends to be overpriced and mediocre. Honourable exceptions are the meals served on longer routes or overnight sailings. On the short, daytime hops between the various islands of the Dodecanese and East Aegean, it's a good idea to stock up with your own provisions.

Hydrofoils

Hydrofoils – commonly known as *dhelfínia* (dolphins) – are roughly twice as fast (and at least twice as expensive) as ordinary ferries. However, they are a useful alternative if you are pushed for time, and their network seems to be growing each year. The main drawback is that they were originally designed for cruising on placid Russian or Polish rivers, and are quite literally out of their depth on the open sea; those prone to seasickness should beware. Most services don't operate – or are heavily reduced – out of season, and are prone to arbitrary cancellation in spring or autumn if not enough passengers turn up. In recent years, though, time-keeping and mechanical reliability have improved somewhat.

Contrary to popular belief, hydrofoils can actually carry one or two small **mopeds** or scooters strapped to the wings. There may be a certain amount of grumbling from the crew, but they should oblige – at your own risk. It's only worth doing this, however, if you're heading for Foúrni,

Hydrofoil companies: principal routes

Gianmar Lines (home ports: Híos or Mitilíni)

Mitilíni–Alexandhroúpoli–Kavála

Mitilíni–Híos–Sámos–Ikaría–Foúrni–Pátmos

Mitilíni–Límnos–Kavála

Ilio Lines (home ports: Vathí or Kálimnos)

Vathí–Pithagório–Pátmos–Léros–Kós–Kálimnos

Vathí–Pithagório–Agathoníssi–Lipsí–Pátmos, etc

Vathí–Pithagório–Foúrni–Ikaría–Pátmos, etc

Mamidhakis/Dodecanese Hydrofoils (home ports: Rhodes, Kós or Kálimnos)

Rhodes–Kós–Kálimnos–Astipálea

Rhodes–Kós–Níssiros–Kós–Sími–Rhodes

Rhodes–Tílos–Níssiros–Kós

Kós–Sími–Rhodes–Kós

Kálimnos–Kós–Léros–Pátmos–(Foúrni)–Pithagório

Kálimnos–Kós–Léros–(Lipsí)–Pátmos–(Agathoníssi)–Pithagório

NB Reverse itineraries apply in all cases. Ports of call in brackets are supplements to the basic north Dodecanese route, served one or two days weekly. Addresses and contact numbers are given in the island accounts.

Agathoníssi or Sími, which presently have no bike-rental facilities.

Because of their need to hug sheltering landmasses, hydrofoils often sail well inside **Turkish territorial waters**, hooting at fishing boats flying the star and crescent. Despite poor relations between the two countries, this is specifically allowed, and almost unavoidable anyway on the northeast Aegean runs between Lésvos and Alexandhroúpoli on the mainland.

When considering the specimen **routes** in the box, remember that while some of the *Ilio Lines* and *Mamidhakis/Dodecanese Hydrofoils* routes appear to be nearly identical, the former tend to sail south from Pithagório on Sámos in the morning, and north from Kós or Kálimnos in the afternoon, while the latter company does just the opposite. We have excluded those companies that only offer charter services as opposed to scheduled services approved by the Ministry of Transport.

Kaïkia and small ferries

In season, **kaïkia** (caiques) and small ferries sail between adjacent islands and to a few of the more obscure ones. These small boats can be extremely useful and often very pleasant, but if they're classified as tourist agency charters, and not passenger lines controlled by the transport ministry, they tend to be quite expensive, with some pressure to buy return fares.

The more regular *kaïkia* **links** are summarized in the "Travel Details" section following each island account, though departures depend on the whims of local boat-owners or fishermen. The only firm information is to be had on the quayside. Incidentally, chartering fishing boats in emergencies, the semi-mythical fallback of the stranded traveller, is of dubious legality and prohibitively expensive – in excess of 25,000dr for the one-hour trip between Níssiros and Kardhámena (Kós), for example.

Kaïkia and small ferries, despite appearances, have a good safety record; indeed it's the larger, overloaded car ferries that have in the past run into trouble.

Flights

Olympic Airways and its subsidiary *Olympic Aviation* operate most of the **domestic flights** between the Greek mainland and the Dodecanese and East Aegean islands, as well as a growing network of radial links between these islands. Thus far the only private airline to successfully challenge this state-run carrier is *Air Greece*, with service confined to Rhodes at time of writing; prices undercut *Olympic* by a fair margin, though frequencies tend to be sparse. *Olympic* **schedules** can be picked up at their offices abroad (see "Getting There" sections) or through their branch offices and representatives in Greece, which are maintained in almost every town or island of any size; Greek-only small booklets, which include prices for domestic routes, appear three times yearly (March, June & Oct) while English-language books geared more for an international readership are published twice yearly (March & Oct).

Fares for flights to and between the islands work out around three to four times the cost of a ferry journey, but on certain inter-island hauls poorly served by boat (Rhodes–Kastellórizo or Kárpathos–Kássos, for example), you might justify this by the time you've saved.

Island flights are often full in peak season; if they're an essential part of your plans, it is worth trying to make a **reservation** at least a week in advance. Domestic air tickets are non-refundable, but you can change your flight, space permitting, without penalty up to a few hours before your original departure.

Incidentally, the only surviving *Olympic*-run **shuttle buses** between the main town and the airport are on Kós and Límnos; others have long since been axed as a cost-cutting exercise. In two instances (Híos, Rhodes), municipally run services have picked up the slack, but otherwise you're at the mercy of the taxi drivers who congregate outside the arrivals gate.

Like ferries, flights are subject to **cancellation** in bad weather, since many services are on small, 30- or 68-seat prop planes, or even tinier Dornier 18-seaters, none of which will fly in strong winds or after dark. Despite these uncertainties, a flight on a Dornier puddle-jumper is a highly recommended experience. Virtually every seat has a view, and you fly low enough to pick out every island feature – you might even select beaches in advance.

Size restrictions also mean that the 15-kilo **baggage weight limit** is fairly strictly enforced; if, however, you've just arrived from overseas or purchased your ticket outside Greece, you are allowed the 23-kilo standard international limit. All services operated on the domestic network are non-smoking.

Transport on the islands

Most islands have some kind of **bus service**, even if it only connects the port with the main town or village, though on larger islands there is usually an efficient and reliable network. For visitors, the main drawback is that buses are almost always geared to local patterns and, from the remotest villages at least, often leave punishingly early to shuttle people to school or work. Luckily, it is almost always possible to **rent a vehicle**, be it a moped, bike or, on larger islands, a car or jeep. Even for just one day, this will enable you to take the measure of a medium-sized island, and work out where you want to base yourself.

Buses

Buses on most islands are cream-and-turquoise-green *Mercedes* coaches, grouped in a syndicate of companies known as *KTEL*. Services on the major routes – both on the mainland and islands – are highly efficient. Except for Mitilíni Town, which has a dedicated, off-street terminal, central bus stations – even on Rhodes – are little more than a marked (or unmarked) stop at a major intersection or *platía*. As a rule, scheduled departures are amazingly prompt, so be there in plenty of time. Seating is generally first-come, first-served, with some standing allowed, and **tickets** are usually dispensed on the spot by a *ispráktoros* or conductor.

Car rental

Car rental in the Dodecanese and East Aegean costs a minimum of £160/US$240 a week in high season for the smallest, Group-A vehicle, including unlimited mileage, tax and insurance. Brochures, particularly on Rhodes, threaten alarming rates of £220/US$330 for the same period, but except in mid-August, no company expects to fetch that price for a car; even on Rhodes they will settle for £190/US$285 or so. Outside peak season, at the smaller local outfits on less touristed islands, you can often get terms of about £25/$37 per day, all inclusive, with better rates for a rental of three days or more. **Shopping around** agencies in the larger resorts can yield a variation in quotes of up to 15 percent for the same conditions over a four-to-seven-period; the most negotiable variable is whether or not kilometres in excess of 100 per day (a common hidden catch) are free. Open **jeeps**, an increasingly popular extravagance, begin at about £30/$US45 per day, rising to as much as £45/US$68 at busy times and places.

Note that the initial rental prices in Greece almost never include tax, collision damage waiver (CDW) and personal **insurance**. CDW in particular is absolutely vital, as the coverage included by law in the basic rental fee is generally inadequate, so check the fine print on your contract. Be careful of the hammering that cars get on minor roads; tyres, windshield and the underside of the vehicle are almost always excluded from even supplementary insurance policies. All agencies will want either a credit card or a large cash **deposit** up front; minimum age requirements vary from 21 to 25. In theory an **International Driving Licence** is also needed, but in practice European, Australasian and North American ones are honoured.

In peak season only you may get a better price (and more importantly, better vehicle condition) by booking through one of the **international companies** that deal with local firms, rather than arranging the rental once you're in Greece; this

Car rental agencies

UK

Avis ☎ 0181/848 8733; stations on Kós, Lésvos, Sámos, Rhodes, Híos

Budget ☎ 0800/181 181; stations on Híos, Kós, Lésvos, Sámos, Rhodes

Europcar/InterRent ☎ 01345/222 525; stations on Rhodes, Kós, Lésvos, Híos, Sámos

Hertz ☎ 0181/679 1799; stations on Rhodes, Kós, Sámos

Holiday Autos ☎ 0171/491 1111; station on Rhodes only

NORTH AMERICA

Avis ☎ 1-800/331-1084; stations on Kós, Lésvos, Sámos, Rhodes, Híos

Budget ☎ 1-800/527-0700; stations on Hios, Kós, Lésvos, Samos, Rhodes

Dollar ☎ 1-800/421-6868; stations on Rhodes, Kós, Lésvos, Híos, Samos

Euro-Dollar ☎ 1-800/800-6000; stations on Rhodes, Sámos, Lésvos, Kós

Hertz ☎ 1-800/654-3001; (Canada) ☎ 1-800/263-0600; stations on Rhodes, Kós, Sámos

Holiday Autos ☎ 1-800/422-7737; station on Rhodes only

Thrifty ☎ 1-800/367-2277; stations on Rhodes, Kós, Pátmos, Lésvos, Sámos, Híos

may also be the only way to get hold of a car at such times. One of the most competitive companies, which can arrange for vehicles to be picked up at Rhodes airport, is *Holiday Autos* (see box for phone number). In the Dodecanese and East Aegean, *Payless, European, Thrifty, Eurodollar* and *Just* are reliable companies with branches in many towns; all are considerably cheaper than the biggest international operators *Budget, InterRent/Dollar, Hertz* and *Avis*. Specific local recommendations are given in the guide.

In terms of **models**, the more competitive companies tend to offer the Subaru M80 or Subaru Vivio and the Suzuki Alto 800 as A-Group cars, and Opel Corsa 1200 or Nissan Cherry in the B-Group. The Suzuki Alto 600, Fiat Panda 750 and Seat Marbella should be avoided at all costs. More acceptable are the Fiat Cinquecento as an A-Group choice or the Fiat Uno in the B-Group. The standard four-wheel-drive options are Suzuki jeeps – great for bashing down rutted tracks to remote beaches.

Driving in greece

Greece has the highest **accident rate** in Europe after Portugal, and many of the roads can be quite perilous: asphalt can turn into a one-lane surface or a dirt track without warning on secondary routes, and you're heavily dependant on magnifying mirrors at blind intersections in congested villages. Uphill drivers insist on their right of way, as do those first to approach a one-lane bridge – **flashed headlights** mean the opposite to what they do in the UK or North America, here signifying that the driver is coming through or overtaking. Even on the so-called motorways of Rhodes and Kós, there is no proper far-right lane for slower traffic, which is expected to straddle the solid white line at the verge and allow rapid traffic to pass.

Wearing a **seatbelt** is compulsory, and children under the age of 10 are not allowed to sit in the front seats. It's illegal to drive away from any kind of accident, and you can be held at a police station for up to 24 hours. If this happens, you have the right to ring your consulate immediately to summon a lawyer; don't make a statement to anyone who doesn't speak, and write, very good English.

Tourists with proof of membership of their home-motoring organization are given free **road assistance** from *ELPA*, the Greek equivalent, which runs breakdown services on several of the larger islands; in an emergency ring their road assistance service on ☎104. Many car rental companies have an agreement with *ELPA*'s equally widespread competitors *Hellas Service* and *Express Service*, but they're prohibitively expensive to summon on your own – over 25,000 drachmae to enrol as an "instant member".

Buying fuel

Fuel currently costs around 210dr a litre for unleaded (*amólivdhi*), 215dr for super; so-called "regular" is on its way out, and even pricier when available. Beware that most stations in island towns and rural areas close at 7pm sharp. Nearly as many are shut all weekend, and though there will always be at least one pump per district open, it's not always apparent which that is. This is not so much of a problem on the major highways in Rhodes and Kós, but it's a factor everywhere else – so always fill up, or insist on a full tank, at the outset. Filling stations run by international companies (*BP, Mobil* and *Shell*) usually take **credit cards**; Greek chains like *EKO, Mamidhakis* and *Elinoil* don't.

Incidentally, the smallest grade of motor **scooters** (*Vespa, Piaggio, Suzuki*) consume "mix", a red- or green-tinted fuel dispensed from a transparent cylindrical device. This contains a minimum of three percent two-stroke oil by volume; if this mix is unavailable, you brew it up yourself by adding to "super" grade fuel the necessary amount of separately bottled two-stroke oil (*ládhi dhío trohón* in Greek). It's wise to err on the side of excess (say five percent by volume), otherwise you risk the engine seizing up.

Motorbikes, mopeds – and safety

The cult of the **motorcycle** is highly developed in the Greek islands, presided over by a jealous deity apparently requiring regular human sacrifice. **Accidents** among both foreign and local motorbikers are common, with fatalities running into two figures annually on the largest islands. Some package companies have taken to warning clients in print against renting motorbikes or mopeds, but with a bit of caution and common sense – plus an eye to increasingly enforced traffic regulations – riding a bike on holiday should be a lot less hazardous than, say, riding in central London or New York.

Many tourists come to grief on rutted dirt tracks or astride mechanically dodgy machines. In many cases accidents are due to attempts to cut corners, in all senses, by riding two to an underpowered scooter. Don't be tempted by this apparent economy – and bear in mind, too, that you're likely to be charged an exorbitant sum for any repairs if you do have a wipe-out.

One precaution is to wear a **crash helmet** (*kránio*); many rental outfits will offer you one, and may make you sign a waiver of liability if you refuse it. Helmet-wearing is in fact required by law, and though very few people comply at present, it's likely to be more strictly enforced in the future. Above all, make sure your travel **insurance policy** covers motorcycle accidents. Reputable establishments require a full **motorcycle driving licence** for any machine over 75cc, and you will usually be required to leave a passport as security.

Mopeds and small motor scooters, known in Greek as *papákia* (little ducks) after their characteristic noise, are good transport for all but the hilliest islands. They're available for rent in most main towns or ports, and at the larger resorts, for 3000dr a day (mopeds), or 3500–4000dr (scooters). Rates can be bargained down out of season, or if you negotiate for a longer period of rental. Before riding off, make sure you check the bike's mechanical state, since many are only cosmetically maintained. Bad brakes and worn spark plugs are the most common defects; dealers often keep the front brake far too loose, with the commendable intention of preventing you going over the handlebars. If you break down it's your responsibility to return the machine, so it's worth taking down the phone number of the rental agency in case the bike gives out and you can't get it back, or if you lose the ignition key.

As far as **models** go, the three-speed Honda 50, Suzuki Townmate and Yamaha Birdie are workhorse favourites; gears are shifted with a left-foot pedal action, and (very important) they can be push-started if the battery fails. These carry two people easily enough, though if you have a choice, the Cub series give more power at nominal extra cost. A larger *Vespa* scooter is more comfortable, but less stable. The *Suzuki Address*, though easily capable of handling an island the size of Kós, is thirsty on fuel and cannot be push-started. Smaller but surprisingly powerful Piaggio Si or Monte Carlo models can take one person only along almost any road and are automatic. Bungy cords (*khtapódi* in slang) for tying down bundles are supplied on request.

Cycling

Cycling on the Greek islands is not such hard going as you might imagine (except in midsummer), especially on one of the **mountain bikes** that are rapidly replacing boneshakers in rental outlets; prices for either are rarely more than 1000dr a day. You do, however, need nerves of steel, as roads are generally narrow, with no verges or bike lanes except on Kós, and many Greek drivers consider cyclists a lower form of life.

If you have your own mountain or touring bike, you might consider bringing it with you. Bikes travel free on most airlines, if within your 23-kilo limit, and are free on most of the ferries. You would be wise to bring any spare parts you might need, however, since the only specialist bike shops in this guide are on Sámos, Kós and Rhodes.

Hitching

Hitching carries the usual risks and dangers, especially for solo women, but overall the Greek islands are one of the safer places in which to do it. As ever, the more lightly travelled and remote the road, the greater the possibility of a lift, though increasingly there's the expectation that foreign tourists should be renting their own transport. From most island towns it's just a short walk to the main road out, where numerous trucks and vans are good bets for thumbing. Hitching on commercial vehicles is nominally illegal, so if you're offered a ride in a large van or lorry, don't be offended if you're set down just before an upcoming town and its potential police checkpoints.

Taxis

Greek **taxis** are among the cheapest in western Europe – so long as you get an honest driver who switches the meter on. Use of the meter is mandatory within city or town limits where Tariff "1" applies, while in rural areas or between midnight and 5am, Tariff "2" is in effect. On certain islands, such as Kássos, Kálimnos and Léros, set rates apply on certain set routes. Otherwise throughout Greece the meter starts at 200dr (though expect this figure to inch up in the near future); any baggage not actually on your lap is charged at 50dr apiece. Additionally, there are **surcharges** of 200dr for leaving (but not entering) an airport, and 100dr for leaving a harbour area. If you summon a taxi by phone, the meter starts running from the moment the driver begins heading towards you. For a week or so before and after Orthodox Easter, and Christmas, a *filodhórima* or gratuity is also levied.

Any or all of these extras will legitimately bump up the basic meter reading of about 1200dr for ten rural kilometres.

Accommodation

There are vast quantities of beds available for tourists in the Dodecanese and East Aegean islands, so that most of the year you can turn up pretty much anywhere and find a room – if not in a hotel, then in a private house or block of rooms (the standard island accommodation). Most of the larger islands have at least one campsite, too, which tend to be basic but inexpensive.

Only in the major resorts during July and August, the high season, are you likely to experience problems. At these times, if you don't have a room reserved in advance, you'd be wise to strike well off the main tourist trail, turning up at each new place early in the day and taking whatever is available – you may be able to exchange it for something better later on. However, reports indicate that in the wake of poor occupancy levels in recent years, many room blocks and hotels formerly monopolized by north European package operators should again be easily available to independent, walk-in travellers.

Out of season, there is a slightly different problem: most private rooms – and campsites – operate only from April to October, leaving hotels your only option. During winter you may have no choice but to stay in the main towns or ports. There will often be very little life outside these places anyway, with all the seasonal beach bars and restaurants closed. On many smaller islands, you will often find just one hotel – and perhaps one taverna – staying open year-round.

Private rooms

The most common form of island accommodation is **privately let rooms** – *dhomátia*. These are regulated and officially classified by the local tourist police, who divide them into three classes (A down to C), according to their facilities. These days the bulk of them are in new, purpose-built, low-rise buildings, but a few are still actually in people's homes, where you'll occasionally be treated to disarming hospitality.

Rooms are almost always scrupulously clean, whatever their other amenities. At their simplest, you'll get a bare, concrete room, with a hook on the back of the door and toilet facilities (cold water only) outside in the courtyard. At the fancier end of the scale, they are modern, fully furnished places with an en-suite marble bathroom and a fully equipped kitchen shared by guests. Sometimes there's a choice of rooms at various prices – owners will usually show you the most expensive first. Price and quality are not necessarily directly linked, so always ask to see the room before agreeing to take it.

Areas to **look for rooms**, along with recommendations of the best places, are included in the guide. As often as not, however, the rooms find you: owners descend on ferry or bus arrivals to fill any space they have, sometimes waving photos of the premises. In smaller places you'll often see rooms advertised, sometimes in German (*Zimmer*); the Greek signs to look out for are "ENIKIAZÓMENA DHOMÁTIA" or "ENIKIÁZONTEH DHOMÁTIA". In the more developed island resorts, where package holidaymakers predominate, *dhomátia* owners will often require you to stay for at least three days. If you can't find rooms in an island town or village, ask at the local **taverna** or *kafenío* (coffee house). Even if there are no official places, there is very often someone prepared to earn extra money by putting you up.

It has become standard practice for room proprietors to ask to keep your **passport** – ostensibly "for the tourist police", who do require customer particulars, but in reality to prevent you skipping out with an unpaid bill. Some owners may be satisfied with just taking down the details, as is done in hotels, and they'll almost always return the documents once you get to know them, or if you need them for another purpose (to change money, for example).

In **winter**, designated to begin in November and end in early April, private rooms – except in the old town of Rhodes – are closed pretty much across the board to keep the hotels in business. There's no point in traipsing about hoping to find exceptions – most room-owners obey the system very strictly. If they don't, the owners will find you themselves and, watching out for hotel rivals, guide you back to their place.

Hotels

Hotels in the larger resorts are often reserved for groups by package holiday companies, though there are often vacancies available (at disadvantageous rates) for walk-in trade. Like private rooms, **categories** for hotels are set by the tourist police. They range from "De Luxe" down to the rarely encountered "E-class", and all except the top category have to keep within set price limits. Letter ratings are supposed to correspond to facilities available, though in practice **categorization** often depends on location and other, less obvious criteria. D-class usually have attached baths, while in C-class this is mandatory, along with a bar or breakfast area. The additional presence of a pool and/or tennis court will attract a B-class rating, while A-category hotels must have a restaurant, bar and extensive common areas. De Luxe hotels are in effect self-contained holiday villages, with both they and A-class outfits usually backing a private beach.

In terms of **food**, C-class hotels are required only to provide the most rudimentary of continental breakfasts, while B-class and above will

Room prices

All establishments listed in this book have been price-graded according to the scale outlined below. The rates quoted represent the cheapest available double room in high season. Out of season, rates can drop by up to fifty percent, especially if you negotiate for a stay of three or more nights. Single rooms, where available, cost around seventy percent of the price of a double.

① up to 5000dr ③ 7000–9000dr ⑤ 13000–17000dr

② 5000–7000dr ④ 9000–13000dr ⑥ above 17000dr

£1=370dr; $1= 240dr

Rented private **rooms** on the islands usually fall into the ② or ③ categories, depending on location, facilities and season; a few in the d category are more like plush self-catering apartments. They are not generally available from late October through to the beginning of April, when only hotels tend to remain open.

Old-fashioned rooms on the remoter islets, often without private bath, tend to fall into the ① price category. Standard, en-suite rooms without cooking facilities weigh in at ②; newer, state-of-the-art rooms and self-catering studios occupy the top end of the ③ niche, along with most of the government-rated C-class hotels, the newer among these edging into ④. Most of ④ correspond fairly well to B-class hotel rates, while ⑤ tallies with A-class, and ⑥ with De Luxe class.

Some of the cheap places will also have more expensive rooms with en-suite facilities – and vice versa, with singles often tucked under stairways or in other less desirable corners of the building.

Prices in any establishment should by law be displayed on the back of the door of your room. If you feel you're being overcharged at a place that is officially registered, threaten to report it to the tourist office or police, who will generally adopt your side in such cases. Small amounts over the posted price may be legitimately explained by tax or out-of-date forms. And occasionally you may find that you have bargained so well, or arrived so far out of season, that you are actually paying less than you're supposed to.

Eco-friendly tourism

Much has been said of late about the negative **environmental impact** of mass tourism on fragile Mediterranean destinations. As a phenomenon, package travel is here to stay, but following are a few suggestions – endorsed and in some cases suggested by readers – on how to land more lightly in Greece.

Visiting during the spring or autumn **shoulder seasons** eases pressure on oversubscribed water, power and sewage networks, as well as being a good idea for several other reasons (see "When to Go", in the Introduction to this book). Forego PVC mineral-**water bottles**, which end up littering every beach and roadside, in preference for a permanent canteen/water-bottle; all ferries, hotel bars and restaurants have a tap gushing cold, potable water for serving with *oúzo*, and staff will gladly top up bottles for customers. Similarly, decline the automatic dispensing of **nylon bags** for every tiny puchase that will fit in a day pack or the palm of your hand – the wind-blown bags invariably end up on the beach or in the sea. And last but not least, when possible you should choose the locally produced orange and lemon soda sold in **recyclable glass bottles**, rather than international brands. By doing so, you will keep several people in work at island bottling plants (still operating on Lésvos, Híos, Kós and Rhodes) and prevent more aluminium cans from joining the plastic on the roadside or in the sea.

usually offer some sort of buffet breakfast including cheese, cold cuts, sausages, eggs, etc. With some outstanding exceptions, noted in the guide, lunch or supper at hotel-affiliated restaurants is bland and poor value.

Villas and long term rentals

The easiest – and usually most economical – way to arrange a **villa rental** is through one of the package holiday companies detailed on p.5 and p.10. They represent some superb places, from simple to luxury, and costs can be very reasonable, especially if shared between four or more people. Several of the companies we list will arrange **"multi-centre"** stays on two or more islands.

On the islands, a few local travel agents arrange villa rentals, though they are mostly places the overseas companies couldn't fill. **Out of season**, you can sometimes get a good deal on villa or apartment rental for a month or more by asking around locally, though in these days of EU convergence and the increasing desirability of the islands as year-round residences, "good deal" means anything under 45,000dr for a large studio (*garsoniéra*) or small one-bedroom flat.

Camping

Officially recognized **campsites** in the Dodecanese and East Aegean are restricted to Rhodes (one), Kós (one), Léros (one), Astipálea (one), Pátmos (one), Híos (one) and Lésvos (two); see the guide for full descriptions. Most places cost from 700dr a night per person, the same fee per tent, and 1200dr per camper van, but at the fanciest sites, rates for two people plus a tent can add up to the price of a basic room. Generally, you don't have to worry about leaving tents or baggage unattended at campsites; the Greeks are one of the most honest races in Europe. The main risk comes from other campers.

Freelance camping – outside authorized campsites – is such an established element of Greek travel that few people realize that it's officially illegal. Since 1977 it has actually been forbidden by a law originally enacted to harrass gypsies, and regulations are increasingly enforced. If you do camp rough, it's vital to exercise sensitivity and discretion. Police will crack down on people camping (and especially littering) around popular tourist beaches, particularly when a large community of campers develops. Off the beaten track, however, nobody is very bothered, though it is always best to ask permission locally in the village taverna or café. During high season, when everything may be full, attitudes towards freelance camping are more relaxed, even in the most touristed places. At such times the best strategy is to find a sympathetic taverna, which in exchange for regular patronage will probably be willing to guard small valuables and let you use their facilities.

Eating and drinking

Greeks spend a lot of time socializing outside their homes, and sharing a meal is one of the chief ways of doing it. The atmosphere is always relaxed and informal, with pretensions rare outside major resorts on Kos and Rhodes. Greeks are not prodigious drinkers – what tippling they do is mainly to accompany food – though in the resorts a whole range of bars, pubs and cocktail joints have sprung up principally to cater for tourists.

Breakfast, picnic fare and snacks

Greeks don't generally eat **breakfast**, so the only egg-and-bacon kind of places are in resorts where foreigners congregate; this can be fairly good value (1100–1600dr for the works), especially where there's competition. More indigenous alternatives are yogurts at a *galaktopolío* (milk bar), or cheese pies and pretzel rings from a street stall (see "Snacks", below).

Picnic fare is good, cheap and easily available at bakeries and *manávika* (fruit-and-veg stalls). **Bread** is often of minimal nutritional value and inedible within a day of purchase. It's worth paying extra at the bakery (*foúrnos*) for *olikís* (wholemeal), *sikalísio* (rye bread), *oktásporo* (eight-grain), or even *enneásporo* (nine-grain), which is most commonly baked where large numbers of Germans or Scandanavians are about. When buying **olives**, go for the fat *Kalamáta* or *Ámfissa* ones; they're more expensive, but tastier. **Fétta cheese** is ubiquitous – often, these days, imported from Holland or Denmark, though local brands are usually better and not much more expensive. The goat's milk variety can be very dry and salty, so ask for a taste before buying; if you have a fridge, leaving the cheese in water overnight will solve both problems. This sampling advice goes for other indigenous cheeses as well, the most palatable of which are the expensive gruyère-type *graviéra*. Despite membership of the EU, plus growing personal incomes and exotic tastes, Greece imports very little **garden produce** from abroad aside from bananas. Fruit especially is relatively expensive and available only by season, though in the more cosmopolitan spots it is possible to find such things as avocados (those from Crete are excellent). Reliable picnic fruits include *yiarmádhes*, a variety of peach available during August and September, and *kristália*, tiny, hard, green pears that ripen a month or two later and are heavenly. Greece also has a burgeoning kiwi industry, and while the first crop in October coincides with the end of the tourist season, the harvest carries over into the following April. Salad vegetables are more reasonably priced; besides the famous, enormous tomatoes (June–Sept), there is a bewildering variety of springtime greens, including rocket, dill, enormous spring onions and lettuces. Useful **phrases** for shopping are *éna tétarto* (250g) and *misó kiló* (500g).

Snacks

Traditional **snacks** can be one of the distinctive pleasures of Greek eating, though they are being increasingly edged out by an obsession with *tóst* (toasted sandwiches) and pizzas. However, small kebabs (*souvlákia*) are widely available, and in most larger resorts and towns you'll find *yíros* – doner kebab with garnish in thick, doughy *píta* bread that's closer to Indian nan bread.

Other common snacks include *tirópites* (cheese pies) and *spanokópites* (spinach pies), which can usually be found at the baker's, as can *kouloúria* (crispy pretzel rings sprinkled with sesame seeds) and *voutímata* (biscuits heavy on the molasses, cinnamon and butter).

Restaurants

Greek cuisine and **restaurants** are simple and straightforward. There's no snobbery about eating out; everyone does it some of the time, and it's still reasonable – around 2600–3400dr per person for a substantial meal with a measure of house wine.

In choosing a restaurant, the best strategy is to go where the Greeks go. They eat late: 2pm to 3pm for **lunch**, 9pm to 11pm for **dinner**. You can eat earlier, but you're likely to get indifferent service and cuisine if you frequent establishments catering to tourist timetables. Chic appearance is not a good guide to quality; often the more ramshackle, traditional outfits represent the best value – one good omen is the waiter bringing a carafe of refrigerated water, unbidden, rather than pushing you to order bottled stuff.

In resort areas, it's wise to keep a wary eye on the **waiters**, who are inclined to urge you to order more than you want, then bring things you haven't ordered. They often don't actually write anything down and may work out the **bill** by examining your empty plates. Although cash-register receipts are now required in all establishments, these are often only for the grand total, and even if they are itemized, will probably be illegible. Where prices are printed on menus, you'll be paying the right-hand (higher) set, inclusive of all taxes and usually **service charge**, although a small tip (150–200dr) is standard practice for the lad who lays the table, brings the bread and water, and so on.

Bread costs extra, but consumption is not obligatory; you'll be considered deviant for refusing it (just say you're on a diet or diabetic), but so much Greek bread is inedible sawdust that there's little point in paying extra unless you actually want it. Good restaurant bread is still so remarkable that its existence is noted in establishment listings; at *ouzerís* on Rhodes and Kos, Italian influence has resulted in the emergence of the more appetizing *skordhópsomo* (garlic bread) or even *bruschetta*.

Be assured that if you have children, they'll be welcome wherever you go. No one minds the slightest if they chase the cats or play tag between the tables.

Estiatória

There are two basic types of restaurant: the **estiatório** and the taverna. Distinctions between the two are minimal, though the former is more commonly found in town centres and tends to have slightly more complicated dishes. An *estiatório* will generally feature a variety of oven-baked casserole dishes: *moussakás, pastítsio*, stews like *kokinistó* and *stifádho, yemistá* (stuffed tomatoes or peppers), the oily vegetable casseroles called *ladherá*, and oven-baked meat or fish. Choosing these dishes is commonly done by going back to the kitchen and pointing at the desired steam trays.

Batches are cooked in the morning and then left to stand, which is why the food is often lukewarm or even cold. Greeks don't mind this (most believe that hot food is bad for you), and dishes like *yemistá* are actually enhanced by being allowed to cool off and stand in their own juice. Similarly, you have to specify if you want your food with little or no oil (*horís ládhi*), but once again you will be considered a little strange since Greeks regard good olive oil as essential to digestion.

Desserts (*epidhórpia* in formal Greek) of the pudding-and-pie variety don't exist at *estiatória*, and yogurts only occasionally. Fruit is always available in season – watermelons, melons and grapes are the summer standards. Autumn treats worth asking after in more urban restaurants include *kidhóni* or *akhládhi stó foúrno*, baked quince or pear with some sort of syrup or nut topping.

Tavernas

Tavernas range from the glitzy and fashionable to rough-and-ready huts set up behind a beach, under a reed awning. Really primitive ones have a very limited menu, but the more established will offer some of the main *estiatório* dishes mentioned above, as well as the standard taverna fare. This essentially means *mezédhes* (hors-d'oeuvres) and *tís óras* (meat and fish, fried or grilled to order).

Since the idea of courses is foreign to Greek cuisine, starters, main dishes and salads often arrive together unless you request otherwise. The best thing is to order a selection of *mezédhes* and salads to share, in true Greek fashion. Waiters encourage you to take the *horiátiki* **salad** – the so-called Greek salad with *fétta* cheese – because it is the most expensive. If you only want tomato, or tomato and cucumber, ask for *domatosaláta* or *angourodomáta*. *Láhano* (cabbage) and *maroúli* (lettuce) are the typical winter and spring salads.

Food and drink glossary

Basics

Aláti	Salt
Avgá	Eggs
(Horís) ládhi	(Without) oil
Hortofágos	Vegetarian
Katálogo/lísta	Menu
Kréas	Meat
Lahaniká	Vegetables
Méli	Honey
Neró	Water
O logariazmós	The bill
Psári(a)	Fish
Psomí (olikis)	Bread (wholemeal)
Sikalísio psomí	Rye bread
Thallassiná	Seafood (non-fish)
Tirí	Cheese
Yiaoúrti	Yoghurt
Záhari	Sugar

Cooking terms

Akhnistó	Steamed
Psitó	Roasted
Saganáki	Rich red sauce
Skáras	Grilled
Stí soúvla	Spit roasted
Stó foúrno	Baked
Tiganitó	Pan-fried
Tís óras	Grilled/fried to order
Yahní	Stewed in oil and tomato sauce
Yemistá	Stuffed (suid, vegetables etc)

Soups and starters

Avgolémono	Egg and lemon soup
Dolmádhes	Stuffed vine leaves
Fasoládha	Bean soup
Piperiés florínes	Canned red Macedonian peppers
Kápari	Pickled caper leaves
Kopanistí, Ktipití, tírosalata	Spicy cheese purée
Krítano	Rock samphire
Mavromátika	Black-eyed peas
Melitzanosaláta	Aubergine/eggplant dip
Revithokeftédhes	Chick pea patties
Skordhaliá	Garlic dip for certain fish
Soúpa	Soup
Taramosaláta	Cod roe paté
Tzatzíki	Yoghurt, garlic and cucumber dip

Vegetables

Angináres	Artichokes
Ánitho	Dill
Angoúri	Cucumber
Bámies	Okra, ladies' fingers
Bouréki	Cougette/zucchini, potato and cheese pie
Briám	Ratatouille
Domátes	Tomatoes
Fakés	Lentils
Fasolákia	French (green) beans
Frésko kremídhi	Spring onions
Horiátiki (saláta)	Greek salad (with olives, fétta etc)
Hórta	Greens (usually wild)
Kolokithákia	Courgette/zucchini
Koukiá	Broad fava beans
Maroúli	Lettuce
Melitzána	Aubergine/eggplant
Papoutsákia	Stuffed aubergine/eggplant
Patátes	Potatoes
Pingoúri, pligoúri	Bulgur wheat pilaf
Piperiés	Peppers
Radhíkia	Wild chicory
Rízi/Piláfi	Rice (usually with *saltsa* – sauce)
Rókka	Rocket (roccheta) greens
Saláta	Salad
Spanáki	Spinach
Yemistá	Stuffed seafood/ vegetables
Yígandes	White haricot beans

Meat and meat-based dishes

Arní	Lamb
Biftéki	Hamburger
Brizóla	Pork or beef chop
Hirinó	Pork
Keftédhes	Meatballs
Kokorétsi	Liver/offal kebab
Kotópoulo	Chicken
Kounélí	Rabbit
Loukánika	Spicy home-made sausages
Moskhári	Veal
Moussakás	Aubergine/eggplant, potato and meat pie with bechamel sauce topping
Ortíkia	Quail
Païdhákia	Lamb chops
Pastítsio	Macaroni baked with meat
Patsás	Tripe-and-trotter soup
Salingária	Garden snails
Sikóti	Liver
Soutzoukákia	Mincemeat rissoles/beef patties
Stifádho	Meat stew with tomato sauce
Youvétsi	Baked clay casserole of meat and pasta

Sweets and dessert

Baklavás	Honey and nut pastry
Bougátsa	Creamy cheese pie served warm with sugar and cinammon

Galaktobóureko	Custard pie	**Cheese**	
Halvás	Sesame or semolina sweetmeat	*Fétta*	Salty, white cheese
Karidhópita	Walnut cake	*Graviéra*	Gruyère-type hard cheese
Kréma	Custard pudding	*Kasséri*	Medium cheese
Loukoumádhes	Deep fried baignettes in honey syrup	*Katsikisio*	Goat cheese
Pagotó	Ice cream	*Mizíthra*	Sweet cream cheese
Pastélli	Sesame and honey bar	*Próvio*	Sheep cheese
Rizógalo	Rice pudding		
		Drinks	
Fruit and nuts		*Bíra*	Beer
Aktinídhia	Kiwis	*Boukáli*	Bottle
Fistíkia	Pistachio nuts	*Gála*	Milk
Fráoules	Strawberries	*Gazóza*	Generic fizzy drink
Karpoúzi	Watermelon	*Kafés*	Coffee
Kerásia	Cherries	*Krasí*	Wine
Kidhóni	Quince	*Áspro/levkó*	White
Lemóni	Lemon	*Mávro/kókkino*	Red
Míla	Apples	*Rosé/Kokkinéli*	*Rosé*
Pepóni	Melon	*Limonádha*	Lemonade
Portokália	Oranges	*Metalikó neró*	Mineral water
Rodhákino	Peach	*Portokaládha*	Orangeade
Síka	(Dried) figs	*Potíri*	Glass
Stafília	Grapes	*Stinyássas!*	Cheers!
Kristália	Green miniature pears	*Tsáï*	Tea
		Alisfakiá	Sage tea

The most interesting **mezédhes** are *tzatzíki* (yogurt, garlic and cucumber dip), *melitzanosaláta* (aubergine/eggplant dip), *kolokithákia tiganitá* (courgette/zucchini slices fried in batter) or *melitzánes tiganités* (aubergine/eggplant slices fried in batter), *yígandes* (white haricot beans in vinaigrette or hot tomato sauce), *tiropitákia* or *spanakópittes* (small cheese and spinach pies), *revithóketedhes* (chick pea patties), *okhtapódhi* (octopus) and *mavromátika* (black-eyed peas).

Among **meats**, *souvláki* (shish kebab) and *brizóles* (chops) are reliable choices. In both cases, pork (*hirinó*) is usually better and cheaper than veal (*moskharísio*). The best *souvláki*, though not often available, is lamb (*arnísio*). The small lamb cutlets called *païdhákia* are very tasty, as is roast lamb (*arní psitó*) and roast kid (*katsíki stó fournó*) when obtainable. *Keftédhes* (meatballs), *biftékia* (a sort of hamburger) and the homemade sausages called *loukánika* are cheap and good. *Kotópoulo* (chicken) is also usually a safe bet.

Seaside tavernas also offer **fish**, though the choicer varieties, such as *barboúni* (red mullet), *tsipoúra* (gilt-head bream), or *fangrí* (common bream), are expensive. The price is usually quoted by the kilo, which should be not much more than double the street market rate – eg if squid is 2000dr a kilo at the fishmongers, that sum should fetch you two 250-gramme portions. Standard procedure is to go over to the cooler and pick your own. The cheapest widely available fish are *gópes* (bogue) and *marídhes* (tiny whitebait, eaten head and all, best rolled in salt and sprinkled with lemon juice).

Seafood dishes such as *kalamarákia* (fried baby squid) and *okhtapódhi* (octopus) are a summer staple of most seaside tavernas, and occasionally *mídhia* (mussels), *kidhónia* (cherry-stone clams) and *garídhes* (small prawns) will be on offer at reasonable prices. Keep an eye out, however, to freshness and season – mussels in particular are a common cause of stomach upsets in mid-summer (see also the box on fish, overleaf).

As more conventional species are overfished, **unusual dishes** are putting in a greater appearance on menus: ray or skate (variously known as *plati, seláhi, trígona* or *vátos*) can be fried or used in soup, and is even dried for decoration. Sea urchins (*ehíni*) are also a humble favourite, being split and emptied for the sake of their (reputedly aphrodisiac) roe that's eaten raw. Only the reddish ones are edible; special shears are sold for opening them if you don't fancy a hand full of spines.

Fish story

Fish meals are becoming increasingly rare and expensive as prices climb and Aegean stocks are depleted. Net trawling is prohibited from late May to late October, when only lamp-lure and multi-hook line methods are allowed. Fish caught during these warmer months tend to be relatively scrawny, thus requiring the butter sauce often served with them. Most restaurants import frozen fish at this time, or rely on *ikhthiotrofía* (fish farms) for a supply of *tsipoúra* and *lavráki* in particular. However, farmed fish subsist exclusively on a diet of pellet food made from petroleum by-products, giving them an unmistakable muddy taste.

Following is a chart of the most commonly offered fish, in Greek alphabetical order, with their English equivalent and the best method of preparation – this depends greatly on typical fish size and fat content. For more on individual species and their habits, consult the specialist guide listed in "Books".

SCALY FISH

Atherína	(Sand smelt) Fried whole as an *ouzerí* snack
Bakaliáros	(Hake) Fried in slices, served with *skordhaliá*
Barboúni	(Red mullet) Grilled; famous smokey flavour
Galéos	(Hound shark, dogfish) Fried in slices, served with *skordhaliá*; fatty
Gávros	(Mock anchovy) Fried whole, quite mild-flavoured
Glóssa	(Sole) Lightly sautéd; mild flavour
Gópa	(Bogue) Fried whole; very common
Zargána	(Garfish) Baked in tomato sauce; rich
Kéfalos	(Grey mullet) Grilled; rich and tasty
Koliós	(Club mackerel) Baked in tomato sauce; rich
Koutsomoúra	(Goatfish) Grilled, same taste as *barboúni*
Lavráki	(Sea bass) Baked or grilled; gourmet fare
Lithríni	(Pandora) Not recommended; bony, insipid
Marídhes	(Whitebait) Fried whole; common snack fish
Melanoúri	(Saddled bream) Grilled; good value
Ksifías	(Swordfish) Baked, grilled; beware *galéos* as substitute
Pérka	(Painted comber) Fried in batter; often frozen and rubbery
Rofós	(Grouper) Baked or grilled
Sálpa	(Salema) Not recommended; insipid, cat food
Sargós	(White bream) Grilled; good value
Singagrídha	(Dentex) Baked in sauce; delicious
Skathári	(Black bream) Grilled; the succulent king of fish
Skoumbrí	(Atlantic mackerel) Baked in sauce; *estiatório* standby
Spáros	(Annular bream) Grilled
Stavrídhi	(Horse mackerel) Fried whole; *ouzerí* food
Tsipoúra	(Gilt-head bream) Grilled; gourmet fare
Fangrí	(Common bream) Grilled; gourmet fare
Hánnos	(Comber) Fried; boney but flavourful
Hristópsaro	(John Dory) As soup; rich white flesh, small bones

OTHER SEAFOOD

Astakós	(Aegean lobster) Steamed or baked; gourmet fare
Vátos, seláhi	(Ray, skate) Fried in slices, or as soup
Garídhes	(Shrimp, prawns) Steamed whole; oil/lemon dressing
Ehíni	(Sea urchin) Raw; only the very briny roe eaten
Foúskes	(Mock oysters) Raw, in their own liquor
Kalamária	(Small squid) Lightly fried; overcooking toughens
Karavídhes	(Crayfish) Steamed or grilled; mostly carapace
Khtapódhi	(Octopus) Grilled, stewed in wine
Kidhónia	(Cherrystone clams) Lightly steamed; a delicacy
Mídhia	(Mussels) Steamed, or in *saganáki* sauce
Petalídhia	(Limpets) Steamed; *ouzerí* snack
Soupiés	(Cuttlefish) Grilled, or baked stuffed

Another peculiar delicacy, frequently available on Rhodes, Kálimnos and several nearby islands, are *foúskes* ("blisters"). These marine molluscs, with eyes and vestigial soft shells, taste (and cost) much like oysters. They live on rocks at depths of 20–40m, and are gathered by sponge-divers for extra income; vacuum-bottled in seawater, they improve with age as they steep in their own liquor.

As in *estiatória*, traditional tavernas offer fruit rather than **desserts**, though nowadays these are often available, along with coffee, in tavernas frequented by foreigners.

Specialist tavernas – and vegetarians

Some tavernas specialize. **Psarotavérnes**, for example, feature fish, while **psistariés** serve spit-roasted lamb, pork or goat (generically termed *kondosoúvli*), grilled chicken (*kotópoulo skáras*) or *kokorétsi* (grilled offal). A bare handful of other tavernas offer game (*kinígi*): rabbit, quail or turtle dove during the autumn hunting season, when migrating flocks fly over Greece on their way south.

If you are **vegetarian**, you may be in for a hard time, and will often have to assemble a meal from various *mezédhes*. Even the excellent standbys of yogurt and honey, *tzatzíki* and Greek salad begin to pall after a while, and many of the supposed "vegetable" dishes on the menu are cooked in stock or have pieces of meat added to liven them up. Restaurants wholly or largely vegetarian are slowly on the increase in touristed areas; this guide highlights them where appropriate.

Wines

Both *estiatória* and tavernas will usually offer you a choice of bottled **wines**, and many have their own house variety: kept in barrels, sold in bulk by the quarter-, half- or full litre, and served either in glass flagons or brightly coloured tin "monkey-cups". Not as many tavernas stock their own wine as once did, but always ask whether they have wine *varelísio* or *híma* – respectively meaning **"from the barrel"** and **"bulk"**. Non-resinated bulk wine is almost always more than decent. *Retsina* – pine-resinated wine, a slightly acquired taste – is also usually better straight from the barrel, though the bottled *Mihali Yeoryiadhi* brand from Thessaloniki is excellent (unlike the near-poisonous *Kourtaki* labels).

Among the more common bottled wines, *Cambas*, *Boutari Lac de Roches* and the Rhodian *CAIR* products are good, inexpensive whites, while *Boutari Nemea* is perhaps the best mid-range red. If you want something better but still moderately priced, *Tsantali Agioritiko* is an excellent white or red; *Boutari* has a fine "Special Reserve" red; and the Macedonian vintner *Carras* does both excellent whites and reds, often featured on *Olympic Airways* international flights. Another company deserving mention, based on the mainland but principally available on Kos, is *Kaviros*, which is very good either in plonk or premium grade, especially as *Cimarosa*. In addition, there are various small, premium wineries whose products are currently fashionable: try *Hatzimihali*, *Athanasiadhi*, *Skouras* and *Lazaridhi*, but expect to pay around 2000dr per bottle in a shop, double that at a taverna.

Cafés, patisseries and bars

The Greek eating and drinking experience encompasses a variety of other places beyond restaurants. Most importantly, there is the institution of the *kafenío*, found in every town, village and hamlet in the country. In addition, you'll come across *ouzerís*, *zaharoplastía* (Greek patisseries) and bars.

The kafenío

The **kafenío** is the traditional Greek coffee shop or café. Although its main business is Greek coffee – prepared *skéto* or *pikró* (unsweetened), *métrio* (medium) or *glikó* (sweet) – it also serves spirits such as *oúzo* (see below), brandy (*Metaxa* or *Botrys* brand, in three grades), beer, tea (either herbal tea known as *alisfakiá* or *tsáï vounoú*, or British-style) and soft drinks. Another refreshing drink sold in cafés is *kafés frappé*, a sort of iced instant coffee with or without milk and sugar – uniquely Greek despite its French-sounding name. Like Greek coffee, it is always accompanied by a welcome glass of cold water. Standard fizzy soft drinks are also sold in all *kafenía*.

Usually the only **edibles** available are *gliká koutalioú* (sticky, syrupy preserves of quince, grape, fig, citrus fruit or cherry), and the old-fashioned *ipovríhio*, a piece of mastic submerged in a glass of water like a submarine, which is what the word means in Greek. Peculiar to Níssiros, but sometimes exported to neighbouring islands, is *soumádha*, concentrated almond syrup identical to Italian *orgeat*; diluted two-to-one with cold water, there's nothing more refreshing on a hot day.

Like tavernas, *kafenía* range from the plastic and sophisticated to the old-fashioned, spit-on-the-floor variety, with marble or brightly painted metal tables and straw-bottomed chairs. An important institution anywhere in Greece, they are the central pivot in more remote villages. You get the impression that many men spend most of their waking hours there. Greek women are rarely to be seen in the more traditional places – and foreign women may sometimes feel uneasy or unwelcome in these establishments. Even in holiday resorts, you will find there is at least one coffeehouse that the local men have kept intact for themselves.

Some *kafenía* close at siesta time, but many remain open from early in the morning until late at night. The chief socializing time is 6–8pm, immediately after the siesta. This is the time to take your pre-dinner *oúzo*, as the sun begins to sink and the air cools down.

Oúzo, mezédhes and ouzerís

Oúzo is a simple spirit of up to 48 percent alcohol, distilled from the grape-mash residue left over from wine-making, and then flavoured with herbs such as anise or fennel. There are more than a dozen brands of *oúzo* in Greece; the best are reckoned to come from Lésvos, Tírnavos on the mainland and Sámos, while the worst is reckoned to be the heavily promoted brand *12* – spiked, like all cheaper *oúzo*, with molasses or neat alcohol to "fortify" it. When you order, you will be served two glasses: one with the *oúzo*, and one full of water that's tipped into the latter until it turns a milky white. You can drink it straight, but the strong, burning taste is hardly refreshing if you do. It is increasingly common to add ice cubes; an ice bucket will be provided upon request.

Until not long ago, every *oúzo* you ordered was automatically accompanied by a small plate of **mezédhes**, on the house: bits of cheese, cucumber, tomato, a few olives, sometimes octopus or even a couple of small fish. Unfortunately these days you usually have to ask, and pay, for them.

Though they are confined to the better resorts and select neighbourhoods of the bigger island capitals such as Ródhos, Kós, Híos and Sámos, one kind of drinking establishment specializes in *oúzo* and *mezédhes*. These are called **ouzerís**, and are well worth trying for the marvellous variety of *mezédhes* they serve. Several plates of these plus drinks will effectively substitute for a more involved meal at a taverna (though it usually works out more expensive if you have a healthy appetite). Faced with the often bewilderingly varied menu, you might opt for the *pikilía* (medley, assortment), which usually comes in several sizes, the largest and most expensive one a bit heavier on the seafood.

Eating at an *ouzerí* is often the best way to get an idea of **regional specialities**, which can be fairly elaborate or incredibly simple. An example of the latter is *krítamo* or rock samphire, mentioned in *King Lear* and offered to the discerning on most of the East Aegean islands. A mineral- and vitamin-rich succulent growing on sea-coast cliffs, it is harvested in May or June, pickled and served unadorned or to jazz up salads.

Sweets and desserts

Similar to the *kafenío* is the **zaharoplastío**, a cross between café and patisserie, which serves coffee, alcohol, yogurt with honey, and sticky cakes.

The better establishments offer an amazing variety of pastries, cream and chocolate confections, honey-soaked Greco-Turkish sweets like *baklavás*, *kataïfi* (honey-drenched "shredded wheat"), *loukoumádhes* or *baignettes* (deep-fried batter puffs dusted with cinnamon and dipped in syrup); *galaktoboúreko* (custard pie), and so on.

If you want a stronger slant towards the dairy products and away from the pure sugar, seek out a **galaktopolío**, where you'll often find *rizógalo* (rice pudding – rather better than the English boarding-school variety), *kréma* (custard) and home- or at least locally made *yiaoúrti* (yogurt), best if it's *próvio* (from sheep's milk).

Ice cream, sold principally at the gelaterie which have carpeted Greece (and particularly the Dodecanese) of late, can be very good and almost indistinguishable from Italian prototypes. A scoop (*baláki*) costs 150–200dr; you'll be asked if you want it in a cup (*kípello*) or a cone (*honáki*), or with *santí* (whipped cream) on top. By contrast, mass-produced stuff like *Delta* or *Evga* brand is pretty trashy, with the honourable exception of *Mars/Opal* fruit ices and *Dove Bars*. A sign reading "PAGOTÓ POLÍTIKO" or "KAÏMÁKI" means that the shop concerned makes its own Turkish-style ice cream – as good as or better than the usual Italian version – and that the proprietors are probably of Asia Minor or Constantinopolitan descent.

Both *zaharoplastía* and *galaktopolía* are more family-oriented places than the *kafenío*, and many also serve a basic continental-type **breakfast** of *méli me voútiro* (honey poured over a pat of butter) or jam (all kinds are called *marmeládha* in Greek; ask for *portokáli* – orange – if you want proper marmalade) with fresh bread or *friganiés* (melba-toast-type slivers). You are also more likely to find proper (*evropaïkó*) tea and non-Greek coffee. *Nescafé* has become the generic term for all instant coffee, regardless of brand; it's generally pretty vile, and in resort areas smart proprietors have taken to offering genuine filter coffee, dubbed "*gallikós*" (French).

Bars – and beer

Bars (*barákia*), once confined to towns, cities and holiday resorts, are now found all over Greece. They range from clones of Parisian cafés to seaside cocktail bars, by way of imitation English "pabs" (sic), with MTV-type videos running all day. Once 20-hour-a-day operations, most bars now close between 2 and 3am, depending on the municipality; during 1994 they were required by the Ministry of Public Order to make an admission/cover charge which included the first drink. This decree, met with a storm of street protests and other mass civil disobedience, is presently in abeyance but could be revived at any time.

For that and other reasons, drinks are invariably more expensive than in a café. Bars are, however, most likely to stock a range of **beers**, all foreign labels made locally under licence, since the indigenous *Fix* brewery closed in 1984. *Kronenberg* and *Kaiser* are the two most common of these, with the former available in both light and dark; since 1993 a tidal wave of even pricier, imported German beers, such as *Bitburger* and *Warstein*, has washed over the fancier resorts. *Amstel* and *Henninger* are the two ubiquitous cheapies, rather bland but inoffensive; the Dutch themselves claim that the former is better than the *Amstel* available in Holland. A possible compromise in both taste and expense is the sharper-tasting *Heineken*, universally referred to as a "*prássini*" by bar and taverna staff after its green bottle.

Incidentally, try not to get stuck with the one-third litre cans, vastly more expensive (and more of a rubbish problem) than the returnable half-litre bottles (see the box on Eco-friendly tourism, p.35).

Communications: mail, phones and the media

Postal services

Most **post offices** are open Monday to Friday from about 7.30am to 2pm, though certain large towns – for example Ródhos and Kós – also have evening and weekend hours. They exchange money in addition to handling mail.

Airmail **letters** from the islands take three to seven days to reach the rest of Europe, five to twelve days to North America, and a little longer to Australia and New Zealand. Generally, the larger the island (and the planes serving its airport), the quicker the service. Aerograms are slightly faster, and for a modest fee (about 400dr), you can further cut delivery time to any destination by using the express (*katepígonda*) service. Registered (*sistiméno*) delivery is also available, but it is quite slow unless coupled with express service. If you are sending large purchases home, note that **parcels** should and often can only be handled in the main island capitals.

For a simple letter or card, **stamps** (*grammatósima*) can also be purchased at a *períptero* (kiosk). However, the proprietors charge ten percent commission on the cost of the stamp, and never seem to know the current international rates. Ordinary **post boxes** are bright yellow, express boxes dark red; if you are confronted by two slots, "ESOTERIKÓ" is for domestic mail, "EXOTERIKÓ" for overseas.

Receiving mail

The **poste-restante** system is reasonably efficient, especially at the post offices of larger towns. Mail should be clearly addressed and marked "poste restante", with your surname underlined, to the main post office of whichever town you choose. It will be held for a month and you'll need your passport to collect it.

Telephones

Local **telephone calls** are relatively straightforward. Street-corner call boxes work only with phone cards; these come in three denominations – 100, 500 and 1000 units – and are available from kiosks, *OTE* offices and newsagents. Not surprisingly, the more expensive cards are the best value.

If you won't be around long enough to use up a phone card, it's probably easier to make **local calls** from a *períptero*, or **street kiosk**. Here the phone is connected to a meter, and you pay after you have made the call. While local calls are reasonable (20dr for the first six minutes), long-distance ones have some of the most expensive rates in the EU – and definitely the worst connections, owing to the lack of digitized exchanges in all of the East Aegean and most of the North Dodecanese islands. When using such circuits, you must wait for the critical series of six electrical crunches on the line after dialling the country or Greek area code. By contrast, the phone system for Rhodes and immediately surrounding islands had a state-of-the-art fibre-optic digital system installed in 1993, and it works like a dream. Other options for local calls are from a *kafenío* or **bar** (same 20dr charge as at kiosks), but you won't be allowed to use these for trunk or overseas calls unless the phone is metered: look for a sign saying "TILÉFONO MEH METRITÍ".

For inter-island and **international** (*exoterikó*) **calls**, it's better and cheaper to use either card phones or visit the nearest **OTE** (*Organismós Tilepikinoníon tis Elládhos*) office, where there's

Phoning Greece from abroad

Dial the international access code (given below) + 30 (country code) + area code (minus initial 0) + number

Australia ☎ 0011

Canada ☎ 011

Ireland ☎ 010

New Zealand ☎ 00

UK ☎ 00

USA ☎ 011

Phoning abroad from Greece

Dial the country code (given below) + area code (minus any initial 0) + number

Australia ☎ 0061

Canada ☎ 001

Ireland ☎ 00353

New Zealand ☎ 0064

UK ☎ 0044

USA ☎ 001

Useful Greek telephone numbers

ELPA Road Service ☎ 104

Fire brigade ☎ 199

Operator ☎ 132 (Domestic)

Operator ☎ 161 (International)

Medical emergencies ☎ 166

Police/Emergency ☎ 100

Speaking clock ☎ 141

Tourist police ☎ 171

Phone credit card operator access numbers from Greece

AT&T USA Direct ☎ 00 800 1311

MCI ☎ 00 800 1211

Sprint ☎ 00 800 1411

Canada ☎ 00 800 1611

British Telecom ☎ 00 800 4411

often a digitally wired booth reserved for overseas calls only; make your call and pay afterwards. **Reverse charge** (collect) or person-to-person calls can also be made here, though connections are not always immediate – be prepared to wait up to half an hour. In the larger island capitals, *OTE* is open from 7am to 10pm or 11pm; in smaller towns their offices can close as early as 3pm, though in a few resorts *OTE* operates Portakabin booths that keep weird but useful schedules such as 2–10pm. **Faxes** can also be sent from *OTE* offices, post offices and some travel agencies – at a price. Receiving a fax may also incur a small charge. Avoid making long-distance calls from a hotel, as they slap a 50 percent surcharge onto the already outrageous rates.

Calls through *OTE* booths will **cost** approximately £2.75 for three minutes to all EU countries and much of the rest of Europe, and US$9 for the same time to North America or Australasia. **Cheap rates**, a reduction of 20–30 percent at the most, apply from 3–5pm and 9pm–8am daily, plus all weekend, for calls within Greece.

British Telecom, as well as North American long-distance companies like *AT&T*, *MCI* and *Sprint*, provide **credit-card call** services from Greece, but only back to the home country. As of writing you have to go through an operator to be connected – there are not yet any direct-dial access numbers. Contact the card-issuing company for the latest information.

For details of phone codes and useful numbers, see the box below.

The Media

British **newspapers** are fairly widely available in Greece at a cost of 300–450dr, or 700–800dr for Sunday editions. You'll find day-old copies of the *Independent* and the *Guardian*'s European edition, plus a few of the tabloids, in all the resorts as well as in major towns. American and international alternatives include the turgid *USA Today* and the more readable *International Herald Tribune*; *Time* and *Newsweek* are also widely available. The oldest local English-language paper is the daily *Athens News*, a Lambrakis Foundation organ with a colour format and useful entertainment listings; the only alternative is the Moonie-managed *Greek Weekly News*, an entertaining read as long as you brace yourself for the pervasive editorial slant.

Among **magazines**, the most enduring is *The Athenian*, a four-colour, English-language monthly sold in the biggest resorts. It's generally worth a read for the cultural/festival listings, updates on Greek life and politics, and often excellent features. Rather less recommendable is the expensive, glossy *Odyssey*, produced every other month by and for wealthy diaspora Greeks, and no better than the average in-flight magazine.

Greek publications

Although you will probably be excluded from the **Greek print media** by the double incomprehensibilities of alphabet and language, you can learn a fair bit about your Greek fellow-travellers by their choice of broadsheet, so a quick survey of Greek magazines and newspapers won't go amiss.

Many papers are funded by **political groups**, which tends to decrease the already low quality of Greek dailies. Among these, only the centrist *Kathemerini* – whose former proprietress Helen Vlakhos attained heroic status for her defiance of the junta – approaches the standards of a major European newspaper. *Eleftherotypia*, once a PASOK mouthpiece, now aspires to more independence, with *Avriani* having taken its place as the PASOK cheerleading section; *Ta Nea* is mostly noted for its extensive small ads. On the **Left**, *Avyi* is the Eurocommunist forum with literary leanings, while *Rizospastis* acts as the organ of the KKE (unreconstructed Communists). *Ethnos* was also shown some years back to have received covert funding from the KGB to act as a disinformation bulletin. At the other end of the political spectrum, *Apoyevmatini* generally supports the **centre-right** Néa Dhimokratía party, while *Estia*'s no-photo format and reactionary politics are both stuck somewhere at the turn of the century. The **nationalist**, lunatic fringe is staked out by paranoid *Stokhos* ("Our Goal: Greater Greece; Our Capital: Constantinople"). Given the generally low level of journalism, there is little need for a soft-porn or gutter press, unlike in Germany or the UK.

Among **magazines** not merely translations of overseas titles, *Takhydhromos* is the respectable news-and-features weekly; *Ena* is more sensationalist, *Klik* a crass rip-off of *The Face*, and *Toh Pondiki* (The Mouse) a satirical weekly revue in the same vein as Britain's *Private Eye* or *Spy*; its famous covers are spot-on and accessible to anyone with minimal Greek. More specialized niches are occupied by low-circulation titles such as *Adhesmatos Typos* (a muck-raking journal) and *Andi*, an intelligent bi-weekly somewhat in the mould of Britain's *New Statesman and Society*.

Radio

If you have a **radio**, playing dial roulette can be rewarding. As the government's former monopoly of wavelengths has ended, regional stations have mushroomed and the airwaves are now positively cluttered. On Rhodes, 102 FM International (also on 107.5FM) features foreign DJs and mostly rock, as well as regular news bulletins in English. The Turkish state radio's third channel is also widely (if somewhat unpatriotically) listened to for its classical, jazz and blues programmes, though its English-language news tends to be heavily edited propaganda. The **BBC World Service** broadcasts on short-wave throughout Greece; 15.07 and 12.09 Mhz are the most common frequencies. The **Voice of America**, with its transmitters on Rhodes, can be picked up in most of the Dodecanese on medium wave.

TV

Greece's two centralized, government-controlled **TV stations**, ET1 and ET2, nowadays lag behind private, decidedly right-wing channels – Mega-Channel, New Channel, Antenna, Star and Seven-X – in the ratings. On ET1, news summaries in English are broadcast daily at 6pm. Programming on all stations tends to be a mix of soaps (especially Italian, Spanish and Latin-American), game shows, westerns, B-movies and sports. All foreign films and serials are broadcast in their original language, with Greek subtitles. Except for Seven-X, which begins at 7pm, and Mega and Antenna (24-hr channels), the main channels broadcast from breakfast time, or just after, until the small hours. Numerous **cable and satellite** channels are received, including Sky, CNN, MTV, Super Channel, French Canal Cinque and Italian Rai Due. The range available depends on the area (and hotel) you're in.

Opening hours and public holidays

It is virtually impossible to generalize about Greek opening hours, except to say that they change constantly. The traditional timetable starts at a relatively civilized hour, with shops opening between 8.30 and 9.30am, then runs through until lunchtime, when there is a long break for the hottest part of the day. Things may then reopen in the mid- to late afternoon.

Tourist areas tend to adopt a slightly more northern timetable, with shops and offices, as well as the most important archeological sites and museums, usually open throughout the day.

Business and shopping hours

Most **government agencies** are open to the public on weekdays from 8am to 2pm. In general, however, you'd be optimistic to show up after 1pm expecting to be served the same day. Private businesses, or anyone providing a service, frequently operate a 9am–6pm schedule. If someone is actually selling something, then they are more likely to follow a split shift as detailed below.

Shopping hours during the hottest months are theoretically Monday, Wednesday and Saturday from approximately 9am to 2.30pm, and Tuesday, Thursday and Friday from 8.30am to 2pm and 6 to 9pm. During the cooler months the morning schedule shifts slightly forward, the evening trade a half or even a full hour back. There are so many exceptions to these rules, though, that you can't count on getting anything done except from Monday to Friday, between 9.30am and 1pm. It's worth noting that delis and **butchers** are not allowed to sell fresh meat during summer afternoons (though some flout this rule); similarly **fishmongers** are only open in the morning, as are **pharmacies**, which additionally are shut on Saturday.

All of the above opening hours will be regularly thrown out of sync by the numerous **public holidays and festivals**. The most important, when almost everything will be closed, are listed in the box below.

Ancient sites and monasteries

All the major **ancient sites** are now fenced off and, like most museums, charge admission fees ranging from 200 to 1500dr, on average 600dr. **Reductions** of approximately 25 percent often apply to senior citizens, 50 percent to students with proper identification. In addition, entrance to any state-run site or museum is free to all EU nationals on Sundays and public holidays – non-EU nationals are unlikely to be detected as such on these days unless they go out of their way to advertise the fact. It's free to take **photographs** of open-air sites, though museum photography or the use of tripods or video cameras anywhere requires an extra permit. This must be arranged in advance and in writing with the relevant department of antiquities: for Rhodes and all of the Dodecanese, fax on ☎0241/31 048; for Samos, fax on ☎01/32 51 096; for Lésvos, Híos and Límnos, fax on ☎0251/20 745.

Opening hours vary from site to site. As far as possible, individual times are quoted in the text, but bear in mind that these change with exasperating frequency and at smaller sites may be subject to the whim of a local keeper. The times quoted are generally summer hours, which operate from around late April to the end of September. Reckon on similar days but later opening and earlier closing in winter.

Smaller sites tend to close for a long lunch and siesta (even where they're not supposed to), as do **monasteries**. The latter are generally open from about 9am to 1pm and 5 to 8pm (3.30–6.30pm in winter) for limited visits. Most operate a fairly strict **dress code** for visitors; shorts on either sex are unacceptable, and women are often expected to cover their arms and wear skirts – wraps are sometimes provided on the spot.

Public holidays

January 1

January 6

March 25

First Monday of Lent (Feb/March; see below)

Easter weekend (according to the Orthodox festival calendar; see below)

May 1

Whit Monday (usually in June)

August 15

October 28

December 25 & 26

There are also a large number of local holidays, which result in the closure of shops and businesses, though not government agencies.

Variable religious feasts

	Lent Monday	Easter Sunday	Whit Monday
1997	March 10	April 27	June 16
1998	March 2	April 19	June 8
1999	Feb 22	April 11	May 31

Festivals

Many of the big Greek festivals have a religious basis, so they're observed in accordance with the Orthodox calendar. Give or take a few saints, this is similar to the regular Catholic liturgical year, except for Easter, which can fall as much as three weeks on either side of the western festival.

Easter

Easter is by far the most important festival of the Greek year – infinitely more so than Christmas – and taken much more seriously than elsewhere in western Europe. From Wednesday of Holy Week until the following Monday, the state radio and TV networks are given over solely to religious programmes.

The **festival** is an excellent time to be in Greece, both for its beautiful religious ceremonies and for the days of feasting and celebration that follow. The remote village of Ólimbos on Kárpathos, and Saint John's Monastery on Pátmos, are the prime Easter venues among the islands in this guide, but unless you plan well in advance you have no hope of finding accommodation at that time.

The first great public ceremony takes place on **Good Friday** evening as the Descent from the Cross is lamented in church. At dusk the *Epitáfios*, Christ's funeral bier, lavishly decorated with flowers by the women of the parish, leaves the sanctuary and is paraded solemnly through the streets. In many places this is accompanied by the burning of effigies of Judas Iscariot.

Late Saturday evening sees the climax in a majestic *Anástasis* mass to celebrate Christ's triumphant return. At the stroke of midnight all lights in each crowded church are extinguished, plunging the congregation into the darkness that envelops Christ as he passes through the underworld. Then there's a faint glimmer of light behind the altar screen before the priest appears, holding aloft a lighted taper and chanting *"Avtó to Fós . . . "* (This is the Light of the World). Stepping down to the level of the parishioners, he touches his flame to the unlit candle of the nearest worshipper, intoning *"Dhévteh, láveteh Fós"* (Come, take the Light). Those at the front of the congregation and on the aisles do the same for their neighbours until the entire church is ablaze with burning candles and the miracle reaffirmed.

Even the most committed agnostic is likely to find this moving. The traditional greeting, as an arsenal's worth of fireworks explode around you in the street, is *"Hristós Anésti"* (Christ is risen), to which the response is *"Alithós Anésti"* (Truly He is Risen). In the week up to Easter Sunday you should wish people a Happy Easter: *"Kaló Páskha"*; after the day, you say *"Hrónia Pollá"* (Many Happy Returns).

Worshippers then take the burning **candles** home, and it brings good fortune on the house if they arrive still lit. On reaching the front door it is common practice to make the sign of the cross on the lintel with the flame, leaving a black smudge visible for the rest of the year. The **Lenten fast** is traditionally broken early on Sunday morning with a meal of *mayarítsa*, a soup made from lamb tripe, rice and lemon. The rest of the lamb will be roasted on spits for Sunday lunch, and festivities often take place through the rest of the day.

The Greek equivalent of **Easter eggs** are hard-boiled eggs (painted red on Holy Thursday), which are baked into twisted, sweet bread-loaves (*tsourékia*) or distributed on Easter Sunday. People rap their eggs against their friends', and the owner of the last uncracked one is considered lucky.

The festival calendar

Most of the other Greek festivals are in honour of one or another of a multitude of **saints**. The most important are detailed overleaf: a village or church bearing a saint's name is a sure sign of celebrations – sometimes right across the town or island, sometimes quiet, local and consisting of little more than a special liturgy and banners adorning the chapel in question. Saints' days are also celebrated as **name days**; if you learn that it's an acquaintance's name day, you wish them *"Hrónia Pollá"* (Many Happy Returns). Also detailed overleaf are a few more **secular holidays**, most enjoyable of which are the pre-Lenten carnivals.

In addition to the specific dates mentioned, there are literally scores of **local festivals (paniyíria)** celebrating the patron saint of the village church. With hundreds of possible name-saints' days (liturgical calendars list two or three, however arcane, for each day) you're unlikely to travel around Greece for long without stumbling on something.

It is important to remember the concept of the **paramoní**, or eve of the festival. Most of the events listed below are celebrated on the night before, so if you show up on the morning of the date given you will very probably have missed any music, dancing or drinking.

Festivals

January 1

New Year's Day (*Protohroniá*) in Greece is the feast day of Áyios Vassílios, and is celebrated with church services and the baking of a special loaf, *vassilópitta*, in which a coin is baked which brings its finder good luck throughout the year. The traditional New Year greeting is *"Kalí Hroniá"*.

January 6

Epiphany (*Áyia Theofánia*, or *Fóta* for short), when the *kalikántzari* (hobgoblins) who run riot on earth during the twelve days of Christmas are rebanished to the nether world by various rites of the Church. The most important of these is the blessing of baptismal fonts and all outdoor bodies of water. At seaside locations, the priest traditionally casts a crucifix into the deep, with local youths competing for the privilege of recovering it.

Pre-Lenten carnivals

These span three weeks, climaxing during the seventh weekend before Easter. Amongst the islands covered in this guide, Lésvos (Ayiássos) and Kárpathos (Ólimbos) have the most elaborate festivities.

March 25

Independence Day and the Feast of the Annunciation (*Evangelismós* in Greek) is both a religious and a national holiday, with, on the one hand, military parades and dancing to celebrate the beginning of the revolt against Turkish rule in 1821, and, on the other, church services to honour the news being given to Mary that she was to become the Mother of Christ. There are major festivities at any locality with a monastery or church named *Evangelístria* or *Evangelismós*..

April 23

The feast of **Saint George** (*Áyios Yióryios*), the patron of shepherds, is a big rural celebration, with much dancing and feasting at associated shrines and towns. If April 23 falls before Easter, ie during Lent, the festivities are postponed until the Monday after Easter.

May 1

May Day is the great urban holiday when townspeople traditionally make for the countryside for picnics and return with bunches of wild flowers. Wreaths are hung on their doorways or balconies until they are burnt on Midsummer's eve. There are also large demonstrations by the Left, claiming the *Ergatikí Protomayiá* (Working Class First of May) as their own.

May 21

The feast of **Áyios Konstandínos** and his mother, **Ayía Eléni**, the first Orthodox Byzantine rulers. It is widely observed as the name day for two of the more popular Christian names in Greece.

June 29

The **Holy Apostles** (*Ayíi Apostolí*), Pétros and Pávlos. Two of the more widely celebrated name days.

July 17

The Feast of **Ayía Marína**: a big event in rural areas, as she's an important protector of crops. The eponymous port town on Léros is a good place to be, as is Ayía Marína village on Kássos, and the namesake islet off Sími. Between mid-July and mid-September there are religious festivals every few days, especially in the rural areas, and between these and the summer heat, ordinary business comes to a virtual standstill.

cont. overleaf

Festivals cont.

July 18–20
The feast of **Profítis Ilías** (the Prophet Elijah) is celebrated at the countless hilltop shrines of Profítis Ilías, notably the one on Rhodes.

July 26
Ayiá Paraskeví; celebrated in parishes or villages bearing that name, for example on Lésvos and Sámos.

July 27
Áyios Pandelímon; liveliest and longest festival at the eponymous monastery on Tílos.

August 6
Metamórfosis toú Sotíros (Transfiguration of the Saviour) provides another excuse for celebrations, particularly at Hristós village on Ikaría, at Plátanos on Léros, and on Psará.

August 15
Apokímísis tís Panayías (Assumption or Dormition of the Blessed Virgin Mary). This is the day when people traditionally return to their home village, and in many places there will be no accommodation available on any terms. Even some Greeks will resort to sleeping in the streets. There are especially major festivities at Ayiássos on Lésvos, at Ólimbos on Kárpathos, on Lipsí and at several locations on Kálimnos.

August 29
Apokefálisis toú Prodhromou (Beheading of John the Baptist). Observances at Vrikoúnda on Kárpathos, and the namesake monastery near Kéfalos on Kós.

September 8
Yénisis tís Panayías (Birth of the Virgin Mary) sees special services in churches dedicated to the event; at Vourliótes on Sámos, next to Vrondianí monastery, a particularly lively festival takes place the night before. There's also a major pilgrimage of childless women to Tsambíka monastery, Rhodes.

September 14
A last major summer festival, the **Ípsosis toú Stavroú** (Exaltation of the Cross); most prominent on Hálki.

October 26
The Feast of **Áyios Dhimítrios**, another popular name day. New wine is traditionally tapped on this day, a good excuse for general inebriation.

October 28
Ókhi Day, the year's major patriotic shindig – a national holiday with parades, folk-dancing and speechifying to commemorate Metaxas's apocryphal one-word reply to Mussolini's 1940 ultimatum: "*Okhi*!"(No!).

November 8
Another popular name day, the feast of the **Archangels Michael and Gabriel** (Mihaíl and Gavriíl, or Taxiárhon), marked by rites at the numerous churches named after them, particularly at Arhángelos village on Rhodes, Asómati village on Kós, the rural monastery of Taxiárhis on Sími, and at the big monastery of Mandamádhos, Lésvos.

December 6
The Feast of **Áyios Nikólaos**, the patron of seafarers, with many chapels dedicated to him.

December 25
A much less festive occasion than Greek Easter, **Christmas** (*Hristoúyenna*) is still an important religious feast. In recent years it has acquired all of the commercial trappings of the Western Christmas, with decorations, trees and gifts. December 26 is not Boxing Day as in England, but the **Sínaxis tís Panayías** (Meeting of the Virgin's Entourage), a legal holiday.

December 31
New Year's Eve (*Paramoní Protohroniá*), when, as on the other twelve days of Christmas, children go door to door singing the traditional *kálanda* (carols), receiving money in return. Adults tend to playcards, often for money. The *vassilópitta* is cut at midnight (see January 1).

Water sports

The Greek seashore offers endless scope for water sports. Windsurfing boards can be rented out in most resorts, and larger resorts have waterskiing and parasailing facilities.

The last few years have seen a massive growth in the popularity of **windsurfing** in Greece. The country's bays and coves are ideal for beginners, and boards can be rented in literally hundreds of resorts. Particularly good areas include the coasts of Sámos, Lésvos, Kós, Kárpathos and, of course, Rhodes. You can almost always pay for an initial period of instruction, and rental rates are very reasonable – about £5/US$7.50 an hour.

Waterskiing is available at a number of the larger resorts, such as Faliráki on Rhodes, and a few of the smaller ones. By the rental standards of the ritzier parts of the Mediterranean, it is a bargain, with twenty minutes' instruction often available for around £8–10/$12–15. At many resorts, **parasailing** (*parapént*) is also possible; rates start at £10/$15 a go.

A combination of steady winds, appealing seascapes and numerous natural harbours have long made the Greek islands a tremendous place for **sailing**. Holiday companies offer all sorts of packaged and tailor-made cruises (see p.5 and p.10). Locally, small boats and dinghies are rented out by the day at many resorts. Larger craft can be chartered by the week or longer, either bare-boat or with skipper, from several marinas in the Dodecanese and the East Aegean. Rhodes is by far the busiest (see Rhodes Town "Listings" for local agencies), and justifiably so given the garland of small, interesting islands less than a day's sail away. Kálimnos is also a major sailing centre, while Kós and Sámos have recently acquired new marinas. There is relatively little sailing activity north of Samos owing to the enormous distances of open sea between large islands, and the relatively poor anchorage when you finally arrive. Spring and autumn are the most pleasant and least expensive times; **meltémi** winds make for pretty nauseating sailing between late June and early September, and summer **rates** for the same craft can be two or three times as high as shoulder-season prices. For more details, contact the *Hellenic Yachting Federation*, Akti Navárhou Koundourióti 7, 185 34 Pireás (☎01/41 37 351; fax ☎01/41 31 119).

Because of the potential for pilfering submerged antiquities, **scuba diving** is severely restricted around the Dodecanese and the East Aegean. Its legal practice is confined among these islands to short stretches of coast off Rhodes and Kálimnos. For an update on the situation – permitted areas are slowly being added since a liberalization in policy was announced by the Ministry of Culture – contact the *Union of Greek Diving Centres* (☎01/92 29 532 or ☎41 18 909), or request the information sheet "Regulations Concerning Underwater Activities" from the nearest overseas branch of the GNTO.

Public beaches, sunbeds and umbrellas

Not many people realize that all **beaches** in Greece are public land; that's understandable, given the extent to which luxury hotels encroach on them, and the sunbeds and umbrellas that carpet entire strands. Greek **law**, however, is very clear that the shore from the winter high-tide mark down to the water must be freely accessible, with a right of way provided around hotels or resorts, and that no permanent structures be built in that zone. Accordingly, you should resist pressure to pay rental for unwanted **sunbeds** or **umbrellas**, particularly the latter, which are often anchored with permanent, illegal concrete lugs buried in the sand. Beaches entirely or relatively free of such obstacles are noted in the guide.

Police and trouble

Greece is one of Europe's safest countries, with a low crime rate and an almost unrivalled reputation for honesty. If you leave a bag or wallet at a café, you'll most likely find it scrupulously looked after, pending your return. Similarly, Greeks are relaxed about leaving possessions unlocked or unattended on the beach, in rooms or on campsites. However, in recent years there has been a large increase in theft and crimes, perpetrated mainly by fellow tourists, particularly in the cities and resorts, so it's wise to lock things up and treat Greece like any other European destination. Below are a few pointers on offences that might get you into trouble locally, and some advice on sexual harassment – all too much a fact of life given the classically Mediterranean machismo of Greek culture.

Offences

The most common causes of a brush with authority are nude bathing or sunbathing, and camping outside an authorized site.

Nude bathing is legal on only a very few beaches, and is deeply offensive to the more traditional Greeks. You should exercise considerable sensitivity to local feeling: it is, for example, very bad etiquette to swim or sunbathe nude within sight of a church. Generally, though, if a beach has become fairly established as naturist, or is well secluded, it's highly unlikely that the police are going to come charging in. Where they do get bothered is if they feel a place is turning into a "hippie beach" or nudity is getting too overt on mainstream tourist stretches. Most of the time, the only action will be a warning, but you can officially be arrested straight off – facing up to three days in jail and a stiff fine.

> In an **emergency**, dial ☎ 100 for the police; ☎ 171 for the tourist police; ☎ 166 for an ambulance.

Topless (sun)bathing for women is technically legal nationwide, but specific locales often opt out of this by posting signs, which should be heeded.

Very similar guidelines apply to **freelance camping** – though for this you're still unlikely to incur anything more than a warning to move on. The only real risk of arrest is if you are told to move on and fail to do so. In either of the above cases, even if the police do take any action against you, it's more likely to be a brief spell in their cells than any official prosecution.

Incidentally, any sort of **disrespect** towards the Greek state or Orthodox Church in general, or Greek civil servants in particular, may be construed as offences in the most literal sense, so it's best to keep your comments on how things are working (or not) to yourself. Every year a few foreign louts on Rhodes and Kós find themselves in deep trouble over a drunken indiscretion. This is a society where words count, with a consistent backlog of court cases dealing with the alleged public utterance of *malákas* (wanker). **Drug offences** are treated as major crimes, particularly since there's a growing local use and addiction problem. The maximum penalty for "causing the use of drugs by someone under 18", for example, is life imprisonment and at least a ten-million-drachma fine. Theory is by no means practice, but foreigners caught in possession of even small amounts of grass do get long jail sentences if there's evidence that they've been supplying the drug to others.

If you get arrested for any offence, you have a right to contact your **consulate**, who will arrange a lawyer for your defence. Beyond this, there is little they can, or in most cases will, do.

Sexual harassment

Thousands of women travel independently about the Dodecanese and East Aegean without being **harassed** or feeling intimidated. Greek machismo, however, is strong, if less upfront than in, for example, southern Italy. Most of the hassle you are likely to get is from a small minority of Greek males, known as *kamákia* (fish harpoons), who migrate in summer to the beach bars and discos of the main resorts and towns, specifically in pursuit of "liberated, fun-loving" tourists. Indigenous Greeks, who are increasingly protective of you as you become more of a fixture in any one place, treat these outsiders with contempt. Words worth remembering as unambiguous responses include *pápsteh* (stop it), *afístemeh* (leave me alone) and *fíyeteh* (go away), the latter intensified if followed by *dhrómo*! (road, as in "hit the road"). **Hitching** is not advisable for lone women travellers, but **camping** is generally not a problem, though away from recognized sites it is often wise to attach yourself to a local family by making arrangements to use nearby private land. On the more remote islands you may feel more uncomfortable travelling alone. The intensely traditional Greeks may have trouble understanding why you are unaccompanied, and might not welcome your presence in their exclusively male *kafenía* – often the only place where you can get a drink. Travelling with a man, you're more likely to be treated as a *kséni*, a word meaning both (female) stranger and guest.

Work

Since Greece's full accession to the European Union in early 1993, a citizen of any EU state has (in theory) the right to work in Greece. In practice, however, there are a number of bureaucratic hurdles to overcome. Formerly, the most common job for foreigners was teaching English in the numerous private cramming academies (*frondistíria*), but lately severe restrictions have been put on the availability of such positions for non-Greeks, and you will more likely be involved in a commercial or leisure-orientated trade.

If you plan to work for someone else, you first visit the nearest Department of Employment (in Rhodes, on the Street of the Knights, Odhós Ippotón) and collect two forms: one an **employment application** which you fill in, the other for the formal offer of work by your prospective employer. Once these are vetted, and revenue stamps (*hartósima*, purchased at kiosks) applied, you take them to the Alien's Bureau (Ipiresía Allodhapón) or, in its absence, the central police station, to support your application for a **residence permit** (*ádhia paramonís*). For this, you will also need to bring your passport, two photographs, more *hartósima* and a stable address (not a hotel). Permits are given for terms of three or six months (white cards), one year (green triptych booklets), or even five years (blue booklets) if they've become well acquainted with you. For one- or five-year permits, a **health examination** at the nearest public hospital is required, to screen for TB, syphillis and HIV.

EU nationals who do not wish to work in Greece but still need a residence permit will still get a "white" pass gratis, but must present evidence of financial solvency; personalized pink exchange receipts, travellers' cheques or credit cards are all considered valid proof.

At the present time, **non-EU nationals** who wish to work in Greece do so surreptitiously, with the ever-present risk of denunciation to the police and instant deportation. Having been forced to accept large numbers of EU citizens looking for jobs in a climate of rising unemployment, Greek immigration authorities are cracking down hard on any suitable targets, be they Albanian, African, Swiss or North American. That old foreigners' standby, teaching English, is now available only to TEFL certificate-holders, preferably Greek, non-EU nationals of Greek descent, and EU nationals in that order. If you are a non-EU foreign national of Greek descent, you are termed *"omólogos"* (returned Greek diaspora member) and in fact have tremendous employment and residence rights – you can, for example, open your very own *frondistírio* without any qualifications (something painfully evident in the often appalling quality of English instruction in Greece).

Directory

BARGAINING This isn't a regular feature of life, though you'll find it possible with private rooms and some hotels out of season. Similarly, you may be able to negotiate discounted rates for vehicle rental, especially for longer periods. Services such as shoe, watch and camera repair don't have iron-clad rates, so use common sense when assessing charges (advance estimates are not a routine practice).

CHILDREN Kids are worshipped and indulged in Greece, and present few problems when travelling. Baby foods and nappies (diapers) are ubiquitous and reasonably priced, plus concessions are offered on most forms of transport. Private rooms establishments and luxury hotels are more likely to offer some kind of babysitting service than the mid-range, C-class hotels.

CINEMA Greek **cinemas** show a large number of American and British movies, always in the original language, with Greek subtitles. They are highly affordable, currently 1100–1600dr depending on location and plushness of facilities, and in summer a number are set up outside on vacant lots. An **outdoor movie** is worth catching at least once for the experience alone, though it's best to opt for the earlier screening (approximately 9pm) since the soundtrack on the later show tends to be turned down or even off to avoid complaints from adjacent residences.

DEPARTURE TAX This is levied on all international ferries – currently 1500dr per person *and* the same again for any car or motorbike – within the EU. To non-EU states (Turkey, Egypt and Israel), it's 4000dr per person, sometimes arbitrarily levied twice (on entry and exit). There's also an airport departure tax, currently 2800dr for destinations under 750 miles away, 5600dr for remoter ones, but it's always included in the price of the ticket – there's no collection at the airport itself.

ELECTRICITY 220 volt AC throughout the country. Wall outlets take double round-pin plugs as in the rest of continental Europe. Three-to-two-pin adaptors should be purchased beforehand in the UK, as they can be difficult to find in Greece; the standard five-amp design will allow use of a hair-dryer. North American appliances will require both a step-down transformer and a plug adapter.

FILM *Fuji* and *Agfa* print films are reasonably priced and easy to have processed – you practically trip over "One Hour Foto" shops in some resorts. *Fuji* and *Ektachrome* slide film can be purchased, at a slight mark-up, on the larger islands, but it cannot be processed there – whatever you may be told, it will be sent to Athens, so it's best to wait until you return home.

FOOTBALL (Soccer) By far and away the most popular sport in Greece. The most important (and most heavily sponsored) teams are *Panathanaïkós* and *AEK* of Athens, *Olympiakós* of Pireás, and *PAOK* of Thessaloníki.

GAY LIFE For men, overtly gay behaviour in public is still taboo in rural Greece, and only visible on Rhodes. Eressós on Lésvos, birthplace of Sappho, is (appropriately) an international mecca for lesbians. Homosexuality is legal over the age of 17, and (male) bisexual behaviour quite widely accepted.

HIKING Greeks are just becoming used to the notion that anyone should want to walk for pleasure, yet if you have the time and stamina it is probably the best way to see many of the Dodecanese and East Aegean islands. This guide includes descriptions of a number of hikes, but for more detail you might want to acquire Marc Dubin's *Trekking in Greece* (see "Books" in *Contexts*). For advice on maps, see p.24.

LAUNDRETTES (*plindíria*) are beginning to crop up in most of the main resort towns; sometimes an attended service wash is available for little or no extra charge over the basic cost of 1300–1500dr per wash and dry. Otherwise, ask room owners for a *skáfi* (laundry trough), a bucket (*kouvás*), or the special laundry area; they freak out if you use bathroom washbasins, Greek plumbing and wall-mounting being what they are.

PERÍPTERA These are street-corner kiosks, or sometimes a hole-in-the-wall shopfront. They sell everything from pens to disposable razors, stationery to soap, sweets to condoms, cigarettes to plastic crucifixes – and are often open when nothing else is.

TIME Greek summertime begins at 4am on the last Sunday in March, when the clocks go forward one hour, and ends at 4am the last Sunday in September, when they go back. Be alert to this, as the change is not well publicized, leading scores of visitors to miss planes and ferries every year. Greek time is two hours ahead of Britain, but one hour for a few weeks in October when the countries' respective changes back to wintertime fail to coincide. For North America, the difference is seven hours for Eastern Standard Time, ten hours for Pacific Standard Time, with again an extra hour plus or minus for those weeks in April and October when one place is on daylight savings and the other isn't. A recorded time message (in Greek) is available by dialling ☎141.

TOILETS Public ones in towns are usually in parks or squares, often subterranean; otherwise try a bus station. Except in areas frequented by tourists (such as Ródhos Town), public toilets tend to be pretty filthy – it's best to use those in restaurants and bars. Note that throughout Greece you drop toilet paper in the adjacent wastebins, not in the bowl.

USEFUL THINGS A small alarm clock for early buses and ferries, a flashlight if you're camping out, sunscreen of high SPF (15 and above; generally unavailable in Greece), and ear plugs for noisy ferries or hotels.

The Guide

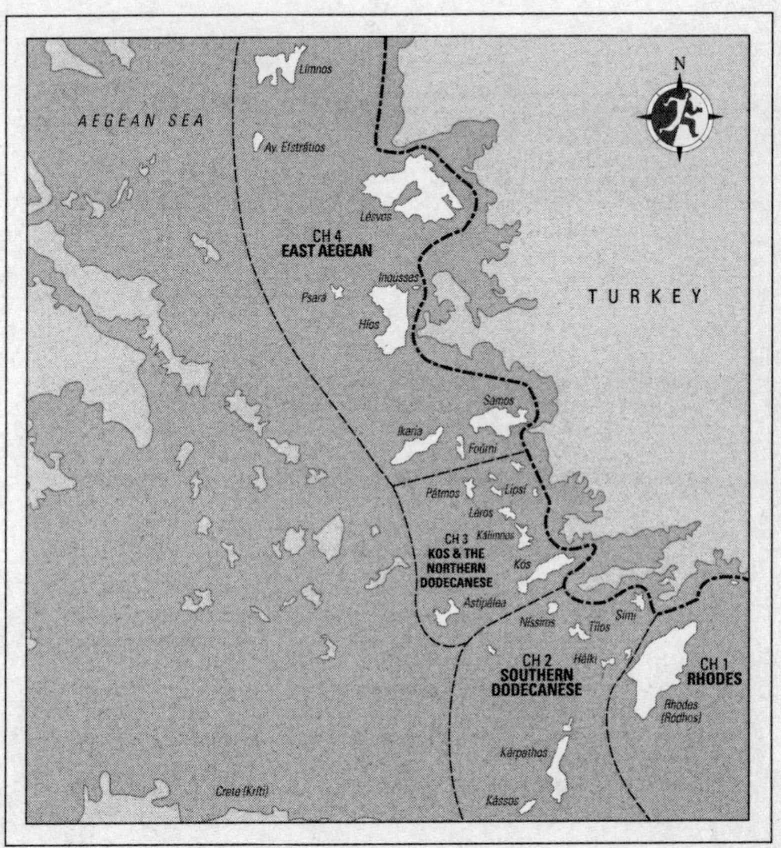

Límnos
AEGEAN SEA
Ay. Efstrátios
Lésvos
CH 4
EAST AEGEAN
Inoússes
Psará
Híos
TURKEY
Sámos
Ikaría
Foúrni
Pátmos
Lipsí
Léros
CH 3
Kálimnos
KOS & THE
NORTHERN
DODECANESE
Kós
Astipálea
Níssiros
Tílos
Sími
CH 2
SOUTHERN
DODECANESE
Hálki
CH 1
RHODES
Rhodes
(Ródhos)
Kárpathos
Kássos
Crete (Kríti)
N

Chapter 1

Rhodes

It's no accident that **Rhodes** (Ródhos) is, along with Crete, the most visited of Greek islands. Not only is its east coast lined with numerous sandy beaches, but the capital's kernel is a beautiful and remarkably preserved medieval city, a legacy of the crusading Knights of St John who used the island as their main base from 1309 until 1522. Add to this a nine-month season with three hundred sunny days annually, and you have all the ingredients for touristic success; the only quibble might concern its precise nature. Dozens of battery-chicken-farm hotels lining the "Golden Mile" between the airport and main town hardly bode well for any degree of good taste, nor does the fact that certain guests wear T-shirts inscribed "SEX 90%, LOVE 1%, RELAX 9%, THIS IS RHODES 100%" without apparent embarrassment. If you're so inclined, you need look no further, but those of a more enquiring nature will discover a hilly, partly forested interior big enough to get lost in, remote castles and Byzantine churches, pleasant ridges and stream canyons, as well as peaceful villages still living at least partly from agriculture.

Rhodes has an official population of over 98,000, more than half the population of the entire Dodecanese. As for the transient and foreign population, several thousand permanent expats are joined in a good year by over one million tourists (up to 100,000 a day in July). Of the foreigners, Germans, Brits, Swedes, Italians and Danes predominate in that order; accordingly smörgåsbord, fish fingers and pizza jostle alongside *moussakás* on tourist-trough menus. Numerous Greeks also frequent the better hotels, as Rhodes is heavily promoted domestically as a chic weekend destination. All the proceeds of tourism sloshing about have engendered a notably decadent, mock-Athenian lifestyle among the townspeople, reflected in the expensive *gelaterie* and designer shops featuring the latest Lacoste, Trussardi and Ralph Lauren gladrags.

Some mythology and etymology

According to **legend**, the sun god Helios (then a separate being from Apollo) was away doing his daily rounds when Zeus appor-

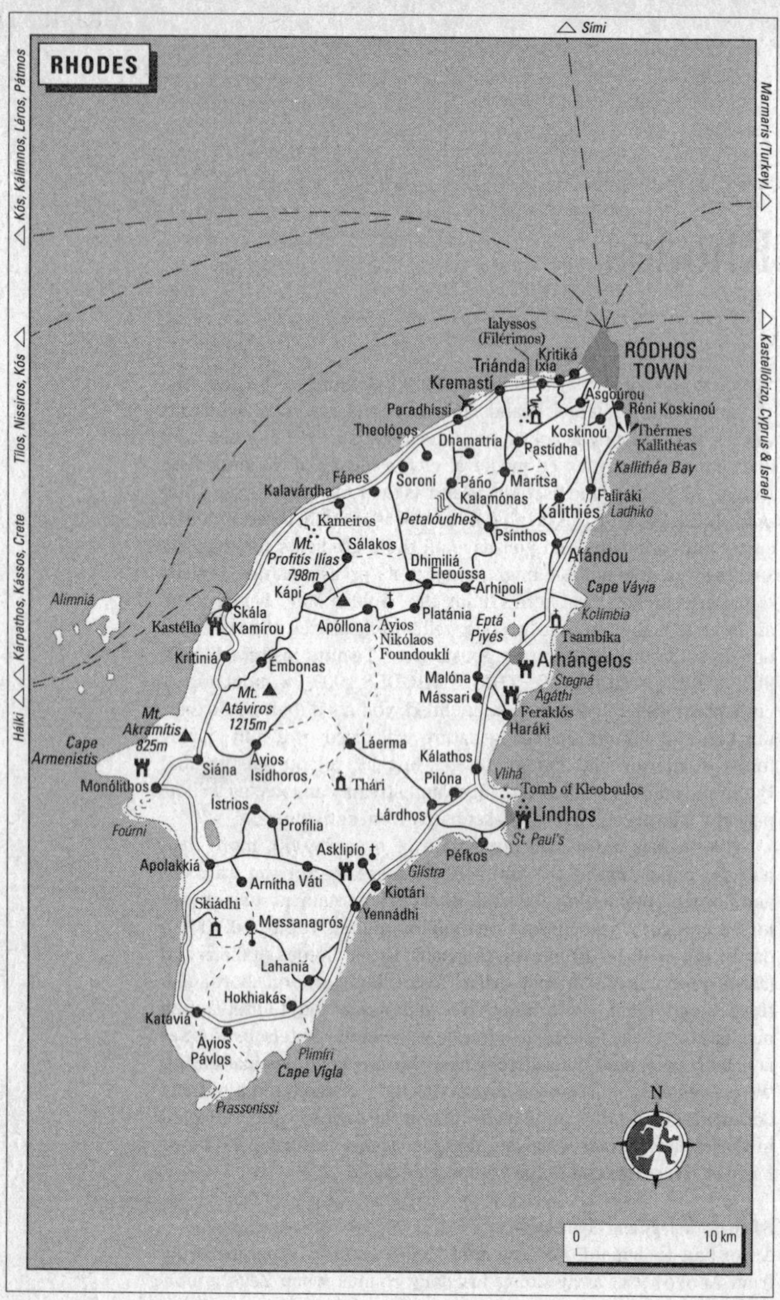
RHODES
Sími
Marmaris (Turkey)
Kastellórizo, Cyprus & Israel
Kós, Kálimnos, Léros, Pátmos
Tílos, Nissiros, Kós
Háiki, Kárpathos, Kássos, Crete
Ialyssos
(Filérimos)
Kritiká
RÓDHOS
TOWN
Triánda
Ixia
Kremastí
Asgoúrou
Paradhíssi
Réni Koskinoú
Theológos
Koskinoú
Thérmes
Kallithéas
Dhamatría
Pastídha
Kallithéa Bay
Fánes
Soroní
Páño
Marítsa
Kalavárdha
Kalamónas
Faliráki
Kameiros
Petaloúdhes
Kalithiés
Ladhikó
Mt.
Profitis Ilías
798m
Sálakos
Psínthos
Afándou
Dhimiliá
Eleoússa
Kápi
Arhípoli
Cape Váyia
Alimniá
Skála
Kamírou
Platánia
Kolímbia
Kastéllo
Apóllona
Áyios
Nikólaos
Foundouklí
Eptá
Piyés
Tsambíka
Kritiniá
Émbonas
Arhángelos
Malóna
Stegná
Mt.
Atáviros
1215m
Mássari
Agáthi
Feraklós
Mt.
Akramítis
825m
Haráki
Cape
Armenistis
Láerma
Kálathos
Siána
Áyios
Isídhoros
Vlihá
Monólithos
Thári
Pilóna
Tomb of Kleoboulos
Ístrios
Lárdhos
Líndhos
Profília
St. Paul's
Foúrni
Asklipío
Péfkos
Apolakkiá
Váti
Glístra
Arnítha
Kiotári
Yennádhi
Skiádhi
Messanagrós
Lahaniá
Hokhiakás
Kataviá
Áyios
Pávlos
Plimíri
Cape Vígla
Prassoníssi
N
0
10 km

tioned the world among his fellow Olympian deities. To make amends, he promised Helios any part of the earth that had not yet emerged from the sea. As it happened, Helios had spied the nymph Rodon, daughter of Poseidon and Amphitrite, under the water off Asia Minor; concentrating his rays, he induced her to rise up, whereupon he married her. In its essentials, this pretty myth deviates little from the Father Sky/Mother Earth prototypes common to many early cultures, though in the case of Rhodes it seems the tale evolved to explain the presence of fossilized seashells up in the Rhodian hills, for indeed the island was thrust up from the sea floor aeons ago by earthquakes and plate tectonics.

The real derivation of the **name** "Rhodes" remains controversial: the tourist board claims that it stems from the ancient Greek word for "rose", though neither the domesticated nor the wild *Cistus* rock species, however abundant now, are native to the island. It is more likely a corruption of *ro(ï)di* or pomegranate, and ancient coins with a pomegranate on one side and the sun god's head on the other are fairly common. A recent, ingenious theory has it that the "rose" is really the hibiscus, which also grows here in profusion but again is not native.

A brief history

Blessed with an equable climate and strategic position, the island of Rhodes was important from earliest times, despite a lack of many good harbours. The best natural port spawned the ancient town of Lindos which, together with the other city-states Kameiros and Ialyssos, united in 408 BC to found the new capital of Rhodes at the northern tip of the island. At various moments the cities allied themselves with Alexander, Persians, Athenians or Spartans as prevailing conditions suited, generally escaping retribution for backing the wrong side by a combination of seafaring audacity, sycophancy and burgeoning wealth as a trade centre. Following the failed siege of Demetrios Polyorketes in 305 BC (see box overleaf), Rhodes prospered even more, displacing Athens as the major venue for rhetoric and the arts in the east Mediterranean. The ancient town, which lies beneath virtually all of the modern city, was initially laid out by early urban planner Hippodamus of Miletus according to a grid layout much in vogue at the time, with planned residential and commercial quarters. Its perimeter walls totalled nearly 15km, enclosing roughly double the area of today's city, and the Hellenistic population exceeded 100,000, a staggering figure for ancient times.

Decline set in when Rhodes became involved in the Roman civil wars and Cassius sacked the town; by late imperial times, it had become a backwater, a status confirmed by numerous barbarian raids during the Byzantine period. The Byzantines were compelled to cede the island to the Genoese, who in turn (after a three-year resistance) surrendered it to the Knights of St John (see box p.72).

The first siege of Rhodes

The first great **siege of Rhodes** in 305 BC, considered the most noteworthy military campaign of ancient times, resulted from power struggles between the generals of Alexander the Great following his death. Owing to their close trade links, Rhodes sided with Egypt, then ruled by Ptolemy. Rival Macedonian general Antigonus ordered Rhodes to attack its ally on his behalf; when the islanders refused, Antigonus, furious at this rebuff, sent his son **Demetrios** to discipline the defiant Rhodians. Nicknamed "Polyorketes" (Besieger of Many Cities) and fresh from the capture of Salamis on Cyprus, Demetrios was one of the military geniuses of his day, with intimidating resources to draw upon: 200 warships, nearly as many supporting craft, and 40,000 seasoned infantrymen. Against these forces the Rhodians could muster just 8000 citizen-soldiers, perhaps 2000 Cretans and Egyptian mercenaries, and 15,000 slaves who were bought up by the municipality and promised their freedom in the event of successful resistance. Additionally, the government guaranteed funerals with full honours for the fallen, plus perpetual subsidy to their surviving relatives. These wise strategies boosted morale, strengthened social cohesion and probably influenced the battle's outcome, as no significant instance of treason was recorded throughout the long siege, in which every able-bodied inhabitant was occupied in the defense.

Having blockaded the city with his fleet, Demetrios initially targetted the apparently vulnerable harbour walls, launching projectiles from a pair of ingenious "tortoises": armoured carapaces slung between two ships and protected by booms to repel ramming attacks by the Rhodians. In a daring sortie, these were sunk by the Rhodians, whose cause was futher helped by the destruction in a storm of a new, land-based siege tower, and the arrival of fresh reinforcements from Ptolemy.

In light of these reverses, Demetrios changed tactics, devoting his attentions to the landward walls and ordering the construction of the so-

The second great siege of Rhodes, during 1522, saw the Ottoman sultan Süleyman the Magnificent oust the stubborn knights, who retreated to Malta; town and island once again lapsed into relative obscurity, though it was heavily colonized and garrisoned until the Italian seizure of 1912.

After 1922, Fascist-ruled Italy selected Rhodes to be the crown jewel of its "Aegean Empire", and lavished great sums on road-building, water-works, reafforestation and the first inklings of a mass tourism industry. More controversially, the Italians engaged in excavation and restoration of archeological sites, as well as indulging their usual edifice complex in new civic structures and restorations of medieval monuments. The Greek Orthodox population benefited little from this, on the contrary enduring sustained cultural persecution (see "History" in *Contexts*). In autumn 1943 the Italians capitulated, and certainly the Jews of the Dodecanese must have preferred the relative leniency of their rule, suffering total genocide at the hands of the Germans who replaced them. The British administered the island from mid-1945 until the 1948 unifi-

called **Helepolis** or "Overthrower of Cities", as yet the largest siege tower the world had seen. Sheathed in metal and animal hides, this measured 27 metres on each side at the base, tapering slightly over a nine-storey height, with windows for launching missiles and drawbridges for depositing commandoes atop the walls; over three thousand men were required to arm and move this wheeled, 125-tonne behemoth.

In response, the tenacious Rhodians doubled their walls and mounted successful forays to break the Macedonian blockade, while Demetrios' many enemies surreptitiously arranged to replenish the city's food supplies. The Helepolis repeatedly damaged the city's fortifications, but the Macedonians failed to gain entry; in one nocturnal raid, the Rhodians almost succeeded in setting the tower alight. Following stalled peace negotiations sponsored by other Hellenic cities, Demetrios opted for a decisive charge on the weakest spot, in conjunction with a general attack along the entire length of the perimeter walls. Some 1500 of his men managed briefly to establish a foothold inside the city, near the theatre, but were surrounded by the Rhodians and cut down almost to a man.

By now the siege had been on for almost a year, with both sides nearly exhausted; Demetrios' father, Antigonos, and Ptolemy began urging their respective protégés to come to honourable terms, as nobody would gain if the wealthiest city in the Aegean were reduced to rubble. This final truce was in fact prompted by an ingenious act of sabotage: a Rhodian engineer directed a team of sappers to tunnel past the walls and undermine the usual path of the Helepolis, causing it to founder and collapse. Demetrios, finally convinced of the islanders' resolve, confirmed Rhodes as an independent city-state, requiring it only to contribute ships towards Macedonian military expeditions as long as hostilities were not directed against Ptolemy, and one hundred noble hostages as security against any breach of the agreement. He also left all his war machinery with the Rhodians to play a crucial role in the saga of the Colossus (see box, p.77).

cation with Greece, thus beginning a long-standing love affair between the UK and Rhodes. Only now are the worst memories of Fascist rule fading, as those who directly experienced it pass away, and grudging acknowledgement is finally being made of the comprehensive and still mostly usable infrastructure inherited from the Italians.

Ródhos Town

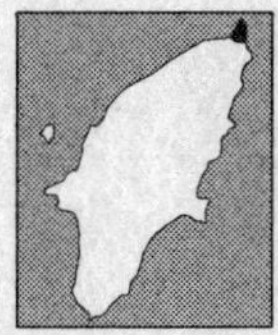

RÓDHOS TOWN, built around the second best natural harbour on the island after Líndhos, is very much the main event on Rhodes, and deservedly so in its exquisite medieval city. Air arrivals miss out on the majestic approach by ferry, usually in the morning light which shows to advantage a fair amount of the old town's five-kilometre ramparts, their contours softened by gardens and accented by turrets. Once the apotheosis of military architecture, today they are merely a decorative backdrop, dividing the town into two unequal parts: the relatively compact walled quarter, and the sprawling modern neighbourhoods surrounding it on three sides.

The separation of new town from old dates from the Ottoman occupation; the Greeks, forbidden to reside in the walled city built by the Knights of St John, founded several suburb villages or *marásia* in the environs. Áyios Ioánnis, Áyii Anáryiri, Ayía Anastasía, Mitrópolis and Áyios Yióryios were initially established due south of the Turkish cemeteries which grew up outside the walls, while Neohóri – synonymous with the sharp promontory to the northwest – was settled last. Since the Italian era they have all merged into one cement-laced conurbation, but the above-named churches still exist, as do the narrow lanes and older houses immediately around them. Even with this filling-in of previously empty spaces, modern Rhodes is still far smaller in both dimensions and population than its Hellenistic precursor.

Tourism is predominant in much of the old town and throughout the Neohóri district west of Mandhráki yacht harbour, where the few buildings that aren't hotels serve as souvenir shops, bars and car rental or travel agencies. Locals mostly live south and west of the walled city, in the older parishes, with students from one of the main campuses of the University of the Aegean supplementing the permanent population of about 40,000.

Arrival, information and transport

The **airport**, currently being expanded, is 13km southwest of town, conveniently near the village of Paradhíssi. Any public **urban bus** coming from Paradhíssi, Theológos, Kalavárdha or Sálakos will stop up on the road opposite the northerly car-park entrance, and services are fairly frequent between 6.30am and 9pm (see "Travel Details"). The bus fare to town is 250dr, versus 2000dr for **taxis**, the latter figure increasing slightly to about 2500dr after midnight; standard fares to the most popular resort destinations are displayed on a placard. Those flying in at an unsociable hour might therefore consider arranging **car rental** in advance of their trip, though at slow times you may be able to get something affordable on the spur of the moment from *Holiday Autos* (☎0241/35 239), who have a booth at the airport.

As of writing, all international and inter-island ferries drop anchor in the mid-most of Rhodes' three ports, the so-called commercial harbour, more properly known as Kolóna. In future, however, some may be diverted to a new terminal planned for the easternmost port, Akándia, so look out for changes. Local boats to and from Sími, plus east-coast excursion boats, currently use the south quay of Mandhráki yacht harbour, while hydrofoils dock at the west quay – occasionally beside the Áyios Nikólaos bastion – but these also are scheduled to move their base of operations, this time to the small jetty in Kolóna where the *Nissos Kalymnos* now calls.

Information and maps

Between the east-coast bus stop and the Mandhráki taxi rank there's a helpful municipal **tourist office** (May–Oct daily 9am–9pm; ☎0241/35 945), while 200m up Papágou, on the corner of Makaríou, is the less organized **EOT** office (Mon–Fri 8am–2pm; ☎0241/23 255); both dispense bus and ferry schedules plus information sheets on the archeological sites. Situated next to the EOT, the multilingual **Tourist Police** (☎0241/27 423; 24hr) deal with general information and complaints; officers wear a badge or flag indicating languages spoken.

The free island **maps** supplied by information offices or car-rental firms are as good as any you can buy; all are based on the work of the same cartographer, Tsopelas. Ródhos Town is another matter; accept no substitute for the A–Z-type mini-atlas "Map of Rhodes Town" (1500dr), which includes an overview poster-map, or "Rhodes, Map of the Old Town" (1200dr), another art-format map of the medieval city that's nonetheless the most accurate available. Both were prepared by long-time resident Mario Camerini; if you're having difficulty finding them, enquire at *Araliki* (see "Old town bars", p.84).

Local buses

Orange-and-cream (as opposed to the usual Greek green-and-cream) *KTEL* **buses** for all points along the east coast leave from and arrive at a terminal on Papágou, just above Platía Rimínis, aka "Sound and Light Square". Identically coloured coaches run by *RODA* depart for the west coast from a stop just around the corner on Avérof, under the sidewalk arcades of the so-called New Market; *RODA* also runs relatively infrequent urban lines from the same terminal, with both services severely reduced on Saturday and Sunday. Tickets for the long-distance *RODA* buses are sold on board, and those for the numbered city routes from special kiosks (for subsequent cancellation in the bus).

Taxis and traffic control

Taxi ranks are numerous and shown on the town maps with a circled 'T'. Even by the standards of Greek tourist resorts, Rhodian taxi drivers can be a source of grief for the inexperienced. Resist their initial gambits to deposit you at inconveniently remote beach-strip hotels, which pay kickbacks to the drivers, and also treat sceptically reports that particular hotels or pensions in the old town are "full", "dirty", "closed", "burnt down", etc. If you are luggage-laden, drivers are obliged by law to take you to the door of your chosen accommodation, even if it is in the old town, which is otherwise off-limits to non-residents' vehicles. In the event of any trouble, refuse to pay until delivered to your destination, and if necessary note down licence numbers; the tourist police are happy to investigate such incidents.

As noted above, all wheeled **traffic** is banned within the medieval walls, except for residents' cars and scooters; this law is strictly enforced eighteen hours a day by a warden manning a chain at each gate. Parking within any reasonable distance of the old town is a challenge, and the closest most will get is along Filellínon, just outside the Ayíou Athanasíou gate. At night, there may also be space along the walls facing the commercial harbour. Neohóri, the northern extension of the new town, is a nightmare, though surprisingly you can sometimes find a parking spot along Platía Eleftherías, the western esplanade at Mandhráki.

Accommodation

Inexpensive pensions abound in the **old town** and are found almost entirely in the quad bounded by Omírou to the south, Sokrátous to the north, Perikléous to the east and Ippodhámou to the west; in addition, there are some more upmarket hotels in the heart of the old Jewish quarter, east of Perikléous. Anyone arriving without a reservation in peak season or late at night would be prudent to accept the offers of proprietors meeting the ferries and change base next day if necessary; it frequently is, since on closer acquaintance, many "rooms" turn out to have facilities (and hygienic standards) little changed since the age of the Knights. Recommended establishments are those most likely to have firm beds, consistent hot water, relatively restrained decor, nocturnal calm and no cockroaches.

The **new town** offers modern, purpose-built hotels, less likely to be open in winter, as well as a few colourful pensions installed in

Accommodation prices

All establishments in this book have a symbol that corresponds to one of six price ranges:

① up to 5000dr	② 5000–7000dr	③ 7000–9000dr
④ 9000–13000dr	⑤ 13000–17000dr	⑥ above 17000dr

1£=370dr; 1$= 240dr

The rates quoted for each category represent the cheapest available double room in high season. Out of season, room prices can drop by up to fifty percent, especially if you negotiate a stay of three or more nights. Single rooms, where available, cost around seventy percent of the price of a double.

Accommodation on Rhodes tends to fall into categories ② and above, the former representing standard, en-suite rooms without cooking facilities. Newer, state-of-the-art rooms and self-catering studios occupy the ③ niche, along with most of the government-rated C-class hotels, the newer of which also edge into ④. Category ④ corresponds fairly well to the government-assigned B-class for hotels, ⑤ with A-class and ⑥ with De Luxe; incidentally, establishments in the latter category are exempt from price control.

former Italian villas. Few of the hotels have vacancies for independent travellers, and many are plagued by after-hours noise from the dozens of bars lining nearby streets – though uninterrupted sleep is unlikely to be a priority of many among the hotel clientele. The establishments listed here have been selected for value and relative peace.

The old town

Andreas, Omírou 28D (☎0241/34 156; fax ☎74 285). Perennially popular, this hotel is the most imaginative of the old-house restorations. All rooms have sinks, there's a terrace bar with a view, plus French and English are spoken. Also two family suites with lofts; singles negotiable. ③.

Apollo, Omírou 28C (☎0241/35 064). Basic but clean and friendly "rooms" place. Self-catering kitchen makes this good for longer stays. ②.

Casa de la Sera, Thisséos 38 (☎0241/75 154). One of several Jewish-quarter renovations, with wonderful floor tiles in the en-suite rooms and a ground-floor breakfast bar. ④.

Cava d'Oro, Kistiníou 15 (Phone/fax ☎0241/36 980). Another refurbishment job in a 700-year-old house, with a small ground floor bar and a garden. Michael Palin stayed here during his 1992 BBC "Pole to Pole" jaunt. Open all year. ④.

Kastro, Platía Ariónos (☎0241/20 446). Vassilis, the proprietor, is a famous eccentric artist renowned for his royalist leanings, but the hotel offers acceptable budget (not en-suite) facilities; rooms facing the garden (adorned with Vassilis' statuary, and a tortoise named Papandreou after the ex-prime minister) are quieter than those overlooking the square with its tavernas. ②.

Iliana, Gavalá 1 (☎0241/30 251). This hotel, formerly a Jewish mansion, exudes a Victorian boarding-house atmosphere, but is clean and quiet enough with private facilities. ③.

Minos, Omírou 5 (☎0241/31 813). Modern, purpose-built pension and hence a bit sterile, but neat as a pin and with great views. ③.

Niki's, Sofokléous 39 (☎0241/25 115). Friendly "rooms" establishment, whose units are on the small side, but ground-floor rooms have showers, and upper-storey ones fine views. Recommended by FOTA (see "Tílos", p.143) as a stop-over for members en route to their favourite island. A snip at ②–③, according to season.

Sotiris Nikolis, Ippodhámou 61 (☎0241/34 561; fax ☎32 034). A top-of-the-range establishment in a restored building, whose rates (⑤) include a huge, rooftop breakfast. Sotiris and his Danish partner, Marianne, also manage nearby self-catering apartments (④) and a simple pension (③). Advance reservations essential for hotel and apartments, but accepted only with a credit-card number as a safeguard against no-shows. Open Apr–Nov except by special arrangement.

Spot, Perikléous 21 (☎0241/34 737). Not the most inspired renovation, but this hotel is spot-less, and you won't find en-suite rooms elsewhere for this price, except at *Niki's*. ②.

The new town

Anastasia, Ikostiogdhóïs Oktovríou 46, Neohóri (☎0241/21 815). A pension with high-ceilinged but unplumbed rooms in an interwar building. ③.

Angela, Ikostiogdhóïs Oktovríou 7, Neohóri (☎0241/24 614; fax ☎22 614). Reasonably quiet hotel for its central location; B-class comfort and breakfast on the sixth-floor roof terrace. ⑤.

Annitsa, Ayíou Ioánnou 44, Áyios Ioánnis (☎0241/32 106). Well-placed hotel on a calm street between the Monte Smith acropolis and the old town, offering self-catering units as well as en-suite rooms. Open April–Oct. ④.

Capitol, Dhilberáki 65–67, Neohóri (☎0241/74 154). Rambling pension in another Italian-era building, quiet enough en-suite rooms considering its proximity to the bar district. ③

Marietta, Ikostiogdhóïs Oktovríou 28, corner Fanouráki, Neohóri (☎0241/36 396). Yet another Italianate pension, this one with en-suite rooms. ④.

New Village Inn, Konstandopédhos, off Íonos Dhragoúmi, Neohóri (☎0241/34 937). High standard, en-suite rooms, some self-catering. ②–③.

Plaza, Ieroú Lóhou 1, Neohóri (☎0241/22 501, fax ☎22 544). Probably the most luxurious hotel within Rhodes city limits, in the heart of Neohóri. Pool, sauna/jacuzzi, buffet English breakfast. Open all year; available at advantageous rates, particularly in winter, through *Argo Holidays*. ⑤.

Royal, Theméli, corner Sofokléous Venizélou, Neohóri (☎0241/24 601). Medium-sized, family-run hotel on quiet side street; no tour groups, so a good bet for last minute vacancies. Open April–Nov, though its future is uncertain as of 1996. Unusually furnished rooms ③–⑤ according to season.

The old town

Simply to catalogue the principal monuments and attractions cannot do full justice to the infinitely rewarding **old town**. There's ample gratification to be derived merely from slipping through the eleven surviving gates and strolling the streets, under flying archways built for earthquake resistance, past warm-toned sandstone and limestone walls painted ochre and blue, and over *hokhláki* (pebble) pavements, arranged by colour into mosaics in certain courtyards. Getting lost in the maze of alleys is part of the experience, but if you'd rather not, accurate map-placards are posted at strategic junctions.

As a walled medieval city, the old town invites favourable comparison with Jerusalem, Carcassonne, or Ávila; both the European Heritage Commission and UNESCO agree, having designated it as a World Heritage Site. All structural alterations are strictly controlled, and efforts are now being made to place utility lines underground and ban obtrusive TV aerials. Such strictures, however, don't apply to the tacky souvenir displays, especially around the intersection of Ippodhámou and Orféos; the numerous portrait artists plying their trade under the plane trees along Orféos proper are considerably more innocuous.

The town today is effectively a legacy of the Knights of St John, who in fact frequently adhered to Hippodamus' grid-plan: Pithagóra, Omírou and Ayíou Fanouríou are among the most important streets which follow exactly their ancient predecessors. The Ottomans added little to the urban fabric other than a bare handful of purpose-built mosques, minarets and the graceful clock tower just south of the Grand Masters' palace. Though not of strategic importance in itself, the old city suffered heavy bomb damage at the hands of the Allies during 1943–45 owing to German military installations in the adjacent commercial harbour.

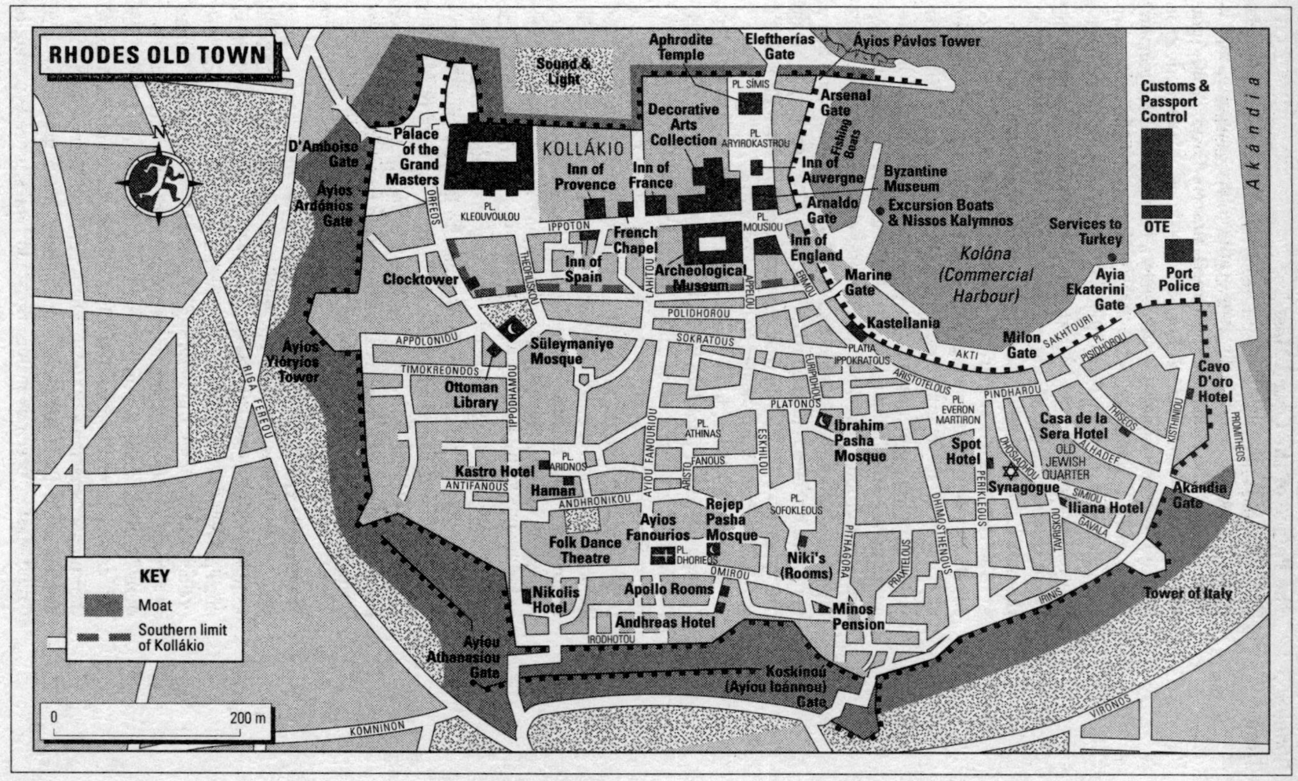
RHODES OLD TOWN
Sound & Light
Aphrodite Temple
Eleftherías Gate
Áyios Pávlos Tower
PL. SÍMIS
Arsenal Gate
Fishing Boats
Customs & Passport Control
Akándia
Palace of the Grand Masters
D'Amboise Gate
Áyios Ardónios Gate
ORFEOS
PL. KLEOUVOULOU
KOLLÁKIO
Inn of Provence
Inn of France
Decorative Arts Collection
PL. ARYIROKASTROU
Inn of Auvergne
Byzantine Museum
Arnaldo Gate
Excursion Boats & Nissos Kalymnos
Services to Turkey
OTE
IPPOTON
French Chapel
PL. MOUSIOU
Inn of England
Inn of Spain
Archeological Museum
Kolóna (Commercial Harbour)
Port Police
Clocktower
THEOFILISKOU
LAHITOU
APPELOU
ERMOU
Marine Gate
Ayia Ekaterini Gate
POLIDHOROU
Kastellania
SOKRATOUS
APPOLONIOU
Süleymaniye Mosque
Milon Gate
SAKHTOURI
AKTI
PL. PISIDHOROU
Áyios Yióryios Tower
TIMOKREONDOS
PLATIA IPPOKRATOUS
EURIPIDHOU
ARISTOTELOUS
PINDHAROU
Cavo D'oro Hotel
Ottoman Library
IPPODHAMOU
PLATONOS
PL. EVERON MARTIRON
THISEOS
KISTHINIOU
RIGA FEREOU
Ibrahim Pasha Mosque
Casa de la Sera Hotel
PROMITHEOS
PL. ATHINAS
ESKHILOU
AYIOU FANOURIOU
Spot Hotel
OLD JEWISH QUARTER
ALHADEF
PL. ARIDNOS
FANOUS
ARISTO
DHOSIADHOU
Kastro Hotel
Synagogue
Akándia Gate
ANTIFANOUS
Haman
PERIKLEOUS
SIMIOU
ANDHRONIKOU
PL. SOFOKLEOUS
DHIMOSTHENOUS
Iliana Hotel
Rejep Pasha Mosque
Ayios Fanourios
TAVRISKOU
GAVALA
Folk Dance Theatre
PL. DHORIEOS
Niki's (Rooms)
PITHAGORA
PRAXITELOUS
KEY
Moat
Southern limit of Kollákio
OMIROU
Nikolis Hotel
Apollo Rooms
IRINIS
Tower of Italy
Minos Pension
Andhreas Hotel
IRODHOTOU
Ayíou Athanasíou Gate
Koskinoú (Ayíou Ioánnou) Gate
0
200 m
KOMNINON
VIRONOS

The Palace of the Grand Masters

The Kollákio (Collachium), or fort-within-a-fort, lies in the northern sector of the city's originally fourteenth-century ramparts, and is dominated by the **Palace of the Grand Masters** (Mon 12.30–7pm, Tues–Fri 8am–7pm, Sat & Sun 8.00am–3pm; 1200dr, free on Sunday). Almost completely destroyed by a lightning-sparked gunpowder magazine explosion in 1856 (which also levelled much of the town and killed over eight hundred), this was hastily reconstructed by the Italians between 1937 and 1939 as a summer home for Mussolini and Victor Emmanuel III ("King of Italy and Albania, Emperor of Ethiopia"), though neither of them ever stayed on Rhodes.

The building's exterior, of middling authenticity, is based largely on medieval engravings and accounts. Inside, matters are on an altogether more grandiose scale, rivalling many a European palace with its ponderous period furnishings; fortunately they are not integral to the building's fabric. A monumental marble staircase leads up to rooms paved with **Hellenistic mosaics** from Kós; while one may deplore their plundering, they have certainly fared better here than if they'd remained in the open air. The best panels, all on the upper floor which you tour clockwise, are of a nymph riding a sea-monster, and the so-called *Nine Muses of Kos*.

Though much has been made of its vulgarity (eg, in Durrell's *Reflections on a Marine Venus*), the interior is in fact fairly restrained by the norms of 1930s dictatorships. However, during recent maintenance work, evidence of the Italians' cavalier attitude to history and outright vandalism was uncovered: Hellenistic and Ottoman artefacts were found discarded under rubble used to fill hollows and then bricked or tiled over; considerable artistic licence was taken with the ground floor, which had actually survived the 1856 explosion; and the site topography was altered to make the palace more imposing. Moreover, the materials and workmanship employed by the Italians are not destined to last anywhere near as long as the original; much of the masonry is cladding rather than structural, with the wall-cores consisting of low-quality, reinforced concrete, whose iron mesh is already causing tremendous problems owing to corrosion and expansion.

The Medieval Exhibit

The ground floor is home to the 1994-inaugurated **Medieval Exhibit** (Tues–Sat 8am–2.30pm, same ticket), far and away the best museum on Rhodes in terms of presentation and interpretation. The collection highlights the enduring importance of Christian Rhodes as a trade centre, with exotic merchandise placing the island in a trans-Mediterranean context. By pressing buttons on one exhibit you can see how Rhódhos Town has shrunk since ancient times to the compact ensemble of today. The Knights are represented with a display about their sugar-refining industry and a gravestone of a Grand Master; precious manuscripts and books precede a wing of post-Byzantine icons, moved here permanently from Panayía Kástrou (see below). A snack bar, well placed at the far end of the exhibits, provides seating looking out onto the palace courtyard.

The city walls

On Tuesday and Saturday afternoons, there's a supplementary one-hour tour of the **city walls** (starting 2.45–3pm; separate 1200dr admission), beginning from a gate next to the palace and traversing the western and southern reaches to the Koskinoú Gate. The tour is the only permitted access to the walls, and worth the expense for unique views of an exotic skyline punctuated with minarets, palm trees and the brooding mass of the Palace. Peering down into seldom-traversed alleys and overgrown gardens, you appreciate just how villagey and – since the World War II bombardments – occasionally crumbled the old town really is. The limestone fortifications, at certain points over 12m thick, date in their present form almost entirely from extensive refurbishment following the siege of 1480 (disregarding modern repairs); the various gates and bastions divided the curtain walls into eight sections, one for each of the Order's "Tongues" or nationalities.

The "Street of the Knights"

The Gothic "**Street of the Knights**" (Ippotón) leads due east from Platía Kleovoúlou, in front of the Palace; once the main thoroughfare of the Kollákio, it was heavily restored by the Italians, who stripped the facades of their wooden, Ottoman balconies and repaired the extensive 1856 blast damage. The Inns lining it housed most of the Knights of St John (see box), according to linguistic-ethnic affiliation – those for England and Auvergne are one block away on Apelloú and Platía Aryirokástrou respectively – and their ground floors served as stables for the Knights' horses. Today the Inns (not generally open to the public) contain government offices and foreign cultural institutions vaguely appropriate to their past. Although commercialization is forbidden on this street, the whole effect is predictably sterile and stagey (indeed, nearby streets *were* used in the filming of *Pascali's Island*). The only hint of life, about halfway up on the south side, is an iron-gated garden where a Turkish fountain, surrounded by cannon balls, once gurgled; it has been shut off since 1993 due to renovation, but if it is flowing again, the sound will be startling in the absolute silence here at night. Directly opposite stands the most ornate of the Inns, that of France, embellished with the coats-of-arms of several Grand Masters.

The Archeological Museum

At the very foot of Ippotón, the Knights' Hospital has been refurbished as the **Archeological Museum** (July/Aug Mon 12.30–7pm, Tues–Fri 8am–7pm, Sat & Sun 8am–3pm; 800dr), though the building, with its arches and echoing halls, rather overshadows the

The Knights of St John and the Second Siege of Rhodes

The Order of the Knights Hospitallers of St John was established in eleventh-century Jerusalem as a nursing order tending sick Christian pilgrims. But since their original charter involved protecting as well as ministering to Christians, not a great conceptual leap was involved in them becoming a more militant order after the First Crusade. The Knights were compelled to leave Palestine in 1291 after losing their principal strongholds to the Saracens and a competing chivalric order, the Knights Templar.

Cyprus proved unsatisfactory as a new home, so the Hospitallers migrated further west to Rhodes in 1306, which they captured from the Genoese after a three-year war. Once in possession, the Knights began modifying and shrinking the relatively flimsy Byzantine town fortifications; adequate funds were ensured when their rivals the Templars were suppressed in 1312 and most of their European assets made over to the Hospitallers by Pope Clement. Despite their origins, the Knights became a seafaring Order, aggrandizing themselves with frequent raids on non-Christian shipping. A huge fleet was fitted out for this purpose, its flagship the *Grand Carrack*, an eight-decker galley equipped for hundreds of men for six months of continuous sailing.

There were three classes of membership in the Order, sworn to quasi-monastic vows of chastity, poverty and obedience that were honoured more often than not. Full-fledged knights, never numbering more than 650, were recruited only among the nobility, while brothers, who served as soldiers or nurses, could be commoners. Chaplains were assigned to each of the seven, later eight, nationalities or "Tongues": France, Auvergne, Provence, Italy, Spain, Germany, and England. Each tongue was headed by a prior, who among them chose the Grand Master or general prefect of the order; these were elected for life, though in theory subject to a council of the priors. Of the nineteen Grand Masters, fourteen were French, a reflection of the three Francophone contingents, and the fact that French (with Latin) was one of the two official languages of the order. During the fourteenth century, Spain managed to divide her contingent into the inns of Aragon and Castile, in a ploy to increase Spanish-speaking influence.

After the fall of Constantinople in 1453, the Knights were the only significant obstacle to further Ottoman expansion in the Aegean, as well as a continuing nuisance to their shipping. Although Rhodes withstood

contents. The appallingly presented collection consists largely of painted pottery dating from the sixth and seventh centuries, enlivened at one point by Bronze Age grave jewellery from Ialyssos. Rather more accessible is the Hellenistic statue gallery, located behind the second-storey sculpture garden, where visitors pose for photos with a not-very-naturalistic porpoise-head sculpture. In a rear corner stands *Aphrodite Thalassia*, the so-called "Marine Venus" beloved of Lawrence Durrell, lent a rather sinister aspect by her sea-dissolved face; in the adjacent wing crouches a friendlier *Aphrodite Bathing*, or more precisely wringing out her tresses. Opposite are earlier, fine works of the Rhodian sculpture academy, such as Hygea feeding her familiar serpent and Asklepios leaning on his staff.

two brief Ottoman sieges in 1444 and 1480, Grand Masters Pierre d'Aubusson and Aimerie d'Amboise decided to embark on a final fortification programme to resist any technological advance in Ottoman artillery.

In the spring of 1522, Sultan Süleyman the Magnificent, determined to stamp out the Knights' piracy, landed on Rhodes with a force of 100,000. For six months the Knights and their auxiliaries, outnumbered thirty to one, held out until the Ottomans were ready, like Demetrios before them, to concede defeat. But a traitor among the Knights, piqued at not being elected Grand Master, sent word to the Sultan that the garrison was at the end of its tether and could withstand only a few more concerted attacks. The consequent Turkish offensives in October and November ensured victory, following which Süleyman granted unusually magnanimous terms: the 180 surviving Knights were allowed to take all their movable property and ships with them on New Year's Day 1523, as well as any civilians who preferred not to live under Muslim rule.

For seven years the Knights searched for a new base in the Mediterranean, before settling on Malta, where they successfully repulsed another, four-month Ottoman attack in 1565, and provided crucial aid for the defeat of the Ottomans at Lepanto six years later. However, the English "Tongue" had been dissolved in 1534 by Henry VIII, and subsequently the Knights proved to be an anachronism: large, unified states of the sixteenth century could commission and outfit armadas far more efficiently, and the opening of trade routes to the New World and the Far East lessened the importance of controlling Mediterranean trade. The French branch of the Order was dissolved during the Revolution, and its assets confiscated; Napoleon met little resistance in 1798 when he annexed Malta in a minor diversion en route to Egypt, and dispersed the remaining Knights, apparently for good.

The English "Tongue" was revived in 1831 and re-organized as the St John Ambulance Brigade in 1888. The oldest visible traces of the Order in London's Clerkenwell district are the medieval gate on St John's Lane, all that survives of the twelfth-century priory where English Knights were recruited, and the crypt of the later church facing St John's Square, with a Maltese cross visible outside. In July 1995, today's worldwide Order – also active in Sweden, the Netherlands, Germany and Italy – held its annual four-day convention on Rhodes, with gala events centred (of course) on the Grand Master's Palace.

The Decorative Arts and Byzantine Museums

Nearby on Platía Aryirokástrou, with its Byzantine fountain from Arnítha village, is the **Decorative Arts Collection** (Tues–Sun 8.30am–3pm; 600dr), gleaned from old houses across the Dodecanese. As with its neighbour, there's not much in the way of explanation, but the fine Iznik and Kütahya ceramics, costumes, embroidery and folk pottery are fairly self-explanatory. The most compelling artefacts are carved cupboard doors and chest lids painted with mythological or historical episodes in naïve style.

Across the way stands the **Byzantine Museum** (Tues–Sun 8.30am–3pm; 600dr), housed in the old cathedral of the Knights, who adapted the Byzantine shrine of Panayía Kástrou for their own needs. Medieval icons and frescoes lifted from crumbling chapels on Rhodes and Hálki, as well as photos of art still *in situ*, constitute the exhibits. It's worth a visit since most of the Byzantine churches in the old town and outlying villages are locked, though the collection has been severely depleted by transfers of the best items to the Palace of the Grand Masters.

Ottoman Rhodes

If you head south from the Palace of the Grand Masters, it's hard to miss the most conspicuous Turkish monument in Rhodes, the candy-striped **Süleymaniye mosque**. Rebuilt in the nineteenth century on foundations three hundred years older, it's currently under scaffolding, like most local Ottoman monuments. The old town is in fact well sown with mosques and *mescids* (the Islamic equivalent of a chapel), many of them converted from Byzantine shrines after the 1522 conquest, when the Christians were expelled from the medieval precinct. Among these, the **Ibrahim Pasha mosque**, in the old bazaar quarter (1531) off Sofokléous, retains an ornate portico, while on Platía Dhoriéos, the **Rejep Pasha mosque** (1588), close to collapse until recent first aid, was built from fragments of earlier churches.

The Süleymaniye and Ibrahim Pasha mosques are still occasionally used by the sizeable Turkish-speaking minority here (see box below), but in general, physical evidence of the four-century Ottoman tenure is neglected and closed to the public, with apparently neither the funds nor the political initiative to repair even those mosques re-consecrated for Christian use since 1912. The Süleymaniye mosque's minaret was declared unsafe in 1989, pulled down, and never replaced.

The Turks of Rhodes

The **Turkish community** of Rhodes dates from the 1522, when an Ottoman garrison and civil servants took control of the island, settling principally in and around the main town. They were supplemented between 1898 and 1913 by Cretan Muslims fleeing intercommunal troubles on their native island, who founded the now-dilapidated suburb of Kritiká, on the way to the airport.

Some old-town Turks can still trace their ancestry to the sixeenth-century conquest, and will proudly tell you that they have every right to be considered native Rhodians. Not surprisingly, such a stance fails to impress the Greek authorities, and their bureaucratic treatment tends to function, like in western Thrace on the mainland, as a barometer of the current state of relations between Greece and Turkey. Recent years have seen a sharp decline in the local Turkish population; for example, while there were once four Turkish jewellers at the base of Sokrátous, there is now just one, *Tzivelek*. Although it's still possible to spot Turkish names on the marquees of various sandalmakers, kebab stalls, and *kafenía*, in the main local "Hellene Muslims" (their official designation) maintain a low public profile, gravitating towards service trades where they're less likely to come in contact with outsiders.

Directly opposite the Sülemaniye Mosque stands the **Ottoman library** (Mon–Fri 7.30am to 2.30pm & 6–9pm, Sat 8am–12pm; a tip for the custodian is appropriate), dating from 1794 and endowed with a rich collection of early medieval manuscripts and Korans; two specimens from the fifteenth century, jointly worth 130 million drachmes, went missing in 1990, but were found at a London auctioneer's and returned in 1994 with appropriate ceremony.

The hamam (Dhimotiká Loutrá)

The Ottomans' most enduring civic contribution is the imposing **hamam** or Turkish baths, marked as the "*Dhimotiká Loutrá*" (Municipal Baths), on Platía Ariónos up in the southwest corner of the old town (Tues 1–7pm, Wed & Sat 7am–7pm, often shuts 6.30 or even 6pm by caretaker whim; 500dr most days, 150dr Wed & Sat). Originally constructed in 1558, it was renovated by the builder of the adjacent Mustafa Pasha mosque in 1765, badly damaged during the last war and restored again afterwards.

In their prime, the Rhodes baths were considered among the most elegant in the Aegean, and are now the last working ones in Greece outside of Thrace. They are capable of holding about two hundred people at any given time, and supposedly consume a tonne of olive wood daily in the process of heating the water, which courses through pipes under the floor as well as out of the "hot" taps. There are separate facilities for each sex, men (typically) getting the grander central section, with its lofty dome pierced by star-shaped skylights, and the actual washing facilities tucked into smaller, marble-lined rooms off the main hall. The clientele consists principally of old-town Greeks, who use the *hamam* as a social occasion, supplemented by a smattering of tourists and local Turks.

Unlike *hamams* in Turkey, no towels or sundries are included in the admission price, so bring everything you need; you'll be assigned a free locker for your clothes. Beyond the weighted doors is the cool room, from which you proceed to the steam room, directly above the heating pipes. Massages may be available, performed on the stone platform that's the focus of any *hamam*. In the bathing rooms you sluice yourself down by dipping a bowl into the stone font. In another contrast to Anatolian practice, bathers strut around buck naked. And although the baths are cleaned scrupulously at closing time, don't be too surprised to glimpse the odd cockroach – their name in Turkish, after all, means "*hamam*-bug".

The old Jewish quarter

Heading downhill from the Süleymaniye mosque, **Sokrátous**, once the heart of the Ottoman bazaar, is now the "Via Turista", whose multiple fur and jewellery stores swarm with tourists – conspicuous among them, as one reader memorably put it, "the blue-rinse set vying for gold by the inch".

The Jews of Rhodes

As in much of the rest of Greece, Jews had dwelt in Rhodes since at least the first century AD, and during the Ottoman era were permitted – unlike the Orthodox Greeks – to live inside the walled city, in the easternmost quarter alotted them by the conquerors. Neither under Italian rule did the local Jews suffer especially; only since re-unification with Greece in 1948 has the much-reduced community felt it necessary to consult with the Rhodian Turks on strategies to counter nationalistically motivated official harassment.

It's not widely known that around two thousand local Jews had the prescience to leave Rhodes before 1939, travelling on Italian passports to what was then the Congo, South Africa and the US. Of the 1700 Rhodian and approximately 120 Koan Jews deported by the Nazis in June 1944, barely eighty returned. Today there are less than forty, mostly elderly Jews from Vólos, Kardhítsa and Lárissa on the mainland, who resettled here after 1948 on the orders of Greece's head rabbi so that a living Jewish presence would remain on the island. The caretaker is an exception, a Rhodian woman who survived Auschwitz and – like so many of her generation – speaks Greek, Ladino, Italian and French, but little English. The community is too tiny to support a rabbi, so one comes annually from Belgium or France to conduct Yom Kippur services.

Beyond the tiled centrepiece **fountain** in Platía Ippokrátous, where broad steps lead up to the **Kastellania** or medieval traders' tribunal and stock exchange, Aristotélous leads to the **Platía ton Evréon Martíron** (Square of the Jewish Martyrs), renamed in memory of the local community that was almost totally annihilated in 1944.

Of the two **synagogues** that once stood on Rhodes, only **Kal Kadosh Shalom**, on Simíou (a doorway just beyond Dhosiádhou 16), 100m to the south, survives today. This ornate structure features a beautiful *hokhláki* floor and eight arcaded columns supporting the roof. Rarely used for religious services, it's maintained essentially as a memorial to the two thousand Jews of Rhodes and Kos deported to Auschwitz in summer 1944; plaques commemorating the dead are mostly in French, the preferred language of educated, turn-of-the-century Jews in the east Aegean.

The new town

Nobody comes to Rhodes especially to ogle Italian town planning and civic architecture, but it's difficult to avoid noticing some of the choicer examples of Art Deco and later Fascist Monumental scattered about **Neohóri**. Prominent among these are the town hall and prefecture opposite, the law courts and post office further along Platía Eleftherías, the reconstructed **basilica of Evangelismós** (speculatively modelled on that of Saint John opposite the Grand Master's palace, blown up in 1856) in between, and the rotondas of the nautical club and aquarium on their respective promontories.

The irregularly heptagonal **New Market** or *Néa Agorá* still functions as a produce and fish vendor's, though the cafés and *souvlaki* stalls within are touristy and not especially good value; the best of these, and handy while you're waiting for a bus, are the *Halki* and *Symi*, originally set up by natives of those neighbouring isles.

A less-than-complete separation of old and new towns is most obviously demonstrated by the **Áyios Nikólaos** fortress at the end of relentlessly contemporary Mandhráki harbour's east jetty, itself of ancient vintage and studded with sixteenth-century windmills. The fortress (currently shut but set to become a maritime museum) was built by the Knights after the first Turkish siege of 1480, and last saw service as a World War II gun emplacement; it now supports a modern lighthouse.

The entrance to Mandhráki is also the sentimental favourite candidate-site for the **Colossus of Rhodes** (see box below), an ancient statue of Apollo built to celebrate the end of the 305 BC siege; today two columns surmounted by bronze deer, adopted as the island's mascots, are less overpowering replacements (see box overleaf).

The Colossus of Rhodes

Reproduced ad nauseam on maps, posters, tea towels, T-shirts, etc, as the symbol of the island, the **Colossus of Rhodes**, one of the Seven Wonders of the ancient world, has not actually stood intact for over two millennia. According to legend, Demetrios Polyorketes, upon conceding defeat in 305 BC (see p.62), suggested that his siege paraphernalia be sold and the proceeds used to erect a statue commemorating the campaign. Originally the Peloponnesian sculptor Lysippos was commissioned to fashion a massive Chariot of the Sun, but subsequently gave the job to a local student, Khares of Lindos, who chose to cast a bronze effigy dedicated to the island's patron deity Apollo Helios. This took twelve years to complete, near the end of which time Khares supposedly killed himself in shame upon noticing a serious design flaw, leaving the final phase to a certain Lakhes.

Ancient travellers described the Colossus as being 35m high and weighing in at an estimated 125 tonnes, though their texts are coy on the all-important issue of where and in what pose the statue was placed. This has not prevented medieval and modern artists from depicting him standing astride the mouth of Mandhráki harbour with ships sailing between his legs. Our only clue is that the Colossus collapsed on land, not into the sea, sundered at the knees by an earthquake in 227 BC. The sun god, via his oracle at Delphi, forbade the restoration of the Colossus, and for nearly nine centuries the remains lay untouched. In 654 AD, they were finally purchased by a Jew from Edessa and supposedly hauled away on the backs of nine hundred camels (debunkers say ninety), only to return (according to yet another debatable legend) in the form of Turkish cannon-balls during the 1522 siege. Every so often purported statue fragments are found on the seabed near Mandhráki, but these have always turned out to be more contemporary metallic debris.

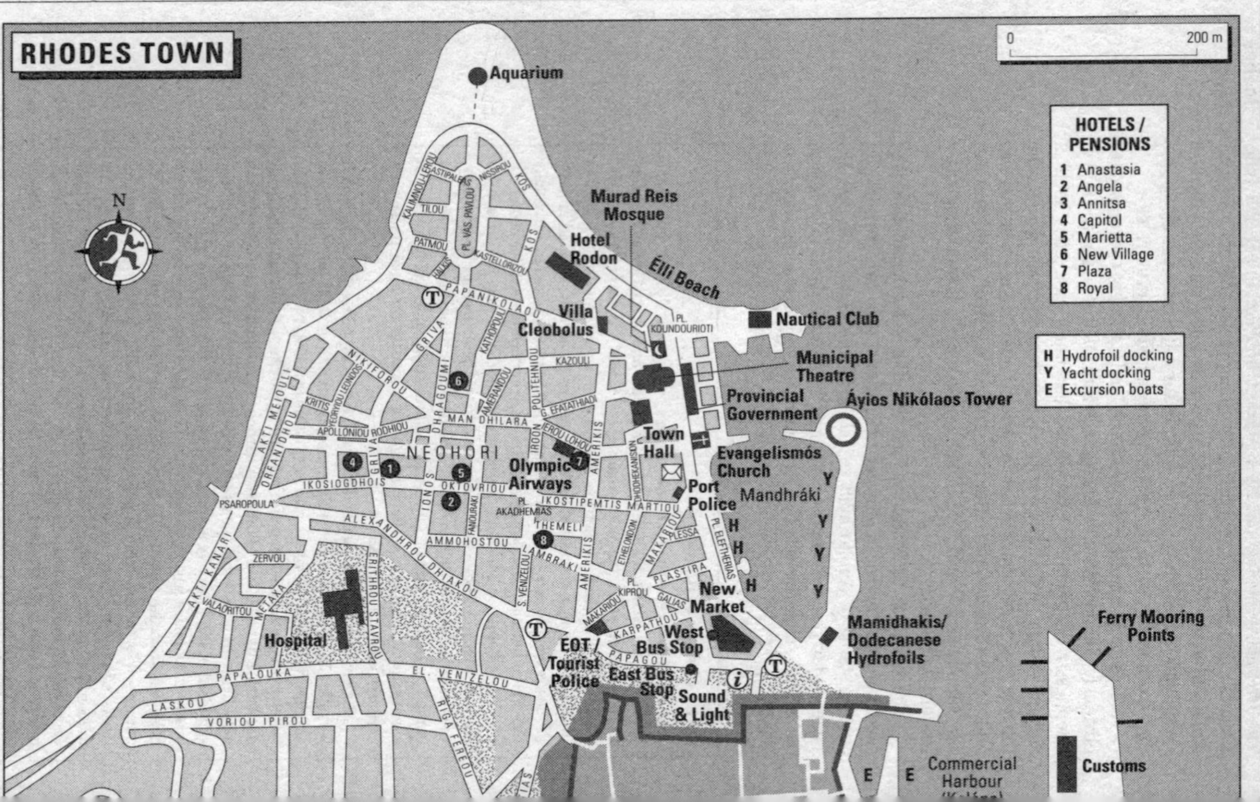

RHODES TOWN
N
0
200 m
HOTELS / PENSIONS
1 Anastasia
2 Angela
3 Annitsa
4 Capitol
5 Marietta
6 New Village
7 Plaza
8 Royal
H Hydrofoil docking
Y Yacht docking
E Excursion boats
Aquarium
Murad Reis Mosque
Hotel Rodon
Élli Beach
Nautical Club
Villa Cleobolus
Municipal Theatre
Provincial Government
Áyios Nikólaos Tower
Town Hall
Evangelismós Church
Mandhráki
Port Police
Olympic Airways
NEOHORI
New Market
West Bus Stop
EOT / Tourist Police
East Bus Stop
Sound & Light
Mamidhakis/ Dodecanese Hydrofoils
Ferry Mooring Points
Commercial Harbour
Customs
Hospital
PAPANIKOLAOU
NIKIFOROU
GRIVA
DHRAGOUMI
KATHOPOULI
KAZOULI
POLITEHNIOU
G. EFSTATHIADI
MAN DHILARA
APOLLONIOU RODHIOU
KRITIS
AKTI MEIOULI
ORFANIDHOU
IKOSIOGDHOIS
28 OKTOVRIOU
IONOS
FANOURAKI
PL. AKADHEMIAS
IKOSTIPEMTIS MARTIOU
THEMELI
AMMOHOSTOU
ALEXANDHROU DHIAKOU
LAMBRAKI
AMERIKIS
S. VENIZELOU
ETHELONDON
MAKARIOU
PLESSA
PL. ELEFTHERIAS
PLASTIRA
PL. KIPROU
GALIAS
KARPATHOU
PAPAGOU
PSAROPOULA
AKTI KANARI
ZERVOU
VALAORITOU
METAXA
ERITHROU STAVROU
PAPALOUKA
EL. VENIZELOU
RIGA FEREOU
LASKOU
VORIOU IPIROU
TILOU
PATMOU
PL. VAS. PAVLOU
KOS
PL. KOUNDOURIOTI

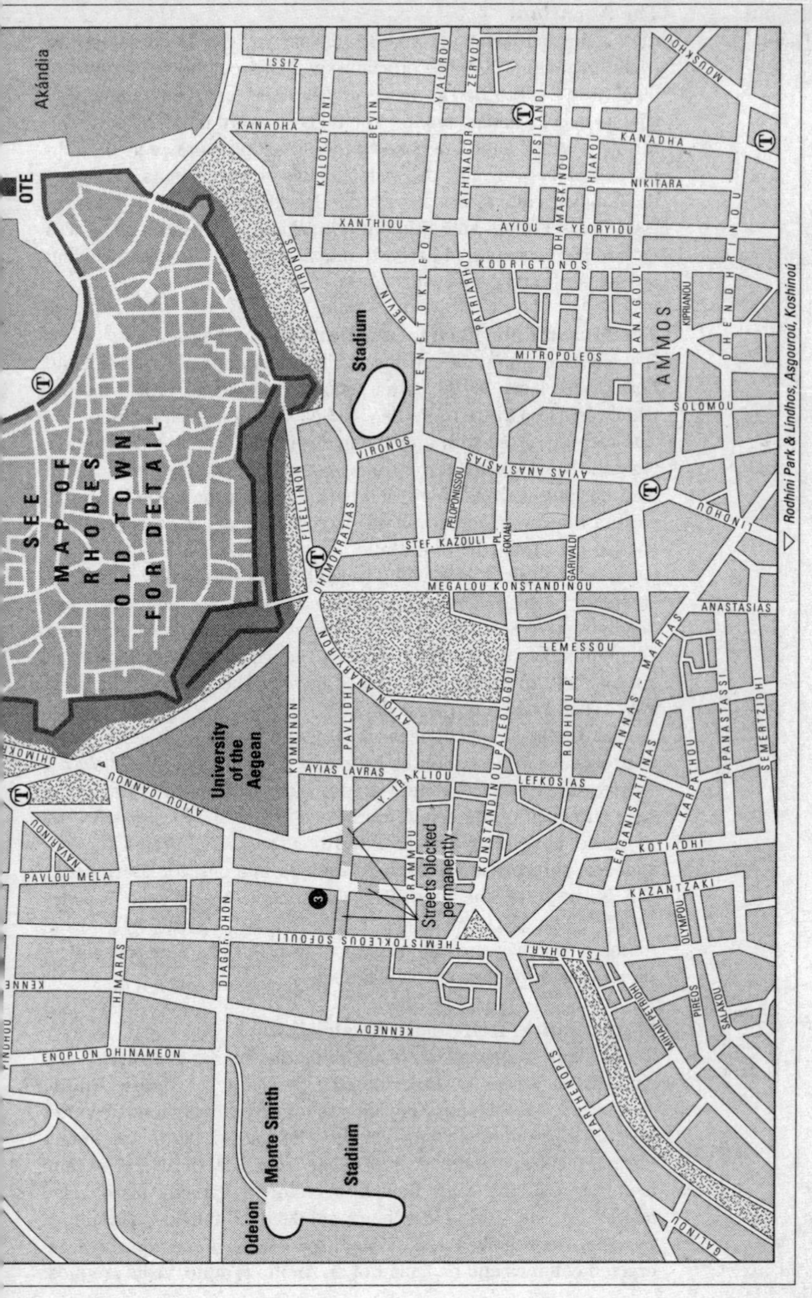
Akándia
OTE
SEE MAP OF RHODES OLD TOWN FOR DETAIL
University of the Aegean
Stadium
AMMOS
Monte Smith
Stadium
Odeion
Streets blocked permanently
Rodhíni Park & Líndhos, Asgouroú, Koshinoú
ISSIZ
KANADHA
KOLOKOTRONI
BEVIN
YIALOROU
ZERVOU
ATHINAGORA
IPSILANDI
MOUSKHOU
XANTHIOU
AYIOU YEORYIOU
DHAMASKINOU
DHIAKOU
NIKITARA
VIRONOS
KODRIGTONOS
VENETOKLEON
PATRIARHOU
PANAGOULI
KIPRIANOU
DHENDRINOU
MITROPOLEOS
SOLOMOU
AYIAS ANASTASIAS
PELOPONISSOU
FILELLINON
DHIMOKRATIAS
STEF. KAZOULI
PL. FOKIALI
GARIVALDI
LINDHOU
MEGALOU KONSTANDINOU
ANASTASIAS
LEMESSOU
AYION ANARYIRON
ANNAS - MARIAS
SEMERTZIDHI
PAPANASTASSI
KOMNINON
PAVLIDHI
RODHIOU P.
KARPATHOU
AYIAS LAVRAS
Y. IRAKLIOU
LEFKOSIAS
KONSTANDINOU PALEOLOGOU
ERGANIS ATHINAS
AYIOU IOANNOU
NAVARINOU
DHIMOKRATIAS
GRAMMOU
KOTIADHI
KAZANTZAKI
PAVLOU MELA
OLYMPOU
THEMISTOKLEOUS SOFOULI
TSALDHARI
DIAGORIDHON
HIMARAS
KENNEDY
MIHAIL PETRIDHI
PIREOS
SALAKOU
LINDHOU
ENOPLON DHINAMEON
PARTHENONOS
GALINOU

The Aquarium

At the northernmost point of the island, an **Art Deco Aquarium** (daily 9am–9pm; 600dr), officially the "Hydrobiological Institute", displays a subterranean maze of seawater tanks containing live specimens of Rhodian sealife. The biggest crowd-pleasers are green turtles, enormous groupers and wicked-looking moray eels; if nothing else, a dusk or rainy-day visit should settle arguments as to what the English equivalents are of the Greek fish offered in tavernas (see also "Eating and drinking" in *Basics*). Upstairs is a less enthralling collection of half-rotten taxidermic specimens, including sharks, seals and even a whale.

The Murad Reis mosque and Durrell's cottage

Between the aquarium and the similarly curvilinear Nautical Club, but much closer to the latter, stands the **Murad Reis mosque**, which, in a departure from the usual pattern of official indifference, was recently fitted with a new minaret by the Greek Archeological Service. Next to this is the tomb of the eponymous admiral, who died during the 1522 siege, and between them the *hokhláki* courtyard of the caretakers' dwelling. To the west extends a eucalyptus-shaded cemetery, the oldest and one of the largest Muslim graveyards on the island, containing several rather battered *türbe*s (free-standing, domed tombs) of Ottoman worthies and also one belonging to a Shah of Persia. On the far side, a plaque on the **Villa Cleobolus** commemorates Lawrence Durrell's residence here from spring 1945 to spring 1947, but otherwise the cottage – hardly a villa – seems neglected these days.

Across the street to the northwest sprawls the even more down-at-heel *Hotel Rodon*, built in 1928 and disused since World War II despite its strategic location across from Élli beach. This Italian structure is currently being refurbished to house a local **casino**, set to move here from the Grand Hotel in 1997. Complete with sunbeds, parasols and showers (standing room only for latecomers), **Élli** is the most sheltered of the mediocre, coarse-sand beaches which, under different names, fringe Neohóri; the westerly, wind-buffeted beaches are the haunts of windsurfers and paragliders rather than swimmers and sunbathers.

Monte Smith: Hellenistic Rhodes

About 2km southwest of Mandhráki, the sparse remains of the Hellenistic acropolis (unenclosed) perch atop **Monte Smith**. Formerly Áyios Stéfanos, this hill was rather bizarrely renamed after the British admiral Sydney Smith, who used it as a watchpoint during the Napoleonic wars. Dating from the third and second centuries BC, the ruins include a restored, garishly marble-clad *odeion* to one side of the more subdued, 200-metre stadium, a peaceful, tree-flanked spot. Above the *odeion* loom the three re-erected columns and pediment of an **Apollo temple**; visits are most

The Deer of Rhodes

The deer found on Rhodes, *Dama dama*, are not actually indigenous to the island. They were first introduced in ancient times at the behest of the Delphic oracle in response to islanders' entreaties as to how best to quell an eruption of snakes. Accounts differ as to how the reptiles were dispatched: the deer either repelled them with the odour of their urine, or impaled the serpents on their antlers. The deer themselves subsequently died out and had to be re-introduced by the Knights; the Italians did likewise, after they were hunted to extinction during Ottoman rule.

For some years, many specimens lived in the dry moat between the inner and outer walls of the old town. However, eight were killed by feral dogs in 1994, prompting a debate on the future of the remaining 55. A proposal to release them into the wild south of the island was vetoed for fear of poachers; instead they will be kept in a special sanctuary to be created at Rodhíni park and funded as part of its upgrade.

rewarding at sunset, when both temple and town are shown to advantage, with Turkey and Sími visible on the horizon.

Infrequent #5 buses run from the New Market if you're not keen on the walk, though from the Ayíou Athanasíou gate of the old town it's hardly more than fifteen minutes on foot. The only other significant reminders of the ancient city are the foundations of an Aphrodite temple in the old town's Platía Símis; gauging the distance between that and the acropolis gives you a fair idea of ancient Rhodes' vast extent.

Rodhíni Park

Vegetated Monte Smith is popular enough with joggers and strollers, but for summer shade and greenery the best spot is probably the **Rodhíni park**, nearly 2km south of town on the road to Líndhos, and served by urban bus route #3. This wooded area lines either bank of a natural ravine and is currently being expensively renovated after years of neglect. On August evenings a **wine-tasting** festival is held here by the municipal authorities (8pm–midnight; wine included in admission fee). Hellenistic rock-cut **tombs** near the south end of the park, rather dubiously attributed to the Ptolemies, constitute a more permanent attraction.

Eating and drinking

Finding good-value **tavernas** in and around Ródhos Town is a challenge, though by no means an insurmountable one. The place is large enough that certain economies of scale apply: tradespeople have to eat somewhere, and a little nosing about in secluded old-town alleys will turn up semi-legal (unlicensed) buffet stalls doling out cheap but sustaining nibbles. However, if you're setting your sights a couple of notches higher, it's possible to find carefully prepared, even exotic meals at not overly inflated prices.

Ródhos Town

Worthwhile establishments are scattered fairly evenly throughout both the old and new towns, though Neohóri fare tends to be more western and snacky, while restaurants in neighbourhoods south of the old city offer a serious Greek feed.

Cafés and bakeries

Dolce Italia, Alexándhrou Dhiákou 16, Neohóri. The longest-established (since 1984) of Rhodes' fancy-pants cafés, this purveys every imaginable permutation of Italian coffee, as well as juices, alcoholic drinks and fifteen flavours of ice cream.

Kringlans Swedish Bakery, Amarándou 20, Neohóri. Stress on Scandanavian goodies and rich filter coffee. Closed Sun evening.

Ömer, Omírou, near corner Pithagóra, old town. Turkish bakery with wholegrain bread and fine cakes.

Tsipillos, Ippodhámou 41, old town. Plenty of turnovers suitable for snacks; the last wood-fired bakery in town, and as such worth supporting.

The old town

Aigaion, Eskhílou 47, corner Aristofánous. Run by a welcoming Kalymniot family, this seafood-biased *ouzerí* features brown bread and seafood curiosities such as *foúskis* (see *Basics*).

Le Bistrot, Omírou 22–24. Always full, with a loyal expatriate clientele, this is a genuine French-run bistro with excellent if slightly pricey food (about 3000dr per person for the works). Open for lunch and supper daily except Sun.

Cleo's, Ayíou Fanouríou 17 (☎0241/28 415). Rather overpriced but tasty nouvelle Italian with a French twist, strong on appetizers and pasta dishes, served in elegant surroundings. Count on 4500dr per person; reservations recommended; closed Sun.

O Meraklis, Aristotélous 32, old town. One of the last Rhodian rough edges not yet filed smooth, this *patsás* (tripe-and-trotter soup) kitchen caters for a nocturnal clientele of post-club lads, Turkish shopkeepers, tarts, pimps, nightclub singers and travellers just stumbled off a ferry. Great free entertainment (including rude staff), and the soup's good, too: the traditional Greek working man's breakfast and hangover cure. Open 3–7am only.

Mikis, in the alley behind Sokrátous 17. Very inexpensive hole-in-the-wall place, serving absolutely nothing but fish, salads and wine.

Nireas, Platía Sofkoléous 22 (☎0241/21 703). Another good, if somewhat pricey, family-run *ouzerí*; reservations advised in the evenings.

Sea Star, Platía Sofokléous. The *Nireas*' adjacent rival, marginally less expensive, with seafood offered by a colourful proprietor.

Yiannis, Apelloú 41, below *Hotel Sydney*. Fair portions of moderately priced Greek oven food, dished out by a family who spent many years in New York.

The new town

Alatopipero/Salt and Pepper, Mihaïl Petrídhi 76, extreme southwest edge of new town, off map (☎0241/65 494). Arch rival of *Palia Istoria* (see below), the waiters at this upmarket *ouzerí* proffer successive trays of oddities such as stuffed cyclamen leaves and *hortópittes* (wild green crêpes), more conventional carniverous and seafood delicacies, plus a few desserts, all accompanied by limited bottlings from Greece's growing number of micro-wineries. Moderate to expensive (2500–3000dr per person for *mezédhes* only, rising to around 4000dr for main course only); dinner only; reservations recommended.

Felicia, Gríva 61. Very low-priced pasta and pizza place.

Makis Grill House, Dhendhrinoú 69, Ámmos district. Every conceivable cut of roast beast here, including *kokorétsi* (offal kebab) and *kefalákia* (sheep's head, if you dare); considered by some to be better value for money than *Palia Istoria* (below).

Palia Istoria, Mitropóleos 108, corner of Dhendhrinoú, in Ámmos district (☎0241/32 421). Managed by Haris, a former actor, this taverna is reckoned to be one of the best on Rhodes, but (not too surprisingly) it's very expensive. Dishes include cauliflower *yiovétsi*, peppered testicles, celery hearts in egg-and-lemon sauce, scallops with mushroom and artichokes, plus more than a hundred types of wine. Evenings only; reservations essential.

Toh Steno, Ayíon Anaryíron 29, 300m southwest of the old town. As the name ("narrow" in Greek) implies, this is a small *ouzerí* with indoor and outdoor seating; all the usual standards but wholesomely executed at normal prices.

Vakhos, Mihaïl Petrídhi 90, off map (☎0241/63 287). Straight-forward, home-style taverna cooking, whose quality is reflected in the slightly bumped-up prices. Reservations usually not necessary but you might want to check.

7.5 Wonder, Dhilberáki 15 (☎0241/39 805). Swedish chefs blend French, Mediterranean and Eastern classics. Their motto is: "Food, drink and party hats since 292 BC" (the year the Seventh Wonder went up).

Suburb villages: Koskinoú and Asgoúrou

KOSKINOÚ, 4km from Ródhos Town, is famous for the ornate doorways and flower-filled *hokhláki* courtyards of its well-preserved traditional houses. The bus service to Koskinoú (from the west station, oddly), often via Asgoúrou, ceases at 9pm so you'll have to take a taxi at least one way.

ASGOÚROU (sometimes Sgoúrou), 5km south of town on a different road, was once populated wholly by Turks. Many have died or converted, but a legacy of the village's past is the enormous Muslim cemetery at its edge, near the pair of almost adjacent *ouzerís* that will be the main attraction for most visitors.

Kalymnos, Asgoúrou, cemetery road. Simple and moderately priced, pitched at a mainly local clientele; the menu, mostly of seafood dishes, is available in English.

Toh Steki, Asgoúrou, cemetery road. The more elaborate, pricier outfit here, with an extensive menu featuring unusual *mezédhes* (cherrystone clams, seafood coquille, *bruschetta*). Meals are served in two phases: first you select from a tray of vegetarian dishes, then of seafood specialities (no meat). The food is rich, and portions fair-sized, so two can satisfy themselves for about 7000dr.

O Yiannis, Koskinoú. To find it, leave transport at the eastern square, by the church with the wedding-cake belfry, and head inland along the lane starting adjacent. Abundant *mezédhes* with a Cypriot/Turkish/Middle-eastern flair, washed down with house wine; extremely reasonable, especially in a group.

Nightlife and entertainment

The old town formerly had a well-deserved reputation for being as silent as a tomb at night, but this has changed with the emergence of more genteel establishments catering to those bored with the dusk-to-dawn circus of the new town. Among the estimated two hundred **bars and clubs** there, theme night and various drinks-with-cover gimmicks predominate. New-town dance clubs and ethnically specialized watering holes are mostly confined to the streets and alleys bounded by Alexándhrou Dhiákou, Orfanídhou (alias "Skandi Street", after the new Vikings), Fanouráki and Nikifórou Mandhilará, with a special concentration on the first two streets.

Sedate by comparison, folk dances approved by the Ministry of Culture (Mon–Fri at 9.20pm, April–Oct; 2500dr, students 1250dr) are presented by the *Nelly Dimoglou Company*, performed in the landscaped **"Old Town Theatre"** off Andhroníkou, near Platía Ariónos. More of a techno extravaganza is the **Sound and Light** show (nightly, English-language screenings vary from 8.15pm to 10.15pm; admission costs 2000dr, with student discount), spotlighting sections of the city walls, performed in a garden just off Platía Rimínis, between the municipal and EOT tourist offices.

There are four **cinemas** screening the latest international films, all with snack bars and a ten-minute interval mid-way through films. Choose from the *Rodon Municipal Theatre*, next to the Town Hall (indoor Nov–April, open-air June–Oct); *Metropol*, opposite the Stadium, corner of Venetokléon/Víronos (indoor year-round plus open-air June–Sept); *Pallas*, Dhimokratías, near the Stadium (Oct–May); *Titania*, Kolokotróni, off Kanadhá (year-round, but may close July/Aug–Sept).

Old town bars

Araliki, Aristofánous 45. The bohemian set hangs out at this old-style *kafenío* on the ground floor of a medieval house; simple *mezédhes* provided by Italian proprietress Miriam accompany drinks, which even include Nissirot *soumádha*. Open all year.

Arhaia Agora, Omírou 70. Very elegant, upmarket bar with good taped music, food and a garden at the rear shared with the affiliated *Sotiris Nikolis* hotel.

Café Chantant, Aristotélous 22. Respected as a long-established music café (Greek popular and *rembétika*), but steel yourself for the inflated drink prices and often ear-shattering sound amplification.

L'Île Flottante (aka *Juan Carlos* after the proprietor), Sofokléous 22, corner of eponymous square. Civilized café/bar/*gelateria*, with music turned down low, and outdoor seating under trees. Open very late.

Mango Bar, Platía Dhoriéos 3. Piped music and a variety of drinks at this established bar on an otherwise quiet square; also a good source of breakfast after 8am, served under a plane tree.

Nyn kai Aei, on a cul-de-sac off Sofokléous 4T. An elegant though slightly pricey live-music bar in a vaulted, thirteenth-century building, attracting a thirty-something clientele; the name means "now and forever" in ancient Greek.

Popeye's, Sofokléous 38, south end of the square. Cheap beer and wine for a collegiate crowd at this outdoor pub; the favourite haunt of yacht hostesses between assignments.

Rolóï, Orféos 1. The baroque clock tower erected by Ahmet Fetih Pasha in 1857 is now the focus of possibly the most exclusive café/bar in the old town.

There's an admission charge to climb the tower, and steeply priced drinks, but you are paying for the terrific view. However, its future is in doubt as it was closed for noise-law violation in 1996.

Valentino, in a tiny, nameless alley south of Sokrátous, just east of Apelloú. Weirdly lit, rather lugubrious gay bar, which seems to operate only sporadically due to police harassment.

Neohóri bars

Blue Lagoon Pool Bar, Ikostipémptis Martíou 2. One of the better theme bars, in this case a "desert island" with palm trees, waterfalls, a shipwrecked galleon – and taped music.

Christos' Garden, Dhilberáki 59. This combination art-gallery/bar/café, run by Christos Voulgaris, occupies a carefully restored old house and courtyard with pebble-mosaic floors throughout. Incongruously classy for the area.

Hard Rock Cafe, Orfanídhou 29. Yes there's one here too, though whether it's the real thing or a trademark ripoff is hard to say. "Hard rock, soft lights, driving music" promised.

Presley's, Íonos Dhragoúmi 27. A small and thus often crowded bar, featuring a wide range of '50s and '60s music despite its obsessive Elvis-orientation (the cocktails are named after his hits).

Shooters, Apolloníou Rodhíou 61. Run by the *Waterhoppers* scuba outfitters, this is a popular haunt of the wet-suit set; live acoustic music Tuesday and Thursday.

Sticky Fingers, Anthoúla Zérvou 6. Long-lived music bar with reasonable drinks; *the* place for rock, often live, nightly from 10pm onwards.

Tropical Oasis, near the EOT. For sheer tackiness, this is unbeatable, providing loud music videos, a "Dancing Waters" show and several bars with exorbitant prices surrounding a pool to which admission is free.

Discos and dance halls

Amazon at La Scala, out of town at Ixiá, behind the *Rodos Palace Hotel*. Open 11pm until dawn.

Jungle at Le Palais, Ikostipémptis Martíou 2. The best disco on Rhodes; cool off in the adjacent *Blue Lagoon* (see above). Open 10pm until dawn.

Minuit, Kastellorízou (off Platía Vasiléos Pávlou, alias Palms Square). Reasonably priced venue with dancing to live Greek and international music.

Listings

Airlines *AVRO*, Papaloúka 31 (☎0241/76 206), for *Monarch*, *Britannia* and most charter lines; *British Airways*, Platía Kíprou 1 (☎0241/27 756); *KLM*, Ammohóstou 23 (☎0241/21 010); *Olympic*, Ieroú Lóhou 9 (☎0241/24 571); *Air Greece*, c/o *Triton Holidays*, Plastíra 9 (☎0241/21 690).

Airport information (☎0241/91 771 or ☎93 838). For the latest on (often delayed) flight arrivals and departures.

Animal Welfare Society Ikostiogdhóïs Oktovríou 28 (☎0241/37 727). To report problems or make cash donations; open Mon–Sat 10am–1pm only.

American Express c/o *Rodos Tours*, Ammohóstou 23 (☎0241/74 022 or ☎21 010). Refund agents for lost/stolen cheques; open Mon–Sat, standard shop hours.

ATMs *Barclays*, Iróön Politehníon, Neohóri; *Trapeza Pisteos/Credit Bank*, Neohóri; *Ioniki Trapeza/Ionian Bank*, Neohóri and the old town near the museums; *Ethniki Trapeza/National Bank*, Neohóri, more or less opposite *Trapeza Pisteos* on Platía Kíprou; or the *Emboriki Trapeza/Commercial Bank*, Neohóri.

Bookstores *Pressbyran*, Íonos Dhragoúmi, opposite *Chevaliers Hotel*. This stocks some fiction and non-fiction paperbacks, but you'd be wise to bring holiday reading with you. Alternatively, try the reasonable lending/exchange library in Líndhos (see p.95).

Car rental Prices at non-international chains are fairly standard (12–13,000dr) but can be bargained down a little out of peak season. More flexible local outfits and smaller chains, all in the new town, include *Alexander*, Afstralías 58 (☎0241/27 547); *Alamo*, Mandhilará 64 & airport (☎0241/75 970); *Express*, Papanikoláou 17 (☎0241/24 672); *Just*, Orfanídhou 45 (☎0241/31 811); *Kosmos*, Papaloúka 31 (☎0241/74 374); *MBC*, Ikostipémptis Martíou 29 (☎0241/28 617); *Orion*, Yioryíou Leóndos 36 (0241/22 137); *Payless*, Íonos Dhragoúmi 29 (☎0241/26 586).

Consulates *UK*, Amerikís 111 (☎0241/27 306); *USA*, in emergency contact the *Voice of America* transmitter offices in Asgoúrou (☎0241/66 731) or Afándou (☎0241/51 225); *Netherlands*, c/o *Ialyssos Tours*, Alexándhrou Dhiákou 25 (☎0241/31 571). All other English-speaking nationals are represented only in Athens.

Exchange Most bank branches are in the new town, and keep weekday evening and Saturday morning hours. At other times use the ATMs (see above) or the representative agencies for your brand of traveller cheque, if pertinent.

Ferries Tourist office handouts list fairly complete schedules, plus the bewildering array of representatives, for the six boat and several hydrofoil companies that operate here. The most useful agencies are *Kydon*, at Ethelondón Dhodhekanisíon 14 (☎0241/23 000), for *G&A* and the *Nissos Kalymnos*; *DANE* at Amerikís 95 (☎0241/77 070); and *Mamidhakis/Dodecanese Hydrofoils* on Platía Neoríou, Mandhráki east jetty (☎0241/24 000). Schedules should be confirmed with the agencies or port police on the Mandhráki esplanade near the post office.

Laundrettes *Express Service*, Dhilberáki 97, corner Orfanídhou, Neohóri; *Lavomatic*, Ikostioghdóïs Oktovríou 32, Neohóri; *Hobby*, Plátonos 32, old town.

Motorbike rental Mopeds will make little impact on Rhodes' huge area, and gain you scant respect from motorists. Sturdier *Yamaha 125s*, suitable for two persons, start at about 5000dr a day. There are plenty of outlets in the new town, especially along and just off of Alexándhrou Dhiákou. If money's no object, and you have the proper driving licence, you may *Rent a Harley*, on Ialissoú (☎0241/95 145). In the old town, *Mandar Moto*, at Dhimosthénous 2, corner Platía Evréon Martíron, has a large stable of medium-sized bikes. *Mike's Rent A Motorbike*, Ioánni Kazoúli 23, Neohóri (☎0241/37 420), has a wide range of new models from 50cc to 500cc, and offers full insurance.

Newspaper The free restaurant/bar advertiser and info sheet, *Rodos News*, appears monthly from April to October and is available virtually everywhere; contents include topical features, news on local scandal, plus periodically amended museum and bus schedules.

OTE Junction of Amerikís and Ikostipémptis Martíou, in the new town (daily 7am–11pm), and at the foot of the jetty in the commercial harbour (daily 8am 10pm); the latter also has several booths for *ATT Direct* and *MCI* services to North America.

Post office Main branch with ougoing mail, poste restante and exchange windows at Platía Eleftherías 1, Mandhráki harbour (Mon–Fri 7.00am–8pm, also Sat & Sun in high season); plus a mobile office on Orféos, in the old town (theoretically daily 7.30am–2pm, but service occasionally suspended).

Scuba diving *Waterhoppers Diving School* touts for business daily on Mandhráki quay (☎0241/38 146, or mobile ☎093/422617). Alternatively, *Dive Med*, also found along Mandhráki (☎0241/33 654, fax ☎23 780). (See box p.88.)

Thomas Cook, Sofokléous Venizélou, Neohóri (☎0241/35 672). Refund agents for lost/stolen travellers' cheques; open seven days, *Thomas Cook* cheques cashed commission-free.

Travel agents *Castellania*, Evripídhou 1–3, corner Platía Ippokrátous (☎0241/75 860), is especially good for *Olympic Airways* and ferry tickets. *Contours*, Ammohóstou 9 (☎0241/36 001), can arrange cheap scheduled and charter flights to all destinations, while *Visa*, Mandhilará 8 (☎0241/33 282), concentrates on low price charter flights. *GEM Travel* at Papaloúka 31 (☎0241/76 206) is good for cheap flights back to the UK, in particular unclaimed return seats or one-way tickets; scheduled return flights are usually exorbitant.

Yacht charter *Vernicos Yachts*, Mandhráki (☎0241/30 241; fax ☎30 838); *Yacht Agency Rhodes*, Víronos 1, corner Kanadhá (☎0241/22 927; fax ☎23 393).

Around the island

Ródhos Town is very much the main event on Rhodes, but while it's conceivable to spend an entire vacation within its confines, that would certainly be inadvisable. The enormous, diamond-shaped **island** offers ample scope for two weeks of excursions, and if you're not on an all-inclusive, one-centre package, it's highly recommended that you change your overnight base at least once; distances are considerable and, despite an ongoing improvements programme, road conditions often leave much to be desired.

With ample winter rainfall and rich soil, Rhodes could easily feed itself if mass tourism were not such a lucrative distraction; the island could also keep its population inebriated indefinitely, with 10 million litres of wine produced annually. Unhappily, much of the scenery inland – predominantly arid, scrubby sand-hills in the east and south – has been made that much bleaker by fire-scorched areas extending from Profítis Ilías in the north to Asklipío, beyond Líndhos in the south.

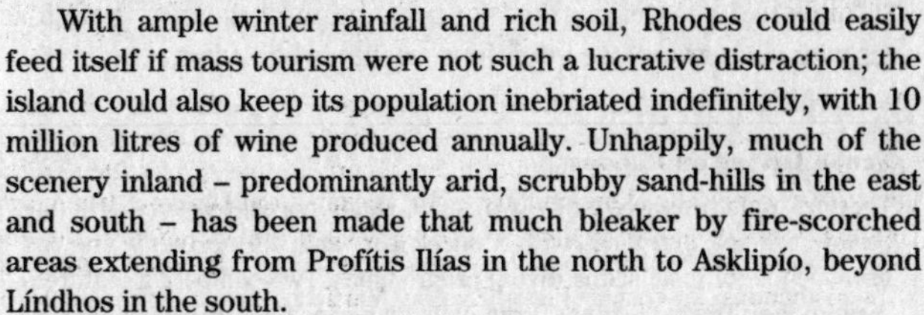

With the exception of the coast between Líndhos and Kiotári, tourist facilities are still concentrated in the upper 25 percent of Rhodes. What the Italians begun, the 1967–74 junta continued, monstrous hotels on the northwest coast between the town and airport being their lasting contribution to posterity. Only during the late 1970s did attention shift to the naturally better endowed east coast. The process continues slowly as bank loans and official permits allow, with facilities spreading towards the south tip of island.

The east coast

Heading down the **east coast** from the capital, you have to proceed some distance before you escape the crowds from local beach hotels at Réni Koskinoú and all along Kallithéa Bay, their numbers swelled by visitors using the regular buses from town or on boat tours out of Mandhráki and Kolóna. However, once past the excesses of Faliráki there is surprisingly little development on this coast until you reach

Líndhos, and a fair number of beaches, most of them sandier and more sheltered than anything on the west coast (see p.96). Incidentally they face the open Mediterranean, not the Aegean, which means that the water tends to be warmer, greener and (usually) cleaner.

Thérmes Kallithéas

Nostalgia buffs might care to look in at the decayed, all-but-abandoned Italian-built spa of **Thérmes Kallithéas** (unrestricted access), in a palm grove 3km south of Réni Koskinoú. This isn't currently signposted, but easy enough to find at the base of a cliff bristling with antennae; look for an unmarked road down through pines, which veers off as soon as the hotels lining Kallithéa Bay heave into sight. If visiting by bus, be sure *not* to get onto a vehicle serving sound-alike Kallithiés – this is an inland village reached by an entirely different road!

Illuminated at night, the spa is hugely enjoyable as a bit of kitsch mock-orientalia. A pair of swooping staircases, the occasional venue for advertising shots, bracket a six-pillared cupola over a now dried-up pool. The springs here were celebrated in antiquity, since Hippocrates of Kós (see p.180) recommended them; whether they have ceased flowing from a natural process or just neglect is unclear. In 1996 the EOT announced that 600 million drachmes in EU funds had been earmarked for restoration of the spa, though as ever with such grandiose intentions, seeing is believing.

Scuba Diving on Rhodes

Thérmes Kallithéas overlooks two small, sandy coves, the southerly one (below the spa entrance) with a snack bar, and the northerly one the usual venue for local **scuba diving** programmes. Two competing outfitters (see Ródhos Town, "Listings") run daily dive-trips here in season, departing Mandhráki at about 9.15am, arriving an hour later, and heading back by 4pm. On offer are a shallow-water, guided "try dive" for the inexperienced, or two deeper dives for those previously certified, either costing about 10,000dr. The more advanced dive, to a depth of about forty feet, explores a cave and tunnel system on the north side of the bay.

As the dives tend to be short and relatively shallow, and the day long, there could easily be scope for a third dive, but the scuba instructors confess that two plunges just about exhaust the legal territory of exploration – the confines of this little bay are the sole permitted dive area until further notice. In the off season, at some risk to all concerned, advanced dives at a remote offshore wreck are undertaken by special arrangement.

Snacks are available on the dive boat or at the spa cantina noted above, but it's best to bring some food and drink of your own. Diving tends to finish by 2.30pm, but you're more or less stuck here waiting for the boat back as there's no bus service down to Kallithéa spa and it's a hot, twenty-minute walk up to the coast highway (half-hourly bus service once you get there).

Faliráki

FALIRÁKI, at the south end of Kallithéa Bay, may once have been a fishing village, but today it's Rhodes' biggest youth-orientated package playpen, firmly in the mould of a Spanish costa resort. An overwhelmingly British and German clientele's typical nicknames for the place are "Fairly Rocky" or "Feely-Fucky", the latter pretty much reflecting the main interest of those in attendance. As *Rodos News* says, if it's possible or imaginable to do it in, on or over the water, rental equipment is available here. Bungy-jumping (at *New World Bungy*, on the beach) is a Big Thing, not to mention go-karting, water-slides and jet-boating; watersports centres along the beach offer waterskiing and parasailing, as well as renting out windsurf boards, canoes and pedaloes.

So-called "Faliráki North" is smarter, the south end of the developed strip frowsier, while there's also a fair bit of less desirably positioned development on the inland side of the busy highway. In slight mitigation, all this is predominantly low-rise and still fairly low-density, leaving plenty of greenery and low-lying ground in which the local mosquitos breed. There's even an unofficial nudist beach at the far south end of matters, in secluded coves beyond a headland.

Practicalities

Given such a self-explanatory, home-from-home environment, specific recommendations for rooms or restaurants are generally pretty futile. If you decide to take advantage of all the creature comforts by **staying** here, you may as well be hung for a sheep as a lamb, and splash out at the *Faliraki Beach Hotel* (☎0241/85 301, fax ☎85 675; ⑤) or the adjacent *Apollo Beach Hotel* (☎0241/85 513, fax ☎85 823; ⑤), both with prime mid-beach locations and available through *Argo Holidays* (see *Basics*). At the other end of the scale, the island's only surviving **campsite**, *Faliraki Camping* (☎0241/85 358) is here, somewhat pricier than usual but well appointed with a pool, restaurant and bar.

Eating out, most establishments are predictably plastic, but for grills you might try *O Kandas*, near the *Hotel Columbia Beach*, or the English-run *Partners*, near the south end of things just inland from the main highway, for good international cuisine. Other likely prospects include *La Strada*, near the junction of the main coast highway and the side street down to the bus turnaround area, for high quality Italian food; *Akroyali*, beside the beach taxi rank, serving Greek standards in a notably un-Hellenic area; and *Pagoda*, on the main highway, for Thai-slanted Chinese specialities.

Entire streets are devoted to fairly obvious **nightlife**, which can reportedly get a bit rough after hours; this is about the only locale in this book with any pattern of muggings and rape. If you've raved all night, *Eden Pool Bar* (near the go-karts) is good for pre-dawn breakfasts. Among several **car rental** outfits, *J&D* (☎0241/85 885), next to the *Hotel Calypso*, is one of the more reputable, and also the local *Thomas Cook* representative.

Ladhikó and Afándou

The peninsula closing off Faliráki to the south is called **Cape Ladhikó**; one pebbly cove, proclaimed as "**Anthony Queen**" (sic) on many excursion boat marquees, was a location for the film *The Guns of Navarone*, and Quinn supposedly bought coastal property here. If he hasn't yet sold up, he'll be wealthy when he does, as this is now a desirable resort area, less manic than Faliráki. The small, almost landlocked, sandy bay adjacent to "Queen" gets more patronage from land-based beachcombers.

South of the Ladhikó headland extends the sweeping pebble-and-sand expanse of **Afándou bay**, the most undeveloped large beach on east coast, with nary a sunbed or umbrella as yet. Inland spreads an eighteen-hole **golf course**, the only one in the Greek islands aside from Corfu's, and beyond the coast highway lies Afándou ("the Invisible") village, not especially memorable if unobjectionable.

The best local **meals** are to be had at *Taverna Traganou*, immediately south of the Ladhikó headland, overlooking the sea and the north end of Afándou bay. At the southern end, *O Afantis* is an exceptionally good fish taverna.

Kolímbia and Eptá Piyés

Some 5km south of Afándou, a dilapidated church is your first hint of **KOLÍMBIA**, developed as a model farm scheme by the Italians to house colonists during the 1920s. Strange, identical villa-farmhouses with outsized chimneys and exterior ovens dot the coastal plain to the north of the three-kilometre side road. This avenue, lined with around two dozen uninspiring hotels and rows of eucalyptus planted by Italians to drain the marshes here, runs east arrow-straight to volcanic **Cape Váyia**. Upon reaching the sea, a left fork quickly ends at the edge of Afándou beach, with sweeping views north to Ladhikó point; bearing right at this T-junction takes you past a small, rocky cove with a taverna to the more picturesque and protected south beach at the base of Tsambíka promontory (see overleaf), dominated by the *Golden Odyssey* hotel. The more modest and congenially designed *Relax* (☎0241/56 220; ④) and *Mistral* (☎0241/56 350, fax ☎56 293; ⑤) hotels are also within easy walking distance of the sand.

Eptá Piyés

Heading inland from Kolímbia junction on the main highway, it's a four-kilometre walk or drive to **Eptá Piyés** (Seven Springs), a superb oasis with a tiny dam created by the Italians to irrigate their Kolímbia colony. It is also accessible by a marked path/mountain bike track from the village of Arhángelos (see below). A shaded streamside **taverna**, in operation since 1948 and immensely popular at weekends with islanders and visitors alike, serves surprisingly no-nonsense, hearty fare in a setting enlivened by geese, ducks and shrieking peacocks.

A trail, or a rather claustrophobic Italian **aqueduct-tunnel**, both lead from the vicinity of the springs to the reservoir. The 186-metre tunnel is strictly one-way, with just a single combination turna-round-point/air-vent about halfway through – not for claustrophobes. The reservoir at the far end is more of a deep pond, with no prohibitions (as yet) against diving in. Like Thérmes Kallithéas, Eptá Piyés is scheduled for an EU-funded clean-up and facelift in the near future, with uncertain consequences.

Tsambíka: monastery and beach

The enormous, Gilbraltar-like mass of **Tsambíka**, 26km south of Ródhos Town, is actually the eroded flank of a much larger extinct volcano. From the highway, a steep, 1500-metre-long cement drive terminates at a small car park and snack bar, from which concrete steps lead up to the summit monastery of **Panayía Tsambíka** (300m elevation), offering unrivalled views along some fifty kilometres of coastline. It's unremarkable except for the happier consequences of the September 8 festival, when barren women make the climb – sometimes on their hands and knees – to pay homage to an eleventh-century icon and ingest a small piece of the wick from one of the shrine's lamps. Any children born afterwards are called Tsambikos or Tsambika, names that are peculiar to the Dodecanese – and common enough to confound sceptics.

From the top you survey Kolímbia just to the north, and shallow Tsambíka **bay** on the south side of the headland; of all Rhodian beaches, this warms up earliest in the spring. The entire area appears to have been protected by the forest service from any development other than the recent paving of the road down to the bay, and a single, permanent **taverna** to complement several cantina caravans. Although there's no public transport to this excellent beach, it teems with people – and rental umbrellas – all summer. On the seabed at the wilder, southern end of the sand, hundreds of hermit crabs scuttle about in their appropriated shells.

Arhángelos and Stegná

More substantial facilties can be found at **ARHÁNGELOS**, a large citrus-farming village just inland, 29km from Ródhos Town. The place is overlooked by a crumbling fifteenth-century castle, and home to a dwindling leather-crafts industry, much touted in tourist literature but hard to find on the ground; there's more evidence of rag-rug weaving and (at festival times) musical prowess. The courtyard of the main church, with an enormous *hokhláki* dating back to 1845, is the only remarkable sight. Though you might explore the warren of alleys between the main road and the citadel, Arhángelos is now firmly caught up in German package tourism, with a full quota of "mini-markets" and jewellery stores, as well as a **bank** and **post office**. Most commercial life occurs along the single thoroughfare, in the form of a few bars and six tavernas – none superlative, but all a good deal less expensive than in the coastal resorts. The preferred hangout seems to be the **bar** and grill of *George Mavrios*, under the mulberry trees. Recommendable local **hotels**, both well out of Arhángelos but with views over it, are *Katerina* (☎0244/22 169, ③) and *Anagros* (☎0244/22 248, ③).

Stegná, three rather steep kilometres by road below Arhángelos, is the closest **beach**. Rather scrappy development, mostly summer cottages for the locals, straggles behind a kilometre of gravelly coastline punctuated by rocky outcrops which provide a scenic backdrop. There are a few basic **rooms** places and **tavernas** suitable for lunch.

Haráki and Agáthi

A more comfortable overnight base on this stretch of coast is **HARÁKI**, a pleasant if undistinguished, two-street fishing port overlooked by the stubby ruins of Feraklós castle. Originally a Byzantine fortress, this served as the Knights' initial toehold on Rhodes in 1306, later as a POW compound, and was the last of their strongholds to fall to the Ottomans. Among the mostly self-catering **accommodation** here (generally ③), well-positioned outfits include *Savvas* (☎0244/51 287) and *Voula* (☎0244/51 381), adjacent to the track to the castle. Local **restaurants** include *Tommy's*, run by a professional fisherman, whose specialities include fish in garlic sauce, oven baked seafood, and lobsters or mussels cooked in various ways. Perhaps the best all-around taverna in this area is *Efterpi*, 200m south of Haraki at so-called **Massari beach**, next to the army camp; here you can sample such delicacies as Smyrna-style eggplant and *mídhia sagánaki*.

There's swimming off the town beach if you don't mind an audience from the handful of waterfront cafés and tavernas, but most people head north to the secluded **Agáthi** beach. Contrary to expectations, this cannot be accessed from the castle road: you have to backtrack 700m out of village to a separate side road flanked by two pensions, and then proceed another 800m to the short but broad sandy bay overlooked by the chapel of Ayía Agáthi on the far (north) hillside. Although Agáthi is no secret by any means, there's no development other than an abandoned, half-finished hotel just south. As at Tsambíka, numerous hermit crabs can be seen in the shallows.

Líndhos

LÍNDHOS, the island's number-two tourist attraction, erupts from barren limestone surroundings 12km south of Haráki. Like Ródhos Town, its charm is heavily undermined by commercialism and crowds – up to half a million visitors in a typical year. At midday dozens of coaches park nose-to-tail on the narrow access road, with even more on the drive down to the beach. Back in the village itself, those few vernacular houses not snapped up by package operators have, since the 1960s, been bought up and refurbished by wealthy British and Italians. The old *agorá* or serpentine high street presents a mass of fairly indistinguishable bars, crêperies, mediocre restaurants and travel agents. Although high-rise hotels have been prohibited inside the municipal boundaries, it's still a relentlessly mercenary theme park, especially hot and airless in August, and quite ghostly in winter since the village has scarcely any life apart from tourism.

Nonetheless, if you arrive before or after peak season, when the pebble-paved streets between the immaculately whitewashed houses are relatively empty of people, you can still appreciate the beautiful, atmospheric setting of Líndhos. The late Byzantine church, its belfry

Rhodian Village Houses

Vernacular **rural houses** on Rhodes, and to a great extent those on the nearby islands of Tílos, Hálki, Níssiros and Kós, share certain basic characteristics. This is owing to the matrilineal system of inheritance, still common in the Dodecanese, whereby the eldest daughter is given the family house upon marriage. The father is obliged to build similar houses for any younger girls; this makes it inadvisable to build costly, involved structures when so many might be required.

In its most unadorned form, the Rhodian village house interior is a single, undivided, one-storey rectangle or *monóhoro*, built of stone and earth, usually with a corner fireplace indicated from outside by a beaked chimney. Opposite the fireplace, along the rear wall, is a raised sleeping platform or *soufás*, with storage cupboards underneath and an embroidered curtain or *spervéri* around it. This longer wall is generally devoted to racks displaying the celebrated Rhodian collections of household plates, both imported and locally made. Depending on room size, the space is often divided either widthwise or lengthwise by a soaring arch; this helps support a flat roof, traditionally made of cedar beams resting on the wall tops. The gaps in between are filled with successive layers of wild olive or oleander shoots, calamus reeds, seaweed and, finally, hard-packed special earths called *aspropília* or *patélia*, with the walls extending up to form a low surrounding parapet or *koumoúla*.

In wealthier villages, such as Koskinoú and Lahaniá, the basic *monóhoro* unit is found at the rear of an enclosed courtyard. Auxiliary buildings, such as kitchens, ovens, stables, olive presses and (much later) toilets, also face onto the courtyard which is paved in *hokhláki* or pebble mosaic and entered via a *pyliónas* or ornate doorway. Líndhos represents the most elaborate development of this trend, with the *monóhoro* used only on formal occasions; exquisite *hokhláki* paving is often present inside the rooms, ceilings can be decorated with painted plants as well as shrub branches or reed canes, and exceptionally ornate *pyliónes* are adorned with braided relief work reflecting Frankish or Arab influences. Directly above the *pyliónes* can often be found the so-called "captain's room", from which the master of the house used to watch activity at the north harbour, or scan the horizon for pirates.

in scaffolding at present, is covered inside with well-preserved eighteenth-century frescoes. The most imposing fifteenth-to-eighteenth-century **captains' residences** (see box on p.93) are built around *hokhláki* courtyards, their monumental doorways or *pyliónes* often fringed by intricate stonework, with the number of braids or cables supposedly corresponding to the number of ships owned. Several are open to the public, most notably the **Papkonstandis Mansion**, which is the most elaborate and now home to an unofficial museum. Entrance to the "open" mansions is free, but you'll probably come under some pressure to buy something, especially the lace and embroidery for which the place is noted.

The acropolis

On the 115-metre bluff looming above Líndhos, the **acropolis** (Mon–Sat 8.30am–6.40pm, Sat–Sun 8.30am–2.40pm; 1200dr) represents a surprisingly felicitous blend of ancient and medieval culture, though the Knights of Saint John destroyed a considerable quantity of the surviving Hellenistic structures by quarrying them for use in fortification. Once through the tower-gate built by the Knights, you ascend two flights of monumental stairs and a long *propylaion* (monumental gateway) to the high point (in all senses): the **Doric Temple** of Athena Lindia, its six columns perennially swaddled in scaffolding. The unusual southwest-to-northeast orientation was dictated by the limited triangular area of flat ground on the summit, here tapering to its apex.

Before the founding of Rodhos in 408 BC, Lindos with its 16,000 inhabitants was the most important settlement on the island, thanks to its natural defences – the acropolis is a sheer drop on all sides except the north approach – and the two excellent harbours nestling beneath the cliffs. The surrounding craggy countryside was as poor then as it is now, and the population was forced to look to the sea for a living, with an enormous fleet trading as far as present-day Spain; the local tradition of boat-building continued well into the last century. As if in corroboration, a fifth-century BC relief of a trireme clings to the rock face, on the left at the base of the stairs leading up to the castle gate.

Though the ancient city of Lindos and its original temple date from at least 1100 BC, the first stone temple was erected by the tyrant Kleovoulos in the sixth century BC, replaced by the present structure after a 348 BC fire. The word "tyrant" then had not yet assumed its modern, perjorative overtones; Kleovoulos was actually revered as one of the Seven Sages of antiquity, and to him was attributed the Delphic inscription "Measure in All Things", usually rendered as "Nothing in Excess".

A 45-minute walk east of town brings you to the headland and chapel of **Áyios Emilianós**, the latter originally a round, stone-built tomb, purportedly that of Kleovoulos but actually dating from the first century BC.

Local beaches

Líndhos' principal **north beach**, once the main ancient harbour, is overcrowded and will suffer from pollution until the sewage treatment plant, courtesy of the EU, is completed; if you do base yourself here, cleaner, quieter swimming is to be had one cove beyond at **Pállas** beach (with a nudist annexe around the headland), or 5km north at **Vlihá** bay, where the luxurious *Steps of Lindos* hotel, on the hillside just above, is recommended (☎0244/42 263 or 42 249, fax ☎42 267; ⑥ half board).

At the southern flank of the acropolis huddles the small, phenomenally well-sheltered harbour and sandy beach of **Saint Paul**, where the apostle is said to have landed in 58 AD on a mission to evangelize the island. According to legend, the ship bringing Paul to Rhodes, threatened by a storm, was unable to find the main, north harbour; a miraculous bolt of lightning split the rocks asunder and created this almost land-locked bay expressly for the saint's benefit. In all likelihood Paul is spinning in his grave contemplating today's ranks of topless sun worshippers.

Practicalities

On the bus-stop square at the edge of the village, as far as vehicles can go, is the municipal **tourist office**, open all day in season. They can offer little assistance with **accommodation**, almost all of which is booked semi-permanently by overseas tour companies – your best bet is booking through a company such as *Direct Greece* (see *Basics*). The oft-cited exceptions, *Electra* (☎0244/31 226; ④) and *Pension Katholiki*, next door to each other on the way to the north beaches, are both of a relatively low standard and vastly overpriced. It could be more productive to throw yourself on the mercy of *Pallas Travel* (☎0244/31 494, fax ☎31 595) who might be able to roust any stray vacancies. Other useful contacts are *Triton Holidays* (see Ródhos Town "Listings", p.85) or the *Independent Association of Lindian Property Owners* (☎0244/31 221, fax ☎31 571).

As for **restaurants**, they tend to have bland menus served by staff who are wearily short with tourists. It's therefore hard to come up with specific suggestions, though *Agostino's*, by the southerly car park, possesses the important virtues of Émbonas wine, real country sausages (not imported hot dogs) and a partly local clientele. For desserts, try *Gelo Blu*, which serves Italian ice cream and coffee. The apotheosis of **nightlife** is the 1995-inaugurated *Epos Club*, a disco with a capacity of a thousand, a swimming pool and a rooftop bar; *Jody's Flat* is a bar recommended for its video-cinema matinees.

American expat Sheila Markou runs a unique, combination **laundrette/lending library** behind *Pallas Travel*, open during normal shop hours; she both sells and lends second-hand books, and this is truly the only decent source of foreign-language reading matter on Rhodes. Local **car rental** rates tend to be 25 to 30 percent less than in Ródhos Town, though vehicles can accordingly be 25 to 30 percent less roadworthy. There are two proper **banks** offering normal service hours and rates of exchange – which is more than can be said for the exchange facilities at local travel agents.

The west coast

Rhodes' **west coast** is the windward flank of the island, so it's damper, more fertile and more forested; windmills, first introduced by the Italians, irrigate crops from the high water table. Most beaches along the often steep, cliff-hemmed shoreline are exposed and decidedly rocky, but this hasn't deterred touristic development; as in the east, the first few kilometres of the busy shore road south-west from the capital have been surrendered entirely to industrial tourism. From Neohóri's aquarium down to the airport, the asphalt is fringed by an uninterrupted line of 1970s-vintage mega-hotels, though such places as Triánda (8km from the city centre), Kremastí (12km along) and Paradhíssi (15km) are still nominally villages, and appear so in their centres.

This was the first part of the island to be favoured by the package operators, and tends to be frequented in summer by a decidedly middle-aged, sedate clientele that often can't be bothered to stir far from the pool. Several local deluxe hotels remain open during the winter, coining a few extra drachmes from the convention and seminar trade. But for more casual tourists, neither the fierce winds – beach umbrellas consistently point seaward – the planes buzzing over Paradhíssi nor the giant, exhaust-billowing power plant at Soroní offer much inducement to pause here.

Ixiá and Triánda

If it weren't for Ródhos' town-limits sign, you wouldn't be able to tell when you'd left the capital – on the coast road at least – and entered **IXIÁ**, where most of the island's deluxe **hotels** cluster. Of these, the *Miramare Beach Hotel* (☎0241/96 251, fax ☎90 153; ⑥ half-board), 5km along, is the most idyllic, consisting of recently renovated bungalows in a landscaped setting just behind the beach lawn. However, as of writing, the *Miramare Beach* is caught up in protracted lease litigation, so you may have to settle for the beachfront *Rhodos Imperial* (☎0241/75 000, fax ☎76 690, ⑥ half-board).

Among local **tavernas**, the *Marco Polo* – installed within the *Rhodos Imperial* itself – prepares post-nouvelle Sino-Italian (!) dishes to perfection. *Ta Kioupia*, Argonáfton 12 (☎241/91 824 for reservations; closed Sun), attracts a clientele of foreigners and Athenians, particulaly well-heeled celebrities, who tend to go into ecstasies over its cuisine (arty *mezédhes*, no fish); however there's a growing local consensus that it's overrated and – at about 7000dr minimum per head – overpriced. Nearby, *Toh Tzaki*, with occasional live *bouzoúki* music, could be a more reasonable, conventional alternative.

In similarly developed **TRIÁNDA**, often confusingly called Ialyssos (see below), the *Elizabeth Beach Hotel Apartments* (☎0241/92 656, fax ☎33 021; ⑤) and the adjacent *Latin Beach Apartments* (☎0241/94 053; ⑤) are A-class complexes in leafy surroundings, though the beach in question – harsh shingle – could be better. The accordingly misnamed *Sandy Beach Taverna* is a popular and very reliable lunch stop.

Ialyssos and around

At the central junction in Tríanda, you can make a detour inland for the five-kilometre ride up to the site of ancient **Ialyssos** (Tues–Fri 8.30am–6pm, Sat–Mon 8.30am–3pm; 800dr but see note following) on flat-topped, pine-covered Filérimos hill; Filérimos means "lover of solitude" after the Byzantine hermits who founded a monastery (see below) here in the tenth century. Though only 267m above sea level, this has always been a strategic point; the knights installed themselves here during their campaign to oust the Genoese, and from its Byzantine castle Süleyman the Magnificent also directed the 1522 siege of Rhodes.

Foundations of third-century **temples to Zeus and Athena**, built atop a far older Phoenician shrine, sprawl in front of the monastery church, while below, further towards the car park, lies the partly subterranean church of **Áyios Yióryios**. This simple, barrel-vaulted structure contains fourteenth- and fifteenth-century frescoes that are unfortunately not as vivid or well preserved as those at Thári or Asklipío. Just southeast of the parking area, a hillside **Doric fountain** with a columned facade was only revealed by subsidence in 1926.

Filérimos monastery

Heavily damaged during fighting between Italians and Germans in autumn 1943, the **Filérimos monastery** on view today is for once not just an Italian job, but also the result of postwar restoration. Despite the questionable authenticity of the original Italian work, the existing structure is beautiful, consisting of an asymmetric chapel built in stages. Behind several hexagonal, groin-vaulted chambers, lies a small, low-slung cloister overgrown with bougainvillaea, while next to the belfry stands an early baptismal font embossed with the Cross of the Knights. As a concession to the Rhodian faithful, the church alone is open to pilgrims after hours, but as the guard makes clear, you are to light your candles, drop your coins in the box, reverence the icon of the Virgin and make a swift exit.

The cross of Filérimos

Southwest of the monastery and archeological zone, a **"Way of the Cross"**, its fourteen Stations marked out by copper plaques in the Italian era, leads to an enormous concrete crucifix. This has replaced the original, which the Italians erected in September 1934, and destroyed seven years later to prevent allied airmen using it for navigation during air raids. Today's cross, built in 1995 at a cost of 20 million drachmes, is almost identical to the original, standing just under 18m tall with a narrow staircase inside; you're allowed to climb out onto the cross-arms for a supplement to the already amazing view. Illuminated at night, the crucifix is clearly visible from the island of Sími and – perhaps more pertinently – infidel Turkey across the straits.

Kremastí, Paradhíssi and Theológos

KREMASTÍ, back on the coast and 4km beyond Triánda, is notable for its gargantuan church and schoolhouse, funded by expatriated Rhodians in America, and for its 15–23 August festival, one of the biggest in the Dodecanese, with a street fair, amusement park, and dancing on the last day. At other times you might prefer to avoid this large village, as it's home to the biggest military barracks on island.

The airport village of **PARADHÍSSI**, literally just outside the terminal, is often visited when departing flights get delayed (☎0241/91 771 or ☎93 828 for the latest information). The highly regarded *Anixis Taverna*, immediately opposite the airport car park, is open year-round for dinner only, with live music at weekends; it also has its own spring water and a weird decor featuring trees growing through the ceiling.

The relatively calm village of **THEOLÓGOS**, 6km beyond Paradhíssi and then 1km inland, has a beach annexe dominated by a handful of hotels, including the well laid-out *Doretta Beach Hotel* (☎0241/41 441; ⑤). You can get plastered at the eminently reasonable *Billy's Bar*, just opposite.

Ancient Kameiros

Just over 12km southwest of Theológos, the important archeological site of **Kameiros** was, together with ancient Lindos and Ialyssos, one of the three Dorian powers that united late in the fifth century BC to found the powerful city-state of Rodos. Soon eclipsed by the new capital, Kameiros was abandoned; only in 1859 was it rediscovered, then completely excavated after 1929.

As a result it is a particularly well-preserved Doric townscape, doubly worth visiting for its beautiful hillside location (Tues–Sun 8.30am–5pm, until 6pm peak season, may close 3pm Sat/Sun; 800dr). While none of the individual remains are spectacular, you can pick out the foundations of two small temples, the re-erected pillars of a Hellenistic house, and the *stoa* of the upper *agora*, complete with water cistern. There were no fortifications, nor was there an acropolis – partly owing to the gentle slope of the site, and also to the likely settlement here of peaceable Minoans, specifically the half-legendary prince Althaemenes. Unlike Rodos, Lindos and Ialyssos, Kameiros was primarily a town of farmers and craftsmen, a profile borne out by rich finds now in the Rhodes archeological museum and the British Museum.

Practicalities

RODA public buses (see "Travel Details") provide minimal links in season from Ródhos Town; if arriving under your own steam (more likely), park intelligently so that you're not hemmed in by the phalanxes of tour coaches which inevitably show up later. On the beach below Kameiros there are several **tavernas**, ideal while you're waiting for one of the two daily buses back to town. If you're willing to walk 4km east to **KALAVÁRDHA**, you'll have rather better frequencies, since besides having its own service this is where the bus routes descending from Sálakos meet the west coast road.

Skála Kamírou and Kástro Kritiniás

There are more restaurants clustered 15km south at **SKÁLA KAMÍROU** (commonly rendered Skála Kámiros or even Kámiros Skála). This tiny anchorage is somewhat inexplicably the hapless target of coach tours in search of an authentic fishing village – as stickers in the restaurant windows attest. The best of several **fish tavernas** here, *Nikoloudhakis*, is accordingly not on the quay but well inland on the east side of the main highway.

Less heralded is the daily **kaïki to Hálki**, which leaves at 2.30pm, weather permitting, and returns very early the next morning; on Wednesdays and Sundays, daytrips depart at 9am and arrive back at 4pm, though Wednesday services tend to be monopolized by package transfers between the two islands (see "Travel Details").

Kritiniá: castle and village

A couple of kilometres south of Skála, the local castle, officially signposted as **Kástro Kritiniás** but locally known as "Kastéllo", is from afar the most impressive of the Knights' rural strongholds; its access road, though recently paved from the north approach, is too narrow and steep for tour buses. With only a chapel and a rubbish-filled cistern more or less intact inside, Kástro Kritiniás proves close up to be no more than a shell – a glorious shell, though, with fine views west to assorted islets and Hálki. You make a "donation" to the formidable little old lady at the car park in exchange for fizzy drinks, seasonal fruit or flowers.

KRITINIÁ itself, 3km east, is a quiet hillside village with a few rooms and tavernas signposted around a central square. Its name stems from its supposed foundation by emigrants from Crete (*Kríti* in Greek). An interesting little **folklore museum** full of rural oddments stands just north of the village on the main bypass road.

Around Mount Akramítis

Beyond Kritiniá, the main road winds south through dense forest on the lower slopes of **Akramítis**, Rhodes' second highest and arguably most beautiful mountain ridge; along with Atáviros peak, just north-east, it has recently been proposed as a nature reserve by the local Association for the Protection of the Environment.

SIÁNA, just below the 825-metre summit, claims to be the most attractive mountain settlement on the island; the village is less controversially famous for its aromatic pine-and-sage honey and *soúma*, a grape-residue distillate identical to *grappa* or Cretan *ráki*. This is produced clandestinely in most Greek wine-making districts, but only on Rhodes is its local manufacture legal owing to an Italian licence which continues to be honoured. Bus tours call in at the church on the main square, which contains heavily restored eighteenth-century frescoes

Monólithos and around

The tiered, flat-roofed farmhouses of **MONÓLITHOS**, 4km south-west of Siána at the end of the public bus line, are scant justification for the long trip out here. Food at the two tavernas tends to be indifferent owing to tour-group trade, but the view over the bay is striking, and you could use the village as a base by staying in advertised **rooms** or at the *Hotel Thomas* (☎0241/22 741 or 0246/61 291, fax ☎0246/28 834; ③), actually a self-catering affair and supposedly open all year.

Diversions in the area which make showing up worthwhile include yet another **Knights' castle** 2km west of town (unrestricted access), photogenically perched on a 200-metre-high pinnacle (the "monolith" of the village name) and enclosing a couple of chapels. The fine-gravel beach of **Foúrni** is hidden five bumpy, curvy kilometres below the castle, its 800-metre extent unadorned except for a seasonal drinks cantina. Beyond a headland, to the left as you face the water, are some **caves** that were hollowed out by early Christians fleeing persecution; slippery, well-worn steps lead down to them.

The interior

Inland Rhodes is hilly and still mostly wooded, despite the recent depredations of arsonists. You'll need your own vehicle to see its highlights, especially as the enjoyment resides principally in getting away from it all; no single site justifies the tremendous expense of a taxi or the inconvenience of trying to make the best of the sparse bus schedules.

In retrospect it will probably be the soft-contoured, undulating scenery which stands out, along with the last vestiges of agrarian life in the villages, some barely mustering three-digit populations. Most people under retirement age are away working in the tourist industry, returning only at weekends and during winter. The young that do remain behind stay largely to help with the grape harvest in late summer (when there may also be a slight chance of work for foreigners). If you have time to spare, and a bit of Greek at your command, traditional hospitality in the form of a drink at the *kafenío*, or perhaps more, may still be found.

Petaloúdhes: the "Butterfly Valley"

The only highly publicized tourist "attraction" in the island's interior is **Petaloúdhes** or the "Butterfly Valley" (daily Apr–Sept 9am–5pm; 300dr). Actually a rest-stop for Jersey tiger moths (*Panaxia quadripunctaria*), during July and August it might more accurately be christened the "Valley of the Tour Buses".

In all of Greece, only here and at a similar valley on Páros island do the moths come to live out the final phase of their life cycle, attracted for unknown reasons by the abundant European sweetgum trees that flourish in this steep-sided canyon. Peak arrival time is mid-June to August, when the moths roost in droves on the trees in order to conserve energy for mating; they cannot eat during this stage, and die of starvation soon afterwards.

Against the tree trunks, the moths are a well-camouflaged black and yellow, but flash cherry-red overwings in flight. On no account should you clap or shout to scare them into flight, as this causes stress and interferes with their reproduction. Indeed, tours have now been reduced and strict visiting rules instituted to protect the moths.

Visiting the valley

Petaloúdhes is reached by a seven-kilometre paved side road bearing inland from the west coast road between Paradhíssi and Theológos. The canyon is divided into two roughly equal sections by a road crossing it, with an admission booth for each – one ticket is valid for both parts.

Whether the "butterflies" are abundant or not, it's worth visiting just for the sake of the peaceful valley; the Rhodians certainly think so on weekends, packing out the fairly reasonable **taverna** by the parking area just below the lower section. Seats beside the pond-side café, just below the upper section of ravine, are also at a premium. An enjoyable trail threads the length of the valley shaded by conifers as well as sweet gum trees, repeatedly crossing a non-potable stream on rough-hewn wooden bridges. It's a surprisingly brisk 45-minute walk in total; flip-flops or similar footwear won't do.

Above the highest reaches of the canyon stands the tiny monastic church of **Kalópetra**, built on 1782 foundations, but not really worth the extra ten-to-fifteen minute walk beyond the trail system on forestry tracks. The five-kilometre road from the lower taverna to **PSÍNTHOS** passes the monastery anyway, with asphalt pavement resuming just beyond. Psínthos, where the Italians decisively defeated the Turks on May 17, 1912, offers at its outskirts a number of leafy **tavernas** suitable for lunch.

Around Profítis Ilías

At an elevation of 798 metres, **Profítis Ilías** is Rhodes' third highest summit, and its most lushly forested; arsonists have yet to succeed in compromising its appeal. The Italians endowed the area with a number of their typical follies, and several villages in the surrounding foothills also merit brief halts.

From Psínthos, you can proceed 14km southwest via Arhípoli to **ELEOÚSSA**, nestled in the shade of the dense forest at the east end of Profítis Ilías' ridge. The square is flanked by the grandiose former summer residence of the Italian governer; no photos allowed as it's now a Greek military installation.

Two other villages hug the southeast slopes of the mountain: gaily painted **PLATÁNIA** unfortunately overlooks the start of an extensive burnt-out area from a hillside setting; **APÓLLONA**, further west, is surprisingly touristed despite a dull layout enlivened only by domed outside ovens, still in use. Most people, however, head directly west out of Eleoússa for 3km to the late Byzantine, four-apsed church of **Áyios Nikólaos Foundouklí** (St Nicholas of the Hazelnuts). Locals descend in force for picnics on weekends at the partly shaded site adjacent, with a fine view north over cultivated valleys; the frescoes inside, dating from the thirteenth to fifteenth centuries, could use a good cleaning, but various scenes from the life of Christ are recognizable.

Negotiating an unsignposted but fairly obvious welter of dirt tracks beyond the church brings you finally to **Profítis Ilías** itself, where the Italian-built chalet-hotel *Elafos/Elafina* (closed since the 1980s despite appearing on EOT lists) hides in deep woods just to the north. A snack bar nearby is generally open in summer, and there's good, gentle strolling around the summit and eponymous church; the peak itself is an off-limits military watchpoint.

Another popular local walk follows the zigzagging *kalderími* that begins next to the chapel of Áyios Andónis, below the Profítis Ilías church, and leads within forty minutes down to the upper edge of **SÁLAKOS** village, at the heart of which is an irregularly shaped, tree-shaded square, fringed by *kafenía* and tavernas. The village has lately acquired a reputation for the recently introduced Nymph brand of spring water; an old Italian mansion adjoining the bottling plant has been revitalized as the *Nymph Inn* (☎0246/22 206; ④), potentially a wonderful base for touring the interior. The Profítis Ilías area can also be easily approached from Kalavárdha on the west-coast road, via Sálakos.

Around Mount Atáviros

All tracks and roads west across Profítis Ilías converge upon the road up from Kalavárdha bound for **ÉMBONAS**, a large and architecturally nondescript village backed up against the north slope of 1215-metre **Mount Atáviros**, roof of the island. Émbonas, with its two pensions and rather meat-orientated tavernas (of which *Skevos* is the least likely to be swamped by groups), is more geared to handling tourists than you might expect from its unprepossessing appearance, since it's the venue for summer "Greek nights" and daytime wine-tasting excursions from Ródhos Town.

The village lies at the heart of the island's most important grape-growing districts, owing to a combination of granitic soil and cooling sea breezes. *CAIR* – the vintners' cooperative founded by Italians in 1928 – produces a variety of acceptable mid-range wines at its two plants near the capital, the most ubiquitous being the white Ilios and the red Chevalier de Rhodes. However, products of the smaller, family-run *Emery* winery (☎0246/41 208; Mon–Fri 9am–3pm; free tours) at the village outskirts are even more esteemed, in particular the namesake Emery dry white and rosé, the recently introduced Mythiko red and white, and the premium Villaré white.

To see what Émbonas would be like without tourists, carry on clockwise around the mountain past modern, nondescript **Artamíti** monastery – its name is a corruption of "Artemis" after a temple in the forests nearby – to less-celebrated **ÁYIOS ISÍDHOROS**. This has as many vines and tavernas as Émbonas (try *Snag* (sic) *Bar Ataviros*), a more open feel, and the trailhead for the five-hour return ascent of 1215-metre Atáviros. This path, beginning in an olive grove at the very northeastern edge of the village, is the safest and easiest way **up the mountain**, which has extensive foundations of an ancient Zeus temple on the summit; sources advising the steep, cross-country scramble from Émbonas should be disregarded. Most of the mountain itself is bare, except for some enormous oaks on the lower slopes, but dense, unburnt forests extend to the east, beyond Artamíti.

Thári Monastery

The road from Áyios Isídhoros to Siána has recently been paved; not so the fairly appalling one that curves for 12km east to Láerma, though it's worth enduring if you've any interest at all in Byzantine monuments. The area's main attraction is **Thári monastery**, lost in pine forests five well-marked kilometres south. The oldest religious foundation on the island, this was re-established as a community of half a dozen monks in 1990 by a charismatic abbot from Pátmos. The striking *katholikón* (open daily, all day) consists of a long nave and short transept surmounted by barrel vaulting. Despite two recent cleanings, the damp of centuries has irrevocably smudged the frescoes dating from 1300 to 1450, but they are still exquisite. Recently cleaned, and thus the most distinct, are those in the transept depicting the Evangelist Mark and the Archangel Gabriel, while the nave boasts various acts of Christ, including such rarely illustrated scenes as the *Storm on the Sea of Galilee*, *Meeting Mary Magdalene*, and *Healing the Cripple*.

The monastery, dedicated to the Archangel Michael, takes the name "Thári" from its foundation legend, as related by an elderly caretaker. A princess, kidnapped and abandoned here by pirates, was visited in a dream by the Archangel, who promised her eventual deliverance. In gratitude, she vowed to build as many monasteries in his honour as the gold ring cast from her hand travelled in cubits.

This she did but, upon being reunited with her parents, the ring was lost in some bushes. Thus "Thári" comes from *tharévo*, "I hazard, guess, venture", after the family's futile search for the heirloom. In their pique, apparently only one cloister was founded.

The far south

South of a line connecting Monólithos and Lárdhos, you could easily begin to think you had strayed onto another island – at least until the still-inflated prices brought you back to reality. Gone are the five-star hotels and roads to match, and with them the bulk of the crowds. Gone too are most tourist facilities and public transport. Only three weekly buses serve the exceptionally depopulated villages here, approaching along the the east coast, where deserted beaches are backed by sheltering dunes. Tavernas grace the more popular stretches of sand, but aside from the growing package resorts of Lárdhos and Péfkos, there are still few places to stay. A new auxiliary airport has long been mooted for the area, however, so this state of affairs won't persist indefinitely.

Lárdhos and Péfkos

Already massive construction is underway behind the sandier patches south of **LÁRDHOS** village, solidly on the tourist circuit despite an inland position between Láerma and the peninsula culminating in Líndhos. Situated downstream from some of the most fire-ravaged territory on Rhodes, it has endured catastrophic floods during rainy winters since the blaze. The beach 2km south of the village is coarse gravel, and – exceptionally so on Rhodes' eastern shore – the water can be downright filthy; it's better to continue another 3km to **Glístra** cove, a small but delightful crescent of dark sand speckled with fine gravel, which sets the pattern for most of the coast from here on.

Four kilometres east of Lárdhos, on the beach road to Líndhos, **PÉFKOS** (Péfki on some maps) was originally an overflow annexe of the latter, but is now emerging as a fully fledged resort in its own right. The sea is cleaner than at Lárdhos but beaches are small, well hidden and often difficult to park near. **Accommodation**, predominantly in villas, is almost totally controlled by UK-based package operators such as *Direct Greece* (again see *Basics*). **Eating out**, try *Butcher's Grill*, which is exactly what is sounds like with some casserole dishes as well, or the *Shanghai Chinese Restaurant*, open evenings only.

Asklipío and Kiotári

Nine kilometres beyond Lárdhos, a paved side road heads 4km inland to **ASKLIPÍO**, a sleepy village guarded by a crumbling **Knights' castle** and graced by the Byzantine church of **Kímisis Theotókou**. For admission to the latter, call at the priest's house behind the apse, or if that doesn't work, haul on the belfry rope. The building dates from 1060, with a ground plan nearly identical to Thári's, except that two subsidiary apses were added during the eighteenth century, partly to conceal a secret school in a subterranean crypt.

The frescoes here are in far better condition than those at Thári owing to the drier local climate; they are also somewhat later, though the priest claims that the final work at Thári and the earliest here were executed by the same artist, a master from Híos. Their format and subject matter, though common on nearby Cyprus, are rare in Greece: didactic "cartoon strips" which extend completely around the church in some cases, and extensive Old Testament stories in addition to the more usual lives of Christ and the Virgin. There's a complete sequence of Genesis episodes, from the *Creation* to the *Expulsion from Eden*; note the comically menacing octopus among the fishes on the *Fifth Day*. A seldom-encountered *Apocalypse of John the Divine* takes up most of the east transept, and *hokhláki* flooring decorates both the interior and the vast courtyard.

Immediately adjacent to the church is a small **ethnographic museum** (admission by donation), with one room devoted to religious artefacts and another to displays on bygone rural life. Asklipío's other concession to tourism is the *Agapitos Restaurant-Bar*, on the hillside above the village access road; they also have a few **rooms** (☎0244/43 235; ③) for those not requiring a coastal base.

Kiotári

Just beyond the detour for Asklipío, the beachfront hamlet of **KIOTÁRI** gets few foreign visitors, perhaps because it's mysteriously omitted from most maps. It was in fact Asklipío's original site, until Byzantine-era piracy compelled the residents to retreat inland. Most of the area is now owned by the Orthodox Church, which has protected the coast from burgeoning development by refusing to sell it off; as at Stegná, locals have instead built numerous simple cottages for summer use. Facilities for outsiders thus far consist of just a few self-catering **studios** and a line of shorefront **tavernas**, best of these *Tsambicos*. The beach is resolutely gravelly but fine for a dip; rock formations and a small offshore reef lend the coast a bit of definition.

Yennádhi

At **YENNÁDHI**, 4km further south, a featureless dark-sand-and-gravel beach extends for kilometres in either direction. It's clean and serviceable, with sunbeds and rudimentary watersport gear available, plus two virtually indistinguishable tavernas – *Klimis* and *Andonis* – just behind the most accessible part of the shoreline. Despite some Italian monuments and the remains of a brick factory (look for its stack), the actual village up by the road is a dull grid made duller by proliferating cement construction. However

Yennádhi is virtually the only place along this stretch with any **amenities**, including car rental – absolutely essential in this practically bus-free zone – as well as a rash of pensions, bars and a **post office**.

Lahaniá and southeast beaches

South of Yennádhi, you'll see more fine if lonely beaches, often marked just by isolated "taverna-rooms" which function at peak season only. Just 2km inland along a side road, though invisible from the sea, **LAHANIÁ** village, with its eponymous **hotel** (☎0244/43 089; ③) and smattering of "rooms", is a possible base if you don't mind the predominantly German atmosphere; nearly half of the 140 inhabitants are bohemians from Munich and Berlin, who since the 1980s have opened craft shops and bought up the handsome houses lining the hilly streets. On the main square, strangely sited at the lower, eastern end of the village, *Taverna Platanos* is fairly priced and nourishing enough, with seating between the church and two wonderful fountains, one retaining an Ottoman inscription.

You can go directly from Lahaniá to Hokhlakás, which straddles a paved side road leading south to **Plimíri**, an exceptionally well-protected, sandy bay backed by dunes, whose only facility is a good-value rustic **taverna**. Beyond the new concrete jetty which someday may become a yacht marina, a 1980-vintage wreck attracts expert scuba divers.

Áyios Pávlos, 5km beyond Hokhlakás, is close to another Italian-era model farm, complete with belfry, which now merely houses livestock. From here a fair-quality road leads southeast to an unnamed but pristine beach below **Cape Vígla**, which – like mounts Akramítis and Atáviros – will hopefully soon benefit from officially protected status.

Kataviá and Prassoníssi

Shortly beyond Áyios Pávlos the road enters **KATAVIÁ**, over one hundred kilometres from the capital, marooned amidst fields of wheat or barley which are the only crops that thrive locally. Several **tavernas**, pricier than you'd expect for the location, preside over the junction that doubles as the square; a vital **filling station** – the first since Lárdhos – and a few **rooms** to rent, aimed mostly at windsurfers (read on), complete the list of amenities. Like so many villages in the far south, three quarters of the houses here are deserted, their owners having left to find work in Australia or North America.

From Kataviá, a rough but marked track leads through a frequently used military exercise area to **Prassoníssi**, Rhodes' southernmost extremity and site of a lighthouse automated only in 1989. From May to October you can stroll across the wide, low sandspit linking it to the rest of Rhodes, but during winter, storms swamp this tenuous link and make Prassoníssi a true island. Even in summer the prevailing northwesterly winds drive swimmers to the lee side of the spit, leaving the exposed shore to the world-class windsurfers who come here to train. In season the scrubby junipers rustle with tents and caravans; water comes from two **tavernas** flanking the access road, the only facilities or even permanent structures here. The one next to its old windmill has more character, but beware their fish grills – tasty but among the most expensive in the Dodecanese.

Messanagrós and Skiádhi Monastery

From Lahaniá, an alternative route heads 9km northwest along a narrow but paved road to the picturesque hilltop village of **MESSANAGRÓS**. This already existed in some form by the fifth century AD, if the foundations of a ruined basilica at the village outskirts are anything to go by. Within this vast area, amid patches of mosaic flooring, squats a smaller but equally venerable thirteenth-century chapel; any previously existing frescoes are long gone, but there's a *hokhláki* floor and stone barrel arches to admire. You can fetch the key from nearby *Kafenio O Mike*, and buy a candle and/or a coffee as a donation.

The monastery of Skiádhi

The onward road to the **monastery of Skiádhi**, 6km distant, is shown incorrectly on most maps. You should take the Kataviá-bound road initially, then after about 2km bear right onto an unsigned dirt track; these last 4km are quite badly surfaced, but even a puny Category A rental car can get through in dry conditions.

Known formally as Panayía Skiadhení, the monastery – despite its undistinguished modern buildings – was originally founded in the thirteenth century to house a miraculous icon of the Virgin. In the fifteenth century a heretic stabbed the painting, allegedly causing blood to flow from the wound in her cheek; the fissure, and suspicious brown stains around it, are still visible. Needless to say, the offending hand was instantly paralysed.

Except on 7/8 September, the festival of the icon, you can usually stay overnight upon arrangement with the caretaker priest Ioannis Kermaïtzis and his wife (call ☎0244/46 006 in advance to check the monastery is attended). The extremely kind Pater Yiannaki, as he is fondly known, speaks some English as he lived in America for a while before settling here in 1992; he claims to be busier in winter than summer, hosting retreats for stressed-out Rhodian hoteliers, and is the only Orthodox priest you are likely to meet who dispenses business cards.

The immediate surroundings of the monastery are rather dreary since a comprehensive fire in 1992, but the views west are stunning. Tiny **Khténia** islet is said to be a petrified pirate ship, so rendered by the Virgin in answer to prayers from desperate locals about to succumb to yet another raid.

The southwest coast and Apolakkiá

West of Kataviá, the island loop road – now completely paved – emerges onto the deserted, sandy **southwest coast**; Skiádhi can easily be reached from this side too, as the road up from here is better signposted than from Messanagrós. If freelance camping and nudism are your thing, this is the place to indulge, though you'll need your own transport, or lots of supplies, a tent and a stout pair of shoes. There are crashing waves and often a strong undertow along this coast – only strong swimmers should venture far offshore.

The nearest inland village, 7km north of the Skiádhi turning, is nondescript, agricultural **APOLAKKIÁ**, set amid plastic greenhouses and its famous melon patches, and also equipped with a few **pensions** and shops. Several reasonable **tavernas** and *kafenía* surround the badly signposted central junction, where there always seem to be a few stopped motorists scratching their heads over maps. Northwest leads to Monólithos, due south back to Kataviá, and the northeasterly bearing is an enjoyable, paved road cutting quickly back to Yennádhi via Váti. A few hundred metres along this latter option, a proudly signposted side track heads north to a new irrigation dam absent from all maps, oddly scenic as these things go and plainly visible from Siána overhead.

Travel Details

ISLAND TRANSPORT

BUSES

With some important exceptions near Ródhos Town, *RODA* buses serve mostly points on the west coast, while *KTEL* buses ply the east coast. The schedules below are mostly invalid on weekends. Fares are usually 250–800dr one way, and never more than 1300dr. Journey times vary from 10–15 minutes for Koskinoú to almost 2hr for Kataviá in the far south.

RODA

New Market (Néa Agorá) to: airport (Paradhíssi; 11 daily 7am–10pm); Apóllona (2 daily at 1.50 & 3.30pm); Émbona (1 daily at 2.40pm); Kalavárdha (4 daily 6.50am–9pm); Kallithéa hotels (half-hourly 9am–10.30pm); Kameiros ruins (2 daily at 10am & 1.15pm); Koskinoú (11 daily 6am–9pm); Kremastí (8 daily 9.30am–10.30pm); Monólithos (1 daily at 1.15pm); Petaloúdhes Valley (2 daily at 9 & 11am); Sálakos (4 daily 6.50am–3.40pm); Theológos (6 daily 9am–9pm).

KTEL

Platía Rimínis (aka "Sound & Light Square") to: Afándou (15 daily 6.30am–9pm); Apolakkiá (3 weekly at 2.30pm Mon, Weds & Fri); Arhángelos (13 daily 6.45am–9pm); Asklipío (3 weekly at 2.30pm Tues, Thurs & Sat); Faliráki (17 daily 7.45am–9pm); Kataviá (3 weekly at 2.30pm Tues, Thurs & Sat); Kolímbia (6 daily 9am–7.30pm); Láerma (1 daily at 3pm); Lárdhos (3 daily 2.30–6pm); Líndhos (12 daily 7.45am–6pm); Mássari (4 daily 9am–3pm); Mesanagrós (3 weekly at 2.30pm Tues, Thurs & Sat).

INTER-ISLAND TRANSPORT

KAÏKIA AND EXCURSION BOATS

Skála Kámiros to: Hálki (1 daily at 9am Wed & Sun, at 2.30pm all other days, on rivals *Afroditi* and *Chalki*; 1hr 15min).

NB *Afroditi* and *Chalki* leave simultaneously and can each carry one car. At least one of the Wednesday *kaïkia* may be fully booked by Hálki package clients and unavailable to independent travellers.

Mandhráki to: Sími (1 daily at 9.30am on excursion *kaïki*, returning 3.30–4pm; or 4 weekly – usually Mon, Wed, Thurs & Fri – 3–6pm on the less costly islanders' ferries *Symi I* or *Symi II*; 1hr 30min).

NB Unless you can persuade quayside touts to sell you a one-way ticket (difficult in high season) on the excursion boats, they work out expensive for use in island-hopping; current information available at Ethnárhou Makaríou 17 (☎0241/37 769).

FERRIES

Rhodes Commercial Harbour (Kolóna) to: Astipálea (1 weekly on *DANE*; 5hr); Áyios Nikólaos (Crete; 1 weekly on *Ventouris Lines*); selected western Cyclades (usually Folégandhros, Mílos, Santoríni, Serifos, Sífnos; 1 weekly on *Ventouris*); Hálki (2 weekly on *G&A Ferries* or *Ventouris*; 2hr); Iráklio (Crete; 2 weekly on *G&A*); Kálimnos (10 weekly on *DANE*, *G&A* or *Nissos Kalymnos*; 5hr 20min); Kárpathos (Pigádhia; 3 weekly on *G&A* or *Ventouris*, 1 stopping at Diafáni; 4hr 30min–5hr 30min); Kássos (2 weekly on *G&A* or *Ventouris*); Kastellórizo (3 weekly on *G&A* or *Nissos Kalymnos*; 4–5hr); Kós (14 weekly on *DANE*, *G&A* or *Nissos Kalymnos*; 4hr–6hr 30min); Léros (6–8 weekly on *DANE* or *G&A*; 6hr 30min–7hr); Náxos (1–2 weekly on *G&A*); Níssiros (4 weekly on *G&A* or *Nissos Kalymnos*; 3–5hr); Páros (1–2 weekly on *G&A*); Pátmos (7–8 weekly on *DANE* or *G&A*; 8hr 30min–9hr 30min); Pireás (11 weekly on *DANE* or *G&A*; 13–18hr); Sími (3–4 weekly on *G&A* or *Nissos Kalymnos*; 1hr 30min–2hr); Síros (1 weekly on *G&A*); Thessaloníki (1 weekly on *DANE*); Tílos (4 weekly on *G&A* or *Nissos Kalymnos*; 2hr 30min–4hr).

HYDROFOILS

Mandhráki to: Kálimnos (2 weekly on *Mamidhakis/Dodecanese Hydrofoils*); Kós (7 weekly on *Mamidhakis*); Níssiros (2 weekly on *Farmakidhis Lines* or *Mamidhakis*); Sími (3 weekly on *Mamidhakis*); Tílos (2 weekly on *Farmakidhis*, 1 weekly on *Mamidhakis*).

NB Current information on *Mamidhakis/Dodecanese Hydrofoils* available at Platía Neoríon, Mandhráki jetty (☎0241/24 000); on *Farmakidhis Lines* at New Market, Suite 33 (☎0241/78 334). *Ilio Lines* afternoon services for islands between Rhodes and Kálimnos have been suspended since June 1995. If resumed, there are 2 or 3 weekly at most.

DOMESTIC FLIGHTS

Rhodes Paradhíssi Airport to: Athens (6–8 daily in summer, 4–5 daily in winter on *Olympic* or *Air Greece*); Iráklio (Crete; 4–6 weekly year-round on *Olympic* or *Air Greece*); Kárpathos (2–4 daily in summer, 1–2 daily in winter on *Olympic*); Kássos (1 daily in summer, 4 weekly in winter, often via Kárpathos, on *Olympic*); Kastellórizo (6 weekly in summer, 2 weekly in winter on *Olympic*); Kós (2–3 weekly, March–Oct only, on *Olympic*); Míkonos (2–3 weekly, June–Sept only, on *Olympic*); Thessaloníki (4–6 weekly year-round on *Olympic* or *Air Greece*); Thíra (Santoríni; 3–4 weekly, March–Oct only, on *Olympic*).

INTERNATIONAL TRANSPORT

FERRIES AND HYDROFOILS

Ródhos Town to: Cyprus (Limassol; 18hr); Israel (Haifa; 39hr); Turkey (Marmaris; 1–14 weekly on *Farmakidhis Lines*, 1 daily – in theory – on Turkish car ferry; 1hr & 2hr respectively).

NB Specimen prices for Cyprus and Haifa (including taxes but before any applicable student/youth discounts): deck class £52/$78, cheapest cabin £82/$123 to Cyprus, £74/$111 and £112/$168 respectively to Israel. Fares to Turkey with Greek-run *Farmakidhis Lines* are £26/$39 one-way, £43/$65 return, inclusive of Greek (but not Turkish) taxes. The Turkish afternoon car ferry costs £38/$57 one way, £54/$81 round trip, all taxes included. Services to Egypt are suspended until further notice.

Greek script table

Afándou	Αφάντου	ΑΦΑΝΤΟΥ
Agáthi	Αγάθη	ΑΓΑΘΗ
Akándia	Ακάντια	ΑΚΑΝΤΙΑ
Akramítis	Ακραμίτης	ΑΚΡΑΜΙΤΗΣ
Apolakkiá	Απολακκιά	ΑΠΟΛΑΚΚΙΑ
Apóllonsa	Απόλλωνα	ΑΠΟΛΛΩΝΑ
Arhángelos	Αρχάγγελος	ΑΡΧΑΓΓΕΛΟΣ
Arhípoli	Αρχίπολη	ΑΡΧΙΠΟΛΗ
Asgouroú	Ασγουρού	ΑΣΓΟΥΡΟΥ
Asklipío	Ασκληπιείο	ΑΣΚΛΗΠΙΕΙΟ
Atáviros	Αττάβυρος	ΑΤΤΑΒΥΡΟΣ
Áyios Emilianós	Αγιος Αιμιλιανός	ΑΓΙΟΣ ΑΙΜΙΛΙΑΝΟΣ
Áyios Isídhoros Foundouklí	Αγιος Ισίδωρος Φουντουκλή	ΑΓΙΟΣ ΙΣΙΔΩΡΟΣ ΦΟΥΝΤΟΥΚΛΗ
Áyios Pávlos	Αγιος Παύλος	ΑΓΙΟΣ ΠΑΥΛΟΣ
Dhimiliá	Διμυλιά	ΔΙΜΥΛΙΑ
Eleoússa	Ελεούσα	ΕΛΕΟΥΣΑ
Émbonas	Έμπωνας	ΕΜΠΩΝΑΣ
Eptá Piyes	Επτά Πηγές	ΕΠΤΑ ΠΗΓΕΣ
Faliráki	Φαλιράκι	ΦΑΛΙΡΑΚΙ
Filérimos	Φιλέριμος	ΦΙΛΕΡΙΜΟΣ
Foúrni	Φούρνι	ΦΟΥΡΝΙ
Haráki	Χαράκι	ΧΑΡΑΚΙ
Hokhlakás	Χοχλακάς	ΧΟΧΛΑΚΑΣ
Ialyssos	Ιαλυσός	ΙΑΛΥΣΟΣ
Ixia	Ιςιά	ΙΞΙΑ
Kalamónas	Καλαμώνας	ΚΑΛΑΜΩΝΑΣ
Kálathos	Κάλαθος	ΚΑΛΑΘΟΣ
Kalavárdha	Καλαβάρδα	ΚΑΛΑΒΑΡΔΑ
Kalithiés	Καλυθιές	ΚΑΛΥΘΙΕΣ
Kameiros	Κάμειρος	ΚΑΜΕΙΡΟΣ
Kápi	Κάπι	ΚΑΠΙ
Kataviá	Κατταβιά	ΚΑΤΤΑΒΙΑ
Kiotári	Κιοτάρι	ΚΙΟΤΑΡΙ

Kolímbia	Κολύμπια	ΚΟΛΥΜΠΙΑ
Kollákio, Collachium	Κολλάκιο	ΚΟΛΛΑΚΙΟ
Kolóna	Κολόνα	ΚΟΛΟΝΑ
Koskinoú	Κοσκινού	ΚΟΣΚΙΝΟΥ
Kremastí	Κρεμαστή	ΚΡΕΜΑΣΤΗ
Krtiniá	Κρητηνιά	ΚΡΗΤΗΝΙΑ
Ladhikó	Λαδικό	ΛΑΔΙΚΟ
Láerma	Λάερμα	ΛΑΕΡΜΑ
Lahaniá	Λαχανιά	ΛΑΧΑΝΙΑ
Lárdhos	Λάρδος	ΛΑΡΔΟΣ
Líndhos	Λίνδος	ΛΙΝΔΟΣ
Malóna	Μαλώνα	ΜΑΛΩΝΑ
Mandhráki	Μανδράκι	ΜΑΝΔΡΑΚΙ
Marítsa	Μαρίτσα	ΜΑΡΙΤΣΑ
Mássari	Μάσσαρη	ΜΑΣΣΑΡΗ
Messanagrós	Μεσαναγρός	ΜΕΣΑΝΑΓΡΟΣ
Monólithos	Μονόλιθιος	ΜΟΝΟΛΙΘΟΣ
Mónte Smith	Μόυτε Σμίθ	ΜΟΝΤΕ ΣΜΙΘ
Neohóri	Νεοχώρι	ΝΕΟΧΩΡΙ
Paradhíssi	Παραδείσι	ΠΑΡΑΔΕΙΣΙ
Pastídha	Παστίδα	ΠΑΣΤΙΔΑ
Péfkos	Πεύκος	ΠΕΥΚΟΣ
Petaloúdhes	Πεταλούδες	ΠΕΤΑΛΟΥΔΕΣ
Pilónas	Πυλώνας	ΠΥΛΩΝΑΣ
Platánia	Πλατάνια	ΠΛΑΤΑΝΙΑ
Plimíri	Πλημμύρι	ΠΛΗΜΜΥΡΙ
Prassoníssi	Πρασονήσι	ΠΡΑΣΟΝΗΣΙ
Profítis Ilías	Προφήτης Ηλίας	ΠΡΟΦΗΤΗΣ ΗΛΙΑΣ
Psínthos	Ψίνθος	ΨΙΝΘΟΣ
Réni Koskinoú	Ρένι Κοσκινού	ΡΕΝΙ ΚΟΣΚΙΝΟΥ
Rodhíni	Ροδίνι	ΡΟΔΙΝΙ
Ródhos	Ρόδος	ΡΟΔΟΣ
Sálakos	Σάλακος	ΣΑΛΑΚΟΣ
Siána	Σιάνα	ΣΙΑΝΑ
Skála Kamírou	Σκάλα Καμείρου	ΣΚΑΛΑ ΚΑΜΕΙΡΟΥ
Skiádhi Monastery	Μονή Σκιάδι	ΜΟΝΗ ΣΚΙΑΔΙ
Soroní	Σορωνή	ΣΟΡΩΝΗ
Stegnaá	Στεγνά	ΣΤΕΓΝΑ
Thári Monastery	Μονή Θάρι	ΜΟΝΗ ΘΑΡΙ
Theológos	Θεολόγος	ΘΕΟΛΟΓΟΣ
Thérmes Kallithéas	Θέρμες Καλλιθέας	ΘΕΡΜΕΣ ΚΑΛΛΙΘΕΑΣ
Triánda	Τριάντα	ΤΡΙΑΝΤΑ
Tsambíka	Τσαμπίκα	ΤΣΑΜΠΙΚΑ
Váti	Βάτι	ΒΑΤΙ
Vlihá	Βλυχά	ΒΛΥΧΑ
Yennádhi	Γευυάδι	ΓΕΠΠΑΔΙ

Chapter 2

The Southern Dodecanese

The seven **southern Dodecanese** closest to Rhodes not only offer ideal escapes when the "big island" begins to pall, but are worthy destinations in their own right. An increasing number of visitors essentially skip Rhodes, using a flight-only deal to deposit them at Rhódos Town's harbour, where on any given day in season hydrofoils or ferries are on hand to whisk them off to these surrounding islands. If you have the means, and plan well in advance, they are also an excellent and satisfying group to hop by chartered yacht, starting from Mandhráki harbour.

Rhodes' near neighbours offer a variety of escapes in terms of scenery and amenities. Harshly romantic **Kárpathos** is the only really sizeable island of the south Dodecanese, with direct charter-flight access from Europe (plus useful local flights from Rhodes), magnificent beaches of all compositions, and an area in the far north of remarkable ethnological interest. Just next door, melancholy **Kássos** will probably appeal only to misanthropes allergic to other tourists.

The more cheerful duo of **Hálki** and **Sími**, which closely bracket Rhodes to the west and north respectively, are essentially one-town limestone outcrops which, like Kássos, have always been forced to make a living from the sea. Sími is greener, more hikeable, better endowed with pebble beaches, and more geared up for independent travellers – though its spectacular harbour also makes it the most popular daytrip destination from Rhodes among this selection of islands. Hálki's houses have recently been comprehensively restored to provide accommodation for a more gentrified package clientele. By contrast, the most remote and depopulated isle of the Dodecanese, **Kastellórizo**, once represented an extreme example of seafaring resourcefulness spurred by the poverty of on-shore resources. Today the island serves as an idiosyncratic haven for a non-packaged, slightly alternative crowd willing to brave the long trip out from Rhodes and the utter lack of beaches.

Bare but relatively well-watered **Tílos**, least maritime of all the Dodecanese, combines almost overwhelming tranquility and excellent sandy beaches with a growing range of creature comforts,

Accommodation prices

All establishments in this book have a symbol that corresponds to one of six price ranges:

① up to 5000dr ② 5000–7000dr ③ 7000–9000dr
④ 9000–13000dr ⑤ 13000–17000dr ⑥ above 17000dr

£1=370dr; $1= 240dr

The rates quoted for each category represent the cheapest available double room in high season. Out of season, prices can drop by up to fifty percent, especially if you negotiate a stay of three or more nights. Single rooms, where available, cost around seventy percent of the price of a double.

For more accommodation details, see p.34

though occasionally problematic access from either Rhodes or Kós should retard further development in the near future. The round volcano-isle of **Níssiros**, dry but fertile, receives regular excursions from adjacent Kós, but so far these have scarcely affected the convivial ethos in the main port's many tavernas, nor penetrated the picturesque outlying villages or hidden coves.

Kárpathos

A long, narrow island isolated between Rhodes and Crete, wild **Kárpathos** has always been something of an underpopulated backwater, although it is physically the third largest of the Dodecanese. A mountainous spine, habitually cloud-capped as it traps moisture-laden west winds, rises to nearly 1200 metres, and effectively divides the more populous, lower-lying south from an exceptionally rugged north. Despite a magnificent if windswept coastline of cliffs and promontories constantly interrupted by little beaches, Kárpathos has succumbed surprisingly little to tourism. This has a lot to do with the appalling road system – rutted even where paved, unspeakable otherwise – the dearth, save two or three exceptions, of interesting villages, and the surprisingly high cost of food, which offsets reasonable room prices.

On balance, Kárpathos hasn't the most alluring of interiors: the central and northern uplands were badly scorched by 1980s forest fires, and agriculture plays a slighter role than on any other Greek island of comparable size. Although there are in fact good oil-bearing olive groves, and enough livestock to export, the Karpathians are frankly too well off to bother much with farming: massive emigration to America and the resulting remittance economy has transformed Kárpathos into one of the wealthiest Greek islands, even before the recent influx of tourists.

Most foreigners come here for a glimpse of the traditional village life that prevails in the isolated north of the island, and for numerous superb, secluded beaches, among the best in the Aegean.

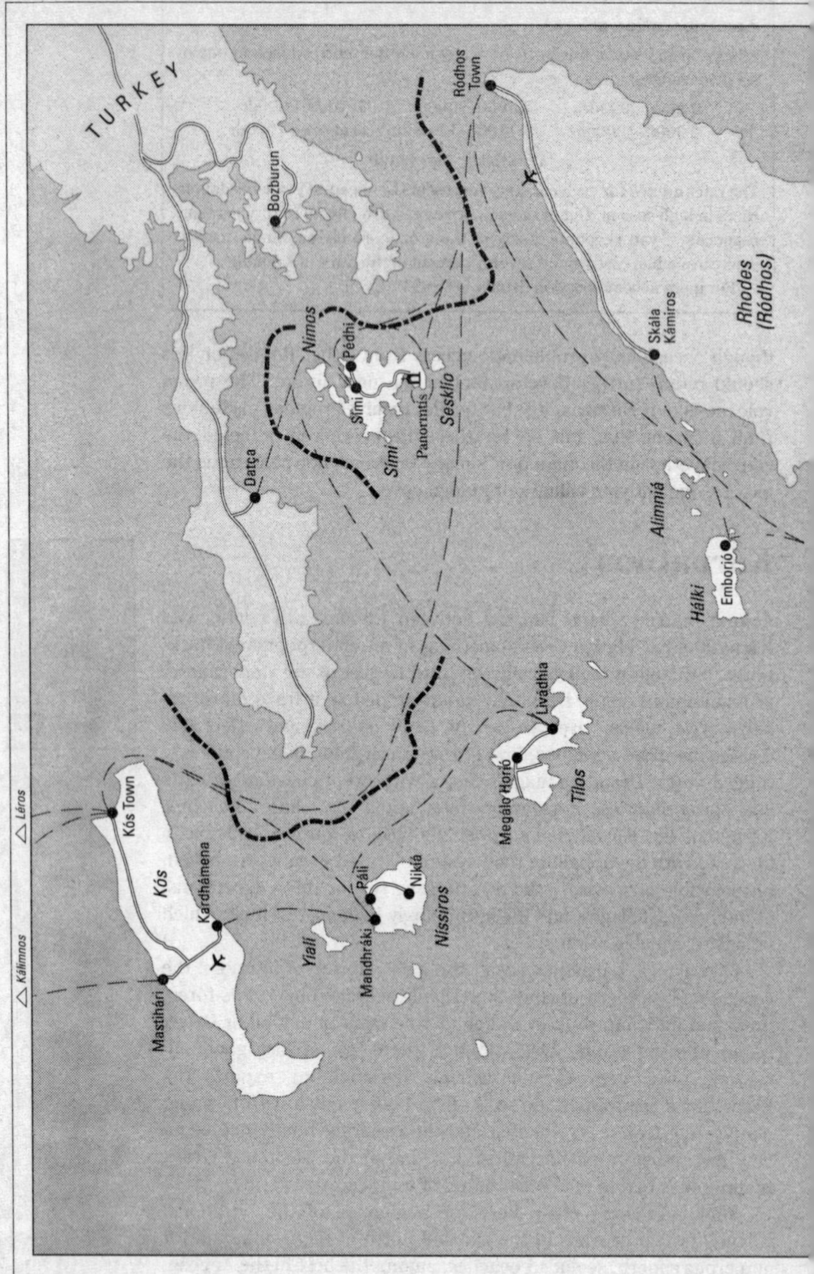

TURKEY
Bozburun
Ródhos Town
Rhodes (Ródhos)
Skála Kámiros
Nímos
Pédhi
Sími
Panormitis
Sesklío
Sími
Datça
Alimniá
Hálki
Emborió
Livádhia
Megálo Horió
Tílos
Léros
Kálimnos
Kós Town
Kós
Kardhámena
Mastihári
Páli
Nikiá
Níssiros
Mandhráki
Yialí

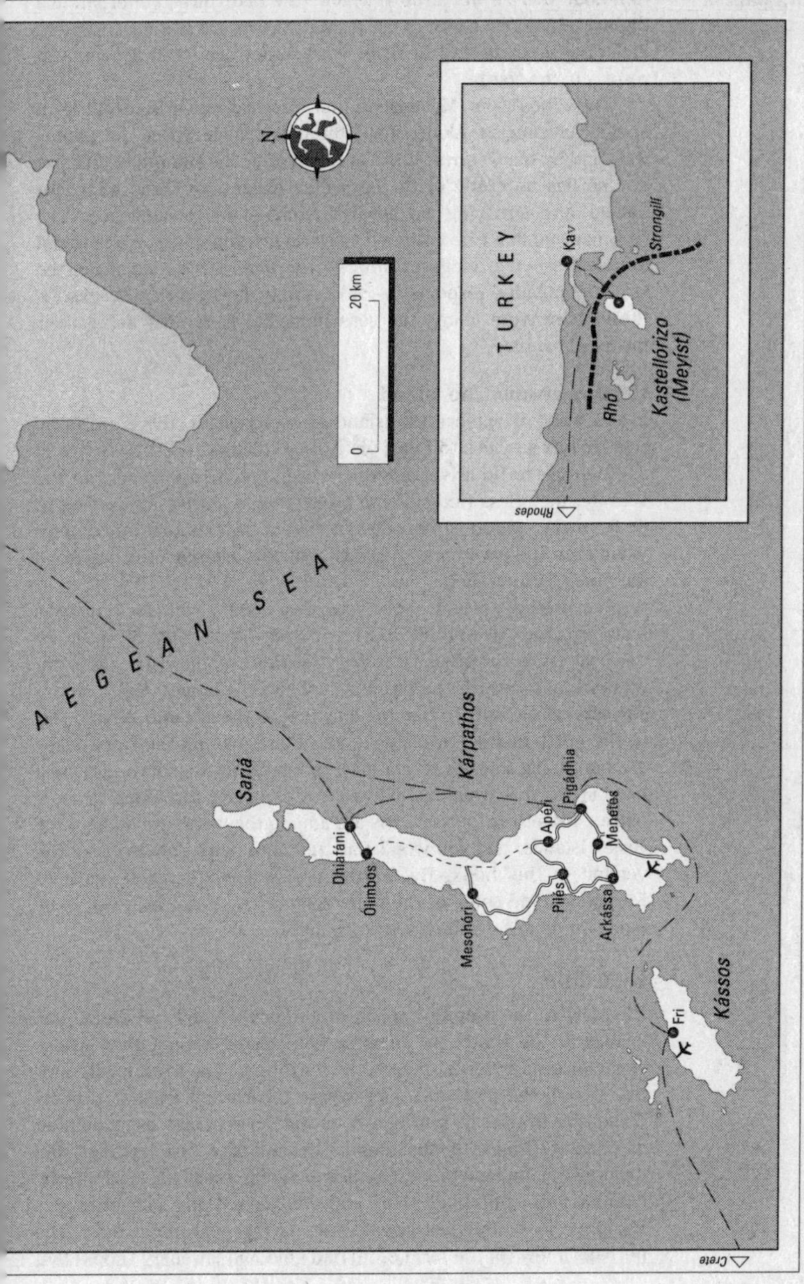

AEGEAN SEA
Sariá
Kárpathos
Dhiafáni
Ólimbos
Mesohóri
Apéri
Pigádhia
Piliés
Menetés
Arkássa
Kássos
Fri
Crete
N
0
20 km
TURKEY
Kav
Strongilí
Kastellórizo
(Meyísti)
Rhó
Rhodes

Although there's an airport which can take direct international flights, only a few charters use it, and visitors – a Euro-assortment, including a smattering of Brits – are concentrated in a couple of resorts in the south.

Kárpathos' four Mycenaean and classical cities figure little in ancient chronicles. Alone of the the major Dodecanese, Kárpathos was held by the Genoese and Venetians after the Byzantine collapse and so has no castle of the crusading Knights of Saint John, nor indeed any surviving medieval fortresses of consequence. The Ottomans couldn't be bothered to settle or even garrison it; instead they left a single judge or *kadi* in the main town, and made the Greek population responsible for his safety during pirate attacks. Of these there were many, the seas immediately around being their favoured haunt.

Getting around the island

If you want to explore the island as a passenger, there are fairly regular **bus** services to Pilés, via Apérí, Voládha and Óthos, as well as Ammopí; to be driven anywhere else, you'll have to rely on the set-rate, meterless **taxis**. These aren't too expensive for getting to or from the airport, 16km distant (about 2500dr one way), or to villages on the paved road network, but they charge a fortune to go anywhere further afield.

For getting around under your own steam, you can **rent cars** from *Holiday* (☎0245/22 813) or *Circle* (☎0245/22 690), up by the post office, or **bikes** from *Hermes Rent a Motorbike* (☎0245/22 090), out towards the beach, which has the biggest fleet and on-site service. Be warned that the only fuel on the island is located just to the north and south of town, and that tanks on the small bikes are barely big enough to complete a circuit of the south, let alone head up north – which is, in any case, expressly forbidden by most outfits. Moreover tourist maps are among the worst available in the Greek islands, and you won't find anything more detailed than the version in this book. By far the easiest way to reach northern Kárpathos, and some of the more remote east coast beaches, is by boat (for details of which see box p.122).

Pigádhia

PIGÁDHIA, the island's capital, often known simply as Kárpathos, nestles at the south end of extremely scenic **Vróndi Bay**, whose sickle of sand extends 3km to the northwest. The town itself, curling around the jetty and quay where ferries and excursion boats dock, is as drab as its setting is beautiful; an ever increasing number of concrete blocks contributes to the air of a vast building site, making the Italian-era port police building seem an heirloom by comparison. Although there's absolutely nothing special to see, Pigádhia does offer just about every facility you might need, and perhaps a few (in the form of myriad gold and jewellery shops) that

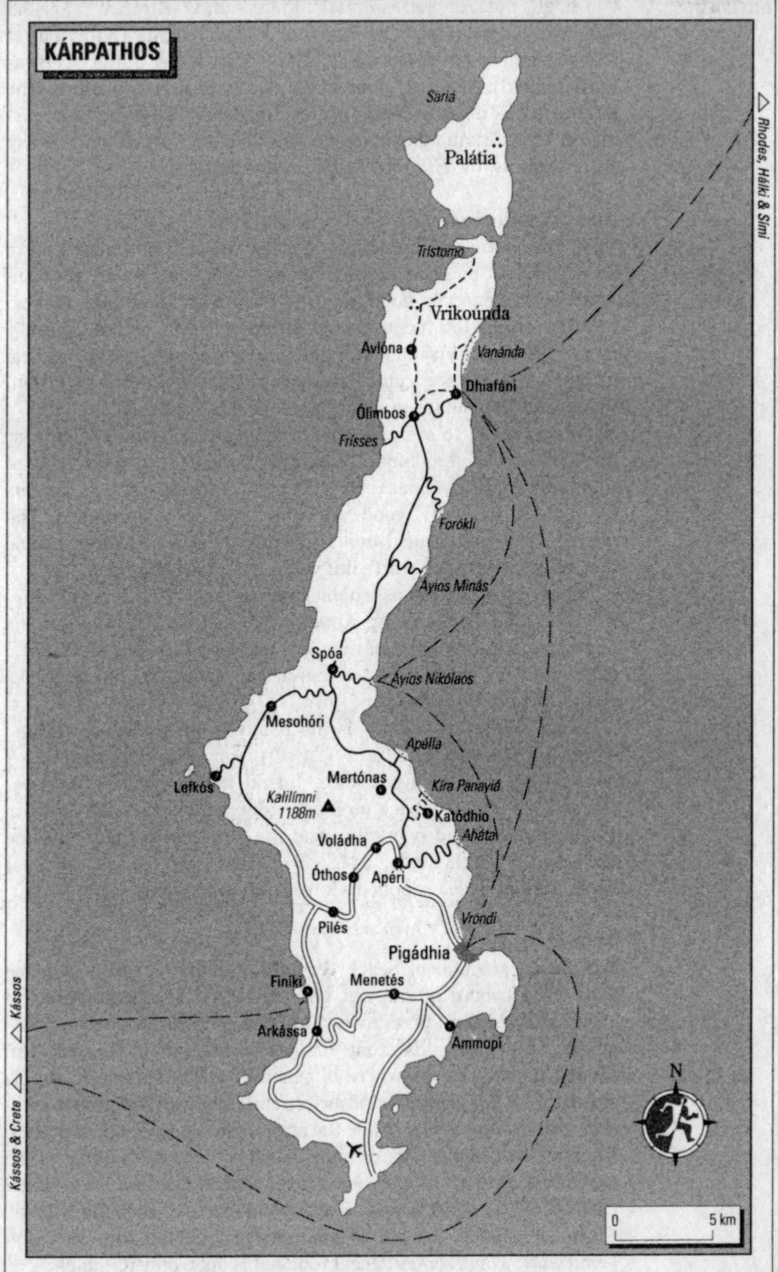
KÁRPATHOS
Sariá
Palátia
Trístomo
Vrikoúnda
Avlóna
Vanánda
Dhiafáni
Ólimbos
Frísses
Forókli
Áyios Minás
Spóa
Áyios Nikólaos
Mesohóri
Apélla
Lefkós
Mertónas
Kíra Panayiá
Kalilímni
1188m
Katódhio
Voládha
Aháta
Óthos
Apéri
Pilés
Vróndi
Pigádhia
Finíki
Menetés
Arkássa
Ammopí
N
0
5 km
Rhodes, Hálki & Sími
Kássos
Kássos & Crete

you might not. Among essentials, there's an **OTE** office (Mon–Sat 7.30am–3.10pm, Sun 9am–2pm) on Platía Pémptis Oktovríou, at the west end of Apodhímon Karpathíon (the "Street of the Overseas Karpathians"); just next door is the *Olympic Airways* office. The **post office** is directly south, on Ikostiogdhóïs Oktovríou, the main inland street running parallel to Apodhímon Karpathíon. Among several **banks**, the *Ethniki/National* has an **ATM**.

Accommodation

Most ferries are met by people offering **rooms**, and unless you've sorted this out in advance, you may as well take up an offer – standards seem generally good, and the town is small enough that no location will be too inconvenient. More expensive places generally lie north towards Vróndi beach and tend to be occupied by package groups as far as the ruined fifth-century basilica of **Ayia Fotiní**, though development is gradually spreading beyond that.

If you prefer to seek out somewhere yourself, possibilities near the jetty end of Apodhímon Karpathíon, signposted past the (not especially recommended) *Hotel Coral*, include *Anna's Rooms* (☎0245/22 313; ②), good value and very well positioned. The nearby *Vittoroulis Apartments* (☎0245/22 639; ③) are available on a weekly basis, but worth it if you're staying that long.

Other, simpler rooms establishments include *Sofia's* (☎0245/22 154; ②), the rambling *Konaki* (☎0245/22 908; ②), on the upper through-road west of the town hall, or *Filoxenia* (☎0245/22 623; ②), on Anastasíou, a cul-de-sac lane off Ikostiogdhóïs Oktovríou, on the east side of town.

Next door to *Filoxenia* is the relatively luxurious, good-value *Artemis Pension* (☎0245/22 724; ②), somewhat misnamed as it consists of self-catering studios. Inland **hotels** include the *Avra* (☎0245/22 388; ②), back on Ikostiogdhóïs Oktovríou, whose main virtue is year-round operation, and the more comfortable en-suite *Karpathos* (☎0245/22 347; ③), near the south end of Dhimokratías which shoots back from the waterfront.

Vróndi beach

Pigádhia's magnificent beach, **Vróndi** ("thunder"), takes its name from an attribute of the sea god Poseidon, who was patron of Pigádhia's ancient precursor. The beach improves towards its centre, where the tidal zone has the least amount of rock-reef, though the water everywhere is generally clean and warm; simple **sports** are possible, with windsurfers and canoes to rent from beachside lean-tos and tables. While the advancing tide of hotels has yet to fill in all the blank spots, camping rough is probably a thing of the past. Just inland, 1500m along from town, the *Blue Bay Hotel* (☎0245/22 479; ③) is well situated and not overwhelmingly huge. Curiously there's just one restaurant right behind the sand, *Toh Limanaki*, which serves decent food but is open only for lunch.

Eating and drinking

Most of Pigádhia's waterfront **tavernas** are indistinguishable and expensive, with a few notable exceptions; *Psistaria Olympia*, on the waterfront, will appeal to carnivores, while fish aficionados should head for *Iy Kali Kardhia*, at the north end of the shoreline boulevard on the way to the beach. Places inland tend to work out slightly cheaper: try the friendly *Mike's*, up a pedestrian way from the stylish *Kafenio Café* on Apodhímon Karpathíon.

Kafenio Halkia, in one of the few surviving old buildings next to the church on Apodhímon Karpathíon, attracts a mixed crowd of locals and tourists for the sake of its nightly live music (not the best on the island); the limited evening menu seems to be a secondary consideration. Among trendier **bars**, *Rocks* and *Symposium*, overlooking the bay from from perches just below Apodhímon Karpathíon, currently seem the most popular.

A particularly well-developed Karpathian institution are the half-dozen **English-breakfast cafés** along Apodhímon Karpathíon, courtesy of returned USA emigrants. Many are overpriced and greasy, but they tend to improve as you head up towards the *Ethniki/ National* bank, where the street veers out of sight of the water.

Southern Kárpathos

The southern extremity of Kárpathos towards the airport is flat and extraordinarily desolate, its natural barrenness exacerbated by recent fires. There are a couple of empty, sandy **beaches**, especially on the southeast coast, but they're not at all attractive, and exposed to prevailing winds; the nicest of these is the tiny cove by the *Hotel Poseidon* (☎0245/22 020; ④), at **Makrís Yialós**, which offers some shelter. You're better off going no further in this direction than **AMMOPÍ**, just 7km from Pigádhia. This, together with the recent development at Arkássa (see below), is the closest thing on Kárpathos to a purpose-built beach resort: two sandy, tree-fringed coves serviced by a couple of tavernas and a few rooms establishments – not exactly pretty, but as yet not quite overcrowded.

Heading west from Pigádhia rather than south along the coast, the road climbs steeply for 9km up to **MENETÉS**, an appealing village with handsome old hilltop houses, a tiny folklore museum and a spectacularly sited church. There's a good **taverna** run by Mihalis Sevdhalis, and a memorial with views back to the east.

The west coast

Kárpathos' west coast seems far less developed than the east coast, since – with the sterling exception of Lefkós – beaches are scanty and exposed, and the shoreline is more bleak than dramatic. For a change the local road system isn't too bad, and it's gradually being improved as the asphalt loop inches around the southern half of the island.

Arkássa and Finíki

Beyond Menetés, the road immediately starts its descent to **ARKÁSSA**, tucked into a ravine on the west coast, with excellent views across to Kássos en route. Arkássa's scenic location and smattering of tiny beaches just south of Paleokástro headland (see below) have made it a prime target for heavy development, with hotels and restaurants sprouting in clusters along the mostly rocky coastline.

A few hundred metres south of where the ravine meets the sea, a signposted cement side road heads towards the whitewashed chapel of Ayía Sofía, five minutes' walk away and built on the spot where **Classical and Byzantine Arkessia** stood. Its visible remains consist of several mosaic floors with geometric patterns, one of which runs diagonally under the floor of a half-buried chapel, emerging from the walls on either side. The headland beyond, known as Paleokástro, was the site of Mycenaean Arkessia, of which sections of Cyclopean wall remain.

Most places **to stay** in Arkássa are aimed squarely at the package market, but the en-suite *Rooms Irini* (☎0245/61 263; ②) and the more opulent *Hotel Dimitrios* (☎0245/61 255; ③), at the south end of the village, are worth contacting. **Eating out**, *Petaloudha Taverna* is reliable and often has seafood.

This may come from the tiny fishing port of **FINÍKI**, just a couple of kilometres north, which offers a minuscule **beach**, three or four **tavernas**, and several **rooms** establishments lining the road to the jetty; the taverna attached to *Fay's Paradise* (☎0245/61 308; ②; open mid–June to mid–Sept) is noted for its squid and stuffed cabbage. In season, weather permitting, there are weekend *kaïki* trips to Kássos.

Lefkós and Mesohóri

The asphalt west-coast road currently runs out 5km short of the attractive resort of **LEFKÓS** (Paraliá Lefkoú). Unless you rent a car, it's not particularly convenient as a touring base, as only three buses a week call here from Pigádhia; if you're on a small motorbike, this is the furthest you can reach and return from without running out of gas. However, your efforts will be rewarded with a striking topography of cliffs, hills, islets and sandspits surrounding a triple bay, making this a delightful spot for flopping on the beach.

If you wish to stay, there are three combination **taverna/rooms** establishments (no phones; ③) perched on the promontory overlooking the two more northerly and progressively wilder bays; on the spit between them lie the badly crumbling remains of medieval fortifications. On the southern cove, the *Sunlight Restaurant* has garnered an enviable tamarisk-shaded position; the food's acceptable, though as ever on Kárpathos, pricier than you'd expect.

Back on the main road, you climb northeast through one of the few sections of Karpathian pine forest not scarred by fire to

MESOHÓRI. The village tumbles down towards the sea around narrow, stepped alleys, amid which stands a medieval church with frescoes and – typical of several villages around Mount Kalilímni – an adjacent working fountain. The only tourist facility of any sort is a snack bar at the top of the village where the access road ends. Otherwise, you can continue along the main road to Spóa, overlooking the east coast (see below).

Central Kárpathos

The **centre** of Kárpathos supports a quartet of villages blessed with superb hillside settings and ample running water – and a cool climate, necessitating warm clothes even in August. Nearly everyone here has "done time" in North America, then returned home with their nest eggs; New Jersey, New York and Canadian car plates tell you exactly where repatriated islanders struck it rich – in many instances, fabulously so.

A little above the Finíki–Lefkós route, **PILÉS** is perhaps the prettiest of these villages, with great sea views west, local honey on sale, and a seasonal snack bar. **ÓTHOS** lies just below the second highest summit of the Dodecanese, 1188-metre **Mount Kalilímni**. The highest (700m) and chilliest settlement on Kárpathos, Óthos is noted both for its heavy red wine and an ethnographic museum installed in a traditional house. From here you cross a saddle often swirling with cloud to reach **VOLÁDHA**, endowed with a pair of nocturnal grills and a tiny Venetian citadel. Seven kilometres east of Pilés lies **APÉRI**, largest, lowest and wealthiest of the four. During the pirate era it served as the island's capital, and is still seat of the local bishop. In addition to an attractive fountain, the village offers two **tavernas** which operate nights only except in high season.

East coast beaches

From Apéri, you can bike 7km east along a very rough side road to the isolated **Aháta** beach, a 200-metre, dramatically backdropped pebble bay with a freshwater spring but no other facilities. North of Apéri, the main road up the east coast is extremely rough in places, but makes a beautiful drive, passing above beaches most easily accessible by boat trips from Pigádhia. The first one encountered is **Kíra Panayiá**, just below Katódhio hamlet, reached via a rutted side road even worse than that at Aháta. There are a surprising number of villas, **rooms** and **tavernas** in the ravine behind the 150m of fine gravel – in peak season hopelessly packed out. That said, the turquoise water is sheltered from most summer winds and exceptionally clear, with caves at the south end providing refuge and shade. Kíra Panayiá can also be reached on foot from the village of Mertónas, overhead; it's a fairly popular hike of less than an hour, with the trail emerging onto the lowest curves of the access road.

Apélla is the best of the beaches you can – just about – reach by road, but has no amenities other than a freshwater spring. The end of this itinerary is **SPÓA**, high above the shore on the island's spine, where the road stops by a snack bar at the edge of the village. From **Áyios Nikólaos**, 5km below, is an excellent beach with tavernas and an ancient basilica.

Northern Kárpathos

Although connected by road with Spóa, much the easiest (and most common) way to get to **northern Kárpathos** is by boat (see box below). Inter-island ferries call at **Dhiafáni** once a week, or there are smaller tour boats daily from Pigádhia. These take a couple of hours, and are met at Dhiafáni by buses for the eight-kilomere trip up to the traditional village of **Ólimbos**, the main attraction in this part of Kárpathos.

Ólimbos and around

High in the mountains, windswept **ÓLIMBOS** straddles a long ridge below slopes studded with mostly ruined windmills. The village was originally founded during the eighth century AD as a refuge from the pirates that plagued the coastal settlements at Vrikoúnda and Sariá, the now-uninhabited islet that hovers just north of Kárpathos like a ball balanced on a seal's nose.

The area has long been a mecca for foreign and Greek ethnologists, who treat it as a living museum of peasant dress, crafts, dialect and music that have long since vanished elsewhere in Greece. But Ólimbos is gradually being dragged into the twentieth century, thanks to the semi-paved road up from Dhiafáni, electricity, and a growing number of tourists; since 1980, the number of daytrippers has increased ten-fold to 30,000 annually, to the extent that they outnumber locals during the day. It's still a very picturesque place, full of (often posed) photo opportunities, but traditions are vanishing by the year – or at least they're hard to witness in season, when the locals must certainly get tired of being ogled like animals in a zoo. Nowadays it's only the older women and those

Boat tours

Olympos Travel (☎0245/22 993), on Pigádhia waterfront near the jetty, offers very good deals on all-in trips (from around 4500dr to Ólimbos, land transfer included), though the rival boat (*Chrisovalandou Lines*; pay on board for best deals) is much more attractive and stable in heavy seas. Less well publicized is the fact that you can use these boats for a one-way trip between the north and the south, in either direction, at about one third of the going rate for daytrips. *Olympos* and other agents also offer excursions to Kássos and to several isolated east coast beaches which have no road access or facilities; enquire as to whether lunch is included, and bring supplies if not.

Ólimbos – a mild debunking

The apparent exoticness of Ólimbos has prompted numerous sensational write-ups in the past, many of them exaggerated, plagiarized from each other, or simply untrue. Much is made of the local matrilineal property inheritance, with houses passing down from mother to eldest daughter – the so-called *kanakára* – upon her marriage, giving rise to claims of some rediscovered Amazonian realm. However, this custom is prevalent on several other of the Dodecanese; it was apparently a method of dodging taxation or confiscation dating from Ottoman times, when women weren't systematically counted on censuses. Still less known is that an oldest son – the *kanakáris*, literally "favourite son" – also inherits all the real property of his father's line; hence the massive emigration of younger brothers, who have literally no prospects in the village.

For at least some of this mystification, the villagers themselves are partly responsible, not being averse to occasional leg-pulling or the natural tendency of telling people what they want to hear. Amateur anthropologists on flying visits are particularly easy, credulous targets: a reporter for the French edition of *GEO Magazine* was recently assured by one disgruntled, divorced woman shopkeeper that most local men were either homosexual or impotent. This remark was printed verbatim, without critique or irony, variously causing scandal and amusement when the news got back to Ólimbos.

Probably the best way to experience Ólimbos at its most authentic involves turning up at one of the seasonal **festivals**, when traditional music is performed by the men; indeed vast crowds descend on August 15 and at Easter. Few outsiders realize, however, that the winter Carnival is nearly as important folklorically; masquers traipse from house to house, performing in return for hospitality and getting thoroughly drunk through straws (no doffing of masks allowed).

The order of precedence of **musical instruments** is slightly unusual: the *tsamboúna* or bagpipe takes the lead, followed by the *lýra*, or three-string spike fiddle, while the *laoúto*, a variant of the lute or oud and used for rhythm, defers to both. The *lýra* is unlike the Cretan models, resembling more a *politikí* or Pontic *lýra*; the bows however do have little bells, as on Crete.

working in tourist shops who wear the striking and magnificently colourful traditional dress.

After a while you'll notice the dominant role that the women play in daily life: tending gardens, carrying goods on their shoulders, or herding goats. Nearly all Ólimbos men emigrate or work elsewhere on the island, sending money home and returning only on holidays. The long-isolated villagers also speak a unique dialect, said to retain traces of its Doric and Phrygian origins; thus "Ólimbos" is pronounced "Élimbos" locally.

Entering the village, you're obliged to run a gauntlet of souvenir shops, from which you can expect some persistent if good-natured sales pitches; beware of Chinese- and Bulgarian-made embroidery touted as "traditional local handicraft". The most genuine articles are unfortunately the least portable: carved wooden doors or furniture, and the flamboyantly painted plaster-relief folk art on houses. Plant and animal, mythic and geometric designs are all represented on balustrades, lintels and eaves, though the most popular motif seems to be the double-headed eagle of the Paleologue dynasty.

Deceptively modern-looking, the main **church of the Assumption** sports seventeenth-century fresco fragments, and the altar screen proved to be gold-leafed after a recent cleaning. Two working **windmills** just beyond, restored in the mid-1980s, grind wheat and barley during late summer only, more for show than anything else. Under one of the mills is tucked a small, unsignposted **museum** (sporadic hours; free), with such wooden oddities as a fez rack (from the days when such headgear was worn) and a vulture trap, baited with carrion, that looks like an oversized garlic press.

Practicalities

The daytime commercialization of Ólimbos provides a good reason for staying overnight – either with an organized excursion or free-lance, in one of several **rooms** establishments. The *Ólimbos* (☎0245/51 252; ②), near the village entrance, is a good bare-bones option, while *Hotel Aphrodite* (☎0245/51 307; ②) offers the only en-suite facilities and a southerly ocean view.

There are nearly as many places to **eat**; *Parthenonas*, on the square by the church, is excellent – try their *makaroúnes*, a local dish of home-made pasta with onions and cheese. During spring-time, *myrgouátana*, a rock-dwelling marine invertebrate (tastier than it sounds), is served up breaded and sauteed as *mezédhes* in Ólimbos *kafenía*, along with *petalídhes* (limpets). Incidentally, there is no bakery in Ólimbos; the village women make their own four or five days a week, at one of several rustic communal ovens (a favourite photo-op). If you need some, you could ask your pension or restaurant proprietor.

Hikes from Ólimbos

Walking from the village, the tiny port and beach at **Frísses** are a dizzy drop below on the west coast, or there are various, signposted **hikes** up into the mountains. The most challenging of these is the route from Ólimbos **to Spóa or Mesohóri** in the south (initially trail, then cross-country or dirt track), a seven-hour trek unfortunately made less scenic by a devastating 1983 forest fire (though new trees are now waist-high).

Perhaps the most attractive option, and certainly the easiest, is to hike **down to Dhiafáni**. The path begins just below the two working windmills, well marked with red paint-dots and rock cairns. About twenty minutes along, bear right up towards the road (the left turn leads to Avlóna; see below), and after ten or so minutes on this, plunge down and left through extensive, unburnt forest, towards the bed of a ravine draining to Dhiafáni. A small stream trickles alongside much of the way, and there's also a spring; at your approach, snakes slither into hiding and partridges break cover. The entire route, mostly on well-kept trails, takes around ninety minutes downhill.

By staying overnight in Ólimbos, you could also tackle the marked trail north to the Byzantine ruins at **Vrikoúnda**, via the seasonally inhabited hamlet of Avlóna. The drop from Avlóna to Vrikoúnda is quite steep, and while there is water at Avlóna, you should take ample food and make a day of it. During the August 28-29 **festival** comemorating the beheading of John the Baptist, this route is busy with Olimbians making a pilgrimage to the saint's remote chapel near Vrikoúnda.

Dhiafáni and around

Although its popularity is growing – and will soar on completion of the new deep-water dock to accommodate ferries – rooms in **DHIAFÁNI** are still inexpensive, and the pace of life slow, except in August when it's overrun by Italians and Germans. Most of the settlement only dates from the postwar years, so don't expect much in the way of architectural character. There are numerous places at which to **stay** and eat, several shops, and even a small travel agency (*Orfanos Travel*; ☎0245/51 410). This has its own en-suite hotel (③), plus a metered phone, money exchange facilities and ferry tickets for sale. The obvious *Golden Beach* (☎0245/51 315; ②) and *Mayflower* (☎0245/51 228; ②) hotels opposite the quay, neither en suite, are noisy; better to try the garrulously friendly *Pansion Delfini* (☎0245/51 391; ②) or *Pansion Glaros* (☎0245/51 259; ②; high season only), up on the southern hillside. Back on the front, the best **taverna** is *Anatoli*, easily recognizable by the folk reliefs that sprout from its roofline, and offering local wine from the barrel, among other home recipes. Outside of August, it's one of just three places open.

Around Dhiafáni

Orfanos Travel organizes **boat trips** to various nearby beaches, as well as to the Byzantine site at **Palátia** on the islet of **Sariá** (Saría), just a stone's throw north of the main island; alternative days out involve negotiating a perilously narrow strait to **Trístomo** anchorage and the ruins of **Vrikoúnda**. Habitation at both Vrikoúnda and Sariá predates the Christian era, as two of Kárpathos' four ancient city states were located here.

There are also a few coves within walking distance. Closest, though not the best, is **Vanánda**, a stony bay with an eccentric, slogan-bedaubed **campsite/snack bar** in the oasis behind. To get there, follow the pleasant signposted path north through the pines, but don't believe the signs that say "ten minutes" – it's over half an hour away. An ugly new road cuts the path in two spots, but it's not too obtrusive and the trail is still quicker.

Better beaches lie south of Dhiafáni, but require more effort to reach, trekking around headlands and scrambling down streambeds; the boat ride in from Pigádhia is an excellent way of spotting likely coves and committing their location to memory. **Forókli** and **Áyios Minás** are two southerly beaches distant enough to justify renting a boat.

Greek script table

Kárpathos	Κάρπαθος	ΚΑΡΠΑΘΟΣ
Aháta	Αχάτα	ΑΧΑΤΑ
Ammopí	Αμμοπη	ΑΜΜΟΠΗ
Apélla	Απέλλα	ΑΠΕΛΛΑ
Apéri	Απέρι	ΑΠΕΡΙ
Arkássa	Αρκάσα	ΑΡΚΑΣΑ
Avlóna	Αυλώνα	ΑΥΛΩΝΑ
Áyios Minás	Αγιος Μηνάς	ΑΓΙΟΣ ΜΗΝΑΣ
Áyios Nikólaos	Αγιος Νικόλαος	ΑΓΙΟΣ ΝΙΚΟΛΑΟΣ
Dhiafáni	Διαφάνι	ΔΙΑΦΑΝΙ
Forókli	Φορόκλι	ΦΟΡΟΚΛΙ
Kíra Panayiá	Κύρα Παναγιά	ΚΥΡΑ ΠΑΝΑΓΙΑ
Lefkós	Λευκός	ΛΕΥΚΟΣ
Menetés	Μενετές	ΜΕΝΕΤΕΣ
Mesohóri	Μεσοχώρι	ΜΕΣΟΧΩΡΙ
Ólimbos	Όλυμπος	ΟΛΥΜΠΟΣ
Óthos	Όθος	ΟΘΟΣ
Pigádhia	Πηγάδια	ΠΗΓΑΔΙΑ
Pilés	Πυλές	ΠΥΛΕΣ
Sariá	Σαριά	ΣΑΡΙΑ
Spóa	Σπόα	ΣΠΟΑ
Vanánda	Βανάντα	ΒΑΝΑΝΤΑ
Voládha	Βωλάδα	ΒΩΛΑΔΑ
Vrikoúnda	Βρυκούντα	ΒΡΥΚΟΝΤΑ
Vróndi	Βρόντη	ΒΡΟΝΤΗ

Kárpathos travel details

ISLAND TRANSPORT

BUSES

Pigádhia to: Ammopí (2–3 daily); Apéri (3–4 daily); Arkássa (1–2 daily); Finíki (1–2 daily); Lefkós (3 weekly Mon, Wed & Sat); Óthos (3–4 daily); Pilés (3–4 daily); Voládha (3–4 daily).

Dhiafáni to: Ólimbos (2 daily each way).

INTER-ISLAND TRANSPORT

KAÏKIA

Pigádhia to: Dhiafáni (at least 1 daily in season; 2hr).

Finíki to: Kássos (irregular service, peak season only).

FERRIES

Pigádhia to: Áyios Nikólaos (Crete); 1 weekly on *Ventouris Lines* or *Vitsentzos Kornaros*; selected western Cyclades (minimum Thíra, Mílos, Sífnos; 1 weekly on *Ventouris*); Hálki (1–2 weekly on *G&A Ferries* or

Ventouris); Iráklio (Crete; 1–2 weekly on *G&A*); Kássos (1 weekly on *G&A*, *Ventouris* or *Vitsentzos Kornaros*); Náxos (1–2 weekly on *G&A*); Páros (1–2 weekly on *G&A*); Pireás (1–2 weekly on *G&A*, 1 weekly on *Ventouris* or *Vitsentzos*); Rhodes (1–2 weekly on *G&A*, 1 weekly on *Ventouris*; 5–6hr); Sími (1 weekly on *G&A* or *Ventouris*); Sitía (Crete; 1 weekly on *Vitsentzos Kornaros*).

Dhiafáni to: Hálki, Iráklio, Kássos, Páros, Pigádhia, Pireás, Rhodes, Sími, Thíra (all 1 weekly on *G&A* or *Ventouris*).

NB All ferry services to Dhiafáni are subject to cancellation in bad weather until the new pier is completed (projected date 1996).

DOMESTIC FLIGHTS

Kárpathos to: Athens (3–4 weekly; 80–90 min); Kássos (3–4 weekly; 15min); Rhodes (10 weekly–2 daily; 40–70min); Crete (Sitía; 1 weekly; 1hr).

NB Flights between Kárpathos and Kássos are not currently subject to airport tax, and – taxi fare to the airport aside – cost about the same as a ferry or *kaïki* passage.

Kássos

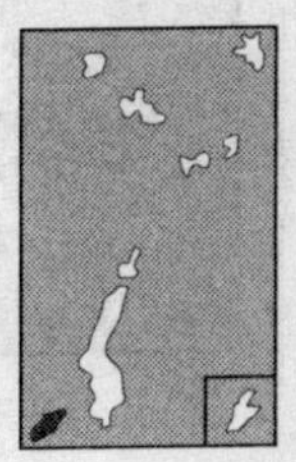

Like Psará islet in the East Aegean (see p.292), **Kássos** bravely contributed its large fleet to the Greek revolutionary war effort, and likewise suffered appalling consequences. In late May 1824, an Ottoman army sent by Ibrahim Pasha, Governor of Egypt, laid siege to the island; on June 7, aided perhaps by a traiter's tip as to the weak point in Kássos' defences, the invaders descended on the populated north coast plain, slaughtered the inhabitants, and put houses, farms and trees to the torch.

Barren and depopulated since then, Kássos attracts few visitors, despite being a regular port of call for large ferries and its regular air links with Rhodes and Kárpathos. What remains of the population is grouped together in five villages under the shadow of Kárpathos, leaving most of the island accessible only on foot or by boat. There's little sign here of the wealth brought to other islands by diaspora Greeks or – since Kássos hasn't much to offer them – by tourists; crumbling houses and disused hillside terraces are poignant reminders of better days.

Kássos is more productive than it appears from the sea, though it's not a fertile island by any stretch of the imagination; as on Psará, wild trees have never taken root again since the holocaust. Sheer gorges slash through lunar terrain, and fenced smallholdings of wind-lashed midget olives provide the only permanent relief. Springtime grain crops briefly soften the usually empty terraces, and livestock somehow survives on a thin furze of thornbush.

Especially after the 1824 holocaust, Kassiots distinguished themselves as skilled pilots (see *Contexts* p.346); the rough, almost harbourless coast here was perhaps the best training-ground imaginable. Ironically, in view of Ibrahim Pasha's Egyptian origins, islanders

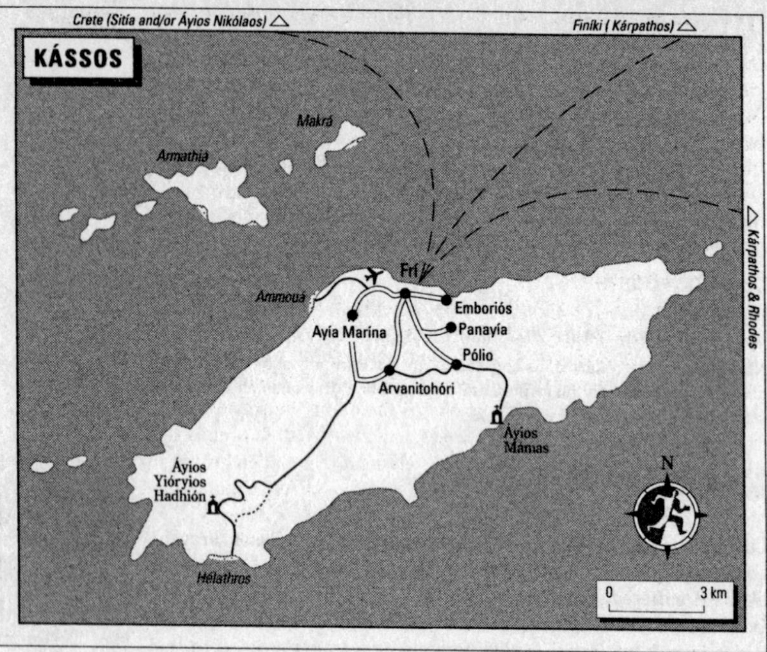

were also instrumental in digging the Suez Canal, and there was for many decades a substantial Kassiot community in Port Said. These days, evidence of emigration to the USA is everywhere: American-logo T-shirts and baseball caps are *de rigueur* in summer, and the conversation of vacationing expatriates is spiked with Americanisms.

Arrival and getting around

Kássos can be a pain to reach; Frí's anchorage, at the dock just west of Boúka fishing port, is so poor that passing **ferries** won't stop if an appreciable wind is up. In such cases you have to disembark at Kárpathos and fly the remaining distance in light aircraft, which are less sensitive to gales. No airport tax is charged for such a short trip, so the cost of the air ticket and taxi fare to Kárpathos airport is comparable to the Kárpathos-based excursion boats which can manoeuvre into Boúka in most weathers. The abandoned works of a new jetty that came to nothing are visible just east of Boúka.

The **airport** lies a single kilometre west of Frí, an easy enough walk if lightly laden, otherwise a cheap (400dr) ride on one of the island's three **taxis**. Except in high season, when you can take advantage of an unreliable bus service, motorbike rental and boat excursions, the only other method of exploring the island's more remote corners is by hiking along fairly arduous, shadeless tracks.

Frí and Emboriós

Most of the capital **FRÍ**'s appeal is confined to the immediate environs of the wedge-shaped fishing port of **Boúka**, protected from the sea by the two crab-claws of a breakwater and overlooked by the town cathedral of **Áyios Spirídhon**. On June 7, a memorial service for the victims of the 1824 massacre is held here. Inland, Frí is engagingly unpretentious, one might even say down-at-heel; no attempt has been made to prettify what is essentially a dusty little town poised halfway between demolition and reconstruction.

Accommodation can be found at the seafront hotels *Anagenissis* (☎0245/41 323 or 41 495; fax ☎41 036; ③ en suite, ② without) and, just behind, at the less expensive *Anessis* (☎0245/41 201 or 41 234; fax ☎41 730; ② en suite), both with partial sea views. The manager of the *Anagenissis*, Emmanuil Manoussos, also has a few pricier apartments, and runs the all-in-one travel agency just below (though *Olympic Airways* occupies separate premises at the far end of the building). Both hotels tend to be noisy owing to morning bustle on the waterfront and the phenomenal number of small but lively bars, one right under the *Anessis*. During high season a few **rooms** operate, for example those owned by Elias Koutlakis (☎0245/41 363; ④); these tend to be in the suburb of Emboriós (see below), fifteen minute's walk east, and also more expensive than Frí lodgings.

Perched in a spectacular location overlooking Boúka, *Iy Oraia Bouka* is easily the best of Frí's **tavernas**, and reasonably priced if you shun the imported Rhodian prawns. *Ouzeri Toh Meltemi*, on the way to Emboriós, is an honourable runner-up, while *Iy Kassos* – serving simple grills on the town-hall *platía* – is a distinct third. Unlikely to generate much enthusiasm are two pokey tavernas at **Emboriós**, the former commercial port, today partly silted up and useless to larger ships. **Shops** in Frí are fairly well stocked for self-catering, and two stalls sell imported fruit, remedying Kássos' former dire lack of fresh produce.

Northern beaches

Frí's **town beach**, if you can call it that, is at **Ammouá** (Ammoudhiá), half-an-hour's walk west of the airport along the coastal track. This sandy cove, just before the landmark chapel of **Áyios Konstandínos**, is often caked with seaweed and tar, but persevere five minutes more and you'll find much cleaner gravel coves. Otherwise, it's well worth shelling out for high-season boat excursions to far better beaches on a pair of islets visible to the northwest. **Armathiá** boasts no less than five beaches – two small ones on the southeast flank, plus three larger ones on the more exposed northwest shore; **Makrá** has one large sandy cove at its northeast tip, facing Kássos. There are no amenities (or shade) on either islet, so bring water, a picnic and some sort of sun protection.

Inland villages

Kássos' **inland villages** cluster in the agricultural plain just inland from Frí, and are linked to each other by road; all, except arguably the dull grid of Arvanitohóri, are worth a passing visit, manageable on foot in a single day.

Larger than Frí in extent and also more rural, **AYÍA MARÍNA**, the village 1500m inland and uphill, is attractive, especially when seen from the south, with its two belfries poking above scraggly olive groves; one of these churches is the focus of the island's liveliest **festival**, on July 17. Just beyond the hamlet of Kathístres, a further 500m southwest, the cave of **Ellinokamára** is so named for the Hellenistic wall partially blocking the entrance; from there a path continues for another ninety minutes in the same direction to the larger, more natural cave of **Seláï**, which has impressive stalactites.

On the opposite side of the plain, above Emboriós but more easily reached by a two-kilometre road from Frí, **PANAYÍA** is famous for the architecture of its now-neglected mansions – many of Kássos' wealthiest ship captains hailed from here – and the oldest surviving church on the island, the eighteenth-century **Panayía tou Yióryi**, though the relatively modern, larger church is venue for the other major island **festival** on August 15. Just adjacent stands an intriguing Siamese-sextuplet chapel complex, with dedications to six separate saints. From **PÓLIO**, 3km above Panayía and site of the island's badly deteriorated medieval **castle**, a track leads southeast within ninety minutes more to **Áyios Mámas**, one of Kássos' two important rural monasteries.

The southwest: Hélathros and Áyios Yióryios

A dirt track heads southwest from the paved road linking the villages of Ayía Marína and Arvanitohóri; having skirted a fearsome gorge, you are unlikely to see another living thing aside from goats or an occasional wheeling hawk. After about an hour, the Mediterranean appears to the south, a dull expanse ruffled only by the occasional ship bound for Cyprus and the Middle East. When you finally reach a fork, it's wisest to adopt the upper, right-hand turning, following derelict phone lines and some initial cement paving towards the rural monastery of **Áyios Yióryios Hadhión**, 11km (or 3hr on foot) from Frí, and only frequented during its festival in late April or perhaps in summer when caretakers and/or overseas Kassiots may be resident. There are a few open guest cells and cistern water if you need to fill up flasks; the only other water en route is from a well at the path's high point, soon after the fork.

From the monastery it's another 3km or 45min – bikes can negotiate all but the last 500m – to **Hélathros**, a lonely cove at the mouth of one of the larger, more forbidding Kassiot canyons. The beach itself is small and mediocre, gravel and pebbles on a sand base, but the water is pristine and – except for the occasional fishing boat – you'll probably be alone. Incidentally, the lower, left-hand option at the fork is the direct track to Hélathros, but this is only 2km shorter and, following severe storm damage, impassable to any vehicle; even hikers face some daunting scrambling on all fours, so it's probably not worth pursuing.

Greek script table

Kássos	Κάσος	ΚΑΣΟΣ
Ayía Marína	Αγία Μαρίνα	ΑΓΙΑ ΜΑΡΙΝΑ
Áyios Yióryios Hadhión	Άγιος Γεώργιος Χαδιών	ΑΓΙΟΣ ΓΕΩΡΓΙΟΣ ΧΑΔΙΩΝ
Emboriós	Εμπορειός	ΕΜΠΟΡΕΙΟΣ
Frí	Φρύ	ΦΡΥ
Hélathros	Χέλαθρος	ΧΕΛΑΘΡΟΣ
Panayía	Παναγία	ΠΑΝΑΓΊΑ
Pólio	Πόλιο	ΠΟΛΙΟ

Kássos travel details

INTER-ISLAND TRANSPORT

FERRIES

Kássos to: Áyios Nikólaos (Crete); 1–2 weekly on *G&A Ferries* or *Ventouris Lines*, 1 weekly on *Vitsentzos Kornaros*/Iráklio; 1–2 weekly on *G&A* or *Ventouris*/Sitía; 1 weekly on *Vitsentzos Kornaros*); selected Cyclades (1–2 weekly on *G&A* or *Ventouris*); Dhiafáni (1 weekly on *G&A* or *Ventouris*); Hálki (1–2 weekly on *G&A* or *Ventouris*); Iráklio (Crete; 1–2 weekly on *G&A* or *Ventouris*); Kárpathos (2 weekly on *G&A* or *Ventouris*, 1 weekly on *Vitsentzos Kornaros*; 1hr 30min); Pireás (1–2 weekly on *G&A* or *Ventouris*, 1 weekly on *Vitsentzos Kornaros*); Rhodes (1–2 weekly on *G&A* or *Ventouris*; 6hr 30min); Sími (1 weekly on *G&A* or *Ventouris*); Sitía (Crete; 1 weekly on *Vitsentzos Kornaros*); Thíra (1–2 weekly on *G&A* or *Ventouris*).

NB In rough seas all ferries will skip the poor mooring at Boúka.

DOMESTIC FLIGHTS

Kássos to: Crete (Sitía; 1 weekly; 30min); Kárpathos (3–4 weekly; 15min); Rhodes (1 daily; 40–50min).

Hálki

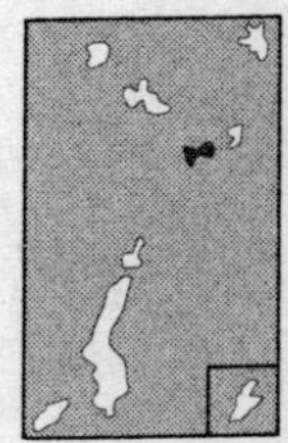

Hálki, a tiny (20 square kilometres), waterless, limestone speck west of Rhodes, is a fully fledged member of the Dodecanese, though all but three hundred of the former population of three thousand have decamped (mostly to Rhodes or to Tarpon Springs, Florida) in the wake of a devastating viral sponge blight early in this century. Despite a renaissance through tourism in recent years, the

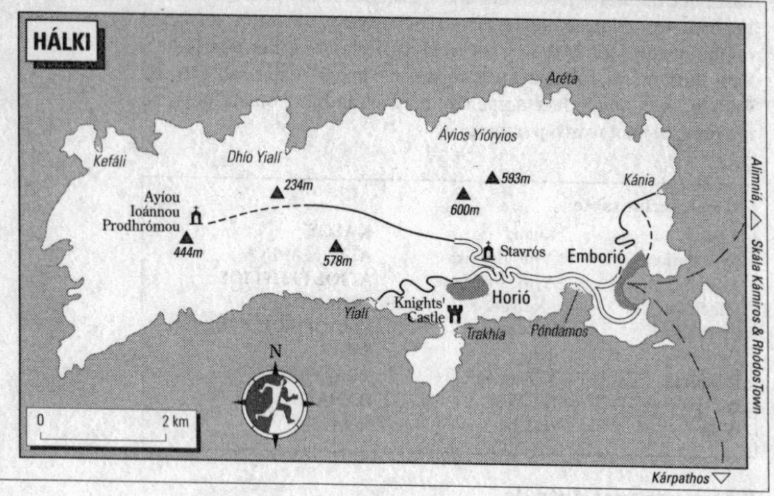

island is tranquil compared to its big neighbour, with a slightly weird, hushed atmosphere; in front of the town hall, the freestanding clock tower – largest in the Dodecanese – is permanently stopped at 12.32, and mirrored architecturally by the even taller campanile of Áyios Nikólaos church below. The big event of the day is the arrival of the regular afternoon *kaïki* from Skála Kámiros on Rhodes; the island is just a bit too remote for the sort of daytrips that plague Sími. Besides people, Hálki is home to about 5000 sheep and goats, plus a 30-strong fishing fleet which sends most of its catch to Rhodes: together, the only significant economic activity aside from summer tourism.

The first hint of development came in 1983, when UNESCO designated Hálki as the "isle of peace and friendship", and made it the seat of an annual summer international youth conference. (Tílos was approached first but declined the honour.) As part of the deal, 150 crumbling houses were to be restored as guest lodges for the delegates and other interested parties, with UNESCO footing the bill. As of 1987, only one hotel had been completed, by converting the former sponge-processing plant; the only tangible sign of "peace and friendship" was an unending stream of UNESCO and Athenian bureaucrats occupying every available bed and staging drunken, musical binges under the guise of "ecological conferences". The islanders, fed up with what had obviously turned out to be a scam, sent the freeloaders packing at the end of that year.

Since then, in conjunction with specialist British tour operators, most (though not all) of the designated houses in **EMBORIÓ**, the port and only area of habitation, have been restored by their owners, creating several hundred guest beds. However, these are pretty much block-booked from April to October by the tour companies and occupied by a rather staid, well-mannered clientele. Independent travellers will be lucky to find anything at all, even early or late in the year, and if alone should expect to pay the full double rate.

Accommodation

One good place to start your hunt for **accommodation** is the five-room *Captain's House* (☎0241/45 201; ②; one bona fide single; ③), a wonderful, quiet spot where you're in close contact with your hosts, Alex (ex-Greek Navy captain) and Christine Sakelaridhes. Owing to its small size, pre-booking is mandatory, but if they're full, they will point you in other likely directions. For more en-suite comfort, try *Pension Cleanthe* (☎0241/45 334; ③), inland near the school; the hill-side studios of *Pension Argyrenia* (☎0241/45 205; ③), below the municipal cistern; and *Hotel Manos* (☎0241/45 295; ③), the converted sponge works at the south end of the bay. Those wishing to rent **studios** in the restored houses should check with *Halki Tours* and *Zifos Tours* (see below) for availability.

Eating and drinking

If lodging works out relatively expensive, **eating out** is surprisingly reasonable, especially compared to any neighbouring isle. Of the several tavernas on Emborió's waterfront, *Maria's* (whose triplet daughters serve) is good for casserole dishes, and is the only place open for lunch; *Omonia* offers the best range of seafood and meat grills; while reasonably priced *O Houvardhas* has the best food on the island, as long as Lefkosia is in the kitchen.

Bars and **cafés** sit all in a row at mid-quay. Adjacent *Bokolia* and *Areti* are essentially cake-and-coffee shops that also offer reasonable breakfasts; *Kostas* is an old standby with foreign beer on tap, while *Toh Steki* is usually the most musical.

Other practicalities

Other essential facilities include a **post office** (the best place to change money – there's no bank), three stores amply stocked for self-catering, a very good bakery which cranks out pies and pizzas, and two **travel agencies**: *Halki Tours* (☎0241/45 281), the representative of *Laskarina*, which deals mostly with houses and villas; and *Zifos Tours* (☎0241/45 241), which handles *Direct Greece* properties (these tend to be smaller studios). Both agencies also sell ferry tickets and will change money at a pinch – for a hefty commission.

The interior

Three kilometres inland, 45 minutes' walk west from Emborió, lies the old pirate-proof village of **HORIÓ**, abandoned in the 1950s. The recent laying down of power lines, and a few restored cottages, suggest that Horió may eventually benefit from the same attentions as Emborió. Except during the August 14–15 festival (*paniyíri*), the liveliest on the island, the church is kept securely locked to protect its medieval frescoes; from just behind it a clear path climbs for about ten minutes to the dilapidated **castle**, built largely from ancient masonry. Inside this, traces of Byzantine frescoes still cling to an otherwise ruined chapel – the archeological authorities in Rhodes will eventually spirit these away to safety in their museum. Across the valley, the little monastery of **Stavrós** is the venue for another *paniyíri* on September 14.

There's little else to see or do inland, though you can spend three enjoyable hours (one way) **walking** across the island from Emborió; the terrain en route is monotonous, but enhanced by views over half the Dodecanese and Turkey. A newly bulldozed dirt road picks up where the cement "Tarpon Springs Boulevard" mercifully ends, near Stavrós. The pavement was donated by the expatriate community in Florida to ensure easy Cadillac access to the Stavrós *paniyíri* grounds, though the money might have been better spent on a proper sewage system and salt-free water supply – like most essentials, fresh water has to be brought from Rhodes by tanker, and often runs out in peak season. At the end of the route, (the last half hour on a path), you'll come to the monastery of **Ayíou Ioánnou Prodhrómou**. The caretaking family there can put you up in a cell (except around August 29, another big festival date), but you'll need to bring supplies.

Island beaches

Póndamos, fifteen minutes' walk west of Emborió, is the only sandy beach on Hálki, and even this has been artificially supplemented. Longish but narrow, its sunbeds and pedaloes are completely packed in summer, though you can escape the crowds for some excellent snorkelling. The sole facility is the somewhat pricey *Nick's Pondamos Taverna*, which serves lunch only and also lets **rooms** (☎0241/45 295; ②), though these are usually booked by *Direct Greece*.

Small and pebbly **Yialí**, west of and far below Horió, lies an hour's hike away from Póndamos, down a jeep track. There's absolutely no shade, and the sea can be rough in this exposed setting. Half an hour's walk north of Emborió lies **Kánia**, with a rocky foreshore but sandy bay bottom; there's no shade in the morning, and a rather industrial ambience from both the power lines coming in from Rhodes, and the island's only petrol pump off to one side.

These three coves are within easy walking distance but no great shakes, so it's well worth signing on at Emborió's quay for boat excursions to more remote beaches nearly impossible to reach by land. More or less at the centre of Hálki's southern shore, directly below Horió's castle, **Trakhía** consists of two coves on either side of an isthmus, one or the other providing shelter in any wind. North-coast beaches figuring as excursion-boat destinations include pretty **Aréta**, **Áyios Yióryios** just beyond, and the remote double bay of **Dhío Yialí**.

Alimniá islet

The most interesting boat excursion is to the deserted islet of Alimniá (Alimiá), roughly halfway between Hálki and Rhodes, a favourite swimming and barbecueing venue with both islanders and tour clients. Despite the presence of reliable fresh water, the village here, overlooked by a couple of palm trees and yet another Knights' castle, was never re-inhabited after World War II. It is said that the villagers were deported after they admitted to assisting British commandos sent to sabotage the Italian submarines who used the deep harbour here. The commandos themselves were captured by the Nazis, bundled off to Rhodes and summarily executed as spies rather than regular POWs; Kurt Waldheim allegedly countersigned their death sentences. If you go snorkelling, you can still glimpse outlines of the submarine pens to one side of the deep bay. Most of the houses are now boarded up; some buildings bear the sombre trace lines of bullet holes, while inside others you can glimpse crude paintings of ships and submarines sketched by bored Italian soldiers. Nowadays just one is inhabited on a seasonal basis, when Alimniá is used by shepherds grazing livestock.

Greek script table

Hálki	Χάλκη	ΧΑΛΚΗ
Alim[n]iá	Αλιμ[ν]ιά	ΑΛΙΜ[Ν]ΙΑ
Ayíou Ioánnou Prodhrómou	Αγίου Ιοάννου Προδρόμου	ΆΓΙΟΥ ΙΟΑΝΝΟΥ ΠΡΟΔΡΟΜΟΥ
Emborió	Εμπορειό	ΕΜΠΟΡΕΙΟ
Horió	Χωριό	ΧΩΡΙΟ

Hàlki travel details

INTER-ISLAND TRANSPORT

KAÏKIA

Hálki to: Rhodes (Skála Kámiros; 1 daily on rivals *Afrodhiti* and *Halki*; each can carry one car).

NB The Wednesday *kaïki* may be fully booked by package clients.

FERRIES

Hálki to: Crete (2 weekly on *G&A Ferries* or *Ventouris Lines*); selected western Cyclades (minimum Thíra, Mílos, Sífnos; 1–2 weekly on *G&A* or *Ventouris*); Kárpathos (2 weekly on *G&A Ferries* or *Ventouris Lines*); Kássos (1–2 weekly on *G&A* or *Ventouris*); Rhodes (Ródhos Town; 2 weekly on *G&A* or *Ventouris*); Sími (1–2 weekly on *G&A* or *Ventouris*).

NB Boats nominally calling at Hálki will skip the island in bad weather, as Emborió's dock is very exposed.

HYDROFOILS

Irregular service from Rhodes, 2 weekly at most; as with *kaïkia*, organized tour or package clients may have priority, and no one-way tickets are sold.

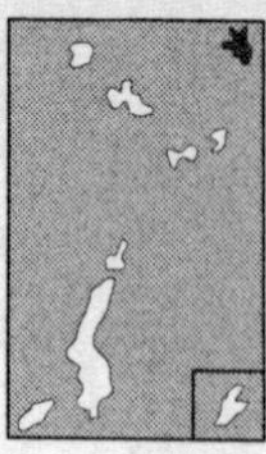

Sími

Sími's most pressing problem, lack of water, is in many ways also its saving grace. As with so many dry, rocky Dodecanese islands, if the rain cisterns don't fill during the winter, water has to be imported at great expense from Rhodes. As a result the place can't hope to support more than a handful of large hotels; instead, hundreds of people are shipped in daily during the season from its larger neighbour, relieved of their money and sent back. This arrangement suits both the islanders and those visitors lucky enough to stay longer. Many foreigners return regularly, or even own houses here – indeed since the mid-1980s the more desirable dwellings, ruined or otherwise, have been sold off in such numbers that the island has essentially become the Ídhra of the east Aegean.

Incredibly, less than a hundred years ago the island was richer and more populous (30,000) than Rhodes, its wealth generated by shipbuilding and sponge-diving, skills nurtured since pre-Classical times. Under the Ottomans, Sími, like many of the Dodecanese, enjoyed considerable autonomy in exchange for a yearly tribute in sponges to the sultan; but the new, Italian-imposed frontier, the 1919–22 war, the advent of synthetic sponges and the gradual replacement of the crews by Kalymniots spelt doom for the local economy. Vestiges of past nautical glories remain at the still-active *karnáyia* (boatyards) at Pédhi and in Haráni district, but today the souvenir-shop sponges come mostly from overseas, and many of the magnificent nineteenth-century mansions stand roofless and empty, their windows gaping blankly across the outstanding natural harbour.

Sími Town

SÍMI, the island's capital and only proper town, consists of Yialós, the port, and Horió, which leads a socially separate existence on the hillside above. The 3000-strong Simiot population is scattered fairly evenly throughout the mixture of surviving Neoclassical and more typical island dwellings; outsiders have preferred to build anew rather than restore derelict properties accessible only by donkey or on foot. As on Kastellórizo, a wartime blast – this time set off by the retreating Germans – shattered hundreds of houses up in Horió. Shortly afterwards, the official surrender of the Dodecanese to the Allies was signed here on May 8, 1945: a plaque marks the spot at the present-day *Restaurant Les Katerinettes*, and each year on that date there's a fine festival with music and dance.

Sími's port, an architecturally protected area since the early 1970s, is deceptively lively, especially between noon and 4pm when the spice-and-sponge stalls throng with Rhodes-based daytrippers, and exhaust pollution envelopes the quay. Just one street back from the water, however, the more peaceful pace of village life takes over. Two massive stair-paths, the Kalí Stráta and Katarráktes, effectively

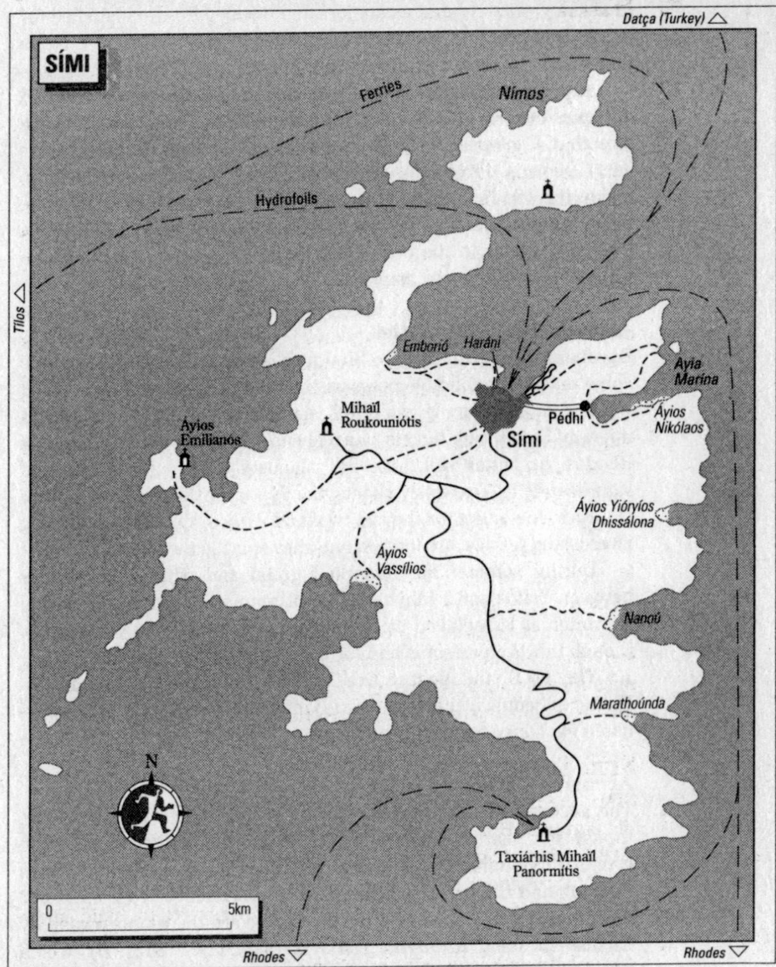

deter many of the daytrippers and are most dramatic around sunset; massive ruins along the lower reaches of the Kalí Stráta are lonely and sinister after dark, home only to wild fig trees, owls and nightjars.

A series of blue arrows through Horió leads to the excellent local **museum** (Tues–Sun 10am–2pm; 400dr). Housed in a fine old mansion at the back of the village, the collection concentrates on Byzantine and medieval Sími, with a gallery of medieval icons and exhibits on frescoes in isolated, locked churches. In addition there are antiquarian maps and the inevitable ethnographic wing of costumed mannequins, embroidery and furniture. As you head back to central Horió, it's worth taking a look at the nineteenth-century

pharmacy, with its apothecary jars and wooden drawers labelled for exotic homeopathic and herbal remedies; it still functions (after a fashion), in tandem with the adjacent clinic.

At the very pinnacle of things, a castle of the **Knights of St John** occupies the site of Sími's ancient **acropolis**, and you can glimpse a stretch of Cyclopean wall on one side, as well as the Grand Master's escutcheon. A dozen churches grace Horió; that of the **Ascension**, inside the fortifications of the acropolis, is a successor to the one blown to bits when the Germans torched the munitions cache there. One of the bells in the new belfry is the nose-cone of a thousand-pound bomb, hung as a memorial.

Arrival and practicalities

Excursion boats run daily to Sími from Ródhos Town, where you'll come under considerable pressure to buy an expensive return ticket – not what you want if you're off island-hopping. Either insist on a one-way ticket, buy tickets more cheaply through travel agents on Rhodes, or better still, take the islanders' own unpublicized and significantly less expensive boats, the *Symi I* or the catamaran *Symi II*. *Anes*, the outlet for the last two, and *Psihas*, the agent for all big inter-island **ferries**, are located one alley apart in the marketplace.

During summer an unmarked green and white van shuttles between Yialós and Pédhi via Horió at regular intervals until 11pm; in winter, it is replaced by a blue van. There are also three **taxis**, though this is a perfect island for boat and walking excursions.

The **OTE** and **post office** operate the standard Monday-to-Friday schedules; there are two **banks** (but no ATMs) and designated exchange agents for odd hours.

Accommodation

The **accommodation** situation for independent travellers is tough, though not nearly so bad as on Hálki. **Studios**, rather than simple rooms, predominate, most controlled by package operators such as *Kosmar* and *Laskarina*; if there are any vacancies, proprietors will meet arriving boats. Among the best value are the rooms owned by English-speaking *Katerina Tsakiris* (☎0241/71 813; ③), which have kitchen facilities and a grandstand view over the harbour – reservations essential. Rather more basic are two establishments down by the market area: the *Glafkos* (☎0241/71 358, fax ☎76 800; rooms ②, studios ③), on the square, and the fairly cramped *Egli* (☎0241/71 392; ②), a last resort located just a few steps in from the taxi rank.

With a bit more to spend, you could try the rooms, studios and houses managed by the *Jean & Tonic* bar (☎0241/71 819; ③–④); or the *Hotel Horio* (☎0241/71 800; ④) and adjacent *Hotel Fiona* (tel/ fax ☎0241/72 088; ④) – both good, mock-traditional outfits at the top of the Kalí Stráta in Horió. If money's no object, the *Aliki* (☎0241/71 665; ⑤), a few paces to the right of the clock tower, is also a famous monument, and slightly more affordable if reserved in advance from Britain as a package. Failing these, your best strategy is to appeal for help from *Sunny Land* (☎0241/71 320, fax ☎71 413), the first agency you encounter after disembarking; their weekly, off-peak rates for villas, houses and apartments are highly competitive (③–④), even if you don't stay the full seven days.

Eating and drinking

You're best off avoiding entirely the **tavernas** on the north and west sides of the port, where menus, prices and attitudes have been terminally warped by the daytrip trade. Honourable exceptions include *Tholos*, an excellent, female-run *ouzerí* out beyond the Haráni boatyard, with a menu that changes daily; and *Elpidha*, an *ouzerí*–breakfast café near *Sunny Land*, which looks straight across the water at *Tembeloskala*, another good *ouzerí*-bar – both with unbeatable views. *Tembeloskala* (The Lazy Step) takes its name from the adjacent stairway, where loafers used to take advantage of the cool breeze that funnelled down it.

Matters improve perceptibly as you press further inland or up the hill. At the very rear of what remains of Sími's traditional marketplace, *O Meraklis* has polite service and well-cooked dishes, such as the indigenous baby shrimps, though prices have climbed and portions shrunk of late; *Neraïdha*, well back from the water and near the OTE, is delicious and still reasonably priced despite its discovery by tour operators. Up in Horió, *Georgios* is a supper-only institution that's been going for decades, serving up large portions of Greek nouvelle cuisine in its pebble-mosaic courtyard. Specialties such as chicken breast in wine-and-mushroom sauce, squid and spinach, and feta-stuffed peppers are excellent value.

There are nearly half a dozen **bars** in Yialós, plus a few more up in Horió. With such a large ex-pat community, some of these are predictably run by foreigners: in Horió, convivial *Jean & Tonic* caters to a mixed clientele all year round, while *Vapori*, down at Yialós, is the oldest bar on the island, welcoming customers with breakfasts, desserts and complimentary newspapers in several languages, in addition to trompe l'oeil tables and varied music.

Around Sími Town

Sími has no big sandy **beaches**, but there are plenty of pebbly stretches in the deep, narrow bays along the coastline. **PÉDHI**, 45 minutes' walk from Yialós, retains some of its former identity as a fishing hamlet, and is able to cultivate a few vegetable gardens thanks to fresh water beneath the plain behind – the island's largest. The beach is poor, though, and the giant, pricey *Pedhi Beach* package hotel (☎0241/71 870, fax ☎71 982; ⑤) has considerably bumped up prices at the three local tavernas, of which the most reasonable and authentic is *Iy Kamares*.

Most visitors will elect to tackle the half-hour walk along a rough but obvious path (lace-up shoes required) along the south shore of this almost landlocked bay to **Ayios Nikólaos**. The only all-sand beach on Sími, this offers sheltered swimming, tamarisks for shade, and a mediocre taverna behind its 50-metre extent. Alternatively, a paint-splodge-marked path on the north side of the inlet leads within an hour to **Ayía Marína**, where there's another, somewhat better taverna, and a monastery-capped islet to which you can easily swim.

Virtually in Yialós, ten minutes beyond Haráni, you'll find the tiny **Nós** "beach", but there's sun here only until lunchtime and it's usually packed with daytrippers. Instead, you can continue along the coastal track past tiny gravel coves and rock slabs popular with nudists and snorkellers, or cut inland from the Yialós square past the former site of the desalination plant, to appealing **Emborió** bay, with the well-placed and peaceful *Nirrides Apartments* (☎0241/71 784; ④) on the way, a taverna at one end, and an artificially strewn sand beach at the other.

Inland from the bay, up a stream bed and some steps, is a Byzantine **mosaic** fragment under a protective shelter, next to Siamese-triplet chapels. Much has been obliterated, but you can discern a man leading a camel, a partridge, and a stag in flight from a boar. Beyond a lone pine beside the chapels, a faint trail marked by painted arrows and letters leads 100m further to a slight rise ringed by a collapsing chain-link fence. Inside the enclosure, a hole in the ground gives access to a subterranean complex known locally as **Dhódheka Spília** (Twelve Caves), either catacombs or the crypt of a basilica which once stood here.

Remote bays and monasteries

Plenty of other, more secluded coves are accessible by energetic walkers with sturdy footwear, or by those prepared to pay a modest sum (return fares only) for the **taxi-boats** moored in front of the *Ionian Bank*. These operate daily in season, roughly hourly from 10am to 1pm, returning from their destinations between 4 and 5pm.

They are the best way to reach the southern bays of **Marathoúnda** and **Nanoú**, and the only method of getting to the spectacular, cliff-girt fjord of **Áyios Yióryios Dhissálona**. Dhissálona lies in shade after 1pm or so, and Marathoúnda lacks a taverna, making Nanoú the most popular destination for daytrips. The beach there is a 200-metre stretch of gravel, sand and pebbles, with sunbeds and umbrellas, good snorkelling, a scenic backdrop of unique pines and a taverna – the latter probably the best and most reasonable of Sími's more remote eateries.

From Sími, it's a two-hour walk southwest across the island – through patches of natural juniper forest – to **Áyios Vassílios**, the most scenic of the gulfs. The trek to **Áyios Emilianós**, at the island's extreme west end, takes a little longer, but you can stay the night (bring supplies) here in an otherwise empty, wave-lashed cloister. On the way here you might look in at the monastery of **Mihaïl Roukouniótis**, Sími's oldest, with lurid eighteenth-century frescoes and a peculiar ground plan: the *katholikón* is actually two stacked churches, the one currently in use built atop an earlier structure abandoned to the damp.

If you don't trust the indifferent island map on sale, guided walks to several beaches are led regularly by Hugo Tyler (☎0241/71 670), with groups generally met by a boat for the ride home. Hugo, resident since 1977, sets off at 7.30am to avoid the heat and allow time for generous libations en route.

The only means of reaching **Nímos**, the satellite islet skirted by hydrofoils or ferries approaching Sími from the north, is by boat. Daytrips call here for a beach barbecue and a visit to its monastery; otherwise Nímos is bare, and lonely except for grazing goats.

Taxiárhis Mihaïl Panormítis

At the southern point of the island looms the huge, eighteenth-century monastery of **Taxiárhis Mihaïl Panormítis** ("Panormítis" for short), Sími's biggest rural attraction. It's generally the first port of call for the excursion boats from Rhodes, but these allow you just a quick half-hour tour; if you want more time, you'll have to come on a "jeep safari" from Yialós or arrange to stay the night in the *ksenónas* (inn) set aside for pilgrims. There are many of these in summer, as Mihaïl has been adopted as the patron of sailors in the Dodecanese. The only monk permanently in residence, Father Gavriïl, lived in Australia for a while and so speaks a little English – certainly enough to chat up single women visitors; he is occasionally assisted by novices from the big monastery on Pátmos, of which the place is a dependency. Overnighting is on a donation basis – you'll be chided if you're stingy.

Like many of Sími's monasteries, Panormítis was thoroughly pillaged during the last war, so don't expect too much of the building or its treasures. An appealing pebble-mosaic court surrounds the central *katholikón*, tended by Gavriïl, lit by an improbable number of oil lamps and graced by a fine *témblon*, though the frescoes are recent and mediocre. The small **museum** (nominal fee) contains a strange mix of precious antiques, junk (stuffed crocodiles and koalas), votive offerings, models of ships named *Taxiarhis* or *Panormitis*, and a chair piled with messages-in-bottles brought here by Aegean currents – the idea being that if the bottle or toy boat arrived, the sender's wish would be granted. Amenities consist of a tiny beach, a shop/*kafenío* and a taverna; near the latter stands a grandiose memorial commemorating three Greeks, including the monastery's former abbot, executed in February 1944 by the Germans for aiding British commandos.

Greek script table

Sími	Σύμη	ΣΥΜΗ
Áyios Emilianós	Αγιος Αιμηλιανός	ΑΓΙΟΣ ΑΙΜΗΛΙΆΝΟΣ
Mihaïl Roukouniótis	Μιχαήλ Ρουκουνιότης	ΜΙΧΑΗΛ ΡΟΥΚΟΥΝΙΟΤΗΣ
Áyios Nikólaos	Αγιος Νικόλαος	ΑΓΙΟΣ ΝΙΚΟΛΑΟΣ
Áyios Vasílios	Αγιος Βασίλειος	ΑΓΙΟΣ ΒΑΣΙΛΕΙΟΣ
Áyios Yióryios	Αγιος Γεώργιος	ΑΓΙΟΣ ΓΕΩΡΓΙΟΣ
Dhissálona	Δυσσάλονα	ΔΥΣΣΑΛΟΝΆ
Emborió	Εμπορειό	ΕΜΠΟΡΕΙΟ
Horió	Χωριό	ΧΩΡΙΟ
Marathoúnda	Μαραθούντα	ΜΆΡΑΘΟΥΝΤΆ
Nanoú	Νανού	ΝΑΝΟΥ
Nímos	Νίμος	ΝΙΜΟΣ
Nós	Νός	ΝΟΣ
Pédhi	Πέδι	ΠΕΔΙ
Taxiárhis Mihaïl Panormítis	Ταξιάρχης Μιχαήλ Πανορμίτης	ΤΆΞΙΑΡΧΗΣ ΜΙΧΑΗΛ ΠΑΝΟΡΜΙΤΗΣ
Yialós	Γιαλός	ΓΙΑΛΟΣ

Sími travel details

INTER-ISLAND TRANSPORT

KAÏKIA AND EXCURSION BOATS

Sími to: Rhodes (4 weekly year-round on *Symi I* or *Symi II*, 1–2 daily in season on excursion boats – see p.138).

FERRIES

Sími to: Kálimnos (1 weekly on *G&A Ferries*, 2 weekly on *Nissos Kalymnos*); Kastellórizo (2 weekly on *Nissos Kalymnos*); Kós (1 weekly on *G&A*, 2 weekly on *Nissos Kalymnos*); Léros (1 weekly on *G&A*); Lipsí (1 weekly on *G&A*); Náxos (1 weekly on *G&A*); Páros (1 weekly on *G&A*); Pátmos (1 weekly on *G&A*); Pireás (1 weekly on *G&A*); Níssiros (1 weekly on *G&A*, 2 weekly on *Nissos Kalymnos*); Rhodes (2 weekly on *Nissos Kalymnos*); Tílos (1 weekly on *G&A*, 2 weekly on *Nissos Kalymnos*).

HYDROFOILS

Sími to: Kálimnos (1–2 weekly on *Ilio Lines*); Kós, Níssiros, Rhodes, Tílos (all 1–2 weekly on *Ilio* or *Mamidhakis/Dodecanese Hydrofoils*).

NB *Ilio Lines* and *Mamidhakis/Dodecanese Hydrofoils* services usually run on different days, thereby providing fairly well-spaced coverage during the week.

INTERNATIONAL TRANSPORT

FERRIES

Sími ranks as an official port of entry, and there are now ferry services to Turkey (Datça) for approximately 10,000dr return plus 4000dr port tax. However these are irregular (at best 2 weekly) and problematic, since local souvenir merchants, protective of their monopolies, often attempt to prevent them sailing.

Tílos

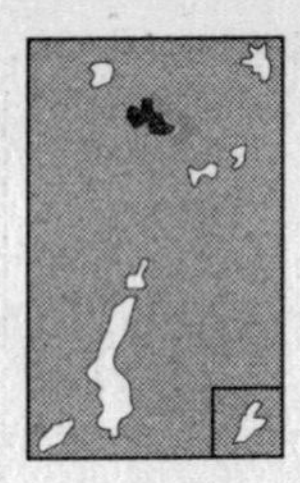

The small, blissfully quiet island of **Tílos**, with a population of only 350 (shrinking to 80 in winter), is one of the least frequented of the Dodecanese, though it can be visited as a daytrip by hydrofoil once or twice a week. Why anyone should want to come for just a few hours is unclear: while it's a great place to rest on the beach or go walking, there is nothing very striking at first glance. After a few days, however, you may have stumbled on several of the seven small castles of the Knights of St John that stud the crags, or gained access to some of the inconspicuous medieval chapels, often frescoed or with *hokhláki* courtyards, clinging to the hillsides.

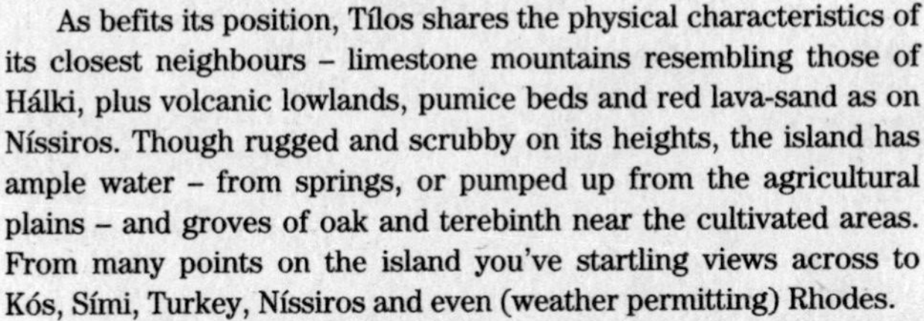

As befits its position, Tílos shares the physical characteristics of its closest neighbours – limestone mountains resembling those of Hálki, plus volcanic lowlands, pumice beds and red lava-sand as on Níssiros. Though rugged and scrubby on its heights, the island has ample water – from springs, or pumped up from the agricultural plains – and groves of oak and terebinth near the cultivated areas. From many points on the island you've startling views across to Kós, Sími, Turkey, Níssiros and even (weather permitting) Rhodes.

Stranded midway between Kós and Rhodes, Tílos has always been a backwater, and among all the east Aegean islands has the least developed nautical tradition. With ample groundwater and rich volcanic soil, the islanders could afford to turn their backs on the sea, and instead made Tílos the breadbasket of the Dodecanese. Until the 1970s, approaching travellers were greeted by the sight of blond, shimmering fields of grain bowing in the wind; today the hillside terraces languish abandoned.

Since the late 1980s, Tílos has arrived touristically in a small way; the current number (250–300) of guest beds on the island would be doubled if all the "rooms" blocks and hotels at foundation or skeleton stage were completed. *Laskarina Travel* bookings account for just a fraction of this capacity, and the island principally attracts an independent, disparate, return clientele. A battle over the direction of future development has joined between rival factions: northern Europeans who wish to walk and beachcomb in peace, versus raucous Italians and Greeks itching to exercise their dirt bikes and 4WD vehicles. Welts of new, useless bulldozer tracks scarring the slopes around the port would indicate that the latter group, supported by the megalomaniac management of the *Hotel Irini*, is prevailing for the moment, though a Green-ish pressure group of foreigners – FOTA (Friends Of Tílos Association) – has been formed as a voice for the opposition. So far their most tangible accomplishments include the publication of an astonishingly accurate local map by Baz "Paris" Ward, sold at island shops, and perhaps tipping the balance of local opinion in a decision not to bulldoze a road over the superb path to Lethrá beach.

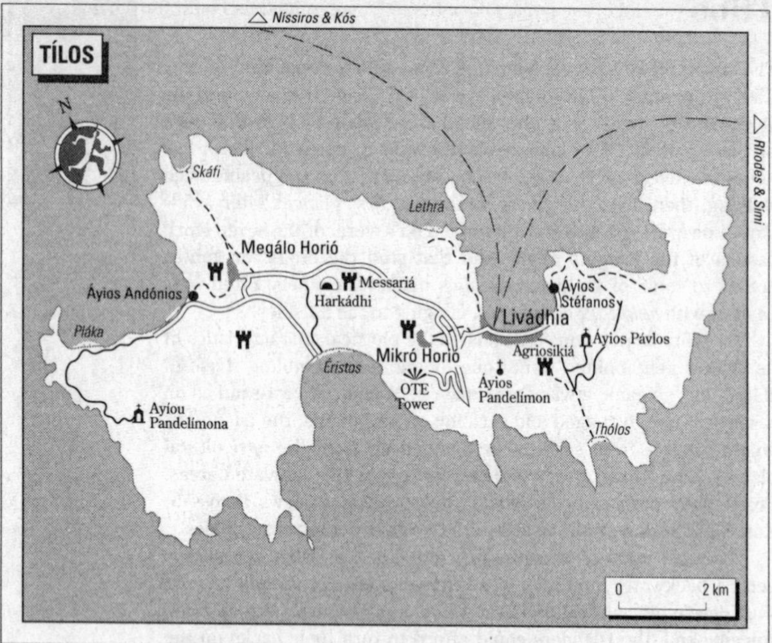

Getting around the island

Tílos' main paved road runs 7km from the ferry port of Livádhia and Megálo Horió, the island's capital and only other significant habitation. When boats arrive, a rust- or cream-coloured **public minibus** links the two, and accommodation proprietors from Éristos beach or Megálo Horió provide their own vehicles. At other times the bus adheres to a schedule of up to five departures daily in high season along the Livádhia–Éristos stretch. You can also rent a **motorbike** in the post office square at Livádhia, but beware that the only **fuel** is sold out of jerry-cans at the *Ikonomou* supermarket in Megálo Horió. Boat trips advertised to remote beaches are offered solely during high season; otherwise you have to walk.

Livádhia and around

Of the two main island settlements, **LIVÁDHIA** is more equipped to deal with tourists and closer to the best remaining hikes. The village retains an overall feel of 1970s Greece – though a mushrooming of new hotels and half-finished building sites behind the long pebble beach is an ominous trend. Despite its currently peaceful profile, the bay of Livádhia saw a certain amount of action during World War II. About 30m in front of *Sofia's* taverna, you can snorkel over the wreck of a submerged German patrol boat, chased aground by a British submarine early in 1944 and subsequently bombed to bits.

At the west end of the quay, above the jetty, you might also hunt for the white memorial plaques in honour of two Greek resistance fighters who, in autumn of the same year, machine-gunned dozens of Germans before being themselves overpowered.

Accommodation

If they have vacancies, rooms and hotel owners will meet the ferries, but in high season it may be worth phoning ahead. Budget options include the rather spartan *Stamatia's* (☎0241/44 334 or 44 255; ②), on the waterfront, or the recently refurbished and good-value *Hotel Livadhia* (☎0241/44 266 or 44 202; ②), with en-suite rooms and two "penthouse" units; the latter also runs *Studios Sofia*, just behind (③). Nearby stands the newly built *Pension Periyali* (☎0241/44 398; ②), open June to September only, with a pleasant breakfast bar and light evening snacks; or you might try *Kastello* (☎0241/44 292; ③), east down the beach, then inland. Luxury on this side of the island means the *Hotel Irini* (☎0241/44 293; fax ☎44 238; ④), a lushly landscaped low-rise complex 200m inland from mid-beach; *Laskarina Holidays* tends to monopolize many of the rooms, but even in mid-season individual travellers can usually secure a vacancy with advance notice.

Eating, drinking and nightlife

Among seafront tavernas, *Sofia's* is a convivial meeting place with Greek island music on tape; it's now virtually the house taverna of *Laskarina* patrons, resulting in smaller portions and blander recipes of late. For a better, more robustly Greek meal, you can usually rely on *Irina* (aka *Yiorgos*). The best place for fish grills is *Blue Sky*, an unmissable eyrie perched above the ferry dock. For breakfast or pre-dinner **drinks**, *Omonia* – under the trees strung with fairy lights, near the post office – is enduringly popular and has recently expanded its menu to include daily specials. Local **nightlife** is restricted to a handful of bars: *La Luna*, at the ferry pier (moving soon to garish new premises at the tiny eastern anchorage of Áyios Stéfanos), the already operating *Tilos Oasis*, at the same anchorage, and a music pub in Mikró Horió (see below).

Other practicalities

The **post office** is the only reliable place to change money; **OTE** consists of a metred **phone** at *Stefanakis Travel*, which divides the **ferry-ticket** trade with a rival agency on the jetty – and takes full advantage of phone customers, as there's not yet a card-phone on the island. A bakery off the square does decent bread and *píttes*, and all the shops, especially *Yannis* on the square, stock a range of produce.

Around Livádhia

From Livádhia you can hike north for a little over an hour to the pebble bay of **Lethrá**, along the endangered path noted previously, or for slightly longer south to the sandy cove of **Thólos**. The track to the latter begins by the cemetery and the chapel of **Áyios Pandelímon** with its Byzantine mosaic court, then curls around under the seemingly impregnable castle of **Agriosikiá**; once up on the saddle overlooking the descent to Thólos, a cairned route hairpins back and upwards to the citadel in twenty minutes. Views are wonderful, especially early in the morning, but there no longer seems an easy way into the half-ruined castle itself.

Mikró Horió

It's less than an hour's walk west by trail up to the ghost village of **MIKRÓ HORIÓ**, whose 1200 inhabitants left for Livádhia during the 1950s owing to water shortages. The name (meaning "Little Village") is rather a misnomer as it was once more populous than Megálo Horió (Big Village); the interesting ruins, also accessible by dirt road, include threshing cirques strewn with grain millstones. A *Club Med* scheme to restore the houses seems to have evaporated, and virtually the only intact structures are the castle-guarded church (locked except for the festival on August 15) and an old house which has been restored as a late-hours **music pub** (Greek tunes until 2am, disco thereafter).

Megálo Horió and around

The rest of Tílos' inhabitants live in or near **MEGÁLO HORIÓ**, and until recently had very little to do with the Livadhians, with whom they were not on the best terms. The village's simple, vernacular houses, arranged in tiers, enjoy an enviable perspective over a vast agricultural plain stretching down to the bay of Éristos; just under half of them are inhabited, so the village is no metropolis by any standard.

Your choices for **accommodation** in Megálo Horió are the *Pension Sevasti* (☎0241/44 237; ③), at the lower end of the village, *Miliou Apartments* (☎0241/44 204; ③), in the centre, or *Studios Ta Elefandakia* (☎0241/44 213; ③) by the car park. Of the two restaurants, that attached to the *Pension Sevasti* has the most reliable lunchtime opening hours and the best view.

The Knights' castle and Harkádhi cave

Megálo Horió is overlooked by a vast **Knights' castle**, which encloses a sixteenth-century **chapel** with rather battered frescoes. The castle is reached by a stiff, half-hour climb that begins on the lane behind the *Ikonomou* supermarket and threads its way up through a vast jumble of cisterns, house foundations and derelict chapels – hints of Megálo Horió's much greater medieval size. A massive gate-tower incorporates Classical masonry, and a block in front of the chapel bearing Greek inscriptions provides additional proof that the *kástro* was built over the ancient acropolis.

From the Knights' castle, two other fortresses are visible across the plain; the easterly one of **Messariá** helpfully marks the location of **Harkádhi** cave, where Pleiocene midget elephant bones were discovered in 1971. Hidden for centuries until exposed by a World War II artillery barrage, the cave can now be reached by a trail from the road which ends just beyond the spring-fed cypress below the cave-mouth. The bones themselves have been transferred to a small museum in Megálo Horió; at the time of writing this was not yet open to the public, though you may be able to glimpse the exhibits through the window.

Local beaches: Skáfi and Éristos

From Megálo Horió you can reach the most easily accessible of Tílos' remote beaches, sandy but often windy **Skáfi**; this lies over an hour's walk away along a path that begins below the *Ikonomou* supermarket and leads directly up the valley to the north.

South of and below Megálo Horió, a sign points left along the six-kilometre paved side road to the long **Éristos** beach; historically the left (east) portion has been nudist, though lately bare skin seems to have spread across the whole strand. Opening of the relatively comfortable *Eristos Beach Hotel*, directly behind the pinkish sand, is scheduled for late 1996. A small, nameless **snack bar** near the new hotel provides unexceptional food, with more of the same at *Taverna Tropikana*, hidden well back from the sand, among the citrus orchards; the latter also has a few simple **rooms** (☎0241/44 242; ②). The *Tropikana's* perennial rival on the far side of the access road, *Navsika*, closed down in 1995, but new proprietors may re-activate it in the future.

The far northwest

The main cement road beyond Megálo Horió hits the coast again at **ÁYIOS ANDÓNIOS**, with a single **hotel/taverna** (the *Australia*, ☎0241/44 296; ③), an abandoned filling station and a very exposed, average beach which is uncomfortably close to Megálo Horió's sewage outlet. At low tide you can find a row of lava-trapped human skeletons strung in a row – presumably sailor victims of a Nissirian eruption in 600 BC – discovered by the same archeologists who found the miniature elephants.

There's better swimming and afternoon shade from exotic century plants at isolated **Pláka** beach, 2km west of Áyios Andónios. People pitch tents among the olive trees behind, despite a lack of toilet facilities and a brackish well; there have been recent initiatives towards transforming this area into an official campsite.

Ayíou Pandelímona monastery

The road finally ends 8km west of Megálo Horió at the fortified monastery of **Ayíou Pandelímona**, founded in the fifteenth century for the sake of its miraculous spring. These days the place is usually deserted except for July 25–27, when long cement tables on the terrace below host the island's biggest festival. Its tower-gate and oasis setting more than two hundred forbidding metres above the west coast are the most memorable features, though the eminently photogenic inner court boasts a *hokhláki* surface, and the church a fine tesselated marble floor. On the walls of the *katholikón*, an early eighteenth-century fresco shows the founder-builder holding a model of the monastery, while behind the ornately carved altar screen is a fresco of the Holy Trinity. To guarantee access, you need to visit with the regular Sunday-morning minibus tour from Megálo Horió (fare 1000dr, an hour to look around), as the place has been bereft of monks for years and has no resident caretaker.

Greek script table

Tílos	Τήλος	ΤΗΛΟΣ
Áyios Andónios	Αγιος Αυτώνιος	ΑΓΙΟΣ ΑΝΤΩΝΙΟΣ
Éristos	Εριστος	ΕΡΙΣΤΟΣ
Lethrá	Λεθρά	ΛΕΘΡΑ
Livádhia	Λιβάδια	ΛΙΒΑΔΙΑ
Megálo Horió	Μεγάλο Χωριό	ΜΕΓΑΛΟ ΧΩΡΙΟ
Mikró Horió	Μικρο Χωριό	ΜΙΚΡΟ ΧΩΡΙΟ
Moní Ayíou Pantelímona	Μονή Αγίου Παντελείμονα	ΜΟΝΗ ΑΓΙΟΥ ΠΑΝΤΕΛΕΙΜΟΝΑ
Pláka	Πλάκα	ΠΛΑΚΑ
Skáfi	Σκάφι	ΣΚΑΦΙ
Thólos	Θόλος	ΘΟΛΟΣ

Tílos travel details

ISLAND TRANSPORT

BUS

The minibus schedule is posted in Livádhia's central square; not to be implicitly trusted, so confirm with *Yiorgos' Kafe–Bar* adjacent!

INTER-ISLAND TRANSPORT

FERRIES

Tílos to: Kálimnos (3–4 weekly on *G&A Ferries* or *Nissos Kalymnos*); Kastellórizo (1–2 weekly on *G&A*); Kós (3–4 weekly on *G&A* or *Nissos Kalymnos*; 3hr); Léros (1–2 weekly on *G&A*); Lipsí (1–2 weekly on *G&A*); Níssiros (3–4 weekly on *G&A* or *Nissos Kalymnos*; 1hr 30min); Pátmos (1–2 weekly on *G&A*); Pireás (1–2 weekly on *G&A*); Rhodes (3–4 weekly on *G&A* or *Nissos Kalymnos*; 2hr 30min non-stop); Sími (3–4 weekly on *G&A* or *Nissos Kalymnos*; 2hr); Síros (1–2 weekly on *G&A*).

HYDROFOILS

Tílos to: Kálimnos (1 weekly on *Ilio Lines*); Kós (1 weekly on *Ilio*, 1 weekly on *Mamidhakis/Dodecanese Hydrofoils*); Níssiros (1 weekly on *Mamidhakis*); Rhodes (1 weekly on *Ilio*, 1 weekly on *Mamidhakis*); Sími (1 weekly on *Ilio*).

NB *Ilio Lines* have historically called here on Wednesday, *Mamidhakis/Dodecanese Hydrofoils* on Sunday.

Níssiros

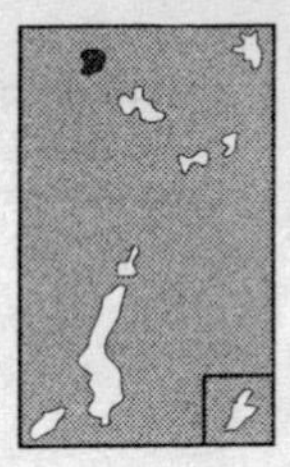

Volcanic **Níssiros** is noticeably greener than its southern neighbours Tílos, Hálki and Sími, and unlike them has proven attractive and wealthy enough to retain more of its population, staying lively even in winter. While remittances from abroad (particularly Astoria, New York) are still important, much of the island's income is derived from quarrying; offshore towards Kós, the islet of Yialí is essentially a vast lump of gypsum and pumice on which the miners live while slowly chipping it away.

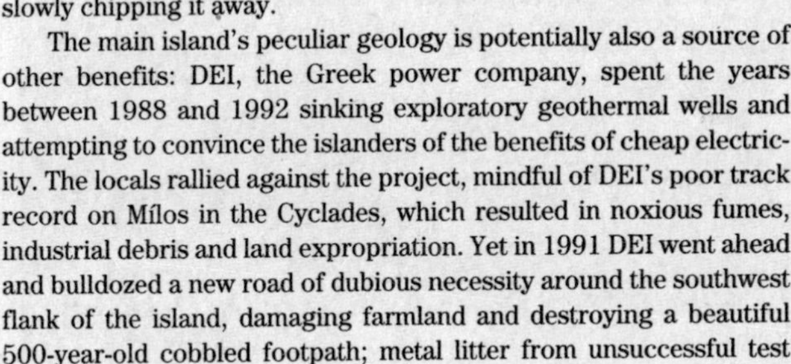

The main island's peculiar geology is potentially also a source of other benefits: DEI, the Greek power company, spent the years between 1988 and 1992 sinking exploratory geothermal wells and attempting to convince the islanders of the benefits of cheap electricity. The locals rallied against the project, mindful of DEI's poor track record on Mílos in the Cyclades, which resulted in noxious fumes, industrial debris and land expropriation. Yet in 1991 DEI went ahead and bulldozed a new road of dubious necessity around the southwest flank of the island, damaging farmland and destroying a beautiful 500-year-old cobbled footpath; metal litter from unsuccessful test bores also did little to endear them to the local populace.

In 1993, a local referendum went massively against the scheme, and DEI, together with its Italian contractor, took the hint and packed up. The desalination plant, reliant on expensive power from the fuel-oil generator, scarcely provides enough fresh water to spur a massive growth in package tourism. The relatively few tourists who stay the night, as opposed to the daytrippers from Kós, still find peaceful villages with a minimum of concrete eyesores, and a friendly if rather tight-knit population. Níssiros also offers wonderful hiking opportunities, and wherever you stroll you'll hear the contented grunting of pigs as they gorge themselves on acorns from the many oak trees. Autumn is a wonderful time, especially when the landscape has perked up after the first rains, and the late-January almond-blossom is one of the island's glories.

Mandhráki

MANDHRÁKI is the deceptively large port and capital of the island, where wooden balconies and shutters on its tightly packed white houses provide splashes of bright colours, with blue swatches of sea often visible at the ends of the narrow streets. Except for the drearier fringes near the ferry dock, the bulk of the place is cheerful enough, arrayed around the community orchard or *kámbos*, portions of which are rather ominously up for sale to developers. Another, less alarming, harbinger of gentrification was the stone-paving of the narrow lanes in 1995.

The town is overlooked by two ancient fortresses which also protect Mandhráki somewhat from the wind. Into a corner of the

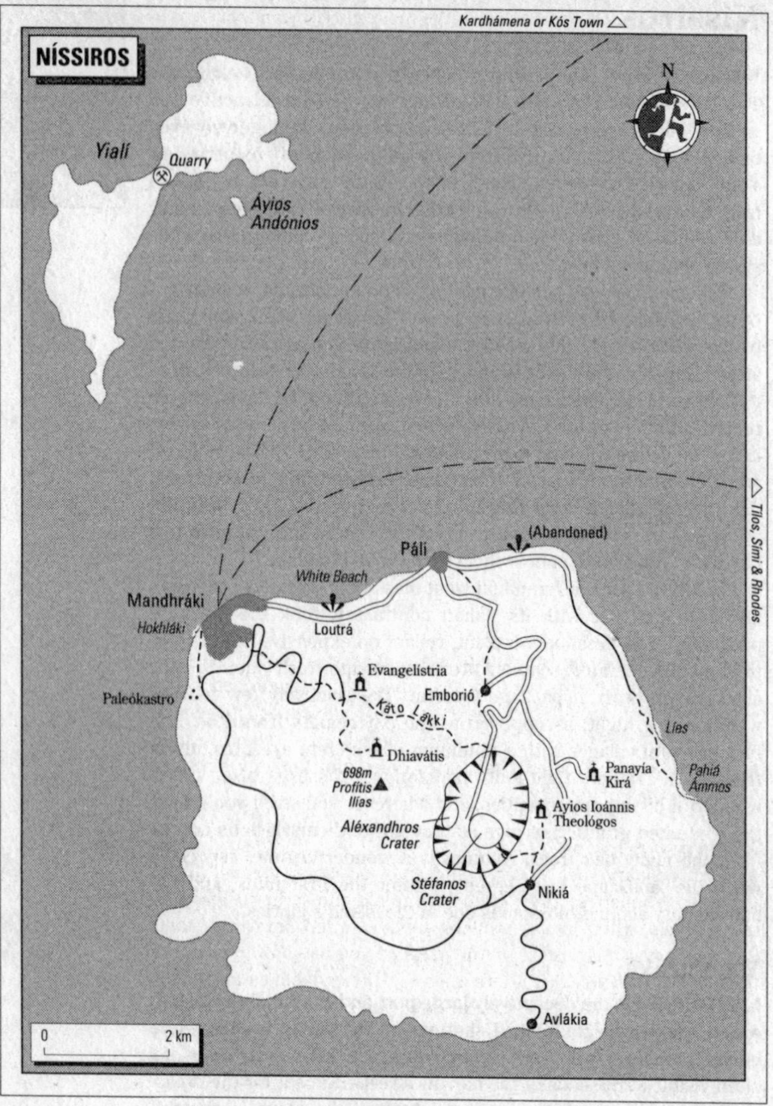

first of these, the predictable, fourteenth-century **Knights' castle**, is wedged the little monastery of **Panayía Spilianí**, built on this spot in accordance with instructions from the Virgin Herself, who appeared in a vision to one of the first Christian islanders. The monastery's prestige grew after raiding Saracens failed to discover the vast quantities of silver secreted here in the form of a rich collection of

Byzantine icons. On the way up to the monastery, you might stop in at the house designated as the **Historical and Ethnographic Museum** (erratic hours; free), two small rooms full of archival photos, heirlooms and other ethnographic memorabilia.

As a defensive bastion, the 2600-year-old Doric **Paleókastro** (unrestricted access), twenty minutes' well-signposted walk out of the Langadháki district, is infinitely more impressive than the Knights' castle, and counts as one of the more underrated ancient sites in Greece. You can clamber up onto the massive, Cyclopean-block walls by means of a broad staircase beside the still-intact gateway.

Accommodation

You'll see a handful of port **hotels** to your left as you disembark; best of these, helpful and friendly, are the *Three Brothers* (☎0242/31 344; ③) and the *Romantzo* (☎0242/31 340; ③), both with affiliated restaurants. Most popular budget option in town itself is the basic *Pension Iy Dhrosia* (☎0242/31 328; ②), tucked right under the castle on the shore; enquire at Mihalis Orsaris' butcher shop on the main street. If it's full, Hartofilis and Irini Pakhos (same phone; ②) also have en-suite rooms over their residence inland; these facilities are well-worn and ripe for an overhaul, but the family is welcoming and their pension open most of the year.

Also set back from the sea, but overlooking the *kámbos*, is Mandhráki's luxury accommodation, the *Porfyris* (☎0242/31 376; ④), with gardens, views over the orchards and a large, deep swimming pool. Just uphill from the *Panorama* restaurant, the small *Hotel Ipapanti* (☎0242/31 485; ③) is a good bet of recent vintage but in traditional architectural style, quiet and with even better views than the *Porfyris*.

Eating and drinking

Nissirian culinary specialities include pickled caper greens, *pittiá* (chickpea croquettes) and *soumádha*, an almond syrup identical to Italian orgeat, which is only available by the bottle from Irini Sakalli, in Áyios Sávvas district, or by the glass at tavernas *Romantzo* and *Karava*. Curiosities aside, there are a few dependable eating establishments on the shoreline, but the best places for **food and nightlife** are on or near the lively, inland Platía Ilikioméni, shaded by its two giant rubber trees. Here *Irini* serves arguably the best food and most generous portions on the island, while *Panorama*, over towards the *Hotel Porfyris*, will tempt you (or not) with delicacies such as snails, sausages and (in autumn) suckling pig.

Dependable shoreline restaurants include *Kleanthis*, a popular local hangout at lunchtime, and adjacent *Mike's*, which looks tacky but isn't. Just inland, *Nissiros*, the oldest taverna on the island, is moderately priced and always packed after dark, whereas the *Karava*, at the port end of town, is relatively expensive and usually empty – a sea view and unusually extensive menu are compensation. The focus of **nightlife**, oddly enough, is not the shore but the various bars and cafés on and around Platía Ilikioméni; most durable of these is *Cactus Bar*, with garden seating.

Other practicalities

Just beyond the public toilets on the lane into town from the jetty is *Enetikon Travel*, the older travel agency (☎0242/31 180), though you may find *Dhiakomihalis*, further inland, more useful as it's the bank agency and also the rep for the *Nissos Kalymnos*. There's a short-hours **OTE** near Platía Ilikioméni, and a **post office** at the harbour. Also by the jetty is a small **bus** station, with (theoretically) early morning and early afternoon departures into the interior, and more frequent jaunts as far as Páli. In practice, these are prone to cancellation, so you might consider renting a **motorbike**: minimum rates offered by an inland tourist shop (about 2000dr per day) are better than those of the *Hotel Romantzo*.

East of Mandhráki: the coast

Beaches on Níssiros are in even shorter supply than water, so much so that the tour agency here can successfully market excursions to a sandy cove on **Áyios Andónios** islet, just next to the mining machinery on **Yialí**. Closer at hand, the black-rock beach of **Hokhláki**, behind the Knights' castle, is useless if the wind is up, and the town beach of **Miramare** at the east edge of the harbour would be a last resort in any weather. Better to head out east along the main road, passing the recently restored spa of **Loutrá** (hot mineral-water soaks by prior arrangement) and the smallish **"White Beach"** (aka Yialiskári), 2km along from Mandhraki and dwarfed by an ugly, eponymous **hotel** (☎0242/31 498; ④), generally fully booked by tour groups. The beach is actually misnamed, as its high percentage of black sand creates a decidedly salt-and-pepper appearance.

A kilometre or so further, 45 minutes' walk or 4km in all from Mandhráki, the fishing village of **PÁLI** makes a more attractive base. Here you'll find the *Hotel Hellenis*, (☎0242/31 453; ③), two **rooms** places (the fanciest at the west end of the quay), a bakery stocking brown bread (a rarity in Greece), and one of the better **tavernas** on the island, *Afroditi* (aka *Nikos & Tsambika*), featuring Cretan wine from the barrel and home-made desserts.

Another stretch of dark sand extends east of Páli to an apparently abandoned new spa, but to reach Níssiros' best **beaches**, continue in that direction for an hour on foot (or twenty minutes by moped along the partly surfaced road), past an initially discouraging seaweed- and cowpat-strewn shoreline, to the delightful cove of **Líes**, where the track ends near a single, seasonal **cantina** (*Oasis*). From here, walking a further ten to fifteen minutes along a trail past the headland brings you to the idyllic, 300-metre expanse of **Pahiá Ámmos** bay. The grey-pink sand here, though coarse, even forms dunes, and the beach can easily accommodate a high-season batch of tourists.

The interior

It is the dormant volcano at the centre of the island that gives Níssiros its special character and fosters the growth of abundant vegetation – and no stay would be complete without a visit. When excursion boats arrive in Mandhráki from Kós, the *Polyvotis Tours* coach and usually one of the public buses are pressed into service to take customers into the interior. Tours tend to set off at about 10.30am and also 2.30pm, so if you want relative solitude, time your visit around these, and use either the early morning or late afternoon scheduled buses to Nikiá village, a moped or your own feet.

Emborió and Panayía Kirá

The road up from Páli winds first past the virtually abandoned village of **EMBORIÓ**, where pigs and cows far outnumber people, though the place is slowly being bought up and restored by Athenians and foreigners. New owners are often surprised to discover natural saunas, heated by volcanic vents, in the basements of the crumbling houses; at the outskirts of the village, right by the access road, there's a public **steam bath** in a grotto, whose entrance is outlined in white paint. If you're descending to Páli from here, an old cobbled way offers an attractive short cut of the four-kilometre road.

About half way between Emborió and Nikiá, a signposted side road leads down to the island's third major monastery (after Spilaní and Áyios Ioánnis, below), **Panayía Kirá**. Unfortunately the place is locked most of the time, but you can still enjoy the fine setting on fertile terraces overlooking Pahiá Ámmos (to which there is no obvious way down). Over the gate to the courtyard looms a fortification tower; the medieval *katholikón* stands off-centre, on the south side of the compound.

Nikiá and Áyios Ioánnis Theológos

NIKIÁ, the large village on the east side of the volcano's caldera, occupies a spectacular location 14km from Mandhráki, with views out to Tílos. Of the three **cafés** here, the one on the engaging, round *platía* is rarely open, while the one in the middle of town usually has food. There is also accommodation in a municipal **inn**, though this tends to be substandard and expensive.

By the bus turnaround area, signs point to the 45-minute trail descending to the crater floor; a few minutes downhill, you can make a brief detour to the eyrie-like monastery of **Áyios Ioánnis**

Theológos, with a shady tree and yet another perspective on the volcano. The picnic benches and utility buildings come to life at the annual festival on the evening of September 25.

Incidentally, it is not worth following small signs towards **Avlákia**, 5km south of Nikiá. This is an abandoned fishing hamlet of about a dozen houses around the unspectacular monastery of **Áyios Nikólaos**. Its surroundings are dreary and barren, with no beach or swimming opportunities, and the road down is rough – in short, a complete waste of time and petrol.

The volcano

To **drive** directly to the volcanic area, 13km in total from Mandhráki, you have to take the unsignposted road which veers off to the right just past Emborió. Whether you approach from this direction or on foot from Nikía, a sulphurous stench drifts out to meet you as the fields and scrub gradually give way to lifeless, caked powder. The sunken main crater of **Stéfanos** is extraordinary, a Hollywood moonscape of grey, brown and sickly yellow; there is another, less visited double crater (dubbed **Aléxandhros**) to the west, equally dramatic visually, with a clear trail leading up to it from the access road. The perimeters of both are pocked with tiny blowholes from which jets of steam puff constantly and around which form little pincushions of pure sulphur crystals.

The whole floor of the larger crater seems to hiss, and standing in the middle you can hear something akin to a huge cauldron bubbling away below you. According to legend this is the groaning of Polyvotis, a titan crushed here by Poseidon under a huge rock torn from Kós. Hardly less prosaic are the facts of the 1422 eruption, when the volcano apparently blew its top Krakatoa-style; the most recent hiccups, which produced steam, ash and earthquakes, occurred in 1873 and 1933. A small **café** in the centre of the wasteland opens up when tourists are around.

Walks

Since the destruction of the old direct trail between the volcano and Mandhráki, pleasant options for **walking** back to town are limited. If you want to try, backtrack along the main crater access road for about 1km to find the start of a clear but unmarked path which passes the volcanic gulch of **Káto Lákki** and the monastery of **Evangelístria** on its two-hour course back to the port.

Evangelístria also marks the start of the two-hour, round-trip detour up **Profítis Ilías**, the island's summit; the path is rough, and faint in spots, but it's hard to get lost since the way is marked with cairns and white-painted arrows or crosses. A few minutes before the shrine on the peak, the farm and chapel of **Dhiavátis**, tucked into a small hollow with huge trees, makes a good picnic spot or emergency bivouac.

Greek script table

Níssiros	Νίσυρος	ΝΙΣΥΡΟΣ
Avlákia	Αυλάκια	ΑΥΛΑΚΙΑ
Áyios Ioánnis Theológos	Αγιος Ιοάννης Θεολόγος	ΑΓΙΟΣ ΙΟΑΝΝΗΣ ΘΕΟΛΟΓΟΣ
Emborió	Εμπορειό	ΕΜΠΟΡΕΙΟ
Hokhkláki	Χοχλάκι	ΧΟΧΛΑΚΙ
Líes	Λίες	ΛΙΕΣ
Loutrá	Λουτρά	ΛΟΥΤΡΑ
Mandhráki	Μανδράκι	ΜΑΝΔΡΑΚΙ
Nikiá	Νικιά	ΝΙΚΙΑ
Pahiá Ámmos	Παχιά Αμμος	ΠΑΧΙΑ ΑΜΜΟΣ
Páli	Πάλοι	ΠΑΛΟΙ
Panayía Kirá	Παναγία Κυρά	ΠΑΝΑΓΙΑ ΚΥΡΑ
Yialí	Γυαλί	ΓΥΑΛΙ

Níssiros travel details

ISLAND TRANSPORT

BUSES

Mandhráki to: Emborió (2 daily); Nikiá, (2 daily); Páli (5 daily); none to Líes or the volcano.

INTER-ISLAND TRANSPORT

KAÏKIA AND EXCURSION BOATS

Níssiros to: Kardhámena (Kós; daily in season on a tour boat, 2–4 days weekly on the unpublicized islanders' shopping *kaïki Chrysoula*); Kós Town (Kós; 2–4 weekly in season on *Nissos Kos* or similar craft).

FERRIES

Níssiros to: Astipálea (1 weekly on *G&A Ferries*); Kálimnos (2 weekly on *G&A* or *Nissos Kalymnos*); Kastellórizo (1 weekly on *G&A*, 2 weekly on *Nissos Kalymnos*); Kós (1 weekly on *G&A*, 2 weekly on *Nissos Kalymnos*); Léros (1 weekly on *G&A*); Lipsí (1 weekly on *G&A*); Náxos (1 weekly on *G&A*); Páros (1 weekly on *G&A*); Pátmos (1 weekly on *G&A*); Pireás (2 weekly on *G&A*); Rhodes (1 weekly on G&A, 2 weekly on *Nissos Kalymnos*); Sími (1 weekly on G&A, 2 weekly on *Nissos Kalymnos*); Síros (1 weekly on *G&A*); Tílos (1 weekly on G&A, 2 weekly on *Nissos Kalymnos*).

HYDROFOILS

Níssiros to: Kálimnos (2 weekly in season on *Ilio Lines*); Kós, Rhodes, Sími, Tílos (all 2 weekly in season on *Ilio*, 1–2 weekly on *Mamidhakis/Dodecanese Hydrofoils*).

Kastellórizo

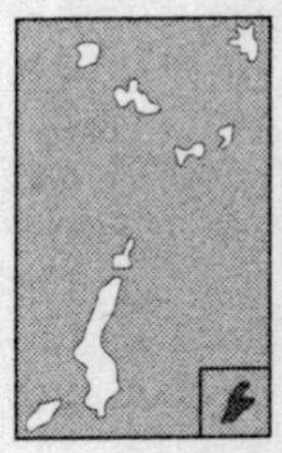

Kastellórizo's official name, Meyísti (Biggest), seems more an act of defiance than a statement of fact. While the largest of a tiny group of islands, it is actually the smallest of the Dodecanese, over seventy nautical miles from its nearest Greek neighbour (Rhodes), yet barely one mile from the Turkish coast at the narrowest straits. At night its lights are quite outnumbered by those of the Turkish town of Kaş, about four miles across the bay, with whom Kastellórizo has long had excellent relations.

Less than a century ago there were about 14,000 people here, supported by a fleet of schooners that made fortunes transporting goods, mostly timber, from the then Greek towns of Kalamaki (now Kalkan) and Andifelos (Kaş), on the Anatolian mainland just opposite. But withdrawal of autonomy after the 1908 "Young Turk" revolution, the Italian seizure of the other Dodecanese in 1912 and an abortive revolt against the Ottomans in 1913 sent the island into decline. The French, not the Italians, were masters here from 1914 and 1920 when they needed a staging post for the Syrian front, which made Kastellórizo a hapless target for Ottoman artillery on the Anatolian mainland. (On January 9, 1917, the British seaplane carrier *Ben-My-Chree*, among the first such craft ever built, was sunk by a well-aimed Turkish shell while at anchor here.)

Local shipowners failed to modernize their craft upon the advent of steam power late in the nineteenth century, preferring to sell their fleets to the British for the Dardanelles campaign; the new frontier drawn up between Kastellórizo and republican Turkey, combined with the expulsion of all Anatolian Greeks in 1923, deprived any remaining vessels of their trade. During the 1930s Kastellórizo enjoyed a brief renaissance when it became a major stopover point for French and Italian seaplanes en route to the Middle East, but events at the close of World War II put an end to any hopes of the island's continued viability.

When Italy capitulated to the Allies in the autumn of 1943, Kastellórizo was occupied by a few hundred Commonwealth commandos, who left of their own accord during late spring of 1944. In early July of that year, a harbour fuel depot caught fire and exploded, taking with it more than half of the 2000 houses on Kastellórizo. Postwar enquiries concluded that although a small minority of British officers had engaged in some haphazard looting before their departure, it was probably Greek pirates engaged in pillaging of their own who accidentally or deliberately caused the conflagration. The British government, without admitting guilt, agreed in the 1950s to pay compensation for the missing items; however, the settlement was delayed for three decades, and then only the 850 surviving applicants in Athens were considered eligible for compensation – those who had emigrated to Australia and the few who had chosen to stay on the island after 1945 were excluded. As a result, the British are not especially popular here.

Even before these events, most of the population had left for Rhodes, Athens, Australia (particularly Perth) and North America; ironically, when the long-sought union of the Dodecanese with Greece occurred in 1948, there were less than seven hundred islanders remaining. Today there are scarcely more than two hundred people living year-round on Kastellórizo, largely maintained by remittances from the 30,000-plus emigrants and by subsidies from the Greek government, which fears that the island will revert to Turkish sovereignty should their numbers diminish any further. With so few inhabitants, life is inevitably claustrophobic, especially in winter when feuds and vendettas are resumed after suspension for the tourist season.

Yet Kastellórizo may have a future of sorts, thanks to expat Kassies who have begun renovating their crumbling homes with a view to resuscitating the island as a retirement or holiday venue. Each summer the population is swelled by returnees of Kassie ances-

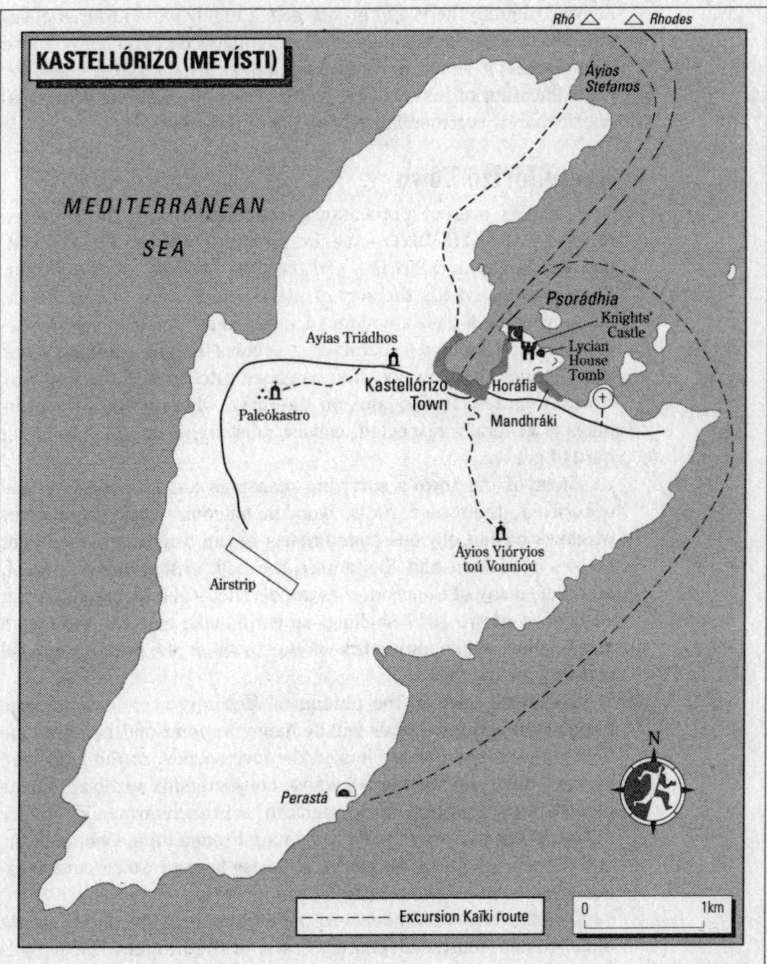

try, some of whom celebrate traditional weddings in the Horáfia's Áyios Konstandínos cathedral, which incorporates ancient columns pilfered from Patara in Asia Minor. Access to the island has also improved; during the 1980s the government dredged the harbour to accommodate larger ferries, completed an airport for flights to and from Rhodes, and briefly contemplated making Kastellórizo an official port of entry, a measure – like the optimistic sign on the quay boldly proclaiming "Europe Begins Here" – calculated to appeal to the numerous, mostly Israeli yachties who drop anchor.

Perhaps the biggest recent boost for Kastellórizo was its role as the setting for the film *Mediterraneo*, which has resulted in a tidal wave of Italians; locals routinely chant "*stanze*" (rooms) to all new arrivals, though the island in fact gets a highly varied tourist clientele. Visitors to the island seem divided between two camps: those who dismiss it as a human zoo maintained by the government for the edification of nationalists, and others who celebrate an atmospheric, barely commercialized outpost of Hellenism.

Kastellórizo Town

The island's present population is concentrated in the northern town of **KASTELLÓRIZO** – the finest natural harbour, it is claimed, between Beirut and Pireás – and the little "suburb" of **Mandhráki**. Even in summer, it's the sort of place where, after two strolls up and down, you'll have a nodding acquaintance with your fellow visitors and all the island's characters – such as the pub-crawling priest Papa Yiorgis, who on occasion has been pitched into the water by rowdy yachties. Traffic jams on the quay, where a ban on motorbikes is generally respected, consist most frequently of a strutting herd of geese.

Most of the town's surviving mansions are ranged along the waterfront, their tiled roofs, wooden balconies and tall, narrow windows having obvious counterparts in the originally Greek-built houses of Kalkan and Kaş across the bay. Just one street back, however, many of the properties are derelict – abandonment having succeeded where 1917 shelling, an earthquake in 1926 and fire in 1944 failed. Sepia postcards of the town in its prime bear sad witness to its decline.

Locations used in the filming of *Mediterraneo* have become popular attractions. Locals will be happy to point out the light-blue house by the hotel which hosted the love scenes, or the neglected graveyard beyond Mandhráki, whose non-Orthodox section contains tenants worthy of the movie scenario: a French–Armenian soldier killed in action nearby in 1917, a young French hippie who met his end here in 1974, and Riccardo, Milanese house-restorer and drop-out, dead of an overdose in 1988.

The fire-blasted hill between the harbour and Mandhráki sports a half-ruined, fourteenth-century **castle of the Knights**. The keep is now home to the local **museum** (Tues–Sun 7.30am–2.30pm; free), whose displays include plates from a Byzantine shipwreck, frescoes rescued from decaying churches, a reconstruction of an ancient basilica on the site of today's gaudy Ayíou Yioryíou tou Louká (in Horáfia district between the port and Mandhráki), plus the more usual ethnographic mock-ups. Just below and beyond the museum, in the cliff-face opposite Psorádhia islet, is tucked Greece's only Lycian **house-tomb**; it's unmarked, but you can find it easily enough by following the shoreline walkway, then climbing some steps opposite the first wooden lamp standard. House tombs were the common burial places of Lycian nobles and are scattered all along the Turkish coast opposite.

Accommodation

Despite its recent strut in front of the cameras, Kastellórizo is not prepared for – nor, except in high season, does it get – more than a few dozen visitors per day. *Laskarina Holidays* operated here as the lone tour company for a while, but terminated its arrangement owing to still tenuous links with Rhodes and the scarcity of amenities. **Pensions** installed in the old houses tend to be fairly basic, with long climbs up and down stairs to a shared bathroom. If you're not met off the boat, the best budget option is the restored mansion-pension managed by Australian–Greek brothers Jimmy and Damian *Mavrothalassitis* (☎0241/49 202; ②), the only one with baths en suite; otherwise try *Paradhisos* (☎0241/49 074; ②), at the west end of the seafront, *Barbara* (☎0241/49 295; ②), at the opposite end, or the more modern *Kristallo* (☎0241/41 209; ②). More luxury is available, for a hefty price, at the *Hotel Meyisti* (open April–Oct; ☎0241/49 272; fax ☎49 221; ⑤), at the far northwestern end of town.

Eating and drinking

Apart from fish, and whatever can be smuggled over from Kaş, Kastellórizo has to import foodstuffs and often also potable water from Rhodes; taverna prices are consequently higher than the norm, rendered even more expensive by the island's new-found celebrity status.

The waterfront **eateries** in particular have had a long and detrimental acquaintance with the yacht market; only *Little Paris*' seafood is at all affordable or reliably fresh. Two restaurants that can be more enthusiastically recommended are both found inland: *Iy Orea Meyisti*, run by the Mavrothalassitis brothers (they of the pension), and *Ouzeri O Meyisteas*, behind the arcades of the disused municipal market building, which specializes in reasonably priced and generous helpings of goat chops. *Ta Platania*, beside two scrawny plane trees opposite Áyios Konstandínos in Horáfia, has a menu that changes daily and includes home-made desserts, but its role as the film crew's canteen has predictably nudged prices up. **Nightlife** at the three adjacent harbour bars spills out onto the quay and occasionally into the water.

Other practicalities

The **post office** stands at the northwestern end of town, behind *Hotel Meyisti*; there's no OTE or bank. Most ferry companies are represented by one of several grocery stores along the quay, while the only travel agency, grouchy *DiZi Travel*, has made itself unpopular locally by monopolizing all air tickets back to Rhodes; currently you cannot book a return flight at *Olympic Airways* in Rhódos Town.

Lately it has been possible to arrange a ride **to Turkey** (Kaş) on the supply boat *Varvara*, run by the *Taverna Apolavsi*. It's a bit of a racket for the scant distance involved, intended partly to protect the Rhodes–Marmaris shuttle operators: since Kastellórizo is not yet an official port of entry/exit, non-"Kassies" must pay a hefty, 8000-drachma "special visa fee" to customs. The ride itself, however, may be free on certain days, depending on whether the *Varvara's* crew are going shopping anyway – 5000dr round trip otherwise.

The rest of the island

Kastellórizo's austere hinterland is predominantly bare rock, flecked with stunted vegetation made leaner by a serious bush-fire in summer 1994. Incredible as it may seem, two generations ago much of the countryside was carefully tended, producing wine of some quality. A rudimentary road system links points between Mandhráki and the airport, but there are not many specific places to go and no vehicles to rent. The island is fringed by sheer karst cliffs, and offers no anchorage except at the main town.

Áyios Stéfanos and the grotto of Perastá

Swimming is complicated by a total absence of beaches and an abundance of sea urchins and razor-sharp limestone reefs; the safest place to swim near town lies beyond the cemetery at **Mandhráki**, or at the tiny inlet of **Áyios Stéfanos**, a forty-minute walk north of town along the obvious trail beginning behind the post office. Once you swim away from the shore, you're rewarded by clear waters graced by a rich variety of marine life.

Over on the southeast coast, accessible only by a 45-minute boat ride from town, the grotto of **Perastá** is famous for its stalactites and strange blue light effects; the low entrance, negotiable only by inflatable raft, gives little hint of the enormous chamber within. Splashing about in its depths is magic, though claims of rivalry to Capri's grotto are a bit overblown since the blue tint doesn't reflect well on the walls. Two-hour raft trips (2000dr per person) visit the cave only, or for 5000dr, on a larger *kaïki*, you can take it in as part of a five-hour tour that includes Rhó islet (see below).

Rural monasteries and ruins

Heat (infernal in summer) permitting, you can hike south for forty minutes up the obvious, zigzag stair-path from town, then through desolate, recently fire-charred vineyards, to the monastery of **Áyios Yióryios tou Vounioú**. The sixteenth-to-eighteenth-century church boasts fine groin vaulting and a carved *témblon*, but its highlight is a crypt, with the frescoed, subterranean chapel of **Áyios Harálambos** off to one side; access is via a narrow, steep passage descending from the church floor – bring a flashlight and scrambling clothes. The only way to gain access is to go early in the morning with the key-keeper, who lives behind the taverna *Little Paris*.

Alternatively, a fifteen-minute track-walk west of the port leads to the peaceful monastery of **Ayías Triádhos**, perched on the saddle marked by the OTE tower; committed Orthodox can arrange with its eccentric caretakers, Pater Ioannis and Dhespina, to stay in one of four spartan cells overlooking the chicken coops.

The onward path to the ancient Doric citadel of **Paleokástro** leaves the track just beyond the monastery; after a twenty-five minute walk, your arrival is signalled by masonry from Classical to medieval times, a warren of vaulted chambers, tunnels and cisterns, plus another, ruined monastery with a pebble-mosaic courtyard. From any of the heights above town you've tremendous views north over sixty kilometres of Anatolian coast and the elephant's-foot-shaped harbour, east to tiny gull-roosts dribbled like batter drops on the griddle of the sea, and west to larger islets, including **Rhó**.

Rhó: Lady and islet

Until her death, *Iy Kyrá tis Rhó* (**The Lady of Rhó**), aka Dhespina Akhladhiotis (1893?–1982), resolutely hoisted the Greek flag each day on the islet of that name, in defiance of the Turks on the mainland. In her waning years, an honorary salary, a commemorative stamp and television appearances lent her glory and fame which she revelled in; by most accounts she was a miserly curmudgeon, known to have refused passing sailors emergency rations of fresh water.

Should you take a *kaïki* daytrip out to Rhó, her **tomb** is the first thing you see when you dock at the sandy, northwestern harbour; from here a path heads southeast for 25 minutes to the islet's southerly port, past the side trail up to an intact Hellenistic **fortress** on the island's very summit. There are no facilities on Rhó – just one caretaker, four dogs and hundreds of goats – so bring your own food and water.

Klimis the caretaker, a middle-aged Athenian as genial as "The Lady" was alleged to be ornery, continues her flag-raising duties on a government stipend and, like his predecessor, stays here for months on end in a twenty-square-metre cottage. Only a cassette collection and visits from daytrippers or mainland friends vary his self-imposed exile at the furthest point of Greece.

Greek script table

Kastellórizo	Καστελλόριξο	ΚΑΣΤΕΛΛΟΡΙΖΟ
Ayías Triádhos	Αγίας Τριάδος	ΑΓΙΑΣ ΤΡΙΑΔΟΣ
Áyios Yióryios toú Vouniού	Αγιος Γεώργιος τού Βουνιού	ΑΓΙΟΣ ΓΕΩΡΓΙΟΣ ΤΟΥ ΒΟΥΝΙΟΥ
Meyísti	Μεγίστη	ΜΕΓΙΣΤΗ
Paleokástro	Παλαιοκάστρο	ΠΑΛΑΙΟΚΑΣΤΡΟ
Perastá	Περαστά	ΠΕΡΑΣΤΑ
Rhó	Ρώ	ΡΩ

Kastellórizo travel details

INTER-ISLAND TRANSPORT

FERRIES

Kastellórizo to: Piréas (1 weekly on *G&A Ferries* via selected Dodecanese & Cyclades; 28hr); Rhodes (3 weekly with *G&A* or *Nissos Kalymnos*; 4hr–5hr 30min).

DOMESTIC FLIGHTS

Kastellórizo to: Rhodes (4–7 weekly in season; 45min).

INTERNATIONAL TRANSPORT

FERRIES

Kastellórizo to: Turkey (Kaş; subject to local conditions as described on p.160).

Chapter 3

Kós and the northern Dodecanese

Compared to teeming Rhodes and its often cosy neighbours, **Kós and the northern Dodecanese** fall somewhere in between. Though by no stretch of the imagination unspoilt, sandy **Kós** feels calmer than Rhodes, partly because in roughly one-third the area and population, there's perhaps one sixth as much going on. It is still, however, the seat of an *eparhía* (a Greek county) and transport hub of the region, with the only international airport; all packages arranged on its neighbours are of necessity routed through here. If you choose to spend your entire vacation on Kós, you'll find it has the best beaches of these half-dozen isles, creature comforts and distractions, plus surprisingly wild scenery on the slopes of the third-highest mountain in the Dodecanese.

The smaller islands fanning out northwest from Kós, except for disappointing **Psérimos** – overrun with organized daytrips – lack the intimacy of the southern Dodecanese, though their larger scale means reliable bus services, consistent moped rentals, and a wider choice of resorts.

Kálimnos, just across the straits from sandy Kós, could hardly be more different: a limestone-core, seafaring island famous for its sponge-gathering tradition that has only lately developed any semblance of a tourist industry at its westerly beaches and on the peacefully car-free islet of **Télendhos** just opposite. **Léros**, a geological continuation immediately northeast of Kálimnos, across an even narrower channel, has long had local tourism inhibited by a sinister institutional reputation, but up close it proves welcoming and varied in its landscapes and townscapes, the latter including some of the best Italian Art Deco buildings in the Dodecanese.

Astipálea and Pátmos, out at the western fringes of this group, are more typical of the adjacent Cyclades in terms of architecture and general ambience. **Astipálea**, to all intents and purposes synonymous with its stunningly picturesque *hóra*, is protected from blatant exploitation by its problematic access and skeletal amenities, while **Pátmos**, with its imposing medieval monuments and

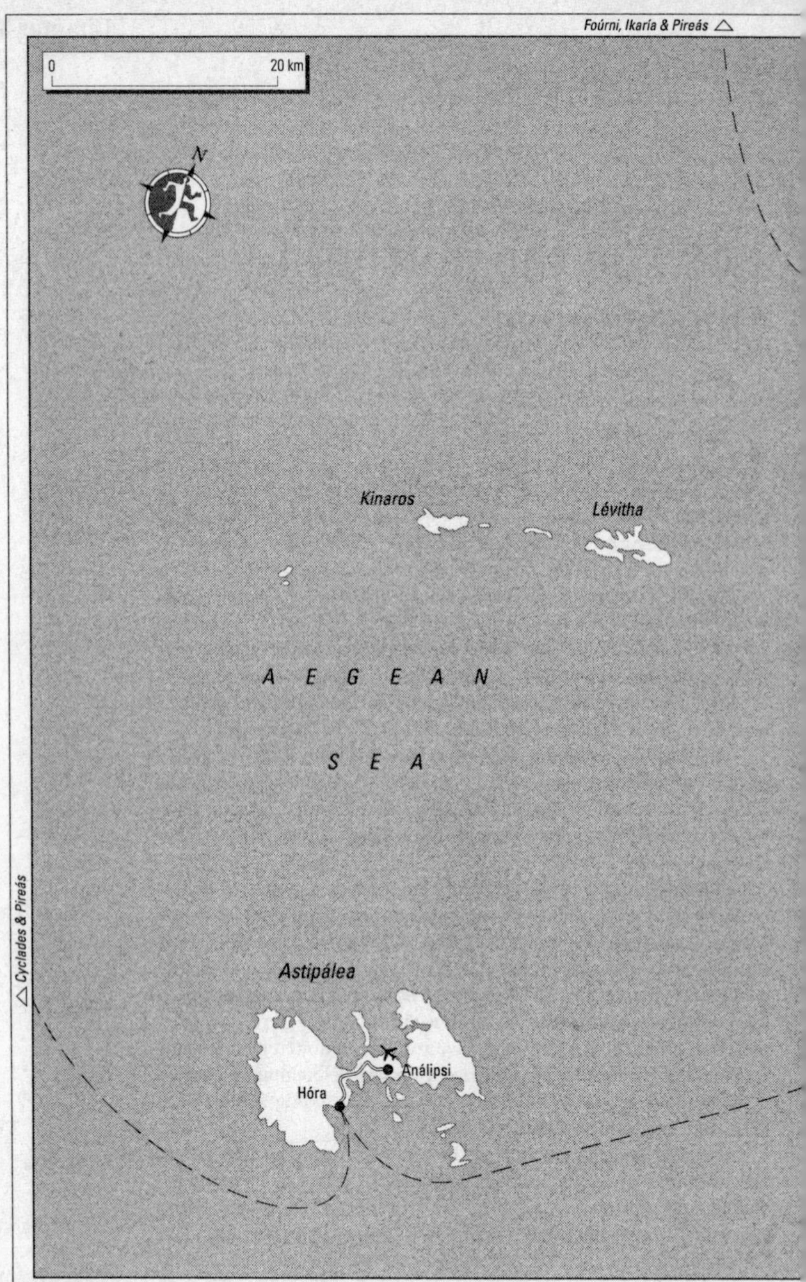
Foúrni, Ikaría & Pireás
0
20 km
N
Kinaros
Lévitha
A E G E A N
S E A
Astipálea
Análipsi
Hóra
Cyclades & Pireás

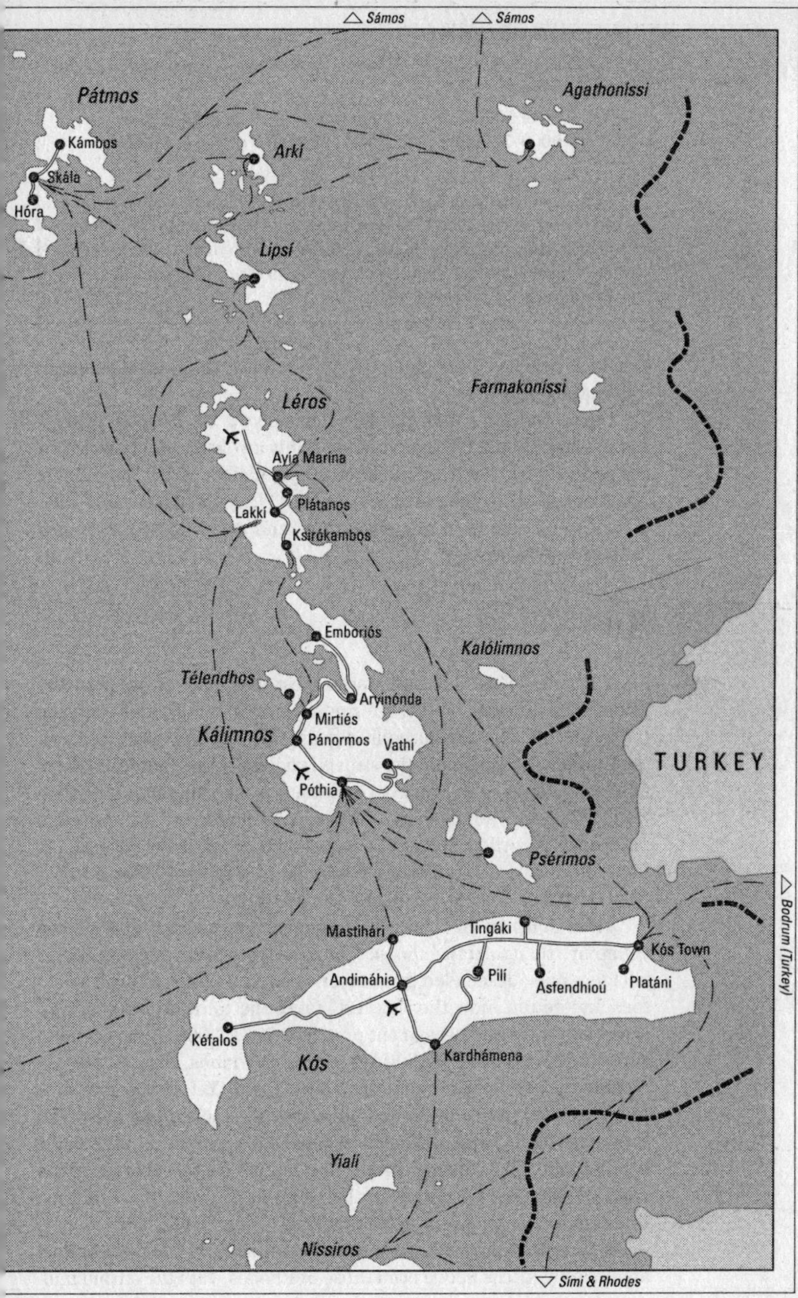
Sámos
Sámos
Pátmos
Kámbos
Skála
Hóra
Arkí
Agathoníssi
Lipsí
Farmakoníssi
Léros
Ayía Marína
Plátanos
Lakkí
Ksirókambos
Emboriós
Kalólimnos
Télendhos
Aryinónda
Mirtiés
Kálimnos
Pánormos
Vathí
TURKEY
Póthia
Psérimos
Bodrum (Turkey)
Mastihári
Tingáki
Kós Town
Andimáhia
Pilí
Asfendhíoú
Platáni
Kéfalos
Kós
Kardhámena
Yialí
Nissíros
Sími & Rhodes

Accommodation prices

All establishments in this book have a symbol that corresponds to one of six price ranges:

① up to 5000dr	② 5000–7000dr	③ 7000–9000dr
④ 9000–13000dr	⑤ 13000–17000dr	⑥ above 17000dr

£1=370dr; $1= 240dr

The rates quoted for each category represent the cheapest available double room in high season. Out of season, prices can drop by up to fifty percent, especially if you negotiate a stay of three or more nights. Single rooms, where available, cost around seventy percent of the price of a double.

For more accommodation details, see p.34

excellent beaches, is not surprisingly the most frequented island in this chapter after Kós.

Lipsí, formerly a backwater dependency of Pátmos, with a single village and a few beaches, has lately awoken to tourism with a vengeance; by contrast, neither depopulated **Arkí** nor lonely **Agathoníssi** off to the north are are ever likely to attract more than a handful of visitors at any given time, and accordingly make ideal peak-season hideaways.

Kós

After Rhodes, **Kós** is the second largest and most popular of the Dodecanese islands, and there are superficial similarities between the two. Here also the harbour is guarded by an imposing castle of the Knights of Saint John, the streets are lined with grandiose Italian public buildings, and minarets and palm trees punctuate extensive Hellenistic and Roman ruins. Although its hinterland for the most part lacks the wild beauty of Rhodes' interior, acre for acre Kós is the most fertile of the islands described in this book, blessed with partly volcanic soil and abundant ground water.

Mass tourism has largely destroyed the former agricultural economy, though transhumance of a sort persists: whereas inland villagers once descended in summer to coastal plains to farm tomatoes and cotton, now the "harvest" takes the form of tourists, who seasonally swell the permanent population of 22,000. A memorial of sorts to the vanished way of life is the enormous, disused tomato cannery at the harbour mouth in Kós Town. Yet in the lowlands there are still plenty of tended olive groves, stacked hay bales and browsing cattle, and delicious sheeps' milk yogurt is still made locally. Like Tílos further south, Kós never had to make its living from the sea and consequently has little in the way of a maritime tradition or a contemporary fishing fleet.

Kós' increasing reliance on the tourist industry has pushed food and lodging prices above even those of Rhodes, with the strong mili-

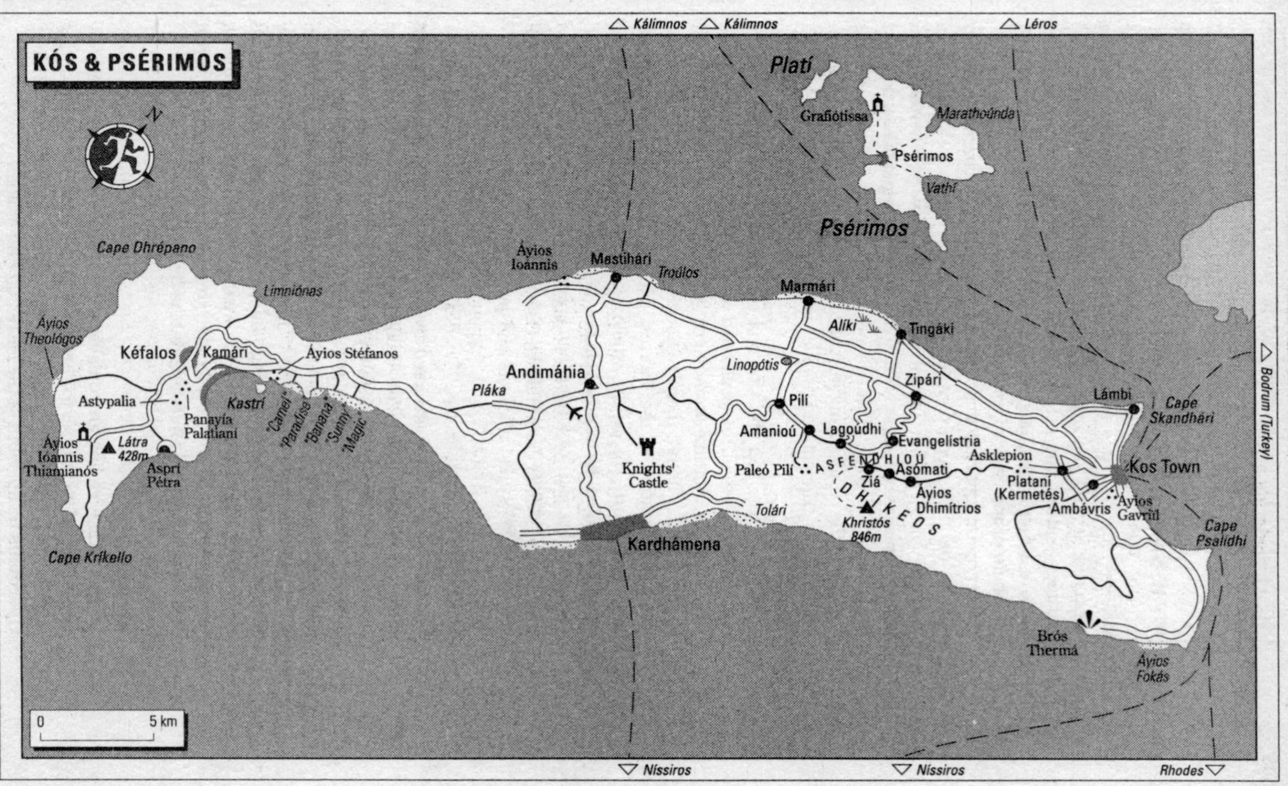
KÓS & PSÉRIMOS
Kálimnos
Kálimnos
Léros
Bodrum (Turkey)
Nissiros
Nissiros
Rhodes
Platí
Grafiótissa
Marathoúnda
Psérimos
Vathí
Psérimos
Cape Dhrépano
Áyios Ioánnis
Mastihári
Troúlos
Marmári
Alikí
Tingáki
Límniónas
Áyios Theológos
Kéfalos
Kamári
Áyios Stéfanos
Andimáhia
Linopótis
Zipári
Lámbi
Cape Skandhári
Astypalia
Kastrí
Panayía Palatianí
Pláka
Pilí
Amanioú
Lagoúdhi
Evangelístria
Asklepion
Kos Town
"Camel"
"Paradise"
"Banana"
"Sunny"
"Magic"
Áyios Ioánnis Thiamianós
Látra 428m
Aspri Pétra
Knights' Castle
Paleó Pilí
ASFENDHIOÚ
Ziá
Asómati
Áyios Dhimítrios
Plataní (Kermetés)
Ambávris
Áyios Gavriíl
DHÍKEOS
Khristós 846m
Tolári
Cape Psalídhi
Cape Kríkello
Kardhámena
Brós Thermá
Áyios Fokás
0
5 km

tary presence here only adding to the pressure on these resources. Except for the far southwest, this is not an island that attracts many independent travellers, and from early July to early September you'll be lucky to find any sort of room at all without advance reservations or a pre-booked package.

For these and the following reasons, Kós is the isle travel writers love to hate, often savaging the place without having ventured beyond the main town. It is faulted for being flat and boring – indeed, the centre of the island is so low-lying that the peak of Níssiros can be glimpsed above it from Kálimnos – as well as for its dismal lack of architectural or culinary distinction. To its credit, one might add that tourism is handled uncharacteristically slickly on Kós, courtesy of (by Greek island standards) a well-developed public infrastructure: the city bus service is a marvel, cyclists are actively catered for with marked bike lanes, and the biological sewage plant east of town is proudly signposted – this last partly the result of an unusual continuity in local administration, thanks to an efficient and popular mayor who has been re-elected a dozen times.

If Kós were half the size and contained the same number of attractions, it would be acclaimed as one of the most interesting Greek islands. But like an indulgently edited movie, Kós drags a bit in the middle, though there's enough to hold your interest for the one-week duration of the shortest package. Swimming opportunities, for a start, are on the whole excellent – virtually the entire coast is fringed by sandy beaches of various sizes, colours and consistencies. But for longer than a week, you'd be better off with a multi-centre holiday, taking in one or more of the surrounding islands as well.

Kós Town

Minoan settlers were attracted by the island's only good, natural harbour, opposite ancient Halikarnassos (today Bodrum), and despite regular and devastating earthquakes throughout history, **KÓS TOWN** has remained on this site, prospering from sea trade. The contemporary city, home to most of Kós' population, spreads in all directions from the almost landlocked port. Apart from the Knights' castle, the first thing you see arriving by boat, its most compelling attraction lies in the wealth of Hellenistic and Roman remains, many of which were only revealed by the earthquake of 1933 and excavated afterwards by the Italians.

Arrival

Large **ferries** anchor just outside the harbour at a special jetty by one corner of the castle; **excursion boats** to and from neighbouring islands sail right in and dock all along Aktí Koundouriótou. **Hydrofoils** tie up south of the castle, on Aktí Miaoúli.

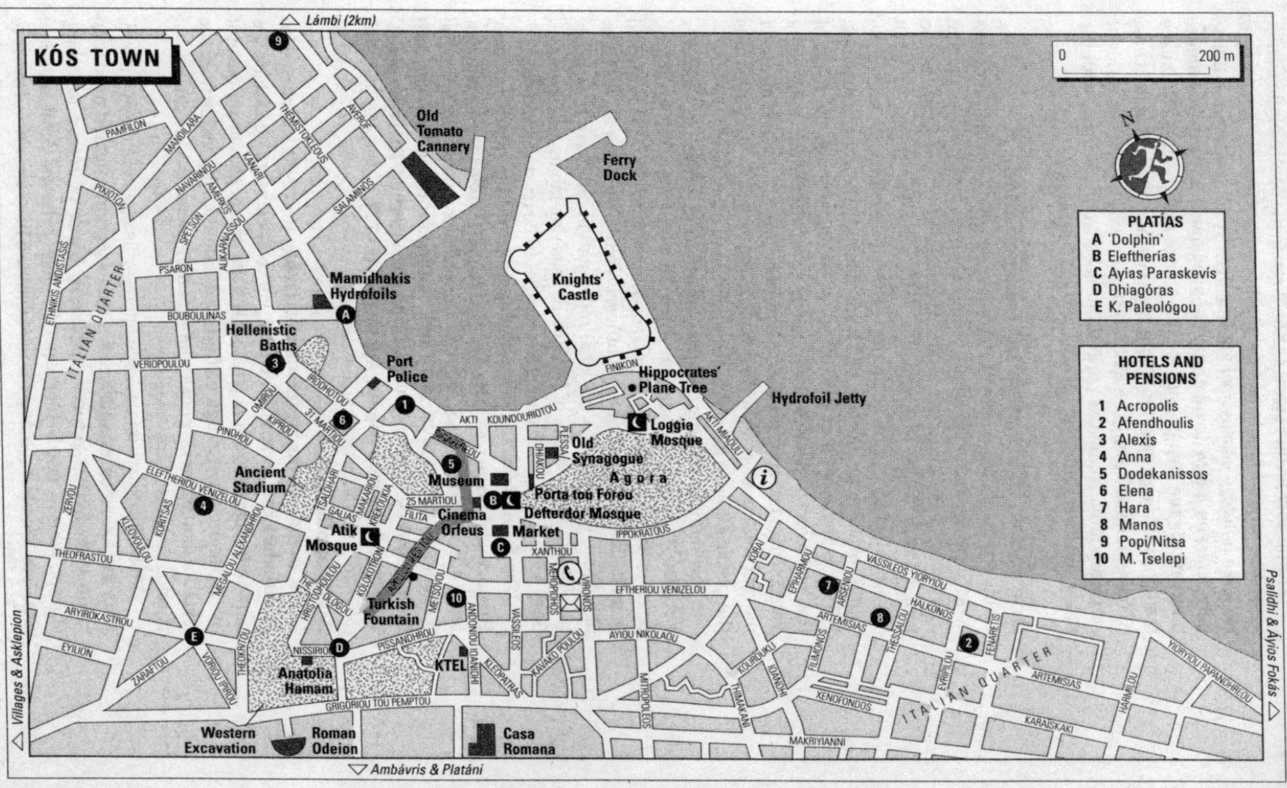

KÓS TOWN
0
200 m
N
PLATÍAS
A 'Dolphin'
B Eleftherías
C Ayías Paraskevís
D Dhiagóras
E K. Paleológou
HOTELS AND PENSIONS
1 Acropolis
2 Afendhoulis
3 Alexis
4 Anna
5 Dodekanissos
6 Elena
7 Hara
8 Manos
9 Popi/Nitsa
10 M. Tselepi
Lámbi (2km)
Psalidhi & Áyios Fokás
Villages & Asklepion
Ambávris & Plataní
Old Tomato Cannery
Ferry Dock
Knights' Castle
Hippocrates' Plane Tree
Loggia Mosque
Hydrofoil Jetty
Mamidhakis Hydrofoils
Port Police
Hellenistic Baths
Ancient Stadium
Museum
Cinema Orfeus
Old Synagogue
Agora
Porta tou Forou
Defterdar Mosque
Market
Atik Mosque
Turkish Fountain
KTEL
Anatolia Hamam
Western Excavation
Roman Odeion
Casa Romana
ITALIAN QUARTER
ITALIAN QUARTER
AKTI KOUNDOURIOTOU
AKTI MIAOULI
FINIKON
PLESSA
DHIAKOU
IPPOKRATOUS
XANTHOU
MEROPIDHOS
VIRONOS
VASSILEOS
ANDONIOU IOANIDHI
KLEOPATRAS
KAVAKO POULOU
METSOVOU
25 MARTIOU
31 MARTIOU
FILITA
KREKOUKIA
MAKARIOU
GALIAS
TSALDHARI
KOLOKOTRONI
HRISTODHOULOU
THEOLOGOU
PISSANDHROU
NISSIRIOU
GRIGORIOU TOU PEMPTOU
THEOKRITOU
VORIOU IPIROU
MEGALOU ALEXANDHROU
ELEFTHERIOU VENIZELOU
EFTHERIOU VENIZELOU
AYIOU NIKOLAOU
MITROPOLEOS
THIMAKANI
KOURDUKLI
IOANDHI
MAKRIYIANNI
XENOFONDOS
FILIMONOS
EPIHARMOU
KORAI
ARSENIOU
ARTEMISIAS
THESSALOU
HALKONOS
VASSILEOS YIORYIOU
EVRIPILOU
FENARETIS
ARTEMISIAS
KARAISKAKI
HARMILOU
YIORYIOU PAPANDHREOU
AVEROF
SALAMINOS
THEMISTOKLEOUS
KANARI
ALIKARNASSOU
AMERKIS
NAVARINOU
SPETSON
PSARON
BOUBOULINAS
VERIOPOULOU
IRODHOTOU
OMIROU
KIPROU
PINDHOU
MANDILARA
PAMFILON
PIXIOTON
ETHNIKIS ANDISTASIS
KORITSAS
KLEOVOULOU
ZERVOU
THEOFRASTOU
ARYIROKASTROU
EVILION
ZARAFTOU

The **airport** is 26km west of Kós Town in the centre of the island; an airline shuttle bus is laid on for *Olympic Airways* flights, and package holidays usually include transfers. If you arrive on a flight-only deal, you'll have to take a taxi or head towards the giant roundabout outside the airport gate for the orange and cream *KTEL* **buses** that pass through here en route between Mastihári, Kardhámena, Kéfalos and Kós Town. The *KTEL* terminal in Kós Town is a series of stops around a triangular park 400m back from the quay, with the ticket and information booth officially at Kleopátras 7.

Orientation, information and transportation

Thanks to the Italian planners, driving or pedalling around Kós Town is quite painless, despite a fairly comprehensive one-way system and a growing pedestrian-only zone. At the back of the harbour, the round Platía Iróön Politehníou – informally known as "Dolphin Square" after its central sculpture – effectively marks one end of the tourist esplanade; Finíkon or "Palm Avenue" the other. Vassiléos Pávlou is the most unrestricted street cutting through the heart of the commercial district from north to south, while Eleftheríou Venizélou and its continuation, Artemisías, provide the best means of moving west to east. From the waterfront, Megálou Alexándhrou is the quickest way to get out to the main island trunk road.

The municipally run **tourist information office** at Vassiléos Yioryíou 3 (July–Aug daily 7am–9pm, Nov–Apr Mon–Fri 8am–3pm, intermediate schedules in spring/autumn; ☎0242/28 724) is housed in an Italian-era hotel: once an officers' club, then a crêche, and now also home (upstairs) to the local radio station. Staff are reasonably helpful and keep stocks of local maps, bus timetables and specimen ferry schedules (which they stress are not to be trusted implicitly).

The main **taxi** stand lies at the east end of Koundouriótou, near Hippocrates' plane tree. The Kós municipality runs its own efficient **local bus** service, *DEAS*, through the beach suburbs and up to the Asklepion, with a ticket and information office at Aktí Koundouriótou 7. Owing to the island's notorious flatness, **pedal-bike rental** is a very popular option (see p.177).

Accommodation

If you're just in transit, then there's really no viable alternative to staying in Kós Town. But even if you're sticking to the island for one or two weeks, the capital makes an excellent touring base; it offers the broadest range of food and nightlife, the majority of the island's motorbike or pedal-bike rental agencies, and is the hub of public transport.

Most hotels are on package operator lists, and relatively expensive; the following establishments are exceptions, geared to walk-in trade even if they reserve a seasonal block of rooms for tours. Except where noted, they operate only between April and late October. Families looking for a beach-base in or near Kós Town are best off at more luxurious accommodation en route to Cape Psalídhi and Áyios Fokás.

The relatively pricy but very well-appointed **campsite** also lies 2500m east towards Cape Psalídhi, and can be reached by the city bus service (or its own minibus which meets ferries), but functions only during the warmer months. You may well find yourself out there unintentionally, since in July and August absolutely every town bed is booked up months in advance by Greeks and Italians. During this season some hotels even rent out balconies for a few thousand drachmas, with or without the permission of the room's tenants, and apparently with the approval of the tourist authorities.

Centre

Acropol, Tsaldhári 4 (☎0242/22 244). An older hotel, with en-suite rooms and a garden. ③.

Alexis, Irodhótou 9, corner Omírou (☎0242/28 798 or ☎25 594). Deservedly popular backpacker's pension in an inter-war villa overlooking the Hellenistic baths. No en-suite rooms, but a self-catering kitchen, garden, terrace, pedal-bike hire and extremely helpful management. Open late March–early Nov most years. ②.

Anna, Venizélou 77 (☎0242/23 030). Pension with largish balconies for the en-suite rooms and in a fairly quiet location well inland. ③.

Dodekanissos, Ipsilándou 2 (☎0242/28 460). Despite a promising position on a pedestrian zone, this hotel is noisy and not so well maintained; a last resort. ③.

Elena, Megálou Alexándhrou 5–7(☎0242/22 740). Well-positioned hotel on a relatively quiet side street; clean rooms, all with balconies and some with baths, have partial views of an archeological area. ③.

Moustafa Tselepi, Venizélou 29, corner Metsóvou (☎0242/28 896). These well-furnished rooms are a good choice for longer stays, and some have cooking facilities. ③.

The east Italian quarter

Afendoulis, about 600m east of the ancient *agora* at Evripílou 1 (☎0242/25 321, fax ☎25 797). Hotel under the same management as *Pension Alexis*; more comfortable, en-suite rooms, most with balconies. Cool, cave-like basement rooms are a haven in summer. No tour alottment. ③.

Hara, Hálkonos 6, corner Arseníou (☎0242/22 500). Smallish, friendly, en-suite hotel, with minimal tour agency allotment. One of the spots where the *Hotel Afendhoulis* management sends its frequent overflow. ③.

Manos, Artemisías 15 (☎0242/28 931). Hotel open high season only; of a similar standard to *Hara*, with which it shares overflow from *Afendoulis*. ③.

North of the port

Alice Springs, almost in Lámbi, at far end of Kanári, near *Disco Heaven* (☎0242/23 473). Hotel set slightly inland and so not deluged by tour groups; no prizes for guessing where the management spent some years. ③.

Nitsa, Avérof 41 (☎0242/25 810). Pension with self-catering facilities and nocturnal noise from bars across the way. ③.

Popi, Avérof 37 (☎0242/23 475). Similar pension to *Nitsa*. ③.

Psalídhi and Áyios Fokás

Dimitra Beach, Áyios Fokás (☎0242/28 581). An attractive hotel (⑤) and bungalow village (⑥) with its own beach.

Niridhes Beach, Psalídhi, just west of the *Ramira Beach* (☎0242/23 380). Another small beachfront hotel, with pool and ball-sports facilities. ⑤.

Ramira Beach, Psalídhi, 3km from town (☎0242/28 489 or ☎22 891). Well-landscaped medium-sized hotel, with tennis court and pool. ⑤.

Theodhorou, Psalídhi, 1200m from town (☎0242/23 364). A good, small mid-range option, right off the bike path. ④.

The town

Despite a population of 15,000, Kós Town feels remarkably low density, thanks to it sprawling, flat layout. Vast areas of open space alternate with a wonderful hotchpotch of surviving Ottoman monuments and Italian-era mock-medieval and Art Deco buildings (a good example of which is the old synagogue, see box p.179). Despite central appearances, this is mostly a planned town, with the pines and shrubs planted by the Italians now fully matured, especially in the garden suburb extending east of the central street grid.

The Knights' castle

For most visitors, the obvious first port of call is the **Knights' Castle** (Tues–Sun 8.30am–3pm; 600dr), reached by a causeway over its former moat; this has long since been filled in and planted with palms, giving rise to the avenue's name, Finíkon. The original Knights' castle, which existed here between 1314 and 1450, has vanished without trace, replaced by the existing inner castle (1450–78). This in turn nestles within the outer citadel, built to formidable thickness between 1495 and 1514 to withstand new artillery technology following unsuccessful Ottoman sieges in 1457 and 1477.

A fair proportion of ancient Kós, in the form of masonry fragments and tumbled columns, has been incorporated into the walls of both strongholds or, more recently, piled up loose in the southeast forecourt. A bewildering array of escutcheons and coats-of-arms on the various walls and towers will appeal to aficionados of heraldry, as the period of construction spanned the terms of several Grand Masters and local governors. For example, the south corner of the older castle bears two Grand Masters' escutcheons, best admired from the massive, most technically advanced southwest bastion identified with del Caretto, the Grand Master who finished the job. There are also dozens of canonballs lying about, few if any ever fired in anger, since this castle surrendered without resistance in accordance with the terms ending the marathon siege of Rhodes (see p.62). The biggest explosion that ever occured here was orchestrated for the grand finale of Werner Herzog's first black and white feature, *Signs of Life* (1966), in which a low-ranking *Wehrmacht* officer goes berserk and torches an ammunition dump inside the castle.

Hippocrates' plane tree and the Loggia Mosque

Rather sterile steel scaffolding has replaced the ancient pillars that once propped up the sagging branches of **Hippocrates' plane tree**, immediately opposite the causeway leading into the Knights' castle. At seven hundred years of age, this venerable tree has a fair claim to being one of the oldest in Europe, though not really elderly enough to have seen the great healer. Its trunk has split into four sections, which in any other species would presage imminent demise, but abundant suckers from its roots promise some sort of continuation. Adjacent stand a hexagonal Turkish pillar fountain and the imposing eighteenth-century mosque of Hassan Pasha, also known as the **Loggia Mosque** after its covered portico on the north side. This three-storey building is locked and in poor repair, especially the tracery of its upper windows. The ground floor – like that of its near-contemporary the **Defterdar mosque** on nearby Platía Eleftherías – is taken up by rows of shops.

The ancient town

The largest single excavated section of ancient Kós is the **agora**, a sunken zone reached via steps from either Ippokrátous or Nafklírou. The latter, a pedestrian street (and nightlife mecca, see p.176), leads away from Platía Eleftherías under the **Pórta toú Fórou**, all that's left of the outer city walls built by the Knights between 1391 and 1396.

What you see is confusing and jumbled owing to successive earthquakes in 142, 469 and 554 AD; the most easily distinguishable items are the foundations of a massive double Aphrodite sanctuary roughly in the centre of the site, some columns of a *stoa* that once surrounded the so-called Harbour Basilica near the Loggia Mosque, plus two re-erected columns and the architrave of the Roman *agora* itself, in the far west of the archeological zone.

Another, more comprehensible section of the ancient town, the so-called **western excavations**, abuts the ancient acropolis approximately where Platía Dhiagóras lies today. Intersecting marble-paved **Roman streets** (named Cardo and Decumana) dating from the third century AD lend definition to this area, as does the **Xisto** or colonnade of a covered running track. Inside the Xisto squat the hulking brick ruins of a bath alongside the original arch of its furnace room. South of this stands the restored doorframe of a baptistry belonging to a Christian basilica erected above the baths after 469 AD. The floor of the basilica and of an unidentified building at the northern end of these excavations retain well-preserved fragments of **mosaics**, although the best have been carted off to the Palace of the Grand Masters in Rhodes (see p.70). What remains tends to be under several inches of protective gravel, or – in the case of the famous **Europa mosaic** house, to the north of the east-to-west Decumana street – currently off-limits to visitors. Secreted in a cypress grove just across Grigoríou toú Pémptou is a fourteen-row

Roman **odeion**, which at one time hosted musical events associated with the Asklepieia festivals (see below).

The Archeological Museum

The Italian-built **Archeological Museum**, on Platía Eleftherías (Tues–Sun 8.30am–3pm; 600 dr), is a none too subtle propaganda exercise, with a distinct Latin bias in its choice of exhibits. Four rooms containing good, though not superlative, statuary are grouped around a central atrium where a mosaic shows Hippocrates welcoming Asklepios to Kós. The most famous exhibit, a statue thought to portray Hippocrates, is in fact Hellenistic, but most of the other highly regarded works – Hermes seated with a lamb, Hygeia offering an egg to Asklepios' serpent, a boxer with his arms bound in rope, statues of wealthy townspeople – are emphatically Roman.

The Ottoman old town: Haluvaziá

Kós also boasts a medieval "old town", the former Turkish district of **Haluvaziá**, lining either side of a pedestrianized street running from behind the covered produce market on Platía Eleftherías as far as Platía Dhiagóras and the orphaned minaret overlooking the western archeological zone. This begins life as Iféstou, then becomes Apelloú further on. It was long considered an undesirable area, but while all the rickety townhouses nearby collapsed in the 1933 earthquake, the sturdily built stone dwellings and shops here survived. Today they are crammed with highly commercial tourist boutiques – especially for silver jewellery – and snack bars; one of the few genuinely old things here is a dry **Turkish fountain** with an inscription, found where the walkway cobbles cross Venizélou; another juts from the wall of the barber shop at the corner of Hristodhoúlou and Passanikoláki, lodged next to the minaret-less but still-functioning **Atik mosque**.

Continuing in same direction, you should certainly make the detour west of Platía Dhiagóras to Nissiríou 3, where the **Anatolia Hamam** was acquired in 1992 and lovingly restored by an Athenian couple. During the Ottoman period this was the mansion of a local pasha, whose descendants left for Izmir in 1950; the small Turkish bath (the *hamam* of the name) inside functioned as the neighbourhood spa until 1970 or so, after which the premises operated sporadically as a brothel before falling into complete disrepair. The new owners have preserved the original cedar floors, painted ceilings and of course the tiny *hamam* as an intimate part of this very classy bar. There are four separate upstairs dining salons, plus an outdoor terrace; even if you don't eat here, it's well worth the price of a drink to look around.

The Casa Romana

The Greeks have attempted to dampen Italian "public relations" by signposting the **Casa Romana** (same hours and fees as castle and museum), on Grigoríou toú Pémptou at the rear of town, as

"Restored House of Kós, 3rd Century AD". Already the 1930s reconstruction work on this palatial Roman house is beginning to deteriorate, providing grist for future archeology; of the three fee-entry, restricted-hours sites in town, it's probably the one to skip if you're short of time.

This building, devastated by the 554 AD earthquake, was evidently the villa of a wealthy citizen, and is arrayed around three atria with mosaic floors. The smallest one, by the ticket booth, features panthers attacking a stag; the largest courtyard shows another panther and a tiger on opposite sides; while the pool of the third atrium is surrounded by dolphins, plus a damaged nymph riding a horse-headed sea-monster, possibly a representation of Poseidon.

Eating

Despite an overwhelming first impression of Euro-bland cuisine aimed at the chartered masses, it is easy to eat well, and sometimes even reasonably, in Kós Town. Virtually all the better-value places are a few blocks inland, and scattered fairly evenly throughout the town grid. You can pretty much write off most of the waterfront tavernas, though the long-established *Limnos*, one of the first as you come from the ferry jetty, is probably the best of a bad bunch.

Cafés and desserts

Fontana di Gellato, Venizélou just west of Apelloú and the dry Turkish fountain. Top-notch Italian ice cream to take away.

Helena's House, corner Avérof and Porfiríou. Friendly, Dutch-run café serving pancake breakfasts and light snacks as well as drinks.

O Kivotos, Voríou Ipírou, within sight of the Roman *odeion*. A tea house specializing in herbal teas and less expensive pastries, run by a young Greek couple.

O Platanos, opposite Hippocrates' Plane Tree. Atmospheric café with fancy cakes and classical music; priced accordingly.

Toh Rodhon, Platía Ayías Paraskevís, behind the municipal produce market off Vassiléos Pávlou. Marginally less expensive than its fairly indistinguishable rivals here; pancake/croissant breakfasts, hot drinks and juices served under giant Indian fig trees – little hope, though, of a decent cappuccino.

Central and Italian quarter

Barba George, Píndhou 21. Taverna with garden seating and standard grills; in fierce competition with *Theodhoros*, below.

Chinese Express, corner Krekoukiá and Passanikoláki, opposite the Atik mosque. Cheap, quick take-away, or eat in at the diner tables; open quite late.

Limnos, Aktí Koundouriótou. Not brilliant, but acceptable as a long-established harbour-view eatery. All the Greek oven standards; open most of the year.

Olympiada, Kleopátras 2, near the *KTEL* terminal. Good for a quick, Greek lunch; open till mid-November.

Peking, corner Halkónos and Arseníou. Regarded as the most authentic of the half-dozen Chinese eateries on the island; not grossly inflated for the set meal.

Theodhoros, Píndhou 22. Taverna serving similar food to its cross-street rival *Barba George*.

North of the port

Toh Hani, Amerikís 29. Slightly more locally orientated and less expensive than *Toh Kohili*; portions aren't huge, but the food – old standards with a twist – is excellent. Four *mezédhes* plates required to satifsy each diner, plus foreign beer on draught; indoor seating, so may be open out of season.

Toh Kohili, Alikarnassoú 64, corner Amerikís. New *ouzerí*, whose expensive menu is worth it for such delicacies as quail, squid stuffed with *manoúri* cheese, skillfully rendered eggplant, and imported beers. Summer only.

Nikolaos O Psaras, corner Alikarnassoú and Avérof. Cheap and cheerful side-walk taverna that does fish dishes reasonably and abundantly by resort standards.

Noufara, Kanári 45. Carnivore heaven, with roast chicken, *kondosoúvli*, etc; considered the best grill in town. Indoor and sidewalk seating, open most of the year.

Suburbs

Ambavris, in the eponymous hamlet, 800m south of the Casa Romana. Efficient service, impeccable island recipes and reasonably priced, large portions make this arguably the best taverna in the town vicinity. The "Greek (medley) Plate" is excellent value, and vegetarians are catered for. Count on a short wait for the outdoor seating in the courtyard of this converted farmhouse. Open Apr–Oct only.

Mavromatis, Yioryíou Panandhréou 15, about 2km out on the coast road towards Cape Psalídhi. Good-value, hybrid western-Greek cuisine (ie stuffed chicken breast washed down with imported beer), and gravel-court seating outside overlooking the beach and Turkey. Open during the warmer months only.

Drinking and nightlife

For loud (120-decibel) **nightlife**, you need look no further than "Bar Street", officially Nafklírou and Dhiákou, two roughly parallel pedestrian lanes joining Platía Eleftherías and the castle. Every address is a bar, just choose according to the crowd and the (techno and house) noise level. It is sobering (though not literally) to reflect that in Ottoman and Italian times this was a gritty bazaar quarter, domain of the blacksmiths and socially on par with Haluvaziá; today it is your eardrums, not your hooves, that will get a hammering after 10pm.

Bars off "Bar Street"

Anatolia Hamam, Nissiríou 3. Elegant bar, as well as international-cuisine restaurant (see p.174). Often live music until 11pm; open most of the year.

Beach Boys Dance Bar, Kanári 57. Happy hours and yes, a tiny dance floor; people spill out on the sidewalk.

Blues Brothers Cafe, Aktí Koundouriótou, corner Iróön Politekhníou (Dolphin Square). Doyen of the waterfront bars, with rock and blues soundtrack and a very mixed crowd. Stick to the beers and bottled drinks; the special cocktails tend to be weak.

Jazz Opera, Arseníou 5, near corner Artemisías. Jazz plus blues, funk, rock, reggae for a thirty-something crowd.

Discos

Heaven, 2km northwest of the town centre in Lámbi. Outdoor, garden venue, so open June–Sept only.

Playboy, north side of the port, Kanári 2. The most impressive indoor venue, famous for its light shows.

Listings

Airlines *Air 2000* c/o *Karis Travel*, Irodhótou 8 (☎0242/23 327); *Monarch* c/o *Aeolos Travel*, Artemisías 17 (☎0242/26 203); *Olympic*, Vassiléos Pávlou 22 (☎0242/28 331).

Bike rental Of a huge number of establishments, *Motorent*, at Kanári 49, is about the largest and most conspicuous. Expect to pay a minimum 3000dr for a single-person moped, about 2000dr for a mountain bike, and much less for a balloon-tyre pedal-bike.

Car rental Not absolutely essential on smallish, mostly flat Kós unless you're a family or group; rates start at about 8000dr per day. *Marion*, at Vassiléos Yioryíou 12 (☎0242/26 293), provides a good service; if they're out of vehicles, try *Alpha*, Bouboulínas 23 (☎0242/22 488) or *Autorent*, Kanári 31 (☎0242/28 882).

Cinemas *Orfevs* screens a varied programme in an Art Deco building diagonally opposite the archeological museum in winter, in summer in premises on Fenarétis at the east end of Halkónos. The indoor building also hosts concerts and other special events. The *Kentriko* cinema, at Ayíou Nikoláou 8, appears to have closed down.

Exchange The *Trapeza Pisteos/Credit Bank* on the waterfront opens Saturday mornings; some other banks keep evening hours, and there are four ATMs (*Ethniki/National*, *Emboriki/Commercial*, *Pisteos/Credit*, *Ioniki/Ionian*). *Ethniki* and *Pisteos* also have machines that change foreign notes.

Ferry agents Virtually all ferry and excursion boat agents sit within 50m of each other at the intersection of Vassiléos Pávlou and the waterfront. *Exas*, Aktí Koundouriótou, on the corner of Vassiléos Pávlou, and also at Vassiléos Pávlou 4 (☎0242/28 545), is generally switched-on and helpful; it's the main agent for *G&A Ferries* and the exclusive agent for *Ilio Lines*. *Python Tours*, Vassiléos Pávlou 1 (☎0242/22 217), specialize in trips to Turkey; *Stefamar*, Avérof 23 (☎0242/26 388), deals strictly with day excursions to neighbouring islands. Staff at the *Mamidhakis/Dodecanese Hydrofoils* office on "Dolphin Square" can be extremely rude, so you may prefer to book tickets elsewhere.

Laundrettes Three to choose from: *Happy Wash* at Mitropóleos 14; *Laundry Center* on Mandhilará 47; *Laundromat Center*, Alikarnassoú 124.

Map The most accurate locally sold map, for both the island and the town, is that published by Pandelis Vayianos; don't be put off by its 3-D matchbox art.

OTE Víronos 6, corner Xánthou (Mon–Fri 7.30am–10pm).

Post office Venizélou 14; sporadic Saturday morning hours in high season.

Around Kós Town

All coastal points between Lámbi, to the north of Kós Town, and Áyios Fokás, to the east, are connected by the *DEAS* bus line; alternatively you can rent a pedal-bike and take advantage of the designated cycle paths extending as far east as Cape Psalídhi.

The closest beaches that answer to the description are at and beyond **LÁMBI**, 3km north towards Cape Skandhári with its military watchpoint, the last vestige of a vast army camp which has deferred to the demands of tourism. However, north-facing beaches beyond the point are not the best: narrow, scrappy and closely hemmed by a frontage road.

East of Kós Town, the strands around Cape Psalídhi are grey-gravel and uninspiring. Possibly more interesting hereabouts are a few re-erected columns in the fourth-century basilica of Áyios Gavriïl, just inland from the road as you clear the edge of Kós Town. Similar beaches, functional at best, line Cape Fokás, further east, whose focal point is the planned resort of Áyios Fokás, 9km from town.

The unusual and remote hot springs of **Brós Thermá** emerge 5km beyond Áyios Fokás, and though nominally served by *DEAS* bus, they are most easily reached by hired vehicle; take the dirt side road off the pavement, marked by a sign announcing an impending multinational project to "improve" the springs. For the moment these issue from a tiny grotto, trickling down to the sea through a trench that's periodically redug after winter storms. The trench water itself is too hot to bear fully immersed, so most visitors bathe in the tidal zone inside a crescent of boulders, feasible during most of the year. There's a small seasonal taverna above the springs, but no other facilities until the development project gets off the ground.

Platáni

The Greek–Turkish village of **PLATÁNI** lies 2km south of Kós Town, on the road to the Asklepion. Until 1964 it was most commonly known as Kermetés (*Germe* in Turkish), and the Turkish community had its own primary school, but in the wake of the Cyprus crises of that year, the village was officially renamed and the school converted to a Greek-only format. Subsequent emigration to Anatolia caused Turkish numbers on the island to drop from around 3000 to less than 1000. Only those Turks owning real property and businesses have stayed, but as on Rhodes, the long-term outlook is bleak. Underlying tensions were highlighted by the virulently nationalistic graffiti that appeared on Ottoman fountains and gravestones in 1994.

Platáni's older domestic architecture is strongly reminiscent of styles in rural Crete, from where some of the village's Muslims came between 1898 and 1913; there's even a working Ottoman fountain near the crossroads. This junction is dominated by a collection of tavernas, several of which are run by local Turks. The Turkish-style

The Jews of Kós

Just outside Platáni on the road back to the harbour, a Jewish **cemetery** stands in a dark conifer grove, 300m from the Muslim graveyard. Dates on the headstones, inscribed in a mix of Hebrew and Italian, stop ominously after 1940. The remaining local community of about 120 was transported to Rhodes in summer 1944 by the Nazis, and thence, together with the Rhodian Jews, to Auschwitz for extermination. Just one Koan Jew, who died recently, survived the war; according to Jewish communal law he inherited all the real property of his deceased co-religionists, supposedly selling it for a small fortune when tourism reached Kós in the 1970s.

The former **synagogue**, disused since 1944, is a marvellously orientalized Art Deco building in Kós Town, at Alexándhrou Dhiákou 4, between the ancient *agora* and the waterfront; it was recently refurbished and a plaque now identifies it as the "municipal multipurpose hall". In 1994 the synagogue and Jewish cemetery got the same blue-graffiti treatment as the Turkish monuments, an act as ugly as it is inexplicable, given the manner and completeness of the local Jews' disappearance.

mezédhes and kebabs at *Arap* (outdoor tables, summer only) and *Gin's Place* (indoor seating, all year) are much better food than most on offer in Kós Town, and are best enjoyed in a group, when you can pass the various plates around.

The Asklepion

Native son **Hippocrates** is justly celebrated on Kós; not only does he have a tree, a street, a statue and a new international medical institute named after him, but the Hellenistic **Asklepion** (Tues–Sun 8.30am–3pm; 800dr) 4km south of town, one of just three in Greece, is a major tourist attraction. City buses make the trip via Platáni between 8am and 2pm, to Platáni only between 4 and 10.30pm; otherwise you've a 45-minute walk. Incidentally, there is no food or drink available here, so come equipped or pause in Platáni en route.

The Asklepion was actually founded just after the death of Hippocrates, but it's safe to assume that the methods used and taught here were his. Both a temple to Asklepios (god of medicine, son of Apollo) and a renowned curative centre, its magnificent setting on three artificial hillside terraces overlooking Anatolia reflects early recognition of the importance of the therapeutic environment. Until recently a fountain provided the site with a constant supply of clean, fresh water, and extensive stretches of clay piping are still visible, embedded in the ground.

Today very little remains above ground owing to chronic earthquakes and the Knights' use of the site as a quarry. The lower terrace never did have many structures anyway, as this was the main venue for the observance of the *Asklepieia* – quadrennial celebrations and athletic or musical competitions in honour of the healing god. Sacrifices to Asklepios were conducted at an **altar**, the

Hippocrates

Hippocrates (c. 460–370 BC) is generally regarded as the father of scientific medicine, and still influences doctors today through the Hippocratic oath – which probably has nothing to with him and is in any case much altered from its original form. Hippocrates was certainly born on Kós, probably at Astypalia near present-day Kéfalos, but otherwise details of his life are few and disputed; what is certain is that he was a great physician who travelled throughout the Classical Greek world but spent part of his career teaching and practising at the Asklepion on his native island. A vast number of medical writings have been attributed to Hippocrates, only a few of which he could actually have written; *Airs, Waters and Places*, a treatise on the importance of environment on health, is widely thought to be his, but others were probably a compilation from a medical library kept on Kós. This emphasis on good air and water, and the holistic approach of ancient Greek medicine, seems positively modern in the late twentieth century.

oldest structure on the site, whose foundations can still be seen near the middle of the second terrace. Just to its west, the Corinthian columns of a second-century **Roman temple** were partially re-erected by nationalistically minded Italians. A monumental **staircase** flanked by exedrae (display niches) leads from the altar up to the second-century BC **Doric temple** of Asklepios on the topmost terrace, the last and grandest of a succession of the deity's shrines at this site.

The north coast

The two neighbouring resorts of Tingáki and Marmári are separated from each other by a salt marsh called **Alikí**, which retains water until June after a wet winter. Between January and April it's host to hundreds of migratory birds, and most of the year you'll find tame terrapins to feed near the outlet to the warm, shallow sea. There's almost always a breeze along this coast, making it a popular destination for windsurfers, who can hire boards at either resort.

Both Tingáki and Marmári are served by *KTEL* bus from Kós Town, but if you're travelling under your own steam, especially on a bike of any sort, it's safest and most pleasant to take the obvious **minor road** from the southwest corner of town as far as Tingáki; most of this route is paved, and involves about the same distance as travelling the main trunk road and marked turn-off. Similarly, a grid of paved rural lanes links the inland portions of Tingáki and Marmári.

Tingáki

TINGÁKI, the shore annexe of the Asfendioú villages (see below), lies 12km west of Kós Town. It's pleasant enough for a busy resort, with most of its half-dozen, medium-sized **hotels** scattered inland among fields and cow pastures. One of the better choices is *Hotel*

Ilios (☎0242/29 411; ③–④ according to season), a well-designed bungalow complex about 1500m back from the water; closer to the seafront turnaround square is the *Meni Beach* (☎0242/29 217; ④), perhaps more convenient if less peaceful. The *Tingaki Taverna*, on the square, is the oldest and still the best **restaurant** here. The **beach** itself is white-sand, long and narrow; it improves, and veers further out of earshot from the frontage road, as you head southwest, with the best patches to either side of the drainage from Alikí. The profiles of Kálimnos, Psérimos and Turkey's Bodrum peninsula on the horizon all make for spectacular scenery.

Marmári

The traditional annexe of Pilí village (see below), **MARMÁRI** (15km from town) has a smaller built-up area than Tingáki, and the beach itself is broader, especially to the west where it forms mini-dunes. The *Apollonia Bungalows* (☎0242/41 412; ④) are one of the nicer places to **stay** locally, but you may have a hard time squeezing in between German tour groups. For **food**, *Exohiki Psistaria Apostolis*, on west side of the access road down from the island trunk road, is a real find, offering fresh fish, meat grills, an amazing wine list, engaging decor and reasonable prices. Open daily in season, it also operates on Sundays from November to April for the benefit of the islanders.

A unique attraction of the area is the **Marmari Riding Centre** (☎0242/41 783), on the east side of the usual access road from the island trunk route. This has 24 horses and ponies available for one-hour shoreline excursions (5000dr), including a dry-marsh gallop after June, and half-day trips along the beach and foothills between Pilí and Kardhámena (15,000dr).

Around Mount Dhíkeos

The main interest of inland Kós resides in the villages on **Mount Dhíkeos** (the ancient Oromedon). This handful of settlements, collectively referred to as **Asfendhioú**, nestle amid the island's only natural forest and are worth visiting for a glimpse of what Kós looked like before tourism and concrete took hold. They can be reached from the main island trunk road via the extremely curvy side road from Zipári, 8km from Kós Town; a badly marked but paved minor road to Lagoúdhi; or the shorter access road to Píli.

The Asfendhioú villages

The most accessible Asfendhioú village from Kós Town is **EVANGELÍSTRIA**, up the side road from Zipári. Next to its name-sake parish church stands the *Taverna Asfendiou*, while behind extends a neighbourhood of low, whitewashed houses, now two-thirds abandoned in the mad rush down to the coast; the remainder are being bought up and restored by outsiders.

Further up the road from Evangelístria, **ZIÁ**'s spectacular sunset **views** make it the hapless target of up to six tour buses per evening. Perhaps a dozen or so islanders still dwell in the village, but otherwise any building on the main street that isn't a taverna is probably a souvenir shop. Their wares include throw-rugs in hideous shades of purple and blue, fortunately unique to the area. Best of the eight view **tavernas**, which trade largely on their position, are the adjacent, co-owned *Avli* and *Vouno*. But *Olympiada*, situated at the base of the pedestrian walkway snaking through the upper quarter, is indisputably one of the better tavernas on the island, and open in winter too (always a good sign). Since it's the one taverna here without a view, the food has to be good and reasonably priced to make up for this deficiency. Dishes not usually associated with tourist resorts, like chickpeas, bulgur pilaf (*pinigouri* in Koan dialect) and *spédzofaï* (sausage and pepper stew), are washed down by Caviros wine from the bottle or barrel, product of an excellent mainland winery.

Asómati and Áyios Dhimítrios

East of Ziá the way deteriorates to dirt as it continues to two more Asfendhioú settlements. The first you'll come to is **ASÓMATI**, home to around thirty villagers plus a handful of foreigners and Athenians renovating houses. There's just one tiny store where you can get a drink, and the place really only comes to life at the November 8 festival celebrated around the **church of Arkhángelos**, whose courtyard harbours a fine *hokhláki* mosaic.

ÁYIOS DHIMÍTRIOS, 2km beyond along an exceedingly rough track, is shown on some maps by its old name of Haïhoúdhes. It was abandoned entirely during the junta years, when the inhabitants went to Zipári or further afield. Today just one farmer lives here beside the recently restored namesake **monastery**. Most maps show a road continuing from Áyios Dhimítrios to the Asklepion, a few kilometres further, but it's fairly rough and really only suitable for a sturdy mountain bike or jeep.

Up Khristós peak

Ziá (see above) is the preferred trailhead for the ascent to the summit of 846-metre **Khristós** peak, the highest point on Kós. Taking less than half a day, this is within the capabilities of any reasonably fit, properly shod person, and offers what are arguably the best views in the Dodecanese.

From the *Olympiada* restaurant you should head up the paved walkway to the top of the village, then continue south up steps past a few houses. At the top of these stone stairs gushes a fountain, the outlet of the famous local Kefalóvrisi spring that keeps Ziá and Evangelístria well watered. Top up your water bottle here; the lone spring further up the mountain is unreliable. Just above this point you follow a narrow track through a glen, passing the chapel of

Isódhia tís Theotókou with its vaulted roof and covered porch. Bear right at the junction behind it and head west past the last house in Ziá. On your right, a fifteen-minute walk above the restaurant, the chapel of **Áyios Yióryios** houses a few frescoes. The rough track, now scarcely passable to vehicles, curls gradually south past isolated farm cottages and sheep-pens, then through two gates.

Just over half an hour out of Ziá you'll reach the true trailhead amid a grove of junipers. The spot is fairly obvious, with the path flanked by red and blue paint splodges, and a trilingual sign requesting that you take your garbage with you. The distinct trail zigzags eastwards up the mountainside, leaving the juniper forest within fifteen minutes and arriving in about an hour at the ridge leading east-northeast to the summit. The grade slackens, and three or four shattered cisterns, once used by shepherds, are visible north of the path. From the point where the ridge is attained, it's another twenty minutes to the summit along the watershed, usually just to its north; the little pillbox-like chapel of the **Metamórfosis toú Sotírou**, visible most of the time now, stands about 40m northeast of the altitude survey marker. Once up top, Turkey's Knidos Peninsula dominates the view to the southeast; Níssiros, Tílos and Hálki float to the south; Astipálea closes off the horizon on the west; Kálimnos (and on a good day, Léros) spread out to the north; and the entire west and north portions of Kós are laid out before you.

The south flank of the mountain is a sheer drop to the Aegean, and the summit ridge northeast can only be tackled by technical climbers – too many knife-edge saddles and arrêts. So the only viable descent is back the way you came, which takes only about ten minutes less than the climb up owing to the rough surface.

Pilí: new and old

Further along the main island road is **Linopótis**, a sunken pond fed by a permanent spring, always swarming with terrapins, ducks and eels. From the junction here, a signposted access road leads left to contemporary **PILÍ**, which divides into two districts. In the upper neighbourhood, 100m west of the upper square and church, the simple *Taverna Piyi* serves inexpensive village fare in a superb setting overlooking trees, a tankful of carp and frogs, and (best of all) a giant cistern-fountain, the *piyí* of the name, decorated with four carved lion-head spouts.

Pilí's other monument is the so-called **Harmilio** (Tomb of Harmylos); from the upper church, head 300m along the Kardhámena-bound road, turn left on the minor road to Amanioú, then left again after about 200m. The Harmilio consists of a subterranean vault with twelve niches, probably a Hellenistic family tomb. Immediately above it, traces of an ancient temple foundation have been incorporated into the medieval chapel of Stavrós.

Paleó Pilí

Paleó (medieval) **Pilí**, roughly 3km southeast of its modern descendant, was the Byzantine capital of Kós, inhabited from about the tenth century until the Ottoman conquest. The way there is signposted rather inconspicuously (if at all) on a house in Amanioú, the next hamlet east of lower Pilí. The trick is to barrel straight through the T-junction presided over by a church; left takes you to Lagoúdhi. By this point the fortifications of old Pilí will be visible dead ahead on its crag.

The road continues up to a wooded canyon, dwindling to a dirt track just before a spring whose environs make a great picnic venue. From opposite the fountain, a stair-path leads within fifteen minutes to a **Byzantine castle** dating from the eleventh century, whose partly intact roof affords superlative views. En route you pass the ruins of the abandoned village, as well as two fourteenth-century **churches** (Ipapandí and Mihaïl) usually kept locked to protect their scanty fresco fragments. A third chapel, dedicated to the Arkhángelos and open at last inspection, retains more substantial traces of wall art. Some five minutes uphill from the fountain along the dirt track, the remains of a **watermill** sit in the ravine just west.

Central Kós

Near the **centre of the island**, a pair of giant roundabouts by the airport funnels traffic northwest towards Mastihári, northeast back towards town, southwest towards Kéfalos, and southeast to Kardhámena. The fairly dry, desolate countryside hereabouts provides ample ammunition for those who would dismiss Kós as dull or unattractive, and additionally the area is well sown with military installations guarding the airport.

Mastihári

The least developed of the northern shore resorts, **MASTIHÁRI** was a permanent village long before tourist times, as well as the historic summer quarters of Andimáhia (see below). Though shorter than those at Marmári or Tingáki, the local beach extending to the west is broader, with less frequented dunes (and no sunbeds) towards the south end. A kilometre or so east is the secluded beach of **Troúlos**, reached by a dirt track. The fifth-century basilica of **Áyios Ioánnis** lies about 1500m down the west beach, past the *Kanari Beach Hotel*; it's fairly typical of Kós' several early Christian churches, with a row of column bases separating a pair of side aisles from the nave, a tripartite narthex, and a baptistry tacked onto the north side of the building.

Mastihári, 25km from the capital by the most direct route, is also the **ferry port** for the shortest crossing to Kálimnos; throughout the year there are morning and early evening sailings, plus a late-night departure when flight schedules warrant it. Boats can be fully occupied by package clients in high season, so booking in advance then is recommended (see "Travel Details", p.191)

Practicalities

Mastihári has a higher proportion of non-block-booked **rooms** than other coastal resorts; examples overlooking the west beach include *Studios Diana* (☎0242/51 282; ③) and the slightly quieter *Filio* (☎0242/51 518; ③) or *Studios Irini* (☎0242/51 269; ③). **Eating out**, *O Makis*, one street inland from the centre of the waterfront, is about the best of half a dozen **tavernas** here, well regarded for moderately priced fresh fish and *mezédhes*. The foreign-run *Gelateria Arcoballeno*, at the entrance to the village, sells the real thing as well as decent cappuccinos and espressos (a rarity in Greece). *Christo's Bar*, on the front, is the place for harder stuff.

Andimáhia and Pláka

The workaday village of **ANDIMÁHIA**, 5km southeast of Mastihári, straggles over several of the ridges that extend from here to the far southwestern tip of Kós. The only "sight" and concession to tourism is a much-photographed **windmill** on the main street, the last surviving of more than thirty mills that once dotted the ridges here and at Kéfalos (see p.188). It's now preserved as a working museum and unfurls its sails during daylight hours. For 100dr you can climb up to the mast-loft and watch wholewheat flour being ground on the lower floor.

One worthwhile diversion from the main trunk road, immediately west of the airport and Andimáhia, is **Pláka**, a forested ravine with picnic grounds, a spring and a flock of semi-tame peacocks. The unmarked but paved side road leads off from a small white chapel opposite the forest of radio masts in the airport precinct, and its dirt-surface continuation out of the Pláka vale emerges again on the main road, just before Kós' southwestern beaches.

The Knights' castle

East of Andimáhia, an enormous, triangular **Knights' castle** overlooks the islands of Níssiros, Tílos and Hálki. Access is via a marked, three-kilometre, mostly dirt side road that begins next to a Greek army barracks 700m northeast of the twin roundabouts, and ends in an informal parking area with a seasonal snack bar just before.

Enormous when seen from afar, the fortifications (unrestricted entry) prove less intimidating close up; once through the imposing double north gateway, surmounted by the arms of Grand Master Pierre d'Aubusson, you can follow the well-preserved crenellated west parapet. The badly crumbled eastern wall presides over a sharp drop to badlands draining towards Kardhámena (see below), to which it's around a two-hour walk in cooler weather. Inside the walls stand **two chapels**: the westerly, dedicated to Áyios Nikólaos, retains a surviving fresco of Áyios Hristóforos (Saint Christopher) carrying the Christ Child, while the eastern one of Ayía Paraskeví, though devoid of wall painting, boasts fine rib vaulting. The castle was originally built during the fourteenth century as a prison for misbehaving knights, then modified during the 1490s in tandem with the fortification programme at the citadel in Kós Town.

Kardhámena

KARDHÁMENA, on the southeast coast, 31km from town, is the island's second-largest package resort after the capital itself, with visitors (mainly Brits) outnumbering locals by twenty to one in season. Runaway development has banished whatever redeeming qualities it may once have had, reducing the town to a seething mass of Carling Black Label and Foster's signs. Darts, bingo and karaoke competitions are staged regularly, and, rather disconcertingly, safe-deposit boxes are prominently offered for rent. Names like the *Bubble and Squeak Bistro*, exhortations to "Avoid Hangovers, Stay Drunk", and the ten-toes-up, ten-toes-down logo of *Bonkers' Bar* pretty much epitomize the tone of the place.

A hefty sand **beach** stretches to either side of the town, to the east hemmed in by ill-concealed military bunkers and a road as far as **Tolári**, where the massive *Norida Beach Hotel* is the largest all-inclusive complex on the island. By forking left before reaching Tolári you'll reach Pilí after 9km – a paved, useful shortcut, if narrow and potholed in spots.

Practicalities

Kardhámena is mostly worth knowing about as a place to catch a **boat to Níssiros**. There are supposedly two daily sailings in season: the morning tourist excursion boat at approximately 9.30am, and another, less expensive one at 2.30pm. In practice the afternoon departure of the *Chryssoula*, the Nissirians' postal and shopping *kaïki*, can really only be relied upon to run Mondays and Thursdays. Arrivals from Níssiros coincide fairly well with bus departures to Kós Town.

Outside high season there are generally a few **rooms** not taken by tour companies. Prices are not outrageous (②–③), and accommodation tends to be about fifteen percent cheaper than in Kós Town. If you decide to stay, search out (or pre-book) quieter premises west of the riverbed, beyond the *Valinakis Beach Hotel* – not that sleep is a particularly high priority for most holidaymakers here.

Restaurants here in general serve predictably poor and unauthentic food, but the one reasonable, most Greek and longest-running **taverna** is *Andreas*, right on the harbour. Inland and northeast, a **bakery** (the way signed with red arrows) does home-made ice cream, brown bread and filled pies, while *Peter's* **rent-a-bike** (☎0242/91 487), across the street, is one of the more flexible outfits.

Southwestern Kós

The portion of Kós **southwest** of Andimáhia and the airport is the least developed and most thinly populated part of the island, with its permanent inhabitants confined to the lone, blufftop village of Kéfalos. Besides being the only area where non-package tourists might happen upon a vacancy in high season, it also offers the most secluded and scenic beaches on island, plus a number of minor ancient sites.

South coast beaches

The south-facing **beaches** between the airport and Kéfalos, shown as separate extents on most tourist maps, are essentially one long stretch at the base of a cliff, interrupted only between "Paradise" and Áyios Stéfanos. The sections, described from east to west, are often given fanciful names on the signboards for their individual access roads.

"**Magic**", also known as Poléni, is the longest, broadest and wildest section; "**Sunny**", the next along and an easy walk from "Magic", has sunbeds and a seasonal taverna. "**Banana**" (officially Langádha), also with sunbeds to rent, is the cleanest and most scenic, with junipers tumbling off the dunes almost to the shore. "**Paradise**", often dubbed "Bubble Beach" in boat-trip jargon owing to volcanic gas vents in the tidal zone, is overrated; the sandy area is small for the hordes descending upon its wall-to-wall sunbeds and two tavernas, while boats attached to the paragliding and banana-ride outfits buzz constantly offshore. "**Camel**" is the smallest and loneliest of these strands, flanked by weird rock formations (but no humped beasts) and protected somewhat from crowds by an unusually steep drive down to a small drinks cantina.

Limniónas

Just east of the turning for Áyios Stéfanos, another marked, paved side road leaves the main route, bound for **Limniónas** (Limiónas), the only north-facing beach and fishing port in this part of Kós. After about 3km along this, bear right at the obvious dirt track, signposted not for Limniónas but for its two rival **tavernas**. Of this pair, the welcoming *Limionas*, closer to the anchorage, serves fish lunches and dinners that justify the trip out here. Swimming is actually a secondary consideration, though there are two compact patches of sandy **beach** to either side of a peninsula that ends in an islet now tethered to Kós with a breakwater.

Áyios Stéfanos

Uninterrupted beach resumes at **Áyios Stéfanos** and continues 5km west to Kamári (see below). This area is overshadowed by a huge, 1970s-vintage **Club Med** complex of well-landscaped bungalows around a less attractive main hotel – but at least the development has its own sewage treatment plant, which is more than can be said for the haphazard development at Kamári. Less commendable is the management's tendency to imply that both local beaches are private.

The badly marked public access road to the public westerly beach begins near the bus stop and cuts through the Club Med grounds, fizzling out just before a peninsula crowned with the exquisite remains of two triple-aisled, sixth-century **basilicas**. Though still the best preserved on the island, these have not been faring well of late, with several columns toppled over since the 1980s. But the entire floors are decorated with excellent **mosaics**, most of them under a protective layer of sand. Visible south of the apse, two peacocks perch upon and drink from a goblet; in the north chapel's aisle, next to the baptistry and font, two mosaic ducks can be seen paddling about.

The basilicas overlook the tiny but striking islet of **Kastrí**, sporting a chapel and a distinct volcanic pinnacle. From the sandy cove west of the peninsula it's just a short swim away; in spots you can even wade across. The sea here warms up early in the year and is shallow enough to stay that way into November. As at "Paradise", gas bubbles up from the ocean floor, which offers the best snorkelling on an island not known for it owing to a sandy seabed.

Kamári

Essentially the shore annexe of Kéfalos (see below), **KAMÁRI** is a growing resort of scrappy, rapidly multiplying breeze-blocks, pitched a few notches above Kardhámena, though even here the British tour operator *Thomson* has a hammerlock on much of the place. The developed strip, a myriad of lower-rise rooms, self-catering studios and tavernas, thins out a bit as you head south towards the fishing port; in addition to offering all water sports, in season Kamári serves as an alternative departure point for Níssiros excursions.

More independent **hotels or pensions** that can be recommended include *Sydney* (☎0242/71 286; ④) and the adjacent *Maria* (☎0242/71 308; ③), on the seafront west of the road up to Kéfalos, and *Eleni* (☎0242/71 318; ④), in a quiet inland location on the Áyios Stéfanos side of the bay. *Stamatia's*, at the broadest part of the fairly average beach, is one of the better **tavernas**.

Kéfalos

The end of the line for buses, 43km from Kós Town, is the inland settlement of **KÉFALOS**, which squats on a flat-topped hill looking northeast down the length of Kós. Kéfalos itself, as densely planned as Andimáhia is open, has little to attract the hordes from Kamári other than a few shops, the region's only **post office**, and a few basic **tavernas**. Even the **Knights' castle** here, downhill beside the Kamári-bound road, is rudimentary and unimpressive; the Knights must have thought so too, abandoning it in 1504. But for better or worse, the village makes a staging point for expeditions south into the rugged peninsula that terminates at dramatically sheer Cape Kríkello.

Cape Kríkello

The first point of interest on a tour of the south peninsula is Byzantine **Panayía Palatianí**, 1km south of Kéfalos; a marked path east from the roadside leads within five minutes to this chapel, which incorporates generous chunks of an ancient temple. Some 500m past this, a less conspicuous sign reading 'PALATIA' points down a broader, shady lane to the the site of ancient **Astypalia**, the original capital of Kós until abandoned in 366 BC. The main artefact here is a late Classical amphitheatre with two rows of seats remaining, enjoying a fine prospect over the curve of Kamári Bay.

Immediately past the detour for Astypalia, a dirt track leaves the paved but narrow ridge road and heads west towards the chapel at **Áyios Theológos**, 7km from Kéfalos. This spot offers a seasonal taverna as well as good beaches to either side, though it's a long, bumpy way down – a jeep could be handy – and waves batter the shore when the wind is up.

Further along the ridge route you can make a detour to the cave of **Asprí Pétra**, inhabited in Neolithic times; the side road is well marked, but the final approach path will prove impossible to find, so get precise local directions before venturing this far.

On the western flank of 428-metre Mount Látra with its telecom tower, the appealing monastery of **Áyios Ioánnis Thimianós** (7km from Kéfalos) is pretty much the end of the road for non-4WD vehicles. Set on a natural balcony under two plane trees, the church is locked except during the festival on August 28–29.

Psérimos

PSÉRIMOS would be an idyllic little island were it not so close to Kós and Kálimnos; throughout the season, both of these dispatch daily excursion boats, which compete strenuously to dock at the undersized harbour. In mid-summer, daytrippers blanket the main sandy **beach**, which stretches around the bay in front of the thirty or so houses of the single village; even during April or October you can be guaranteed at least a hundred outsiders daily (nearly double the permanent population). Not surprisingly the islanders are apt to respond to visitors in a rather surly fashion.

There are a couple of other, less attractive beaches to hide away on during the day: sandy **Mathiés**, half an hour east, or pebbly **Marathoúnda**, a forty-five-minute walk to the north. Nowhere on Psérimos, including the monastery of **Grafiótissa**, whose festival takes place on August 15, is much more than an hour's walk away.

Practicalities

When the daytrippers have gone you can, out of season, have the place to yourself, and the islanders become much better humoured. Even during the season there won't be too many overnighters since there's a limited number of **rooms** available. Pick of the several small pensions would be either *Tripolitis* (☎0243/23 196; ③), over Saroukos' taverna, or rooms managed by *Katerina Xyloura* (☎0243/23 497; ③), above her taverna on the eastern side of the harbour. Katerina also acts as postmistress if you want to write home since the island can't support a full-scale post office. There's just one small **store**, not very well-stocked, and most of the island's supplies are brought in daily from Kálimnos. **Eating out** in the evening won't break the bank, and there's plenty of fresh fish in the handful of tavernas. However, in keeping with the islet's Jekyll-and-Hyde personality, lunchtime is a different story, and service has become so bad that excursion boats (see below) now schedule their lunches at Kálimnos tavernas instead.

Getting there and back

Partly because of these recent programme changes, Psérimos is no longer so easy to visit as a full day's trip, from either Kálimnos or Kós. Virtually all boats based at Kós harbour operate daily triangle tours, departing between 9.30 and 10am; stopping for a swim on either Psérimos or adjacent **Platí** islet; lunching in Póthia, the port of Kálimnos; and then pausing for another swim at whichever islet wasn't visited in the morning. If you want to spend the entire day on Psérimos, you'll have to ride one-way on a boat scheduling it as the first stop, and then cadge a lift back on another boat which calls at Psérimos in the afternoon, around 4pm. You should pay no more than forty percent of the full excursion price (currently about 5000dr) for each leg of the journey, and it would probably be a good idea to pack basic overnight gear if the afternoon boat refuses to take you back to Kós for any reason.

The islanders themselves don't bother with the excursion boats but use their own small craft, the *Grammatiki*, to visit Kálimnos for shopping on Monday, Wednesday and Friday (returns early afternoon); if you've been staying a few days, you may well be able to wangle a ride on this or your host's own boat.

Greek script table

Kós	Κός	ΚΩΣ
Andimáhia	Αντιμάχεια	ΑΝΤΙΜΑΧΕΙΑ
Asfendhioú	Ασφενδιού	ΑΣφΕΝΔΙΟΥ
Asómati	Ασώματοι	ΑΣΩΜΑΤΟΙ
Asprí Pétra	Ασπρή Πέτρα	ΑΣΠΡΗ ΠΕΤΡΑ
Áyios Dhimítrios	Αγιος Δημήτριος	ΑΓΙΟΣ ΔΗΜΗΤΡΙΟΣ
Áyios Fokás	Αγιος Φωκάς	ΑΓΙΟΣ ΦΩΚΑΣ
Áyios Ioánnis Thimianós	Αγιος Ιοάννις Θυμιανός	ΑΓΙΟΣ ΙΟΑΝΝΗΣ ΘΥΜΙΑΝΟΣ
Áyios Stéfanos	Αγιος Στέφανος	ΑΓΙΟΣ ΣΤΕΦΑΝΟΣ
Áyios Theológos	Αγιος Θεολόγος	ΑΓΙΟΣ ΘΕΟΛΟΓΟΣ
Brós Thermá	Μπρος Θερμά	ΜΠΡΟΣ ΘΕΡΜΑ
Cape Kríkello	Ακροτήρι Κρίκελο	ΑΚΡΟΤΗΡΙ ΚΡΙΚΕΛΟ

Greek script cont.

Dhíkeos	Δίκεος	ΔΙΚΕΟΣ
Evangelístria	Ευαγγελίστρια	ΕΥΑΓΓΕΛΙΣΤΡΙΑ
Kamári	Καμάρι	ΚΑΜΑΡΙ
Kardhámena	Καρδάμαινα	ΚΑΡΔΑΜΑΙΝΑ
Kermetés	Κερμετές	ΚΕΡΜΕΤΕΣ
Khristós	Χριστός	ΧΡΙΣΤΟΣ
Lámbi	Λάμπι	ΛΑΜΠΙ
Limniónas	Λιμνιώνας	ΛΙΜΝΙΩΝΑΣ
Marmári	Μαρμάρι	ΜΑΡΜΑΡΙ
Mastihári	Μαστιχάρι	ΜΑΣΤΙΧΑΡΙ
Pilí	Πυλί	ΠΥΛΙ
Pláka	Πλάκα	ΠΛΑΚΑ
Platáni	Πλατάνι	ΠΛΑΤΑΝΙ
Psalídhi	Ψαλίδι	ΨΑΛΙΔΙ
Tingáki	Τιγκάκι	ΤΙΓΚΑΚΙ
Ziá	Ζιά	ΖΙΑ
Zipári	Ζιπάρι	ΖΙΠΑΡΙ
Psérimos	Ψέριμος	ΨΕΡΙΜΟΣ
Grafiótissa	Γραφιότισσα	ΓΡΑΦΦΙΟΤΙΣΣΑ
Marathoúnda	Μαραθούντα	ΜΑΡΑΘΟΥΝΤΑ
Mathiés	Μαθιές	ΜΑΘΙΕΣ

Kós travel details

ISLAND TRANSPORT

CITY (*DEAS*) BUSES

Kós Town to: Asklepion (8 daily); Áyios Fokás (half-hourly); Brós Thermá (9 daily); Lámbi (16 daily); Platáni (14 daily).

KTEL BUSES

Kós Town to: Andimáhia, Kardhámena, Kéfalos (3–6 daily); Marmári (10–12 daily); Mastihári (3–4 daily); Pilí (4–5 daily); Tingáki (10–12 daily); Ziá via Evangelístria (2–3 daily).

INTER-ISLAND TRANSPORT

SMALL FERRIES

Kardhámena to: Níssiros (2 weekly on *Chrysoulla*; 55min).

Kós Town to: Kálimnos (1 daily on *Kourounis*).

Mastihári to: Kálimnos (Póthia; 3 daily most of the year on *ANEM – Shipping Company of Mastihari Anonymous*; 1hr). Sailings geared vaguely to arrivals of *Olympic Airways* flight from Athens (☎0242/51 407 for current information).

EXCURSION BOATS

Kardhámena to: Níssiros (1 daily; 1hr).

Kós Town to: Kalimnos (1 daily; 1hr 10min); Níssiros (3–5 weekly; 1hr 30min); Pátmos (3–7 weekly).

NB These are not good value if all you want is transfer to another island; even when sold, one-way tickets work out expensive.

LARGE FERRIES

Kós Town to: Astipálea (1 weekly on *G&A Ferries*); Kálimnos (5–6 weekly on *DANE*, 3–4 weekly on *G&A*; 1–2hr); Kastellórizo (1 weekly on *G&A*); Léros (5–6 weekly on *DANE*, 3–4 weekly on *G&A*; 2hr 30min); Lipsí (1 weekly on *G&A*); Náxos (1 weekly on *G&A*); Níssiros (1 weekly on *G&A*); Páros (1 weekly on *G&A*); Pátmos (5–6 weekly on *DANE*, 3–4 weekly on *G&A*; 4hr); Pireás (5–6 weekly on *DANE*, 3–4 weekly on *G&A*; 12–14hr); Rhodes (5–6 weekly on *DANE*, 5–8 weekly, mostly direct, on *G&A*; 4hr); Sími (1 weekly on *G&A*); Síros (1 weekly on *G&A*); Thessaloníki (1 weekly on *DANE*); Tílos (1 weekly on *G&A*).

NB The *Nissos Kalymnos* calls twice weekly, going north and south, at Kós Town; see Kálimnos "Travel Details" for a summary of its movements.

HYDROFOILS

Kós Town to: Agathoníssi (2 weekly on *Ilio Lines* or *Mamidhakis/ Dodecanese Hydrofoils*); Astipálea (1 weekly in season on *Mamidhakis*); Foúrni (1–2 weekly on *Ilio*, 1 weekly on *Mamidhakis*); Ikaría (1–2 weekly on *Ilio*); Kálimnos (4–7 weekly on *Ilio*, 2 weekly on *Mamidhakis*; 35min); Léros (4–7 weekly on *Ilio* or *Mamidhakis*); Lipsí (1–4 weekly on *Ilio*, 1 weekly on *Mamidhakis*); Níssiros (2 weekly on *Mamidhakis*; 45min); Pátmos (4–7 weekly on *Ilio* or *Mamidhakis*); Pithagório (Samos; 4–14 weekly on *Ilio* or *Mamidhakis*); Rhodes (1 daily in season on *Mamidhakis*; 2hr–2hr 30min); Sími (3 weekly on *Mamidhakis*; 1hr 30min); Tílos (1 weekly on *Mamidhakis*; 1hr 15min); Vathí (Samos; 4–14 weekly on *Ilio* or *Mamidhakis*; 5–6hr).

NB All afternoon itineraries are carried out by *Ilio Lines*. As of writing, *Ilio Lines* schedules from Kós south towards Rhodes had been suspended, but historically they have dovetailed well with *Mamidhakis/Dodecanese Hydrofoils* services.

DOMESTIC FLIGHTS

Kós to: Athens (1–3 daily; 50min); Rhodes (2–3 weekly, Apr–Oct only; 30min).

INTERNATIONAL TRANSPORT

FERRIES

Kós Town to: Turkey (Bodrum; 1–2 weekly in winter, 2 daily in peak season; 45min). Greek-run morning boat accepts foot passengers only; afternoon Turkish boat takes a few cars. Passenger fares are £13.50/$20 one-way or day return, £27/$41 open return, plus the same punitive 8000dr tax as at Rhodes.

Astipálea

Geographically, historically and architecturally, **Astipálea** would be more at home among the Cyclades – on a clear day you can see Anáfi or Amorgós in the west far more easily than any of the other Dodecanese (except the west tip of Kós), and it looks and feels more like these two than its neighbours to the east. Anecdotes relate that the island was mistakenly re-assigned to the Ottomans after the Greek Revolution only because the French, English and Russians had such a poor map at the 1830 and 1832 peace conferences.

Despite its butterfly shape, Astipálea does not immediately impress visitors as the most beautiful of islands. The heights, which

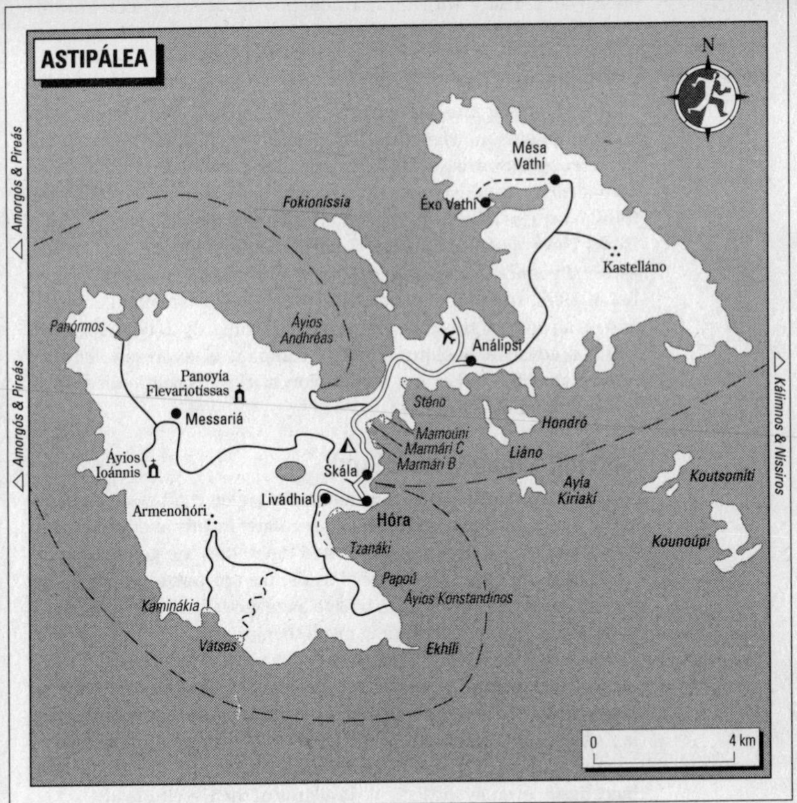

offer modest opportunities for walking, are bleak and covered in thornbrush. Yet the herb *alisfakiá*, made into a tea, flourishes too, and somehow hundreds of sheep survive – as opposed to snakes, which are (uniquely in the Aegean) entirely absent. Lush citrus groves and vegetable patches in the valleys signal the presence of a relatively ample water supply, hoarded in a new reservoir above Livádhia. The few beaches of the generally featureless coastline are sadly often stony or strewn with seaweed.

In antiquity the island's most famous citizen was Kleomedes, a boxer disqualified from an early Olympic games for causing the death of his opponent. He came home so enraged that he demolished the local school, killing all its pupils. Things have calmed down a bit in the intervening 2500 years, and today Astipálea is renowned mainly for its honey and fish; the abundant local catch has only been shipped to Athens since the late 1980s, a reflection of the traditionally poor ferry links in every direction. These have improved recently with the introduction of new services towards Pireus via selected Cyclades, but you still risk being marooned here for an extra day or three outside July or August.

Despite this relative isolation, plenty of people find their way to Astipálea during the particularly short, intense mid-July-to-early-September season, when the 1200 permanent inhabitants are all but overrun by upwards of 7000 guests a day; most are Athens-based Astipaleans, supplemented by a large number of Italians plus the foreign owners of restored second homes in understandably popular Hóra. There are relatively few English-speakers among the arrivals, especially since *Laskarina Holidays* deleted the island from their list in 1995, frustrated by chronically unreliable connections to Kós and its airport. At this time you would be foolhardy to hope for a bed without advance booking – rough camping is expressly frowned upon – and the noise and commotion at the densely built port in particular defies belief.

Getting around the island

A single, overworked **bus** runs along the paved road system linking Hóra, Skála, Livádhia and Análipsi, regularly in July and August, less frequently out of season – the posted timetables are generally reliable. There are only three official **taxis**, far too few to cope in high season when you may have to trudge baggage-laden some distance to your arranged lodgings, adding insult to injury caused by the ungodly arrival times of ferries. Taxis are easier to find at the island's tiny **airport**, up behind Análipsi, where they await daytime domestic flight arrivals. The most reliable of several places that **rent mopeds** is *Lakis & Manolis*, with branches on the dock and just below the square in Hóra. The Astipálea **map** sold locally is often hilariously inaccurate, even by the lenient standards of the Greek islands.

Skála and Hóra

The main harbour of **SKÁLA** or Péra Yialós dates from the Italian era; Astipálea was the first Dodecanesian island they occupied in 1912. Most of the settlement between the quay and the line of nine windmills is even more recent – and, it must be said, neither terribly attractive nor peaceful in summer.

As you climb up beyond the port towards **HÓRA**, the island's official capital and main business district, the neighbourhoods get progressively older. Steep streets are enlivened by the *poúndia*, or colourful wooden balconies, of whitewashed houses draped around the base of the **kástro**, one of the finest in the east Aegean. Originally erected in the thirteenth century, not by the Knights of Saint John but the Venetian Quirini clan, the castle was remodelled in its present form by the Turks who took over the island in 1522. Until well into this century over three hundred souls dwelt within its walls, but depopulation and wartime damage have combined to leave only a desolate shell. The fine groin vaulting over the castle's entrance supports the church of **Evangelístria Kastrianí**, one of two intact here, the other being **Áyios Yióryios** (both usually locked). In contrast to the ongoing renovation activity outside the walls, restoration of the few interior dwellings is forbidden, as they're now the property of the archeological authorities.

Accommodation

Astipálea boasts **accommodation** in all ranges, from spartan, 1970s-vintage rooms with hallway baths to luxury studios. Owing to its layout, high-season noise – particularly the sound of ferries dropping anchor at 3am – reverberates mightily in Skála, so if uninterrupted sleep is a priority, you might want to insist on more atmospheric rooms and restored villas (③–④) in Hóra.

Otherwise, there are two moderately priced, en-suite **hotels** down in the port: the recently refurbished *Astynea* (☎0243/61 209; ④), behind a pedestrian zone, and the *Paradisos* (☎0243/61 224; ③), at the base of the ferry dock – hardly a paradise but open much of the year. *Iy Monaxia* (☎0243/61 290; ③), aka *Viki's* after the proprietress who lived 16 years in Australia, is one lane inland above the dock, beside the former power plant, and has relatively quiet rooms above its taverna. Further up the scale are the *Hotel Vangelis* (☎0243/61 281; ③), above an excellent restaurant, and *Karlos Studios* (☎0243/61 330; ④), both well-appointed units on the east shore of Skála port. A seasonal **campsite** operates among the calamus reeds and tamarisks behind Marmári B' (see p.197), a bay in the slender middle section of the island, 4km along the road to Análipsi and easily reached by bus. However this is low-lying and water-logged all winter, and consequently ridden with mosquitoes during the summer.

Eating and drinking

Being so Athenian-orientated, the restaurant scene is quite distorted seasonally; during August, upwards of 45 eateries operate across the island, few of them high quality and most priced expressly to make a quick buck. The following is a selection of the more reliable or locally orientated restaurants.

Toh Akroyiali sits behind Skála's tiny beach, and though service tends to be haphazard, the food is good. Its inland rival, *Australia*, has a less tasty menu, but the friendliness of the managing family has earned it a following. The *Psitopolio Galini*, up some steps behind the *Hotel Astynea*, is a reliable option for carniverous dinners; another recommendable grill, *Dionysos*, sits near the base of the main uphill pedestrian lane in Hóra. Fish specialists include *Babis* (July–Aug only), on the way to Análipsi, and *Dimitris*, just above the downhill road from Hóra in the area's one-way traffic system. Finally, for excellent home-cooking, *Iy Monaxia* (see above) is open year-round. The best **café/bar** in Skála is currently *Siroko*, beside the antique shop on the quay.

Most of the area's **nightlife** revolves around more atmospheric Hóra, where two traditional *kafenía* on the square are worth a mention: *Kafenio Ouzeri Aigaion* is the spacious alternative to *Kafenio Myli*, the original, unsignposted corner spot with a terrace, opposite the public clinic; at either you can sample *alisfakiá*, the local variant of mountain tea. Relatively subdued **clubs** include *Kastro Bar*, below the east wall of the castle, classiest and longest-lived but open only during peak season, and *La Luna*, with a view terrace, on the road to Livádhia.

Other practicalities

The **post office** and main shopping area are located in Hóra, though the **OTE** is down in the port next to the *Hotel Paradisos*. You can change money at the post office or a bank agent; the island's first proper bank is scheduled to open in late 1996, but until then there are no credit card facilities whatsoever.

The southwest and beyond

Half an hour's walk (or a short, frequent bus journey) west from the capital lies **Livádhia**, a fertile valley with a popular, good beach but a rather ramshackle collection of restaurants immediately behind. You can rent a **room** or **bungalow** in the beach hamlet – for example from the *Nikos Kondaratos* family (☎0243/61 269; ②), who have been known to offer a mattress in the local orchards when rooms are full. For more comfort, *Studios Electra*, near the water (☎0243/61 270 or ☎61 535; ③), has views up to the castle. Among the **tavernas**, *Thomas* and *Kalamia* are among the more durable and decent.

Beaches

If the busy beach here is not to your liking, continue southwest along the footpath that begins near the foundations of the knolltop **basilica** at Livádhia's west end. After a fifteen-minute walk you'll come to **Tzanáki**, where three small shingle coves huddle at the base of sculpted cliffs, with nose-to-nose views of Hóra. The first two are easy to reach, the third more difficult, but their beauty and relative convenience means that you'll share them with upwards of two hundred fully naked others on a typical August day.

Beyond the Tzanáki trio, the coves of Moúra, slimey-rocked and seaweed-strewn, or Papoú, accessible only by boat, are a complete waste of time, and accordingly they're omitted from the map. However the third bay beyond Tzanáki, **Áyios Konstandínos**, just reachable by motorbike along 6km of rough dirt road from Livádhia, is rather more worth an effort. Here you'll find 200m of partly shaded sand and gravel hemmed in by spring-nurtured orchards, as well as a good seasonal taverna.

Around Ekhíli promontory from Áyios Konstandínos lie two south-facing beaches, Vátses and Kaminákia, neither with any permanent amenities. Both are best visited by boat, though the regularity of excursions depends on client numbers and the captain's mood regarding the destination. **Vátses** also has trail access, and slightly better **Kaminákia** lies at the end of a bone-jarring road descending from **Armenohóri**, a ransacked archeological site in the centre of this portion of Astipálea, signposted at a junction above Tzanáki.

Áyios Ioánnis: monastery and waterfall

A favourite outing in the west of the island is the two-hour walk or 45-minute motorbike ride from Hóra to the oasis of **Áyios Ioánnis**, 10km distant. Proceed northwest along the dirt track beginning from the fifth or sixth windmill, passing high above the reservoir, then keep left when a side track goes right towards the remote monastery of **Panayía Flevariotíssas**. Beyond this point the main track (this time ignore a left) curls north at the base of ridge, where the overflow of a spring seeps across the road. After skirting high above the half-dozen isolated farms in the valley of **Messariá**, you reach a junction with gates across each option. Go through the left-hand one, and soon the securely walled orchards of the uninhabited farm-monastery Áyios Ioánnis come into view.

From the balcony of the church, the island of Anáfi can be seen on the horizon, and a steep, faint path leads down to the base of a ten-metre waterfall whose deep bathing pools are currently silted up. Below this, a rather arduous, pathless trek down the valley ends at a fine, pebbly bay. For those walkers who fancy a different route back to Hóra, there's a faint path east towards Armenohóri.

Minor islets

On opposite sides of Astipálea lie a pair of islets; both are accessible by boat from their big neighbour, though usually the only visitors are passing yachts. **Sírna**, southeast of the main island, has a single family of shepherds in permanent residence owing to the spring near its south-facing anchorage. **Lévitha** (Levítha), way off to the north, also has a lone family as wardens, but with school-age children they're only here during summer, spending the winter on Amorgós.

The northeast

Northeast of Skála, a series of bays nestle in the narrow "body" of the "butterfly". Of the three coves known as **Marmári A', B' and C'**, the first is home to the local power plant, while the next one hosts the island's only organized **campsite** (see p.195). The third, reasonably attractive bay is also the start of a path east to the unfortunately named but perfectly swimmable coves of **Mamoúni** ("Bug" or "Critter" in Greek). Beyond Marmári C', **Stenó** takes its name ("Narrow") from the island's width at this point – a mere hundred metres or so; the middle beach east of the isthmus, with clean sand and a seasonal taverna, is the best.

Análipsi (Maltezána) and beyond

ANÁLIPSI, widely known by its alias, Maltezána (after medieval Maltese pirates), is a ten-kilometre bus trip or taxi ride from town. Although it's the second-largest settlement on Astipálea, there's surprisingly little for outsiders besides a narrow, sea-urchin-speckled **beach** (there are other, better beaches east of the main bay) and a nice view south to a horizon dotted with islets. Despite this, blocks of **rooms** are going up at a terrific pace, since the airport lies a mere 700m away. At the edge of the surrounding olive groves are the well-preserved remains of **Roman baths**, with floor mosaics of zodiac signs and personifications of the seasons. Facilities are limited: of the two small **tavernas**, *Obelix* is better than *Asterix*, plus night-owls can enjoy a high-season **disco** (*Ostria*) that's more heavily attended than rival *Faros* in Skála.

Many maps show a fully fledged village of **Kastelláno**, reached by a side road about 8km past Maltezána, while other sources fancifully describe an opulent villa for Mussolini at this spot. There is in fact nothing here besides a pair of camouflage-painted, Italian-built concrete bunkers, standing barely tall enough to cast a shadow for sheep and goats sheltering from the sun.

The motorable road ends at Mésa Vathí, from where an appalling track continues to **ÉXO VATHÍ**, a sleepy fishing village with a single decent taverna and a superb small-craft harbour. However, following several accidents, ferries no longer dock here in winter; instead, foot passengers (no vehicles) are transferred ashore by launch at **Áyios Andhréas**, just west of Marmari C'. Neither place has lights on the quay nor good anchorage, which can result in Astipálea being effectively cut off for days during winter, when Skála is buffeted by prevailing southerlies.

Greek script table

Astipálea	Αστυπάλαια	ΑΣΤΥΠΑΛΑΙΑ
Análipsi	Ανάληψι	ΑΝΑΛΗΨΙ
Armenohóri	Αρμενοχώρι	ΑΡΜΕΝΟΧΩΡΙ
Áyios Andhréas	Αγιος Ανδρέας	ΑΓΙΟΣ ΑΝΔΡΕΑΣ
Áyios Ioánnis	Αγιος Ιοάννης	ΑΓΙΟΣ ΙΟΑΝΝΗΣ
Áyios Konstandínos	Αγιος Κωνσταντίνος	ΑΓΙΟΣ ΚΩΝΣΤΑΝΤΙΝΟΣ
Éxo Vathí	Έξο Βαθύ	ΕΞΟ ΒΑΘΥ
Hóra	Χώρα	ΧΩΡΑ
Kaminákia	Καμινάκια	ΚΑΜΙΝΑΚΙΑ
Lévitha	Λέβιθα	ΛΕΒΙΘΑ
Maltezána	Μαλτεζάνα	ΜΑΛΤΕΖΑΝΑ
Marmári	Μαρμάρι	ΜΑΡΜΑΡΙ
Mésa Vathí	Μέσα Βαθύ	ΜΕΣΑ ΒΑΘΥ
Skála	Σκάλα	ΣΚΑΛΑ
Sírna	Σύρνα	ΣΥΡΝΑ
Stenó	Στενό	ΣΤΕΝΟ
Tzanáki	Τζανάκι	ΤΖΑΝΑΚΙ
Vátses	Βάτσες	ΒΑΤΣΕΣ

Astipálea travel details

INTER-ISLAND TRANSPORT

FERRIES
Astipálea to: Amórgos (2–4 weekly on *G&A Ferries*); Kálimnos (1–2 weekly on *G&A*, 2 weekly on *Nissos Kalymnos*; 2hr 30min–3hr); Náxos (2–4 weekly on *G&A*); Níssiros (1–2 weekly on *G&A*); Páros (2–4 weekly on *G&A*); Pireás (2–4 weekly on *G&A*); Rhodes (1–2 weekly on *G&A*); Síros (1–2 weekly on *G&A*); Tílos (1–2 weekly on *G&A*).

HYDROFOILS
Astipálea to: Kálimnos (1 weekly, July–Aug only).

DOMESTIC FLIGHTS
Astipálea to: Athens (3–4 weekly; 1hr).

Kálimnos

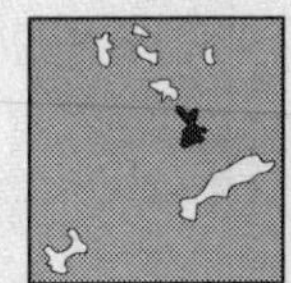

Most of the population of **Kálimnos** lives in or around the large port of Póthia, a wealthy but not conventionally beautiful town famed for its sponge divers. Unfortunately almost all the Mediterranean's sponges, with the exception of a few deep-water beds off Italy, have been devastated by a viral disease, and only three or four of the fleet of thirty-odd boats are still in use. To compensate for this disaster, the island has recently established a tourist industry – so far confined to one string of beach resorts – and customized its sponge boats for deep-sea fishing. The warehouses behind the harbour still process and sell sponges all year round, though most of these are now imported from Asia and America. There are also still numbers of elderly gentlemen about who rely on two canes or walking frames, stark evidence of the havoc wrought in their youth by the "bends", long before divers understood its crippling effects.

The departure of the remaining sponge fleet, usually just after Easter, is preceded by a week of festivities known as *Iprogrós*; the fleet's return, approximately six months later, is the occasion for more uproarious, male-orientated celebration in the port's bars. If you see musicians playing on Dodecanese ferries at these or other times, it's a fair certainty that they are either natives of Kálimnos or on their way there; with two festival seasons per year guaranteed, the island has preserved a vital and idiosyncratic musical tradition.

Kálimnos essentially consists of two cultivated and inhabited valleys sandwiched between three limestone ridges, harsh in the full glare of noon but magically tinted towards dusk. The climate, especially in winter, is alleged to be drier and healthier than that of neighbouring Kós or Léros, since the quick-draining limestone strata, riddled with many caves, retain less moisture. They do, however, admit seawater, which has tainted Póthia's underground wells; drinking water must be brought in by tanker truck from the pure bores at Vathí. In the cultivated valleys, mosquitoes (*kounoúpia*) can a problem, but chemical or electrical remedies are sold locally.

Since Kálimnos is an important hub of two hydrofoil lines, the home port of the very useful local namesake ferry (see "Travel Details"), and also the place where long-distance ferry lines from the Cyclades and Astipálea join up with the main Dodecanesian routes, many travellers only pause here en route to other islands. Yet Kálimnos has sufficient attractions to justify a stay of several days – or even longer, as witnessed by the package industry at the western beaches. Local legend, common to several other spots in Greece, asserts that if you drink island water (salty or otherwise),

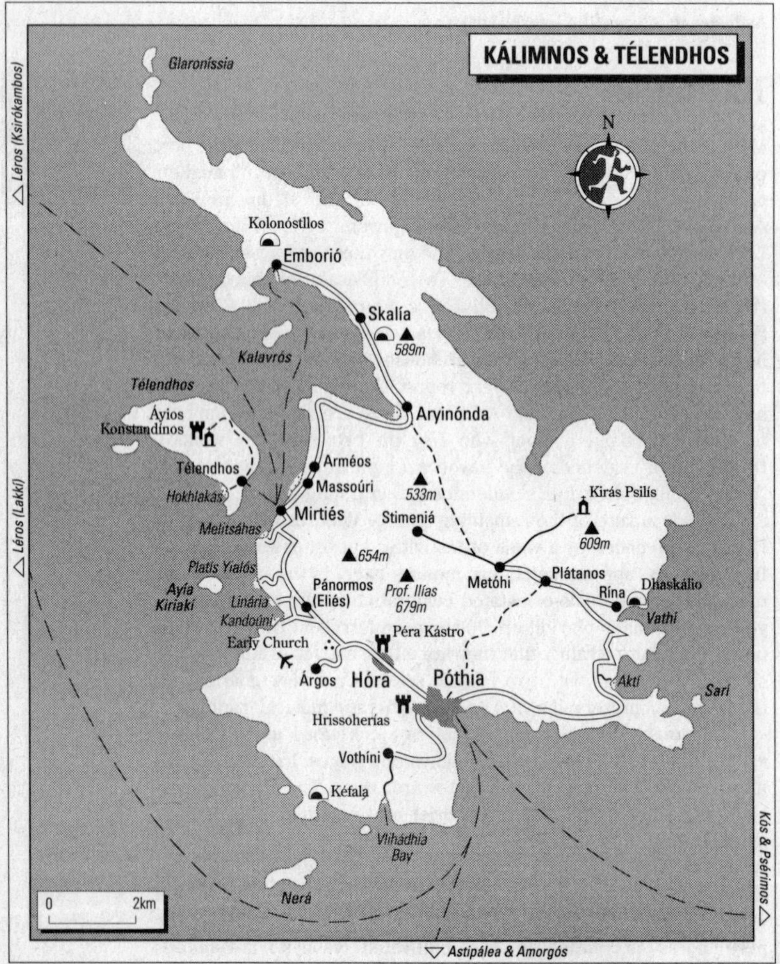

Sponges and sponge-diving

Sponges are colonies of microscopic marine organisms which excrete a fibrous skeleton, increasing its size by about thirty percent annually. When alive, they are dark – almost black – in colour, and can be seen throughout the Dodecanese and east Aegean as melon-sized blobs, anchored to rocks in three to ten metres of water. However, these are mostly wild sponges, impossible to clean or shape with shears; Kalimnian divers are after the so-called *ímero* or "domesticated" sponges, which are much softer, more pliable, and dwell at greater depths.

Before the late nineteenth century, sponge-fishers free-dived for their quarry; weighted with rocks, they descended to the seabed to spear as many sponges as possible on a single breath of air before being hauled to the surface by a safety line. The industrial revolution signalled momentous changes: divers were fitted with insulated suits and breathing apparatus filled by an air-feed line connected to primitive, hand-operated compressors on board the factory boats. This resulted in the first cases of the "bends", or nitrogen embolism; divers working at depths of over 40m and at pressures of several atmospheres would rise too quickly to the surface, so that the dissolved air in their bloodstream bubbled out of solution – with catastrophic results. Not until after World War II was the physiological effect well understood and the first decompression chambers made available; by then hundreds of Kalimnians had been paralyzed, lost their hearing or even died. Furthermore, the new technology enabled the seabed to be stripped with ruthless efficiency; the sponge fleets were forced to hunt further and further from home, finally ending up in Libyan territorial waters until Colonel Gadaffi imposed punitive duties.

In its natural form, even the "domestic" sponge is unusable until processed. First the sponges have the smelly organic matter thrashed out of them, often by being trodden on the boat deck; next they are tossed in a rotary vat with hot sea water for a day or so, to complete the process. In Póthia you can still see a workshop or two where the sponge-vats still spin; in the old days, the divers simply made a "necklace" of their catch and trailed it in the sea behind the boat. A third, optional processing step, that of bleaching the sponges with nitric acid to a pale yellow colour, has been added to accord with modern tastes. But the bleaching process weakens the fibres, so it's best to buy the more durable natural brown ones. In line with the risks, and competition from the production of synthetics, natural sponges are not cheap, even on Kálimnos; a good, hand-size bath sponge with a dense network of small holes will cost the equivalent of about £3/$5 in Greek drachmes.

you'll return to live here one day. And indeed there is an unusually large number of resident foreigners, either married to locals or in business for themselves, presumably attracted by the unpretentious ethos of the main town.

Póthia

Its houses arrayed in tiers up the sides of a natural rock amphitheatre, **PÓTHIA** (sometimes Pothiá), without being particularly picturesque, is colourful and authentically Greek. Your first, and

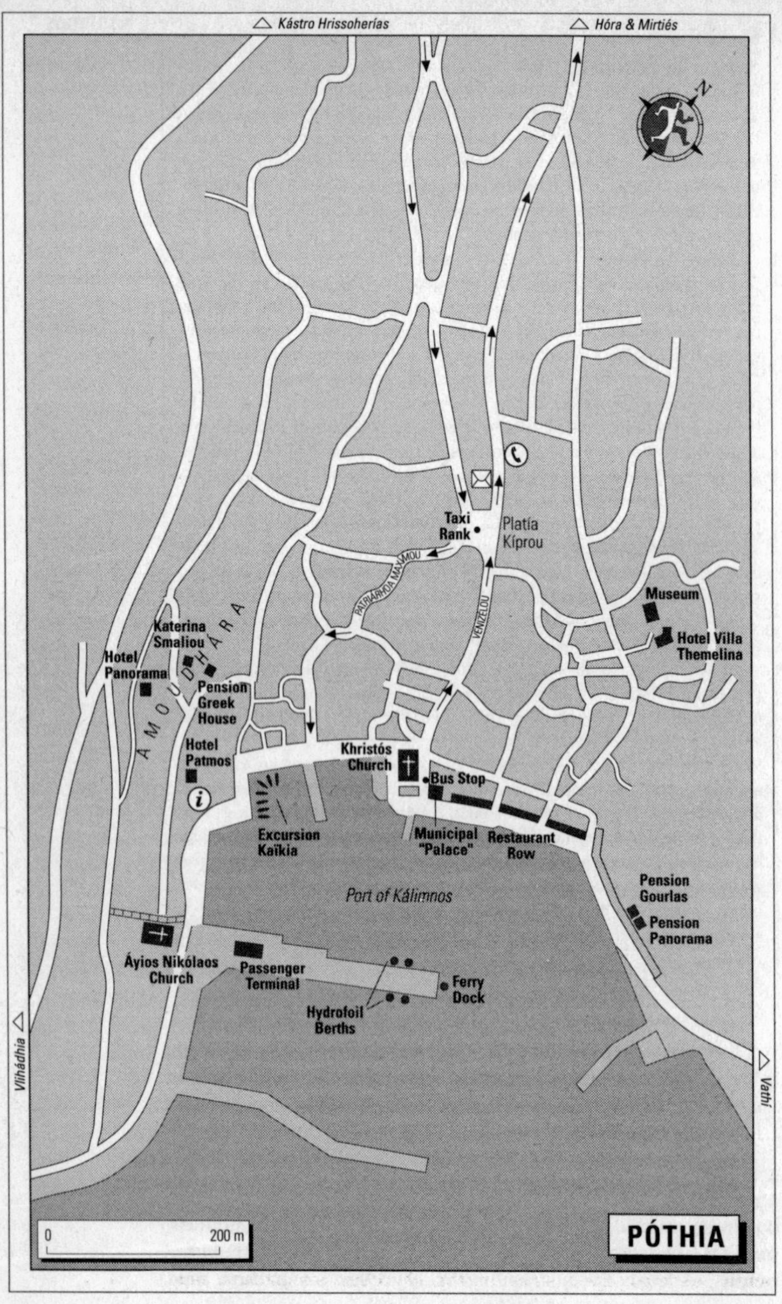
Kástro Hrissoherías
Hóra & Mirtiés
N
Taxi Rank
Platía Kíprou
PATRIÁRHOU MAXÍMOU
VENIZÉLOU
Museum
Hotel Villa Themelina
Katerina Smaliou
AMOUDHÁRA
Hotel Panorama
Pension Greek House
Hotel Patmos
Khristós Church
Bus Stop
Excursion Kaïkia
Municipal "Palace"
Restaurant Row
Port of Kálimnos
Pension Gourlas
Pension Panorama
Áyios Nikólaos Church
Passenger Terminal
Ferry Dock
Hydrofoil Berths
Vlihádhia
Vathí
0
200 m
PÓTHIA

overwhelming, impression will likely be of the phenomenal noise created by exhibitionist motorbike traffic and the cranked-up sound systems of a dozen waterfront cafés. This is not entirely surprising, since with about 11,000 inhabitants, Póthia ranks as the third largest town in the Dodecanese after the main ports of Rhodes and Kós. The effects of package tourism are quarantined well away on the west coast, with the only hint of it here being some yacht flotillas at anchor and a few chandleries catering to them.

Accommodation

Accommodation in town is rarely a problem, since pension proprietors usually meet the ferries (though it must be said that some of the premises touted are less than desirable). The Pothians have so far remained indulgent of short stays, perhaps realizing that the port won't hold most people's interest for more than a day or two. If you prefer to hunt for yourself, the following establishments are worth contacting in advance.

Gourlas (☎0243/29 087). Pension at the start of the Vathí road in the Vouvalis district; sea views but also a bit of road noise. ③.

Greek House (☎0243/23 752 or 29 559). Pension situated in Amoudhára district, 200m north of the *Patmos*. Very friendly, voluble proprietress whose rooms are all en suite, with kitsch decor. Best is the "penthouse", up a terrifying spiral staircase. Open year-round. ② .

Katerina Smalliou (☎0243/22 186), 100m above *Greek House*. No en-suite facilities, but a communal kitchen, better views than lower down, and more subdued interiors. Open March–Nov. ②.

Panorama (☎0243/23 138). Hotel above *Katerina Smalliou*, slightly to the south; well-appointed rooms with balconies living up to the name. Open Apr–Oct. ③.

Panorama (☎0243/29 249). Pension in the Vouvális district, adjacent to *Gourlas*. ③.

Patmos (☎0243/22 750). Hotel in a relatively quiet side street at the west end of the front near the municipal tourist office; just a few rooms, so fills quickly, but open year-round. ②.

Villa Themelina (☎0243/22 682). Close to the museum, another Vouvális family mansion has been converted into the most characterful and elegant hotel on the island, with a pool and two modern extensions in vernacular style. Block-booked by *Sovereign/First Choice* (☎01293/599909) May–Oct, with independent trade accepted only during April. ④.

The town

The most rewarding way to acquaint yourself with Póthia is simply to wander its backstreets, where elegant Neoclassical houses are surrounded by surprisingly large gardens, or craftsmen ply their trade in a genuine, workaday bazaar. During the Italian occupation, local houses were painted blue and white to irritate the colonial overlords, and though the custom is beginning to die out, the Greek national colours are still evident among the otherwise pink and ochre buildings. Even some of the churches are painted blue, though not the eighteenth-century **Khristós** cathedral, whose interior is noteworthy as a sort of impromptu gallery for Kalimnian painters. Other public artworks, in the form of numerous bronze statues dotted about the town, are the works of contemporary sculptors Mikhalis Kokkinos and his daughter Irini.

More formal edification is provided by the local **museum** (Tues–Sun 10am–2pm; 500dr; guided tours only), installed in a grand former residence of the Vouvális family, local sponge magnates. The rather uninspiring, eclectic collection includes a kitsch-furnished *belle époque* parlour and small troves from the island's several caves.

Eating, drinking and nightlife

When **eating out**, the best strategy is to follow the waterfront 500m northeast past the Italian-built municipal "palace" to a line of **fish tavernas** and *ouzerís*. The local seafood speciality is octopus croquettes, more tender than you'd expect. *Minore tis Avyis*, one of the first establishments you'll come to, offers a good mix of meat, seafood, and vegetarian *mezédhes*. At the far east end of the quay, *Barba Petros* (aka *Adherfi Martha*), serves fair-sized if plainly presented portions of some of the best and most reasonable seafood anywhere. Good oven dishes can be enjoyed at *O Ksefteris*, a hole-in-the-wall, traditional taverna well signposted inland east of Khristós church; it's pricier than it looks – perhaps because of too many appearances in guidebook listings. For those with a sweet tooth, *Zaharoplastiki O Mihalaras*, just west of *Psarouzeri O Kambourakis* on the front, is sticky-cake heaven, and occasionally serves puddings. Local ice cream and frozen tortes are on offer at Florentzis, immediately east of Khristós church; there are few outlets in Greece offering such fare, so support this one.

Most night-owls congregate at almost a dozen loud music **cafés** concentrated at the first kink in the harbour quay, opposite the berthing place for the Kós *kaïkia*. At least two of Póthia's old buildings have recently been given a new lease of life as **clubs**: *Apothiki* (Warehouse) east of the church, redesigned as a live music venue, and the bar *Blues Brothers*, in a hundred-year-old house near the sponge shops.

Other practicalities

The **OTE** and the **post office** are virtually opposite each other inland on Venizélou; all **boat** and **hydrofoil agents** line the first hundred or so metres of waterfront as you bear right out of the pier-area gate, and there's an *Olympic Airways* office at Patriárhou Maxímou 17, 200m inland from the quay. **ATMs** can be found at the waterfront branches of the *Ethniki/National* and *Ioniki/Ionian* banks.

The main **taxi** rank is inland on Platía Kíprou, where some of them function as "taxi-buses" (set-route, set-rate, may not depart until full), but **bona fide buses** (regular service as far as Aryinónda in the northwest and Vathí in the east) depart from a stop beside the municipal "palace", with schedules helpfully posted. Except for the line to the main western resorts, services are not terribly frequent, so for any unusual explorations you might consider **hiring a moped** from one of the outlets on the waterfront.

The castles: Hrissoherías and Péra Kástro

From Póthia, the island's main road leads northwest to its main beach resorts. The first place you come to after 1200m en route is a castle of the Knights of St John, **Kástro Hrissoherías**, in the suburb of Míli. Huddled inside the whitewashed battlements is a small monastery, whose usually locked church contains some battered frescoes. The castle's location permits wonderful views southeast over the town to Kós, and north towards Hóra and Péra Kástro.

The island's old capital, **HÓRA** (aka Horió), 1500m further along the main road, is still a village of two thousand or so inhabitants. Steep steps ascend from its highest easterly point to the walled precinct of the Byzantine citadel-town **Péra Kástro**, appropriated by the Knights of Saint John and inhabited until late in the eighteenth century. Inside the imposing gate, all is rubble now except for several well-maintained, whitewashed chapels, some unlocked to permit a glimpse of late medieval fresco fragments.

About 250m beyond Hóra, on the left just past the turning for Árgos village, you can view floor **mosaics** of a ruined, fifth-century church built of masonry from a Hellenistic temple.

Vlihádhia and the Kéfala cave

Some 6km southwest of Póthia, the small bay of **Vlihádhia** is reached via the nondescript village of Vothíni, from which a narrow ravine leads down to the sea. The sand-and-pebble **beach** here, divided into two separate coves, is too unsecluded and litter-strewn to justify a special trip. Its only distinction is the locally based **scuba-diving** operation, since Vlihádhia is one of a limited number of legal diving areas in Greece. During high season there are dives at 2.30pm every weekday, with two (11am and 3pm) on weekends.

Local *kaïkia* also make well-publicized excursions to **Kéfala cave**, a bit to the west. You have to walk thirty minutes from where the boats dock, but the vividly coloured formations are ample reward; the cave was inhabited before recorded history, and later served as a sanctuary of Zeus (who is fancifully identified with a particularly imposing stalagmite in the biggest of six chambers).

West coast resorts: "Brostá"

From the ridgetop pass at Hóra, the road dips into a pine- and eucalyptus-shaded valley leading to the consecutive **beach resorts** of Kandoúni, Mirtiés and Massoúri. Islanders refer to these collectively as "*Brostá*" (Forward), the leading side of Kálimnos, as opposed to "*Píso*" (Behind), the Póthia area.

Kandoúni and Platís Yialós

Kandoúni, some 200m of brown, hard-packed sand favoured by locals, is effectively the shore annexe of the rich agricultural valley-village of **PÁNORMOS** (aka Eliés), with all the trappings of the package-holiday industry scattered between the two. The north end of the same bay, **Linária**, has better sand and is separated from Kandoúni proper by a rock outcrop. Curiously, there is virtually no **accommodation** overlooking the water; the best inland choice here is the *Hotel Elies* (phone/fax ☎0243/47 160; ④), in a garden setting. Decent local **restaurants** include *Taverna Marinos*, serving reasonable Greek food, or *Epicure*, which mixes in western music and more western (vegetarian) fare along with the standard Greek dishes.

If you'd prefer seaview **accommodation**, take the side road to **Platís Yialós**, where *Studios Oceanis* (☎0243/22 789) and *Studios Mousselis* (☎0243/47 757) are possibilities when not block-booked. The sandy **beach** itself, though a bit shorter than Kandoúni, is arguably the best on the island: cleaner than its southern neighbours, more secluded, and scenically situated opposite Ayía Kiriakí islet. Those after even more privacy can hunt out tiny, foot-access-only coves in the direction of Linária. A lone **taverna** at the base of the cliff behind Platís Yialós serves lunches.

Mirtiés and Massoúri

The main road, descending in zigzags, finally meets the sea again 8km from Póthia at **MIRTIÉS**, which shares Kálimnos' tourist trade with **MASSOÚRI**, 1km to the north; both have their fair share of neon-lit music bars, "spesial menus" (sic), souvenir boutiques and the like. The **beach** at Mirtiés is narrow, pebbly and cramped by development, though it does improve to nearly the same standard as Platís Yialós as you approach Massoúri. The closest really good beach to Mirtiés lies 500m south, at **Melitsáhas** cove. Possibly this coast's most appealing feature is its position opposite the evocatively shaped islet of Télendhos (see below), which frames some of the more dramatic sunsets in Greece. It's also possible to go from Mirtiés directly to Léros aboard the daily mid-morning *kaïki* (see "Travel Details").

For **accommodation** (April–Oct only), the *Atlantis Hotel*, on the landward side of the road in Mirtiés, is reasonably good value (☎0243/47 497; ③), while the smallish *Pension Hermes* (☎0243/47 693; ③) overlooks the sea and can be reserved through *Island Wandering* (see *Basics*). A bit more remote, but enjoying the best views of all, is *Niki's Pension* (☎0243/47 201; ③), up the hill between Mirtiés and Massoúri.

Eating out, *Toh Iliovasilema*, owned by the local butcher, is a fine carniverous option despite its tacky decor; for its antithesis, *Nectar*, at Mirtiés, has an extensive western/vegetarian menu, plus free mosquito repellent for clients seated in the garden, while homely, standard-Greek *Barba Yiannis*, at Massoúri, is one of the last tavernas to shut in autumn.

Télendhos

The trip across the strait to the striking, volcanic islet of **Télendhos** is arguably the best reason to come to Mirtiés; little boats shuttle to and fro constantly throughout the day and into the night. Local legend declares that Télendhos is a petrified princess, gazing out to sea after her errant lover; the woman's-head profile is most evident at dusk. According to geologists, the islet split from Kálimnos proper during a cataclysmic earthquake in 554 AD; traces of a submerged town are said to lurk at the bottom of the strait.

Télendhos is car-free and thus blissfully tranquil, though even here increasing numbers of brick-and-concrete constructions are sprouting up. For diversion or sustenance you'll find the ruined, thirteenth-century monastery of **Áyios Vasílios**, a castle at remote **Áyios Konstandínos**, a tiny beach and several tavernas and inexpensive pensions, all in or near the single village. If you want to book ahead (mandatory in summer), try *Pension Uncle George* (☎0243/47 502; ②), above an excellent taverna; *Pension Rita* (☎0243/47 914; ②) next door, with its welcoming café; *Dhimitris Harinos* (☎0243/47 916; ②), at the north end of the waterfront, or *Foukena Galanomati* (☎0243/47 401; ②), with another taverna, away beyond the ruined monastery. A ten-minute walk west along a well-signposted path leads over the ridge to **Hokhlakás** beach, small and pebbly but very scenic, with sunbeds for hire; *Barba Stathis* taverna en route is the closest option for lunch.

Northern Kálimnos

Some 5km beyond Massoúri, **ARYINÓNDA** has a pebble beach backed by a bare minimum of facilities which include the *Sea Breeze Taverna*. **SKÁLIA**, 3km further, has very little to delay you other than a **cave** that's more accessible though less famous than the one at Kéfala. End of the line is **EMBORIÓ**; an irregular bus service covers the 19km between here and Póthia, otherwise you can catch the occasional shuttle boat from Mirtiés. Emborió offers **tavernas** and **accommodation** – *Harry's Taverna Paradise* (☎0243/47 434; ④), with attached garden apartments, and *Themis* (☎0243/47 277; ③), much further inland – but a rather shingly though scenic beach. Beyond Emborió there's another cave, **Kolonóstilos**, with column-like formations after which it's named ("Column–Pillar" in Greek).

Vathí: fjord and valley

Heading east from Póthia, excursions seem initially unpromising, if not downright grim; along the first 4km the road passes some boatyards, a power plant, the gas works, a quarry and the local rubbish dump. None of this prepares you for a sudden bend in the road and the dramatic view over Vathí, a sharp descent below, whose colour provides a startling contrast to the lifeless grey rock elsewhere on

Kálimnos. This long, fertile valley, carpeted with orange and tangerine groves, forms a continuation of the cobalt-blue fjord that penetrates the landscape here. A veritable maze of tracks, drives and lanes threads through these orchards, where numerous 'for sale' signs suggest that citrus cultivation is no longer as profitable as before.

Rína

The simple fjord port of **RÍNA**, 8km from Póthia, makes a reasonable base, especially for walking holidays (see below). You can **stay** here at the *Hotel Galini* (☎0243/31 241; ②), overlooking the boatyard, or the *Pension Manolis* (☎0243/31 300; ②), on the slope to the south, which has cooking facilities and a helpful proprietor. If necessary, there are a few simple rooms at adjacent **tavernas** *Panormitis* and *Popy's*. There's little to distinguish between these establishments, though both are pricier than you'd expect owing to patronage from the numerous yachts that call here.

The steep-sided inlet has no beach to speak of; the closest, about 3km back towards Póthia, is **Aktí**, a functional pebble beach with sunbeds and a single snack bar, reached by a steep cement driveway. Boat excursions from Rina – and strong swimmers – sometimes visit the Neolithically inhabited stalactite cave of **Dhaskálio**, out by the fjord mouth.

Vathí walks

For **walkers**, the lush Vathí valley immediately behind Rína may prove an irresistible lure. However, the most popular hikes (which could be linked back to back to make a very long day) actually begin further up the valley at the hamlets of Plátanos and Metóhi, following old ridgetop paths southwest to Póthia and northwest to Aryinónda. Either hike, involving total elevation changes of 800m, will take between three and four hours; you should carry all essentials with you, especially water as there's no shade once you're out of the orchards. Despite inaccurate tracings in other guides and local maps, the Aryinónda-bound trail avoids Stimeniá. This latter route may be easier to find from the Aryinónda end; the path is marked by orange paint splodges, and vaguely follows the telegraph poles.

Greek script table

Kálimnos	Κάλυμνος	ΚΑΛΥΜΝΟΣ
Aktí	Ακτή	ΑΚΤΗ
Aryinónda	Αργυνώντα	ΑΡΓΥΝΩΝΤΑ
Dhaskálio	Δασκάλειο	ΔΑΣΚΑΛΕΙΟ
Eliés	Ελιές	ΕΛΙΕΣ
Emborió	Εμπορειο	ΕΜΠΟΡΕΙΟ
Hóra	Χώρα	ΧΩΡΑ
Horió	Χωριο	ΧΩΡΙΟ
Kandoúni	Καντούνι	ΚΑΝΤΟΥΝΙ

Greek script cont.

Kástro Hrissoherías	Κάστρο Χρυσοχερίας	ΚΑΣΤΡΟ ΧΡΥΣΟΧΕΡΙΑΣ
Kéfala	Κέφαλα	ΚΕΦΑΛΑ
Kolonóstilos	Κολονόστυλος	ΚΟΛΟΝΟΣΤΥΛΟΣ
Massoúri	Μασούρι	ΜΑΣΟΥΡΙ
Melitsáhas	Μελιτσάχας	ΜΕΛΤΤΣΑΧΑΣ
Metóhi	Μετόχι	ΜΕΙΟΧΙ
Mirtiés	Μυρτιές	ΜΥΡΤΙΕΣ
Pánormos	Πάυορμος	ΠΑΥΟΡΜΟΣ
Plátanos	Πλάτανος	ΠΛΑΙΑΝΟΣ
Platís Yialós	Πλατύς Γιαλός	ΠΛΑΤΥΣ ΓΙΑΛΩΣ
Póthia	Πόθια	ΠΟΘΙΑ
Rína	Ρίνα	ΡΙΝΑ
Skália	Σκάλια	ΣΚΑΛΙΑ
Télendhos	Τέλενδος	ΤΕΛΕΝΔΟΣ
Vathí	Βαθύ	ΒΑΘΥ
Vlihádhia	Βλυχάδια	ΒΛΥΧΑΔΙΑ
Vothíni	Βοθύνοι	ΒΟΘΥΝΟΙ

Kálimnos travel details

ISLAND TRANSPORT

BUSES

Póthia to: Emborió (2 daily on Mon, Wed, Fri); Massoúri (12 daily); Mirtiés (12 daily); Vathí (3 daily in summer only); Vlihádhia (3 daily in summer only).

INTER-ISLAND TRANSPORT

KAÏKIA AND EXCURSION BOATS

Mirtiés to: Léros (Ksirókambos; 1 daily); Télendhos (constantly from dawn till after dark).

Póthia to: Kós Town (1 daily); Psérimos (1 daily).

SMALL FERRIES

Kálimnos to: Kós (Mastihári; 3 daily on *ANEM*).

NB *ANEM* ferries to Kós (☎0242/51 407) have limited or no space for vehicles on their craft.

LARGE FERRIES

Kálimnos to: Agathoníssi (2 weekly on *Nissos Kalymnos*); Astipálea (1–2 weekly on *G&A Ferries*, 2 weekly Mar-Dec on *Nissos Kalymnos*); Kastellórizo (1 weekly on *G&A*, 2 weekly on *Nissos Kalymnos*); Kós (1 daily on *DANE* or *G&A*, 2 weekly on *Nissos Kalymnos*; 1hr 30min); Léros (1 daily on *DANE* or *G&A*, 2 weekly on *Nissos Kalymnos*); Lipsí (1–2 weekly on *G&A*, 2 weekly on *Nissos Kalymnos*); Náxos (1 weekly on *G&A*); Níssiros (1 weekly on *G&A*, 2 weekly on *Nissos Kalymnos*); Páros (1 weekly on *G&A*); Pátmos (1 daily on *DANE* or *G&A*, 2 weekly on *Nissos Kalymnos*; 3hr); Pireás (1 daily on *DANE* or *G&A*; 12hr); Rhodes (1 daily on *DANE* or *G&A*, 2 weekly on *Nissos Kalymnos*; 6hr); Sámos (Pithagório; 2 weekly on *Nissos Kalymnos*); Sími (1 weekly on *G&A*, 2 weekly on *Nissos Kalymnos*); Síros (1 weekly on *G&A*); Tílos (1 weekly on *G&A*, 2 weekly on *Nissos Kalymnos*).

NB The *Nissos Kalymnos*, based at Póthia (☎0243/29 612), operates between March and December.

HYDROFOILS

Kálimnos (Póthia) to: Agathoníssi (1–2 weekly on *Ilio*, 1 weekly on *Mamidhakis*); Astipálea (1 weekly on *Mamidhakis*); Foúrni (1–2 weekly on *Ilio*, 1 weekly on *Mamidhakis*); Ikaría (1–2 weekly on *Ilio*); Kós (4–7 weekly on *Ilio Lines*, 2 weekly on *Mamidhakis*); Léros (4–14 weekly on *Ilio Lines* or *Mamidhakis*); Lipsí (1–4 days weekly on *Ilio*, 1 weekly on *Mamidhakis*); Pátmos (4–14 weekly on *Ilio Lines* or *Mamidhakis*); Sámos (Pithagório; 4–14 weekly on *Ilio Lines* or *Mamidhakis*); Sámos (Vathí; 4–7 weekly on *Ilio Lines*); Sími (1 weekly on *Mamidhakis*); Rhodes (2 weekly on *Mamidhakis*).

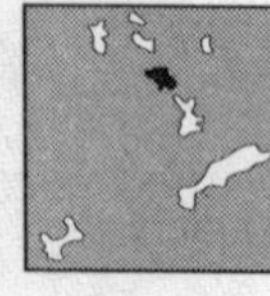

Léros

Léros is so indented with deep, sheltered anchorages that during the last world war it harboured – in turn – the entire Italian, German, and British Mediterranean fleets. Unfortunately, many of these magnificent fjords and bays seem to absorb rather than reflect light, and the island's relative fertility can seem scraggly and unkempt when compared to the crisp lines of its more barren neighbours. These characteristics, plus the island's lack of spectacularly good beaches, meant that until the late 1980s just a few thousand foreigners (mostly Italians who grew up on the island), and not many more Greeks, came to visit each year.

Such a pattern is now history, with at least three package-tour operators forming the vanguard of those "discovering" Léros; the island still offers such understated pleasures as gentle walks, springtime botanizing and the company of islanders unjaded by mass tourism. Moreover, things probably won't change unless the long-mooted extension of the airport runway to accommodate jets takes place.

Not that Léros needs, or strenuously encourages, tourism; various prisons and sanitoria have dominated the Lerian economy since the 1950s, providing direct or indirect employment for over one third of the population. During the junta era, the island supported a notorious detention centre (at Parthéni); today, two mental hospitals are the repository for many of Greece's more intractable psychiatric cases, and another asylum is home to hundreds of mentally handicapped children. The island's domestic image problem is compounded by its name, the butt of jokes by mainlanders who pounce on its similarity to the word *léra*, connoting rascality and unsavouriness.

In 1989 a major scandal emerged when it was discovered that EC maintenance and development funds for the various asylums had been embezzled by administrators and staff, with inmates kept in degrading conditions. Since then, an influx of EC inspectors, foreign psychiatrists and extra funding have resulted in drastic improvements. An infamous courtyard where patients were chained naked has been shut, and other substandard wards phased out in favour of halfway houses scattered across the island, much to the

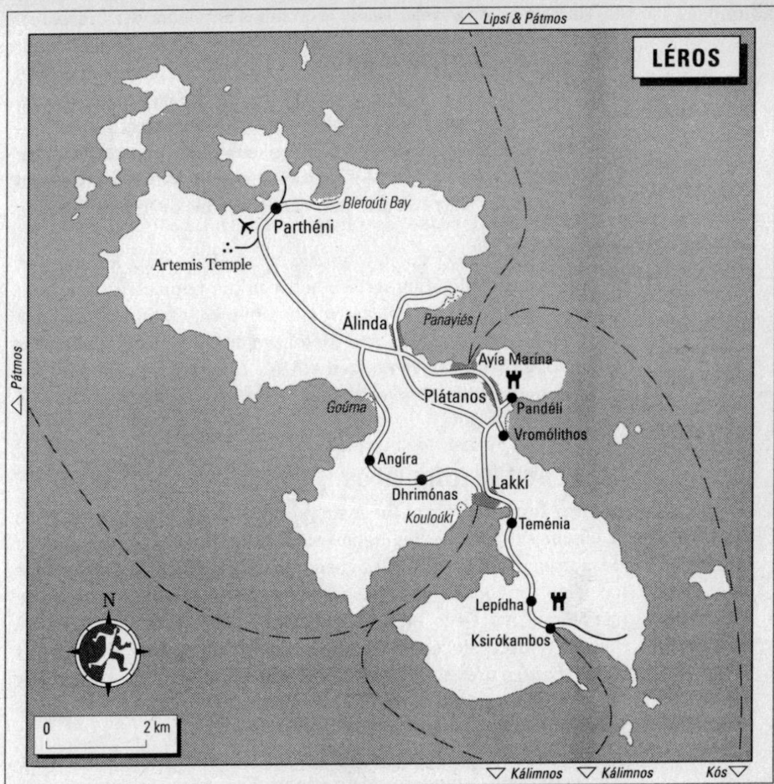

alarm of less tolerant individuals in the nascent tourism trade. Sensational foreign press coverage and a lurid British Channel 4 documentary have ensured that Léros will be a long time overcoming the stigma of its institutional identity, though in fact you have to know where to look to find evidence of it.

More obvious is the legacy of the **Battle of Léros** on 12–16 November 1943, when overwhelming German forces displaced a British division which had landed prematurely on the island following the Italian capitulation. Churchill devoted a page or so of *The Second World War* to this debacle; in a mini-reprise of the Battle of Crete, German paratroopers and supporting aircraft descended unexpectedly on the outnumbered Commonwealth garrison. Bomb nose cones and shell casings have found a second lease of life as gateposts or gaily painted garden ornaments in the courtyards of churches and tavernas. Each year for three days following 26 September, memorial services and a naval festival – one of the island's biggest – commemorate the sinking of the Greek battleship *Queen Olga* during the German attack.

Unusually for a small island, Léros has abundant ground water, channelled into cistern-springs at strategic points, including an enomous capped reservoir marked by a poplar at the Plátanos bus stop. These, plus low-lying ground staked with avenues of eucalyptus trees planted by the Italians, make for an even more horrendous mosquito contingent than on Kálimnos, so come prepared with an anti-bug kit. Some sort of reef or rock-climbing shoes wouldn't go amiss either, as entry to the sea can often be over foot-bruising rocks.

Léros is compact enough for the energetic to walk around, but there is a reasonable bus service between the populated areas, and several outlets for motor- and mountain-bike rental, including a conspicuous one in Lakkí and *Motoland* in Pandéli. The island is hilly enough to make motorized wheels a better bet, though you could manage with a mountain bike between Álinda and Lakkí if you're reasonably fit.

Lakkí and Ksirókambos

All large **ferries** arrive at the main port of **LAKKÍ**. This was once the headquarters of a bustling Italian naval base, which accounts for the extraordinary, rather overdesigned look of the place. Boulevards far too wide for today's paltry amount of traffic are lined with some marvellous Art Deco edifices, including the round-fronted movie theatre (closed since 1985), the primary school and the defunct *Leros Palace Hotel*. Most of them are crumbling if not actually abandoned, the neglect said to be a deliberate policy of the Greeks who would just as soon forget the Italian legacy.

Buses don't meet the ferries; instead, there's a **taxi** rank, charging set fares to standard destinations. Few people stay in Lakkí, preferring to head straight for the resorts of Vromólithos, Pandéli or Álinda (see below). If you do get stuck here, the three local **hotels** are inland and fairly indistinguishable (all ③ and en-suite); the *Katerina* (☎0247/22 460) is likely to be the quietest. You can eat well at *Sotos*, a Swedish–Greek venture with plenty of choice for vegetarians. Lakkí bay, with its leaden waters and a busy boatyard at Teménia, will not appeal to bathers, but the sand-and-gravel beach of **Kouloúki**, just 600m west, has a seasonal snack bar and some pines for shade.

Ksirókambos

From Lakkí, a main road runs 5km south to **KSIRÓKAMBOS**, another possible point of arrival if you're coming by *kaïki* from Mirtiés on Kálimnos. Although billed as a resort, it's essentially a fishing port where people also happen to swim – the beach here is mediocre, though it improves as you head west. Alternatively, there are minuscule, hard-to-reach coves below the coastal track that heads southeast.

Accommodation is available at *Villa Maria* (☎0247/22 827; ③) or, a bit inland, at *Yianoukas Rooms* (☎0247/23 148; ②); the island's **campsite** is in an olive grove at the village of **LEPÍDHA**, 750m back up the road to Lakkí, which also has its own small castle, containing the mosaic floor of an early church as well as Roman and Byzantine house foundations. **Meals** can be had at *Taverna Tzitzifies*, just by the jujube trees at the east end of Ksirókambos, where the road hits the shore.

Pandéli and Vromólithos

Just less than 3km north of Lakkí, Pandéli and Vromólithos together form the fastest-growing resort on the island – and are certainly the most attractive and scenic places to stay.

PANDÉLI (Pandelí) is still very much a working port; a cement jetty was finished in 1994, primarily to benefit the local fishermen rather than the increasing numbers of yachts calling here. The negligible beach is compensated for by a relative abundance of non-package **accommodation**. In ascending order of comfort, choose from the basic, central *Pension Roza* (☎0247/22 798; ②); the *Pension Kavos* (☎0247/23 247; ③), further east, with a pleasant breakfast terrace; the quiet *Pension Afroditi* (☎0247/23 477; ③), inland on the way to *Motoland* bike rental; or, up on the ridge dividing Pandéli from Vromólithos, the *Hotel Rodon* (☎0247/23 524 or ☎22 075; ③), whose peace is disturbed only by wafts of R&B or soul from the *Beach Bar* on a rock terrace some distance below.

The other, long-established **bar** is the civilized *Savana*, at the opposite end of Pandéli, but the soul of the place is the row of waterfront **tavernas**, which come alive after dark. These become less expensive and pretentious as you head east, culminating in *Maria's*, a local institution, decked out in coloured lights and whimsically painted gourds – food often seems a secondary consideration, but the grilled octopus is reliable. About halfway along the front, *Zorba's* offers large portions of well-prepared food, with a good choice for vegetarians.

Vromólithos

VROMÓLITHOS boasts the best easily accessible **beach** on the island, hemmed in by hills studded with massive oaks. The shoreline is mixed gravel and coarse sand, and the sea here is fine, but you have to cross a nasty reef before reaching deeper water. Two **tavernas** behind the beach, *Paradisos* and *Frangos*, trade more on their location than their cuisine (which improves when Greek weekenders are about), but the standard of **accommodation** here is higher than at Pandéli, so Vromólithos tends to be monopolized by package companies. If you're choosing a base in advance through tour-operator brochures, *Castle Vigla*, perched upon a hill to the south, is well worth reserving. Otherwise try *Tony's Beach Rooms & Studios* (☎0247/27 742 or ☎25 226; ④), right behind the water, or *Pension Margarita* (☎0247/22 889; ③), inland.

Plátanos and Ayía Marína

The Neoclassical and vernacular houses of **PLÁTANOS**, the island capital 1km west of Pandéli, are draped gracefully along a saddle between two hills, one of them crowned by the inevitable Knights' castle. Locally known as the **Kástro**, this is reached either by a paved but potholed road peeling off the Pandéli road, or by a more scenic stair-path from the central square. The army has decamped to a neighbouring summit, so you are now allowed to take photos of the view and battlements – as ever, most dramatic at sunrise or sunset. The medieval church of **Panayía toú Kástrou**, inside the gate, houses a small **museum** (daily 8.30am–12.30pm, plus Weds, Sat and Sun 4–8pm; token admission), though its carved *témblon* and naïve oratory are more remarkable than the sparse exhibits, which incongruously include a certified chunk of the Berlin Wall.

Except for *Hotel Eleftheria* (☎0247/23 550 or 23 145; ③), with en-suite rooms at a peaceful hillside location in town, Plátanos is not really a place to stay or eat, although it does have good **amenities** – including no less than seven hairdressers. *Leros Travel*, the main representative for *G&A Ferries*, is conveniently located next door to *Olympic Airways*, near the central stop and posted schedule for the **bus**. The **post office** and short-hours **OTE** lie just a few hundred metres down the road towards Ayía Marína.

Ayía Marína

Plátanos merges seamlessly with **AYÍA MARÍNA**, a port 1km north on the shore of a fine bay. If you're travelling to Léros on an excursion boat from Pátmos and Lipsí, or on any hydrofoil, this may well be your point of entry. **Accommodation** in Ayía Marína is rather informally arranged: ask for rooms at the kiosk opposite the middle school or at the *Dhelfini Snack Bar*, and for apartments at *Garbo's*, just up the road to Plátanos. The adjacent *DRM* and *Kastis* **travel agencies** can book rooms elsewhere, and between them arrange tickets for most ferries and both hydrofoil companies. *DRM*, as well as some of the package operators, issue clients with useful sketch maps and information sheets detailing isolated beaches and short walks on Léros.

On the waterfront, *Taverna Ayia Marina* has the broadest and freshest menu of standard Greek dishes, while three musical café-bars on the quay constitute the local **nightlife**. For more unusual **dining**, British-run *Garbo's* (see above), open year-round but evenings only in summer, has hit upon a winning formula of exotic food (including curries) and movie-poster decor to attract a sizeable, year-round local clientele.

Álinda and nearby beaches

ÁLINDA, 3km northwest of Ayía Marína, ranks as the longest-established resort on Léros, with development just across the road from a narrow strip of pea-gravel beach. Most of the half-dozen **hotels** and pensions here – with more under construction – are block-booked by package companies; of these, the hotel *Yianna* (☎0247/23 153; ③) is worth reserving in advance. If showing up on spec, you'll probably have better luck at pensions *Papa Fotis* (☎0247/22 247; ②), on the Ayía Marína side of things, or *Karina* (☎0247/22 716; ②), set in its own gardens.

Good **eating** options at Álinda may not be immediately obvious. *Toh Steki*, next to the cemetery (see below), is arguably the best-value taverna on the island, especially in the evenings for grills and *mezédhes*. The diner at the *Hotel Alinda* serves up much fancier cuisine at prices that are not grossly inflated, a sterling exception to the rule of atrocious hotel-affiliated restaurants in Greece.

An **Allied War Graves cemetery** for the casualties of the 1943 battle occupies a walled enclosure near the south end of the beach; immaculately maintained, it serves as a moving counterpoint to the holiday hubbub outside. The other principal sight at Álinda is the privately run historical/ethnographic **museum** (daily 9am–noon and 6–9pm), housed in the Bellini mansion near the *Pension Karina*. Along with the usual rural impedimenta, you'll find extensive exhibits on the printing trade, including rare documents and clippings.

Panayiés and Goúrna

At the north end of the main Álinda beach strip, you can follow a sign ("**Panayiés** 600m") the stated distance east, past a spring, to a well-situated snack-bar overlooking several gravel coves, the most isolated of which is naturist.

Otherwise, the road towards the north end of the island takes off from the centre of Álinda; within a few hundred metres you pass the well-marked turn-off to **Goúrna**. This is Léros' biggest sandy **beach**: long, hard-packed and gently shelving, with a view west over some islets. But it's also wind-buffeted, strewn with flotsam and currently fringed with rubble and an impromptu car park. Nor are there any facilities, though a paved road loops back over the hills to Lakkí via the tiny hamlets of Angíra and Dhrimónas. Better, if far smaller, beaches can be found by walking along the coast from Goúrna in either direction.

The far north

Seven kilometres from Álinda along the main route north, a marked side track on the left leads to the **Temple of Artemis**, atop a slight rise just west of the airport runway. In ancient times, Léros was sacred to the goddess, and the temple here was supposedly inhabited by guinea fowl – the grief-stricken sisters of the ancient hunter-hero Meleager, who were metamorphosed thus by Artemis following their brother's death. All that remains now are some jumbled walls, no more than two masonry courses high, but the setting is superb.

The onward road skims the shores of sumpy, reed-fringed **Parthéni Bay** before arriving at the eponymous hamlet and army base; in its former capacity as a political prison during the junta era, this must have been a dreary place to be detained, and it's still an unpopular posting for conscripts.

Just over 11km from Plátanos, the paved road runs out at **Blefoúti**, a rather more inspiring sight with its huge, virtually land-locked bay enclosed by greenery-flecked hills. The beach surface and tidal zone are the Lerian norm, but there are tamarisks to shelter under and a decent taverna, *Iy Thea Artemi*, for lunch.

Greek script table

Léros	Λέρος	ΛΕΡΟΣ
Álinda	Αλυντα	ΑΛΥΝΤΑ
Ayía Marína	Αγία Μαρίνα	ΑΓΙΑ ΜΑΡΙΝΑ
Blefoúti	Μπλεφούτι	ΜΠΛΕΦΟΥΤΙ
Goúrna	Γούρνα	ΓΟΥΡΝΑ
Kouloúki	Κουλούκι	ΚΟΥΛΟΥΚΙ
Ksirókambos	Ξηρόκαμπος	ΞΗΡΟΚΑΜΠΟΣ
Lakkí	Λακκί	ΛΑΚΚΙ
Panayiés	Παναγιές	ΠΑΝΑΓΙΕΣ
Pandéli	Παντέλι	ΠΑΝΤΕΛΙ
Parthéni	Παρθένι	ΠΑΡΘΕΝΙ
Plátanos	Πλάτανος	ΠΛΑΤΑΝΟΣ
Vromólithos	Βρομόλιθος	ΒΡΟΜΟΛΙΘΟΣ

Léros travel details

ISLAND TRANSPORT

BUSES

Plátanos to: Parthéni via Álinda in the north, and Ksirókambos via Lakkí in the south (4–6 daily).

INTER-ISLAND TRANSPORT

KAÏKIA AND EXCURSION BOATS

Léros (Ayía Marína) to: Lipsí (1 daily May–Oct); Pátmos (occasionally May–Oct).

Léros (Ksirókambos) to: Kálimnos (Mirtiés; 1 daily May–Oct).

FERRIES

Léros to: Kálimnos (9 weekly on *DANE*, *G&A Ferries* or *Nissos Kalymnos*); Kós (9 weekly on *DANE*, *G&A* or *Nissos Kalymnos*); Lipsí (3 weekly on *G&A* or *Nissos Kalymnos*); Míkonos (1 weekly on *G&A*); Náxos (1 weekly on *G&A*); Níssiros (1 weekly on *G&A*); Páros (1 weekly on *G&A*); Pátmos (9 weekly on *DANE*, *G&A* or *Nissos Kalymnos*); Pireás (9 weekly on *DANE* or

G&A); Rhodes (8 weekly on *DANE* or *G&A Ferries*); Sími (1 weekly on *G&A*); Síros (1 weekly on *G&A*); Tílos (1 weekly on *G&A*); Tínos (1 weekly on *G&A*).

HYDROFOILS

Ayía Marína to: Agathoníssi (1 weekly on *Ilio Lines* or *Mamidhakis/ Dodecanese Hydrofoils*); Foúrni (1–2 weekly on *Ilio*, 1 weekly on *Mamidhakis*); Ikaría (1–2 weekly on *Ilio*); Kálimnos (4–7 weekly on *Ilio* or *Mamidhakis*); Kós (4–7 weekly on *Ilio* or *Mamidhakis*); Lipsí (4–7 weekly on *Ilio*, 1 weekly on *Mamidhakis*); Pátmos (4–7 weekly on *Ilio* or *Mamidhakis*); Sámos (Pithagório and often Vathí; 4–7 weekly on *Ilio* or *Mamidhakis*).

DOMESTIC FLIGHTS

Léros to: Athens, 6–10 weekly in summer, 5 weekly in spring, 4 weekly in winter.

Pátmos

Arguably the most beautiful and certainly the best known of the smaller Dodecanese, **Pátmos** has a distinctive, immediately palpable atmosphere. It was in a cave here that Saint John the Divine (in Greek, *O Theologos* or "The Theologian"), received the New Testament's Revelation and unwittingly shaped the island's destiny. The monastery commemorating him, founded here in 1088 by the Blessed Khristodhoulos (1021–1093), dominates Pátmos both physically – its fortified bulk towering above everything else – and, to a considerable extent, politically. While the monks inside no longer totally control the island as they did for more than six centuries, their influence has nonetheless stopped Pátmos from going the way of Rhodes or Kós.

Despite vast numbers of visitors and the island's established presence on the cruise, hydrofoil and yacht circuits, tourism has not been allowed to take over Pátmos completely. Although there are a number of clubs and even one disco around Skála, the port and main town, drunken rowdies are virtually unknown, and this is one island where you really do risk arrest for nude bathing. Package clients have only recently begun to outnumber independent visitors, and are pretty much confined to Gríkou and a few newish mega-hotels at the west end of Skála. Daytrippers still far outnumber those staying here overnight, and Pátmos seems an altogether different place once the last ship has gone at sunset (except perhaps during July or August). Among those staying, no one nationality predominates, lending Pátmos a healthy mixed feel unique in the Dodecanese. Away from Skála, development of any kind is appealingly subdued if not deliberately retarded, thanks to the absence of an airport. On outlying beaches, little has changed since the early 1980s, though "for sale" signs on a number of seafront fields would suggest that such days are numbered.

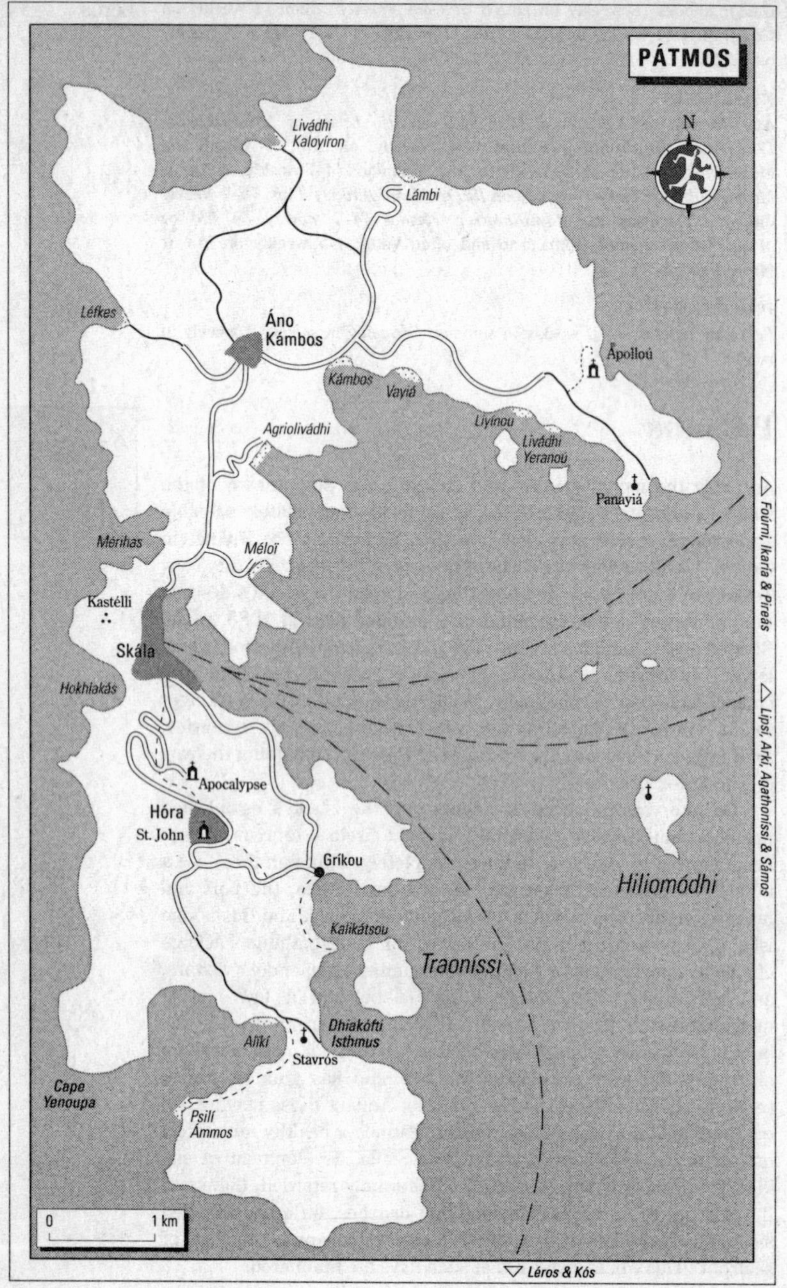

PÁTMOS
N
Livádhi
Kaloyíron
Lámbi
Léfkes
Áno
Kámbos
Apolloú
Kámbos
Vayiá
Agriolivádhi
Liyínou
Livádhi
Yeranoú
Panayiá
Fourni, Ikaría & Pireás
Mérihas
Méloï
Kastélli
Skála
Hokhlakás
Lipsí, Arkí, Agathoníssi & Sámos
Apocalypse
Hóra
St. John
Gríkou
Hiliomódhi
Kalikátsou
Traoníssi
Alíkí
Dhiakófti
Isthmus
Stavrós
Cape
Yenoupa
Psilí
Ámmos
0
1 km
Léros & Kós

Skála and around

SKÁLA seems initially to contradict any solemn, otherworldly image of Pátmos; the waterside, with its ritzy cafés and clientele, is a bit too sophisticated for its own small-town good, and it must be said that some of the world-weary personnel are none too civil at times. During peak season, the quay and commercial district heave by day with hydrofoil excursionists and cruise-ship passengers souvenir-hunting or being shepherded onto coaches for the ride up to the monastery; after dark there is still considerable traffic in the form of well-dressed, overnight visitors. In winter, the town assumes a moribund air as most shops and restaurants close when their owners and staff leave for Rhodes or Athens.

If you feel like heading out straight away, the most obvious possibility is **Méloï beach** (see p.225), 1500m to the north, and one of the most convenient and popular coves on the island; Hóra, a bus- or taxi-ride south up the mountain, is a more attractive base but has few rooms. Yet given time – especially out of peak season – Skála reveals some more enticing corners in the residential fringes to the east and west, where vernacular mansions hem in pedestrian lanes creeping up the hillsides. The town itself dates only from the 1820s, when the Aegean had largely been cleared of pirates, but at the summit of the westerly rise, known as **Kastélli**, you can examine the extensive foundations of the island's ancient acropolis.

Accommodation

Numerous persistent **rooms** touts meet all ferries and hydrofoils. Their offerings tend to be a long walk distant and/or inland – not necessarily a bad thing, as any location near the waterfront, which essentially doubles as the busy road north towards Kámbos, will be plagued by noise. The calmest areas are to the east, along the relatively quiet road to Gríkou; north of town near Mérihas bay, beyond the power plant; and west towards the pebble shore of Hokhlakás. In general, Skála's accommodation is above average in quality, though correspondingly higher priced.

Bona fide **hotel** proprietors sometimes join the fray on the quayside, though it's wisest to reserve such lodgings in advance. In the centre, the *Rex* (☎ 0247/31 242; ③) is a rather well-worn fall-back; the *Galini* (☎ 0247/31 240 or ☎ 31 740; ④), in a cul-de-sac behind the *Rex*, is considerably more upmarket and a good bet for vacancies despite a package-tour presence.

To the east, facing the fishing anchorage, stand the adjacent *Delfini* (☎ 0247/32 060; fax ☎ 32 061) and the smaller *Captain's House* (☎ 0247/31 793; fax ☎ 32 277), both ④ peak season but ③ otherwise; they're reasonably good value, with an assortment of rooms facing the water or inland. Some 150m further towards Gríkou, truly out of town, the *Blue Bay* (☎ 0247/31 165; fax ☎ 32 303; ④) is even more comfortable and completely free of port-related noise.

Saint John on Pátmos

Pátmos is intimately associated with early Christianity, for around AD 95, John the Evangelist – later known as John the Divine – was exiled here from Ephesus on the orders of the emperor Domitian. While John was on Pátmos, supposedly dwelling in a grotto up the hill from the harbour, an otherworldly voice from a cleft in the ceiling bid him set down in writing what he heard. By the time John was allowed to return home, that disturbing finale to the New Testament, the Book of Revelations (or the Apocalypse), had supposedly been disseminated in the form of a pastoral letter to the Seven Churches of Asia Minor.

Revelations, whoever really wrote it, belongs squarely within the Judeo-Christian tradition of apocalyptic books, with titanic battles in heaven and on earth, supernatural visions, plus lurid descriptions of the fates awaiting the saved and the damned following the Last Judgement. As with other similar books in the Old Testament, Revelations is a product of troubled times, when the religion of the elect – whether Judaism or Christianity – was powerless and thus humiliated in secular terms. Some cosmological justification had to be found for this, so emphasis was laid on the imminence of the Last Days. Of all the chapters of the Bible, Revelations is still among the most amenable to subjective application by fanatics, and was in use as a rhetorical and theological weapon within a century of appearing. Its vivid imagery lent itself easily to depiction in frescoes, adorning the refectories of numerous Byzantine monasteries and the narthexes of Orthodox churches, conveying a salutary message to illiterate medieval parishioners.

In addition to transcribing the Apocalypse, John supposedly wrote his Gospel on Pátmos, and also expended considerable effort combating paganism, most notably in the person of an evil local wizard, **Kynops**. In an episode related by John's disciple Prokhoros, Kynops challenged the saint to a duel of miracles; the magician's stock trick involved retrieving effigies of the deceased from the seabed, so John responded by petrifying Kynops while he was underwater. A buoy near the edge of Skála harbour today marks a submerged rock that is supposedly the remains of the wizard. Mechanical efforts to remove this marine hazard have all failed, and it is claimed that fish caught in the vicinity taste bad. In the far southwest of the island, a foul-smelling volcanic cave has also been identified as a favourite haunt of the magician, whose name lives on as Cape Yénoupa (the modern form of "Kynops").

Forever after in the Orthodox world, desolate, volcanic topography has become associated with Saint John, and Pátmos with its monitory landscape of igneous outcrops is an excellent case in point. Other nearby examples include the isle of Níssiros, where one of the saint's monasteries overlooks the volcano's caldera, and Lésvos, where another monastery dedicated to him sits atop an extinct volcano, gazing at lava fields.

Best of a cluster north of the power plant are the *Australis* (☎ 0247/31 576; ③) and *Villa Knossos* (☎ 0247/32 189; ③), run by the same family, plus the adjacent *Pension Sydney* (☎ 0247/31 139; ③), whose rooms have attractive terraces. In the same area but closer to Mérihas cove, the newish *Hotel Asteri* (☎ 0247/32 465 or ☎ 31 347; ④) is well laid out and boasts some sea views.

Out towards Hokhlakás, most easily reached by following the main commercial pedestrian street inland from the municipal "palace", good-value options include the comfortable, hillside *Summer* (☎ 0247/31 769; ④) or the more modest *Sunset* (☎ 0247/31 411; ③). Hokhlakás cove itself is not especially good for swimming; if you're keen to stay nearer a proper beach, there's a good but overpriced **campsite** at Méloï, together with some **rooms** – best are those run by *Loula Koumendhourou* (☎ 0247/32 281; ③), on the slope south of the bay – and a couple of **tavernas**. Of the latter, *Melloi* (alias *Stefanos'*) is excellent, reasonably priced, friendly and open late in the season; in spring or autumn you may find that this is the closest place to Skála that's open for lunch.

Eating and drinking

Normally there are more than enough places for **eating out** in Skála, though they are subject to sudden crowds when the cruise boats arrive. Prices are pretty similar across the board, with location and style the distinguishing factors. A contender for first prize is *O Grigoris*, serving big portions on the waterfront at the junction with the road up to Hóra; runners-up might be *O Vrahos*, a traditional, barrel-wine-type taverna opposite the yacht anchorage, and *Gorgonas*, a popular seafood *ouzerí* near the fishing port, whose portions tend to be on the small side. *Pandelis* – one lane back from mid-waterfront – is surly and overpriced, but the food is good. For lighter snacks or breakfast, French-run *Skorpios Creperie*, on the way to Hóra, makes a convenient stop, though its opening hours are rather erratic. The *Astoria Cafe*, next to the eponymous travel agency on the quay, is good for reasonable ice cream and coffee; while *Polar Gelateri*a, on the main market thoroughfare, is one of several places selling filled croissants but nearly unique for fruit-and-yoghurt breakfasts.

The biggest **bar** has long been the wood-panelled, barn-like *Café Arion* on the waterside, where the local youth hang out and play cards. Lately a few other clubs have appeared on the scene; *Byblos*, inland, is the place to be seen, while *Kafe Aman*, near the fishing anchorage, has music and outdoor seating.

Other practicalities

Everything else of importance can be found within, or within sight of, the Italian, wedding-cake-style municipal "palace": large ferries anchor directly opposite, the port police occupy the front of the building, the **post office** one of its corners, and the fairly helpful municipal **tourist information** office (daily except Sun, 9am–1pm & 5–8pm) takes up the back, with **bus and boat timetables** posted outside.

Moped and **motorbike rental** outfits are sufficiently numerous, with lowish rates owing to Pátmos' modest size and limited road network. **Excursion boats** to Psilí Ámmos, Lipsí and Arkí/Maráthi all leave at about 10am from just in front of *Astoria Travel*, one of several agencies handling *Gianmar Lines* and *Mamidhakis/ Dodecanese* hydrofoil tickets. *G&A Ferries* and *Ilio Lines* are represented jointly at the back of the central square, while at the south end of the quay, the *Nissos Kalymnos* and *Miniotis Lines* are handled by *DRM*. There are **two banks** (including an *Ethniki Trapeza/National Bank* ATM) and an **OTE** (inland, closed at weekends).

In keeping with its upmarket clientele, Pátmos' alias might be the Isle of the High-Class Souvenirs; numerous **arty boutiques** offer designer jewellery and pottery, batik clothing and fabric, puppets, driftwood art, and so forth.

The monasteries and Hóra

For all visitors to Pátmos, the first order of business is likely to be the hilltop capital of **Hóra**, where the Monastery of Saint John shelters behind its massive defences. Both this monastery, and the Monastery of the Apocalypse (below) are on cruise itineraries, becoming hopelessly crowded in the hour or two after the ships have docked, so keep an eye on the harbour and time your visit accordingly. Both public buses and tour coaches make the climb up here, but the half-hour walk along a beautiful old cobbled path shortcutting the road puts you in a more appropriate frame of mind.

In 1088, the soldier-cleric Ioannis "The Blessed" Khristodhoulos was granted lifetime title to Pátmos by Byzantine Emperor Alexios Komnenos. It had long been Khristodhoulos' ambition to establish a religious community near the site of Saint John's Revelation, and within three years he and his followers had completed the framework of the monastery now visible, as well as a smaller one around the Grotto of the Revelation. The double threats of piracy and the Selçuk Turks meant that from the outset the main monastery was heavily fortified, with buttresses added later to make its hilltop position virtually impregnable.

The original imperial grant also included provisions for tax exemption and the right of the monks to engage in sea trade, clauses exploited to the full by the monastery and usually respected by later Turkish and Venetian rulers. A commercial fleet and extensive landholdings across the Balkans made the monastic community immensely wealthy, enabling it steadily to augment the library inaugurated by Khristodhoulos, which in its prime contained far more than today's 4000 books and rare manuscripts.

The Monastery of the Apocalpyse

Over halfway up the path, pause at the **Monastery of the Apocalypse** (Mon, Wed & Fri 8am–2pm & 4–6pm, Tues, Thur, Sat & Sun 8am–2pm; free) built around the grotto where Saint John heard the voice of God and dictated His words to a disciple,

Prokhoros – yet again supernaturally, it would seem, since Prokhoros apparently lived some centuries after the Evangelist. For many years, a leaflet left for pilgrims pointed out that the "fissure . . . (divides) the rock into three parts, thus serving as a continual reminder of the Trinitarian nature of God" and moreover admonished visitors "to ask yourself whether you are on the side of Christ or of Antichrist". This provocative literature has now vanished, but in the cave wall the presumed nightly resting place of the saint's head is fenced off and outlined in beaten silver.

The Monastery of Saint John

The grotto compound is merely a foretaste of the **Monastery of Saint John** (erratic hours, but theoretically Mon, Tues, Thur & Sun 8am–2pm & 4–6pm, Wed, Fri & Sat 8am–2pm; free; "modest" dress essential). A warren of interconnecting courtyards, chapels, stairways, arcades, galleries and roof terraces (the latter regrettably off-limits), it offers a rare glimpse of Patmian interior architecture, strongly influenced by medieval Crete, owing to the large numbers of Cretans in Khristodhoulos' original working party. Hidden in the walls are fragments of an ancient Artemis temple which stood here before being destroyed by Khristodhoulos.

Off to one side, the **treasury** (same hours; separate 500dr admission fee) merits a leisurely visit for its magnificent array of religious treasures, mostly medieval icons of the Cretan School – including Saint John Damascene wearing what appears to be a *kefiya* – and liturgical embroidery of the same era, particularly two satin shrouds threaded with gold for the *epitáfios* or bier of Christ, carried in solemn procession on Good Friday. Among the multiple donations of the pious from across the Orthodox world, with Russia particularly well represented, a filigreed cross of incredible delicacy stands out. Yet pride of place goes to the eleventh-century parchment *chrysobull* of Emperor Alexios Komnenos, granting the entire island to Khristodhoulos; even earlier are various precious manuscripts and an unusual mosaic icon of Saint Nicholas.

This tallies just a small fraction of the museum's contents; if you get hooked, the well-stocked gift shop at the end offers a catalogue and high-quality reproductions of favourites. The famous **library** is unfortunately off-limits to all except credentialled ecclesiastical scholars.

Hóra

The promise of security afforded by Saint John's stout walls spurred the growth of **HÓRA** immediately outside the fortifications from the late thirteenth century onwards. Despite earthquakes and the Italians' demolition of buildings to create open space, it remains an architecturally homogenous village, with cobbled alleys sheltering dozens of shipowners' mansions, most dating from Pátmos' seventeenth- and eighteenth-century heyday. High, almost windowless walls and monumental wooden doors betray nothing of the opulence within: painted ceilings, pebble-mosaic terraces, flagstoned kitchens with carved cistern heads, carved furniture and embroidered bed-curtains.

Inevitably a certain amount of touristic tattiness disfigures the main ramps approaching the monastery gate, but away from the principal throughfares you stumble upon passages no wider than one person, lined with ruins, blocked by rubble or overgrown with spicey-scented plants rarely disturbed by foot traffic. At night, when the monastery ramparts are floodlit to startling effect, it is tempting to nominate Hóra as the most beautiful settlement in the Dodecanese.

Neither should you miss the **view** from Platía Lódza, named after the remnant of an adjacent Venetian *loggia*. Easiest glimpsed at dawn or dusk, the landmasses to the north – going clockwise – include Ikaría, Thímena, Foúrni, Sámos with the brooding mass of Mount Kérkis, Arkí, Lipsí and the double-humped Samsun Daq (ancient Mount Mycale) in Turkey.

There are over forty "minor" churches and monasteries in and around Hóra, many of them containing beautiful icons and examples of local wood carving; almost all are locked, to prevent thefts, but someone living nearby will have the key. Among the best are the church of **Dhiasózousa**, the convent of **Zoödhóhou Piyís** due west of the village, and the convent of **Evangelismoú**, at the southwest edge of village (daily 9–11am); follow the wall-arrows.

Practicalities

You can **eat** well at *Vangelis*, on the inner square, which usually has a slight edge over nearby *Olympia* in terms of freshness and variety – and a wonderful jukebox. Just below the village, *Aloni* is fairly well regarded as as an evening venue for folk-dance extravaganzas. There are, however, very few places **to stay**; foreigners here are mostly long-term occupants, who have bought up and restored almost a third of the crumbling mansions since the 1960s. Getting a short-term room can be a pretty thankless task, even in spring or autumn; one strategy is to contact *Vangelis* taverna early in the day, or phone ahead for reservations at *Yioryia Triandafyllou* (☎ 0247/31 963; ④) or *Marouso Kouva* (☎ 0247/31 026; ④).

The rest of the island

Pátmos, as a locally published guide once memorably proclaimed, "is immense for those who know how to wander in space and time". For lesser mortals, the island is easy to negotiate on foot or by bus; there's still plenty of scope for **walking** despite a dwindling network of paths, otherwise a single **bus** offers a surprisingly reliable service between Skála, Hóra, Kámbos and Gríkou – the terminal, with a timetable posted up, is right in front of the main ferry dock.

Southern beaches

After the extraordinary atmosphere and magnificent scenery, Pátmos' main attraction is its **beaches**. From Hóra, a paved road (partly shortcut by a path) winds east to the sandiest part of rather overdeveloped **GRÍKOU** (Gríkos), the main venue for Patmian package tourism, such as it is. You may glimpse hapless Gríkou clients walking the 5km to Skála rather than waiting for the infrequent bus. Of the **hotels** here, the *Panorama* (☎ 0247/31 209; ④) is, as the name suggests, one of the best positioned. The beach itself forms a narrow belt of hard-packed sand giving way to large pebbles as you head south toward the strange volcanic outcrop of **Kalikátsou**, honeycombed with caves fashioned by Paleo-Christian hermits. En route you pass the hillside *Flisvos* taverna, the oldest and most reliable one here, which also has a few simple **rooms** (☎ 0247/31 380 or 31 290; ③).

A moped is probably the best mode of transport along the dirt roads from Hóra as far as **Stavrós** chapel on the Dhiakófti isthmus. On the northwest shore of this sprawls **Alikí** beach (no facilities), but most people who've made it out here opt for a thirty-minute walk along the trail southwest to **Psilí Ámmos** beach. This is the only pure-sand cove on the island, with shade lent by tamarisks and a good, lunch-only **taverna**. Cliffs and hills to either side create a dramatic backdrop, though the seabed itself shelves gently. In summer Psilí Ámmos can also be reached by a *kaïki* service, which departs from Skála at about 10am and returns at 3.30pm.

Northern beaches

More, even better beaches can be found in the north of the island, a few still accessible on foot via stretches of old paths that follow the startling, indented eastern shore, though mostly along side roads off the main route north from Skála.

Méloï is not only handy but usually quite appealing: there are tamarisks behind the narrow belt of sand, and good snorkelling offshore. The first beach beyond Méloï, **Agriolivádhi**, is wider at its sandy centre, if less shaded; sunbeds are available, and two tavernas function at high season.

The next beach, **Kámbos**, is popular with Greeks, and the most developed remote resort on the island, with seasonal watersports facilities and two tavernas, though its appeal is diminished somewhat by a rock shelf in the shallows and the road directly behind. **ÁNO KÁMBOS**, 600m west and uphill, is the only proper village on Pátmos besides Skála and Hóra; this is the northernmost stop for the bus, which turns around at the cobbled *platía* beside the church and two *kafenía*.

East of Kámbos beach, there are several more coves. **Vayiá** (pebbles) and **Livádhi Yeranoú** (sand and gravel) are less visited but arguably more attractive; Yeranoú can offer shade from tamarisks and a seasonal drinks cantina, but is prone to drifting rubbish.

Between them, around the Liyínou headland, lie two pebbly coves popular with naturists and accessible by trail only.

From Kámbos you can also travel north to the bay of **LÁMBI**, best for swimming when the prevailing wind is from the south, and renowned for an abundance of multicoloured volcanic stones. A hamlet of sorts here has **rooms** (☎ 0247/31 778; ②) and one of the best tavernas on the island: *Estiatorio Lambi*, closest to road's end and open late into the year. Weather permitting, Lámbi is also the most northerly port of call for the daily excursion *kaïkia* that ply the east coast in season.

Lipsí

Of the various islets to the north and east of Pátmos, **Lipsí** is the largest, most interesting and most populous, and the one that is beginning to establish a significant tourist trade: Germans in early summer, hordes of Italians later on, plus a recently inaugurated smattering of British package clients. Given all this, plus the regular main-line ferries calling here en route between the Cyclades and the larger Dodecanese, the place can get crowded out in July or August.

During the quieter months, however, Lipsí still makes an idyllic halt, the sleepy pace of life making plausible a purported link between the island's name and that of Calypso, the local nymph who legendarily held Odysseus in thrall for several years. Deep wells from a single spring nurture many small, well-tended farms in the interior, but pastoral appearances are deceptive – four times the relatively impoverished year-round population of six hundred is overseas (principally in Tasmania, for some reason). Most of those who remained behind live around the fine harbour where most of the food and lodging is located; an awful lot (in both senses) of new building is going on at the fringes of the port settlement.

Practicalities

Prime **accommodation** choices include *Rooms Panorama* (☎0247/41 279; ③), *Angeliki Petrandi* (③) and *Studios Barbarosa* (☎0247/41 312; ③), just up the stairway into the town centre. The best **tavernas** are the *Mangos Brothers*' premises, affiliated to the (not especially recommended) *Hotel Kalypso*, and *Toh Dhelfini*, next to the police station. On the waterfront to either side of the *Kalypso*, idiosyncratic *kafenía* and *ouzerís* with non-existent decor offer grilled seafood *mezédhes* in outdoor seating; though not as cheap as they used to be, they're still atmospheric and an almost obligatory pre-dinner social ritual. On or near the elevated village square, behind the cathedral, you'll find the **post office** and an **OTE**; nearby, the combination **tourist office** and **Ecclesiastical Museum** is hilariously indiscriminate, featuring such "relics" as oil from a sanctuary on Mount Tabor and water from the Jordan River. Lipsí is in fact a dependency of the Monastery of Saint John on Pátmos, and is as well sown with blue-domed country chapels as any of the larger Dodecanese.

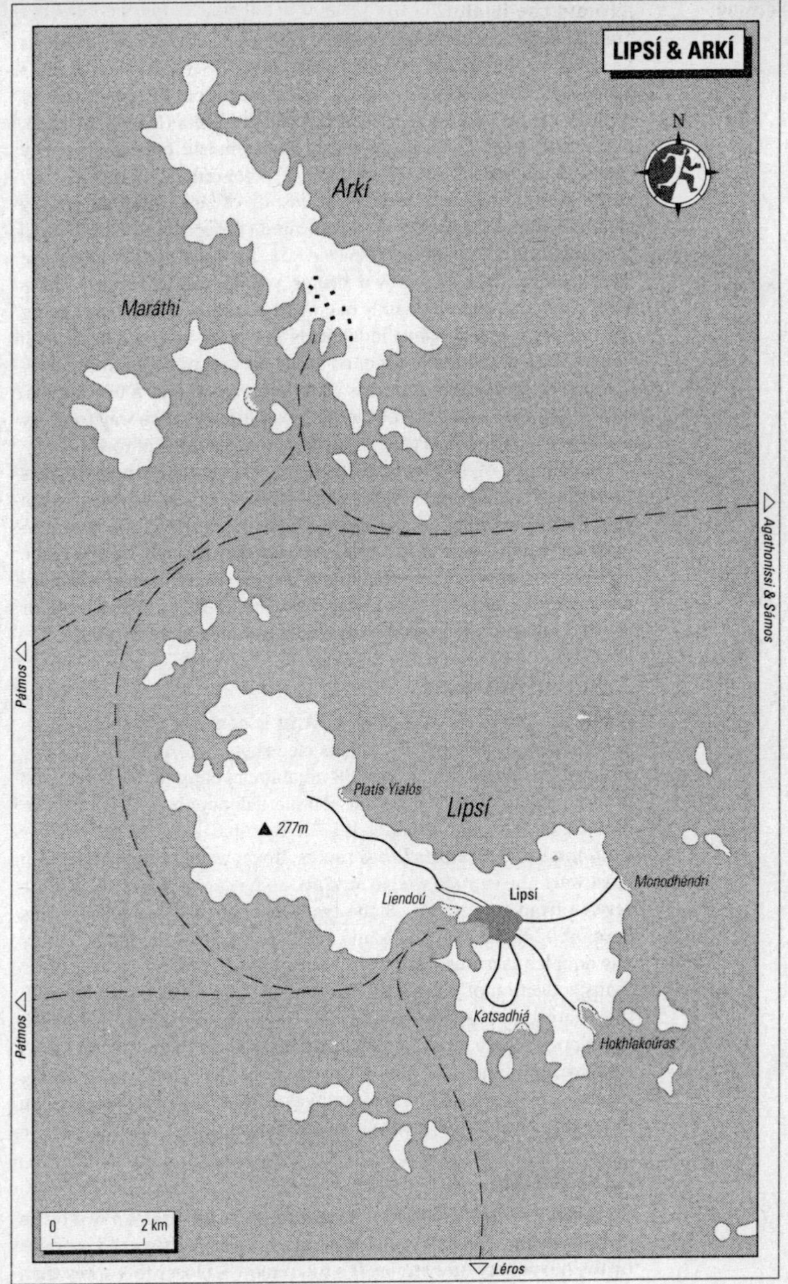
LIPSÍ & ARKÍ
N
Arkí
Maráthi
Agathoníssi & Sámos
Pátmos
Platís Yialós
Lipsí
277m
Monodhéndri
Liendoú
Lipsí
Pátmos
Katsadhiá
Hokhlakoúras
0
2 km
Léros

Around the island

The island's **beaches** are rather scattered. Closest to town is **Liendoú**, immediately to the west, but the most attractive is **Katsadhiá**, a collection of small, sandy coves about 2km south of the port. Here you'll find a very good taverna, *Andonis* (May–Sept only), just inland from *Dilaila*, an eyesore of a music bar which partly redeems its existence by running a semi-official **campsite**. By contrast, **Hokhlakoúra**, at the southeast tip of Lipsí, is rather grubby shingle with no facilities; more appealing (especially to naturists) is **Monodhéndhri**, on the northeast coast. An hour's walk along the road leading west from town brings you to well-protected **Platís Yialós**, a small, shallow, sandy bay with a seasonal snack bar. During high season, enterprising individuals run pick-up-truck-taxis with bench-seats in the load space, or small excursion boats to the various coves. **Motorbike rental** is also now available at a few outlets, paralleling the expansion of the dirt-road network; the way to every beach is (initially at least) well signposted at the edge of town.

A handful of surviving paths often shortcut the newer roads through the undulating countryside – whichever you follow, you can walk from one end of Lipsí to the other in less than two hours. A **carpet-weaving school** for girls operates sporadically on the quay, and on certain summer evenings a *santoúri* (Levantine hammer-dulcimer) player performs. Other than that there's nothing to do or see, but Lipsí is among the better places in which to do nothing.

Arkí and Maráthi

About two-thirds the size of Lipsí, **Arkí** is considerably more primitive, lacking drinking water, mains electricity, a ferry dock, and any discernible village centre. Just 39 inhabitants cling to life here, most of them engaged in fishing, but complete depopulation is conceivable within the next decade. It's an optional stop on the *Nissos Kalymnos* and *Miniotis Lines* routes: if you want to alight here, you must warn the captain well in advance so he can radio for the shuttle service from the island. Of the two seasonal **tavernas-with-rooms** here (☎0247/32 371, the island's only phone; ②), the more remote one doubles as a music pub after hours, courtesy of the owner's enormous collection of jazz tapes. There's also no proper beach on Arkí; the nearest one is just offshore on the islet of **Maráthi**, to which daytrippers come a couple of times a week from Pátmos – links with Arkí are unreliable. The pair of **tavernas** here have fairly comfortable **rooms** (②) for rent, making Maráthi as good or better an option than Arkí for acting out Robinson Crusoe fantasies.

Agathoníssi

The small, steep-sided islet of **Agathoníssi** is still often known by its medieval name Gaídharo, and like Lípsi was formerly owned outright by the monastery on Pátmos. It's too remote – closer to Turkey than its Greek neighbours, in fact – for most day excursions, though some are rather half-heartedly advertised in Pithagório on Sámos. Lately a few intrepid backpackers (mostly German and Italian) have started including Agathoníssi on their itineraries, and since hydrofoil connections dovetail fairly well with the appearances of the *Nissos Kalymnos*, you needn't be marooned here for more than two or three days during the tourist season. "Marooned" is perhaps too harsh a word, as the island has reasonable swimming, a friendly feel and a large enough summer clientele to keep things interesting.

There are no springs on Agathoníssi, so rain-catchment basins and cisterns are ubiquitous, supplemented in dry years by water imported from Rhodes. Nevertheless, the island's 13 square kilometres are greener and more fertile than they appear from the sea; mastic and carob bushes are interspersed with small oaks on the heights, and two arable valleys lie to the west of Mikró Horió hamlet – the largest known accurately enough as Megálos Kámbos (Big Field). Goats, sheep and chickens far outnumber the human islanders for whom they provide the main livelihood, but fresh produce is chronically absent from the few stores, so bring your own. Indeed the principal intrusions of the outside world seem to be a helipad, a pair of fish nurseries and a garrison of six conscripts who may sometimes be found waiting tables in the harbour restaurants in an attempt to alleviate their boredom.

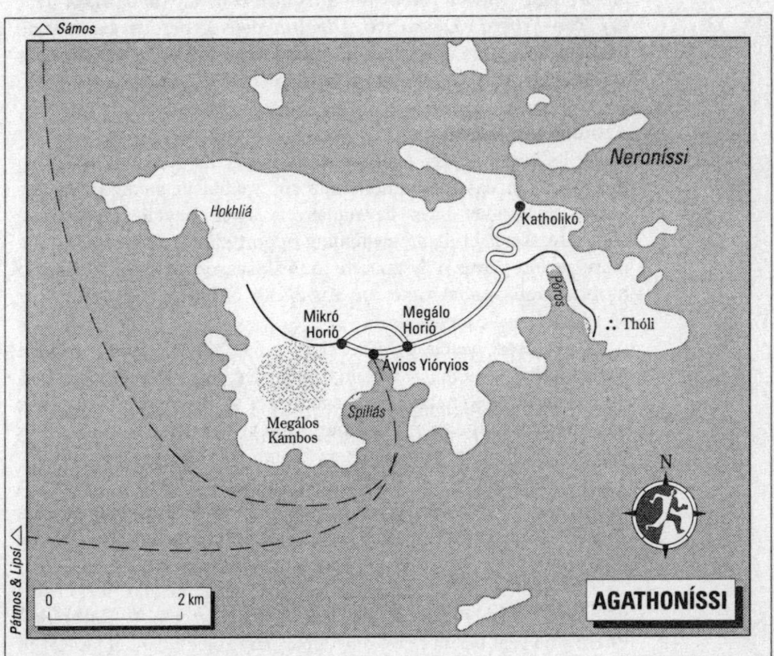

Practicalities

Three of the island's four places to stay, mustering all of sixty beds among them, are down in the port hamlet of **ÁYIOS YIÓRYIOS**. In descending order of preference – distinguished more by location than intrinsic luxuries – they are seafront *Theoloyia Yiameou* (☎0247/23 692 or ☎23 687; ②), with kitchen facilites; the welcoming *Maria Kamitsi* (☎0247/23 690; ②), also just behind the water; and some rooms inland above *George's Taverna* (☎0247/24 385; ②). For **eating** out, either *George's* or *Ioannis* are good bets; proprietor George serves meat and game casseroles, while Ioannis offers fish and meat grills. In addition, he operates a fleet of three *kaïkia* for shopping trips to Sámos (passengers taken), emergency transfers to Pithagório, or shuttles to remote beaches for when you tire of the pebble strand here, which is fine for a dip if you don't mind the lack of privacy.

Of two inland settlements, the fairly attractive hamlet of **MEGÁLO HORIÓ** can muster just over a hundred people (considerably more than its counterpart Mikró Horió, with a population of eleven). Numbers have dropped from several hundred since the last war, but those who've stayed seem determined to make a go of it, and in contrast to so many other islands, there are virtually no abandoned or neglected houses here. **Amenities** consist of two rather haphazardly stocked shops, the *Kafenio Irini* (light snacks only) and a single pension run by the *Katsoulieri* family (☎0247/24 385; ②). The *Kafenio Dhekatria Adhelfia* does generous, home-style lunches, about the only place on island serving food at midday. Not surprisingly, there is no post office, bank or OTE here or at the port.

Around the island

Along its south shore, Agathoníssi is nearly as indented as Léros, making it an excellent anchorage for yachts in summer. At the heads of various bays lie numerous small **beaches**, providing adequate, if not brilliant, swimming opportunities. Boat trips to the more remote coves only operate in peak season; at other times you have to walk – sometimes on roads but often by faint path – or scramble cross-country.

The closest beach to Áyios Yióryios is **Spiliás**, a twenty-minute walk southwest along a recently bulldozed road; this shingle-and-gravel strand is so named for a small cave at its far end. Continuing southwest over the cave headland, without benefit of a trail, brings you to another cove that's quieter, though not necessarily superior.

In the far northwest of the island, ninety minutes away, **Hokhliá** bay provides a more challenging target; there are tracks across the Megálos Kámbos and a trail for a short while thereafter, but the final approach is difficult – seek local advice when setting out.

The cement-paved road heading east out of Megálo Horió leads within 45 minutes (give or take a few trail shortcuts) to **Katholikó**. There's no real beach here, only a partially ruined fishing hamlet of a half-dozen houses under some tamarisks, with an equal number of fishing boats at anchor. A fish farm, owned by an Athenian supermarket chain, floats just offshore in the lee of **Neroníssi**. The closest proper beaches lie twenty minutes' walk south, along **Póros** bay, accessible via a dirt track veering southeast a few minutes before Katholikó. The one at the head of the bay is usually filthy, but the Agathoníssi's best swimming spot – relatively speaking – is found an hour from Áyios Yióryios at **Thóli**. Snorkelling here is rewarding, thanks to a tiny reef, and the beach is partly shaded.

Thóli cove takes its name from the internal arcades of a mysterious late Byzantine or early **medieval structure** just inland, by far the most remarkable sight on the island and unique in the east Aegean. It is neither a public bath nor a manor house, and seems to have no obvious military use; nor does it appear to be part of a monastery, since no church is associated with it. However, its location at the head of a still-used agricultural valley with two threshing cirques just above, plus the discovery of amphorae in the bay below, suggest that it was most probably a trading post and grain warehouse. The architecture matches that of similar Byzantine buildings at Miletus, an important ancient city just out of sight on the Turkish coast.

Farmakoníssi

Off by itself to the south of Agathoníssi, the isle of **Farmakoníssi** often excites the curiosity of travellers who glimpse it from the hydrofoil speeding between Léros and Pátmos. A tiny, scrub-covered dot on the map, it has scant **Roman ruins**; indeed Julius Caesar was supposedly held prisoner here by pirates for some weeks in 77 BC. The island was inhabited by an old shepherd and his dog until the early 1990s, when the shepherd fell ill and was taken off the island to hospital. Someone remembered the dog weeks later and went back expecting the worst, only to discover that the animal had survived by eating wild figs. Recently Farmakoníssi has been selected as a candidate for foreign resettlement under a Greek government scheme (see *Contexts*) that focuses on remote, deserted islands. If you're interested in retiring from the world, contact your nearest Greek consulate or embassy.

Greek script table

Pátmos	Πάτμος	ΠΑΤΜΟΣ
Agriolivádhi	Αγριολειδάδι	ΑΓΡΙΟΛΕΙΒΑΔΙ
Gríkou	Γροίκου	ΓΡΟΙΚΟΥ
Hókhlakás	Χόχλακας	ΧΟΧΛΑΚΑΣ
Hóra	Χώρα	ΧΩΡΑ
Kámbos	Κάμπος	ΚΑΜΠΟΣ
Lámbi	Λάμποι	ΛΑΜΠΟΙ
Livádhi Yeranoú	Λειβάδι Γερανού	ΛΕΙΒΑΔΙ ΓΕΡΑΝΟΥ
Méloï	Μέλοϊ	ΜΕΛΟΪ

Greek script cont.

Monastery of the Apocalypse	Αποκάλυψη	ΑΠΟΚΑΛΥΨΗ
Monastery of St John	Αγιος Ιοάννης Θεολόγος	ΑΓΙΟΣ ΙΟΑΝΝΗΣ ΘΕΟΛΟΓΟΣ
Psilí Ámmos	Ψιλή Αμμος	ΨΙΛΗ ΑΜΜΟΣ
Skála	Σκάλα	ΣΚΑΛΑ
Vayiá	Βαγιά	ΒΑΓΙΑ
Lipsí	Λειψοί	ΛΕΙΨΟΙ
Hokhlakoúra	Χοχλακούρα	ΧΟΧΑΚΟΥΡΑ
Liendoú	Λιεντού	ΛΙΕΝΤΟΥ
Katsadhiá	Κατσαδιά	ΚΑΤΣΑΔΙΑ
Monodhéndhri	Μονοδένδρι	ΜΟΝΟΔΕΝΔΡΙ
Platís Yialós	Πλατύς Γιαλός	ΠΛΑΤΥΣ ΓΙΑΛΟΣ
Arkí	Αρκοί	ΑΡΚΟΙ
Maráthi	Μαράθι	ΜΑΡΑΘΙ
Agathoníssi	Αγαθονήσι	ΑΓΑΘΟΝΗΣΙ
Áyios Yióryios	Αγιος Γεώριος	ΑΓΙΟΣ ΓΕΩΡΓΙΟΣ
Farmakoníssi	Φαρμακονήσι	
Hokhliá	Χοχλιά	ΧΟΧΛΙΑ
Katholikó	Καθολικό	ΚΑΘΟΛΙΚΟ
Megálo Horió	Μεγάλο χωριο	ΜΕΓΑΛΟ ΧΩΡΙΟ
Mikró Horió	Μικρο Χωριό	ΜΙΚΡΟ ΧΩΡΙΟ
Spiliás	Σπηλιάς	ΣΠΗΛΙΑΣ
Thóli	Θόλοι	ΘΟΛΟΙ

Pátmos travel details

ISLAND TRANSPORT

BUSES

Skála (Pátmos) to: Hóra (7 daily); Gríkou (5 daily); Kámbos (3 daily).

KAÏKIA

Skála (Pátmos): daytrips to most east coast beaches & Maráthi.

INTER-ISLAND TRANSPORT

KAÏKIA AND EXCURSION BOATS

Pátmos to: Arkí (sporadically); Kós (1 daily); Léros (sporadically); Lipsí (1 daily); Sámos (1 daily).

Lipsí to: Léros (1 daily May–Oct on *Anna Express*); Pátmos (1 daily May–Oct on *Rena* or *Black Beauty*).

Agathoníssi to: Sámos (Pithagório; sporadically, as passenger traffic or grocery shopping demands).

FERRIES

Pátmos to: Agathoníssi, 2–4 weekly on *Nissos Kalymnos* or *Miniotis Lines*; Foúrni (1 weekly on *Miniotis*); Híos (1 weekly on *Miniotis* or *NEL*); Ikaría (1 weekly on *Miniotis*); Kálimnos (10–11 weekly on *DANE*, *G&A* or *Nissos Kalymnos*); Kavála (1 weekly on *NEL*); Kós (10–11 weekly on *DANE*, *G&A*

or *Nissos Kalymnos*); Léros (10–11 weekly on *DANE*, *G&A* or *Nissos Kalymnos*); Lésvos (1 weekly on *NEL*); Límnos (1 weekly on *NEL*); Lipsí (4–5 weekly on *G&A*, *Nissos Kalymnos* or *Miniotis*); Meyísti (1 weekly on *G&A*); Míkonos (1 weekly on *G&A*); Náxos (1 weekly on *G&A*); Níssiros (1 weekly on *G&A*); Páros (1 weekly on *G&A*); Pireás (8–9 weekly on *DANE* or *G&A*; 9–10hr); Rhodes, (8–9 weekly on *DANE* or *G&A*); Sámos (Pithagório; 2 weekly on *Nissos Kalymnos*, 1 weekly on *Miniotis*); Sámos (Vathí; 1 weekly on *NEL*); Sími (1 weekly on *G&A*); Síros (1 weekly on *G&A*); Thessaloníki (1 weekly on *DANE*); Tílos (1 weekly on *G&A*); Tínos (1 weekly on *G&A*).

Lipsí to: Kálimnos (3 weekly on *G&A* or *Nissos Kalymnos*); Kós (3 weekly on *G&A* or *Nissos Kalymnos*); Léros (3–5 weekly on *G&A*, *Miniotis* or *Nissos Kalymnos*; 1hr 15min); Méyisti (1 weekly on *G&A*); Míkonos (1 weekly on *G&A*); Náxos (1 weekly on *G&A*); Níssiros (1 weekly on *G&A*); Páros (1 weekly on *G&A*); Pátmos (3–5 weekly on *G&A*, *Miniotis* or *Nissos Kalymnos*; 1hr); Pireás (2 weekly on *G&A*); Rhodes (1 weekly on *G&A*); Sámos (Pithagório; 1 weekly on *Minotis*); Sími (1 weekly on *G&A*); Síros (1 weekly on *G&A*); Tílos (1 weekly on *G&A*); Tínos (1 weekly on *G&A*).

Agathoníssi to: Kálimnos, Kós, Léros, Lipsí, Pátmos, Sámos (all 2 weekly April–Dec on *Nissos Kalymnos*).

NB Between January and April, when the *Nissos Kalymnos* is in dry dock, *Miniotis* craft often take over its route and schedule for all points between Sámos and Kálimnos.

HYDROFOILS

Pátmos to: Agathoníssi (1 weekly on *Mamidhakís/Dodecanese Hydrofoils* or *Ilio Lines*); Foúrni (1 weekly on *Mamidhakís*, 3–7 weekly on *Ilio* or *Gianmar Lines*); Ikaría (4–7 weekly on *Gianmar* or *Ilio*); Kálimnos (4–7 weekly on *Mamidhakís* or *Ilio*); Kós (4–7 weekly on *Mamidhakís* or *Ilio*); Léros (4–7 weekly on *Mamidhakís* or *Ilio*); Lipsí (1 weekly on *Mamidhakís*, 2 weekly on *Ilio*); Sámos (Pithagório or Vathí; 4–7 weekly on *Mamidhakís* or *Ilio*); Sámos (Vathí; 4–7 weekly on *Gianmar*).

Lipsí to: Agathoníssi, Kálimnos, Kós, Léros, Pátmos, Sámos (all 1 weekly on *Mamidhakis*, 2–6 weekly on *Ilio*).

Agathoníssi to: Kálimnos, Kós, Léros, Lipsí, Pátmos, Sámos (all 1 weekly on *Ilio* or *Mamidhakis*).

Chapter 4

The East Aegean Islands

The five substantial islands and four minor islets scattered off the north Aegean coast of Turkey form a rather arbitrary archipelago. Although a passing similarity in terms of architecture and landscape can be detected, virtually the only common denominator is the strong individual character of each island. Despite their proximity to modern Turkey, the members of this group bear few signs of an Ottoman heritage, especially when compared to Rhodes and Kós. There's the occasional mosque, with or without battered minaret, and some of the domestic architecture betrays obvious influences from Constantinople, Macedonia and further north in the Balkans, but by and large the enduring Greekness of these islands is testimony to the 4000-year Hellenic presence in Asia Minor just opposite, which only ended in 1923.

This heritage is regularly referred to by the Greek government in its propaganda war with Turkey over the sovereignty of these far-flung outposts – as well as the disputed straits between them and the Turkish mainland. The tensions here are, if anything, worse than in the Dodecanese, aggravated by potential undersea oil deposits. The Turks have also persistently demanded that Límnos, strategically astride the sea lanes to and from the Dardenelles, be demilitarized, but so far Greece has shown no signs of backing down.

The heavy military presence can be disconcerting, especially for lone woman travellers, and large tracts of land are off-limits as military reserves. Yet as on Rhodes and Kós, local tour operators do a thriving business shuttling passengers for inflated tariffs (owing to punitively high docking fees at both ends) between these islands and the Turkish coast, with its amazing archeological sites and teeming resorts. Most of the East Aegean's main ports and towns are not the quaint, picturesque spots you may have become used to in other parts of Greece, but rather heavily urbanized bureaucratic, military and commercial centres. In all cases you should suppress an initial impulse to take the next boat out, however, and delve instead into the worthwhile interiors.

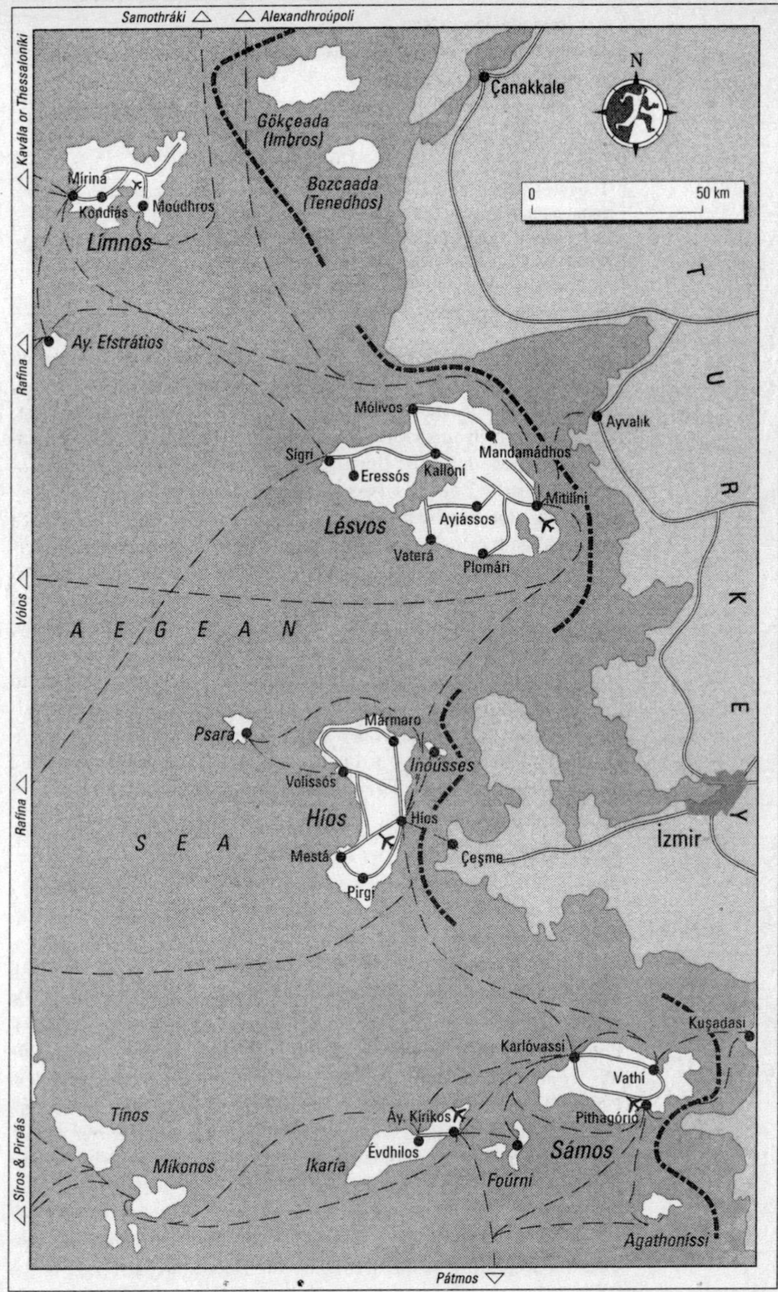
Samothráki
Alexandhroúpoli
Kavála or Thessaloníki
Rafína
Vólos
Rafína
Síros & Pireás
Pátmos
N
Çanakkale
0
50 km
Gökçeada
(Imbros)
Bozcaada
(Tenedhos)
Mírina
Kondiás
Moúdhros
Límnos
Ay. Efstrátios
T
U
R
K
E
Y
Mólivos
Ayvalık
Mandamádhos
Sígri
Eressós
Kalloní
Mitilíni
Lésvos
Ayiássos
Vaterá
Plomári
A E G E A N
S E A
Psará
Mármaro
Inoússes
Volissós
Híos
Híos
Çeşme
İzmir
Mestá
Pirgí
Kuşadası
Karlóvassi
Vathí
Pithagório
Tínos
Áy. Kírikos
Évdhilos
Sámos
Mikonos
Ikaría
Foúrni
Agathoníssi

Accommodation prices

All establishments in this book have a symbol that corresponds to one of six price ranges:

① up to 5000dr ② 5000–7000dr ③ 7000–9000dr
④ 9000–13000dr ⑤ 13000–17000dr ⑥ above 17000dr

£1=370dr; $1= 240dr

The rates quoted for each category represent the cheapest available double room in high season. Out of season, prices can drop by up to fifty percent, especially if you negotiate a stay of three or more nights. Single rooms, where available, cost around seventy percent of the price of a double.

For more accommodation details, see p.34

Sámos, just north of the Dodecanese, is the most frequented island of the group, but if you leave the considerable crowds behind, is still arguably the most verdant and beautiful. **Ikaría**, to the west, remains relatively unspoiled, if a minority taste, with a recently inaugurated airport that's too tiny to have much effect on the number of visitors. Nearby **Foúrni** serves as a haven for determined solitaries, as do the Hiot satellites **Psará** and **Inoússes**, neither of these with any package-tour facilities. **Híos** itself offers far more cultural interest than any of its southern neighbours, but its natural beauty has been ravaged by wildfires, and the development of tourism has until recently been deliberately retarded. **Lésvos** may not impress initially, though once you grasp its old-fashioned, Anatolian ambience, you may find it hard to leave – a substantial number of visitors return to the island. By contrast virtually no foreigners and few Greeks visit remote **Áyios Efstrátios**, and with good reason. **Límnos**, the northernmost of this chain, is a bit livelier, but its appeal is confined mostly to the area immediately around the attractive port town.

Sámos

Lush, seductive and shaped like a pregnant guppie, **Sámos** seems to swim away from Asia Minor, to which the island was joined until Ice Age cataclysms sundered it from Mount Mycale on the Turkish mainland. The resulting 1500-to-2500-metre strait is now the second narrowest distance between Greece and Turkey, and accordingly military installations bristle on both sides, though as you ride in from the airport, signs reassuringly announce "SAMOS UNNUCLEAR ISLAND" (sic). In its variety of mountainous terrain, beaches and vegetation, Sámos has the feel of a much larger island, and before recent development and wildfires took their toll it was indisputably among the most beautiful in the Aegean; yet much of value remains, testimony to its ample natural endowments.

There's little physical evidence for this now, but Sámos was also once the wealthiest island in the Aegean. Under the patronage of the local tyrant Polycrates, it became home to a thriving intellectual community, which included the philosophers Epicurus and Pythagoras, the astronomer Aristarchus and the bard Aesop. Decline ensued when the star of Classical Athens was in the ascendant, though the island's status improved somewhat during early Byzantine times when Sámos headed its own *theme* (imperial administrative district).

Towards the end of the fifteenth century, the Genoese – who controlled Sámos from their base on Híos – abandoned the island to the mercy of Venetian and Turkish pirates. Following their pillaging and massacring, Sámos remained almost completely desolate until 1562, when an Ottoman admiral, Kiliç Ali Paşa, got permission from the sultan to repopulate it with Greek Orthodox settlers recruited from every corner of Greece and Asia Minor. The population was further supplemented after 1923 with an influx of refugees from Anatolia.

This heterogenous descent of today's islanders largely explains an enduring identity crisis and a rather thin topsoil of indigenous culture, and is reflected in village names, which are either clan surnames or adjectives indicating origins elsewhere. Consequently there is no genuine Samiot music, dance or dress, and little that's original in the way of cuisine and architecture (the latter a blend of styles from northern Greece and the Asia Minor coast). The Samians compensated for this by struggling fiercely for independence during the 1820s, but the Great Powers (Britain, France and Russia) handed the island back to the Ottomans in 1830, with the proviso that it be semi-autonomous and ruled by an appointed Christian prince. This period, referred to as the *Iyimonía* (Hegemony), was marked by a mild renaissance in fortunes courtesy of the tobacco and hemp trade, but union with Greece, a bitter World War II occupation and subsequent mass emigration effectively reversed that, until the arrival of tourism during the early 1980s.

Today the Samian economy is increasingly dependent on package tourism, especially in the eastern half of the island, which has borne most of the onslaught. By contrast, the rugged western part is less developed and has retained much of its natural grandeur, despite the persistent efforts of arsonists; since 1990, Sámos has lost roughly one third of its original forest cover, and in some areas – particularly Marathókambos in the southwest – the devastation is total. This is not to put you off the countryside, where there still survive unique and extensive forests of black pine on the peaks and Calabrian pine lower down, but you should brace yourself for seemingly endless vistas of charred tree-trunks, and pay heed to fire-damage warnings when deciding where to spend a two-week package.

The rather sedate clientele is overwhelmingly Dutch, German or Scandinavian, and couples-orientated. The absence of an official campsite on such a large island, and phalanxes of recent self-catering villas and smallish hotels, hint at the sort of custom expected.

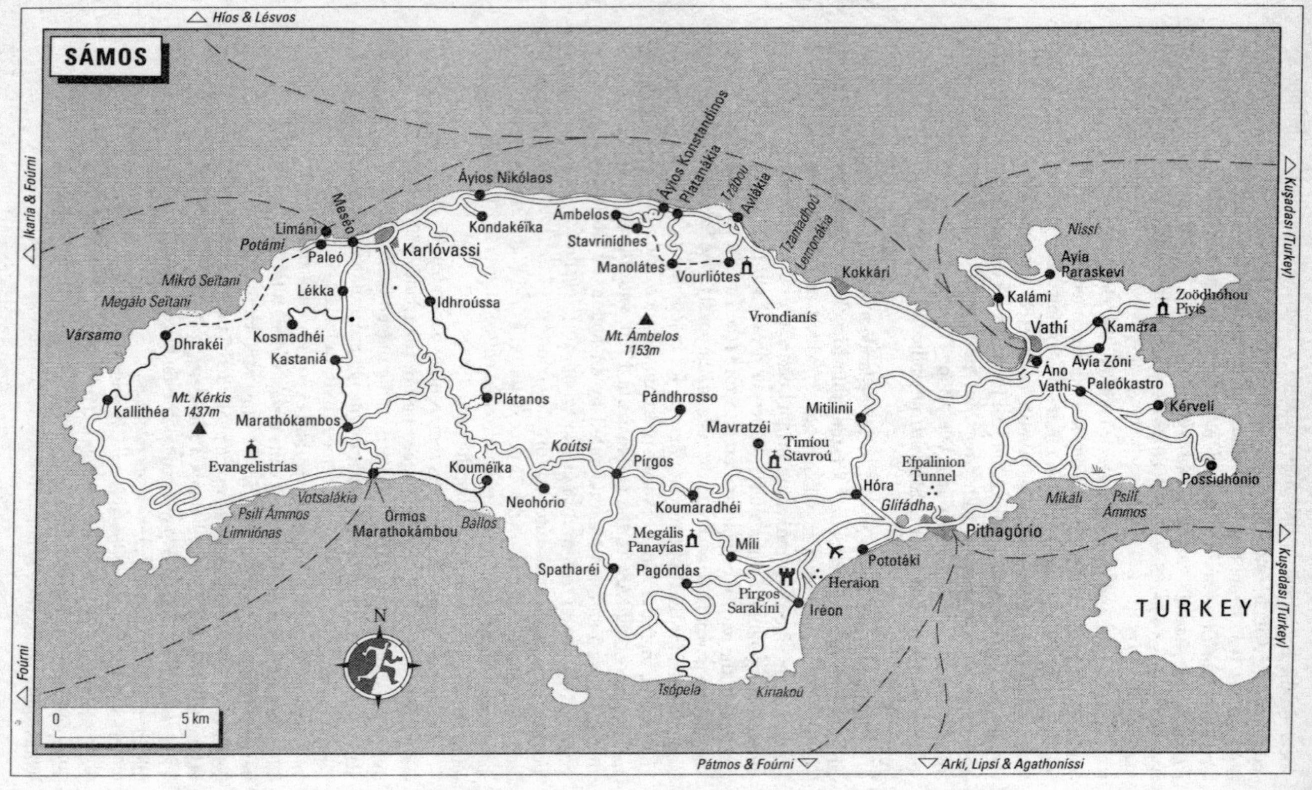
SÁMOS
Híos & Lésvos
Ikaría & Foúrni
Foúrni
Kuşadası (Turkey)
Kuşadası (Turkey)
Pátmos & Foúrni
Arkí, Lipsí & Agathoníssi
TURKEY
Vársamo
Megálo Seïtani
Mikró Seïtani
Potámi
Limáni
Paleó
Meséo
Karlóvassi
Áyios Nikólaos
Kondakéïka
Ámbelos
Stavrinídhes
Áyios Konstandínos
Platanákia
Tzábou
Avlákia
Tzamadhoú
Lemonákia
Manolátes
Vourliótes
Vrondianís
Kokkári
Lékka
Idhroússa
Kosmadhéi
Kastaniá
Dhrakéi
Mt. Ámbelos 1153m
Nissí
Ayía Paraskeví
Kalámi
Zoödhóhou Piyís
Vathí
Kamára
Áno Vathí
Ayía Zóni
Paleókastro
Kérveli
Possidhónio
Kallithéa
Mt. Kérkis 1437m
Marathókambos
Evangelistrías
Plátanos
Pándhrosso
Mitilinií
Mavratzéi
Tímiou Stavroú
Efpalinion Tunnel
Koútsi
Pírgos
Kouméïka
Neohório
Koumaradhéi
Hóra
Glifádha
Mikáli
Psilí Ámmos
Pithagório
Votsalákia
Psilí Ámmos
Limniónas
Órmos Marathokámbou
Ballos
Megális Panayías
Míli
Pototáki
Spatharéi
Pagóndas
Heraion
Pírgos Sarakíni
Iréon
Tsópela
Kiriakoú
N
0
5 km

Arrival

Sámos has no less than three **ferry ports** – Karlóvassi in the west, plus Vathí and Pithagório in the east – as well as an **airport** which lies 14km southwest of Vathí and just 3km west of Pithagório. All ferries between Pireás, the Cyclades and Sámos call at both Karlóvassi and Vathí, as do the smaller *Miniotis Lines* ferries linking the island with Híos, Foúrni, Ikaría and Pátmos. Vathí also receives the weekly *NEL* sailing between northern Greece and the northern Dodecanese, via all intervening islands, the *Ilio Lines* and *Gianmar* hydrofoils to the Dodecanese and north Aegean, plus most hydrofoils and small ferries from Kuşadası in Turkey. Pithagório receives two regular weekly sailings of the *Nissos Kalymnos* from Kós or Kálimnos, and the reliable *Mamidhakis/ Dodecanese Hydrofoils* from as far south as Kós.

Getting around the island

The **bus terminals** (there are no covered stations, just ticket booking offices) in Pithagório and Vathí lie within walking distance of the ferry dock; at Karlóvassi a bus is occasionally on hand to take you the 3km into town from the port. There is no *Olympic Airways* shuttle bus from the airport; you are at the mercy of the numerous taxi drivers, whose meters should not read much more than 2300dr for the trip to Vathí. In high season, **taxis** to the airport or docks must be booked several hours in advance (☎0273/28 404 in Vathí) – best get your hotel to arrange one.

The bus service itself is excellent along the corridors Pithagório–Vathí and Vathí–Karlóvassi via Kokkári, but poor otherwise; you are virtually expected to **rent a motorbike or car**, and with numerous outets, it's easy to find a good deal. An increasing number of **mountain bikes**, ideal for the island's network of dirt tracks, are available for hire, or even for sale; see Vathí "Listings".

Vathí

Lining the steep northeast shore of a deep bay, **VATHÍ** – often confusingly and officially referred to as Sámos – is a busy provincial town which grew from a minor anchorage after 1830 when it replaced Hóra as the island's capital.

The provincial authorities have big plans for the waterfront – green space, a sports centre, outdoor amphitheatre – though these have stalled in mid-execution due to lack of funds and the unwillingness of the coast guard to relinquish a small base. Thus the divided shore highway, equipped with arty lamp standards and baby palm trees, ends ingnominiously in a dangerous diversion. Near the much-needed car park and new fishing harbour you can see fishermen (and -women) peddling their catch before 10am. The dumping of raw sewage in the bay has ceased, but still nobody in their right mind goes swimming at Vathí; the closest appealing beaches are a few kilometres away.

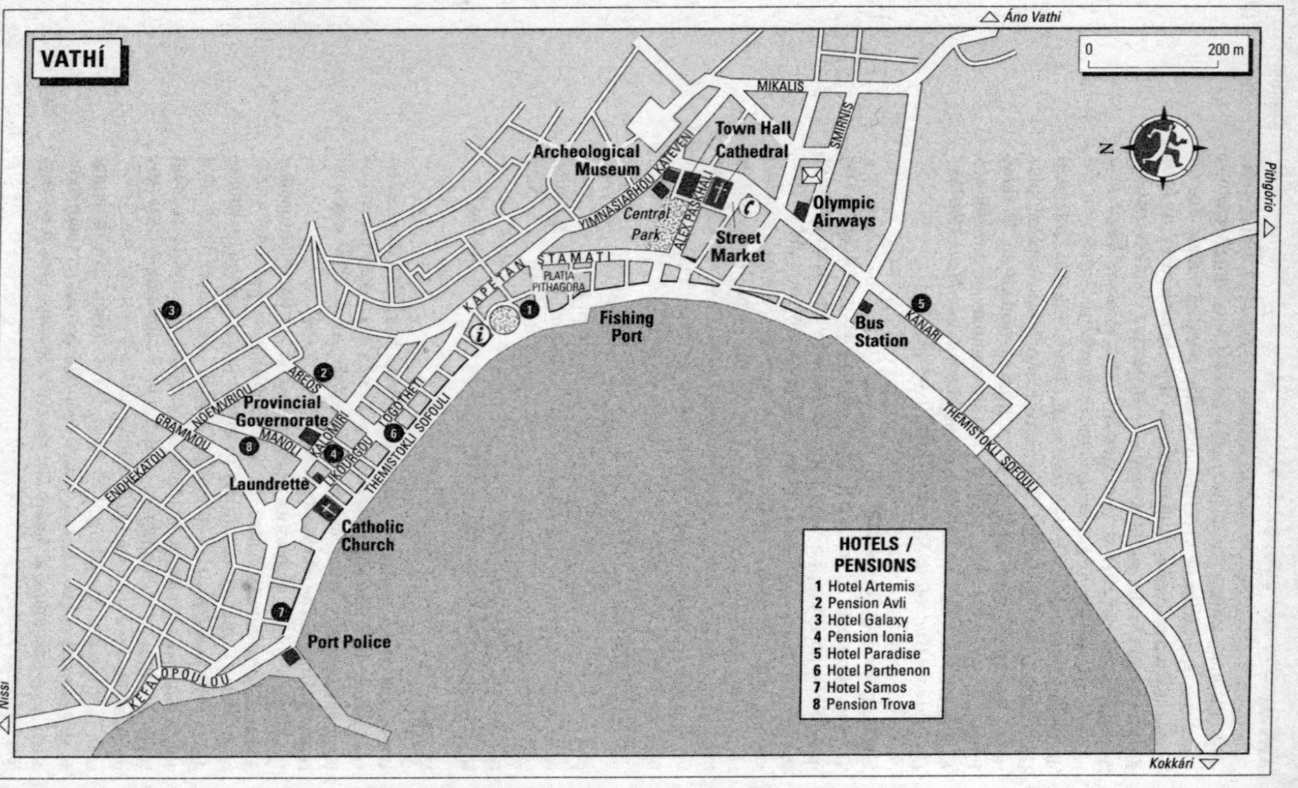
VATHÍ
Áno Vathi
0
200 m
N
Pithgório
Kokkári
Nissi
MIKALIS
SMIRNIS
Town Hall
Cathedral
Archeological Museum
YIMNASIARHOU KATEVENI
ALEX PASKHALI
Central Park
Olympic Airways
Street Market
STAMATI
PLATIA PITHAGORA
KAPETAN
Fishing Port
Bus Station
KANARI
THEMISTOKLI SOFOULI
AREOS
Provincial Governorate
NOEMVRIOU
GRAMMOU
MANOLI
KALOMIRI
LOGOTHETI
LIKOURGOU
ENDHEKATOU
Laundrette
Catholic Church
Port Police
KEFALOPOULOU
HOTELS / PENSIONS
1 Hotel Artemis
2 Pension Avli
3 Hotel Galaxy
4 Pension Ionia
5 Hotel Paradise
6 Hotel Parthenon
7 Hotel Samos
8 Pension Trova

Orientation and information

The main Vathí reference point is the shore boulevard, **Themistoklí Sofoúli**, which describes a 1300-metre arc around the bay. From its northern end at the ferry dock, it's 400m to the traffic circle of **Platía Pithagóra**, universally known as "Lion Square" after its giant feline statue, and about 800m to the major turning inland to the bus terminal, a perennially cluttered intersection next to the ticket booking office. The municipal **tourist information office** is on Ikostipémptis Martíou (July–Aug Mon–Fri 8am–8pm, Sat–Sun 9am–1pm; rest of year as funding permits), not especially cheerful but worth a stop for their large stock of information leaflets, comprehensive bus and ferry schedules and accommodation listings – though staff do not make reservations for you.

Accommodation

Most establishments catering for independent travellers cluster in the hillside district of Katoúni, more or less directly above the ferry dock, and, with the exception of August, you'll have few problems finding affordable **accommodation**. For more luxury you'll have to spread your nets a bit wider, either in the town proper or in the shoreline suburb of Kalámi, to the northwest, where most of Vathí's package industry is based.

Budget

Artemis, just off the "Lion Square" (☎0273/27 792). Basic hotel with en-suite rooms, some with harbour view. ③.

Parthenon, on Themistoklí Sofoúli, about halfway between "Lion Square" and the ferry jetty (☎0273/27 234). This hotel is the oldest (and probably cheapest) place in town, but clean and acceptable aside from bar noise from below. ②.

Avli, Aréos 2 (☎0273/22 939). This wonderful period pension, up a stair-street, is the former convent school of the French nuns (see below), so the rooms, arrayed around a courtyard (*avlí* in Greek), are appropriately institutional; one wing with en-suite units is often reserved by a British package outfit, but it's worth asking. Open May–Oct. ②, ③ for en-suite.

Ionia, Manóli Kalomíri 5 (☎0273/28 782). Recently renovated pension inland, across from the provincial governorate. ②.

Trova, Kalomíri 26 (☎0273/27 759). A pension up the hill from the provincial headquarters. Open May–Oct. ②.

Moderate to expensive

Christiana, Potamáki district (☎0273/23 084; fax ☎28 856). The only accommodation in Áno Vathí, with a large pool and good rustic views. Open April–Oct. ④–⑤ according to season.

Galaxy, Angéou 1, near the top of Katoúni (☎0273/22 665; fax ☎27 679). A surprisingly affordable hotel in garden surroundings with a small pool; frequent vacancies despite appearances on package-group lists. Open May–Oct. ③.

Ionia Maris, Gangoú beach (☎0273/28 428; fax ☎23 108). Among the best hotels in Vathí for service and facilities. Only drawback is the low-lying site: despite effectively monopolizing tiny Gangoú beach, there are no views to speak of. Open May–Oct. ⑤.

Mirini, Kalámi, above Gangoú beach (☎0273/28 452). Easily the most attractive mock-traditional hotel premises, with half-timbering and recycled-tile roof; knock-out bay views too. Open April–Oct. ④.

Panthea, Kalámi, 3km from port (☎0273/22 275). Small and rather remote hotel, but mountain-bike hire and windsurfing school on the premises. Often block-booked by German tour groups. Open April–Oct. ④.

Paradise, Kanári 21 (☎0273/23 911; fax ☎28 754). Hotel with front rooms overlooking the bus stop; side and rear rooms have views of orchards and its pool. Open May–Oct. ④–⑤ according to season.

Samos, the obvious behemoth at the base of the ferry dock (☎0273/28 377; fax ☎28 482). Drops its rates by a category in lean times; popular with Japanese tour groups in winter. ③.

The town

A prominent waterfront curiosity near the ferry jetty is the old French Catholic **church**, labelled "ECCLESIA CATOLICA", disused except for monthly Masses since 1974, when the last nuns departed Sámos after having schooled the elite for nearly a century. Their male compatriots, incidentally, re-introduced the art of wine-making to the island, though the contemporary tipple must bear little resemblance to the ancient stuff acclaimed by Byron ("Dash down you cup of Samian wine..."). The local *oúzo* – particularly the *Yiokarinis* brand – is more highly regarded.

Strolls inland can be more rewarding; you might first visit the museum-like (but expensive) **antique and watch shop** of Mihalis Stavrinos, just off the "Lion Square", where you can invest in assorted precious baubles or rare engravings. The pedestrianized marketplace just beyond – two-thirds authentic, one-third tourist schlock – and tiers of **Neoclassical houses** on stair-lanes are also of interest.

Áno Vathí

The best target on foot, a twenty-minute walk south and 150m above sea level, is the atmospheric hill village of **Áno Vathí**, an officially preserved community of tottering, tile-roofed houses. The village's late medieval churches are neglected but still worth a look: the tiny chapel of **Áyios Athanásios**, immediately behind the municipal offices and crêche, boasts a fine *témblon* and naïve frescoes, while the quadruple-domed double church of **Aï Yannáki**, in the vale separating the two hillside neighbourhoods of the village, has an intriguing ground plan that compensates for its lack of decoration. A terrace-park is being laid out above it, potentially a pleasant vantage to admire the eighteenth-century structure.

The Archeological Museum

If you're pressed for time, the only must in Vathí is the excellent **Archeological Museum** (Tues–Sun 8.30am–3pm; 800dr), set behind the small central park beside the Neoclassical town hall (under restoration). One of the best provincial collections in Greece is housed in the old Paskallion building and the modern wing immediately opposite, the latter specially constructed for the star exhibit: a majestic, five-metre-high **kouros**, discovered – like most of the items – out at the Heraion sanctuary (see p.248). The opening of this wing was delayed for years, since the roof had to be raised twice as more bits of this statue were found; when the building was finally inaugurated in 1987, the president of the German Federal Republic – whose archeological institute controls the Heraion digs – flew out to attend the ceremonies. The *kouros*, the largest free-standing effigy to survive from ancient Greece, was found together with a devotional mirror to the Egyptian goddess Mut (syncretized with Hera) from a Nile workshop, only one of two such mirrors discovered in Greece.

In the equally compelling collection of small objects in the Paskallion, more votive offerings of Egyptian design – a hippo, a dancer in Nilotic dress, Horus-as-Falcon, an Osiris figurine – prove trade and pilgrimage links between Sámos and the Nile valley going back to the eighth century BC. The Mesopotamian and Anatolian origins of other artwork confirm the exotic trend at the Heraion, most tellingly in a case full of ivory miniatures: Perseus and Medusa in relief, a kneeling, perfectly formed mini-*kouros* which once adorned a lyre, a pouncing lion, and a *rhyton* or drinking horn terminating in a bull's head. The most famous local artefacts are the dozen or so bronze **griffin-heads**, for which Sámos was the major centre of production in the seventh century BC; mounted on the edge of bronze cauldrons, they were believed to ward off evil spirits.

Eating and drinking

Vathí's **restaurant** profile has improved somwhat in recent years, as chefs from elsewhere in Greece or even overseas assume management (often fleetingly) of formerly stagnating establishments. Skip the obvious rip-off merchants near the dock in favour of more remote tavernas.

Agrambeli, in Áno Vathí, within sight of the *Hotel Christiana*. Popular, noisy and quick-serving, this is the oldest eatery in the village. Menu varies nightly and can include such plates as rabbit stew. Open year round.

Apanemia, at the far west end of the shore boulevard. Above-average prices at this *ouzerí* are justified by appetizing fare from the Athenian chef, a veteran of swish restaurants in Athens and Rhodes. Open May–Oct.

Ta Dhiodhia, 1km south along Themistoklí Sofoúli from the jetty, next to the military headquarters. Indoor and outdoor dining on reasonable, well-prepared seafood and *mezédhes* with local bulk wine. Dinner only; daily in summer, sporadically (ie weekends) off season.

Grigoris, corner of Smírnis and Mikális. Vegetarian's nightmare: grills and more grills, done simply and inexpensively. Occasional live music sessions; open all year.

Toh Steki, at Panayítsa in Áno Vathí, just below the wall fountain. A new *ouzerí*, featuring unusual delicacies (skate, shrimp, snails) served on an open terrace.

Stelios, 150m north of the dock on the right. Virtually the only exception to the above rule; not especially cheap, but ideal for a no-nonsense, pre-ferry meal.

Nightlife

Vathí **nightlife** revolves around a dozen waterfront cafés and a roughly equal number of often posey bars, with frequent parties and theme nights aimed at the local clientele.

Cleary's Pub, inconspicuously marked just behind Platía Pithagóra. An inexpensive standby run by Dutch Desireé, a local character who played one of the witches in Polanski's *Macbeth*. Open May–Oct.

Club Gallery, on Themistoklí Sofoúli near *Ta Dhiodhia*. Art gallery/bar, whose genial owner justifies the name by occasionally hosting exhibition openings. Open most of the year.

Escape, formerly *Number Nine*, at Kefalopoúlou 9 (north of the jetty). The oldest of Vathí's watering holes, with a seaview terrace; new owners have introduced outdoor videos. Open May–Sept.

Metropolis, in the orchards behind the *Hotel Paradise*. Vathí's rather tame disco. Open May–Oct.

Listings

ATMs At three waterfront banks: *Emboriki/Commercial*, *Ethniki/National*, and *Pisteos/Credit*.

Car rental Among seven or so agencies, four to be recommended are ranged along Themistoklí Sofoúlon: try *Budget*, at no. 31 (☎0273/28 856), *Aramis/Eurodollar*, at no. 5, near the jetty (☎0273/22 682), Samorama, at no.15 (☎0273/22 641), or *Autoplan* at no. 67 (☎0273/23 555). Reservations must be made two days in advance in summer.

Ferry/travel agents Two versatile ones, also with good money exchange facilities, are *By Ship*, halfway along the front (☎0273/27 337), and *ITSA*, Themistoklí Sofoúli 5 (☎0273/23 605), right at the base of the ferry jetty. *By Ship* handles *Ilio Lines* domestic hydrofoils as well as the international one to Kuşadası, plus *Arkadhia Lines*, *Nissos Kalymnos* and *Miniotis Lines* ferries. *ITSA* is the current *Gianmar* hydrofoils agent. *Samina Tours* at Themistoklí Sofoúli 67 (☎0273/28 841 or ☎28 842), under the *Hotel Artemis*, is the only fully computerized agency in town and sells well-priced air tickets on *Olympic* or other airlines. *NEL* ferries are handled by *Tzoutzakis*, under the Catholic church, and *Agapitos* and *G&A* ferries to the Cyclades and Pireás have their own outlets near the foot of the jetty.

Laundrettes *Lavomatique*, at the far north end of the pedestrianized marketplace.

Motorbike rental Vathí is chock-a-block with franchises, which keeps rates reasonable. *Aramis*, on Kefalopoúlou, north of the jetty (separate from the car division) has the largest fleet of bikes and mechanical support team, but you may find *Europe Rent a Car* (one outlet near the bus station, one by the

Escape pub) or *Louis* (just behind the waterfront about 400m south of the dock) more congenial.

Mountain bike rental Mountain bikes are increasingly popular for exploring the towns and the growing network of dirt tracks. The stand at the *Hotel Panthea* is open to all, and *Ippokratis Pandelis* (☎0273/22 278), behind the *Frantzeskos oúzo* distillery on the shore road, sells a variety of models at competitive prices.

Olympic Airways On Kanári, corner Smírnis, south of the cathedral.

OTE Across the way from the cathedral and street produce market; open daily 7am–10pm.

Post office On Smírnis, 150m inland from *Olympic Airways;* open weekdays only.

Around Vathí

In the immediate **environs of Vathí** are some modest beaches and small hamlets with tavernas, all ideal targets for daytrips.

Two kilometres east of and above Vathí spreads the vast inland plateau of Vlamarí, devoted to vineyards and home to a pair of hamlets, **AYÍA ZÓNI** and **KAMÁRA**. The former can offer only a fortified monastery with overgrown courtyard, since the adjacent tavernas have closed down; of the two simple tavernas in Kamára, *O Kriton* is recommended. From Kamára you can climb a partly cobbled path to the ridge-top monastery of **Zoödhóhou Piyís** (open at all times) for views across the end of the island to Turkey.

Heading north out of Vathí, the narrow, tour-bus-clogged street threads through beachless **KALÁMI** – formerly the summer retreat of rich Vathiots, now home to package hotels – before ending after 7km at the pebbly bay and fishing port of **AYÍA PARASKEVÍ** (aka Nissí), with two tavernas and good (if rather unsecluded) swimming.

As you head southeast from Vathí along the main island loop road, the triple chapel at **Trís Ekklisíes** marks an important junction, with another fork 100m along the left-hand turning. Bearing left twice takes you through the hilltop village of **PALEÓKASTRO**, remarkable only for its dinnertime **taverna** *Ta Dhilina*, open October to May, so good and reasonable that Vathiots regularly make the six-kilometre trip out here. After another 6km you reach the quiet, striking bay of **Kérveli**, with a small gravel beach, a pair of expensive tavernas and two new luxury hotels. It's hardly worth continuing to the road's end at **Possidhónio**, whose beach is negligible and tavernas generally mediocre, though the left-hand taverna (as you face the sea) has recently acquired new management and is reported to have improved.

The right-hand option at the second junction at Trís Ekklisíes leads to the beaches of Mikáli and Psilí Ámmos, which draw crowds partly by virtue of their views of Mount Mycale (today Samsun Dağı) in Turkey. These are the only spots in this section served by public transport, with a bus service running here up to five times a day in season.

Mikáli, a kilometre or so of rather windswept sand and gravel, has been recently developed and fire-scorched (the two phenomena seem to go together); if you choose to stay out here, the *Oceanida Bay* (☎0273/61 620; fax ☎61 621; ④) is the smallest and best equipped of three similar local hotels. Winter rains fill a salt marsh just behind, a stop-over for migrating flamingoes between December and April.

Psilí Ámmos, further east around the headland, is a crowded, sandy cove that's on every local tour operator's signboard. The most savoury, longest-established namesake taverna stands on the far right as you arrive. If you swim out to nearby **Vareloúdhi** islet, a logical target, beware of strong west-to-east currents, which sweep through the narrow straits even in the shallows.

Pithagório

Most traffic south of Vathí heads for **PITHAGÓRIO**, the island's premier resort – jam-packed and rather tacky at peak season. Formerly known as Tigáni (Frying Pan), for reasons that become obvious in midsummer, it was renamed in 1955 to honour native ancient mathematician, philosopher and mystic Pythagoras. The sixth-century BC tyrant Polycrates established his capital here, now the subject of acres of archeological excavations which have forced modern Pithagório to expand northeastward and uphill. Findings are on display in a minuscule collection in the town hall (Tue–Sun 8.30am–2pm; free), on Platía Irínis, just north of the main thoroughfare Likoúrgou Logothéti. The village core of cobbled lanes and thick-walled mansions is fronted by a small harbour, which fits almost perfectly into the confines of Polycrates' ancient port and still uses his jetty. Today, however, it's devoted almost entirely to pleasure craft and overpriced cocktail bars.

Sámos' best-preserved attempt at a castle, the nineteenth-century *pírgos* (tower-house) of **Lykourgos Logothetis**, overlooks both the town and the shoreline where that local chieftain, together with a certain "Kapetan Stamatis" and Admiral Kanaris, oversaw decisive naval and land victories over the Turks in the summer of 1824. The final battle was won on Transfiguration Day (6 August), and accordingly the church beside the half-ruined tower bears a huge sign in Greek announcing that "Christ Saved Sámos 6 August 1824".

Accommodation

If there are any vacancies – and it's best not to count on it in mid-season – proprietors of the less expensive grades of **accommodation** tend to meet incoming ferries and hydrofoils. Otherwise it's a matter of tramping the streets or (if possible) phoning ahead. The friendly **tourist information** booth, on the left up the main thoroughfare Likoúrgou Logothéti as you face west (☎0273/61 389; fax ☎61 022), can help with finding rooms.

Nocturnal noise can be a problem in Pithagório, so it's worth heading along Pithagóra to its quiet, seaward end, south of Likoúrgou Logothéti; here you'll find the modest pensions *Tsambika* and *Sydney* (②). *Lambis Rooms* (☎0273/61 396; ③), on Íras, 50m back from the water, can also be recommended. Another peaceful area is the hillside north of Platía Irínis, where the *Hotel Galini* is one of the better small outfits (☎0273/61 167; winter 01/98 42 248; ④), attracting a repeat, non-tour clientele. Further uphill, on the road to Vathí, the rear units of *Studios Anthea* (☎0273/62 086; ④) are fairly quiet and allow self-catering.

Eating and nightlife

Eating out can be frustrating in Pithagório, with value for money often a completely alien concept. However, there are a few decent alternatives to the obvious tourist mills: away from the water, you can get a relatively inexpensive, quick and simple lunch at *Taverna Platania*, under two eucalyptus trees opposite the town hall; for dining at the water's edge, you're best off at the extreme east end of the quay at either of two *ouzerís* – *Remataki* (the more expensive and fancier) or *Odysseas*. At the base of the ferry jetty is *Varka*, a beached wooden boat converted into a kitchen, which serves up seafood platters under the adjacent tamarisks – not especially cheap, but fun. Night-owls divide their time between the old stalwart **discos** *Labito*, in the town centre near the namesake hotel, and *San Lorenzo*, 1500m out on the road to Vathí.

Other practicalities

The **bus stop** to get you away is just west of the intersection of Likoúrgou Logothéti and the road to Vathí. Also on Likoúrgou Logothéti are two **banks** (no ATMs) and the **post office**, while the **OTE** is on the quay below the overpriced *Hotel Damo*. The flattish country to the west of the town is ideal for pedal-bike touring, a popular activity; if you want to rent motorized transport, *Evelin* – 1500m out by the airport junction and namesake hotel – is reasonably priced and helpful.

Around Pythagório: ancient sites and beaches

Aside from the archeologists' potholes, visible remains of ancient Sámos are scattered in a broad zone just beyond the current town limits. Just 400m west of Pithagório, on the main road, lie the remains of the **Roman baths** (Tues, Weds, Fri 9am–2.30pm; Thurs & Sun 11.30am–2.30pm; Sat 10.30am–2.30pm; free), fairly dull though nocturnally lit to good effect. Considerably more interesting is the **Efpalínion tunnel** (Tues–Sun 8.30am–2pm; 500dr, 300dr students), a 1040-metre aqueduct bored through the mountain just north of Pithagório; built by slave labour at the behest of Polycrates, it remained in use until this century. To get there, take the well-signposted path heading inland off the shore boulevard just west of town, which meets the access road towards the end of the 20-minute walk. Visits consist of traversing a hewn rock ledge used to transport the spoil from the water channel far below; there are guard-grilles over the worst drops, and lighting for the first 650m, though there are plans to open the entire length of the tunnel. Although the work crews started from opposite sides of the mountain, the eight-metre deviation from true, about halfway along, is remarkably slight: a tribute to the competence of the era's surveyors.

You can also climb to the five remaining chunks of the Polycratian **perimeter wall** enclosing the tyrant's hilltop citadel. There's a choice of routes: one leading up from the Glifádha lagoon, 700m west of Pithagório, past an **ancient watchtower** now isolated from other fortifications; the other approach (easier) leading from the well-signposted monastery of **Panayía Spilianí**, just off the road to the Efpalínion tunnel, and the adjacent ancient **amphitheatre**. The monastery grounds themselves, now bereft of nuns and monks, are a travesty of insensitive restoration and lined with souvenir kiosks, but behind the courtyard, the raison d'etre of the place is magnificent: a cool, illuminated, hundred-metre **cave**, at the drippy end of which is a subterranean shrine to the Virgin (open daylight hours; free). It is thought that this was the residence of the ancient oracular priestess Fyto, and a hiding place during the pirate-ridden medieval era.

Potokáki

The main local **beach** stretches for several kilometres west of the Logothetis "castle", punctuated about halfway along by the end of the airport runway, and the cluster of hotels known as **Potokáki** (not served by public transport). If you don't mind the crowds or occasionally being buzzed by low-flying jets, the central zone is equipped with the usual amenities like kayaks and sunbeds. Most of the sand-and-pebble shore here is well groomed, and the water clean; misanthropes will have to head out towards the end of the road for more seclusion.

Just before the turn-off to the heart of the beach, about 700m from the western edge of Pithagório, sprawls the massive, ultra-luxurious *Doryssa Bay* complex (☎0273/61 360; fax ☎61 463; ⑥), which includes a meticulously concocted fake village guaranteed to confound archeologists of future eras; there's a square with an expensive café, and Sámos' only indoor concert and theatre venue, the *Aithoussa Sibylla*. A more affordable option is The *Fito Bungalows Hotel* (☎0273/61 582; fax ☎62 045; ⑤), whose rates vary slightly depending on season.

Ancient Heraion

The Potokáki beachfront road is a dead end, with the main island loop road contining west from the turn-off for the airport. Along this you'll find signs to the **Heraion Sanctuary** (Tues–Sun 8.30am–3pm; 600dr), once linked to the ancient city of Pithagório by a five-kilometre Sacred Way that's now buried beneath alluvial mud and a bit of today's runway.

Much touted in tourist literature, this massive shrine to Hera, the Mother Goddess, assumes humbler dimensions on approach, with just one surviving column and assorted foundations. Yet once inside the fenced precinct you can sense the former grandeur of the largest ancient temple known, never completed owing to Polycrates' untimely death at the hands of the Persians. The site chosen, near the mouth of the still-active Ímvrassos stream, was Hera's legendary birthplace and the spot for her trysts with Zeus; in a far corner of the fenced-in zone you can see a large, exposed patch of the paved processional Sacred Way.

Just 1km inland from the Heraion stands the sixteenth-century **Pírgos Sarakíni**, a fortified tower-house of a type seen elsewhere in Greece only in the Máni, on the mainland; it is the last surviving of a presumed half-dozen which formerly graced Sámos.

Modern Iréon

Adjacent to Heraion is the modern resort of **IRÉON**, a nondescript grid of dusty streets behind a coarse-shingle beach, attracting a younger, more active and less packaged clientele than Pithagório. Here you'll find more independent **rooms** and a pair of good, small **hotels** that might have spur-of-the-moment vacancies: *Venetia* (☎0273/61 195; ③) and *Heraion* (☎0273/61 180; ③), both within sight of the water. *Irini*, the northeasternmost **taverna** on the shore, serves largish portions of meaty and vegetarian fare; for more traditional seafood, try *Ireon*, at the opposite end of the waterfront. In between are a series of music and breakfast bars, of which the longest lived is the *Varka*, with a real fishing boat serving as the focus.

Just out of town on the track to Kiriakoú, a **horse-riding** centre organizes three-hour jaunts through the hills and orchards behind. A rival stables, *Iron Bridge*, 3km north of Pithagório on the way to Vathí, offers two-hour excursions in the valley leading up to the Efpalínion tunnel (☎0273/61 687 evenings for details).

Hóra and Mitiliní

Three kilometres northwest of Pithagório, the island loop road comes to a junction at long, narrow **HÓRA**, the island's medieval capital. It's still a large, noisy village, worth knowing about principally for the tavernas *Iy Sintrofia*, on the road in from Pithagório, *O Andonis* on the little square with the running fountain, and a grill on Platía Ayías Paraskevís. Though none represents tremendously good value, they are all more down to earth than anything in Pithagório.

Heading 4km north from the crossroads takes you through a ravine to **MITILINÍ**, which initially seems an amorphous, workaday sprawl. A brief exploration, however, reveals a fine main square with some atmospheric *kafenía*, the unmarked taverna *Dionyssos* opposite them – alone worth the trip up from the coast – and *Cine*

Rex, the island's last remaining indoor cinema (open Oct–May), down a side street. It's reasonably priced for the benefit of the numerous local conscripts, with art-house fare on Sundays.

At the southern edge of town, a local worthy has endowed a new **Paleontological Museum** (daily 9am–2.30pm; free) to house bones recovered from a place nearby where Ice-Age animals came to die; so far, however, the exhibits are long on wall space and short on fossils.

Southern Samian villages

Since the circum-island bus passes through or near these villages only once or twice a day, you'll need your own vehicle to explore them all.

Some 4km west of Hóra, an inconspicuous turning leads uphill to the still-functioning monastery of **Timíou Stavroú** (Holy Cross), whose annual festival on 14 September is more an excuse for a tatty open-air market than any music or feasting. One kilometre further on, another detour wends its way to **MAVRATZÉI**, one of two Samian "pottery villages"; this one specializes in the *Koúpa toú Pithagóra* or "Pythagorean cup", supposedly designed by the sage himself to leak onto the user's lap if he indulged beyond the "fill" line. More practical wares can be found at three shops in **KOUMARADHÉI**, back on the main road, 2km further along.

At Koumaradhéi you can descend a paved road through burnt forest to the sixteenth-century monastery of **Megális Panayías** (nominal hours daily 10am–noon), re-opened after a lengthy restoration and containing the finest frescoes on the island. You can continue along this road to **MÍLI**, a village submerged in citrus groves, also accessible from the Iréon road. Four kilometres above Míli sprawls **PAGÓNDAS**, a large hillside community with a splendid main square and an unusual communal fountain-house on the south hillside.

From here, a scenic, paved road curls 9km around the hill to **SPATHARÉI**, rather pokey – more so since the area was devasted by a fire in 1993 – but set on a natural balcony offering the best sea views this side of the island. From Spatharéii, the road continues 6km till it joins up with the main road at **PÍRGOS**, a village lost in pine forests at the head of a ravine, and the centre of Samian honey production. A short distance down the gorge, **Koútsi** is a small roadside oasis of plane trees (supposedly 17) shading a gushing spring and a taverna that makes a convenient lunch stop if tour buses haven't got there first.

The southern coast

The rugged and beautiful coastline south of the Pagóndas–Pírgos route conceals a number of largely inaccessible beaches, seen only fleetingly by most visitors from their incoming airplane. They are now being developed in a low-key way, but still suffer nothing like the crowds of the more obvious beaches.

Kiriakoú

Furthest east of the more accessible coves, the 250-metre sand-and-gravel bay of **Kiriakoú** lies just 5km southwest of Iréon via a well-marked but rough track (jeeps or dirt bikes only). Bring food and water as there's only a diminutive drinks stand, which also rents out a few umbrellas and sunbeds. The water is pristine, the olive-and-pine hinterland unspoiled and unburnt, and the solitude disturbed only by groups of boat-trippers from Iréon. There is also a slightly longer and less steep but unmarked track from Pagóndas.

Tsópela

Tsópela, very near the southernmost point on the island, also has marked road access. Matters begin reasonably enough about 4km beyond Pagóndas on the Spatharéi-bound road, but once past the tiny monastery of Evangelistrías, the five-kilometre track deteriorates until it's too rutted and steep for most 2WDs. Your reward for persevering is a highly scenic sand-and-gravel bay at the mouth of a gorge, with views towards the satellite islet of Samiopoúla, rock overhangs under which to shelter, and curious freshwater seeps on the seabed. A seasonal taverna under the pines, just to the east, serves cheaper and better fare (including fish) than you'd expect for such an isolated spot.

Kouméïka and Bállos

The western reaches of this shoreline, which suffered comprehensive fire damage in 1994, are approached via the small village of **KOUMÉÏKA**, which has a massive inscribed marble fountain and a pair of *kafenía* on its square. Below extends the long, pebbly bay at slightly charred **BÁLLOS**, with sand, a cave and naturists at the far east end. Bállos itself is merely a sleepy collection of summer houses, several rooms to rent and a few tavernas, best of which is the *Cypriot*, although the garrulous couple running it prefer you to book in advance (☎0273/36 394).

Returning to Kouméïka, the dubious-looking side road just before the village marked "Velanidhiá" is in fact quite passable by any vehicle, and a very useful short cut to the beaches beyond Órmos Marathókambos (see "Western Sámos", below).

Kokkári

Leaving Vathí on the north coastal section of the island loop road, there's little to stop for until you reach **KOKKÁRI**, 12km along, the third major Samian tourist centre after Pithagório and the capital. It's also the prime source of nostalgia for Sámos regulars; while lower Vathí and Pithagório had little compelling beauty to sacrifice, much has been irrevocably lost here. The town's profile, covering two knolls behind twin headlands, remains unaltered, and several families still doggedly untangle their fishnets on the quay, but in general its identity has been altered beyond recognition, with constant inland expansion over vineyards and the fields of onions that gave the place its name. However, Kokkári's German promoters have made a virtue of its exposed, rocky beaches buffeted by near constant winds, developing it as a successful windsurfing resort.

Practicalities

As at Vathí and Pithagório, a fair proportion of Kokkári **accommodation** is block-booked for the season by tour companies. One establishment not completely devoted to package tours is the pleasant *Hotel Olympia Beach* (☎0273/92 353; ④), on the western beach road, and the affiliated *Olympia Village* (☎0273/92 420; fax ☎92 457; ⑤ for apartments). Otherwise *Yiorgos Mihelios* (☎0273/92 456) has a wide range of rooms and flats to rent (③–④), as well as the *Pension Green Hill*; for a guaranteed view of the quiet fishing port, try *Pension Alkionis* (☎0273/92 225; ③). If you get stuck, you might seek assistance from the seasonal **EOT post** (Mon–Sat 8.30am–1.30pm; ☎0273/92 217), housed in a portakabin near the main church on the through-road.

Most **tavernas** are along the waterfront and charge above the Greek norm, but these are becoming increasingly outnumbered by breakfast or after-hours bars. At the eastern end of things, *Ta Adhelfia* is as close as you'll get to a simple, unpretentious *psistariá*, while for a blowout, Athenian-run *Kariatidha*, some five doors west from there, is worth the bit extra. Inland, *Farmer's* – on the village through-road, a few steps east of the open-air summer **cinema** – is esteemed for its locally grown food; portions, though not huge, are carefully prepared and reasonably priced. In autumn, *moustalevriá* (grape-must pudding) is on offer by prior arrangement with the proprietor, Nikos Nitsolas, a native of nearby Vourliótes and a subtle comedian.

Other amenities include a short-hours **bank** on the through-road, a **post office** in a portakabin on a lane to seaward, and a **laundrette** next to that. Note that absolutely everything mentioned in this account is shut between late October and mid-April, when scarcely a grocery shop stays open in Kokkári.

West of Kokkári: the north coast

The nearest partly sheltered beaches are thirty to forty minutes' walk west from Kokkári, all with permanently anchored umbrellas and loose sunbeds. The first beach, **Lemonákia**, is a bit too close to the road, with an obtrusive café; 1km beyond, the graceful crescent of **Tzamadhoú** (rhymes with Coleridge's *Xanadu*) figures in virtually every EOT poster of the island. With path-only access, it's a bit less spoilt than Lemonákia, and the far ends of the pebble beach are nudist zones. Unfortunately, a spring just inland has been fenced off to discourage campers from congregating here and to encourage everyone to patronize the fairly pricey taverna signposted up in the vineyards. There's one more large, pebbly stretch west of Avlákia (a mostly Greek resort 6km from Kokkári) called **Tzábou**, but unless you're passing by and want a quick dip, this is not worth a special detour as it faces on to the prevailing northwest wind.

Áyios Konstandínos and around

The next spot of any interest along the coast road is **PLATANÁKIA**, at a plane-shaded bridge by the turn-off for Manolátes (see below). It's essentially just a handful of tavernas and rooms for rent; for oven-cooked specialities and wine from the barrel, visit the excellent *Café Restaurant Apolafsi*, while for rooms you might try *Kalypso* (☎0273/94 124; ③), near what passes for the beach here.

Platanákia is actually the eastern suburb of **ÁYIOS KONSTANDÍNOS**, 1500m distant, a case study in arrested touristic development. The surf-pounded esplanade has at long last been repaved, but there are no usable beaches within walking distance, so the collection of warm-toned stone buildings (increasingly adulterated by concrete structures) constitutes a more peaceful alternative to Kokkári. In addition to modest, long-established **hotels** such as the friendly *Ariadne* (☎0273/94 206; ③), *The Four Seasons* (③), or the *Atlantis* (☎0273/94 329; ③), along the highway, there's a small, well-designed bungalow complex, *Apollonia Bay*, and newer rooms establishments, for example *Maria's* (☎0273/94 460; ③). For food, you can eat at *Toh Kyma*, virtually the only full-menu taverna here, or head out to Platanákia.

Once past "Áyios", as it's known locally, the mountains hem the road in against the sea, and the terrain doesn't relent until near **KONDAKÉÏKA**, whose *kafenío*-lined square is worth a visit at dusk for its fabulous sunset views. Afterwards you can descend to the diminutive shore annexe of **ÁYIOS NIKÓLAOS** for excellent fish dinners, particularly at *Iy Psaradhes*, the westernmost of the two tavernas. Though not visible from the upper road, a reasonable beach here lies a ten-minute walk east past the last clutch of studio accommodation, perennially occupied by a German clientele in summer.

Inland from Kokkári: hill villages

Inland between Kokkári and Kondakéïka lies an idyllic landscape of pine, cypress and orchards overawed by dramatic, often cloud-shrouded mountains, so far hardly touched by fire. Despite destructive nibblings by bulldozers, some of the trail system linking the various **hill villages** is still intact, and you can walk for as long or as little as you like, returning to the main highway to catch a bus home. Failing that, most of the communities can provide a bed on short notice.

Vrondianís

The monastery of **Vrondianís** (Vrónda), directly above Kokkári, is a popular destination for walkers, but since the army now uses it as a barracks, the place only really comes alive during the festival on 7–8 September, when *yiórti* – a special cereal-and-meat porridge –

may be served; this is the one really lively and musical Samian celebration, which spills over into the nearby village of Vourliótes.

Vourliótes

VOURLIÓTES, 2km west of the monastery, has beaked chimneys and brightly painted shutters sprouting from its typical tile-roofed houses. On the photogenic central square, the best of several tavernas is *Snack Bar Iy Kiki*, under new management since 1995, which serves two local specialities: *revithokeftédhes* (chickpea patties), and homemade *moskháto*, a dessert wine so syrupy that it's best drunk with soda as a spritzer. (The other Samian delicacy worth trying if you've a kitchen are the excellent sausages available from select butchers between September and May). Otherwise, similar fare is served at *Iy Pera Vrysi*, at the entrance to the village; with its enormous plane tree and glimpses of the sea below, this is a popular weekend venue for Athenian Greeks.

Manolátes

MANOLÁTES, an hour-plus walk uphill from Vorliótes via a deep river canyon, has a pair of simple snack bars and is the most popular trailhead for the five-hour round-trip up **Mount Ámbelos** (Karvoúnis), the island's second highest summit. From Manolátes you can no longer easily continue on foot to Stavrinídhes, the next village, but should plunge straight down, partly on a cobble path, through the shady valley known as "**Aïdhónia**" (Nightingales) to Platanákia (about an hour's walk). Aïdhónia has a couple of mock-rustic tavernas under its trees, popular targets of "Greek Nights" and thus doling out fairly undistinguished cusine.

Villages of Jehovah

STAVRINÍDHES, should you fight your way on foot or by bike through the deplorable mess of bulldozer tracks beyond Manolátes, has little in the way of tourist facilities and much in the way of recent notoriety. To the infinite chagrin of Sámos' archbishop, many local villagers have become Jehovah's Witnesses, a sect abhorred and actively persecuted in Greece. A similar process has occurred at neighbouring ÁMBELOS, more spectacularly perched on a natural balcony above the sea. Its setting has prompted numerous foreigners to buy and renovate houses here, but again there are no specific delights for outsiders.

Karlóvassi and western Sámos

KARLÓVASSI, 37km west of Vathí and the second town of Sámos, is decidedly sleepier and more old-fashioned than the capital, despite having roughly the same population. Though lacking much aesthetic distinction, it's popular as a base from which to explore western Sámos' excellent beaches, a smattering of medieval ruins and some rewarding walks.

The name, incidentally, despite a vehement lack of Ottoman legacy elsewhere on Sámos, appears to be a corruption of *karlıova*, Turkish for "snowy plain" – the plain in question being the conspicuous saddle of Mount Kérkis overhead, which is indeed snow-capped in harsh winters.

The town divides into no less than four straggly neighbourhoods: Néo, well inland, whose untidy growth was spurred by the influx of post-1923 refugees from Asia Minor; Meséo, across the usually dry riverbed, draped appealingly on a knoll; and picture-postcard Paleó (or Áno), perched above Limáni (or Limín), the small harbour district.

Limáni

The port of **LIMÁNI**, its quay pedestrianized at night, is an appealing place with a working boatyard at the west end. **Ferry-ticket agencies** are scattered within a short distance of each other on the through-road and at the jetty; often a shuttle bus service operates from Néo Karlóvassi, timed to coincide with boat arrivals and departures. Just inland from the shorefront road, slightly to the east, sprawls the **EOS** (Union of Samian Wine-producers) plant, open for tours of the production line (and a sample glass) during normal weekday working hours. The best wines are reckoned to be the Doryssa white and the Selana rosé. Fokianos is a cheaper though equally smooth rosé, and comes in 500ml bottles of plonk or 750ml corked bottles of slightly better stuff.

Most visitors to the area **stay** in or near Limáni, which has a handful of rooms and several fairly expensive hotels. The **rooms**, all in the inland pedestrian lane behind the through-road, are quieter: try those of *Vangelis Feloukatzis* (☎0273/33 293; ③) or *Yiorgos Moskhoyiannis* (☎0273/32 812; ③). Otherwise, the comfortable *Samaina Port Hotel* (☎0273/34 988; ④), co-managed with the *Samaina Bay Maison* apartments slightly inland, overlooks the quay.

Tavernas and bars are abundant, but by far the best and most reasonable waterfront place to **eat** is the easternmost establishment *Steve's* (April–Nov), named after its genial South-African Greek proprietor. Limáni also boasts the island's second outdoor **cinema**, just seaward of the through-road, not far from the *Samaina Bay Maison*.

Paleó and Meséo

Immediately overhead perches the partly hidden hamlet of **PALEÓ**, whose hundred or so houses line both sides of a leafy ravine. The only facilities are the sporadically functioning café *Toh Mikro Parisi*, which sometimes prepares food in summer, and a seasonal taverna on the path down towards **MESÉO**. The latter could be an alternative to Limáni for an overnight stop, with one comfortable hotel, the *Aspasia* (☎0273/32 363; fax ☎34 777; ④), near the wood-fired bakery, and other rooms scattered along the half-kilometre between here and the sea. On the small square some 200m east of the *Aspasia* there's a small, year-round bar-*ouzerí*, *Para Pende*, with a mixed clientele of locals and tourists. Following the street linking the square to the waterfront, you pass one of the improbably huge turn-of-the-century churches, topped with twin belfries and a blue-and-white dome, which dot the coastal plain here. Just at the intersection with the shore road you'll find the friendly, good-value *Ouzerí Toh Kima*, going strong (April–Oct) since 1985 and the best place in town to watch the sunset over a *pikilía* (medley dish).

Néo

NÉO has little to recommend it besides a wilderness of derelict stone warehouses and mansions on the east bank of the river mouth, reminders of the extinct leather industry which flourished here during the first half of this century. However, if you're staying at Limáni, you'll almost certainly visit one of the three **banks** (the *Emboriki/Commercial* has the only ATM), the **post office**, the **OTE** or the one-tree **bus stop** on the main lower square. Some, though not all, buses from Vathí continue down to the harbour; ask for details. While waiting for a bus, one of two traditional **kafenía** might interest you: *O Kleanthis*, on the lower *platía*, or *O Kerketevs*, by the upper square.

Potámi sites

The closest decent beach to Karlóvassi beckons at **POTÁMI**, forty minutes' walk via the coast road from Limáni or an hour by a more scenic trail from Paleó. This broad arc of sand and pebbles, flecked at one end with tide-lashed rocks (and a hideous clifftop chapel), gets crowded at summer weekends, when virtually the entire population of Karlóvassi descends here. Near the end of the trail from Paleó stands *Toh Iliovasilima*, a reasonable and friendly **fish taverna**; there are also a very few **rooms** signposted locally, but many individuals who stay here camp rough (in defiance of prohibition signs) along the lower reaches of the river which gives the beach its name.

A streamside path leads twenty minutes inland, initially past the exquisite eleventh-century church of **Metamórfosis** – the oldest on Sámos, its dome supported on four ancient columns – to an apparent dead end. Beyond this point, you must swim and wade 100m further in heart-stoppingly cold water through a series of fern-tufted rock pools (home to harmless eels and fresh-water crabs), before reaching a low but vigorous waterfall. Bring trainers with good tread and maybe rope if you want to explore above the first cascade; you probably won't be alone until you dive in, since this canyon is well known to locals and also included in the "Jeep Safari" trips of certain tour agencies.

Just above the Metamórfosis church, a clear if precipitous path leads up to a small, contemporaneous **Byzantine fortress**. There's little to see inside other than a cistern and a badly crumbled lower curtain wall, but the views out to sea and up the canyon are terrific, enhanced in October by a carpet of pink autumn crocus. Some islanders claim that a secret tunnel links the castle grounds with the church just below.

The Seïtáni coves

The coast beyond Potámi ranks among the most beautiful and unspoilt on Sámos; this has been an officially designated refuge for monk seals since the early 1980s, though most recent sightings have been at other points of the island (see box). The dirt track at the west end of Potámi bay ends after twenty minutes on foot (or five by car), from which you backtrack a hundred metres or so to find the well-cairned side trail running parallel to the water. Within twenty minutes along this you'll arrive at **Mikró Seïtáni**, a small pebble cove guarded by sculpted rock walls. A full hour's walk from the trailhead, through partly fire-damaged olive terraces, will bring you to **Megálo Seïtáni**, the island's finest beach, at the mouth of the intimidating Kakopérato gorge. You'll have to bring food and water, though not necessarily a swimsuit – there's no dress code at either of the Seïtáni bays.

Southwestern beach resorts

Heading south out of Karlóvassi on the island loop road, the first place you'd be tempted to stop off at is **MARATHÓKAMBOS**, a pretty, amphitheatrical village overlooking the eponymous gulf; there's a taverna or two, but no short-term accommodation.

Órmos Marathokámbou

ÓRMOS MARATHOKÁMBOU, a small harbour 18km from Karlóvassi, has recently been pressed into service as a tourist resort, though some of its original character still peeks through in its backstreets. The port has been improved, with *kaïkia* offering daytrips to Foúrni and the nearby islet of Samiopoúla, while the pedestrianized quay has become the focus of attention; a curiosity at its west end is the island's only set of traffic lights, controlling entry to a one-lane alley. An indifferent beach extends immediately to the east of the quay. The three or four tavernas here are pretty indistiguishable, although *Trata* at least offers bulk wine, always worth asking for on Sámos as it's laced with fewer chemicals than the bottled stuff.

Votsalákia

For better beaches, continue 2km west to **VOTSALÁKIA** (officially signposted "KÁMBOS"), Sámos' fastest-growing resort, which straggles a further 2km behind the island's longest, if not its most beautiful, beach. The place's appeal has been diminished in recent years

The monk seals of Sámos

Along with certain remote islets in the North Aegean, Sámos is one of the last remaining Greek habitats of the Mediterranean monk seal (*Monachus monachus*). Within living memory they were a fairly common sight, even inside Vathí Bay, but their numbers throughout the Aegean began to dwindle alarmingly in the 1960s when steadily reduced fish stocks saw them in increasing competition with humans. Seals can eat nearly their own weight in fish each day and often damage fishnets to get at "ready meals"; until recently, aggrieved fishermen did not hesitate to kill them, despite their protected status. In addition, the isolated beaches used by the seals for giving birth have now been invaded by humans, forcing the shy creatures to retire for this purpose to remote sea caves, preferably with a submerged entrance to keep land-based predators away.

Efforts to preserve the diminished Samian seal community, today estimated at less than ten, began during the mid-1970s when a Swiss–English team attempted to have the area around Megálo Seïtáni declared a natural refuge, with all shoreline construction prohibited. However, Samian villagers were unable to reconcile the pair's hippie garb and lifestyle with expensive Zodiac rafts and other sophisticated equipment, concluding that they were in the pay of a foreign power. The two were denounced as spies and expelled, though an official refuge was eventually designated and the Englishman got his own back in a book chronicling the episode (*The Monk Seal Conspiracy*, London: Heretic Books, 1988, o/p).

Conservationists feared that the local seals had gone for good – they can swim up to 200km a day if necessary – and that the Seïtáni area would be decommissioned as a reserve and officially opened to roads, power lines and hotels; illegal summer cottages already proliferate unchecked at Megálo Seïtáni, and despite strictures from the forest service, a road creeps down from Dhrakéi. So it was with considerable excitement that the spring of 1995 featured several sightings of at least three individuals – including a 1.7-metre-long, several-hundred-kilo adult – basking on pebble beaches at the opposite end of the island, between Vathí and Ayía Paraskeví. Why the seals should have begun surfacing so far from their former haunts is unclear; it may be that they have found inadvertent protection from fishermen's potshots in the regular coastguard patrols mounted to prevent landings of Kurdish refugees from Turkey. If you're lucky enough to see a basking seal, you may find that it will tolerate you from a discreet distance, though on no account should it be touched.

by wall-to-wall rooms, apartments and often rather poor tavernas, plus extensive forest-fire damage of 1993 and 1994, just inland. But for most tastes Votsalákia is still a considerable improvement on the Pithagório area, and the hulking mass of 1437-metre Mount Kérkis overhead rarely fails to impress.

As for **accommodation**, Emmanouil Dhespotakis (☎0273/31 258; ③) seems to control a good quarter of the beds available here, with most of his premises towards the quieter, more scenic western end of things. Also in this vicinity is *Akroyialia*, the oldest and most traditional **taverna** hereabouts, with courtyard seating and a selection of fish and meat grills; *Loukoullos*, on the ocean side of the road near the last of the Dhespotakis rooms, is a fancier, enjoyable bistro-bar. Other facilities include branches of nearly all the main Vathí travel agencies, offering vehicle rental (necessary, as only two daily buses call here) and money exchange to the overwhelmingly family clientele.

Psilí Ámmos and Limniónas

If Votsalákia doesn't suit, you can continue 3km further to the 600-metre sandy beach at **Psilí Ámmos**, more picturesque and not to be confused with its namesake beach in the southeast corner of Sámos. The sea shelves gently here – ridiculously so, as you're still only knee-deep a hundred paces out – and cliffs shelter clusters of naturists at the east end. Surprisingly, there is as yet little development: only one fair-sized apartment complex up in the pines halfway along the beach, plus two tavernas back up on the road as you approach, either of these fine for a no-frills lunch.

German interests have more or less completely taken over **Limniónas**, a smaller cove 2km further west, by constructing a large villa complex rather grandiosely labelled "SAMOS YACHT CLUB". Yachts do occasionally call at the protected bay, which offers decent swimming away from a rock shelf at mid-strand, two **tavernas** at the east end and a very few short-term **accommodation** facilities.

Mount Kérkis

A limestone/volcanic oddity in a predominantly schist landscape, **Mount Kérkis** (Kerketévs) – the Aegean's second highest summit after Sáos on Samothráki – attracts legends and speculation as easily as the cloud pennants that usually wreath it. Hermits colonized and sanctified the mountain's many caves in Byzantine times; the *andártes* (resistance guerrillas) controlled it during the last war; and mariners still regard it with superstitious awe, especially when mysterious lights – presumably the spirits of the departed hermits, or the aura of some forgotten holy icon – are glimpsd at night near the cave-mouths.

Climbing the peak

Gazing up from a supine seaside posture, some people are inspired to go and **climb the peak**. The classic route begins at the west end of the Votsalákia strip, along the bumpy jeep track leading inland towards the convent of **Evangelistrías**. After an initial half-hour through fire-damaged olive groves and past charcoal pits (a major industry hereabouts), the path begins, more or less following power lines steeply up to the convent. One of four friendly nuns will proffer an *oúzo* in welcome and point you up the sporadically paint-marked trail continuing even more steeply up to the peak.

The views are tremendous, though perhaps less than you'd expect since the mountain is rather blunt-topped and the climb itself is humdrum once you're out of the trees. About an hour before the top, there's a chapel with an attached cottage for sheltering in emergencies and, just beyond, a welcome spring that's most reliable after a wet winter. Elation at attaining the summit may be tempered somewhat by the knowledge that one of the worst aviation disasters in Greek history occurred here on August 3, 1989, when an aircraft flying out of Thessaloníki slammed into the mist-cloaked peak, with the loss of all 34 aboard. All told, it's a seven-hour outing from Votsalákia and back, not counting rest stops.

Around the mountain

Less ambitious walkers might want to circle the flanks of the mountain, first by vehicle and then by foot. The road beyond Limniónas to Kallithéa and Dhrakéi, truly back-of-beyond villages with views across to Ikaría, has been paved as far as Kallithéa, making it possible to venture out here on an ordinary motorbike. Buses are better during school termtime, when these more remote spots are accessible by a service that departs from Karlóvassi just after noon every weekday; in summer it only operates two days a week (currently Mon & Fri).

From **DHRAKÉI**, the end of the line, with just a pair of very simple *kafenía* to its credit, a ninety-minute trail descends through partly burned forest to Megálo Seïtáni, from where it's an easy two-and-a-half hour walk to Karlóvassi. People attempting to reverse this itinerary often discover to their cost that the bus (if any) returns from Dhrakéi early in the day, at 2pm, compelling them to stay overnight at one of two rather expensive **rooms** establishments (summer only) in **KALLITHÉA**, and to dine at either the simple *psistariá* on the square or the newer, more versatile taverna on the west edge of the village.

From Kallithéa, you can follow a newer jeep track (starting beside the cemetery) or walk for 45 minutes along an older trail to a spring, rural chapel and plane tree on the west flank of Kérkis. From here it's a half-hour, path-only walk to a pair of **cave-churches**. **Panayía Makriní** stands detached at the mouth of a high, wide but shallow grotto, whose balcony affords terrific views of Sámos' western extremity. A ten-minute scramble overhead will take you to **Ayía Triádha**, whose structure by contrast is largely composed of cave wall. Just adjacent yawns a narrow volcanic cavern; with a flashlight you can explore some hundred metres into the mountain, perhaps further on hands and knees and with proper equipment.

After these subterranean exertions, the closest spot for a swim is **Vársamo** (Válsamo) cove, 4km below Kallithéa and reached via a well-signposted dirt road. The beach here consists of wonderful multicoloured volcanic pebbles, and there are two caves to shelter in on one side of the bay, plus a lone rooms/snack bar establishment just inland.

Greek script table

Sámos	Σάμος	ΣΑΜΟΣ
Ámbelos	Αμπελος	ΑΜΠΕΛΟΣ
Áno Vathí	Ανω Βαθύ	ΑΝΩ ΒΑΘΥ
Ayía Paraskeví	Αγία Παρασκευή	ΑΓΙΑ ΠΑΡΑΣΚΕΥΗ
Ayía Zóni	Αγία Ζώνη	ΑΓΙΑ ΖΩΝΗ
Áyios Konstandiínos	Αγιος Κωνσταντίνος	ΑΓΙΟΣ ΚΩΝΣΤΑΝΤΙΝΟΣ
Bállos	Μπάλλος	ΜΠΑΛΛΟΣ
Dhrakéi	Δρακαίοι	ΔΡΑΚΑΙΟΙ
Evangelistrías	Ευαγγελιστρίας	ΕΥΑΓΓΕΛΕΛΙΣΤΡΙΑΣ
Hóra	Χώρα	ΧΩΡΑ
Iréon	Ηραίον	ΗΡΑΙΟΝ
Kalámi	Καλάμι	ΚΑΛΑΜΙ
Kallithéa	Καλλιθέα	ΚΑΛΛΙΘΕΑ
Kamára	Καμάρα	ΚΑΜΑΡΑ
Karlóvassi	Καρλόβασι	ΚΑΡΛΟΒΑΣΙ
Kérkis	Κέρκης	ΚΕΡΚΗΣ
Kérveli	Κέρβελη	ΚΕΡΒΕΛΗ
Kiriakoú	Κυριακού	ΚΥΡΙΑΚΟΥ
Kokkári	Κοκκάρι	ΚΟΚΚΑΡΙ
Koumaradhéi	Κουμαραδαίοι	ΚΟΥΜΑΡΑΔΑΙΟΙ
Kouméïka	Κουμέϊκα	ΚΟΥΜΕΪΚΑ
Limniónas	Λιμνιώνας	ΛΙΜΝΙΩΝΑΣ
Manolátes	Μανολάτες	ΜΑΝΟΛΑΤΕΣ
Mavratzéi	Μαυρατζαίοι	ΜΑΥΡΑΤΖΑΙΟΙ
Megális Panayías	Μεγάλης	ΜΕΓΑΛΗΣ ΠΑΝΑΓΙΑΣ
Mikáli	Μυκάλη	ΜΥΚΑΛΗ
Mitiliní	Μυτηλινοί	ΜΥΤΗΛΙΝΙΟΙ
Órmos Marathokámbou	Όρμος Μαραθοκάμπου	ΟΡΜΟΣ ΜΑΡΑΘΟΚΑΜΠΟΥ
Pagóndas	Παγώντας	ΠΑΓΩΝΤΑΣ
Paleókastro	Παλαιόκστρο	ΠΑΛΑΙΟΚΑΣΤΡΟ
Pírgos	Πύργος	ΠΥΡΓΟΣ
Pithagório	Πυθαγόρειο	ΠΥΘΑΓΟΡΕΙΟ
Posidhónio	Ποσειδώνειο	ΠΟΣΕΙΔΩΝΕΙΟ
Potámi	Ποτάμι	ΠΟΤΑΜΙ
Potokáki	Ποτοπάκι	ΠΟΤΟΚΑΚΙ
Psilí Ámmos	Ψιλή Αμμος	ΨΙΛΗ ΑΜΜΟΣ
Seïtáni	Σεϊτάνι	ΣΕΪΤΑΝΙ
Spatharéi	Σπαθαραίοι	ΣΠΑΘΑΡΑΙΟΙ
Stavrinídhes	Σταυρινήδες	ΣΤΑΥΡΙΝΗΔΕΣ
Timíou Stavroú	Τιμίου Σταυρού	ΤΙΜΙΟΥ ΣΤΑΥΡΟΥ
Tsópela	Τσόπελα	ΤΣΟΠΕΛΑ
Tzamadhoú	Τζαμαδού	ΤΖΑΜΑΔΟΥ
Vathí	Βαθύ	ΒΑΘΥ
Votsalákia	Βοτσαλάκια	ΒΟΤΣΑΛΑΚΙΑ
Vourliótes	Βουρλιότες	ΒΟΥΡΛΙΟΤΕΣ
Vrondianís	Βροντιανής	ΒΡΟΝΤΙΑΝΗΣ
Zoödhóhou Piyís	Ζωοδόχου Πηγής	ΖΩΟΔΟΧΟΥ ΠΗΓΗΣ

Sámos travel details

ISLAND TRANSPORT

BUSES

Vathí to: Karlóvassi (7–9 daily Mon–Fri, 4–5 Sat/Sun); Kokkári (7–9 daily Mon–Fri, 4–5 Sat/Sun); Mitiliní (3–4 daily Mon–Fri, 1–2 Sat); Pithagório (8–9 daily Mon–Fri, 6–7 Sat/Sun); Psilí Ámmos (2–5 daily).

Pithagório to: Iréon (4–6 daily Mon–Sat July–Aug); Karlóvassi (2 daily Mon–Fri); Pírgos (2 daily Mon–Fri).

Karlóvassi to: Dhrakéi (1 daily Mon–Fri Sept–May, Mon/Fri only June–Aug); Votsalákia (3 daily July/Aug, 1 daily June/Sept).

NB All frequencies are for the period June–Sept except where noted.

INTER-ISLAND TRANSPORT

KAÏKIA AND EXCURSION BOATS

Karlóvassi to: Foúrni (2 weekly).

Pithagório to: Lipsí (1 weekly); Pátmos (4–5 weekly in season).

FERRIES

Vathí to: Agathoníssi (1–2 weekly on *Miniotis Lines*); Arkí (1–2 weekly on *Miniotis*); Foúrni (3–5 weekly on *Agapitos*, *G&A Ferries* or *Miniotis*); Híos (2–4 weekly on *Miniotis* or *NEL*; 4–5hr); Ikaría (Áyios Kírikos or Évdhilos; 5–8 weekly on *Agapitos*, *Arkadia* or *Miniotis*; 2hr 30min); Kavála (1 weekly on *NEL*); Lésvos (1 weekly on *NEL*); Límnos (1 weekly on *NEL*); Lipsí (1–2 weekly on *Miniotis*); Míkonos (2–3 weekly on *Arkadia* or *G&A*); Náxos (2–4 weekly on *G&A*; 5hr); Páros (3–7 weekly by *Agapitos*, *G&A* or *Arkadia*); Pátmos (2–3 weekly on *Miniotis* or *NEL*); Pireás (3–7 weekly on *Agapitos*, *Arkadia* or *G&A*; 12–14hr); Síros (1–2 weekly on *Agapitos* or *G&A*); Thessaloníki (1 weekly on *NEL*).

Karlóvassi: as from Vathí, except no services to Lésvos, Límnos, Pátmos and northern mainland, with *NEL*.

Pithagório to: Agathoníssi (2 weekly on *Nissos Kalymnos*; 1hr 30min); Foúrni (1–2 weekly on *Miniotis*); Ikaría (1–2 weekly on *Miniotis*); Kálimnos (2 weekly on *Nissos Kalymnos*); Léros (2 weekly on *Nissos Kalymnos*); Lipsí (2 weekly on *Nissos Kalymnos*); Pátmos (1–2 weekly on *Miniotis*; 3hr; 2 weekly on *Nissos Kalymnos*; 7hr 30min).

NB The *Nissos Kalymnos* connects with onward services the following day to other Dodecanese islands.

HYDROFOILS

Vathí to: Agathoníssi (1 weekly on *Ilio Lines*); Foúrni (3 weekly June–Sept on *Gianmar Lines*; 1–3 weekly on *Ilio*); Híos (3 weekly June–Sept on *Gianmar*); Ikaría (3 weekly June–Sept on *Gianmar*; 1–3 weekly on *Ilio*); Kálimnos (4–7 weekly May–early Oct on *Ilio*); Kós (4–7 weekly May–early Oct on *Ilio*); Léros (4–7 weekly May–early Oct on *Ilio*); Lésvos (3 weekly June–Sept on *Gianmar*); Lipsí (1–4 weekly on *Ilio*); Pátmos (4–7 weekly May–early Oct on *Ilio*).

NB All *Ilio Lines* services make a stop in Pithagório with both inward and outward journeys; in rough weather the hydrofoil may omit Vathí altogether, beginning and ending its run in Pithagório.

Pithagório to: Agathoníssi (1 weekly on *Mamidhakis/Dodecanese Hydrofoils*); Kálimnos (1 daily in season on *Mamidhakis*); Foúrni (1 weekly on *Mamidhakis*); Kós (1 daily in season on *Mamidhakis*); Léros (1 daily in season on *Mamidhakis*); Lipsí (1 weekly on *Mamidhakis*); Pátmos (1 daily in season on *Mamidhakis*);

NB *Mamidhakis/Dodecanese Hydrofoil* itineraries run every other day during April and late October, once weekly in winter as conditions permit.

DOMESTIC FLIGHTS

Sámos to: Athens (3–5 daily April–Oct, 2–3 daily Nov–March; 1hr).

INTERNATIONAL TRANSPORT

FERRIES

Vathí to: Turkey (Kuşadası; 1 daily late April–late October, 3–5 weekly late May–late September; otherwise approximately 1 weekly or by demand in winter; 1hr 30min).

Morning Greek craft takes passengers only; afternoon Turkish vessels take 2 cars apiece. Rates approximately £33/$50 one way including both Greek and Turkish port taxes, £42/$63 round trip in total; no special day return rate. Small cars £30/$45 one way.

Pithagório to: Turkey (Kuşadası; 3–4 weekly in high season only with Greek morning boat; 1hr 45min). Passenger fares the same as from Vathí.

HYDROFOILS

Vathí to: Turkey (Kuşadası; 2 daily June–Sept in theory; 45min). Fares, especially early or late in the season, are much the same as with the conventional craft.

Ikaría

Ikaría, a narrow, windswept landmass between Sámos and Míkonos, not surprisingly has the geographical characteristics of both the Cyclades and east Aegean. So far it's little visited (except by Germans) and invariably panned by travel writers who usually haven't even been to see it for themselves. The name supposedly derives from the legendary Icarus, who fell into the sea just offshore after the wax bindings on his wings melted; as some locals are quick to point out, the island is clearly wing-shaped.

For years, the only substantial tourism was generated by a few radioactive hot springs on the south coast, some reputed to cure rheumatism and arthritis, others to make women fertile, though a few are so potent that they've been closed for some time. The unnerving dockside sign "WELCOME TO THE ISLAND OF RADIATION" has now been replaced by one proclaiming "WELCOME TO ICARUS' ISLAND".

Ikaría, along with Thessaly on the mainland, western Sámos and Lésvos, has traditionally been one of the Greek Left's strongholds. This tendency dates from long decades of right-wing domination in Greece, when (as in prior ages) the island was used as a place of exile for political dissidents; apparently the strategy backfired, with the transportees outnumbering and even proseletyzing their hosts.

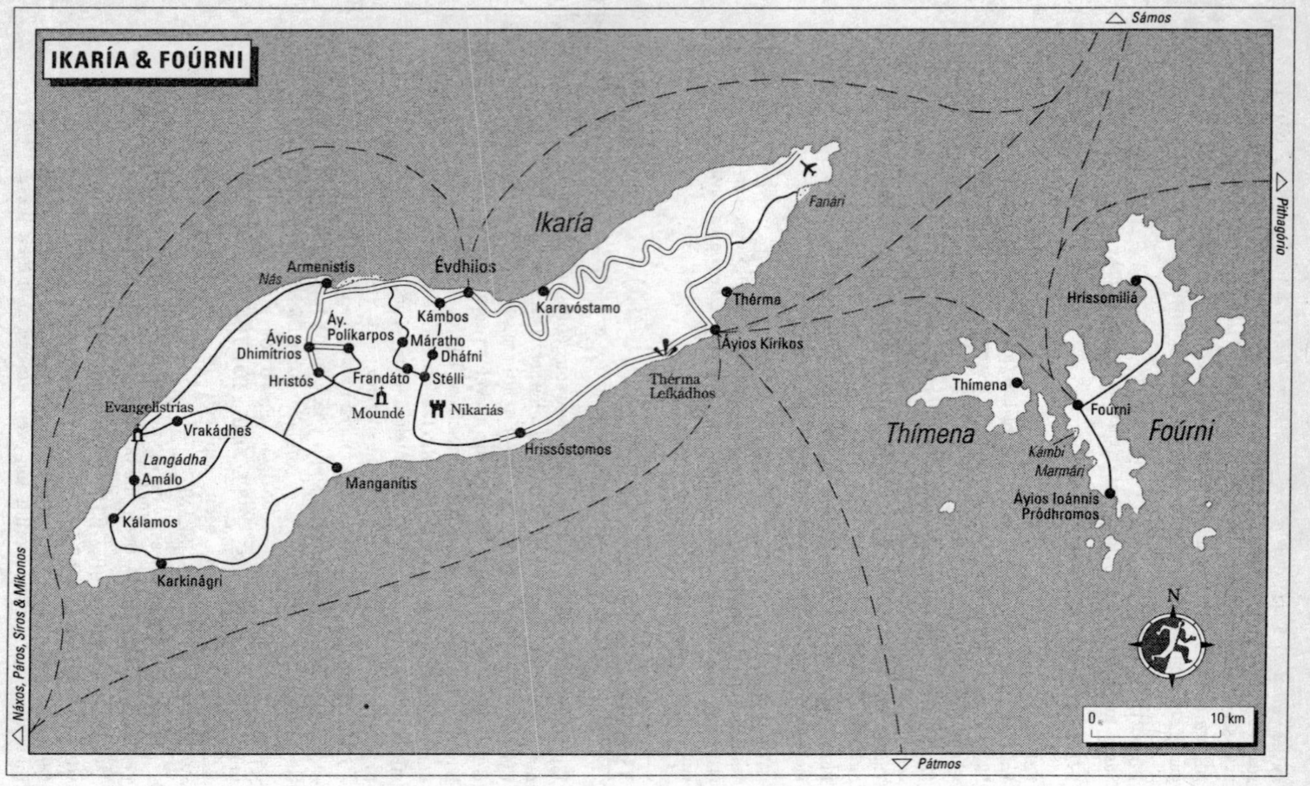

IKARÍA & FOÚRNI
Sámos
Pithagório
Pátmos
Náxos, Páros, Síros & Míkonos
Ikaría
Fanári
Armenistís
Nás
Évdhilos
Karavóstamo
Thérma
Kámbos
Áy. Polikarpos
Áyios Dhimítrios
Máratho
Dháfni
Áyios Kírikos
Hristós
Frandáto
Stélli
Thérma Lefkádhos
Moundé
Nikariás
Evangelistrías
Vrakádhes
Langádha
Amálo
Manganítis
Hrissóstomos
Kálamos
Karkinágri
Thímena
Hrissomiliá
Foúrni
Kámbi
Marmári
Áyios Ioánnis Pródhromos
N
0
10 km

At the same time, many Ikarians emigrated to North America, and, ironically, their capitalist remittances help keep the island going. It can be a bizarre experience to receive a lecture on the evils of US imperialism delivered by a retiree in perfect Alabaman English.

These are not the only Ikarian quirks, and for many outsiders, the place is an acquired taste. Even its most ardent partisans admit that the island hasn't nearly as much to offer as its neighbours. If you've spent any amount of time on adjacent Sámos, Ikaría can come as either quite a shock or the perfect antidote, as the two could hardly be more different.

Except for the forested area in the northwest, it's not a strikingly beautiful island, with most of the landscape being scrub-fringed schist, despite the presence of abundant ground water. The mostly desolate south coast is fringed by steep cliffs, while the north shore is less sheer but furrowed by deep canyons which deflect the road system into terrifying hairpin bends. Nor are there many picturesque villages, since the rural schist-roofed houses are generally scattered so as to be next to their famous apricot orchards, vineyards and fields.

The islanders have resisted most attempts to develop Ikaría for conventional tourism, which splutters along almost exclusively between July and September. Though an airport finally started operating in 1995, with a runway graded across Ikaría's northeast tip to permit approaches in any wind, it wasn't built to accommodate jets. Long periods of seemingly punitive neglect by Athens (and provincial big brother Sámos) have made the islanders profoundly self-sufficient and idiosyncratic, and tolerant of the same in others. Moreover, local pride and integrity dictates that approval from outsiders matters not a bit, and the Ikarians often seem to have little idea of what "modern tourists" expect. It is this very lack of obsequiousness which some visitors mistake for unfriendliness.

Áyios Kírikos and the spas

Most ferries call at the island's south-coast port and capital, **ÁYIOS KÍRIKOS**, a nondescript though inoffensive enough place. Because of the spa trade in nearby Therma, beds are at a premium here, so if you arrive in the evening, you'd be wise to accept any reasonable offers of rooms or proposals of taxi rides to the north coast, which won't be much more than 6000dr *per vehicle* to Armenistís. A cream-and-green **bus** sets out from the main square across the island to Armenistís in theory daily at 10am (in practice it can be any time between 9 and 11am), plus at 1.30pm on weekdays; the service to Evdhilos only departs at noon Monday to Saturday.

The baths in **Thérma**, 1km northeast of the harbour, are rather old-fashioned stone tubs, predictably institutional with hovering attendants, and open 8am–1pm only (preference given to those with doctor's prescription); there is also a grotto-sauna. A better bet for a less formal soak are the more natural hot springs at **Thérma**

Lefkádhos, 3km southwest of Áyios Kírikos, below a cluster of villas. Here the seaside spa is derelict, leaving the water to boil up in the shallows, mixing between giant volcanic boulders to a pleasant temperature. The only drawback is the landward setting; a fire in 1993 devastated all the trees hereabouts, besides killing fourteen people.

Accommodation

If you decide to **stay**, there are several hotels – for example the *Isabella* (☎0275/22 839; ③), or the friendly, basic but spotless *Akti* (☎0275/22 694; ②), on a knoll east of the fishing quay, with views of Foúrni from the garden. Rented rooms or pensions fill fast, and prices are not especially competitive: *Adam's Pension* (☎0275/22 418; ③) is about the fanciest and open all year, while those of *Ioannis Proestos* (☎0275/23 496; ③), above the sweet shop next to *Iy Sinandisis* (see below), are squeaky clean and excellent value. In the quietest and best location, uphill to the left (west) on Artemídhos as you face inland from the foot of the dock, are *Pension Maria Elena* (☎0275/22 835; ③) and a nearby rival. As a last resort you might try three unmarked, spartan outfits grouped around the post office on Dhionísou, the inland high street.

Eating and drinking

When **eating out**, there is a fair choice of establishments. On the way from the ferry to the main square you'll pass the barn-like *Ta Adhelfia* and *Ta Votsala*, open only in the evenings; *Ouzerí Psistaria*, inland toward the post office, is a very good and reasonable combination *ouzerí* and *loukoumádhiko*. Just around the corner from the latter, *Iy Klimataria* is no culinary marvel but worth noting because, unlike most of the others, it's open year-round. Finally, the giant *Iy Sinandisis* on the tree-lined esplanade is utterly unlike any other *kafenío* in the Greek islands: in a reversal of the norm, young adults play *távli* and cards inside, while outside their elders and assorted foreigners suck on sweets or watch each other – better entertainment than anything dished up at the nearby summer cinema.

Other practicalities

There are two **banks**, a limited-hours **OTE**, and assorted **ferry agents**, such as *Ikariadha* and *Dolihi Tours*, all of them coy about giving details of the midday *kaïki* to Foúrni, whose tickets are only sold on board. You can **rent** motorbikes and cars here too, though you may find better deals in Armenistís.

Évdhilos and around

The twisty, 41-kilometre road from Áyios Kírikos to Évdhilos is one of the steepest and most hair-raising on any Greek island, and the long ridge which extends the length of Ikaría often wears a coiffure of cloud, even when the rest of the Aegean sky is clear. **KARAVÓSTAMO**, with its tiny, scruffy port, is the first substantial place on the north coast, and is joined by a series of three beaches to **ÉVDHILOS**. Though the island's second town and a ferry stop at least three times weekly in summer, Évdhilos is considerably less equipped to deal with visitors than Áyios Kírikos. There are two **hotels**, the *Evdoxia*, on the slope west of the harbour (☎0275/31 502; ④), and the Neoclassical *Atheras* (☎0275/31 434; fax ☎31 426; ④), plus a few **rooms**. Of the trio of waterfront **restaurants**, *O Kokkos* has the fullest menu but works out expensive; try *O Flisvos* next door instead. A **post office** and **OTE**, and a surprisingly good town **beach** to the east, are also worth knowing about.

Kámbos and inland

KÁMBOS, 2km west, boasts a small museum with finds from nearby ancient Oinoe, the twelfth-century church of **Ayía Iríni** next to the museum, the sparse ruins of a **Byzantine palace** (just above the road) which housed exiled nobles and, last but not least, a large **beach**. Rooms are available from the store run by *Vassilis Kambouris* (☎0275/31 300; ②), which also acts as the unofficial tourist office for this part of Ikaría. Meals are served at a **taverna** that keeps bizarre 10pm-to-4am hours.

Kámbos is also the start and end point of a road loop up through the hamlet-speckled valley inland. **MARATHÓ** isn't up to much, but **FRANDÁTO** has a summertime taverna; **STÉLLI** and **DHÁFNI** are attractive examples of the little oases which sprout on Ikaría. From Stélli, another dirt road heads south through a mountain pass guarded by the ruined tenth-century Byzantine castle of **Nikariás**, near the hamlet of Kosikiá; from here you can travel east by jeep or motorbike to the large village of Hrissóstomos and the beginning of asphalt for the remaining 12km back to Áyios Kírikos.

Armenistís and around

Most travellers won't stop until reaching **ARMENISTÍS**, 57km from Áyios Kírikos, and with good reason: this little resort lies in the heart of Ikaría's finest wooded scenery, with two enormous, sandy beaches – **Livádhi** and **Messakhtí** – five and fifteen minutes' walk east respectively. The sea between here and Mikonos is one of the windiest patches in the Aegean, making this one of the few spots in Greece with anything resembling a consistent surf (see warning below).

Numerous campers in the marshes behind each stretch of sand set the tone for the place, but the islanders' tolerance doesn't yet extend to nude bathing, as signs warn you, and a semi-official site is in the process of being set up. A dwindling percentage of older buildings lends Armenistís the air of a Cornish fishing village; it's a tiny place, reminiscent of similar youth-orientated spots on the south coast of Crete, though lately gentrification has definitely set in.

Practicalities

The *Paskhalia* **taverna** and en-suite **rooms** (☎0275/71 302; winter ☎01/24 71 411; ③) are the best value in both categories. For more luxury, there's the *Armena Inn* (☎0275/41 415; ③), way up the hillside, or the luxury *Cavos Bay Hotel* (☎0275/71 381; fax ☎71 380; winter ☎01/76 40 235; ④), 1km west.

A "music bar" operates seasonally behind the nearer beach, but **nightlife** is mostly about extended sessions in the tavernas and cafés overlooking the anchorage. A giant bakery-cum-cake shop caters to sweet teeth for the entire west end of the island, and the *Marabou Travel Agency* changes money as well as renting out dilapidated mopeds and somewhat sturdier jeeps, although you don't really need either, since the best of Ikaría lies within an hour's walk of the fishing anchorage here. The sole drawback to staying in Armenistís is **getting away**: taxis and buses are elusive and even wealthier travellers may find themselves hitching to Évdhilos or beyond. Theoretically **buses** head at least as far as Évdhilos – all the way to Áyios Kírikos on Mondays and Fridays – at 7am, and to Évdhilos daily at 3pm, but school kids have priority on the early departure, and the second one is unreliable even by Ikarian standards.

Inland from Armenistís: Ráhes

Armenistís is actually the shore annexe of three inland hamlets – Áyios Dhimítrios, Áyios Políkarpos and Hristós – collectively known as **RÁHES**. Despite the modern dirt roads in through the pines, they still retain a certain Shangri-La quality, with the older residents speaking a positively Homeric dialect. On an island not short of foibles, Hristós is particularly strange, insomuch as the locals sleep much of the day, but shop, eat and even send their children to school at night; in fact most of the villages west of Évdhilos adhere to this schedule, defying central government efforts to bring them in line with the rest of Greece. Near the pokey main square of Hristós there's a **post office** and a **hotel/restaurant**, but for lunch you'll have to scrounge something at one of two unusual *kafenía*. The slightly spaced-out demeanours of those serving may be due to over-indulgence in the excellent home-brewed **wine** which everyone west of Évdhilos seems to make – strong but not hangover-inducing, and stored in rather disgusting goat-skins. These also make good shoulder bags, and are sold in some shops.

Nás

By tacit consent, Greek or foreign hippies, naturists and dope-fiends have been allowed to shift 4km west of Armenistís to **Nás**, a tree-clogged river canyon ending in a small but sheltered pebble beach. The bay is almost entirely enclosed by weird rock formations, and it's unwise to swim outside the cove's natural limits – there are drownings nearly every year in the open sea here, as well as at Messakhtí, closer to Armenistís.

The crumbling foundations of the fifth-century temple of **Artemis Tavropoleio** (Patroness of Bulls) overlook the permanent deep pool at the mouth of the river; people who used to camp rough just upstream are now encouraged to use the semi-official site at *Snack Bar River*. If you continue inland along this, Ikaría's only year-round watercourse, you'll find secluded rock pools for freshwater dips. Back at the top of the path leading down to the beach from the road are two or three tavernas and as many **rooms** – for instance *Pension Nas* (☎0275/41 255; ②).

The southwest coast

Should you be persuaded by *Marabou* in Armenistís to rent a vehicle or join one of their jeep safaris, you can make a tour through half a dozen villages at the southwest tip of the island. **VRAKÁDHES**, with two *kafenía* and a natural-balcony setting, makes a good first or last stop on a tour. A sharp drop below it, the impact of the empty convent of **Evangelistrías** (not to be confused with a namesake above Hristós, often called Moundé) lies mostly in its setting amid gardens overlooking the sea. Nearby **AMÁLO** has two summer tavernas; just inland, **Langádha** is not a village but a hidden valley containing an enormous and seasonally popular *exohikó kéndro* (rural taverna).

Puny mopeds will go down *from* Langádha *to* Kálamos, not the other way around; in any case it's a tough bike that gets all the way to **KARKINÁGRI**, at the base of cliffs near the southern extremity of Ikaría, and a dismal anticlimax. The only thing likely to bring a smile to your lips is the marked intersection of Leofóros Bakunin and Odhós Lenin – surely the last two such Marxist streets remaining in Greece if not anywhere in Europe – at the edge of the town, which boasts two sleepy, seasonal tavernas and a rooms establishment near the jetty. Before this road was opened (the continuation to Manganítis and Áyios Kírikos is stalled at a difficult-to-dynamite rock-face), Karkinágri's only easy link with the outside world was by ferry or *kaïki*, either of which still call once or twice a week in mid-summer.

Satellite islets: Thímena and Foúrni

The straits between Sámos and Ikaría are speckled with a mini–archipelago of spidery islets, although the only ones permanently inhabited are Thímena and Foúrni. **Thímena**, the more westerly, has one tiny hillside settlement, at which a regular *kaïki* calls on its way between Ikaría and Foúrni, but casual visits are explicitly discouraged and there are no tourist facilities.

Foúrni is home to a huge fishing fleet and one of the more thriving boatyards in the Aegean. Thanks to these, and the 1989 improvement of the jetty to receive car ferries, its population is stable, unlike so many small Greek islands. The islets were once the lair of Maltese pirates, and indeed many of the islanders have a distinctly North African appearance.

Apart from the remote hamlet of **Hrissomiliá** in the north, where the island's main, partly paved road goes, most of Foúrni's inhabitants are concentrated in the **port** and **Kambí**, a hamlet just south. The harbour community is larger than it seems from the sea, with the locals' friendliness adding to a general ambience reminiscent of 1970s Greece.

Getting to Foúrni

The islanders' shopping-and-post *kaïki* leaves Ikaría at about 1pm several days a week, stays overnight at Foúrni and returns the next morning. The twice-weekly *kaïki* from Karlóvassi and the occasional larger car ferries are likewise not tourist excursion boats but exist for the benefit of the islanders. The only feasible way of making a daytrip to Foúrni is to take one of the hydrofoils that run several mornings a week in summer from Sámos (Vathí or Pithagório).

Foúrni port

A tout authorized to act for any of the several **rooms** establishments meets all craft and assigns customers to beds (② low season, ③ peak season) by a rota system. However there's nothing stopping you from phoning ahead to reserve space at the more desirable places, which include the seafront ones run by Manolis and Patra Markakis (☎0275/51 268; ② for cold-water rooms in front, ③ for modernized en–suite units in the rear), immediately to your left as you disembark. If they're full (usually the case in August), try the inland, modern blocks of *Evtyhia Amoryianou* (☎0275/51 364, fax ☎0275/51 290 ③), whose father Nikos Kondylas is a mine of information about the island, or *Maouni* (☎0275/51 367; ③). There's currently at least one British tour operator (*Greek Sun*) with an allotment here, so you could even book rooms through them from overseas.

Of the three waterfront **tavernas**, the local favourite is *Rementzo*, better known as *Nikos*'; if you're lucky the local *astakós* or Aegean lobster, actually an oversized saltwater crayfish, may be on the menu. Otherwise go for the succulent *skathári* or black bream, which thrives in the surrounding waters.

The central "high street", fieldstoned and mulberry-shaded, ends well inland at a handsome square with a traditional *kafenío* under each of two giant plane trees. Between them stands a Hellenistic sarcophagus that was found in a nearby field, and overhead on a conical hill looms the site of the island's ancient acropolis. Nearby is a **post office** where you can change money, but no bank; shops are surprisingly numerous and well stocked, so there's no need to haul in supplies from Foúrni's larger neighbours.

Southern Foúrni: Kambí and Áyios Ioánnis Pródhromos

A fifteen-minute walk south from the port, beginning at the school, skirting the cemetery and then slipping over the windmill ridge, brings you to **KAMBÍ**, a scattered community overlooking a pair of sandy, tamarisk-shaded coves which you'll share with chickens and hauled-up fishing boats – and, in season, quite a few other visitors. There are two cafés; the lower (*Andreas*, tables on the sand) also controls seven **rooms**, which are admittedly spartan but have arguably the best views on the island, and another family also has some cottages to let – ask locally. A path continues to the next bay south, which like Kambí cove is a favourite anchorage for passing yachts.

Continuing south along the coast is problematic on foot; best to arrange boat trips in the harbour to **Marmári** cove, so named for its role as a quarry for ancient Ephesus in Asia Minor – you can still see some unshipped marble blocks lying about. From Marmári a faint trail climbs up to the spine of the island, emerging onto the dirt road just south of Theológos chapel. Most of the old ridge path can still be followed south of the chapel, shortcutting the road as it drops to the hamlet and monastery of **ÁYIOS IOÁNNIS PRÓDHROMOS**. There are no facilities whatsoever here – sometimes not even fresh water from the monastery's courtyard tap – but you'll find two tiny, secluded **beaches** below the hamlet to either side of the jetty.

Northern Foúrni: Hrissomiliá and beaches

Heading north from the harbour via steps, then a trail, you'll find more **beaches**: **Psilí Ámmos**, in front of a derelict fish-processing plant, with a bit of shade at one end, plus two more secluded ones further on at **Kálamos**, reached by continuing along the path.

At the extreme north of the island, idyllic **HRISSOMILIÁ** was more usually approached by boat in the years before the road was improved. The village, split into a shore district and a hill settlement at the top of a canyon, has a decent beach flanked by better but less accessible ones. Near the dock are some very rough-and-ready *kafenía*/tavernas; equally simple **rooms** can be arranged on the spot – just ask around.

Should you decide to walk back to town, it's a full three-and-a-half-hour hike from Hrissomiliá to the port. The first two hours are a dreary tramp along a shadeless road, before the old *kalderími* re-appears for the final hour-plus up to the monastery of **Panayía**, which overlooks the town from a ridge on the north. The last section of the path, with two decent beaches in the bay of **Balí** below Panayía to the north, are the walk's main redeeming features.

Greek script table

Ikaría	Ικαρία	ΙΚΑΡΙΑ
Armenistís	Αρμενιστής	ΑΡΜΕΝΙΣΤΗΣ
Áyios Kírikos	Αγιος Κήρυκος	ΑΓΙΟΣ ΚΗΡΥΚΟΣ
Áyios Políkarpos	Αγιος Πολύκαρπος	ΑΓΙΟΣ ΠΟΛΥΚΑΡΠΟΣ
Évdhilos	Εύδηλος	ΕΥΔΗΛΟΣ
Frandáto	Φραντάτο	ΦΡΑΝΤΑΤΟ
Hristós	Χριστός	ΧΡΙΣΤΟΣ

Greek script cont.		
Kámbos	Κάμπος	ΚΑΜΠΟΣ
Karavóstamo	Καραβόσταμο	ΚΑΡΑΒΟΣΤΑΜΟ
Karkinágri	Καρκινάγρι	ΚΑΡΚΙΝΑΓΡΙ
Nás	Νάς	ΝΑΣ
Ráhes	Ράχες	ΡΑΧΕΣ
Thérma	Θέρμα	ΘΕΡΜΑ
Thérma Lefkádhos	Θέρμα Λευκάδος	ΘΕΡΜΑ ΛΕΥΚΑΔΟΣ
Thímena	Θύμαινα	ΘΥΜΑΙΝΑ
Foúrni	Φούρνοι	ΦΟΥΡΝΟΙ
Áyios Ioánnis Pródhromos	Αγιος Ιοάννης Πρόδρομος	ΑΓΙΟΣ ΙΟΑΝΝΗΣ ΠΡΟΔΡΟΡΟΜΟΣ
Hrisomiliá	Χρυσομηλιά	ΧΡΥΣΟΜΗΛΙΑ
Kambí	Καμπή	ΚΑΜΠΗ
Marmári	Μαρμάρι	ΜΑΡΜΑΡΙ

Ikaría Travel Details

ISLAND TRANSPORT

BUSES

Áyios Kírikos (Ikaría) to: Armenistís (daily at 10am, Mon–Fri 1.30pm); Évidhilos (Mon–Sat at noon).

NB departures are unreliable except July/Aug, and even then must be double-checked!

INTER-ISLAND TRANSPORT

KAÏKIA AND EXCURSION BOATS

Foúrni to: Ikaría (Áyios Kírikos; 4 mornings weekly, returning about 1pm); Sámos (Karlóvassi; 2 mornings weekly, usually Mon/Thurs).

FERRIES

Ikaría (Áyios Kírikos) to: Míkonos (1–2 weekly on *Arkadia Lines* or *G&A Ferries*); Náxos (2–4 weekly on *G&A*); Páros (3–5 weekly on *Agapitos Lines*); Pátmos (1–2 weekly on *Miniotis*); Piréas (5–9 weekly with several companies; 9hr 30min–11hr 30min); Sámos (both northern ports; 5–9 weekly with several companies); Síros (1 weekly on *G&A*).

Ikaría (Évidhilos) to: Páros, Pireás, Sámos (all 4–6 weekly on *Agapitos* or *Arkadia*); Síros (1–3 weekly on *Agapitos*).

Foúrni to: Híos (1–2 weekly on *Miniotis*); Ikaría (Áyios Kírikos; 2 weekly on *Agapitos* or *G&A*); Ikaría (Évdhilos; 1 weekly on *G&A*); Míkonos (1 weekly on *G&A*); Náxos (1 weekly on *G&A*); Páros (2 weekly on *Agapitos* or *G&A*); Pátmos (1–2 weekly on *Miniotis*); Pireás (3 weekly on *G&A* or *Agapitos*); Sámos (both northern ports; 3–5 weekly on *Agapitos* or *G&A*); Sámos (varies between Pithagório & Váthi; 1–2 weekly on *Miniotis*); Síros (1 weekly on *G&A*).

HYDROFOILS

Ikaría (Áyios Kírikos) to: Foúrni, Pátmos, Sámos (Vathí) (all 2–3 weekly June–Oct on *Ilio Lines*, 2–3 weekly on *Gianmar Lines*).

Foúrni to: Ikaría (Áyios Kírikos; 3–6 weekly June–Oct, morning, on *Ilio* or *Gianmar*); Pátmos (3–6 weekly June–Oct, morning, on *Ilio* or *Gianmar*); Sámos (Pithagório; 1 weekly June–Oct, midday with *Mamidhakis/ Dodecanese Hydrofoils*); Sámos (Vathí; 3–6 afternoons weekly June–Oct, on *Ilio* or *Gianmar*).

Ikaría

DOMESTIC FLIGHTS
Ikaría to: Athens (2 weekly; 1hr).

Híos

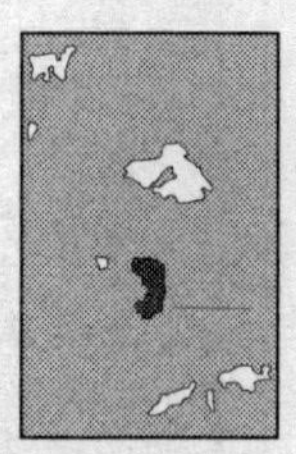

"Craggy **Híos**", as Homer aptly described his (probable) birthplace, has a turbulent history and a strong identity. This large island has always been relatively prosperous: in medieval times through the export of mastic resin, a trade controlled by Genoese overlords between 1346 and 1566, when they held the island in return for services rendered to the faltering Byzantine Empire, and later under the Ottomans, for whom Híos was known as Sakız Adası (Resin Island). Since union with Greece in 1912, several shipping dynasties have emerged here, continuing the pattern of wealth.

These powerful shipowning families and the military authorities did not encourage tourism until the late 1980s, when a worldwide shipping crisis and the saturation of other, more obviously "marketable" islands combined to erode their resistance. Increasing numbers of foreigners are now discovering a Híos beyond its large port capital: fascinating villages, important Byzantine monuments and a respectable, if remote, complement of beaches. While unlikely ever to be dominated by tourism, the local scene definitely has a modernized flavour – courtesy of numerous returned Greek-Americans – and English is widely spoken. All strata of society participate in the maritime way of life, with many people, including women, serving as radio operators or officers in the merchant marine.

Unfortunately, the island has suffered more than its fair share of catastrophes during the past two centuries. The Turks perpetrated their most famous, if not their worst, anti-revolutionary atrocity here in 1822, massacring 30,000 Hiots and enslaving or exiling even more. In 1881, much of Híos was destroyed by a violent earthquake, and throughout the 1980s the natural beauty of the island was severely compromised by devastating forest fires, compounding the effect of generations of tree-felling by boat-builders. Nearly two-thirds of the majestic pines are now gone, with patches of woods persisting only in the far northeast and the centre of Híos.

In 1988, the first charters from northern Europe were instituted, signalling momentous changes for the island. There are now perhaps 10,000 guest beds on Híos, the vast majority of them in the capital or the nearby beach resort of Karfás. So far, tourists seem evenly divided among a babel of nationalities, including a small British contingent brought in by two specialist operators (see

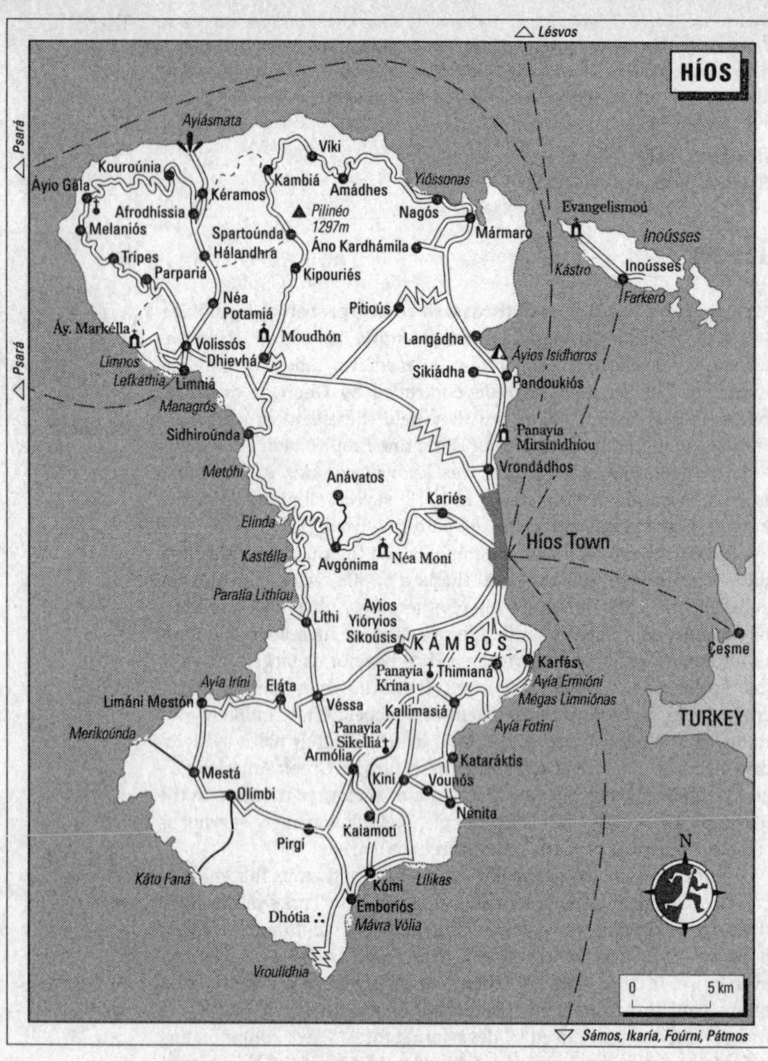

Basics). Further expansion, however, is hampered by the distances and relatively sparse public transport between the port and many of the more interesting villages and beaches, the lack of direct international air links, and the refusal of property owners to part with land for the extension of the airport runway. The provincial authorities have nevertheless completed a new yacht marina at Vrondádhos, home to many professional seafarers, and tourist facilities thus far have tended to be pitched at a fairly sophisticated level.

Híos Town

HÍOS, the harbour and main town, will come as a shock after modest island capitals elsewhere; it's a bustling, concrete-laced commercial centre with little predating the 1881 earthquake. Yet in many ways it is the most satisfactory of the East Aegean ports; time spent exploring is rewarded with a large and fascinating marketplace, a museum or two, some good, authentic tavernas and, on the waterfront, possibly the best-attended evening *vólta* (promenade) in Greece. Old photos show the quay beautifully shaded and paved in red marble; the trees were axed and the marble asphalted over during the 1950s to smooth the rides of imported Cadillacs, but you can still see a few exposed blocks at the water's edge.

Arrival, transportation and information

Large **ferries** dock at the northwest corner of the port, while the smaller ferries, hydrofoils and excursion boats straggle along Egéou. The **airport** lies 4km south along the coast at Kondári; there's no special bus between it and the *Olympic Airways* terminal on the waterfront, but any blue **urban bus** labelled "KONDÁRI KARFÁS", departing from the station on the north side of the park, passes the airport gate. Alternatively, a taxi ride to or from town is not exactly prohibitive (500dr with baggage, against about 200dr for the bus).

The standard green-and-cream **long-distance buses** leave from a parking area on the opposite side of the park, behind the Omirio Cultural Centre; services to the south of Híos are adequate, but those to the centre and northwest of the island are almost nonexistent. To explore these areas it's well worth renting a powerful motorbike (*not* a moped) or a car (see "Listings" for suggestions). Alternatively you could share a taxi, which is common practice here – they're bright red on Híos, not grey as in most of Greece. **Parking** is a nightmare in town; usually the only spaces to be had are northwest of the Kástro walls, along Handhákos, or at the extreme south end of the harbour, in the side streets behind the *Hotel Kyma*.

The helpful **municipal tourist office** (May–Sept Mon–Fri 7am–2.30pm & 6–9.30pm; Sat 10am–1.30pm; Sun 10am–noon; Oct–April Mon–Fri 7am–2.30pm) is at Kanári 18, near the *Ionian Bank*; the conspicuous "Hadzelenis Tourist Information Office" (☎0271/26 743) on the quay is a private entity geared primarily towards accommodation.

Accommodation

Híos Town has a relative abundance of affordable **accommodation**, rarely if ever completely full, and generally open year-round. Most can be found along the water or in the perpendicular alleys and parallel streets behind, and almost all of it is plagued by traffic noise to some degree – we've focused on the more peaceful establishments.

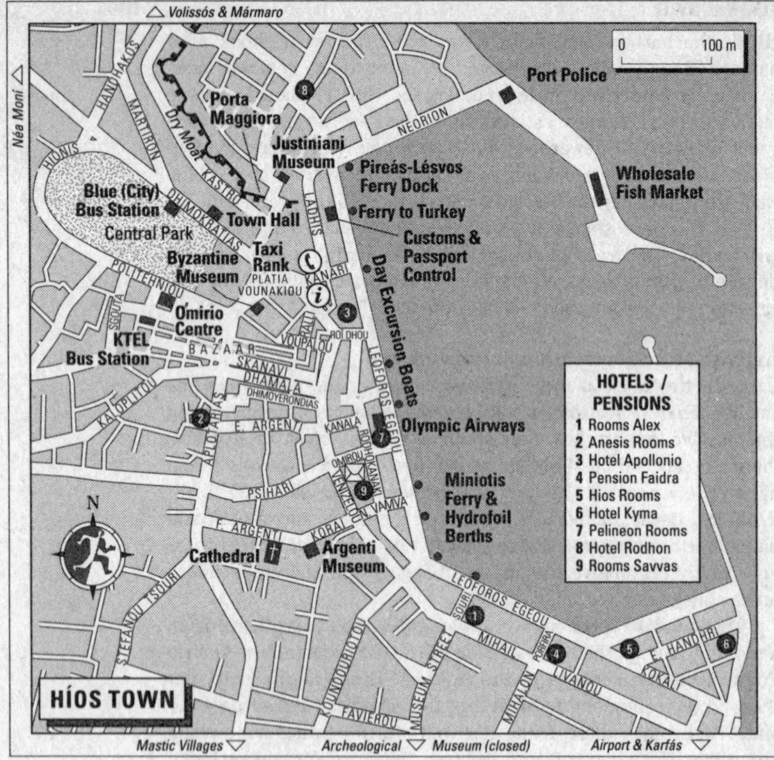

Budget

Rooms Alex, Mihaïl Livanoú 29 (☎0271/26 054). The friendly proprietor tends to meet late ferries; otherwise ring the bell. Roof garden above the well-furnished rooms; ② without bath, ③ en suite.

Híos Rooms, Kokáli 1 corner Egéou (☎0271/27 295 or 26 743). Clean, antique rooms in an old school above a boat chandler's; relatively quiet for a seafront locale. ②.

Pelineon Rooms, Omírou 9, corner Egéou (☎0271/28 030). Many rooms have sea views, and the owner also does bike and car rental; cheap, waterless singles (①), and en-suite doubles (③).

Rooms Savvas, Rodhokanáki 34 (☎0271/41 721). Good value en-suite singles and doubles with high ceilings; also motorbike rental. ②.

Moderate

Anesis, corner Vasilikári and Aplotariás, in the marketplace (☎0271/44 801). Rooms have baths, fridges and air conditioning; quiet after dark. ③.

Apollonio, Roïdhou 5 (☎0271/24 842). Fairly quiet hotel tucked into a tiny square just inland from the water; en suite ③. Also a seaward annexe, the *Acropolis*, with simpler facilities at ②.

Rodhon, Zaharíou 17 (☎0271/24 335). The owners can be crotchety, and the non-suite rooms are rather expensive, but this is virtually the only place inside the *kástro*, and very quiet. ③.

Expensive

Faidra, Mihaïl Livanoú 13 (☎0271/41 130; fax ☎41 128). Well-appointed pension in an old mansion complete with coveted stone arches in the downstairs winter bar; in summer the bar is outside, so ask for a rear room to minimize nocturnal noise. Manolis, the proprietor, is a playwright and an interesting conversationalist. ⑤ in season, ④ for long stays or out of season.

Kyma, east end of Evyenías Handhrí (☎0271/44 500; fax ☎44 600). The hotel building's a bit of a chimera – a Neoclassical mansion with a modern extension – but the service and big breakfasts provided by the kindly Spordhilis family make the place. The old wing saw a critical moment in modern Greek history in September 1922, when Colonel Nikolaos Plastiras commandeered it as his headquarters after the Greek defeat in Asia Minor, and announced the deposition of King Constantine I. ⑤ including breakfast, effectively ③ if booked through *Greek Sun* or *Sunvil* package operators.

The town

Although it's a sprawling town of about 30,000, most things of interest to visitors lie within a hundred or so metres of the water, which is fringed by **Leofóros Egéou**. When this becomes a pedestrian zone at night, traffic circulates on inland parallel streets such as **Rodhokanáki**, **Venizélou** and **Aplotariás**, the latter threading the main commercial district and off-limits to cars by day. **Kanári** links the waterfront with the central park and adjoining main square, officially Plastíra but known universally as **Vounakíou**, to the south and east of which extends the wonderfully lively tradesmen's **bazaar**, where you can find everything from live monkeys to cast-iron woodstoves. Híos must boast more varieties of **bread** than any other island in Greece – corn, whole-wheat, multi-grain, "dark" and "village" – and most of these are on sale from the bakers in the marketplace. Like its neighbours Sámos and Lésvos, Híos also makes respectable **oúzo**; the best brand is reckoned to be *Tetteris*.

The museums

Opposite the Vounakíou taxi rank, in the old **Mecidiye Tzami (Mosque)**, the grandiosely entitled "Byzantine Museum" (Tues–Sun 10am–1pm; free) is merely an archeological warehouse and workshop, awash in marble fragments such as Turkish, Jewish and Armenian gravestones. The official **Archeological Museum**, in the south of the town, is shut indefinitely following 1992 earthquake damage, but its collection was never the most compelling anyway.

More worthwhile is the **Argenti Folklore Museum** (Mon–Fri 8am–2pm plus Fri 5–7.30pm, Sat 8am–12.30pm; 400dr), housed on the top floor of the Koráï Library building at Koráï 2 and endowed by a leading Hiot family. Accordingly there's a rather ponderous gallery of genealogical portraits, showing if nothing else the local aristocracy's compulsion to adopt English dress and artistic conventions in every era. The other wing boasts a hall of costumes and embroidery, kitsch figurines in traditional dress, and carved wooden implements. Among multiple replicas of Delacroix's *Massacre at Hios* are engravings of eighteenth-century islanders as seen by assorted Grand Tourists, plus several views of the Genoese *kástro* which, until the earthquake, was completely intact. Thereafter, developers razed the seaward walls, filled in much of the moat to the south, and made a fortune selling off the resulting real estate around present-day Platía Vounakíou.

The Kástro

You should enter the **Kástro** at the Porta Maggiora, the gate onto the square behind the town hall. The top floor of a medieval mansion just inside is home these days to the **Justiniani Museum** (nominal hours Tues–Sun 9am–7pm; free), housing a satisfying collection of unusual icons and mosaics rescued from local churches. Seventy-five Hiot notables were briefly held hostage in the adjacent small dungeon before their execution by the Ottomans in 1822. It's well worth having a wander around the old **residential quarter** – formerly the Muslim and Jewish neighbourhoods – inside what remains of the castle walls. Among the wood-and-plaster houses you'll find assorted Ottoman monuments in various states of decay, including a cemetery, a small mosque, several inscribed fountains, and a dervish convent that was converted into a church after 1923.

Eating, drinking and nightlife

Eating out in Híos Town can be more pleasurable than the rash of obvious, mostly bogus, *ouzerís* on the waterfront would suggest; it is also usually a fair bit cheaper than on the neighbouring islands of Sámos and Lésvos. There were once more than a dozen traditional, high-ceilinged, wood-floored, mirror-walled *kafenía* along the front; now there is just one, the balance replaced by supernumerary pubs of a trendy style in keeping with the aspirations of most younger Hiots.

Estiatorio Dhimitrakopoulos, corner Sgoúta and Vlatariás, near the *KTEL* station. Simple, inexpensive, oven-cooked fare and an interesting mix of locals and foreign residents in this tiny hole in the wall. Lunch only.

O Hotzas, Yioryíou Kondhíli 3, near intersection of Stefánou Tsoúri, off map. Recently moved to gorgeous new premises with arcaded interior and summer garden, this was long the premier taverna in Híos Town; the cooking has deteriorated of late, but you might still catch them on a good night. Dinner only; closed Sun.

Iakovos Pavtas, beside the wholesale fish market at the far northeast end of the harbour jetty. Go early for the best quality at this *ouzerí*, which serves mostly seafood and is blissfully free of cars and exhaust fumes. Dinner only.

Iviskos The most tasteful café on the quay, with a range of juices, coffees and alcoholic drinks.

O Kavos, towards the south end of the quay, near the "kink" in Egéou. The best (and longest-established) bar in terms of music, decor and crowd.

No-name, immediately behind the *Acropolis/Apollonio* lodgings. This tiny milk shop at the corner of Roïdhou and Venizélou serves sheeps' milk yoghurt from Lésvos, *loukoumádhes* (dough fritters or *baignettes*) and very occasionally rice pudding.

Theodhosiou, junction Leofóros Egéou and Neoríon. A genuine *ouzerí*; good, inexpensive, huge menu, though it's best to wait until after the big ferries have gone from the dock immediately opposite. Dinner only.

Listings

ATMs Numerous banks with ATMs: *Ethniki/National*, *Emboriki/Commercial*, *Pisteos/Credit* and *Ioniki/Ionian*.

Car rental A row of independent agencies along Evyenías Handhrí behind the *Chandris Hotel*; *George Sotirakis/European Rent a Car* at no. 3 (☎0271/29 754) has been tried and can be recommended.

Cinema/revue theatre At Venizélou 92, under *Hotel Diana*; Oct–May only.

Events venue *Omirio*, on the south side of the central park, is an events hall and cultural centre that's well worth a look; aside from frequently changing exhibitions, its large auditorium is a popular venue for foreign musicians.

Ferry/travel agents Whether for the short hop over to Turkey or the long-haul *NEL* ferries, these cluster to either side of the customs building, towards the north end of Egéou and its continuation Neórion. *Miniotis Lines*, at Neoríon 21/23 (☎0271/24 670 or 41 073), is about the most active, with a regular morning service to Çeşme (Turkey), small ferries to many neighbouring islands, and excursions to Inoússes. The Turkish evening ferry to Çeşme is currently handled by *Faros Travel* (☎0271/27 240), while the *Gianmar* hydrofoil agent is *Travel Shop*, Egéou 56 (☎0271/20 160).

Opening hours A Hiot idiosyncracy is the closure of all shops every afternoon during summer – if you want to buy anything, make sure you do so before 2pm.

OTE Directly opposite the tourist office; daily 7am–11pm.

Post office On Omírou, just above Rodhokanáki.

Nearby beaches: Karfás to Kataráktis

Híos Town itself has no beaches worth mentioning; the closest sandy one is at **KARFÁS**, 7km south past the airport and served by frequent blue bus. Since 1988, most of the growth in the Hiot tourist industry has occurred here, to the considerable detriment of the 500-metre-long, minimally shaded beach: massive hotel construction has interfered with natural sand deposition, so that the once gently sloping shore is now steep, rocky and seaweedy, except at its far south end.

Karfás practicalities

The main bright spot is the popular and unique **pension** *Markos' Place* (☎0271/31 990; ③, ② low season, April–Nov, or by arrangement), at the doubly dedicated monastery of Áyios Yióryios and Áyios Pandelímon, on the hillside south of the bay. Markos

Kostalas, who leases the premises from the local municipality, has created a unique environment much loved by the special-activity groups which frequent the place. Guests are housed in the former pilgrims' cells, with self-catering facilities available; individuals (there are several single "cells") are more than welcome, though advance reservations are strongly recommended. The only outfit not specifically geared towards package groups is the long-established seaview hotel, *Karatzas* (☎0271/31 180; ③; open May–Oct), at mid-beach.

Local **eating** options are surprisingly good, considering Karfás' role as a package resort. At the south end of the beach, *O Karfas* (locally known as *Yiamos'* after the proprietor) serves abundant though not especially elegant food at fair prices. The restaurant at the hotel *Karatzas* (see above) has better service and atmosphere, but the best-value taverna is *O Dholomas*, 3km back towards town at Kondári, on a side road between the public swimming pool and the *Morning Star Hotel*; you should overlook the tacky decor and often perfunctory service for the sake of the generally excellent food (open May–Oct; weekends only out of season).

Ayía Ermióni and Ayía Fotiní

Some 2km further along the coast from Karfás, **AYÍA ERMIÓNI** is less of a beach than a fishing anchorage surrounded by a handful of tavernas (best of these is the *Snack Bar Ankira*) and rooms to rent. The actual beach is a few hundred metres further at **Mégas Limniónas**, smaller than Kárfas and beset by road noise, but rather more scenic at its south end where cliffs provide a backdrop. Both Ayía Ermióni and Mégas Limniónas are served by extensions of the blue bus route to either Karfás or Thimianá, the nearest inland village.

The coast road loops up to Thimianá, from where you can (with your own transport only) continue 3km south towards Kalimassiá to the turning for **Ayía Fotiní**, a 700-metre pebble beach with exceptionally clean water. There's no shade, however, unless you count shadows from the numerous blocks of rooms under construction; a few tavernas cluster around the parking area where the side road meets the sea.

Kataráktis

The last settlement on this coast, 5km beyond Kalimassiá and served by long-distance bus, is **KATARÁKTIS**, remarkable mainly for its fishing port, pleasant waterfront of balconied houses and handful of tavernas. The best of these are at the south end of the quay opposite the boats, where *O Tsambos* is hard to fault for inexpensive fish. There are no beaches of any note in the vicinity, but the narrow-alleyed hill villages of **NÉNITA** (same bus service) and **VOUNÓS**, just inland, are worth exploring.

Southern Híos

Besides its olive groves, the gently rolling countryside in the south of the island is also home to the mastic bush, *Pistacia lentisca* to be precise. This rather unexceptional plant, pruned to an umbrella shape to facilitate havesting, grows in much of island Greece, but only here does it produce an aromatic resin of marketable quantity and quality, scraped from incisions made on the trunk during summer. For centuries Hiot mastic was used as a base for paints, cosmetics and chewable jelly beans which became a somewhat addictive staple in the Ottoman harems. Indeed, the interruption of the flow of mastic from Híos to Istanbul by the revolt of spring 1822 was one of the root causes of the brutal Ottoman reaction.

The wealth engendered by the mastic trade supported twenty *mastikhohoriá* (mastic villages) from the time the Genoese set up a monopoly (*maona*) in the substance during the fourteenth and fifteenth centuries. However, the end of imperial Turkey, and the industrial revolution with its petroleum-based products, knocked the bottom out of the mastic market; now it's just a curiosity, to be chewed – try the sweetened *Elma* brand gum – or drunk as a liqueur called *mastíha*. Since ancient times it has also been used for medicinal purposes; contemporary advocates claim that mastic boosts the immune system and thins the blood. Whatever the truth, the *mastikhohoriá* now live mainly off their tangerines, apricots and olives.

The villages themselves, supposedly twenty in total, were the only settlements on Híos spared by the Turks when they put down the local uprising in 1822. Architecturally unique, they were laid out by the Genoese but retain a distinctly Middle-Eastern air. The basic plan consists of a rectangular warren of stone houses, with the outer row doubling as the town's perimeter fortification and pierced by just a few gates. More recent additions, whether in traditional architectural style or not, straggle outside the original defences. All of the *mastikhohoriá* lie on the same trunk route, and more or less share a bus service (see "Travel Details"). However, if you're relying solely on public transport, you'll be hard pushed to see the most interesting villages in single day and have a dip at one of the nearby beaches.

Armólia and Pirgí

ARMÓLIA, 20km from town, is the smallest and least imposing of the mastic villages. Its main virtues are a **pottery industry** – the best shops are the last two on the right, driving southwest – and three **snack bars** open all year round; two are on the road and the other in the centre. (Out of season it can be difficult to find places to eat in the south of the island.)

PIRGÍ, 5km further south, is perhaps the liveliest and certainly the most colourful of the communities, with most of its houses elaborately embossed with *ksistá*, geometric patterns cut into the plaster and then outlined with paint. On the northeast corner of the central square, the twelfth-century Byzantine church of **Áyii**

Apóstoli (Tues–Thurs & Sat 10am–1pm), embellished with much later frescoes, is tucked under an arcade. The giant cathedral of the Assumption on the square itself boasts a *témblon* in an odd folk style dating from 1642, and an equally bizarre carved figure peeking out from the base of the pulpit. All this sits a bit incongruously with the vast number of post-card racks and boutiques that have sprung up lately on every thoroughfare.

Pirgí has a handful of **rooms**, many of them bookable through the *Women's Agricultural and Tourist Cooperative* (☎0271/72 496; ③). Otherwise, try *Rita's Rooms* (0271/72 479; ②), though they're on the main bypass road, with a potentially noisy pub nearby. In the medieval core you'll find a **bank**, a **post office**, a minuscule **OTE** stall on the square, and a couple of **tavernas**, best of which is *Iy Manoula*, right next to OTE.

Emboriós, Kómi and Vroulídhia

Pirgí is actually closest to the two major **beach** resorts in this corner of the island. The nearest of these, 6km southeast, is **EMBORIÓS**, an almost landlocked harbour with a few mediocre tavernas (the most passable of these is *Ifestio*). The only clue to its former importance as a trading post for the ancient Hiots is a scanty, British-excavated archeological site nearby. For swimming, follow the road to its end at an oversubscribed parking lot and initial beach of **Mávra Vólia**, then continue along an obvious trail over the headland to two more dramatic pebble strands, twice as long and backed by impressive cliffs. The red and black volcanic stones absorb the sun, reducing reflective sunburn but becoming quite toasty to lie upon.

If you want pure (brown) sand, you'll have to go to **KÓMI**, 3km northeast of Emboriós, also accessible from Armólia via Kalamotí. It's bidding to become a sort of Greek-pitched Karfás, though so far there are just a few fairly indistinguishable tavernas and summer apartments along the largely pedestrianized beachfront. The bus service is fairly good in season, often following a loop route through Pirgí and Emboriós. If Kómi's not to your taste, you can head just 2km east to the quieter and more pebbly coves of **Lílikas**.

The right fork in the road just before Emboriós leads for 5km past the ruined medieval Dhótia tower, ending in some hair-raising zig zags down to the 150-metre pea-gravel beach of **Vroulídhia**. The dramatically sculptured volcanic bay, 5km from Emboriós, has views south to the very tip of Híos and Ikaría beyond, but gets packed in summer and has no facilities. Women should also beware that the layout of the place means there's no easy escape from lechers.

Olímbi, Mestá and Limáni Mestón

Seven kilometres west of Pirgí is **OLÍMBI**, the least visited of the mastic villages but by no means devoid of interest. The characteristic defensive tower-keep, which at Pirgí stands virtually abandoned away from the modernized main square, here looms bang in the middle, its ground floor occupied by two *kafenía*. A recently improved seven-kilometre side road beginning just east of the village leads to the little beach of **Káto Faná**, a popular spot with Greek summer campers, despite signs forbidding the practice and the lack of any facilities. By the roadside, some 400m above the shore, are the remains of a temple to Apollo, which amount to little more than scattered masonry around a medieval chapel.

The finest example of the *mastikhohoriá* is sombre **MESTÁ**, just 4km further along the road from Olímbi. From its main square, dominated by the **church of Taxiárhis** (the largest on the island), a bewildering maze of cool, shady lanes, with anti-earthquake buttresses and tunnels between and inside the usually unpainted houses, leads off in all directions. Most streets end in blind alleys, except those leading directly to the six gates; the northeast one still has its original iron grate.

If you'd like to **stay**, an EOT-originated scheme of half-a-dozen rooms in restored traditional dwellings is now managed by *Dhimitris Pipidhis* (☎0271/76 319; ③); alternatively, those run by the *Zervoudhi* (☎0271/76 240; ②) and *Yialouri* (0271/76 137; ②) households are somewhat less elaborate. Of the two **tavernas** on the main square, *O Morias sta Mesta* has been written up in numerous international publications for its tasty rural specialities, such as *krítamo* (an edible coastal weed) and the locally produced raisin wine: heavy, semi-sweet and sherry-like.

One drawback to staying in Mestá would be a dearth of good local beaches. Its harbour, **LIMÁNI MESTÓN** (aka Passá Limáni), 3km north, has no beach of any sort and has come down considerably in the world since the ferry service ceased some years ago. You wonder who stays in the handful of rooms (friendliest of these the German-managed *Maria's Labyrinth*, ☎0271/24 452; ②); Limáni is only worth a visit for its two tavernas, which have fish in the right season. The closest beach worthy of the name is at **Merikoúnda**, 4km west of Mestá by dirt track and your own transport.

Central Híos

The portion of Híos extending west and southwest from Híos Town matches the south in terms of interest, and a recently improved road network makes it easy to tour under your own steam. There are also several beaches on the far shore of the island, which, though not the best on Híos (see "Northern Híos" below), are good for a dip at the end of a day's touring.

The Kámbos

The **Kámbos**, a vast, fertile plain carpeted with citrus groves, extends southwest from Híos Town almost as far as the village of Halkío. The district was originally settled by the Genoese during the fourteenth century, and remained a preserve of the local aristocracy until 1822. Exploring it with a bicycle or motorbike is apt to be less frustrating than going by car, since the web of poorly marked lanes sandwiched between high walls guarantee disorientation and frequent backtracking. Behind the walls you catch fleeting glimpses of ornate old mansions built from locally quarried sandstone, masoned in a peanut-brittle pattern. Courtyards are paved in pebbles or alternating light and dark tiles, and most still contain a *mánganos* or water-wheel once used to draw water from wells up to 30m deep.

Accommodation

Many of the sumptuous, three-storey dwellings, constructed in a hybrid Italo-Turko-Greek style unique in the country, have languished in ruins since 1881, but a few have been converted for use as **accommodation**. The most famous of these is the *Villa Argentikon* (☎0271/31 599; fax ☎31 465 or in Milan at ☎02/48 00 82 23), ancestral home of the Italo-Greek counts Argenti de Scio. Initially restored early this century, it has become the most exclusive accommodation in Greece, consisting of four self-contained, meticulously appointed suites in detached villas in orange orchards, plus a few luxury double rooms in the main mansion. If you need to ask how much, you can't afford it, and no casual drop-ins are allowed; suffice to say that if you're in the diplomatic corps or a scion of some deposed European royal family, you'll probably be welcomed by the count himself.

The rest of us can stay at the contrastingly well-signposted and publicized *Hotel Perivoli*, just 100m north of *Villa Argentikon* (☎0271/31 513; fax ☎32 042; ⑤, ④ low season; open April–Oct), whose orchard is also home to a popular restaurant (dinner only). The rooms, no two alike, are mostly en suite and equipped with fireplaces and sofas. Blue urban buses bound for Thimianá pass just 200m to the east. Rather better than *Perivoli* as a straight-forward **restaurant** is *O Kipos ton Oneiron*, in nearby Neohorió, which has a wide range of excellent *mezédhes* and attractive marble decor.

Panayía Krína and Panayía Sikelliá

Not strictly speaking in Kámbos, but most easily reached from it en route from Híos Town to the *mastikhohoriá*, are two outstanding rural Byzantine monuments.

The thirteenth-century Byzantine church of **Panayía Krína**, set apart amid orchards and woods, is well worth the trek through a maze of poorly-marked dirt tracks from the village of VAVÍLI, 9km out of town. It's usually shut for snail's-pace restoration, but a peek through the apse window will give you a fair idea of the finely frescoed interior, sufficiently lit by a twelve-windowed drum. The cloisonné (alternating brick- and stonework) of the exterior alone justifies the trip here, though architectural harmony is marred by the later addition of a clumsy lantern over the narthex.

By contrast, the monastic church of **Panayía Sikelliá** is easy to find, visible from afar in its dramatic clifftop setting south of Tholopotámi, beyond which the three-kilometre dirt access road leading to it is well signposted. Roughly contemporaneous with Panayía Krína, Sikelliá is best visited near sunset, when the cloisonné surface of its blind arches acquires a golden tone. There's nothing much to see inside other than a fine, carved *témblon* and a peculiar late fresco of John the Divine, so it's not essential to time your visit to coincide with that of the key-keeper who may appear at dusk. Except for the festival on September 8, you're likely to have the atmospheric premises to yourself; the monastery outbuildings, save for a perimeter wall and a few fortifications above, have long since vanished, but it's worth climbing the latter for views over the adjacent ravine and the entire south of the island.

Néa Moní

Almost exactly in the middle of the island, the monastery of **Néa Moní** was founded in 1042 by the Byzantine emperor Constantine Monomakhos IX (The Dueller) on the spot where a wonder-working icon was discovered. It ranks among the most beautiful and important monuments on any of the Greek islands; the mosaics, together with those of Dháfni and Ósios Loukás on the mainland, are among the finest art of their age to be found in Greece, and the setting – high in still partly forested mountains 15km west of the port – is no less memorable.

Once a powerful and independent community of six hundred monks, Néa Moní was pillaged during 1822 and most of its residents put to the sword; indeed many of its outbuildings have languished unrepaired since then. The tremor in 1881 caused comprehensive damage (skilfully repaired), while exactly a century later the place was threatened by a forest fire, whose flames were miraculously repelled when the the resident icon was paraded around the perimeter. Today the monastery, with its giant refectory and vaulted water cisterns, is inhabited by just two elderly, frail nuns and a similar number of lay workers; when the last nun dies, Néa Moní will reportedly be taken over by monks again.

Visiting the monastery

Bus excursions are provided by the *KTEL* on Tuesday and Friday mornings only; otherwise you can come by motorbike or walk/hitch from Kariés, 7km northeast, to which there is regular blue-bus service from Híos Town. **Taxis** from town, however, are not prohibitive, charging around 5000dr per carload for a round trip, including a suitable wait while you look around.

Just inside the main gate (daily 8am–1pm & 4–8pm) stands an **ossuary** (currently under restoration) containing the bones of those who met their death here in 1822; axe-clefts in children's skulls attest to the savagery of the attackers. The *katholikón*, with the cupola resting on an octagonal drum, is of a design seen elsewhere only in Cyprus; the frescoes in the exonarthex are comprehensively damaged by holes allegedly made by Turkish bullets, but the **mosaics** further inside are well preserved.

The narthex contains portrayals of the *Saints of Hios* sandwiched between *Christ Washing the Disciples' Feet* and *Judas' Betrayal*, in which the critical kiss has unfortunately been smudged out. In the dome of the sanctuary, which once contained a complete life-cycle of Christ, only the *Baptism*, part of the *Crucifixion*, the *Descent from the Cross*, the *Resurrection* and the Evangelists *Mark* and *John* survived the earthquake. But the *Baptism* and *Resurrection* in particular are exceptionally expressive and go a considerable way to justifying Néa Moní's claim to high rank among Byzantine art.

Avgónima and Anávatos

With your own transport, you can proceed 5km west of Néa Moní to **AVGÓNIMA**, a cluster of dwellings on a knoll above the coast; the name means "Clutch of Eggs", an apt description when viewed from the ridge above. Since the 1980s, the place has been almost totally restored as a summer haven by descendants of the original villagers, though the permanent population is just seven. A returned Greek-American family runs an excellent and reasonable taverna/*kafenío*, *O Pyrgos*, in an arcaded mansion on the main square, but as yet there's no short-term accommodation.

A paved side road continues another 4km north to **ANÁVATOS**, whose empty, dun-coloured dwellings, soaring above pistachio orchards, are almost indistinguishable from the 300-metre-high bluff on which they're built. During the 1822 insurrection, some four hundred inhabitants and refugees threw themselves over this cliff rather than surrender to the besieging Ottomans, and it's still a preferred suicide leap. Anávatos' population now numbers only five, and given a lack of reliable facilities plus an eerie, traumatized atmosphere, it's no place to be stranded at dusk.

The west coast

West of Avgónima, the main road descends 6km to the coast in well-graded loops. Turning right or north at the junction leads first to the much-advertised beach at **Elínda**, which, though alluring from afar, has a rocky shore and murky waters. You're better off continuing towards the more secluded coves to either side of **Metóhi**, or below **SIDHIROÚNDA**, the only village hereabouts, where you'll find a snack bar and views over the entire west Hian shore thanks to the spectacular hilltop setting. All along this coast, as far southwest as Limáni Mestón, loom round **watchtowers** erected by the Genoese to look out for pirates; one of these has lent its name to **Kastélla**, the first swimmable cove you reach by turning left from the junction.

A weekday bus service resumes 7km south of the junction at **LÍTHI**, a friendly village of whitewashed buildings perched on a wooded ledge overlooking the sea. There are tavernas and *kafenía* near the bus turn-around area, but the only place to stay (*Kyra Despina Taverna/Rooms*, ☎0272/73 373; ③) is 2km below at dreary, windswept **Paralía Lithioú**, whose large but garbage-fringed beach makes it a weekend target of Hiot townees.

Some 5km south of Lithí, the valley-bottom village of **VÉSSA** is an unsung gem, more open and less casbah-like than Mestá or Pirgí, but still homogeneous. Its honey-coloured buildings are arrayed in a vast grid punctuated by numerous belfries; there's a simple, inexpensive taverna on the main through-road, or you can follow signs to *Toh Petrino* (☎0271/25 016 or ☎41 097; ④), a converted inn. Among the series of sandy bays along the sixteen-kilometre road west from Véssa to Limáni Meston, only that of **Ayía Iríni** has a seasonal taverna, and all suffer from exposure to the northerly winds.

New construction has somewhat spoilt the architectural profile of **ÁYIOS YIÓRYIOS SIKOÚSSIS**, a ridgetop village nearly 8km east of and above Véssa on the way back to Híos Town, but its domed, eleventh-century Byzantine church in the upper, eastern quarter deserves a glance from the outside.

Northern Híos

Northern Híos never really recovered from the Turkish massacre, and the desolation left by fires in 1981 and 1987 will further dampen travellers' spirits. Since early this century the villages have been all but deserted for much of the year, which means that bus services are correspondingly scanty. About one-third of the former population now lives in Híos Town, venturing out here only for major festivals or to tend grapes and olives, for at most four months of the year. Northerners now based in Athens or the US return to their ancestral homes for just a few intense weeks in midsummer, when marriages are arranged between local families and heritable properties thus consolidated.

The road to Kardhámila

Blue city buses run north from Híos Town only up to **VRONDÁDHOS**, an elongated coastal suburb that's a favourite residence of the island's many seafarers. Homer is reputed to have lived and taught here, and in the terraced parkland just above the little fishing port and pebble beach (mostly local bathers) you can visit his purported lectern, more probably an ancient altar of Cybele. Accordingly, most of the buses heading here are labelled "DHASKALÓPETRA" (Teacher's Rock).

If you have your own wheels, you can make a stop 2km further along at the monastery of **Panayía Mirsinidhíou** (Mirtidhiótissis) – of little intrinsic interest but notable for its photogenic setting overlooking the sea, best at first light. After another 5km, the route swoops down to the tiny bayside hamlet of **PANDOUKIÓS**, bereft of amenities but recently grown in economic importance owing to several offshore fish nurseries. A side road just north leads to the stony cove of **Áyios Isídhoros**, the rather inconvenient location of the island's only official campsite, though the site itself is shaded and faces Inoússes islet across the water.

Langádha

Travelling by bus, **LANGÁDHA** is probably the first point on the eastern coast road where you'd be tempted to alight. Set at the mouth of a deep valley, this attractive little harbour looks across its bay to a pine grove and beyond to Turkey. There are three **rooms** establishments, including *Eleni Sidheri* (☎0271/74 637; ③), but most night-time visitors come for the excellent seafood at the two **tavernas** at the start of the quay; the rest of the esplanade has been taken over by the patisseries, bars and breakfast cafés that are now all the rage in Greece. There is no proper beach anywhere nearby; Dhelfíni bay, just north, is an off-limits naval base.

Just beyond Langádha, an important side road leads 5km up and inland to **PITIOÚS**, an oasis in a mountain pass presided over by a tower-keep; 4km further will bring you to a junction allowing quick access to the west of the island and the Volissós area (see below).

Kardhámila and around

Most traffic proceeds to **ÁNO** and **KÁTO KARDHÁMILA**, the latter 37km out of the main town. Positioned at opposite edges of a fertile plain rimmed by mountains, they initially come as welcome relief from Homer's crags. Káto, better known as **MÁRMARO**, is the larger, its waterside streets flanked by the hillside neighbourhood districts of Ráhi and Perivoláki. It's actually the second largest town on the island, with a bank, post office, OTE branch and filling station (the only one in the entire north).

However, there is little to attract a casual visitor other than some pastel-painted Neoclassical architecture: the port, mercilessly exposed to the *meltémi*, is strictly businesslike, and there are few tourist facilities worth mentioning, certainly not the indifferent waterfront tavernas. One exception is the *Hotel Kardamyla* (☎0272/23 353; ⑤ high season, ④ low season, effectively ③ booked through *Sunvil* or *Greek Sun*; open June–Sept), managed along with Híos Town's *Hotel Kyma* by Theodhore Spordhilis; it's situated behind the pebble beach, with a reliable restaurant that also caters for non-guests.

Nagós

For better swimming head west – by car from the signposted junction by the church, on foot past the harbour-mouth windmill for an hour along a cemented coastal driveway – to **Nagós**, a gravel bay at

Híos water: *not* in the pipeline

Travellers may wonder about the silver pipeline that runs parallel to most of the road between Híos Town and Kardhámila. Begun in 1990, this was supposed to solve a chronic water shortage in the south of the island by tapping the spring at Nagós. However, nobody bothered to measure the flow volume at Nagós to confirm that it was sufficient for a town of 30,000 (it isn't); meanwhile, freshwater undersea springs at Pandoukiós, which well up visibly in the bay at a pressure of several atmospheres, were ignored. Secondly, the pipeline follows the highway rather than the most direct route, so that the contractors could make more on the materials. Finally, the pipes were lined internally with abestos-laced tar, which under the typical baking conditions dissolved into the paltry amount of water that trickled through when the tap was finally opened in 1992. Nearly 500 million drachmes in public funds were wasted on the project, with nothing to show for it but a useless aqueduct that's slowly disintegrating pending bids for the fresh contract to haul the mess away. All in all, it's a sad monument to the debilitating corruption that still besets Greece, years after the fall of the junta and subsequent accession to the EU.

the foot of an oasis. The lush greenery is nourished by active springs up at a bend in the road, enclosed in a sort of grotto and flanked by a *psistariá*, all overawed by tall cliffs. The place name is a corruption of *naós*, after a large Poseidon temple that once stood near the springs, but centuries of pilferage and orchard-tending, plus organized excavations after 1912, mean that there are no remains. Down at the shore the swimming is good, if a bit chilly courtesy of the spring water, plus there are two more tavernas, one renting rooms (☎0272/23 540; ③; open June–Sept). Several more are under construction, and your only chance of relative solitude in July or August lies fifteen minutes' walk west at **Yióssonas**. This is a much longer beach, but less sheltered, rockier and with no facilities.

Northwestern villages

Few outsiders venture beyond Yióssonas; on rare occasions an afternoon bus covers the distance between Mármaro and Kambiá village, 20km west. Along the way, Amádhes and Víki are attractive enough villages at the base of 1297-metre **Pilinéo**, the island's summit, most easily climbed from Amádhes. **KAMBIÁ**, overlooking a chapel-strewn ravine, retains an end-of-the-line feel, despite the recent paving of the onward road south through Spartoúnda and Kipouriés to its union with the main trans-island road to Volissós.

The monastery of Moudhón

Some 4km north of this junction, near the village of Dhievhá, you can make a detour to the sixteenth-century monastery of **Moudhón**, once second in rank on the island after Néa Moní before its partial destruction in 1822. Its outbuildings are currently being restored, but the *katholikón* itself is always kept securely locked, and the key (consult the priest in Volissós) is normally only given out to specialists. However the setting and views west make Moudhón worth a short halt.

Should you be lucky enough to glimpse its naïve interior frescoes, the best is one depicting the *Ouranódhromos Klímax* (Stairway to Heaven): a trial-by-ascent, in which ungodly priests are beset by demons hurling them into the mouth of a great serpent symbolizing the Devil, while the righteous clergy are assisted upwards by angels. In an era when illiteracy was the norm, such panels were intended quite literally to scare the hell out of simple parishioners.

Ayiásmata and around

If you're on foot, ask at one of the *kafenía* by the main church in Kambiá for directions to the start of a one-hour path across the canyon to the abandoned hamlet of Agrelopó; from the church here a system of jeep tracks leads in another ninety minutes to the tumbledown pier and seaweed-strewn beach at **AYIÁSMATA**. This is one of the strangest spots on Híos, consisting of perhaps twenty buildings (four of them churches), including the miraculous (indoor) hot springs after which the place is named. The **spa** is currently in the throes of restoration, so it's best not to count on staying or eating here.

Paved roads south of Ayiásmata pass through strikingly beautiful countryside up to the villages of Kéramos and **AFRODHÍSSIA**, the latter the more attractive. Here the surfaced road system splits: the southerly turning continues south through Hálandhra and **NÉA POTAMIÁ**, the latter an ugly prefab village built to replace an older one destroyed by landslide. From here it's another 20km to Volissós.

The northwest coast

More worthwhile is the northwesterly turning from Afrodhíssia which takes you onto something resembling a coastal road. **KOUROÚNIA**, 6km along, is beautifully arranged in two separate neighbourhoods and set amid thick forest.

After 10km more, you reach **ÁYIO GÁLA**, which has a disproportionate number of old ladies in headscarves and a single telephone in the *kafenío*; anyone receiving a call is summoned by the proprietor over a loud-hailer. The place's claim to fame is a **grotto-church** complex, built into a palisade at the bottom of the village. For access, except at the festival on August 23, you'll need to find the key-keeper, who lives beside a eucalyptus tree at the top of the stairs leading down into it. Of the two churches inside the cave, the larger, at the mouth of the complex, dates from the fifteenth century but resembles a recent villa since an unfortunate pink exterior paint job in 1993. Inside, however, a fantastically intricate *témblon* vies for your attention with a tinier, older, free-standing chapel, built entirely within the rear of the cavern. Its frescoes are badly smudged, except (in the apse) for a wonderfully mysterious and mournful Virgin, surely the saddest in Christendom, holding a knowing Child.

Beyond Áyio Gála, bleak scenery is redeemed mostly by fantastic sunset views across to Psará, but overshadowed by a huge, unaesthetic wind farm at **MELANIÓS**, typical of the four scrappy villages along the 25km road to Volissós.

Volissós and around

VOLISSÓS, 42km from Híos Town by the most direct route, was once the market town for the northwestern villages, and its old stone houses still curl appealingly beneath the crumbling hilltop Byzantine fort. The towers were improved by the Genoese, from whose era also dates the utterly spurious "House of Homer" near the top of the village. Volissós can make a depressing first impression, with the bulk of its 250 mostly elderly (permanent) inhabitants living in newer buildings around the square; however opinions improve with longer acquaintance.

Practicalities

Grouped around the square you'll find a **post office** (but no bank), two comparatively well-stocked shops and three uniformly mediocre, evening-only **tavernas**; by far the best eatery in town is *Pirgos*, up in the eponymous district directly opposite the church. A **filling station**, the only one in northwestern Híos, finally opened in 1995 some 2500m south of town.

Without your own transport, it's difficult to visit Volissós in a day from Híos Town; **buses** make a return trip on Sundays only, and the schedules of the two market-orientated trips on Monday and Thursday do not allow you to return to port on the same day. Taxis are pricey at roughly 6000dr per carload against 800dr per person for the bus (both fares one-way). You should therefore plan on an overnight stay – no great hardship, since the area boasts the best beaches on Híos, unspoiled because most inland property owners have refused to sell land to developers.

Houses in the village itself *are*, however, for sale, with renovated ones forming the basis of both a thriving expat community and a delightful **accommodation** scheme. Eleven units up in the Pírgos district have been meticulously restored by *Stella Tsakiri* (☎0274/21 421; fax ☎21 521; ④ high season, ③ low) and house from two to four persons; all have terraces, fully equipped kitchens and original features such as tree trunks upholding sleeping lofts. Stella, a transplanted Athenian sculptor, speaks perfect English and welcomes direct bookings – she's seldom completely full.

Limniá and local beaches

LIMNIÁ, the port of Volissós, lies 2km south; it's a lively fishing anchorage, and also the place for passenger *kaïkia* to and from

Psará (Mon, Wed & Fri at mid-morning June–Sept only). There is nowhere to stay on the harbour, though there are several **tavernas**; best of these are the long-established *Limnia* on the jetty, where the emphasis is on oven-cooked food, and newcomer *Toh Limanaki* at the rear of the cove, which is better for fish.

At Limniá you're not far from the fabled **beaches**. A 1500-metre walk southeast over the headland brings you to **Managrós**, a seemingly endless sand-and-pebble beach where nudism goes unremarked at the remote south end. The nearest lodgings, among the half-dozen constructions behind the shore, are the bungalows of *Marvina Alvertou* (☎0274/21 335; ③).

The more intimate sandy cove of **Lefkáthia** lies just a ten-minute stroll along a jeep track threading over the headland north of the harbour; amenities are limited to a summer-only snack bar on the sand, and the apartments of *Ioannis Zorbas* (☎0274/21 436; ③), just where the jeep track joins a paved road down from Volissós. This is headed for **Límnos** (not to be confused with Limniá), the next protected bay 400m east of Lefkáthia, where a seasonal *psistariá* operates behind the sand.

Ayía Markélla: beach and monastery

Ayía Markélla, 5km further west of Límnos, stars in many local postcards: a long, stunning beach fronting a monastery dedicated to the patron saint of Hiós. The latter is not especially interesting to outsiders, as its cells are reserved for Greek Orthodox pilgrims. Only religious souvenirs are allowed to be sold within the holy precincts, while all manner of plastic junk is on offer just outside. There's a snack bar as well, and around July 22 – the local saint's festival and biggest island celebration – the "NO CAMPING" signs doubtless go unenforced.

Some old maps show hot springs at one end of the beach; these, actually twenty minutes' walk north around the headland, turn out to be tepid dribbles into pot-sized cavities, not worth the bother and indicative only of the geological unity of this part of Híos with volcanic Lésvos. More useful is the fact that the dirt road heading north from the monastery grounds is passable to any vehicle and emerges at the paved road between Melaniós and Volissós.

Satellite islets: Psará and Inoússes

There's a single settlement, with beaches and an isolated rural monastery, on both of Híos' satellite islands, but each is markedly different from the other and, of course, from their large neighbour. To Inoússes, the nearer and smaller (3km x 10km) of the two, small boats run daily from Híos Town in season; Psará (11km x 6km) has less regular services subject to weather conditions, and is too remote to be done justice on a daytrip. (See p.297 for travel details.)

Psará

The birthplace of the Greek revolutionary war hero Admiral Kanaris, **Psará** devoted her merchant fleets – the third largest in 1820s Greece after Ídhra and Spétses – to the cause of independence, and paid dearly for it. Vexed beyond endurance, the Turks landed overwhelming forces in 1824 to stamp out this nest of resistance. Perhaps 3000 of the 30,000 inhabitants escaped in small boats and were rescued by a French fleet, but the majority retreated to a hilltop powder magazine and blew it (and themselves) up rather than surrender. The nationalist poet Dionysios Solomos immortalized the incident in famous stanzas:

On the Black Ridge of Psará,
Glory walks alone.
She meditates on her heroes,
And wears in her hair a wreath
Made from a few dry weeds
Left on the barren ground.

Today, it's a sad, stark place, never having really recovered from the holocaust, and the permanent population barely exceeds four hundred. The only positive recent development was a decade-long revitalization project instigated by a French-Greek descendant of Kanaris and a Greek team. The port was improved, mains electricity and pure water provided, a secondary school opened, and cultural links between France and the island established, though so far this has not been reflected in increased tourism or tourist facilities.

Since few buildings in the east-facing harbour community predate this century, the architecture here is a strange hotchpotch of ecclesiastical and domestic, with a distinct southerly feel reminiscent of the Dodecanese or Cyclades.

Practicalities

Getting to Psará from Híos can be something of an ordeal: the regular **ferry** from Híos Town takes four hours to cover the 57 nautical miles of habitually rough sea, though the trip from Limniá takes half the time at just over half the price.

If you **stay** overnight, your choices are limited to a single studio behind the dockside string of *kafenía* and tavernas; some rooms let by the priest's wife; the municipal inn, overpriced even at ②; and the EOT *ksenónas* in a restored prison (☎0274/61 293; ④). For **eating**, the best and cheapest place by far is the EOT-run *Spitalia*, housed (as the name indicates) in a restored medieval hospital at the edge of town. The more obvious tavernas tend to be uninspiring and expensive. A **post office**, bakery and shop complete the tally of amenities; there's no bank.

Around the island

Psará's **beaches** are decent, improving the further northeast you walk from the port. You quickly pass **Káto Yialó**, **Katsoúni** and

Lazarétta with its off-putting power station, before reaching **Lákka** (meaning "narrow ravine"), fifteen minutes along, which seems to be named after its grooved rock formations in which you may have to shelter; much of this coast is windswept and there's a heavy swell offshore. **Límnos**, 25 minutes along the coastal path, is big and pretty, but there's no reliable taverna here or at any of the other beaches. The one other thing to do on Psará, really, is to walk north across the island to the monastery of the **Assumption**; uninhabited since the 1970s, this comes to life only during the first week of August, when its revered icon is carried in ceremonial procession to town and back on August 6.

Inoússes

Inoússes has a permanent population of about three hundred – less than half its pre-war figure – and a very different history from Psará. For generations this medium-sized islet has provided the Aegean with many of her wealthiest shipping families: the richest Greek shipowner in the world, Kostas Lemos, was born here, and virtually every street or square on Inoússes is named for one member or other of the huge Pateras shipping clan. This helps explain the large villas and visiting summer yachts on an otherwise sleepy Greek backwater – as well as a sporadically open **Maritime Museum** near the quay, endowed by various shipping magnates. At the west end of the quay, the bigwigs have also funded a large nautical academy.

Two church-tipped islets, each privately owned, guard the unusually well-protected harbour; the **town** itself is surprisingly large, draped over hillsides enclosing a ravine. Despite the wealthy reputation, its appearance is unpretentious and similar to Ildır across the water in Turkey, with the houses displaying a mix of vernacular and modest Neoclassical style. Quite a few of these are currently for sale.

Practicalities

Only on Saturdays and Sundays can you make an inexpensive **daytrip** to Inoússes from Híos with the locals' ferry *Inousses*; other days of the week this arrives at 3pm, returning early the next morning. On weekdays during the tourist season you have to participate in the pricey excursions offered by such Híos-based *kaïki* as the *Maria* or the *Olga*, with return tickets running up to three times the cost of those on the *Inousses*. All that's really possible on a typical six-hour excursion is a look around the single town, a swim at one of Inoússes' attractive beaches and perhaps a meal.

Since most seasonal visitors stay in their ancestral or holiday homes, there is just one, fairly comfortable **hotel**, the *Thalassoporos* (☎0272/51 475; ④), on the main easterly hillside lane. **Eating out** is limited to *O Glaros*, a simple *ouzerí* just below the nautical academy; the conspicuous *Pateronissia*, at the base of the disembarkation jetty, is currently shut. There are three shops, one on the waterfront and two up the hill, but you're probably better off bringing your own picnic materials. Beside the museum is a **post office** and a **bank**, with the **OTE** a few paces further west.

Around the island

The rest of this tranquil island, at least the southern slope, is suprisingly green and well tended; there are no springs, so water comes from a mix of fresh and brackish wells, though public works signs indicate a reservoir in the offing. The sea is extremely clean and calm on the sheltered southerly shore; among the **beaches** here, choose from **Zepága**, **Biláli** or **Kástro**, five, twenty and thirty minutes' walk west of the port respectively. More secluded **Farkeró** lies a 25-minute walk east, first along a cement drive to a seaside chapel, then by path past pine groves and over a ridge. As on Psará, there are no reliable facilities at any of the beaches.

At the end of the westerly road, beyond Kástro, stands the somewhat macabre convent of **Evangelismoú**, endowed by the Pateras family. Inside reposes the mummified body of the lately-canonized Irini, whose prayers to die of cancer in place of her terminally ill father Panagos were answered early in the 1960s; he's entombed here also, having outlived his daughter by some years. The abbess, presiding over some twenty novices, is none other than Mrs Patera. Only modestly attired women are allowed admission, and even then casual, tour-group-type visits are not encouraged.

Greek script table

Híos	Χίος	ΧΙΟΣ
Afrodhísia	Αφροδίσια	ΑΦΡΟΔΙΣΙΑ
Anávatos	Ανάβατος	ΑΝΑΒΑΤΟΣ
Áno Kardhámila	Ανω Καρδάμυλα	ΑΝΩ ΚΑΡΔΑΜΥΛΑ
Armólia	Αρμόλια	ΑΡΜΟΛΙΑ
Avgónima	Αυγώνυμα	ΑΥΓΩΝΥΜΑ
Ayía Fotiní	Αγια Φωτεινή	ΑΓΙΑ ΦΩΤΕΙΝΗ
Ayía Markélla	Αγια Μαρκέλλα	ΑΓΙΑ ΜΑΡΚΕΛΛΑ
Ayiásmata	Αγιάσματα	ΑΓΙΑΣΜΑΤΑ
Áyio Gála	Αγιο Γάλα	ΑΓΙΟ ΓΑΛΑ
Áyios Yióryios Sikoúsis	Αγιος Γεώριος Συκούδης	ΑΓΙΟΣ ΓΕΩΡΙΟΣ ΣΥΚΟΥΣΗΣ
Elínda	Ελίντα	ΕΛΙΝΤΑ
Emboriós	Εμπορειός	ΕΜΠΟΡΕΙΟΣ
Evangelismoú	Ευαγγελισμού	ΕΥΑΓΓΕΛΙΣΜΟΥ
Farkeró	Φαρκερό	ΦΑΡΚΕΡΟ
Inoússes	Οινούσσες	ΟΙΝΟΥΣΣΕΣ
Kalamotí	Καλαμωτή	ΚΑΛΑΜΩΤΗ
Kambiá	Καμπιά	ΚΑΜΠΙΑ
Kámbos	Κάμπος	ΚΑΜΠΟΣ
Karfás	Καρφάς	ΚΑΡΦΑΣ
Kariés	Καρυές	ΚΑΡΥΕΣ
Kataráktis	Καταρράκτης	ΚΑΤΑΡΡΑΚΑΚΤΗΣ

Greek script cont.

Káto Faná	Κάτω Φανά	ΚΑΤΩ ΦΑΝΑ
Kéramos	Κέραμος	ΚΕΡΑΜΟΣ
Kómi	Κώμη	ΚΩΜΗ
Kondári	Κοντάρι	ΚΟΝΤΑΡΙ
Langádha	Λαγκάδα	ΛΑΓΚΑΔΑ
Lefkáthia	Λευκάθια	ΛΕΥΚΑΘΙΑ
Limáni Mestón	Λιμάνι Μεστών	ΛΙΜΑΝΙ ΜΕΣΤΟΝ
Limniá	Λημνιά	ΛΗΜΝΙΑ
Límnos	Λήμνος	ΛΗΜΝΟΣ
Líthi	Λίθι	ΛΙΘΙ
Mármaro	Μάρμαρο	ΜΑΡΜΑΡΟ
Melaniós	Μελανιός	ΜΕΛΑΝΙΟΣ
Merikoúnda	Μερικούντα	ΜΕΡΙΚΟΥΝΤΑ
Mestá	Μεστά	ΜΕΣΤΑ
Metóhi	Μετόχι	ΜΕΤΟΧΙ
Moundhón	Μουνδών	ΜΟΥΝΔΩΝ
Nagós	Ναγός	ΝΑΓΟΣ
Néa Moní	Νέα Μονή	ΝΕΑ ΜΟΝΗ
Nénita	Νένητα	ΝΕΝΗΤΑ
Olímbi	Ολύμποι	ΟΛΥΜΠΟΙ
Panayía Krína	Παναγία Κρήνα	ΠΑΝΑΓΙΑ ΚΡΗΝΑ
Panayía Mersindhíou	Παναγία Μερσινιδίου	ΠΑΝΑΓΙΑ ΜΕΡΣΙΝΙΔΙΟΥ
Panayía Sikelliá	Παναγία Σικελίά	ΠΑΝΑΓΙΑ ΣΙΚΕΛΙΑ
Pandoukiós	Παντουκιός	ΠΑΝΤΟΥΚΙΟΣ
Pirgí	Πυργί	ΠΥΡΓΙ
Pitioús	Πιτιούς	ΠΙΤΙΟΥΣ
Psará	Ψαρά	ΨΑΡΑ
Sidhiroúnda	Σιδηρούντα	ΣΙΔΗΡΟΥΝΤΑ
Véssa	Βέσσα	ΒΕΣΣΑ
Volissós	Βολισσός	ΒΟΛΙΣΣΟΣ
Vounós	Βουνός	ΒΟΥΝΟΣ
Vrondádhos	Βροντάδος	ΒΡΟΝΤΑΔΟΣ
Vroulídhia	Βρουλίδια	ΒΡΟΥΛΙΔΙΑ
Yióssonas	Γιόσωνας	ΓΙΟΣΩΝΑΣ

Híos travel details

ISLAND TRANSPORT

BUSES

BLUE URBAN

Híos Town to: Airport, Karfás, Mégas Limniónas (11 daily 6.30am–8.30pm); Karfás via the airport (roughly hourly 6.30am–8.30pm); Mégas Limniónas, Ayía Ermióni, continuing to Karfás (9 daily 9am–8pm); Vrondádhos (up to 3 hourly 7am–8.30pm Mon–Sat, 2 hourly Sun).

GREEN LONG-DISTANCE

Híos Town to: Anávatos (Tues/Fri at 9am); Armólia (7 daily Mon–Fri, 4 Sat, 1 Sun); Avgónima (1 daily Mon/Thurs 1.30pm, Sun 8.30am); Ayía Markélla (1 daily Mon/Thurs 1.30pm, Sun 8.30am); Emboriós (6 daily Mon–Fri, 3 Sat, 1 Sun); Kataráktis (7 daily Mon–Fri, 3 Sat, 2 Sun); Langádha (6 daily Mon–Fri, 3

Sat, 1 Sun); Lithí (2–3 daily Mon–Fri); Mármaro (6 daily Mon–Fri, 3 Sat, 1 Sun); Mestá (5 daily Mon–Fri, 3 Sat, 1 Sun); Néa Moní (Tues/Fri at 9am); Nénita (7 daily Mon–Fri, 3 Sat, 2 Sun); Pirgí (8 daily Mon–Fri, 4 Sat, 1 Sun); Véssa (2–3 daily Mon–Fri); Volissós (1 daily Mon/Thurs 1.30pm, Sun 8.30am).

GREEN-BUS LOOP ROUTES/LOCAL SHUTTLES
Emboriós–Pirgí–Mestá (2–4 Mon–Fri, 1–3 Sat); **Kómi–Pirgí–Emboriós** (5 daily Mon–Fri, 3 Sat, 1 Sun); **Mármaro–Nagós** (4 daily Mon–Fri, 2 Sat, 1 Sun).

NB All above frequencies are for the period June–Sept.

INTER-ISLAND TRANSPORT

KAÏKIA AND EXCUSION BOATS
Híos to: Inoússes (minimum 1 daily Mon–Fri 2pm, Sat–Sun 9am, returning early morning Mon–Fri, 4pm weekends). Other excursion boats as demand warrants.

Limniá to: Psará (Mon/Weds/Fri 11am–noon June–Sept; 2hr).

FERRIES
Híos to: Áyios Efstrátios (2–3 weekly on *NEL*); Foúrni (1–2 weekly on *Miniotis Lines*); Ikaría (1–2 weekly on *Miniotis*); Kavála (1–2 weekly on *NEL*, summer only); Lésvos (4–7 weekly on *NEL*; 3hr 30min); Límnos (2–3 weekly on *NEL*;10hr 30min); Pátmos (2–3 weekly on *Miniotis* or *NEL*); Pireás (4–7 weekly on *NEL*; 10hr); Psará (3 weekly on *Miniotis*; 4hr); Sámos (both northern ports; 2–4 weekly on *Miniotis*, or Vathí only on *NEL*; 4–5hr); Thessaloníki (2–3 weekly on *NEL*).

HYDROFOILS
Híos to: Foúrni (3 mornings weekly on *Gianmar Lines*); Ikaría (3 mornings weekly on *Gianmar*); Lésvos (3 evenings weekly on *Gianmar*); Pátmos (3 mornings weekly on *Gianmar*); Sámos (3 mornings weekly on *Gianmar*).

DOMESTIC FLIGHTS
Híos to: Athens (3–5 daily April–Oct, 3 daily Nov–March; 50min); Lésvos (2 weekly year-round, 30min); Thessaloníki (2 weekly year-round, 2hr).

INTERNATIONAL TRANSPORT

FERRIES
Híos to: Turkey (Çesme; 1–7 mornings weekly Nov–April, 3–4 weekly May/Sept/Oct on *Miniotis Lines*; 1–7 afternoons weekly on *Ertürk Lines*; 45min). Fares (including tax) one way currently £33/$50, round trip £44/$66 on *Miniotis*, slightly cheaper on *Ertürk*. Small car £41/$62. No tax on the Turkish side. Charters (foot passengers only) on demand through *Akhileas Tetteris*, Neoríon 13, work out cheaper at £29/$44 return; in practice they tend to depart only two or three days weekly

Lésvos

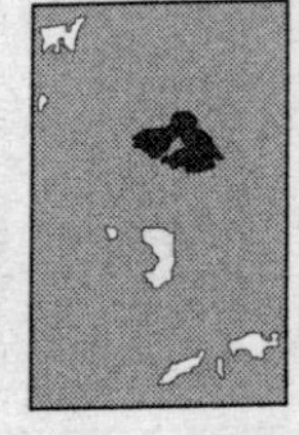

Lésvos (Mitilíni), the third largest Greek island after Crete and Évvia, is not only the birthplace of Sappho, but also of Aesop, Arion, and – more recently – the primitive artist Theophilos, the poet Odysseus Elytis and the novelist Stratis Myrivilis. Despite these artistic associations, Lésvos may not at first strike the visitor as

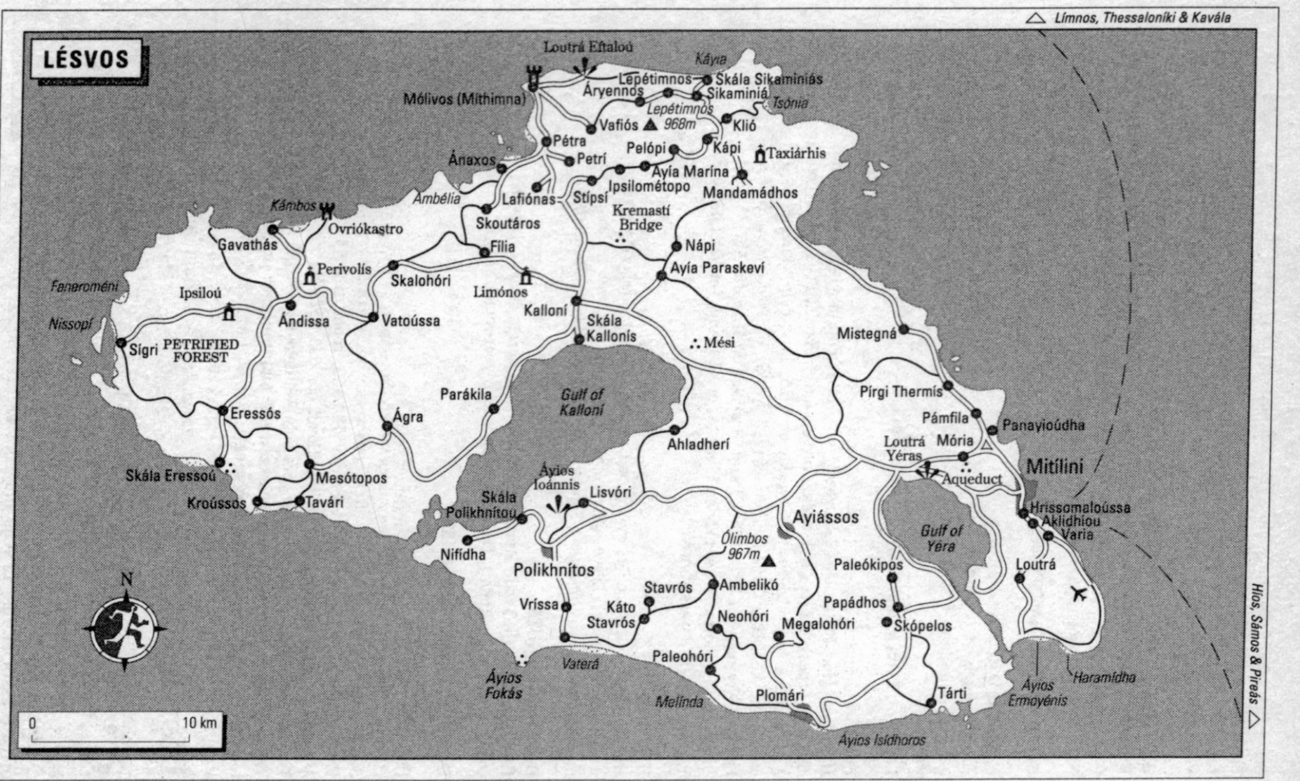
LÉSVOS
Límnos, Thessaloníki & Kavála
Híos, Sámos & Pireás
Mólivos (Míthimna)
Loutrá Eftaloú
Pétra
Petrí
Lafiónas
Ánaxos
Ambélia
Skoutáros
Fília
Limónos
Kalloní
Skála Kallonís
Stípsi
Ipsilométopo
Kremastí Bridge
Áryennos
Vafiós
Lepétimnos
Lepétimnos 968m
Sikaminiá
Skála Sikaminiás
Kávia
Tsónia
Klió
Kápi
Pelópi
Ayía Marína
Taxiárhis
Mandamádhos
Nápi
Ayía Paraskeví
Mési
Mistegná
Pírgi Thermís
Pámfila
Panayioúdha
Mitilíni
Hrissomaloússa
Aklidhíou
Variá
Loutrá
Haramídha
Áyios Ermoyénis
Mória
Aqueduct
Loutrá Yéras
Gulf of Yéra
Paleókipos
Skópelos
Papádhos
Tárti
Áyios Isídhoros
Ayiássos
Megalohóri
Plomári
Ólimbos 967m
Ambelikó
Neohóri
Paleohóri
Melínda
Ahladherí
Gulf of Kalloní
Lisvóri
Áyios Ioánnis
Stavrós
Káto Stavrós
Vaterá
Polikhnítos
Vríssa
Áyios Fokás
Skála Polikhnítou
Nifídha
Parákila
Skalohóri
Vatoússa
Ágra
Ovriókastro
Perivolis
Kámbos
Gavathás
Ándissa
Ipsiloú
PETRIFIED FOREST
Sígri
Fanaroméni
Nissopí
Eressós
Skála Eressoú
Mesótopos
Tavári
Kroússos
N
0
10 km

particularly beautiful or interesting; much of the landscape is rocky, volcanic terrain, dotted with thermal springs and alternating with vast grain fields, salt pans or even near-desert. But there are also oak and pine forests as well as vast olive groves, some of these over five hundred years old. With its balmy climate and suggestive contours, the island tends to grow on you with prolonged acquaintance.

Historically, the olive plantations, *oúzo* distilleries, animal husbandry and fishing industry supported those inhabitants who chose not to emigrate; but with these enterprises relatively depressed since World War II, mass-market **tourism** has made considerable inroads – olive-mill grindstones have found a new lease of life as hotel decor. Yet there are still few large hotels outside the capital or Mólivos, rooms just outnumber villa-type accommodation, and the first official campsites opened only in 1990. While Lésvos is far more developed touristically than Híos, it is rather less so than Sámos, a happy medium that will accord with many people's tastes. Tourist numbers have in fact dropped significantly in recent years, the result both of stalled plans to expand the airport runway and at least one resort (Mólivos) simply pricing itself out of the lower end of the market.

Some history

Lovers of medieval and Ottoman architecture certainly won't be disappointed on Lésvos. Byzantine/Genoese castles can be found at the main town of Mitilíni, Mólivos, Eressós, and near Ándissa; these date from the latter half of the fourteenth century, when the island was given as a dowry to a Genoese prince of the Gateluzzi clan on his marriage to the niece of one of the last Byzantine emperors.

Apart from Crete and Évvia, Lésvos is the only Greek island where Turks settled appreciably in rural villages (they usually stuck to the safety of towns), which explains the odd Ottoman bridge or crumbling minaret often found in the middle of nowhere. That these have survived at all can be ascribed to the relative tolerance of contemporary islanders; the first two centuries of Ottoman rule were particularly harsh, with much of the Orthodox population sold into slavery or deported to the imperial capital, and most physical evidence of the Genoese or Byzantine period demolished.

Again unusually for the Aegean islands, Ottoman reforms in the eighteenth century encouraged the emergence here of a Greek Orthodox land- and industry-owning aristocracy, who built rambling mansions and tower-houses, some of which have survived the thoughtless destruction that claimed the rest during this century. Out in the country, especially at Mólivos, Turks and Greeks got along, relatively speaking, right up until 1923; the Turkish authorities favoured Greek *kahayiádhes* (overseers) to keep the peons in line. However, large numbers of the lower social classes, oppressed by the Ottoman pashas and their Greek lackeys, fled across to Asia

Minor during the nineteenth century, only to return again after the exchange of populations.

Social and economic idiosyncracies persist: anyone who has attended one of the extended village *paniyíria* here, with music for days on end and outdoor tables piled with food and drink, will not be surprised to learn that Lésvos has the highest alcoholism rate in Greece. Breeding livestock, especially horses, is disproportionately important, and traffic jams caused by mounts instead of parked cars are not unheard of – signs reading "Forbidden to Tether Animals Here" are still very much part of the picture. Until recently, another local quirk was a marked tendency to vote Communist, in part a reaction to the late medieval quasi-feudalism here. But lately there's been a shift to the right, with *KKE* incumbents being chucked out in favour of *Néa Dhimokratía* (1990) candidates, who were in turn supplanted by *PASOK* (1993). But whatever their politics, you'll find the islanders fairly religious, with old-fashioned manners and – by Greek standards – a strong sense of community. In contrast to certain neighbouring islands, infrastructure improvement projects do get completed (eventually), and forests are well cared for, with permanent firebreaks backed up during dangerous seasons by 24-hour surveillance crews. As a result, Lésvos has in recent years had only one devastating blaze, and that was attributed to foreign (ie Turkish) saboteurs.

Getting around the island

Public buses tend to radiate out from the harbour for the benefit of working locals, not daytripping tourists. Carrying out such excursions is next to impossible anyway, owing to the size of the island – about 70km by 45km at its widest points – and some appalling roads (at long last being improved, along with their signposting). Furthermore, the topography is complicated by the two deeply indented gulfs of Kalloní and Yéra, which means that going from A to B usually involves an obligatory change of bus at either Mitilíni, on the east shore, or at the town of Kalloní, in the middle of the island. In short, it's best to decide on a base and stay there for at least a few days, exploring its immediate surroundings on foot or by rented vehicle (see p.304). Mopeds or even proper motorbikes make little impact on this huge island, and will certainly go for a spill on some of the rougher dirt roads.

Mitilíni Town

MITILÍNI, the port and capital, sprawls between and around two broad bays divided by a fortified promontory, and in Greek fashion often doubles as the name of the island itself. Most visitors find its general urban bustle somewhat off-putting, and get out as soon as possible; the town returns the compliment by being in fact a fairly impractical and expensive place to base yourself. However, there are several diversions to help you while away a few hours, particu-

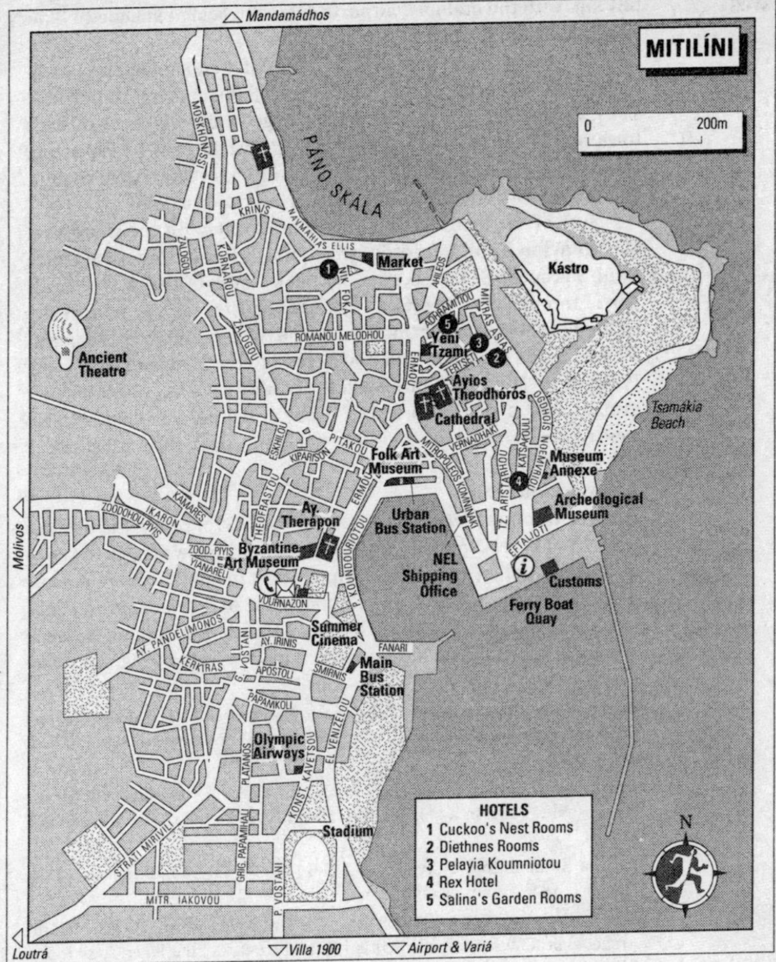

larly the marketplace and a few museums, all located within a few minutes' walk of the waterfront.

Arrival, information and orientation

When arriving or leaving by **public transport**, bear in mind that, as on Híos, there are two bus stations in town. Marquees in the middle of the quay stake out the *astikó* (blue urban bus) terminal, while *iperastikó* (standard *KTEL*) buses have a small station near Platía Konstandinopóleos at the southern end of the harbour. Service frequency has improved slightly in recent years, with up to six weekday departures in summer for the major resorts. There is no bus link with the cramped **airport** (currently being expanded), 7km away, but sharing a taxi is common practice.

Arriving by ferry, you should pause long enough at the jointly housed **EOT/tourist police post** (daily 8.30am–9pm; ☎0251/22 776), behind the customs building, to get hold of their excellent town and island map-brochures. EOT's East Aegean headquarters (Mon–Fri 8am–2.30; ☎0251/42 511), 300m away at Aristárhou 6, deals more with administrative matters than information.

Most of the facilities you'll need are located on the waterfront along **Pávlou Koundouriótou**, which wraps itself around the entire south harbour. **Ermoú** begins one block west of this and threads north through the heart of the marketplace. If you're driving, **Ogdhóïs Oktovríou**, starting just behind the ferry quay, is the quickest way to the north harbour and beyond to the Mandamádhos road. **Parking** in Mitilíni is problematic to say the least; best hunting grounds are at the south end of town, in the perpendicular streets west of Kavétsou, or to either side of Mikrás Asías, near the castle.

Accommodation

Finding **accommodation** is difficult at the best of times: the obvious waterfront hotels are noisy and exorbitant, with few singles to speak of. If you insist on staying in town, it's best to hunt for more modest rooms between the castle and Ermoú; some of the quietest and least expensive establishments are located past the Yeni Tzami, between the north harbour and fortress, and are advertised by signs on telegraph poles.

Cuckoos Nest, past the Yéni Tzamí, near the corner of Navmahías Ellís and Nikifórou Foká (☎0251/23 901; ②, not en suite). Rooms with kitsch decor, and a roof terrace.

Dhiethnes, Yioryíou Tertséti 1 (☎0251/24 968; ③, en suite). Relatively comfortable rooms in a side street off Mikrás Asías, between the castle and Ermoú.

Pelayia Koumniotou, Yioryíou Tertséti 6 (☎0251/20 643; ②, not en suite). Friendly, basic, rooms establishment.

Rex, at Katsakoúli 3 (☎0251/28 523; ③). This Neoclassical hotel behind the Archeological Museum looks inviting from the outside, but its en-suite rooms (no singles) are gloomy and overpriced.

Salina's Garden Rooms, Fokéas 7 (☎0251/42 073; ③). Located behind the Yéni Tzamí.

Villa 1900, P. Vostáni 24 (☎0251/43 437; ④ but negotiable). A restored Neoclassical mansion in the far south of town; all rooms are en suite, with period furnishings and even ceiling murals in a few cases.

The town

The main street, **Ermoú**, links the town centre with the little-used north harbour and crumbled breakwater of Páno Skála, following the course of a canal that used to join the two ports until the Byzantine era. Beginning at one of the more vivid **fish markets** in the Aegean, with flying fish, scorpionfish and other rarely-seen species on sale, Ermoú forges north past half a dozen antique shops – the best in the islands by a long way, with high prices to match – and the roofless **Yéni Tzamí** (New Mosque), once heart of the Turkish quarter and now an occasional venue for art exhibitions. Between Ermoú and the castle lies an enticing maze of atmospheric lanes lined with grandiose *belle époque* mansions and elderly vernacular houses.

The town's skyline is dominated by two churches standing at opposite ends of the marketplace; the Germanic spire of **Áyios Theodhóros** and the mammary dome of **Áyios Therápon** are imposing expressions of the nineteenth-century Ottoman–Greek bourgeoisie's post-Baroque taste. The interior decor of Áyios Therápon in particular seems more appropriate to an opera house than a church, not least because of the most excessive chandelier in the East Aegean.

The **Byzantine Art Museum** (Mon–Sat 10am–1pm; 100dr), just behind Áyios Therápon, contains various icons, including one by Theophilos (see p.306). The small **Folk Art Museum** (sporadic hours, usually 9am–1pm; 250dr), on the quay next to the blue city-bus stop, is a single room of mannequins in traditional dress, embroidery and kitsch pottery – frankly not worth the admission fee.

On the promontory between the bays sits the Byzantine–Genoese–Ottoman **fortress** (Tues–Sun 8.30am–3pm; 500dr), its mixed pedigree reflected in the Ottoman–Turkish inscription immediately above the Byzantine double eagle at the southern outer gate. Inside you can make out the ruins, variously preserved, of the Gatelluzi palace, a Turkish *medresse* (Koranic academy), a dervish cell and a Byzantine cistern. Just below the fortress, at **Tsamákia**, is the fee-entry town "beach".

Tucked away on the westerly hill, and assiduously signposted, the **Hellenistic theatre** (no set hours or admission fee) proves resoundingly anticlimactic on arrival; most of its masonry was pilfered for use in the castle, or reduced to plaster in Ottoman lime kilns.

The Archeological Museum

Formal stimulation is provided by the excellent **Archeological Museum** (Tues–Sun 8.30am–3pm; 500dr), currently housed partly in the mansion of a large estate just behind the ferry dock. Among the more interesting of the well-labelled exhibits are a complete set of mosaics from a Hellenistic dwelling, rather droll terracotta figurines, votive offerings from a sanctuary of Demeter and Kore excavated in the castle, and Neolithic finds from present-day Thermí. A specially built annexe at the rear contains stone inscriptions of various edicts and treaties, and – more interesting than you'd think – *stelae* featuring *nekródhipna* or portrayals of funerary meals. Yet another annexe has been built 150m up the hill at the base of Ogdhóïs Noemvríou, but this is not yet fully operational.

Eating and drinking

Eating out can be daunting, owing to a limited number of tourist-orientated eateries, though resourceful hunting turns up some surprises. Stumbling off a ferry, you might sort yourself out with *patsás* (tripe soup), the traditional Greek hangover cure, at the *Averof*, next to the *Credit Bank*, though the best lunches are to be had at *Iy Lesvos*, on Ermoú, which serves oven-cooked food. Further down, beside the Yéni Tzamí, *Albatross* provides fare such as pickled *krítamo* (rock samphire) and grilled sardines washed down by wine of indeterminate origin and vintage, but the food seems incidental to the bizarre surroundings; a stuffed peacock, plastic cobra and portraits of Jesus juxtaposed with those of the deposed royal family are just some of the items in an eccentric collection that, along with the wild-eyed owner and local clientele, lends a singular ambience to the place.

Another example of a dying breed is the *Ouzeri Krystal*, on Koudouriótou, between the *Ionian Bank* and the *Bank of Greece*. The cavernous, wood-floored interior, heated by a wood-stove in winter, has mirror-lined walls, bench seats and gaming tables; there's more contemporary seating outside. Unless and until it becomes a video-game arcade, this is probably the last place in these islands where you can enjoy an *oúzo* with a large *mezédhes* plate for less than 500dr.

For a more conventional alternative, the line of four **fish tavernas** on the southerly quay known as *Fanári* are the obvious choice for a seafood blowout. All are pretty comparable in price and fare, though *Stratos* and *Strofi*, at the seaward end, seem the most popular. Towards the opposite end of the waterfront, at Koundouriótou 56, the *Asteria* is a safe option for more involved casseroles.

Nightlife and entertainment

If you're stuck here while awaiting a dawn ferry, some consolation can be derived from the town's good **nightlife** and **entertainment**. *Hot Spot* is a fairly accurate self-description of the bar with good music at Koundouriótou 63, near the *NEL* agency; their rival, at no. 59, is *Amadeus*, a café/music bar with an appealing atrium interior. More formal musical events make up the *Lesviakó Kalokéri* **festival**, held in the castle from mid-July to mid-September. The summer **cinema**, *Pallas*, is between the post office and the park on Vournázon, plus there's a winter venue as well as a weekly cinema club of art films pitched at the university crowd.

Listings

ATMs *Ethniki/National* and *Pisteos/Credit* are on Koundouriótou; *Emboriki/Commercial* is on Ermoú.

Car rental Most agents are along Koundouriótou: try *Payless*, at no. 49 (☎0251/43 555); *Budget*, next door (☎0251/25 846); *Thrifty*, at no. 69

(☎0251/41 464); or, failing these, the small independent *AutoTravel*, Aristárhou 9–11 (☎0251/24 357).

Ferry/travel agencies If you're intent on getting over to Ayvalık in Turkey, book short-hop ferry tickets through either *Aeolic Cruises* (☎0251/23 960) or *Mytilana Travel* nearby at Koundouriótou 69 (☎0251/41 318). The main-line ferry agencies are also found along Koundouriótou: *NEL* at no. 47 (☎0251/28 480), and *Gianmar* hydrofoils at *Dimakis Tours*, no. 73 (☎0251/27 865).

Olympic Airways Southwest of the bay and central park, at Kavétsou 44.

OTE/Post office Next to each other on Vournázon, a block behind the central park; OTE open 7am–midnight daily.

Around Mitilíni

If you are based in Mitilíni, there are a few diversions within reach of the blue urban bus line, or (in the case of the beaches described below) just beyond. Of these, the Variá **museums** and the **Yéras spa** are the most rewarding targets.

North of Mitilíni: Panayioúdha, Mória and Pírgi Thermís

The coast road heading **north** from Mitilíni towards Mandamádhos (see p.325) follows a rather nondescript coastline, but offers startling views across the straits to Turkey. Virtually the only appealing spot en route is **PANAYIOÚDHA**, 8km away, with quayside tavernas buzzing at weekends and a church resembling a miniature Áyios Therápon (see p.303).

Just past Panayioúdha you can make a detour to a valley 1km south of **MÓRIA**, the site of a second-century AD Roman **aqueduct** that used to bring water from Mount Ólimbos; the eight remaining spans of the 26-kilometre extent are currently under scaffolding. A little further along the coastal road you may glimpse various *pírgi* (tower-mansions), relics of the nineteenth-century gentry, at **PÁMFILLA** and **PÍRGI THERMÍS**. Also near Pírgi Thermís stands the well-preserved twelfth-century Byzantine church of **Troullotí**, one of the few Byzantine monuments to escape Ottoman ravages.

South of Mitilíni: the Variá museums

Just south of town, on the road to the airport, you glimpse more tower-mansions at Hrissomaloússa and Aklidhíou. But the most rewarding targets in this direction are a pair of unlikely museums in the elegant suburb of **VARIÁ**, 3km from town; blue buses cover the distance every half an hour.

The Theophilos Museum

The recently restored **Theophilos Museum** (Tues–Sun 9am–1pm & 4.30–8pm; 500dr), well signposted on the southern edge of Variá, honours this regional painter with several rooms of wonderful, little-known canvases specifically commissioned by his patron Thériade (see overleaf) during the years leading up to his death.

Theophilos Hadzimihaïl (1873–1934): the Rousseau of Greece?

The "naïve" painter Theophilos Hadzimihaïl was born and died in Mitilíni Town, and both his eccentricities and talents were remarkable from an early age. After a failed apprenticeship as a shoemaker, he ran away to Smyrna, then to Mount Pílion on the Greek mainland in 1894 after allegedly killing a Turk. Wandering across the country from Pílion to Athens and the Peloponnese, Theophilos became one of the characters of turn-of-the-century Greece, dressing up as Alexander the Great or various revolutionary war heroes, complete with *tsaroúkhia* (pom-pommed shoes) and *fustanélla* (pleated skirt). A recluse who (it is claimed) neither drank, swore, smoked nor attended church, Theophilos was ill and living in reduced circumstances back on Lésvos when he was introduced to Thériade in 1919; the latter, virtually alone among critics of the time, recognized his peculiar genuis and ensured that Theophilos was supported both morally and materially for the rest of his life.

With their childlike perspective, vivid colour scheme and idealized mythical and rural subjects, Theophilos' works are unmistakable. Relatively few of his works survive today, because he executed commissions for a pittance on relatively makeshift surfaces such as *kafenío* counters, horsecarts, or the walls of long-vanished houses. Facile comparisons are often made between Theophilos and Henri Rousseau, the roughly contemporaneous French "primitive" painter. Unlike "Le Douanier", however, Theophilos followed no other profession, eking out a precarious living from his art alone. And while Rousseau revelled in exoticism, Theophilos' work was deeply and exclusively rooted in Greek mythology, history and daily life.

In this Thériade-sponsored collection, Theophilos' personal experience of pastoral Lésvos is evident in the wealth of accurate sartorial detail of such elegiac scenes as fishing, reaping, olive-picking and baking; there are droll touches too, such as a cat slinking off with a fish in *The Fishmongers*. The *Sheikh-ul-Islam* with his hubble-bubble seems drawn from life, as does a highly secular Madonna merely titled *Mother with Child*; as an ethnographic document, *The Albanian Dancer* is of most value. However, in classical scenes – such as *Sappho and Alkaeos*, a landscape series of Egypt, Asia Minor and the Holy Land, and episodes from wars historical and contemporary – Theophilos was clearly on shakier ground; *Abyssinians Hunting an Italian Horseman*, for instance, resembles New World Indians chasing down a Conquistador. The sole concessions to modernity are the airplanes sketched in as an afterthought over various island landscapes.

The Thériade Museum

The **Thériade Museum** (Tues–Sun 9am–2pm & 5–8pm; 250dr), its palatial extent contrasting with the adjacent, cottage-like Theophilos gallery, is the brainchild of native son Stratis Eleftheriades. Leaving Mitilíni for Paris at an early age, he Gallicized his name to Thériade and went on to become a renowned avant-garde art publisher, convincing some of the leading artists of the twentieth century to participate in his ventures. The displays here consist of lithographs, engravings, woodblock prints and watercolours by the likes of Miró, Chagall, Picasso, Léger, Rouault and Villon, either annotated by the painters themselves or commissioned as illustrations for the works of prominent poets and authors – an astonishing collection for a relatively remote Aegean island.

Beaches: Haramdíha and Áyios Ermoyénis

Beyond the airport and Krátigos village, the paved road peters out and you face a bumpy 7km more to the sand-and-pebble double beach of **Haramídha** (14km in total from town). The eastern bay boasts three tavernas and a medium-sized hotel, but the superior western strand has no shade or facilities.

Remote as it seems, the more scenic double beach at **Áyios Ermoyénis**, 4km due west of Haramídha, can get very crowded at weekends with excursion-boat trade from town. The patron saint's chapel perches on the cliff separating the two coves; there's no taverna or place to stay, merely a café. If you're driving from Mitilíni, the most direct (12km) road, recently improved, is via Loutrá.

Loutrá Yéras

For other pleasant immersions near Mitilíni, it's worth heading for **Loutrá Yéras**, 8km west along the main road to Kalloní. Just the thing after a sleepless night on a malodorous ferry, these **public baths** (daily summer 8am–7pm, winter 10am–6pm; 150dr) comprise three ornate spouts that feed 38-degree-C water into a marble pool in a vaulted chamber; there are single-sex facilities. A seasonal café on the roof of the bath house overlooks the gulf, and there's an old inn adjacent (☎0251/21 643; ②) for hydro-cure fanatics.

Southern Lésvos

The southernmost portion of Lésvos is indented by two great inlets, the gulfs of **Kalloní** and **Yéra**. The former curves in a northeasterly direction, the latter northwesterly, creating a fan-shaped peninsula at the heart of which is pine-cloaked, 967-metre-high **Mount Ólimbos**. Both shallow gulfs are in turn almost landlocked by virtue of very narrow outlets to the open sea. This is some of the most verdant and productive territory on Lésvos; the best oil-bearing olives are grown here, and the stacks of mills, many still functioning, are a familiar sight on the skyline.

Plomári

Due south of Ólimbos and perched on the edge of the "fan", **PLOMÁRI** is the only sizeable coastal settlement in the south, and indeed the second largest town on Lésvos. It presents an unlikely juxtaposition of scenic appeal and its famous *oúzo* distilling industry; among several local brands, *Varvayianni* (distillery visits Mon–

Oúzo!

Oúzo is the Greek version of a grape-mash spirit found across the Mediterranean from Cyprus to France. The residue of grape skins, pips and stalks left after wine-pressing, called *stémfyla* in Greek, is boiled in a copper still. *Oúzo* was unknown until late medieval times, since before the perfection of copper-sheet technology, such spirits could not be mass-produced. The resulting distillate was known under the Ottomans as *rakí*; its popularity grew during the nineteenth century, when shortages at distilleries in Smyrna, Constantinople and Lésvos tempted the unscrupulous to concoct pseudo-*rakí* by simply dumping pure acohol into flavoured water. This was countered by the official, compulsory addition of dye to incoming alcohol shipments, necessitating disillation to remove it.

The modern term *oúzo* probably derives from the Italian *uso Massalia*, used to tag early shipments leaving the Ottoman empire for Marseille. Today it means a *rakí* base flavoured with various aromatic spices, usually star anise or fennel; exact flavourings and proportions are closely guarded secrets of each distiller. *Oúzo's* alcohol content varies from 38 percent to 48 percent, with 44 percent strenth considered the minimum for any quality. Mediocre commercial *oúzo* is often fortified with molasses, or even alcohol as in Ottoman days. *Oúzo* has the harmless property of turning milky white when water or ice cubes are added; this results from the binding of anethole, an aromatic compound found in fennel and anise.

Fri 8am–8pm, Sat 8am–3pm; free) is reckoned one of the best. This and its rivals can also be sampled at the phenomenal number of traditional *kafenía*, interspersed with a few more contemporary bars, which crowd the old marketplace around the central plane tree.

The local *paniyíri* season kicks off in mid-July with an **oúzo festival**, and culminates towards the end of the month in celebrations honouring Áyios Harálambos, which feature such rural activities as horse races and a bull sacrifice.

Practicalities

Plomári is linked to Mitilíni by a direct **bus** route, which runs past the pretty villages of Paleókipos and Skópelos (as well as Áyios Isídhoros); if you're hitching or have your own two-wheeler, you can take a slight shortcut by using the daytime-only **ferry** (no cars) from Pérama, across the neck of the Yéra Gulf.

Despite a lack of sandy beaches in the immediate vicinity, Plomári is besieged in summer by hordes of Scandinavian package tourists, but you can usually find a **room** – they are signposted literally everywhere – at the edge of the charmingly dilapidated old town, which fills both sides of the Sidhoúndas ravine. The quietest and most attractive area for lodging is the western suburb of **Ammoudhélii**, 1km along the road to Melínda, poised above a church and little gravel **beach**. The single, central hotel, the *Okeanis* (☎0252/32 469; ③), principally catering for package groups, is also one of several local car rental outlets and runs boat-trips to the sandy beaches of **Tárti** (24km east, with food and lodging) and **Vaterá** (see below). There are two **banks**, but as yet no ATMs. Most tourists actually stay in **Áyios Isídhoros**, 3km east, merely a cluster of hotels at the west end of a long gravel beach.

Unfortunately, rustling up a decent **meal** in Plomári is considerably harder; the dinner-only *Platanos* taverna at the central plane tree is often unbearably busy, and nothing special at that. Of the mediocre bunch on the waterfront, most passable is the Danish-run *D'Annelise*, within sight of the bus stop. Ammoudhélli boasts one culinary bright spot: *Toh Ammoudhelli*, overlooking the sea, best for ample seafood and grills washed down by local *oúzo* in the mixed company of tourists and locals. At Áyios Isídhoros you could try *Iy Mouria*, where the road turns inland to cross the creek draining to the long, popular pebble beach.

Melínda

MELÍNDA, 6km west of Plomári on a road under construction, consists of a 700-metre sand-and-shingle **beach** at the mouth of a canyon choked with olive trees. Development in the hamlet just behind means three **taverna/rooms** outfits, including *Maria* (☎0252/93 239; ②) or the more basic *Melinda* (☎0252/93 234; ②). Once the road surfacing is finished, the wild eastern half of the beach will probably become a vast building site, but for the moment it's a beautiful place, with sweeping views west towards the Vaterá coast and the cape of Áyios Fokás, and south (in clear conditions) to Mount Pineléo on Híos and the Turkish Karaburun peninsula.

Ayiássos

AYIÁSSOS, nestled in a remote, wooded valley under the crest of Mount Ólimbos, is the most beautiful hill town on Lésvos, with narrow cobbled streets and ranks of traditional houses that are protected by law. Its Shangri-la quality is heightened on the more usual northerly approach from Mitilíni town, 26km away, which gives no clue of the enormous village until you see huge knots of parked cars at the southern edge of town (where the bus drops you).

Don't be intimidated by the seemingly endless ranks of kitsch souvenirs, aimed mostly at Greeks, but continue uphill to the old marketplace, with its *kafenía*, yoghurt shops and unusually graphic butcher stalls. Regrettably, redundant video-game arcades have marred the traditional ambience, but in certain cafés, bands of *santoúri*, with clarinet, lap-drum and violin, play on weekend afternoons, accompanying spontaneous, inebriated dance performances on the cobbles outside.

Rather more packaged are the products of *santoúri* player Ioannis "Kakourgos" Sousamlis, who plays and sells home-made cassettes in his little studio underneath the central church of the **Panayía Vrefokratoússa**, originally built in the twelfth century to house a wonder-working icon supposedly painted by the Evangelist Luke. (The practice of leasing commercial stalls underneath a place of worship has age-old Greek antecedents, through it's currently far more common in Turkey). With such a venerable icon as a focus, the local **festival** on August 15 is one of the liveliest in Lésvos (let alone Greece), and vividly illustrates the country-fair element in a traditional *paniyíri*, where pilgrims come to buy and sell as well as perform devotions. Ayiássos also takes **Carnival** very seriously; there's a club dedicated to organizing it, opposite the post office.

Practicalities

To reach Ayiássos from Mitilíni you have a choice of several buses a day. Access from Plomári is slightly more complicated; there's asphalt and public transport only as far as Megalohóri, dirt and your own conveyance thereafter, though the surface should improve in future years. The area between Megalohóri and the summit ridge was severely charred by a forest fire during late summer 1994, and though the road was unaffected, the countryside's appeal has taken a tumble.

Of the very few **rooms** available for the increasing number of visitors, the fanciest is the pension *Agia Sion* (☎0252/22 242; ③), run by the pilgrimage church. The best **restaurants** are *Dhouladhelli*, on your left as you enter the village from the extreme south (bus-terminal) end, or *Dhayielles*, 70m further along and less monopolized by Greek tour groups. At either of these spots you can eat well and at a fraction of the prices asked at the coastal resorts.

Polikhnítos and around

A different bus route from Mitilíni leads to the inland village of **POLIKHNÍTOS**, also accessible from Kalloní by a shortcut via the coast guard base at Ahladherí. The spa here has long been shut for repairs, but if you're after a bath, try the working **hot springs** of **Áyios Ioánnis**, fairly well signposted 2km below the village of **LISVÓRI**, in turn 4km east of Polikhnítos. Flanking the eponymous chapel are two vaulted-chamber pools, though the water is odoriferous, iron-stained and best enjoyed on a cool evening (100dr fee to the caretaker).

From Polikhnítos, you can also proceed north to the small, gravelly **beaches** at **Skála Polikhnítou** and **Nifídha** at the road's end, both of which have creditable seafood tavernas; otherwise you can head south, via the attractive village of Vríssa, to Vatéra.

Vaterá

VATERÁ, 55km from town on the Polkhnítos bus route, is a seven-kilometre clean sandy **beach** backed by verdant hills, offering some of the warmest, cleanest simming on Lésvos. A direct coastal road from Melínda is on the cards, though Plomári is opposing this for fear of losing tourist trade to Vaterá's infinitely superior beach, notwithstanding the huge increase in ordinary business it stands to gain as the local market town.

The western end of the resort has more conventional room-type **accommodation** and fewer studios; the nicest of several hotels clustered here is the Greek- and American-run *Vatera Beach* (☎0252/61 212; fax 61 164; open winter by arrangement; ⑤ peak season, ④ shoulder). It also has a good **restaurant** attached, from where you can gaze on the cape of **Áyios Fokás**, 3km to the west, whose **temple of Dionysos** and early Christian basilica are finally being properly excavated. Áyios Fokás also boasts a pair of popular **fish tavernas**.

The **campsite** (*Dionyssos Club*) lies slightly inland from the portion of the beach east of the T-junction, where studio/villa units predominate. Several more **tavernas** line the eastern shore road, and because the clientele are mostly local weekenders, they're reasonable and good – for example *Ta Kalamakia*. **Nightlife**, thus far a couple of pubs and the *Arena Disco*, is rather low-key, reflecting Vaterá's status as a family resort. If you intend to stay here you'll certainly want your own transport as the closest shops are 4km away at Vríssa and the bus appears only a few times a day.

Western Lésvos

The main road west of Loutrá Yéras is surprisingly devoid of settlement, with little of interest before you glimpse the Gulf of Kalloní. The nondescript, eponymous town at its head is the gateway to a mostly treeless, craggy region whose fertile valleys offer a sharp contrast to the bare ridges. River mouths form little oases behind a handful of beaches, a few of which justify the resorts of Skála Kallonís, Sígri and Skála Eressoú. A trio of monasteries lining the road west of Kalloní, in addition to occasionally striking inland villages, provide monumental interest.

Kalloní and Skála Kallonís

KALLONÍ itself is an unembellished agricultural and market town more or less in the middle of the island. You may end up spending some time here since it's the intersection of most bus routes and has a bank with a precious ATM – the only full-service credit-card facility outside of Mitilíni Town.

If you have time to spare, you might make the three-kilometre detour to **SKÁLA KALLONÍS**, Lésvos' fifth-ranking package resort, with a principally Dutch, German and English clientele. Besides the long, coarse-sand beach on the lake-like gulf, there are more luxury facilities here than at either Skála Eressoú or Plomári. However, none of the handful of restaurants rates a mention, and pedal-bike hire – ideal for the flat terrain hereabouts – and a small windsurf/Hobie-Cat school seem the only distinctions of a resort that looks cheap and is probably pitched cheap overseas.

Mési, Ayía Paraskeví and the Kremastí bridge

Signposted just east of the Ahladherí shortcut, some 14km east of Kalloní, are the traces of an ancient **Aphrodite temple** (Tues–Sun 8.30am–3pm; free) at **MÉSI** (Messon). Just the original eleventh-century BC foundations and a few later column stumps remain, plus the ruins of a fourteenth-century Genoese basilica built within; it was once virtually on the sea but a nearby stream has silted things up in the intervening millennia. All told, it's not worth a special trip, but certainly make the short detour if passing by – and brace yourself for the manically voluble caretaker.

Some 7km west of Mési, back towards Kalloní, lies the turning for **AYÍA PARASKEVÍ**, an intriguing tableau of nineteenth-century bourgeois architecture. The place is famed for its **bull-sacrifice rite** on Pentecost Saturday (seven weeks after Orthodox Easter, usually June).

Another, perhaps more compelling, reason to pass through is to visit the **Kremastí bridge**, the largest and best preserved medieval bridge in the east Aegean. This stands 3km west of Ayía Paraskeví, beside a dirt road taking off from the main road to Nápi. However, it is easier to find from the Kalloní–Mólivos road, and since all junctions are unsignposted, exact distances are given: head 3700m south from the turn-off to Stípsi, bear left (east) onto the unmarked dirt track, and then proceed 4300m – the bridge is obvious just to the north.

The monastery of Limónos

West of Kalloní, the road winds 4km uphill to the monastery of **Limónos**, founded in 1527 by the monk Ignatios. It is a huge complex, with just a handful of monks and lay workers to maintain three storeys of cells around a giant, plant-filled courtyard; the north wing, where Ignatios' cell is preserved as a shrine, is the oldest section. The *katholikón*, with its carved-wood ceiling and archways, is built in Asia-Minor style and traditionally off-limits to women. A sacred spring flows from the church's west foundation wall; request a look at the church interior when you visit the ecclesiastical exhibit.

A former abbot established a **museum** (daily 9am–7.30pm; 200dr) on two floors of the west wing. The ground-floor ecclesiastical collection is fine enough, but you should prevail upon the warden (easier done in large groups) to open the upper, ethnographic hall. The first room is a recreated Lesvian *salóni* (sitting room), while the next is crammed with an indiscriminate mix of kitsch and priceless objects – Ottoman copper trays to badly stuffed, rotting egrets by way of brightly painted trunks – donated since 1980 by surrounding villages. An overflow of farm implements is stashed in a corner storeroom below, next to a chamber where giant *kioupiá* (urns) for grain and olive oil are embedded in the floor. Just west, through an archway, one of the two affiliated asylums shares space with a mini zoo filled with patrolling peacocks, ducks and deer.

Beyond, the road heading west passes through **FÍLIA**, with its truncated minaret and pre-1923 mosque, where you can turn off for a shortcut to Skoutáros and the north of Lésvos; the dirt surface has only recently been regraded and should be passable to any car. Most traffic continues through to the unusually neat village and battered minaret of **SKALOHÓRI**, its houses stacked in tiers at the head of a valley facing the sea and the sunset, and **VATOÚSSA**, the most landlocked but also the most beautiful of the western settlements.

The monastery of Perivolís

Eight kilometres beyond Vatoússa, a short track leads down to the sixteenth-century monastery of **Perivolís** (daily 8am–7pm; pull on the bell rope for admission if necessary), built in the midst of a riverside orchard. You should appear well before sunset as only natural light is available to view the fine if faded frescoes in the narthex. On the south wall, in an Apocalyptic panel worthy of Bosch (*The Earth and Sea Yield Up Their Dead*), the Whore of Babylon rides her chimera, and assorted sea-monsters disgorge their victims. On the north side you see a highly unusual iconography of *Abraham, the Virgin, and the Penitent Thief of Calvary in Paradise*. Further interest is lent by a humanized icon of Christ under glass at the *témblon*, and by the friendly old lady (Greek-speaking only) who acts as caretaker.

Ándissa and around

ÁNDISSA, 3km beyond Perivolís, nestles attractively under the only pine grove in the west of the island. At the edge of the village a sign implores you to "Visit our Central Square", and that's not a bad idea, if only for the sake of its three enormous plane trees, shading several cafés and tavernas.

Directly below Ándissa, a paved road leads 6km north toward the fishing hamlet of **GAVATHÁS**, all of 25 buildings, with a narrow, partly protected beach and a few places to eat and stay – such as the *Hotel Restaurant Paradise* (☎0253/56 376; ③). A dirt side track leads one headland east to the huge, duney, wave-battered beach of **Kámbos**. You can keep going in the same direction, following signs pointing to "Ancient Andissa", though they actually lead you to **Ovriókastro**, the most derelict of the island's Genoese castles, evocatively placed on a promontory within line of sight of Mólivos and a goodly swathe of coast to either side. The dirty, exposed beaches here are unlikely to appeal, though there is a small snack-bar. The locals mistakenly identify the castle with the ancient town, but the latter is actually on the next hillock east, formerly an islet; little remains besides the stubby foundations of its walls.

The monastery of Ipsiloú

Just west of modern Ándissa there's an important junction. Carrying straight on leads you past the monastery of **Ipsiloú**, founded in 1101 atop the extinct volcano of Órdimnos (511m), and still home to four monks. The *katholikón*, tucked in one corner of a large, irregular courtyard, has a fine wood-lattice ceiling, but its frescoes were repainted to considerably detrimental effect in 1992. More intriguing are the bits of Iznik tiles stuck into the facade, and the exquisite double gateway. Upstairs you can visit a fairly rich **museum** of ecclesiastical treasure (daily 8am–6pm; donation in exchange for a postcard). Ipsiloú is dedicated to Saint John the Theologian, as is typical for monasteries overlooking apocalyptic landscapes like the surrounding parched, boulder-strewn hills here, some of the most desolate terrain in Greece.

The petrified "forest"

Signposted just to the west of here is one of the main concentrations of Lésvos' rather overrated **petrified "forest"**, indicated by placards which also warn of severe penalties for pilfering souvenir chunks. For once, contemporary Greek arsonists cannot be blamed for the state of the trees, created by the combined action of volcanic ash from Órdimnos and hot springs between 15 and 20 million years ago. The other main cluster is south of Sígri (see below), but locals seem amazed that anyone would want to trudge though the barren countryside in search of them; upon discovery you may agree, since the mostly horizontal, two-to-three-metre-long sequioa trunks aren't exactly one of the world's wonders. If you're curious but unenergetic, there are a fair number of petrified logs strewn about the courtyard of Ipsiloú.

Sígri

SÍGRI, near the western tip of Lésvos, has an appropriately end-of-the-line feel, accentuated in the wake of the general Lesvian tourism slump. At the best of times it had a limited future as a resort, owing to its prior status as an important NATO naval base – there are often as many as a half-dozen battleships moored here. The bay is guarded by a Turkish castle and by the long island of **Nissopí**, which stretches across its mouth and acts as a buffer to the prevailing winds. Once a week a *NEL* ferry calls here on its way between Límnos and Rafína, on the Greek mainland.

The eighteenth-century **castle** sports the sultan's monogram over its entrance; rarely seen outside Istanbul, this was a token of the high regard in which productive Lésvos was held. The vaguely Turkish-looking church is in fact a converted **mosque**, while the town itself is an uneasy mix of old and cement dwellings. The nearest **beach**, south of the castle headland, is narrow and scrappy, but there's the superior one of **Faneroméni**, 3km north at a river mouth, as well as an even better strand 2km south at another creek mouth, just off the one-lane track to Eressós (use of which saves a bit of fuel but no time).

Practicalities

If you want **to stay** in Sígri, there's just one hotel (☎0253/22 340; ③) and a handful of rooms, including *Nelly's Room and Apartments* (☎0253/54 230; ③) which overlook the castle. Most English-speaking customers at Sígri are clients of *Direct Greece*, the latest in a succession of small, specialist operators who have tried to make a go of peddling holidays here. Among several **tavernas**, *Remezzo* may have the best view of the town beach and the fanciest menu, but *Galazio Kyma* – the unmarked white building with blue trim, opposite the jetty – gets first pick of the fishermen's catch and offers fresh seafood at unbeatable prices. If you wish to catch the rare *NEL* ferry, ring ☎0253/54 430 for current information.

Eressós and Skála Eressoú

The southerly option of the T-junction between Ándissa and Ipsiloú leads to the inland town of **ERESSÓS**. This is home to a contented colony of expatriates who have bought or rented property, and a stroll along lanes flanked by the vernacular houses is rewarding during the cooler hours of the day. During summer, half the population is down at Skála, only resettled last century after medieval piracy prompted the settlement of Eressós.

The peaceable modern visitors to western Lésvos park themselves 4km further south at the idyllic beach resort of **SKÁLA ERESSOÚ**, behind which stretches the largest and most attractive agricultural plain on Lésvos, a welcome green contrast to the volcanic ridges above. The three-kilometre beach here, given additional character by an islet within easy swimming distance, runs a close second to Vaterá; consequently the place is beginning to rival Plomári and Mólivos in numbers of visitors – an odd mix of Brits, Nordic types, Greek families, die-hard hippies, and lesbians attracted by the Sappho connection (see below).

Accommodation

Skála has countless **rooms**, but the best ones near the sea fill early in the day or are block-booked by tour companies though often not actually occupied; recent years have seen a merry-go-round of tour operators trying their luck for a season and then pulling out. Other vacancies – like those touted at the bus stop – can be attributed to the fairly appalling standard of some units. The best and quietest rooms tend to be inland, overlooking the plain. If you arrive independently in season, therefore, don't leave the search till late in the day; as a last resort, you might entrust the task to an agency such as *Exersis Travel* (☎0253/53 044), near the bus stop, but you'll pay a hefty surcharge on the room rate.

There are few bona fide **hotels**; longest established of these is *Sappho the Eressia* (☎0253/53 233; ③), in a central, if rather noisy, location on the front. Otherwise, there's a semi-official, free **campsite** with basic facilities at the west edge of town, under some trees behind the sand. The resort's profile may change in the near future as a self-contained, luxury complex is due to commence operation west of the river in 1996. Its main effect will probably be the discomfiture of naturists on the beach below.

The town

There's not much to Skála – just a roughly rectangular grid of perhaps five streets by eight, including the waterfront pedestrian lane (officially Papanikolí). The café-lined square at mid-waterfront is dominated by a bust of Theoprastos, a renowned philosopher and botanist who hailed from **ancient Eressos**. This was not, as you might suppose, on the site of the modern village, but atop Vígla hill at the east end of the beach; you can still see some crumbled bits of citadel wall from a distance. Once on top, the ruins prove even scantier, but it's worth the scramble up for the views – you can discern the ancient jetty submerged beyond the modern fishing anchorage.

Another famous reputed native of ancient Eressos was **Sappho**, the ancient poetess and reputed lesbian, and there are usually appreciable numbers of gay women paying homage here, particularly at the campsite and in the 1700-metre, clothing-optional zone of the beach west of the river mouth. In the river itself live about a hundred terrapins who have learned to come ashore for bread-feedings – watch your fingers as they have a nasty bite!

Ancient Eressos lingered on into the Byzantine era, whose main legacy is the basilica of **Áyios Andhréas**, behind the modern church. The surviving foundations are oddly aligned southwest-to-northeast rather than the usual west-to-east; a notable floor mosaic is currently hidden under sand and plastic until a permanent sunshade is built. A one-room archeological museum (Tues–Sun 8.30am–3pm; free), immediately behind the basilica, is of minimal interest.

Eating, drinking and nightlife

Most **tavernas**, with elevated wooden dining platforms, crowd the beach. The most recommendable, both on the eastern walkway, are *Iy Gorgona*, with friendly service and a large menu of Greek standards at fair prices, and the British-run, partly vegetarian *Bennett's*, at the extreme east end opposite the islet, assuaging cravings for lasagne, garlic mushrooms and apple crumble. Inland, on the way to the museum, the *Aphrodite Home Cooking* taverna lives up to its name, with fair-sized portions and comfortable garden seating. The Canadian-run *Yamas Snack Bar*, on the waterfront, is the place for pancake breakfasts, filter coffee, veggie burgers and homemade bread; they also rent out mountain bikes and function as an Anglophone bar at night. *Sympathy*, a few doors down, is coolly musical, with a mostly Greek-bohemian, stoned clientele. The gay women contingent favours *Blue Horizon*, on the Theophrastos square, while *kamákia* patrol for straight, foreign women at *Glaros*. A summer **cinema** rounds off the nightlife.

Other practicalities

Skála's amenities include an adjacent **post office** and **OTE**, a coin-op, a self-serve **laundry** near the church, and a mobile **bank** van on Tuesdays and Fridays; take advantage of this or the post office, as exchange facilities at the two travel agencies have poor exchange rates as well as commission charges.

Beaches near Skála: Kroússos and Tavári

Excursion boatmen at Skála Eressoú have a hard time convincing customers to leave the beautiful beach here, but if you get restless, there are two potential targets a little further east; both are also accessible by dirt road from Mesótopos (see below).

Kroússos, the first attractive bay along, is medium-sized and sandy, though with no shade at all. In springtime there's good bird-watching in the reedbeds of the rivermouth, and during summer a simple cantina installed in a derelict *KTEL* bus serves up drinks, watermelons and fried fish.

Tavári, the next cove along, is by contrast emphatically not worth the extra bother: apart from the stones and sea urchins, the frontage road runs right along the beach.

East to Kalloní

If you're returning to the main island crossroads at Kalloní, you can complete a loop from Eressós along the western shore of the Gulf of Kalloní via the hill villages of Mesótopos and Ágra; this route is currently all paved except for the first 11km out of Eressós, with that stretch scheduled for completion by 1996.

The only settlement of any consequence on the Kalloní gulf's west shore is **PARÁKILA**, which boasts a ruined mosque, an Ottoman bridge and a fair proportion of Lésvos' citrus groves; nearby beaches are not worth stopping for.

Northern Lésvos

The main road **north of Kalloní** winds up a pine-flecked ridge and then down the other side into increasingly attractive country stippled with poplars and blanketed by olive groves. Long before you can discern any other architectural detail, the cockscomb silhouette of Mólivos castle indicates your approach to the oldest established tourist spot on Lésvos, and still the island's third most populous town.

> **The olives of Lésvos**
>
> No other Greek island is as dominated by **olive production** as Lésvos, which boasts approximately 11 million olive trees. Most of these vast groves date from after a killing frost in 1851, though a few hardy survivors are thought to be over five hundred years old. During the first three centuries after the Turkish conquest, production of olive oil was a monopoly of the ruling pasha, but following eighteenth-century reforms in the Ottoman Empire, extensive tracts of Lésvos (and the oil trade) fell into the hands of the new Greek bourgeoisie, who greatly expanded the industry.
>
> As in most of Greece, olives are harvested on Lésvos between late November and late December, the best ones coming from the hillside plantations between Plomári and Ayiássos. Each grower's batch is brought to the local *triveío* (mill) – ideally within 24 hours of picking – pressed separately and tested for quality. Good first-pressing oil, some 40 percent of that available in the fruit, is greenish and low in linoleic acid (by EU law, less than 1 percent acidity is required to earn the label "extra virgin"). In general, Greek oil tends to be better than Spanish or Italian, owing to hotter, drier summers which promote low acid levels in olives.

Mólivos

MÓLIVOS (officially **MÍTHIMNA**), 61km from Mitilíni, is arguably the most beautiful spot on Lésvos, with tiers of sturdy, red-tiled houses mounting the slopes between the picturesque harbour and the castle, some standing defensively with their rear walls to the sea. Modern dwellings and hotels have been banned from the preserved municipal core and the surrounding countryside – a powerful Athenian watchdog group, "Friends of Molyvos", has seen to that – but this has not surprisingly engendered tweeness and sapped all the authentic life from the Y-shaped market place. Just one lonely tailor still plies his trade among the redundant souvenir shops, and the last locals' *ouzerí* shut down in 1989. Having been cast as an upmarket resort, there are no phallic postcards or other tacky accoutrements, but you are constantly being reminded that, however tasteful, you are still strolling through a stage-set for mass tourism. Yet except in August, the vine-canopied streets seem to absorb easily the package clientele and individual tourists who make their way here, and tour-group custom has lately been reduced by the insistence of some hotels on mandatory half-board.

Arrival and information

If you're driving, beware that cars are banned from the upper village and that parking space is limited; there is a single **parking** area up by the castle, shrunken considerably since a 1994 pedestrian pavement project, and a larger one opposite the tourist office. It is inadvisable to drive further in towards the harbour on the shorefront road.

The municipal **tourist office** (daily minimum hours 9am–1pm, 2.30–4pm, 6–8pm), by the bus stop, stocks large quantities of useful literature, including a town plan of Mólivos, and can help with accommodation (see below). Around the tourist office are an automatic **foreign-money-changing machine**, and several **motorbike and car rental** places. The **post office** is near the top of the upper commercial street, Kástrou, while the **OTE** and a **bank** stand opposite each other on the lower market lane, Dhekátou Évdhómou Noemvríou, at the intersection with the shore road. Note, however, that this is not a full-service bank, and credit-card cash advances can only be processed in Pétra at the *Ethniki Trapeza/National Bank* during normal banking hours.

Accommodation

The principle duty of the tourist office is to provide a no-fee telephone placement service for nearly two thousand rooms (② & ③) in the village, with oral descriptions of the premises available. It's worth taking advantage of this as staff appear to be relatively unbiased and clued up on current vacancies, and it will save you a fair bit of trudging around.

If you don't coincide with their opening hours, you could always try hunting by yourself; the street heading upwards just beyond the tourist office is lined with houses letting rooms – just look for placards with the blue-on-white official EOT logo of a face in profile. **Hotels** are all lower down, along or just off the main sea-level thoroughfare, which heads straight past the tourist office towards the harbour. The official **campsite**, *Camping Methymna*, is 2km northeast of town, on the way to Eftaloú.

Adonis, near the tourist office (☎0253/71 866; fax ☎71 636). Pension in quiet, comfortable garden premises. ④.

Amfitriti, immediately behind the *Olive Press* (see below) (☎0253/71 741; fax ☎71 744). This has its own pool in a calm garden setting. Heavily subscribed to by the tour trade, so book in advance. ⑤.

Milelja, 2km southwest of town (☎0253/72 030, fax ☎71 335, or write to Ayía Kiriakí, 14, 811 08 Mólivos). A self-catering retreat for groups of up to 25–30 persons, lovingly designed and built by Detlef and Gisa Siebert-Bartling, a German couple long resident in Mólivos. Though mainly for prearranged yoga, dance or arts seminars, occasionally solo travellers can be accommodated.

Olive Press, behind the town beach to the south (☎0253/71 646; fax ☎71 647). The most distinctive of the large hotels along here, this occupies the former olive mill – the giant stack marks the spot. Popular with the tour trade, but you may strike lucky with advance notice. ⑤.

Poseidon, near the tourist office (☎0253/71 570). Pension in a peaceful location overlooking the beach; only six rooms. ④.

Sea Horse, overlooking the port (☎0253/71 320; fax ☎71 374). Acceptable if you're not interested in making an early night of it, and can be pre-booked at a discount through some British package agents.

Varvara Kelesi, near the castle (☎0253/71 460). Just three units, fairly representative of rooms in Mólivos; pleasant, inexpensive, quiet – but very high up. ②.

The town

The perimeter walls of the Byzantine–Genoese **castle** (summer Tues–Sun 7.30am–sunset, winter Tues–Sun 8.30am–5pm; free) provide interesting rambles and views of Turkey across the straits. Closer examination reveals a dozen weathered Turkish fountains along flower-fragrant and cobblestoned alleyways, a reflection of the fact that before 1923 Turks constituted thirty-five percent of the population here and owned most of the finest mansions. You can try to gain admission to the Greek-built **Krallis** and originally Turkish **Yiannakos mansions**, or the municipal **art gallery** (Tues–Sun 8.30am–3pm; free) occupying the former residence of local novelist Argyris Eftaliotis.

The local **archeological museum** (Tues–Sun 8.30am–3pm; free), in the basement of the town hall, features finds from ancient Mithymna, just northwest. Although the collection is well labelled and lit, space is limited and the best bits have inevitably been sent to Mitilíni. Besides numerous sea-life encrusted amphorae, there are a clutch of blue Roman beads to ward off the evil eye, demonstrating just how old belief in this affliction is around the Mediterranean. Of more contemporary interest are archive photos showing the Greek Army's victorious advance across the island, beginning 8 November 1912; a month later it was all over for the Ottomans, with the last image showing their prisoners being bundled into *kaïkia* at Mólivos harbour for transfer to Anatolia.

Until excavations resume (unlikely), the site of Mithymna remains of essentially specialist interest, though a **necropolis** has been unearthed next to the bus stop; it's mainly the use of the Classical name that has been revived. The motivation for this, as so often in the Balkans, is political; *Mólivos* ("Graphite", of which there is none locally) is a Hellenicization of the Turkish name *Molova*.

Beaches

Despite a plethora of organized activities and sunbeds to rent, the shingly town beach is mediocre, with rocks and sea urchins in the shallows, though it improves somewhat as you head towards the south end and clothing-optional zone. (This is accessible from the main road only via a track signposted for the "pool–tennis court" of the *Hotel Delfinia*.) Otherwise, you can venture out to bays as remote as Ánaxos and Tsónia (see p.322 & p.324) by taking advantage of advertised boat excursions or the minibus shuttle service (not listed on printed bus schedules) that runs eight times daily in season between Ánaxos and Eftaloú .

Eating and drinking

Choose carefully when **eating out**; the obvious seaview tavernas on the initial uphill grade from the tourist office are all expensive, with miniature portions. Instead, you should head down towards the picturesque harbour to which the centre of nocturnal gravity has recently shifted, partly in response to complaints from hillside residents. In contrast to the variety of night-time options, getting a meal at midday can be nearly impossible as everyone is on the beach – Pétra is the closest and most reliable place for lunches.

The Captain's Table, at the far end of the quay, near the boatyard. Co-managed by Melinda of the now-defunct *Melinda's*, this offers reasonable seafood, *mezédhes* and meat grills.

El Greco, on the lower shopping street. Traditional pudding-and-cake shop; Panayiotis the proprietor is a wonderful raconteur (in several languages) and acts as mother hen to aspiring foreign artists, as the numerous dedicated paintings testify.

Gorgona/Mermaid, on the seaview road, about halfway from the bus stop to the port. A reliable bet after a decade or so in business, with proprietor Kostas enjoying a certain notoriety for his "fish in Lesbian sauce".

Toh Khtapodhi, by the entrance to the port. Perched in an unbeatable location, this is the oldest outfit here and for years featured affordable seafood, but new management has had its rent quintupled, so expect changes in fare and price.

Medusa, behind *Toh Khtapodhi* (see above). A relatively new *ouzerí* with some unusual dishes such as seafood turnovers and cream-stuffed peppers.

Taverna Vafios, Vafiós village, 5km east. Well worth heading out here for the extensive menu of reasonably priced delicacies and local wine from the barrel, served to a largely Greek clientele. Recipes are on the rich side and portions generous, so go hungry.

Nightlife

In terms of formal events, midsummer sees a short **festival** of music and theatre up in the castle. There's also a summer **cinema** next to the tourist office; the old **mosque** spanning the shopping street sporadically functions as a film venue in winter.

In terms of **tippling**, be advised that Mólivos is as expensive in this regard as in everything else. Both beer and drinks by the shot run to 1000dr or more, though there are some happy hours.

Conga Bar, below the shore road, near the *Olive Press Hotel*. Slightly livelier crowd and music than *Skala Bar*, but with similar outdoor seating.

Gatelouzi, about two thirds of the way to Pétra. State-of-the-art outdoor disco on a cantilevered platform like a ship's deck; *the* place to be seen on Saturday nights.

Q, down near the old port. Most durable of several "dancing bars" in the area.

Skala Bar, directly above the harbour, in a former blacksmith's. Doubles as an art gallery; ideal for a more sedentary evening accompanied by 1950s–70s music.

Pétra

Since there are both practical and political limits to the expansion of Mólivos facilities, many package companies are now shifting emphasis to **PÉTRA**, 5km south and marginally less busy. The place is beginning to sprawl untidily behind its broad, sandy beach and seafront square, and diners on the square receive the full brunt of exhaust fumes from waiting buses, but the core of old stone houses, many with Levantine-style balconies overhanging the streets, remains.

Pétra takes its name from the giant volcanic monolith located some distance inland and capped by the seventeenth-century church of **Panayía Glikofilloússa**, reached via 103 rock-hewn steps on the northeast side. The walled compound at the top is of little intrinsic interest, but you should climb up at dawn or dusk for the sake its superb views of the surrounding agricultural plain. More intriguing local sights include the sixteenth-century church of **Áyios Nikólaos**, at the foot of the rock, sporting three phases of well-preserved frescoes up to 1721, and the intricately decorated **Vareltzídhena mansion** (Tues–Sun 8.30am–3pm; 400dr), whose southwest upper room features a painted *trompe-l'œil* ceiling.

Practicalities

For **accommodation**, there are a few small hotels, such as the seafront *Studios Paliria* (☎0253/41 647; ④), and, as at Pirgí on Híos, plenty of **rooms** available through a *Women's Agricultural Tourism Cooperative*, formed by Pétra's women in 1984 to provide a more unusual option for visitors. In addition to operating an upstairs **restaurant** on the square (which also serves as a **tourist office**, crafts shop and general information centre; open Mon–Sat 9am–3.30pm), they arrange accommodation where it's possible to participate in the proprietors' daily routine and learn a bit about village life. Advance reservations are usually required (☎0253/41 238 or ☎41 340; fax ☎41 309; ②–③). Otherwise, you might contact *Pension Katerina* (☎0253/41 024; ③), at the foot of the Glikofilloússa rock.

Aside from the co-operative's excellent eatery, **tavernas** (such as those behind the north beach) are generally a bit tatty, and you're better off either at the *Ouzeri Pittakos* (dinner only), 100m south of the square, or the tersely named *Grill Bar*, on the square itself, ideal for a quick, tasty and reasonable *souvláki* or octopus tentacle. At **Avaláki**, 1500m southwest on the way to Ánaxos, there's a decent namesake taverna immediately behind the tiny, eel-grass-festooned beach.

With the *Gatelouzi* disco looming on the hillside to the north, **nightlife** in town is not surprisingly very modest; the old olive press on the coast road has been converted into a "dance bar", *Mihani/ Machine*, with the industrial apparatus in situ – hence the name.

In addition to a proper **bank**, Pétra's amenities include a jointly housed **OTE** and **post office**, next to Áyios Nikólaos.

Outlying beaches: Ánaxos and Ambélia

ÁNAXOS, 3km southwest of Pétra, is a bit of a higgledy-piggledy mess, but it fringes by far the cleanest beach in the area. The kilometre stretch of sand is dotted with pedaloes and sunbeds, and lined with several not especially memorable snack bars. The blocks of rooms inland are increasingly monopolized by tour companies, making Ánaxos less of a good bet than previously for short-notice accommodation in high season; there may also be mosquitoes from the river mouth. From anywhere along here you enjoy beautiful sunsets behind three offshore islets.

For something utterly different, head 1km south, then 3km west along a badly signposted side road (right at the only fork) to **Ambélia**, an idyllic, 700-metre beach with just a freshwater spring at road's end, and a single taverna at the rivermouth. There's some flotsam, but generally the place is fairly clean, with an attractive valley for a backdrop.

Loutrá Eftaloú

From Mólivos, the shuttle-bus runs 5km northeast to the rustic **thermal baths at Loutrá Eftaloú**, at the end of the road passing the campsite. The hot springs are housed in an attractive, traditional, domed structure, which has (along with the adjacent guesthouse) recently been renovated: a nominal fee and locking hours are in force only if the warden is about. Bring candles and/or a torch for nocturnal visits, and some sort of scoop or pot to sluice yourself down – even after a cool dip at the clothing-optional pebble beach just outside, the spa is just too hot to submerge yourself in. The shoreline west of here is seaweed-strewn and unattractive, hardly justifying a considerable number of luxury hotels and bungalow complexes, some of which are quite reasonably priced – for example the smallish, well-designed *Aeolis* (☎0253/71 772; fax ☎71 773; ⑤) – though generally packed out by German tour groups.

Around Mount Lepétimnos

East of Mólivos, the villages of 968-metre **Mount Lepétimnos**, marked by tufts of poplars, provide a day or two of rewarding exploration. The main road around the mountain first heads 6km east to Vafiós before curling north around the base of the peaks. Though this stretch is in the process of being surfaced, the asphalt and twice-daily bus service back toward Mitilíni currently resume only at Áryennos. Six kilometres further lies the enchanting hill village of **SIKAMINIÁ** (Sikamiá), birthplace of regional novelist Stratis Myrivilis, whose childhood home is identified among the imposing basalt-block houses below the "Plaza of the Workers' First of May", with its two traditional *kafenía* and direct views north to Turkey.

Skála Sikaminiás

A signposted trail shortcuts the twisty 2500-metre road down to **SKÁLA SIKAMINIÁS**, easily the most picturesque fishing port on Lésvos. Myrivilis used it as the setting for his best-known work, *The Mermaid Madonna*, and the tiny rock-top chapel at the end of the jetty will be instantly recognizable to anyone who has read the novel (see "Books" in *Contexts*).

On a practical level, Skála has a few **pensions**, such as the central *Gorgona*, (☎0253/55 301; ③), and the quieter, seaview *Rooms Anna* (☎0253/55 242; ③), west of the chapel. It also boasts three **tavernas**, best and longest-lived of these *Iy Mouria* (aka *Iy Skamnia*), with seating under the mulberry tree in which Myrivilis used to sleep on hot summer nights. In addition to good seafood, courtesy of the active local fleet – *gávros* (mock anchovy) in June or July, sardines in August – you can try the island's summer speciality of *kolokitholoúloudha yemistá* (stuffed squash blossoms).

The only half-decent local **beach** is the rather stony one of **Káyia** (one nightclub, one cantina) just east, so Skála is perhaps better as a lunch stop than an overnight base. A fairly rough, roller-coaster track follows the coast west back to Eftaloú and Mólivos, its condition not deterring a steady stream of vehicles.

Klió and Tsónia

Continuing east from upper Sikaminiá, you soon come to **KLIÓ**, whose single main street leads down to a square with a plane tree, fountain, *kafenía* and views across to Turkey. The village is set attractively on a slope, down which a six-kilometre, easily passable dirt road leads to the 600 metres of beautiful pink volcanic sand at **Tsónia** beach, with just a single taverna and another café at the fishing-anchorage end. The jerry-built prefab cottages just inland essentially form the summer annex of Klió, whose entire population migrates here on weekends in season – a custom still observed to a diminishing degree at all shoreline colonies around the island.

South slope villages

Just beyond Klió, the route forks at Kápi, from where you can complete a loop around the mountain by bearing west along a partly paved road tracing its southern flank. The asphalt runs out after 5km at **PELÓPI**, ancestral village of the unsuccessful 1988 US presidential candidate Michael Dukakis; the main square sports an old mosque now used as a warehouse. Garden-hidden **IPSILOMÉTOPO**, the next village 5km further along, is punctuated by a minaret (but no intact mosque) and hosts revels on July 17, the feast of Ayía Marína. By the time you reach sprawling **STÍPSI**, 13km from Kapí, you're almost back to the main Kalloní–Mólivos road; consequently there's a sporadic bus service here, as well as a large **taverna** at the edge of town to which coachloads of tourists descend in season for "Greek Nights".

There are also **rooms** to let, so Stípsi makes a good base for rambles along Lepétimnos' steadily dwindling network of **trails**; throughout the north of the island you'll see advertisements for donkey- or **mule-trekking**, which in recent years has become even more popular than walking. The Mitlíni EOT has lately jumped into the fray, having marked four long-distance paths across the island with yellow diamonds and documented them in its brochure "*Trekking Trails on Lesvos*", but these rely almost exclusively on vehicle tracks or roads, and are considered locally as something of a bad joke.

Mandamádhos: village and monastery

The main highway south from Klió to the capital runs through **MANDAMÁDHOS**, 6km along. This attractive inland village is famous for its pottery, including the Ali-Baba style *kioupiá* (olive-oil urns) seen throughout Lésvos, but more so for the "black" **icon of the Taxiárhis** (Archangel Michael), whose enormous eponymous **monastery** (summer daily 6am–10pm, winter 6.30am–7pm), just to the north, is the powerful focus of a thriving cult, and a popular venue for baptisms. The image – said to be made from a mixture of mud and the blood of monks slaughtered in a massacre – is really more idol than icon, both in its lumpy three-dimensionality and in the former mode of veneration which seems a vestige of pagan times. First there was the custom of the coin-wish, whereby you pressed a coin to the Archangel's forehead; if it stuck, then your wish would be granted. Owing to wear and tear on the image, the practice is now forbidden, with supplicants referred to a substitute icon by the main entrance.

It's further believed that in carrying out his various errands to bring about the desires of the faithful, the Archangel wears through enough footwear to stock a small shoe shop. Accordingly the icon used to be surrounded not by the usual *támmata* (votive medallions) but by piles of miniature gold and silver shoes left by those he had helped; the shoes were removed in 1986 by the ecclesiastical authorities, perhaps out of embarrassment at the "primitive" nature of the practice. Of late, a token substitute has re-appeared in the form of several pairs of tin slippers which can be dedicated (ie filled with money) and left before the icon. Just why his devotees should want to encourage these peripatetics is uncertain, since in Greek folklore the Archangel also appears to claim the souls of the dying.

Greek script table

Lésvos	Λέσβος	ΛΕΣΒΟΣ
Ahladherí	Αχλαδερή	ΑΧΛΑΔΕΡΗ
Ambélia	Αμπέλια	ΑΜΠΕΛΙΑ
Ambelikó	Αμπελικό	ΑΜΠΕΛΙΚΟ
Ánaxos	Αναξος	ΑΝΑΞΟΣ
Ándissa	Αντισσα	ΑΝΤΙΣΣΑ
Ayía Marína	Αγία Μαρίνα	ΑΓΙΑ ΜΑΡΙΝΑ
Ayía Paraskeví	Αγία Παρασκεύή	ΑΓΙΑ ΠΑΡΣΚΕΥΗ
Ayiássos	Αγιάσος	ΑΓΙΑΣΟΣ
Áyios Ermoyénis	Αγιος Ερμογένης	ΑΓΙΟΣ ΕΡΜΟΓΕΝΗΣ
Áyios Isídhoros	Αγιος Ισίδωρος	ΑΓΙΟΣ ΙΣΙΔΩΡΟΣ
Eressós	Ερεσός	ΕΡΕΣΟΣ

Greek script cont.

Fília	Φίλια	ΦΙΛΙΑ
Gavathás	Γαβαθάς	ΓΑΒΑΘΑΣ
Haramídha	Χαραμίδα	ΧΑΡΑΜΙΔΑ
Ipsilométopo	Υψηλομέτωπο	ΥΨΗΛΟΜΕΤΩΠΟ
Kalloní	Καλλονή	ΚΑΛΛΟΝΗ
Kápi	Κάπη	ΚΑΠΗ
Klió	Κλειώ	ΚΛΕΙΩ
Kroússos	Κρούσος	ΚΡΟΥΣΟΣ
Lepétimnos	Λεπέτυμνος	ΛΕΠΕΤΥΜΝΟΣ
Lisvóri	Λισβόρι	ΛΙΣΒΟΡΙ
Loutrá Eftaloú	Λουτρά Εφταλού	ΛΟΥΤΡΑ ΕΦΤΑΛΟΥ
Loutrá Yéras	Λουτρά Γέρας	ΛΟΥΤΡΑ ΓΕΡΑΣ
Mandamádhos	Μανταμάδος	ΜΑΝΤΑΜΑΔΟΣ
Megalohóri	Μεγαλοχώρι	ΜΕΓΑΛΟΧΩΡΙ
Melínda	Μελίντα	ΜΕΛΙΝΤΑ
Mesótopos	Μεσότοπος	ΜΕΣΟΤΟΠΟΣ
Míthimna	Μήθυμνα	ΜΗΘΥΜΝΑ
Mitilíni	Μυτιλήνη	ΜΥΤΙΛΗΝΗ
Mólivos	Μόλυβος	ΜΟΛΥΒΟΣ
Moní Ipsiloú	Μονή Υψιλού	ΜΟΝΗ ΥΨΙΛΟΥ
Moní Limónos	Μονή Λειμώνος	ΜΟΝΗ ΛΕΙΜΩΝΟΣ
Moní Perivolís	Μονή Περιβολής	ΜΟΝΗ ΠΕΡΙΒΟΛΗΣ
Mória	Μόρια	ΜΟΡΙΑ
Nifídha	Νυφίδα	ΝΥΦΙΔΑ
Ovriókastro	Οβριόκαστρο	ΟΒΡΙΟΚΑΣΤΡΟ
Paleókipos	Παλαιόκηπος	ΠΑΛΑΙΟΚΗΠΟΣ
Pámfila	Πάμφιλα	ΠΑΜΦΙΛΑ
Panayioúdha	Παναγιούδα	ΠΑΝΑΙΟΥΔΑ
Papádhos	Παππάδος	ΠΑΠΠΑΔΟΣ
Parákila	Παράκοιλα	ΠΑΡΑΚΟΙΛΑ
Pelópi	Πελώπη	ΠΕΛΩΠΗ
Pétra	Πέτρα	ΠΕΤΡΑ
Píri Thermís	Πύργοι Θερμής	ΠΥΡΓΟΙ ΘΕΡΜΗΣ
Plomári	Πλωμάρι	ΠΛΩΜΑΡΙ
Polikhnítos	Πολιχνίτος	ΠΟΛΙΧΝΙΤΟΣ
Sígri	Σίγκρι	ΣΙΓΚΡΙ
Sikaminiá	Σικαμινιά	ΣΙΚΑΜΙΝΙΑ
Skála Eressoú	Σκάλα Ερεσού	ΣΚΑΛΑ ΕΡΕΣΟΥ
Skála Sikaminiás	Σκάλα Σικαμινιάς	ΣΚΑΛΑ ΣΙΚΑΜΙΝΙΑΣ
Skalohóri	Σκαλοχώρι	ΣΚΑΛΟΧΩΡΙ
Skoutáros	Σκουτάρος	ΣΚΟΥΤΑΡΟΣ
Stavrós	Σταυρός	ΣΤΑΥΡΟΣ
Stípsi	Στύψη	ΣΤΥΨΗ
Tárti	Τάρτι	ΤΑΡΤΙ
Tavári	Ταβάρι	ΤΑΒΑΡΙ
Tsónia	Τσόνια	ΤΣΟΝΙΑ
Vafiós	Βαφειός	ΒΑΦΕΙΟΣ
Variá	Βαρειά	ΒΑΡΕΙΑ
Vaterá	Βατερά	ΒΑΤΕΡΑ
Vatoússa	Βατούσσα	ΒΑΤΟΥΣΣΑ
Vríssa	Βρίσα	ΒΡΙΣΑ

Lésvos travel details

ISLAND TRANSPORT

BUSES

Mitilíni to: Ayiássos (6 daily Mon–Fri, 4 daily Sat–Sun); Eressós (3 daily Mon–Sat, 2 Sun); Kalloní (5 daily Mon–Fri, 4 Sat–Sun); Mandamádhos (4 daily Mon–Fri, 2 Sat–Sun); Mólivos (5 daily Mon–Fri, 4 Sat–Sun); Pétra (5 daily Mon–Fri, 4 Sat–Sun); Plomári (5 daily Mon–Fri, 3 Sat–Sun); Sígri (2 daily Mon–Sat, 1 Sun); Vaterá (4 daily Mon–Fri, 2 Sat–Sun).

INTER-ISLAND TRANSPORT

FERRIES

Lésvos (Mitilíni) to: Áyios Efstrátios (1–2 weekly on *NEL*; 5hr 30min); Híos (5–12 weekly on *NEL*; 3hr 30min); Kavála (1–2 weekly on *NEL*; 15hr); Límnos (3–5 weekly on *NEL*; 7hr); Pátmos (1 weekly on *NEL*); Pireás (5–14 weekly on *NEL*; 12hr direct, 14hr via Híos); Sámos (1 weekly on *NEL*); Thessaloníki (1–2 weekly on *NEL*; 17hr); Vólos (1 weekly on *NEL*).

Lésvos (Sígri) to: Áyios Efstrátios (1 weekly on *NEL*); Kavála (1 weekly on *NEL*); Límnos (1 weekly on *NEL*); Rafína (via Skíros some years; 1 weekly with *NEL*).

HYDROFOILS

Lésvos (Mitilíni) to: Alexandhroúpoli (2 weekly; 3hr 45min); Foúrni (3 weekly); Híos (3 weekly); Ikaría (3 weekly); Kavála (3 weekly; 5hr–6hr); Límnos (1 weekly; 2hr 45min); Pátmos (3 weekly; 6hr 30min); Sámos, (3 weekly).

NB All services on *Gianmar Lines*, whose craft are usually based here (some months they may move to Híos).

DOMESTIC FLIGHTS

Lésvos to: Athens (3–4 daily; 45min); Híos (2 weekly; 30 min); Límnos (4–7 weekly; 40 min); Thessaloníki (6–9 weekly; 1–2hr).

INTERNATIONAL TRANSPORT

FERRIES

Lésvos (Mitilíni) to: Turkey (Ayvalık; 5–9 weekly in season, winter link unreliable; Dikili; 1 weekly in season; 1hr 30min). Fares for both £25/$38 one-way, £33/$50 return including Greek taxes; no Turkish tax on this crossing. Small cars cost £30/$45 each way.

Límnos

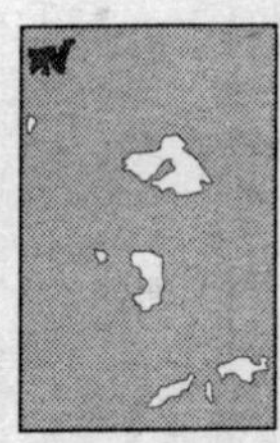

Límnos is a prosperous agricultural and garrison island, whose remoteness and peculiar ferry connections have until now protected it from the worst excesses of industrial-strength tourism. Most summer visitors are Greek, so as an overseas traveller you're still likely to be an object of curiosity and hospitality, though the islanders are becoming increasingly used to numbers of Germans and a smaller British package clientele. Accommodation across the island tends to be comfortable but pricey (④–⑤ is the norm), with a strong

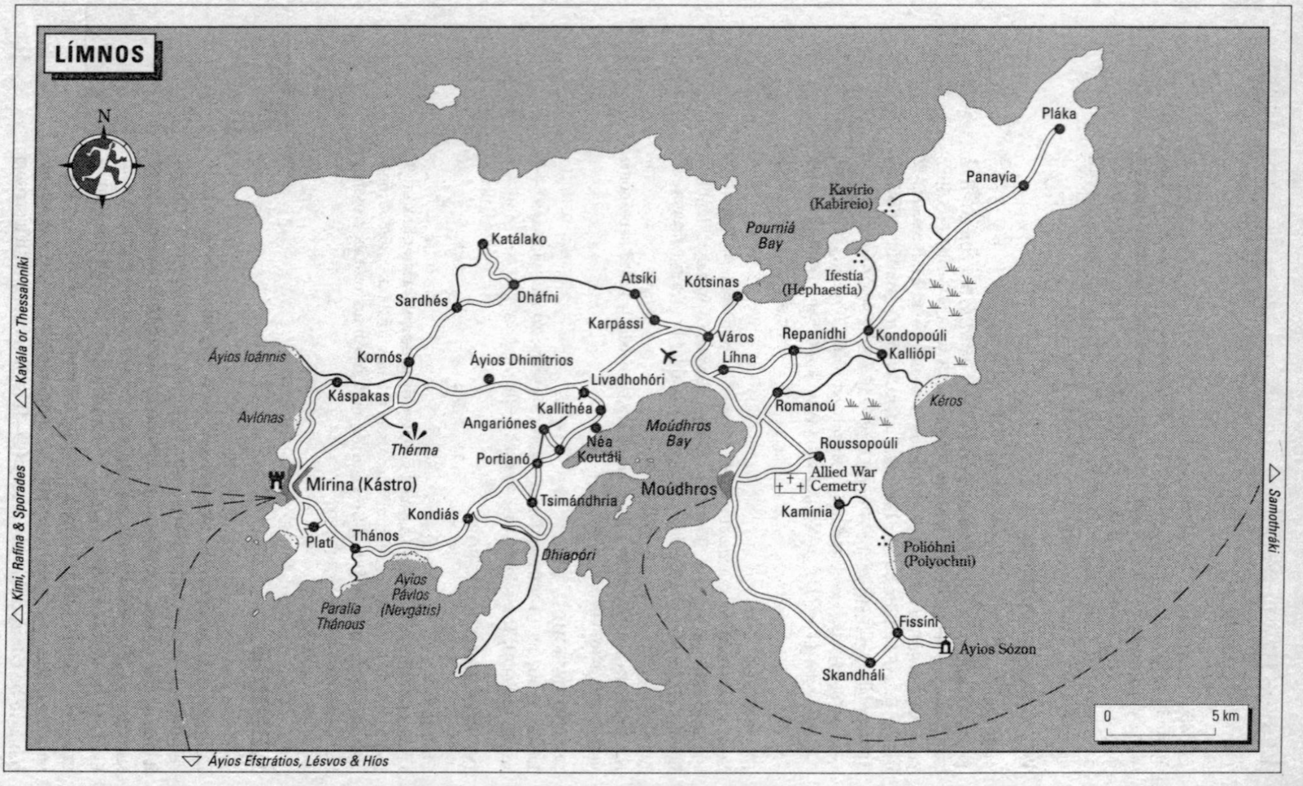
LÍMNOS
N
Samothráki
Kavála or Thessaloníki
Kími, Rafína & Sporades
Áyios Efstrátios, Lésvos & Híos
0
5 km
Pláka
Panayía
Kavírio
(Kabireio)
Ifestía
(Hephaestia)
Kondopoúli
Kalliópi
Kéros
Pourniá
Bay
Repanídhi
Romanoú
Roussopoúli
Allied War
Cemetery
Kamínia
Polióhni
(Polyochni)
Fissíni
Áyios Sózon
Skandháli
Kótsinas
Város
Líhna
Moúdhros
Bay
Moúdhros
Atsíki
Karpássi
Livadhohóri
Néa
Koutáli
Tsimándhria
Dhiapóri
Katálako
Dháfni
Áyios Dhimítrios
Kallithéa
Angariónes
Portianó
Sardhés
Kornós
Kondiás
Thérma
Áyios
Pávlos
(Nevgátis)
Káspakas
Mírina (Kástro)
Thános
Paralía
Thánous
Platí
Áyios Ioánnis
Avlónas

bias towards self-catering units. Having come late to the tourist trade, the Limnians have skipped the backpacker phase entirely and gone straight for the high end of the market.

Among young Greek males, Límnos has a reputation for being dull, largely due to its unpopularity as an army posting. In recent years, the island has been the focus of periodic disputes between the Greek and Turkish governments, resulting in a conspicuous military presence. Turkish aircraft regularly overfly the island, worsening already tense Greek–Turkish relations and prompting "Flying Circus"-type responses from the Greek Air Force.

The gulfs of Pourniá and Moúdhros, the latter one of the largest natural harbours in the Aegean, between them almost pinch H-shaped Límnos in two. The west of the island is dramatically bare and hilly, with the abundant chunks of lava put to good use as street cobbles and building material. Like most volcanic islands, Límnos produces excellent wine: a good dry white and some of the best retsina in Greece, unfortunately neither exported. The low-lying eastern leg of the "H" is occupied by cattle and vast cornfields, and speckled with seasonal ponds or marshes popular with duck-hunters.

The Limnians also proudly tout an abundance of natural food products, including thyme honey and sheep's milk cheese, and indeed the population is almost self-sufficient in foodstuffs. Much of Limnós' countryside consists of rolling hills, with substantial clumps of almond, jujube, poplar and mulberry trees carefully nurtured against constant winds. However, the island is extremely dry, with irrigation water pumped from deep wells, and a limited number of potable springs. The coastline is fringed with terrapin-haunted creeks and long, sandy beaches, so you'll have few problems finding a stretch to yourself – though there's little escape from the stingless but disgusting jellyfish which periodically pour out of the Dardanelles and die here in the shallows. On the plus side, the beaches shelve gently, making them ideal for children and quick to warm up early in summer, with no cool currents except near the river mouths.

Mírina

MÍRINA (Kástro), the capital and port on the west coast, wears the atmosphere of a provincial market town rather than a resort. With five thousand inhabitants, it's pleasantly low key, if not especially picturesque apart from a core neighbourhood of old stone houses dating from the Ottoman occupation. Few explicitly Turkish monuments have survived – there's no mosque, for example – though a fountain at the harbour end of Kídha retains its inscription and is still highly prized for its drinking water.

Arrival, transportation and information

The **airport** is 22km east of Mírina, almost at the exact geographic centre of the island, and shares runways with an enormous air force base. Límnos is one of the few remaining destinations with a shuttle bus to the *Olympic Airways* town terminal. **Ferries** dock at the south end of the town, in the shadow of the castle.

The **bus station**, for what it's worth, is on Platía Eleftheríou Venizélou, at the north end of Kídha. One look at the abysmally sparse schedules (only a single daily afternoon departure to most points, slightly more frequently to Kondiás and Moúdhros) will convince you to **rent your own vehicle**. Cars, motorbikes and bicycles can be hired from either *Myrina Car* (☎0254/24 476), *Petridou Tours* (☎0254/24 787) or the hopefully named *Rent a Reliable Car* (☎0254/24 587); rates for motorbikes are only slightly above the Aegean norm, but cars are expensive. A motorized two-wheeler is generally the best form of transport for exploring the coast and the interior as there are few steep grades but many perilously narrow village streets.

Among three **banks**, the *Ethniki Trapeza*, just off Kídha next to the **OTE**, has an ATM; the **post office** and the *Olympic Airways* terminal are adjacent to each other on Garoufalídhou. Opposite these two is a winter **cinema**, the *Garofallidheion*; a summer venue, the *Maroula*, operates down the street near the intersection with Frínis.

Accommodation

Despite Límnos' upscale reputation, you may still be met off the boat with offers of a simple room. Romeïkós Yialós has several rooms-only **pensions** in its restored houses, all of which are plagued to some extent by evening noise from the bars below. Just north of Romeïkós Yialós, the areas of Ríhá Nerá and Áyios Pandelímon are good bets for **self-catering units**. There's no official **campsite** on Límnos, but Greek caravanners and campers tend to congregate at the north end of Platí and Avlónas beaches (see below).

Afroditi Áyios Pandelímonas (☎0254/23 489; fax ☎24 504; winter ☎01/65 24 022). Apartments in a superb hilltop setting. Substantially discounted if booked in advance through *Sunvil*. ⑤.

Aktaion by the harbour (☎0254/22 258). Simple, friendly hotel in a rather noisy location. Virtually the only outfit open all year. ③.

Akti Myrina at the north end of Romeïkós Yialós (☎0254/22 310; fax ☎22 352; winter ☎01/41 37 907; fax ☎41 37 639). A self-contained, luxury complex of 110 bungalows, with all conceivable diversions and comforts. Walk-in daily rates, based on half-board for two, soar dramatically in season, but are considerably less if booked through package companies *Sunvil* or *Greek Sun*. ⑥.

Apollo Pavillion on Frínis (☎0254/23 712). Hidden away in a cul-de-sac about halfway along Garoufalídhou, this offers a variety of accommodation ranging from pricey hostel-type facilities in the basement (②–③) to large studios on the upper floors (④ high season, ③ otherwise). All rooms have balconies, with views of either the castle or the mountains.

Kosmos Romeïkós Yialós (☎0254/22 050). The best-value pension in these parts; above the namesake pizzeria. ④.

Poseidon Apartments, Ríha Nerá (☎0254/23 982 or ☎51 304). Set back a little from Romeïkós Yialós beach. ④.

Romeïkos Yialos, Sakhtoúri 7 (☎0254; 23 787). A venerable pension in Romeïkós Yialós that's quieter and a bit less expensive than *Kosmos*. ④.

The town

Mírina is fairly large for an island town, but most things of interest are situated on the main shopping street, **Kídha** – stretching from the harbour to **Romeïkós Yialós**, the beach and esplanade to the north of the castle – or on its perpendicular, **Garoufalídhou**, roughly halfway along. As town beaches go, Romeïkós Yialós is not at all bad, and its southerly counterpart, **Tourkikós Yiálos**, beyond the fishing port, provides a decent alternative.

On the headland between Romeïkós Yialós and the south-facing ferry dock stands an originally Byzantine **castle** (access unrestricted), quite ruined despite later additions by the Genoese and Ottomans. It's worth climbing at sunset for views over the town, the entire west coast and – in exceptional conditions – over to Mount Áthos, 35 nautical miles west.

The Archeological Museum

The recently overhauled **Archeological Museum** (Tues–Sun 8.30am–3pm; 500dr) occupies an old mansion behind Romeïkós Yialós, not far from the site of Bronze-Age Myrina in the suburb of Ríha Nerá. Finds are assiduously labelled in Greek, Italian and English, and the entire premises are exemplary in terms of presentation – the obvious drawback being that the best items have been spirited away to Athens. Because of Limnos' fertility and convenient position near the Dardanelles, it was occupied in prehistoric times; exhibits belong predominantly to the Archaic period and before, since the island bcame a mere satellite of Athens during Classical times.

In broad terms, the south ground-floor gallery is devoted to pottery from Polióhni (Polychni); the north wing contains more of the same, plus items from ancient Myrina; while upstairs are galleries of post-Bronze-Age artefacts from Kavírio (Kabireio) and Ifestía (Hephaestia). The star upper-storey exhibits are votive lamps in the shape of sirens, found in an Archaic sanctuary at Hephaestia. Rather less vicious than the harpy-like creatures described by Homer, they are identified more attractively as "muses of the underworld, creatures of superhuman wisdom, incarnations of a nostalgia for paradise".

There are also numerous representations of the goddess Cybele/Artemis, who was revered throughout the island; her shrine was typically situated at a fauna-rich rivermouth – on Límnos this was at at the site of present-day Avlónas. Also noteworthy is an entire room devoted to metal objects, including gold jewellery and bronze items both practical (cheese graters) and whimsical (a vulture and a snail).

Eating and drinking

Mírina's **tavernas** are better value than its lodging. About halfway along Kídha, on an atmospheric little square hemmed in by old houses and a plane tree, *O Platanos* serves traditional oven food; for a pre-ferry meal or evening grill, *Avra*, on the quay next to the port police, makes a good choice.

Seafood on Límnos is excellent thanks to the island's proximity to the Dardanelles and seasonal migrations of fish; accordingly there are no less than five tavernas arrayed around the little fishing port. There's little to distinguish them by price or menu, and all the proprietors are related by blood or marriage. However, it's worth noting that *Psaropoula* seems to attract a mostly German clientele, and that *O Glaros*, at the far end, is considered the best – though it's slightly more expensive.

Not too surprisingly given the twee setting, the restaurants and bars along Romeïkós Yialós are pretty poor value, unless you settle for a drink with views of the nocturnally illuminated castle; a better option for beachfront dining are the tree-shaded tables of *Iy Tzitzifies*, a short walk further north. Finally, worth a mention is an unusual shop next to *O Platanos* on Kídha, devoted to top-grade Cretan products such as wine, honey, oil and spices.

Western Límnos

For more pristine beaches than those at Romeïkós Yialós and Tourkikós Yiálos, you should strike out 3km north from town, past *Akti Myrina*, to the beach at **Avlónas**. This is unspoiled except for a new luxury complex to the south and coolant-water discharge from the local power plant at the north end; however, these have deterred neither the terrapins in the river nor a seasonal colony of freelance campers.

Some 3km further on from Avlónas you work your way through **KÁSPAKAS**, its north-facing houses arranged in pretty, tiled tiers, before plunging down to **Áyios Ioánnis**. Here the island's most unusual **taverna** features seating in the shade of piled-up volcanic boulders, with a sandy beach stretching beyond.

Platí: village and beach

PLATÍ, 2km southeast of Mírina, is a village of some architectural character – and nocturnal activity, which makes rooms here a noisy proposition. However on the smaller square you'll find the *Zimbabwe*, an excellent and popular *ouzerí*, whose food and prices belie its humble appearance – no prizes for guessing where the friendly English-speaking chef spent thirty years. The long, sandy **beach**, 700m below, is popular and usually free of jellyfish; except for the unsightly luxury compound at the south end, the area is still resolutely rural, with sheep parading to and fro at dawn and dusk.

If you wish to stay in Platí, the low-rise *Plati Beach Hotel* (☎0254/23 583; ④) has an enviable position near the middle of the beach; there are also scattered **rooms** here, for example behind *Tzimis Taverna* (☎0254/24 142; ③), which divides lunchtime trade with its neighbour across the way near the south end of the beach. Both of these lose out in the evenings to either the *Zimbabwe* or the nearby poolside bar/restaurant attached to the tastefully landscaped *Villa Afroditi* (☎0254/23 141 or 24 795; fax ☎0245/24 504; winter ☎01/96 41 910; ⑥), co-managed by the same family that runs the *Afroditi Apartments* in Mírina. Hospitable, multi-lingual Panayiotis, Afroditi and George Papasotiriou offer, among other things, what could be the best buffet breakfast in Greece; the rate category for both their premises drops significantly if pre-booked through *Sunvil*.

Thános and Áyios Pávlos beach

THÁNOS, 2km further southeast, is a bigger version of Platí village, with a few tavernas and "rooms" signs in evidence. A one-kilometre rough track below the village leads to **Paralía Thánous**, perhaps the most scenic of the southwestern beaches, with two tavernas, one (*O Nikos*) renting self-catering studios (☎0254/22 787; ③). Beyond Thános, the road curls over to the enormous beach at **Áyios Pávlos** (Nevgátis), flanked by weird volcanic crags to the west and reckoned the island's best for swimming. A typical terrapin-filled river meets the sea at mid-strand, and except for a few umbrellas and wooden shade-pavillions, there are no facilities.

Kondiás

The closest amenities to Áyios Pávlos – such as they are – lie 3km further along (11km from Mírina) and inland at **KONDIÁS**, the island's third largest settlement, cradled between two hills tufted with Limnos' only pine forest. Stone-built, red-tiled houses combine with the setting to make Kondiás the most attractive inland village, though facilities are limited to a few noisy rooms above one of two *kafenía*. You'd be better off eating at one of two simple tavernas 2km east at **Dhiapóri**, the shore annexe of Kondiás; the main attraction here is the narrow isthmus dividing the bays of Kondiás and Moúdhros, though the beach itself is unappealing.

Dháfni, Sardhés and Thérma

From Kondiás it's 11km northeast via Portianó to the junction with the main trans-island road at Livadhohóri. If you've already travelled out on this main highway, you can vary the return to Mírina by continuing northeast to Karpássi, and then bearing northwest towards Atsíki for the "high road" back to Mírina, paved except for the initial stretch. The villages and scenery en route give a good impression of rural Limnian life, though be prepared to reverse in the face of giant grain combines or large flocks of sheep.

DHÁFNI, the first village you'll encounter, challenges stereotypical images of the island's flatness with a hillside setting above a wooded ravine. **SARDHÉS**, 2500m further on, is the highest community on Límnos, providing wonderful views of broody sunsets. Just past Kornós, you rejoin the main road and shortly afterwards pass the easterly turning for **Thérma**, a nineteenth-century Ottoman spa, currently under restoration but due to open in 1996. Unusually for a hot spring, the water is non-sulphurous and the tastiest on the island, so there is always a knot of cars parked nearby under the trees while their owners are filling jerry cans from a public tap.

Eastern Límnos

The shores of **Moúdhros bay**, glimpsed south of the trans-island road, are muddy and best avoided. The bay itself enjoyed considerable importance during World War I, when it served as the staging area for the unsuccessful Allied landings on the Gallipoli peninsula, and later saw Allied acceptance of the Ottoman surrender aboard the British warship *HMS Agamemnon* on 30 October 1918.

Moúdhros and the Allied Cemetery

MOÚDHROS port, the second largest town on Límnos, is a dreary place; only a once-weekly ferry to Samothráki, and a wonderfully kitsch church – looking like a Baroque Iberian church with its two belfries – redeems it. Despite this, there are no less than three **hotels** here: *Toh Kyma* (☎0254/71 333; ⑤) and *Blue Bay* (☎0254/71 041; ④), on the harbour, both with tavernas; the *Filoxenia* (☎0254/71 407; ④), inland; plus some **rooms** (☎0254/71 470 or ☎71 422; ③), just outside the town on the main paved road to Roussopoúli. Any of these would make a suitable base for visiting the archeological sites and beaches of eastern Límnos.

A little further along the Roussopoúli road, you pass an Allied **military cemetery** (unlocked), maintained by the Commonwealth War Graves Commission, its neat lawns and rows of white headstones incongruous in such parched surroundings. In 1915, Moúdhros Bay was the principal base for the disastrous Gallipoli campaign. Of the 36,000 Allied dead, 887 are buried here, with 348 more at another graveyard near Portianó – mainly battle casualties who died after having been evacuated to the base hospital at Moúdhros. Though the deceased are mostly British, there is also a French cenotaph, and – speaking volumes about imperial sociology – a mass "Musalman" grave for Egyptian and Indian troops in one corner, with a Koranic inscription.

Polióhni

Indications of the most advanced Neolithic civilization in the Aegean have been unearthed at **Polióhni** (or Polyochni), 3km by dirt track from the gully-hidden village of **KAMÍNIA**, 7km east of Moúdhros (home to two simple grill-tavernas). Since 1930, ongoing Italian excavations have uncovered four layers of settlement, the oldest from late in the fourth millennium BC, pre-dating Troy on the Turkish coast opposite; the town met a sudden, violent end from war or earthquake in about 2100 BC. Very little of Homeric or Mycenaean vintage has been found yet, though a gold hoard similar to the so-called "Priam's Treasure", recently re-discovered in Russia, was uncovered in 1956.

The actual ruins (daily 9.30am–5.30pm; free) are of essentially specialist interest, though a *bouleuterion* (assembly hall) with bench seating, a mansion and the landward fortifications are labelled. During August and September the Italian excavators are about; if they are free to show you around, the place may become that much more engaging. The site occupies a bluff overlooking a long, narrow rock-and-sand beach flanked by stream valleys, the mouth of one of these being the old port; two wells within the fortifications suggest that reliable fresh water or sieges were major preoccupations.

Ifestía and Kavírio

Ifestía and Kavírio, the other significant ancient sites on Límnos, are most easily reached via the village of Kondopoúli, 7km northeast of Moúdhros. Both sites are rather remote and really only accessible by private transport.

Ifestía

Ifestía (or Hephaistia), in Classical times the most important city on the island, took its name from Hephaistos, god of fire and metal-working. According to legend, he attempted to intercede in a quarrel between his parents Hera and Zeus, and for his troubles was hurled from Mount Olympus by his father. A hard landing on Límnos left Hephaistos permanently lame, but he was adopted by the Limnians and held in high esteem thereafter. Most of the site (daily 9.30am–3.30pm; free) remains unexcavated, but there are scant remains of a theatre and a temple dedicated to the god.

Kavírio

Somewhat more evocative is **Kavírio** (Kabeirio), on the opposite shore of Tigáni Bay from Ifestía, and mercifully out of sight from a new and improbably located luxury complex. The ruins (daily 9.30am–3.30pm; free) are of a sanctuary connected with the cult of the Kabiroi on the island of Samothráki just to the north, although the site on Límnos is probably older. Little survives other than the ground plan – aligned unusually southeast-to-northwest, an orientation dictated by the topography of the headland – but the setting is undeniably impressive. Eleven column stumps stake out a *stoa*, behind eight spots marked as column bases in the main *telestirio* or shrine where the cult mysteries took place.

More engaging, perhaps, is a nearby **sea-grotto** identified as the Homeric *Spiliá toú Filoktíti*, where the Trojan war hero Philoctetes was abandoned by his comrades-in-arms until his stinking, gangrenous leg had healed. Landward access to the cave is via a hundred kilometres of steps leading down from the caretaker's sunshade.

Eastern beaches

One of the best beaches on the island is the east-coast strand at **Kéros**, 4km by dirt road below **KALLIÓPI** (which has two snack bar/tavernas), in turn 2km from Kondopoúli. A long stretch of sand with dunes and shallow water, Kéros attracts a number of Greeks and Germans with camper vans and windsurfers, but is large enough to remain uncrowded. By contrast, the beaches near the village of **PLÁKA**, at the northeastern tip of the island, are not worth the extra effort, and the adjacent hot springs appearing on some maps are actually warm mud baths.

Áyios Efstrátios

ÁYIOS EFSTRÁTIOS ("Aï Strátis" for short) is without doubt one of the quietest and most isolated islands in the Aegean. Historically, the only outsiders to stay here were forced to do so – it served as a place of exile for political prisoners under both the Metaxas regime of the 1930s and the various right-wing governments that followed the civil war. It's still unusual for travellers to show up on the island, and if you do, you're sure to be asked why.

Arrival

Ferries between Límnos and Kavála to either Rafína, Kími or Áyios Konstandínos call at Áyios Efstrátios every few days throughout the year; in summer, there's also a regular *kaïki* from Límnos. The harbour has recently been improved to allow large ferries to dock, replacing the launch method of transferring goods and passengers, but it is still a very exposed anchorage, and in bad weather you could end up stranded here. If an indefinite stay does not appeal, it may be best to get a taste of the island through one of the weekly daytrips advertised on Límnos in high season.

The port

ÁYIOS EFSTRÁTIOS port – the only settlement on the island – is one of the ugliest habitations in Greece. Devastation caused by an earthquake in 1967, which also killed half the population, was compounded by the rebuilding plan; the contract went to a company with junta connections, which prevented the islanders from returning to their old homes and used army bulldozers to raze even those structures that could have been repaired. From the northern hillside, some two dozen remaining houses of the old village overlook its replacement, whose grim rows of prefabs, complete with concrete church and underused shopping centre, constitute a sad monument to the corruption of the junta years. If you're curious, there's an old photograph of the village, taken before the earthquake, in the *kafenío* by the port.

Architecture apart, Áyios Efstrátios still functions as a very traditional fishing and farming community, with the prefabs set at the mouth of a wooded stream valley draining to the sandy harbour beach. Tourist amenities consist of just two very basic **tavernas** and a single **pension** in one of the surviving old houses; it's likely to be full in the summer, so call in advance (☎0254/93 202; ②). No one will object, however, if you camp at the far end of the harbour beach.

The rest of the island

As you walk away from the village – there are few cars and no paved roads – things improve rapidly. A landscape of dry hills and valleys scattered with a surprising number of oak trees is deserted apart from wild rabbits, sheep, an occasional shepherd, and some good beaches where you can camp in desert-island isolation – perhaps the only reason you're likely to visit Áyios Efstrátios. **Alonítsi**, on the north coast, a ninety-minute walk from the village along a track up the north side of the valley, is a two-kilometre stretch of sand with rolling breakers and views across to Límnos.

South of the village, there's a series of greyish sand beaches, most with wells and drinkable water, although with few real paths in this part of the island, getting to them can be something of a scramble. **Lidharío**, at the end of an attractive wooded valley, is the first worthwhile beach, but again, it's a ninety-minute walk from town, unless you can persuade a fisherman to take you by boat. Some of the caves around the coast are home to the rare Mediterranean monk seal (see box, p.258), but you're unlikely to see one.

Greek script table

Límnos	Λήμνος	ΛΗΜΝΟΣ
Avlónas	Αυλόνας	ΑΥΛΟΝΑΣ
Áyios Efstrátios	Αγιος Ευστράτιος	ΑΓΙΟΣ ΣΥΣΤΡΑΤΙΟΣ
Áyios Pávlos	Αγιος Παύλος	ΑΓΙΟΣ ΠΑΥΛΟΣ
Dháfni	Δάφνη	ΔΑΦΝΗ
Dhiapóri	Διαπόρι	ΔΙΑΠΟΡΙ
Ifestía	Ηφαιστεία	ΗΦΑΙΣΤΕΙΑ
Kalliópi	Καλλιόπη	ΚΑΛΛΙΟΠΗ
Kamínia	Καμίνια	ΚΑΜΙΝΙΑ
Káspakas	Κάσπακας	ΚΑΣΠΑΚΑΣ
Kavírio	Καβείριο	ΚΑΒΕΙΡΙΟ
Kéros	Κέρος	ΚΕΡΟΣ
Kondiás	Κοντιάς	ΚΟΝΤΙΑΣ
Kondopoúli	Κοντοπούλι	ΚΟΝΤΟΠΟΥΛΙ
Mírina	Μύρινα	ΜΥΡΙΝΑ

Greek script cont.

Moúdhros	Μούδρος	ΜΟΥΔΡΟΣ
Platí	Πλατύ	ΠΛΑΤΥ
Polióhni	Πολυόχνη	ΠΟΛΥΟΧΝΗ
Portianó	Πορτιανό	ΠΟΡΤΙΑΝΟ
Roussopoúli	Ρουσσοπούλι	ΡΟΥΣΣΟΠΟΥΛΙ
Sardhés	Σαρδές	ΣΑΡΔΕΣ
Thános	Θάνος	ΘΑΝΟΣ

Límnos travel details

INTER-ISLAND TRANSPORT

KAÏKIA

Límnos to: Áyios Efstrátios (1–3 weekly in summer only).

FERRIES

Áyios Efstrátios to: Híos (1–2 weekly on *NEL*); Kavála (1 weekly on *NEL*); Lésvos (1–2 weekly on *NEL*); Límnos (4–5 weekly on *NEL* or *Nomicos Lines*; 1hr 30min); Pátmos (1 weekly on *NEL*); Rafína (Attica; 3–4 weekly on *NEL* or *Nomicos*); Sámos (1 weekly on *NEL*); Skíros (1–2 weekly on *Nomicos*).

Límnos (Mírina) to: Áyios Efstrátios (4 weekly on *NEL*); Áyios Konstandínos (Thessaly; 1 fortnightly on *Nomicos*); Híos (4–5 weekly on *NEL*); Kavála (4–6 weekly on *NEL* or *Nomicos*; 6hr); Kími (Évvia; 1 fortnightly on *Nomicos*; 6hr); Lesvos (Mitilíni or Sígri; 4–5 weekly on *NEL*; 7hr); Pátmos (1 weekly on *NEL*); Pireás (4 weekly on *NEL*); Psará (1–2 weekly on *NEL* or *Nomicos*); Rafína (Attica; 3–5 weekly on *NEL* or *Nomicos*); Sámos (1 weekly on *NEL*); Skíros (1–2 weekly on *NEL* or *Nomicos*); Sporades (all islands; 1 weekly on *Nomicos*); Thessaloníki (2–3 weekly on *NEL*).

Límnos (Moúdhros) to: Samothráki (1 weekly mid–June to mid–Sept on *Arsinoi* or *Saos*).

HYDROFOILS

Límnos to: Kavála (northern mainland) and Lésvos, 1 weekly on *Gianmar Lines*.

DOMESTIC FLIGHTS

Límnos to: Athens (2–3 daily; 1hr); Lésvos (4–7 weekly; 40min); Thessaloníki (4–7 weekly; 50min).

NB Because of heavy use by the Greek armed forces, these flights need to be booked well in advance throughout the year.

Part 3

The Contexts

The historical framework

This section serves merely to lend some perspective to travels in the Dodecanese and East Aegean, and is heavily weighted towards more recent centuries. Although these two island groups are the most recent additions to the modern Greek state, their Hellenic identity has been fairly consistent since ancient times – something the kafenío sages will be only to willing to corroborate in political discussions.

Neolithic, Minoan and Mycenaean ages: c. 5500–1150 BC

It seems that people originally came to the Dodecanese and East Aegean in fits and starts, predominantly from the **Anatolian mainland** just opposite. After the sixth millennium BC, settlement in these islands is fairly well documented by archeological finds on most of the islands, particularly at present-day Thermí, Lésvos; Emboriós, Híos; Líndhos, Rhodes; various sites on Límnos; and in several caves of Kálimnos. In contrast to the exclusively farming communities on the mainland, these were trading posts founded at or near excellent natural harbours.

The years between about **2000 and 1100 BC** were a period of fluctuating regional dominance, based at first upon **sea power**; the Phoenicians in particular lingered briefly at Rhodes en route to Crete from the Middle East. Minoan Crete, which monopolized the eastern Mediterranean trade routes during an era subsequently called the **Minoan Age**, in turn dispatched more permanent colonists during the sixteenth century BC, establishing trading posts at Ialyssos and Kameiros on Rhodes' west-facing Aegean coast.

When the Minoan cities finally succumbed to disaster, natural or otherwise, around 1400 BC, it was the flourishing mainland centre of **Mycenae** that assumed the leading role in these islands, until it in turn collapsed during the twelfth century BC. On Rhodes, the Mycenaean invaders left traces of their distinctive **pottery** (which dominates the town's archeological museum), and founded the cities of Ialyssos, Kameiros and Lindos. By now the island and some of its neighbours (including Kos and Symi) were prominent enough to participate in the semi-legendary **Trojan War**, with their ships included in Homer's roster of those who sailed to Troy.

The Dorian and Archaic eras: c. 1150–500 BC

The collapse of the Mycenaean (or more properly, Late Bronze Age) civilization has traditionally been attributed to the invasion from the north of a fair-skinned "barbarian" people, the **Dorians**, who devastated the existing culture and initiated the first **"Dark Ages"**. These days, archeologists see the influx more in terms of shifting **trade patterns**, though undoubtedly there was major disruption during the **twelfth century**.

Out in the islands, this era saw Límnos apparently retain its indigenous, non-Mycenaean population, and Lesvos play host to **Aeolians** displaced from mainland Thessaly. Meanwhile, the so-called Dorians took over most islands to the south, including Rhodes, where Ialyssos and Kameiros began to grow. Together with Lindos, Astypalia (on Kos), Knidos and Halicarnassos (the latter two on the Anatolian mainland opposite), these six settlements formed the confederacy known as the **Dorian Hexapolis**.

Two cultural trends are salient in this period: the almost total supplanting of earlier mother goddesses by **male deities** (a process begun under the Mycenaeans), and the appearance of an **alphabet** still recognizable by modern Greeks, which replaced the so-called "Linear A" and "Linear B" Minoan/Mycenaean scripts.

Archaic Period

By around **800 BC**, the initially rigorous rule of the Dorians had relaxed on the islands as elsewhere in Greece, perhaps accelerated by the influx from Asia Minor of the so-called Ionians, particularly on Hios, Ikaria and Samos. The twelve-town **Ionian League**, centred at the Panionion shrine on Mount Mycale opposite Sámos, included these islands as members.

Here as elsewhere in the Hellenic world, the ninth century BC ushered in the beginnings of the more democratic Greek **city-state** (*polis*). Citizens – rather than just kings or aristocrats – became involved in government and took part in community activities organizing industry and leisure. Colonial ventures by the wealthier cities (including Lindos) increased, as did commercial dealings, and the consequent rise in the import trade gradually gave rise to a new class of manufacturers.

Each city-state retained both its independence and a distinctive style, with the result that the sporadic attempts to unite against any external enemy were always pragmatic and temporary. The two most powerful states to emerge on the mainland were Athens and Sparta, which exercised a rivalry over the next five centuries. In the Dodecanese and east Aegean, the most important were Lindos on Rhodes, Astypalia on Kos, Molyvos and Mytilene on Lesvos, and the eponymous island capitals, Hios and Samos. Their heyday was the sixth century BC, when Mytilene, Lindos and Samos were ruled by **tyrants** of distinction – Pittakos, Kleovoulos and Polykrates respectively – with the word yet to acquire all of its modern perjorative connotations.

Each city-state had its **acropolis**, or high town, where religious activity was focused. Worship at this stage was **polytheistic**, ordering the Olympic pantheon under Zeus. The proliferation of names and of sanctuary finds on the islands suggests a preference for the divine twins Apollo and Artemis, the latter often merely a thinly Hellenized version of the Anatolian goddess Cybele; Aphrodite and Hera were also well represented, only to be expected bearing in mind the proxmity to Asia with its cults of love goddesses such as Astarte.

The Classical and Hellenistic eras: c. 500–166 BC

Of the outside threats faced by the various city-states, none was greater than that of the **Persians**, who under successive kings Darius and Xerxes made repeated attempts to subjugate both islands and mainland. By virtue of their position, as well as innate sympathies, many of the east Aegean and Dodecanesian city-states took the side of the invaders; though Rhodes successfully resisted Darius' first attack in 491 BC, in the year 480 it contributed nearly forty ships to Xerxes' fleet at the **Battle of Salamis**. It was the decisive Greek naval victory (479 BC) in the Mycale straits off Sámos that finally ended the Persian threat. Shortly thereafter the **Delian Confederacy**, an alliance dominated by Athens, was established, in which many island city-states (including those of Rhodes) were enlisted voluntarily or otherwise.

Athens again was the first to elaborate the concept of **democracy** (*demokratia*), literally "control by the people" – at this stage "the people" did not include women or slaves. In Athens there were three organs of government. The **Areopagus**, composed of the city elders, had a steadily decreasing authority and ended up dealing solely with murder cases. Then there was the **Council of Five Hundred** (men), elected annually by ballot to prepare the business of the Assembly and attend to matters of urgency. Finally, the **Assembly** gave every free man a political voice; it had sole responsibility for law-making and provided an arena for the discussion of important issues. Other "democratic" city-states adopted variations of these institutions, but they were slow to catch on in the eastern islands, where in most cases oligarchies of some sort remained in power.

The power struggles between Athens and Sparta, allied with various networks of city-states, eventually culminated in the **Peloponnesian Wars** of 431–404 BC. The Dodecanese and east Aegean saw little military action, but because of a Dorian heritage shared with Sparta, city-states there tended to defect to the Spartan side when given the opportunity; this was demonstrated by Mytilene, which revolted in 428 (partly to spite pro-Athenian neighbour Molyvos), and Rhodes, Kos and Hios, which changed sides in 412. Only Samos remained a more or less constant Athenian ally to the end of the war. After these conflicts, superbly recorded by Thucydides and nominally won by Sparta, the small city-state ceased to function so effectively.

On Rhodes, this decline was hastened by the founding in 408 BC of a single city intended to replace the three original centres of Ialyssos, Kameiros and Lindos. **Rodos**, the result of this act of union (*synoekismos*) at the northeast tip of the island, was endowed with three natural harbours still in use today. The founding trio slowly withered away over the next few centuries, until only Lindos retained any importance or independence. Quickly growing wealthy from trade – particularly wine to Egypt in exchange for grain – Rodos minted its own currency, which gradually replaced earlier **coinage** from Lindos, Ialyssos and Kameiros.

During this period, the islands of Samos and Hios were at their nadir, intermittently occupied by the resurgent Persians taking advantage of disorder following the Peloponnesian Wars; Kós effected a *synoekismos* of its own in 366 BC, founding the present-day port and capital. Only the largest original city-states of Lesvos remained important during the fourth century BC.

The most important factor in the decline of the city-states was emerging on the northern mainland, in the kingdom of **Macedonia**. Based at the Macedonian capital of Pella, Philip II (359–336 BC) was forging a strong military and unitary force, pushing forward into Thrace and establishing control over the southern mainland. His son, **Alexander the Great**, in an extraordinarily brief but glorious thirteen-year reign, extended these gains into Persia and Egypt as well as parts of modern India and Afghanistan. The east Aegean and Dodecanese islands sided quickly with Alexander, especially mercenary-minded Rhodes, which was granted generous commercial concessions in the conqueror's new Levantine territories.

This unwieldy empire splintered almost immediately upon Alexander's death in 323 BC, and was divided into the three Macedonian dynasties of **Hellenistic Greece**: the Antigonids in Macedonia, the Seleucids in Syria and Persia, and the Ptolemies in Egypt; it was not long before the three fell to fighting among themselves. Their conflicts involved Rhodes, whose islanders had understandably refused an "offer" by Antigonus to join him in attacking Egypt, their long-standing ally and trade partner. Enraged at this defiance, in 305 BC Antigonous sent his son Demetrios to bring the Rhodians to heel; the result was a year-long **siege**, one of the great battles of antiquity (see box on p.62–63). Having fought each other to a standstill, attackers and defenders agreed to a truce, and Demetrios' abandoned war machinery was sold to defray the costs of the **Colossus of Rhodes** (see box on p.77).

Hellenistic Rodos emerged from the war with redoubled prestige and wealth; poets, philosophers, rhetorcians and artists, both native-born and immigrant, made the city home during a **"golden age"** that was to last until the middle of the second century BC. During this time Rhodes' sea-going power was such that her **maritime and trading law** became standard across the Mediterranean, and was adapted by Augustus three centuries later for application throughout the Roman Empire.

The Roman and Bzyantine eras: 166 BC–14th century AD

Until now, **Rhodes** had proved adroit at avoiding political alliances and keeping commercial criteria paramount, but as the second century BC progressed, she became entangled with an expanding **Rome**. The mainland had been subdued by the Romans in a series of campaigns beginning in 215 BC, and by 190 BC their operations extended to the islands, Anatolia and the Middle East. Rome repaid Rhodes for its military assistance with a grant of authority over lands in Lycia and Caria, but the latter complained repeatedly to the Senate. Matters came to a head in 166 BC, when Rome withdrew the Rhodian concession in the two Anatolian realms, and declared the central Aegean islet of Delos a free port, sending Rhodian prosperity into free fall. Rhodes compounded her error by siding against the assassins of Julius Caesar in 42 BC; in retaliation, Cassius plundered and burnt Rodos city, massacring the citizens and forwarding enormous booty to Rome.

Kos' turn had come in 88 BC, at the hands of **Mithridates of Pontus**, who sacked the port town, relieving it of £1 million equivalent in bank deposits; the island was otherwise known for its wine and silk, both long since disappeared. **Samos** had taken Mithridates' part and was punished accordingly, though later it was chosen to host the honeymoon of Anthony and Cleopatra. Of all these islands, **Lesvos** was the Romans' favourite for its lively town life and gentle scenery, with money spent on lavish public works, and imperial visits to its academies and theatres. Following a decree by Emperor

Augustus, these four cities were designated **venues of banishment** for disgraced notables – not too onerous a punishment given their creature comforts.

Christianity and Byzantium

Christianity came early to the east Aegean and Dodecanese; the apostle Paul stopped here in the first century to evangelize Rhodes, Kós, Sámos, Híos and Lésvos, and virtually every island has at least one ruined basilica with mosaic floors, invariably fifth or sixth century, often built atop pagan shrines; these early churches were mostly levelled by Arab raids in the seventh century.

The **decline of the Roman Empire** involved its apportioning into eastern and western empires. In 330 AD Emperor Constantine moved his capital to the Greek city of **Byzantium**, and here emerged Constantinople (modern Istanbul), the "new Rome" and spiritual and political capital of the Byzantine Empire. While the last western Roman emperor was deposed by barbarian Goths in 476, this oriental portion was to be the dominant Mediterranean power for some seven centuries; only in 1453 did it collapse completely.

Christianity had made an influential convert in Constantine, and by the end of the fourth century it was the **official state religion**; its liturgies (still in use in the Greek Orthodox church), creed and New Testament were all written in the **koine**, a form of Greek evolved from the ancient dialect. A distinction was drawn, though, between perceptions of Greek as a language and as a cultural concept. The Byzantine Empire styled itself Roman, or Romios, rather than Hellenic, and moved to eradicate all remaining symbols of pagan Greece, for instance by dismantling ancient temples for use as masonry in building churches.

The seventh century saw **Constantinople** besieged by Persians, and later by Arabs, but the Byzantine Empire survived, losing only Egypt, the least "Greek" of its territories. During the ninth to the early eleventh centuries, culture, confidence and security flourished here. Linked to the Orthodox Byzantine faith was a sense of spiritual superiority, and the emperors saw Constantinople as a "new Jerusalem" for their "chosen people". This was the beginning of a diplomatic and ecclesiastical conflict with the Catholic west that was to have disastrous consequences over the next five centuries. In the meantime the eastern and western patriarchs mutually excommunicated each other.

From the seventh through to the eleventh centuries the Dodecanese and east Aegean became something of a provincial backwater, making little mark in the historical record, with islands such as Ikaría and Lésvos used mostly (as under the Romans) to house banished troublemakers; most illustrious of these was the disgraced **Empress Irene**, exiled to Polykhnítos in 802.

All the islands were ravaged repeatedly by piratical **Saracen raids**, and from these years date numerous castles and watchtowers. Only at the close of this period did two great Byzantine monuments appear: the imperially founded monasteries of **Néa Moní**, on Híos, and **Saint John the Theologian**, on Pátmos. The latter foundation involved an imperial grant of the entire, previously insignificant island to the abbot Khristodhoulos, with the sanctity of the place curiously respected by most subsequent rulers and invaders.

The Coming of the Crusaders

Early in the eleventh century, **Latin Crusaders** began to appear in the region. In 1095 the Normans landed on the Dodecanese, with papal sanction, on their way to liberate Jerusalem. However, these were only a precursor of the rerouted **Fourth Crusade** of 1204, when Venetians, Franks and Germans diverted their armies from the Holy Land to Byzantium, sacking and occupying Constantinople. These Latin princes and their followers, intent on new lands and kingdoms, settled in to divide up the best part of the Empire. All that remained of Byzantium were four small peripheral kingdoms or **despotates**; none of these was based in the islands, though Rhodes was ruled by Leon Gavalas, a wealthy Byzantine governor, for three decades (a street in Ródhos Old Town bears his name).

There followed two centuries of manipulation and struggle between Franks, Venetians, Genoese, Catalans and Turks. In 1261, the **Paleologos** dynasty, provisionally based at Nicaea, recovered the city of Constantinople but little of its former territory and power. Virtually their only Latin Catholic allies were the **Genoese**, whose support came at a heavy price: extensive commercial privileges in the capital itself, and the effective cession, at various moments during the thirteenth and fourteenth centuries, of virtually all the east Aegean and Dodecanese islands to assorted Genoese families.

Within a generation of driving out the Franks the Byzantine Greeks faced a much stonger threat in the expanding empire of the **Ottoman Turks**. Torn apart by internal struggles between their own ruling dynasties, the Paleologi and Cantacuzenes, and unassisted except by the Genoese, they were to prove no match. On Tuesday, May 29, 1453, a date still solemnly commemorated by the Orthodox church, Constantinople fell to the forces of **Sultan Mehmet II** after a seven-week siege.

Genoese and Crusader rule: 1248–1478

From this time onwards the histories of the Dodecanese and East Aegean islands begin to diverge slightly, with often widely varying dates of handover between one conqueror and another, even for neighbouring islands.

Genoese adventurers seized Rhodes from Venetian rivals in 1248, but in 1306 the chivalric order of the **Knights' Hospitallers of St John** (see box on p.72–73), expelled from Palestine and unhappy on Cyprus, landed at Feraklós castle on the east coast of Rhodes. After a three-year war they evicted the Genoese from the island; Genoese-held Kós fell to the Knights in 1314, after which their possession – and prominent fortification – of most of the Dodecanese was a foregone conclusion. The main exceptions were Astipálea, Kárpathos and Kássos, which remained under Venetian rule, and the ecclesiastical idiosyncracy of Pátmos.

From their main bases on Rhodes and Kós, the Knights engaged in both legitimate trade and piracy, constituting a major thorn in the side of the expanding Ottoman empire, and, in the final century of their toehold, the only effective opposition to Ottoman authority in the Aegean. Attempts to dislodge them from these two islands during the fifteenth century were unsuccessful, and it took the Ottoman's acquisition of Kastellórizo as a base in 1512, and then a protracted siege of Rhodes by Sultan Süleyman the Magnificent in 1522 (see box on p.72–73), to send them packing off to Malta, and for all of the Dodecanese to fall into Turkish hands.

Remote Sámos and Ikaría supported garrisons of Venetians plus sundry other adventurers and pirates from the twelfth century onwards, but the Genoese gained undisputed possession of all islands from here north to the Thracian mainland during the fourteenth century. Híos was allotted to the Giustiani clan in 1344, who instituted harsh government through a *maona* or holding company, monopolizing the lucrative gum mastic trade until the Ottoman conquest in 1566. Sámos, essentially deserted since the fifteenth century, and adjacent Ikaría were acquired by the sultan or his representatives in the same decade.

The marriage in 1355 of a Byzantine Emperor to the daughter of the **Gatelluzi family** resulted in Lésvos passing into the hands of the latter. By all accounts they ran a civilized and enlightened principality, except for the unsavoury last of their line, Nicolò, who was defeated and killed by the Ottomans in 1462. Límnos, briefly taken over by the Venetians, followed in 1478.

Ottoman occupation: 1478–1912

Under what Greeks refer to as the **Turkokratía** or years of Ottoman rule, the Dodecanese and east Aegean lapsed into rural provincialism, taking refuge in a self-protective mode of village life that has only recently been disrupted. Only those larger islands with plenty of flat, arable land, such as Rhodes, Kós, and Lésvos, attracted extensive Turkish colonization and garrisoning, and then (except for Lésvos) only in the largest towns, where non-Muslims were forbidden residence in the strategic central citadels. Taxes and discipline were inflicted from Istanbul through resident judges, tax collectors and military personnel, but large enterprises or estates could remain in the hands of local notables, civilian or military, who often enjoyed considerable independence.

By and large, provincial Ottoman government was lethargic if not downright lackadaisical; travellers reported extensive neglect and deterioration on Rhodes in the eighteenth and nineteenth centuries, with discarded weapons and unrepaired damage both still dating from the 1522 siege.

Greek identity, meanwhile, was preserved through the offices of the **Orthodox Church**, which, despite occasional instances of enforced conversion and intermarriage, and the transformation of some churches into mosques, suffered little interference from the Ottomans. All Orthodox people, Greek or otherwise, were officially grouped as one *millet* or **subject nation**, with the patriarch responsible for the behaviour of his flock, collecting taxes and for administering communal and inheritance law. **Monasteries**, often secretly, organized schools and became the trustees of Byzantine culture; this had gone into stagnation after the fall of the empire, whose scholars and artists emigrated west, adding impetus to the Renaissance.

As Ottoman administration became increasingly decentralized and inefficient, individual Greeks rose to local positions of considerable influence, and a number of communities achieved a degree of autonomy. Even on tightly governed Lésvos, much of the lucrative olive-oil trade had passed into Greek Orthodox hands by the eighteenth century; Híos enjoyed special privileges by virtue of its continued monopoly on gum mastic; Sámos produced fine tobacco and rope hemp; while the barren, maritime islets of the Dodecanese, such as Hálki, Kálimnos, Sími and Kastellórizo, made fortunes either by diving for sponges, transporting Anatolian goods on their own fleets, or building boats on Turkish commission. The Ottomans, until relatively late in their history, never bothered to acquire much seamanship, preferring to rely on island crews and shipyards.

A typical anecdote relates how the Symians, on hearing of the fall of Rhodes, sought to allay imperial wrath by presenting Süleyman the Magnificent with a load of their finest sponges. Duly impressed, the sultan declared Sími a duty-free port, and gave the islanders the exclusive right to dive for sponges anywhere in the Aegean, in return for a yearly tribute similar to their introductory gift. These and similar indulgences were mostly honoured until after the establishment of a Greek state in 1830 (see below), with incremental withdrawal of privileges occurring between 1874 and 1908 in response to continued warfare between the Ottomans and "free" Greece.

The struggle for Independence

By the eighteenth century, opposition to Turkish rule on the Greek mainland was becoming widespread, exemplified most obviously by the *klephts* (brigands) of the mountains. It was not until the nineteenth century, however, that a **resistance movement** could muster sufficient support and fire power to prove a real challenge to the Ottomans. In 1770 a Russian-backed uprising enjoyed considerable success out in the islands, with Sámos and Pátmos in particular occupied by Admiral Orlof for three years. On the mainland, however, it was easily and brutally suppressed.

Fifty years later, however, the situation had changed. In Epirus, on the mainland, the Turks were over-extended, subduing the expansionist campaigns of local ruler Ali Pasha; the French Revolution and its propagandists had given impetus, rationale and confidence to national freedom movements; and the Greek fighters were given financial and ideological underpinnings by the **Filikí Etería**, or "Friendly Society", a secret group recruited among the exiled Greek merchants and intellectuals of central Europe. Accordingly, a somewhat motley coalition of *klephts* and theorists launched their insurrection at the monastery of **Ayía Lávra** near Kalávrita in the Peloponnese, where on March 25, 1821, the Greek banner was openly raised by the local archbishop, Yermanos.

The Dodecanese and east Aegean islands participated to varying, often limited degrees in the insurrection; the Aegean was usually not a primary theatre of operations. Pátmos and Sámos had virtually liberated themselves by 1824, though an uprising on Sími was easily quelled and its historic privileges rescinded. At Eressós, on Lésvos, a Turkish frigate was blown up by a kamikaze fire boat, prompting widespread massacre on the island; appalling reprisals were also visited on Híos for rebelling at Samian instigation. Kássos and Psará both harassed Ottoman shipping with their own large fleets, and suffered overwhelming revenge in consequence.

However, even where entire populations (such as on Kós and Rhodes) were restrained en masse by Ottoman garrisons, it was impossible to prevent individual volunteers from slipping away on boats to join the fracas on the mainland – the start of a tradition that was to gather momentum over the next century, commemorated by the Rhodian street Ethelondón Dhodhekanisíon (Dodecanesian Volunteers).

In 1830, **Greek independence** was confirmed by the western powers, and borders drawn up. Within these resided just 800,000 of the six million Greeks living within the Ottoman Empire, and the Greek territories were for the most part the poorest of the Classical and Byzantine lands, comprising Attica, the Peloponnese, the Argo-Saronic islands and the Cyclades. The rich agricultural belt of Thessaly, Epirus in the west, and Macedonia in the north, remained for the moment in Ottoman hands, as did all of the east Aegean islands and the Dodecanese. Alone among the east Aegean islands, Sámos – in recognition of its war efforts – was accorded a special status by the 1832 **Treaty of London**; it ranked as a semi-autonomous Ottoman province overseen by a suitably compliant Christian "prince", who was appointed by the sultan.

The emerging state

From the outset, irredentism was to be the main engine of Greek foreign policy for the next century. The **Megáli Idhéa** (Great Ideal), as it was termed, enshrined the liberation of all ethnic Greek populations residing outside the initially limited Greek state, by expanding its borders to incorporate as much as possible of former Byzantine territories. Among other regions, the east Aegean and Dodecanese were prime targets and beneficiaries of such sentiments.

In 1878, Thessaly, along with southern Epirus, was ceded to Greece by the Ottomans; less gloriously, the Greeks failed in 1897 to achieve *énosis* (union) with **Crete** by attacking Turkish forces on the mainland, and in the process virtually bankrupted the state. The island was, however, granted a status similar to Sámos' (here the prince was appointed by France, England and Russia), eventually becoming part of Greece in 1913.

It was from Crete also that the most distinguished Greek statesman of this century emerged. **Eleftherios Venizelos**, having led a civilian campaign for his island's redemption, was in 1910 elected prime minister of Greece. Two years later he organized an alliance with Serbia, Romanian and Bulgaria to fight the two **Balkan Wars** (1912–13), campaigns that saw the Ottomans all but driven out of Europe and the Aegean islands.

In the east Aegean, the first island to revolt was Ikaría, in July 1912, which in typically idiosyncratic fashion declared itself independent, issuing its own stamps and flying its own flag. This lasted a mere five months, until the Greek fleet showed up in November, en route to landings on Híos, Lésvos and Límnos, whose Ottoman troops resisted for only a few weeks. Already by September, members of the tiny Turkish garrison on Sámos were bundled into *kaïkia* and sent to Asia Minor after the last prince, deemed collaborationist, had been assassinated. With Greek frontiers extended to include central Epirus and western Macedonia (with its capital, Thessaloníki), the *Megáli Idhéa* was approaching reality.

One of its shortfalls, however, lay in the Dodecanese, which had been seized by the Italians in a brief campaign during spring 1912, part of a larger war begun in autumn 1911 to push the Ottomans out of Libya. At first the Italians were acclaimed as Christian liberators by the overwhelmingly Greek Orthodox population, and in turn they undertook not to outstay their welcome. At the outset of **World War I**, however, Italy elected to remain neutral, and was only persuaded to join the Allies by being promised, among other matters, that its sovereignty over the Dodecanese would be recognized – duly codified after the war in the 1920 **Treaty of Sèvres** signed by the last sultan; it's this (and other treaties) that Turkey repudiates today.

Since the Balkan Wars, Venizelos had proved himself a shrewd manipulator of domestic public opinion by revising the constitution and introducing a series of liberal social reforms. Division, however, was to appear with the outbreak of World War I. Venizelos urged Greek entry on the Allied side, seeing in the conflict possibilities for the "liberation" of Greeks in Thrace and Asia Minor. However, the new king, **Constantine (Konstantinos) I**, married to a sister of the German Kaiser, imposed a policy of neutrality. Eventually Venizelos set up a revolutionary government in Thessaloníki, provoking a brief civil war which saw royalist Pireas also menaced by Allied battleships; all of the recently liberated east Aegean islands declared for the Venizelists. In 1917, Greek troops entered the war to join the French, British and Serbian armies in the Macedonian campaign. Upon the capitulation of Bulgaria and Ottoman Turkey, the Greeks occupied Thrace, and Venizelos presented at **Versailles** demands for the predominantly Greek region around Smyrna (now Izmir) on the Asia Minor coast.

The Katastrofí and its aftermath

This marked the beginning of one of the most disastrous episodes in modern Greek history, still referred to in Greece as the **katastrofí** – the same word as in English. Venizelos was authorized to move forces into Smyrna in 1919, but soon afterwards Allied support (except for Lloyd

George's Britain) began to evaporate; in particular the Italians, now consolidating their hold on the Dodecanese, had no wish to be hemmed in on three sides by Greek territory. Within Turkey itself, a new nationalist movement – surreptitiously assisted by the French and Italians – was taking power under Mustafa Kemal, or **Atatürk** as he came to be known.

When Venizelos unexpectedly lost the 1920 elections, monarchist factions took over, their aspirations unmitigated by the Cretan's skill in foreign diplomacy. Greek forces, now led by incompetent and corrupt generals, were ordered to advance upon Ankara in an attempt to crush Atatürk and the Turkish nationalist armies. Greece's Anatolian mandate ignominiously collapsed in August 1922, when Turkish troops forced the Greeks back to the Aegean coast and into a hurried evacuation from Smyrna. After triumphantly entering Smyrna, the Turks systematically massacred much of the remaining Armenian and Greek population before burning most of the city to the ground.

Although an entire Greek army remained intact in Thrace, prepared to fight on, Greece was compelled to accept Atatürk's own terms, formalized by the **Treaty of Lausanne** in 1923. Among other provisions, this ordered the exchange of religious minorities in each country – in effect, the first regulated ethnic cleansing. Turkey was to accept 390,000 Muslims resident on Greek soil. Greece, mobilized almost continuously for the last decade and with a population of under five million, was faced with the resettlement of over 1,300,000 Christian refugees, some tens of thousands of whom were deposited on the east Aegean islands. The *Megáli Idhéa* had ceased to be a viable blueprint for action.

Changes were immediate and far-reaching. Within a few years great agricultural estates of mainland Thessaly were redistributed both to Greek tenants and refugee farmers, and huge shantytowns grew into new quarters around Athens, Pireás and other cities, a spur to the country's then almost nonexistent industry.

Politically, too, reaction was swift. A group of army officers under **Colonel Plastiras** assembled on Híos after the retreat from Smyrna, "invited" King Constantine I to abdicate and, after a show trial, executed five of his ministers held responsible for the *katastrofí*. Democracy was nominally restored with the proclamation of a **republic**, but for much of the next decade changes in government were brought about by factions within the armed forces. Meanwhile, among the urban refugee population, unions were being formed and the **Greek Communist Party (KKE)** was established.

By 1936, the Communist Party had enough electoral support to hold the balance of power in parliament, and would have done so had not the army and the by then restored king decided otherwise. **King Yiorgos (George) II** had been returned by a plebiscite held – and almost certainly manipulated – the previous year, and so presided over an increasingly factionalized parliament.

In April 1936 George II appointed as prime minister **General John Metaxas**, despite the latter's support from only six parliamentary deputies. Immediately a series of KKE-organized strikes broke out, and the king, ignoring attempts to form a broad liberal coalition, dissolved parliament without setting a date for new elections. It was a blatantly unconstitutional move, and opened the way for five years of ruthless **dictatorship**.

Metaxas averted a general strike with military force and proceeded to set up a state based on fascist models of the age. Left-wing and trade union opponents were imprisoned or forced into exile, a state youth movement and secret police set up, and rigid censorship, extending even to passages of Thucydides, imposed. It was, however, at least a Greek dictatorship, and though Metaxas was sympathetic to Nazi organization, he completely opposed German or Italian domination.

Italian rule in the Dodecanese: 1912–43

The **Italian tenure** in the Dodecanese always rested on a flimsy legalistic tissue, which contemporary Turkey has not been slow to criticize in its ongoing dispute with Greek over sovereignty in the Aegean. Briefly, the first **Treaty of Lausanne** (October 1912) stipulated that the Dodecanese were to be returned to the Ottomans when they had evacuated Libya. When Italy and the Ottomans entered World War I on opposite sides, the Italians claimed that this treaty was nullified, to be replaced by the 1915 **Treaty of London** formally acknowledging their possession of the Dodecanese (except for Kastellorizo, occupied by the French for military reasons). Between 1918 and 1923, various conferences agreed that the

Dodecanese were to be handed over to Greece, with the exception of Rhodes, but after the beginning of Fascist rule in Italy, this became progressively more unlikely.

With the rise of **Mussolini**, Italy dropped all altrusitic pretences in the Dodecanese, embarking in stages upon a forced **Latinization** campaign. Land was expropriated for use by Italian colonists, and intermarriage with local Greeks encouraged, though only Catholic ceremonies were recognized. An attempt was made to set up a puppet **Orthodox bishopric**, and when this failed, the Orthodox rite, in all local secular institutions, was suppressed completely. Italian was introduced as the compulsory language of education, and as a result anyone over the age of 65 in the Dodecanese is probably bilingual in Italian and Greek. In response to these strictures there were riots on Kastellórizo during 1933, and on Kálimnos in 1935, with some loss of civilian life. Emigration was not a possible social safety valve as elsewhere in the Greek world; unless one collaborated with the Italian authorities and their assimilation programmes, it was impossible to get a passport, and in any case exit to the USA had been largely closed off by 1930 through racist anti-immigration laws and the onset of the Great Depression. Pressure groups of expatriated Dodecanesians were formed, especially in New York, to lobby anyone who would listen about the Hellenic cause in the Dodecanese.

On the larger islands, massive public works were undertaken to make them the showcases of the "**Italian Aegean Empire**" as Mussolini styled them; roads, monumental buildings and waterworks were constructed, sound and not-so-sound archeology engaged in, and the islands accurately mapped for the first time. The first hotels were built on Rhodes and Kós, and the first tourists arrived by boat or sea plane for stays averaging months rather than weeks. However, smaller islands, except for militarily strategic Léros, were neglected and left punitively undeveloped once the requisite Art Deco **municipal "palace"** had been erected.

World War II and the Greek Civil War

Using a submarine dispatched from a naval base in the Dodecanese, the Italians tried to provoke the Greeks into **World War II** by surreptitiously torpedoing the Greek cruiser *Elli* in Tínos harbour on August 15, 1940. This outrage went unanswered, as Greece was ill equipped to fight; however, when Mussolini occupied Albania, and on October 28, 1940, sent an ultimatum demanding passage for his troops through Greece, Metaxas responded with the apocryphal "óhi" (no). (In fact, his response, in the mutually understood French, was "C'est la guerre"). This marked the entry of Greece into the war, and the gesture is still celebrated as a national holiday.

Galvanized into unity by the crisis, the Greeks drove Italian forces from the country, and in doing so took control of the long-coveted and predominantly Greek-populated northern Epirus (southern Albania). Frittering away its strength in the snowy mountains here, the Greek army failed to consolidate its gains or defend the Macedonian frontier, and coordination with the British never materialized.

Occupation and resistance

In April of the following year Nazi columns swept through Yugoslavia and across the Greek mainland, effectively reversing the only Axis defeat to date. By the end of May 1941, air- and seaborne German invasion forces had completed the occupation of all the other islands, including those of the east Aegean (with the exception of Sámos, Ikaría and Foúrni, which were granted to the Italians). Metaxas died before their arrival, while King George and his new self-appointed ministers fled into exile in Cairo; few Greeks, of any political persuasion, were sad to see them go.

The joint Italian-German-Bulgarian occupation of Greece was among the bitterest experiences of the European war. Nearly half a million Greek civilians starved to death over the winter of 1941–42, as all food was requisitioned, principally by the Germans, to feed occupying armies. In addition, entire villages on the mainland and Crete were burned and the residents slaughtered at the least hint of **resistance** activity.

With a puppet government in Athens – and an unpopular, discredited Royalist group in Cairo – the focus of Greek resistance between 1942 and 1945 passed largely to **EAM**, or National Liberation Front. By 1943 it was in virtual control of most rural areas of the mainland and several islands, working with the British on tactical operations. Initially it commanded widespread popular support, and appeared to offer an obvious framework for a postwar government.

However, most of its members were communist, and British Prime Minister Churchill was determined to reinstate the monarchy. Even with two years of war remaining it became obvious that there could be no peaceful post-liberation regime other than a republic. Accordingly, in August 1943 representatives from each of the main resistance movements – including two non-communist groups – flew clandestinely to Cairo to request that the king not return unless a plebiscite had first voted in his favour. Both Greek and British authorities demurred, and the best possibility of averting civil war was lost.

Subsequently a conflict broke out within EAM between those who favoured taking peaceful control of any government imposed after liberation, and hard-line Stalinist ideologues who forbade participation in any "bourgeois" regime.

In October 1943, with fears of an imminent British occupation following the Italian capitulation, ELAS (the armed wing of EAM) launched full-scale attacks upon its Greek rivals; by the following February, when a ceasefire was arranged, they had wiped out all but EDES, a right-wing grouping suspected of collaboration with the Germans.

The Italian-occupied areas of the Aegean fared slightly better, though scenarios on neighbouring islands varied widely. In the Dodecanese it was business as usual, only more so owing to the exigencies of war. On Foúrni, the Italian garrison and the islanders reached a cosy understanding to have as calm an occupation as possible, while on adjacent Sámos an active resistance contingent on Mount Kérkis prompted a mass reprisal execution in one village. Because of their potential for smuggling people and goods between the islands and Turkey, the use of boats was usually forbidden; this caused fish to disappear from the diet, and guaranteed widespread malnutrition. German-occupied Híos was relatively quiet, though Lésvos – in keeping with its communist sympathies – had like Sámos an active resistance contingent.

When Italy capitulated in September 1943, a brief free-for-all ensued on the islands it had controlled. As elsewhere in Greece, German troops attacked, disarmed and executed their erstwhile allies, particularly on Rhodes. The British quickly occupied Kós, Kastellórizo, Sámos and Léros, but in insufficient strength to repel German attacks; within a few weeks they had to abandon these positions, with considerable losses. Churchill considered the Dodecanese easy pickings, but in the end was denied adequate resources for the job by the Americans, who refused to risk the already precarious advance through Italy proper. The British were unable to return to the Dodecanese until May 1945, reconstructing these islands' infrastructure before a final agreement in late 1947 provided for this archipelago's union with Greece in March 1948.

Civil war

As the Germans began to leave in October 1944, most of the EAM leadership agreed to join a British-sponsored "official" interim government. It quickly proved a tactical error, however: though ninety percent of the countryside was under their control, the communists were given only one-third representation. The king showed no sign of renouncing his claims, and, in November, Allied forces ordered ELAS to disarm. On December 3, members of a civilian demonstration in Athens were shot dead, either by policemen or a provocateur; within days fighting broke out between ELAS and British troops, in the so-called **Dhekemvrianá Battle of Athens**, the only recorded instance of the Allies fighting against a victorious resistance group.

A truce of sorts was negotiated at Várkiza the following spring but the agreement was never implemented. The army, police and civil service remained in right-wing hands, and while collaborationists were often allowed to retain their positions, left-wing sympathizers, many of whom were not communists, were systematically excluded. The elections of 1946 were won by the right-wing parties, followed by a plebiscite in favour of the king's return. By 1947 guerilla activity had reached the scale of a full civil war.

In the interim, King George had died and been succeeded by his brother Paul (with his consort Frederika), while the Americans had taken over the British role and begun implementing the so-called **Truman doctrine**. In 1947 they took virtual control of Greece, their first significant postwar experiment in anti-communist intervention. Massive economic and military aid was given to a client Greek government, whose prime minister needed the countersignature of the American Mission in order to validate any documents.

In the mountains of the mainland, **US military advisers** supervised campaigns against ELAS, and there were mass arrests, court martials and imprisonments – a kind of "White Terror" – lasting until 1951. Over three thousand executions were recorded, including a number of Jehovah's Witnesses, "a sect proved to be under communist domination", according to US Ambassador Grady.

In the autumn of 1949, with the Yugoslav-Greek border closed after Tito's rift with Stalin, the last ELAS guerillas finally admitted defeat and retreated into Albania from their strongholds on Mount Grámmos. Atrocities had been committed on both sides, including – from the Left – wide-scale pillaging of churches and monasteries, and the dubious evacuation of children from "combat areas" to countries behind the new Iron Curtain. Such errors, as well as the hopelessness of fighting an American-backed army, undoubtedly lost ELAS much support.

Reconstruction American-style: 1950–67

It was a demoralized, shattered Greece that emerged into the Western political orbit of the **1950s**. It was also perforce American-dominated, enlisted into the Korean War in 1950 and NATO the following year. In domestic politics, the US Embassy – still giving the orders – foisted a winner-take-all electoral system, which was to ensure uninterrupted victory for the Right over the next twelve years. All overt Leftist activity was banned; those individuals who were not herded into political "re-education" camps or dispatched by legal or vigilante firing squads, went into exile across Eastern Europe, to return only after 1974.

The American-backed, highly conservative **"Greek Rally" party**, led by General Papagos, won the first decisive post-civil war elections in 1952. After the general's death, the party's leadership was taken over – and to an extent liberalized – by **Constantine (Konstantinos) Karamanlis**. Under his rule, stability of a kind was established and some economic advances registered, particularly after the revival of Greece's traditional German markets.

However, the 1950s was also a decade that saw wholesale **depopulation** of villages, as migrants sought work in Australia, America, western Europe and the larger Greek cities. In the east Aegean and the Dodecanese this was especially pronounced – ironically in the case of Rhodes and its neighbours, where the long-sought union with Greece provided merely the freedom to emigrate, mostly denied under Ottoman and Italian rule.

By 1961, unemployment, the Cyprus issue and the installation of US nuclear bases on Greek soil were changing the political climate, and when Karamanlis was again elected prime minister, there was strong suspicion of a fraud arranged by the king and army. Strikes became frequent in industry and even agriculture, and King Paul, with his autocratic, fascist-inclined queen Frederika, were openly attacked in parliament and at protest demonstrations. The far right grew uneasy about "communist resurgence" and, losing confidence in their own electoral influence, arranged the assassination of left-wing deputy Grigoris Lambrakis in Thessaloníki in May 1963. (The killing, and its subsequent cover-up, is the subject of Vassilis Vassilikos's thriller *Z*, filmed by Costa-Gavras.) It was against this volatile background that Karamanlis resigned, lost the subsequent elections and left the country.

The new government – the first controlled from outside the Greek right since 1935 – was formed by **George Papandreou's Centre Union Party**, and had a decisive majority of nearly fifty seats. It was to last, however, for less than two years as conservative forces rallied to thwart its progress. In this the chief protagonists were the army officers and their constitutional Commander-in-Chief, the new king, 23-year-old **Constantine II**.

Since power in Greece depended on a pliant military as well as a network of political appointees, Papandreou's most urgent task in order to govern securely and effectively was to reform the armed forces. His first minister of defence proved incapable of the task and, while he was investigating the right-wing plot that was thought to have rigged the 1961 election, "evidence" was produced of a Leftist conspiracy connected with Papandreou's son Andreas (himself a minister in the government). When the allegations grew to a crisis, George Papandreou decided to assume the defence portfolio himself, a move for which the king refused to give the necessary sanction. He then resigned in order to gain approval at the polls, but the king would not order fresh elections, instead persuading members of the Centre Union – chief among them a certain **Constantine Mitsotakis** – to defect and organize a coalition government. Punctuated by strikes, resignations and street demonstrations, this lasted for a year and a half until new elections were eventually set for May 28, 1967. They failed to take place.

The Colonels' Junta: 1967-74

It was a foregone conclusion that Papandreou's party would win popular support in the polls against the discredited coalition partners. And it was equally certain that there would be some sort of anti-democratic action to try and prevent them from taking power again. Disturbed by the party's leftward shift, King Constantine was said to have briefed senior generals for a *coup d'état*, to take place ten days before the elections. However, he was caught by surprise, as was nearly everyone else, by the **coup of April 21**, 1967, staged by a group of "unknown" colonels. It was, in the words of Andreas Papandreou, "the first successful CIA military putsch on the European continent".

The Colonels' **junta**, having appropriated all means of power, was sworn in by the king and survived the half-hearted counter-coup which he subsequently attempted to mount. It was an ostensibly fascist regime, absurdly styling itself as the true "Revival of Greek Orthodoxy" against Western "corrupting influences", though in reality its ideology was nothing more than warmed-up dogma from the Metaxas era.

All political activity was banned, trade unions were forbidden to recruit or meet, the press was so heavily censored that many papers stopped printing or published blank pages in protest, and thousands of "communists" were arrested, imprisoned, and often tortured. Among them were both Papandreous, the composer Mikis Theodorakis (deemed "unfit to stand trial" after three months in custody), and Amalia Fleming (widow of Alexander). While relatively few people were killed outright – one, dissident lawyer Nikiforos Mandhilaras, found mutilated in the sea off Rhodes, has a street named after him on the island – thousands were permanently maimed physically and psychologically. The best-known Greek actress, Melina Mercouri, was stripped of her citizenship *in absentia*, and thousands of prominent Greeks joined her in exile.

Culturally, the colonels put an end to most popular live music and inflicted ludicrous censorship on literature and theatre, including (as under Metaxas) a ban on production of the Classical tragedies. From this time also dates the gradual, insidious degradation of Greek public discourse; chief colonel Papadopoulos' rambling, illiterate speeches became bywords for obfuscation, bad grammar and Newspeak in general, a trend unfortunately imitated by many elected civilian leaders since then.

The junta lasted for seven years, opposed (especially after the first two years) by the majority of the Greek people, excluded from the European community, but propped up and given massive aid by US presidents Lyndon Johnson and Richard Nixon. To them and the CIA the junta's Greece was not an unsuitable client state; human rights considerations were deemed unimportant, orders were placed for sophisticated military technology, and foreign investment on terms highly unfavourable to Greece was open to multinational corporations. It was a fairly routine scenario for the exploitation of an underdeveloped nation.

Opposition was from the beginning voiced by exiled Greeks in London, the United States and western Europe, but only in late 1973 did demonstrations break out openly in Greece – the colonels' secret police had done too thorough a job of infiltrating domestic resistance groups and terrifying everyone else into docility. On November 17 the students of **Athens Polytechnic** began an occupation of their buildings. The ruling clique lost its nerve; armoured vehicles stormed the Polytechnic gates and a still-undetermined number of students, perhaps as many as four hundred, were killed. (Today they are commemorated throughout the east Aegean and the Dodecanese, in Leftist municipalities, by streets called Iróön Politehníon – "Heroes of the Polytechnic"). Martial law was tightened, and junta chief Colonel George Papadopoulos was replaced by the even more noxious and reactionary General Ioannides, head of the secret police.

Return to civilian rule: 1974–81

The end of the ordeal, however, came within a year as the dictatorship embarked on a disastrous political adventure in **Cyprus**, essentially the last playing of the *Megáli Idhéa* card. By attempting to topple the Makarios government and impose *énosis* (union) on the island, they provoked a Turkish invasion and occupation of nearly forty percent of the Cypriot territory. The army finally mutinied, and Karamanlis was invited to return from Paris to again take office. He swiftly helped negotiate a cease-fire (but no solution) in Cyprus, withdrew temporarily from NATO, and declared that US bases in Attica and on Crete would have to be removed except where they specifically served Greek interest.

In November 1974 Karamanlis and his Néa Dhimokratía **(New Democracy) party** was rewarded by a sizeable majority in elections, with a centrist and socialist opposition. The latter was comprised by the **Panhellenic Socialist Movement (PASOK)**, a new party led by Andreas Papandreou.

The election of *Néa Dhimokratía* was in every sense a safe conservative option, but to Karamanlis's enduring credit it oversaw an effective and firm return to democratic stability, even legalizing the KKE (Communist Party) for the first time in its history. Karamanlis also held a referendum on the **monarchy**; 59 percent of Greeks rejected the return of Constantine II, so he instituted in its place a French-style presidency, which post he himself occupied from 1980 to 1985, and again from 1990 to 1995. Economically there were limited advances, although these were more than offset by inflationary defence spending (the result of renewed tension with Turkey), hastily negotiated entrance into the EC, and the decision to let the drachma float after decades of being artificially fixed at 30 to the US dollar.

Crucially, though, Karamanlis failed to deliver on vital reforms in bureaucracy, social welfare and education; and though the worst figures of the junta were brought to trial and jailed for life, the ordinary faces of Greek political life and administration changed little. By 1981 inflation was hovering around 25 percent, and it was estimated that tax evasion was depriving the state of one-third of its annual budget. In foreign policy, the US bases had remained, and it was felt that Greece, back in NATO, was still acting as little more than an American satellite. The traditional right was demonstrably inadequate for the task at hand.

PASOK: 1981–89

"Change" (*Allayí*) and "Out with the Right" (*Ná Fíyi íy Dhexiá*) were the watchwords of the election campaign that swept **PASOK** and Andreas Papandreou to power on October 18, 1981.

This victory meant a chance for Papandreou to form the first socialist government in Greek history and break a near fifty-year monopoly of authoritarian right-wing rule. With so much at stake, the campaign had been passionate even by Greek standards, and PASOK's victory was greeted with euphoria both by the generation whose political voice had been silenced in the civil war and by a large proportion of the young. They were hopes which ran perhaps naively and dangerously high.

The electoral margin, at least, was conclusive. PASOK won 174 of the 300 parliamentary seats and the Communist KKE – though not a part of the new government – returned another thirteen deputies, one of them composer Mikis Theodorakis. *Néa Dhimokratía* moved into unaccustomed opposition. There appeared to be no obstacle to the implementation of a **radical socialist programme**: devolution of power to local authorities, the socialization of industry, improvement of the woefully skeletal social services, a purge of bureaucratic inefficiency and malpractice, the end of bribery and corruption as a way of life, an independent and dignified foreign policy following expulsion of US bases, and finally withdrawal from NATO and the European Community.

A change of style was promised, too, replacing the country's long traditions of authoritarianism and bureaucracy with openness and dialogue. Even more radically, where Greek political parties had long been the personal followings of charismatic leaders, PASOK was to be a party of ideology and principle, dependent on no single individual member. Or so, at least, thought some of the youthful PASOK cadres.

The new era started with a bang. The wartime resistance was officially recognized; hitherto they hadn't been allowed to take part in any celebrations, wreath-layings or other ceremonies. Peasant women were granted pensions for the first time – 3000 drachmas a month (about US$55 in 1982), the same as their outraged husbands – and wages were indexed to the cost of living. In addition, civil marriage was introduced, family law reformed in favour of wives and mothers, and equal rights legislation was put on the statute book.

These quick, easy and popular reformist moves seemed to mark a break with the past, and the atmosphere had indeed changed. Greeks no longer lowered their voices to discuss politics in public places or wrapped their opposition newspaper in the respectably conservative *Kathimerini*. At first there were real fears that the climate would be too much for the military and they would once again intervene to choke a dangerous experiment in democracy, especially when Andreas Papandreou assumed the defence portfolio himself in a move strongly reminiscent of his father's attempt to remove the king's appointee in 1965. But he went out of his way to soothe military susceptibilities, increasing their salaries, buying new weaponry, and being fastidious in his attendance at military functions. In reality, the resistance of the Polytechnic students to the 1967–74 junta was constantly mythologized, and PASOK activists could be counted on to form human cordons around party headquarters at the first rumour of unrest in the armed forces.

The end of the honeymoon

Nothing if not a populist, Papandreou promised a bonanza he must have known, as a trained and experienced economist, he could not deliver. As a result he pleased nobody on the economic front.

He could not fairly be blamed for the inherited lack of investment, low productivity, deficiency in managerial and labour skills, and other chronic problems besetting the Greek economy. However, he certainly aggravated the situation in the early days of his first government by allowing his supporters to indulge in violently anti-capitalist rhetoric, which frightened off potential investors, and by the prosecution and humiliation of the Tsatsos family, owners of one of Greece's few competitive businesses (Hercules Cement) for the illegal export of capital, something of which every Greek with any savings is guilty. These were cheap victories, not backed by any rational programme of public investment, and the only "socializations" were of hopelessly lame-duck companies.

Faced with this sluggish economy, and burdened with the additional charges of (marginally) improved social benefits and wage indexing, Papandreou's government had also to cope with the effects of world **recession**, which always hit Greece with a delayed effect compared with its more advanced European partners. **Shipping**, the country's main foreign-currency earner, was devastated. Remittances from emigré workers fell off as they joined the lines of the unemployed in their host countries, and tourism diminished under the dual impact of the recession and US President Ronald Reagan's warning to Americans to stay away from allegedly insecure and terrorist-prone Athens airport.

With huge quantities of imported goods continuing to be sucked into the country in the absence of significant domestic production, the **foreign debt** topped £10 billion in 1986, with inflation running at 25 percent and the balance of payments deficit approaching £1 billion. Greece also began to experience the social strains of unemployment for the first time. Not that it didn't exist before, but it had always been concealed as under-employment, by swollen civil service rolls of workers who showed up only to collect salary, by the familial organization of small companies, and the rural structure of the economy – as well as by the absence of reliable statistics.

The second term

A modest spending spree transparently intended to buy votes, continued satisfaction at the defeat of the right, the popularity of his Greece-for-the-Greeks foreign policy, plus some much-needed reforms, saw Papandreou through into a second term with an electoral victory in **June 1985** scarcely less triumphant than the first. But his complacent and, frankly, dishonest slogan was "Vote PASOK for Even Better Days". By October PASOK had imposed a two-year wage freeze and import restrictions, abolished the wage-indexing scheme and devalued the drachma by fifteen percent. Papandreou's fat was pulled out of the fire by none other than his former bogeyman, the European Community, which offered a huge two-part loan on condition that an IMF-style austerity programme was maintained.

The political fallout of such classic right-wing strategies, accompanied by shameless soliciting for foreign investment, was the alienation of the Communists and most of PASOK's own political constituency. Increasingly autocratic (and ironic given the earlier pledge), Papandreou's response to dissent was to fire recalcitrant trade union leaders and expel some three hundred members of his own party.

Assailed by strikes, the government appeared to have lost direction completely. In local elections in October 1986 it lost abundant ground to *Néa Dhimokratía*, including the mayoralties of the three major cities – Athens, Thessaloníki and Pátra.

Papandreou assured the nation that he had taken the message to heart, but all that followed was a minor government reshuffle and a panicky attempt to undo the ill-feeling caused by an incredible freeing of rent controls at a time when all wage-earners were feeling the pinch badly. Early in 1987 he went further and sacked all the remaining PASOK veterans in his cabinet, including his son, though it is said, probably correctly, that this was merely to appease public opinion. The new cabinet was so un-socialist that even the right-wing press called it "centrist".

Similar about-faces were to take place in foreign policy. The initial anti-US–anti-NATO rhetoric was immensely popular, and understandable for a people shamelessly bullied by bigger powers since 1830. There was some high-profile nose-thumbing, like refusing to join EC partners in condemning Jaruzelski's Polish regime, the Soviet downing of a Korean airliner, or Syrian involvement in terrorist bomb-planting.

In stark contrast to these early promises and rhetoric, the "realistic" policies that Papandreou increasingly pursued during his second term were far more conciliatory towards his big Western brothers. This was best exemplified by the fact that US bases remained in Greece until 1994, largely due to the fear that snubbing NATO would lead to Greece being exposed to Turkish aggression, still the only issue that unites the main parties to any degree. As for the once-reviled European Community, Greece had by now become an established beneficiary, and its leader was hardly about to bite the hand that feeds.

Scandal

Even as late as **mid-1988**, despite the many betrayals of Papandreou, it seemed unlikely that PASOK would be toppled in the following year's elections. This was due mainly to the lack of a credible alternative. Constantine Mitsotakis, a bitter personal enemy of Papandreou's since 1965, when his defection had brought down his father's government and set in train the events that culminated in the junta, was an unconvincing and antipathetic character at the helm of *Néa Dhimokratía*. Meanwhile, the liberal centrist parties had disappeared, and the main communist party, KKE, appeared trapped in a Stalinist timewarp under the leadership of Harilaos Florakis. Only the **Ellenikí Aristerá (Greek Left)**, formerly the Euro-wing of the KKE, seemed to offer any sensible alternative programme, and they had a precariously small following.

However, a combination of spectacular blunders, plus perhaps a general shift to the right, influenced by the cataclysmic events in Eastern Europe, conspired against PASOK. First came the extraordinary **cavortings of the prime minister** himself. Towards the end of 1988, the seventy-year-old Papandreou was flown to Britain for open-heart surgery. He took the occasion, with fear of death presumably rocking his judgement, to make public a year-long liaison with a 34-year-old *Olympic Airways* hostess, Dimitra "Mimi" Liani. Widespread depiction in the media of an old man shuffling about after a young blonde, to the public humiliation of Margaret, his American-born wife, did little to bolster his image (Papandreou subsequently divorced Margaret and married Mimi). His integrity was further questioned when he missed several important public engagements – including a ceremony commemorating the victims of the 1987 Kalamáta earthquake – preferring to hit the town with Mimi, reliving his youth in flashy nightspots.

The real damage, however, was done by **economic scandals**. It came to light that a PASOK minister had passed off Yugoslav corn as Greek in a sale to the EC. Then, far more seriously, it emerged that a self-made, Greek-American conman, Yiorgos Koskotas, director of the *Bank of Crete*, had embezzled £120 million (US$190 million) of deposits and, worse still, slipped though the authorities' fingers on a private jet to the US, where he had begun his career as a housepainter. Certain PASOK ministers and even Papandreou himself were implicated in the scandal. Further damage was done by allegations of illegal arms dealings by still more government ministers.

United in disgust at this corruption, the other left-wing parties – KKE and *Ellinikí Aristerá* – formed a coalition, the **Synaspismós**, siphoning off further support from PASOK.

Three bites at the cherry

In this climate of disaffection, an inconclusive result to the June 1989 election was no real surprise. What was less predictable, however, was the formation of a bizarre **"kathársis"** (purging) coalition of conservatives and communists, united in the avowed intent of cleansing PASOK's increasingly Augean stables.

The *Synaspismós* would have formed a government with PASOK but set one condition for doing so – that Papandreou stepped down as prime minister – and the old man would have none of it. In the deal finally cobbled together between the left and *Néa Dhimokratía*, Mitsotakis was denied the premiership, too, having to make way for a compromise choice, Ioannis Tzanetakis, a popular, ex-naval officer who had led an unsuccessful mutiny against the junta.

During the three months that the coalition lasted, the *kathársis* turned out to be largely a question of burying the knife as deeply as possible into the ailing body of PASOK. Andreas

Papandreou and three other ministers were officially accused of involvement in the Koskotas affair – though there was no time to set up their trial before the Greek people returned once again to the polls. In any case, the chief witness and protagonist in the affair, Koskotas himself, was still imprisoned in America, awaiting extradition proceedings.

Contrary to the Right's hope that publicly accusing Papandreou and his cohorts of criminal behaviour would pave the way for a *Néa Dhimokratía* victory, PASOK actually made a slight recovery in November 1989 elections, though the result was again inconclusive. This time the Left resolutely refused to do deals with anyone, and the result was a consensus caretaker government under the neutral aegis of an academic called Zolotas, who was dragged into the prime minister's office – somewhat unwillingly it seemed – from Athens University. His only mandate was to see that the country didn't go off the rails completely while preparations were made for yet more elections.

These took place in April 1990 with the same captains at the command of their ships and with the *Synaspismós* having completed its about-turn to the extent that in the five single-seat constituencies (the other 295 seats are drawn from multiple-seat constituencies in a complicated system of reinforced proportional representation), they supported independent candidates jointly with PASOK. Greek communists are good at about-turns, though; after all, composer Mikis Theodorakis, musical torch-bearer of the left during the dark years of the junta, and formerly a KKE MP, was by now standing for *Néa Dhimokratía*, prior to his resignation from politics altogether.

On the night, *Néa Dhimokratía* scraped home with a majority of one, later doubled with the defection of a centrist, and Mitsotakis finally got to achieve his long-cherished dream of becoming Prime Minister. The only other memorable feature of the election was the first parliamentary representation for a party of the **Turkish minority** in Thrace by activist Ahmet Sadiq, and for the **Greens**, based in Athens – the latter a locus for many disaffected PASOK voters. Sadiq, who had spent as much time in jail for dissident activities as he was to spend in parliament, was eventually winkled out of office on a technicality and killed in suspicious circumstances on July 24, 1995, in his native Thrace.

A return to the right: Mitsotakis

On assuming power, Mitsotakis followed a course of austerity measures to try and revive the chronically ill economy. Little headway was made, though given the world recession, that was hardly surprising. Greek inflation was still approaching twenty percent annually, and at nearly ten percent, unemployment remained chronic. The latter has been exacerbated since 1990 by the arrival of thousands of impoverished Albanians, prompting the first anti-imigration measures with teeth in a country whose population is more used to being on the other side of such laws.

Other conservative measures introduced by Mitsotakis included laws to combat strikes and **terrorism**. The terrorist issue had been a perennial source of worry for Greeks since the appearance in the mid-1970s of a group called **Dhekatoévdhomo Noemvríou** ("November 17", the date of the Colonels' attack on the Polytechnic in 1973). Since 1974, they (and of late, new copycat groups) have killed nearly twenty industrialists, politicians and NATO military personnel, and attacked buildings of foreign corporations in Athens; the lack of any significant arrests has lead to speculation that they were a rogue faction from within PASOK itself. It hardly seemed likely that Mitsotakis's laws, however, were the solution. They stipulated that the typically long and ideological statements of the group could no longer be published, which led to one or two newspaper editors being jailed for a few days for defiance – much to everyone's embarrassment.

The **anti-strike laws** threatened severe penalties but were equally ineffectual, as prolonged breakdowns in public transport, electricity and rubbish collection all too frequently illustrated.

As for the Koskotas scandal, the man himself was eventually extradited and gave evidence for the prosecution against Papandreou and various of his ministers. The trial was televised and proved as popular as any soap opera, as indeed it should have been, given the twists of high drama – which included one of the defendants, Agamemnon Koutsoyiorgas, dying in court of a heart attack in front of the cameras. The case against Papandreou gradually lost steam and he was officially acquitted (by a margin of one vote on the tribunal panel) in early 1992.

The great showcase trial thus went out with a whimper and did nothing to enhance Mitsotakis's position. If anything, it served to increase sympathy for Papandreou, who was felt to have been unfairly victimized. The indisputable villain of the piece, Koskotas, was eventually convicted of major fraud and is serving a 25-year sentence at the high-security Korydallos prison, also home to the ex-junta members.

The Macedonian question

Increasingly unpopular due to the desperate austerity measures, and perceived as ineffective on the international scene, the last thing Mitsotakis needed was a major foreign policy headache. That is exactly what he got when, in 1991, one of the breakaway republics of the former Yugoslavia named itself **Macedonia**, injuring Greek national pride and sparking off vehement protests at home and abroad. Diplomatically, the Greeks fought tooth and nail against anyone's recognizing the breakaway state, let alone the use of the name "Macedonia", but their position became increasingly isolated, and by 1993 the new country had gained official recognition from both the EC and the UN – albeit under the provisional title of the Former Yugoslav Republic of Macedonia (FYROM).

Salt was rubbed into Greek wounds when the FYROM started using the "Star of Vergina" (and of the ancient Macedonian kings) as a national symbol on their new flag, alleged printed a banknote portraying the White Tower of Thessaloniki (Solun in Macedonian), and retained passages in its constitution referring to "unredeemed" Aegean territories. Greece still refuses to call its neighbour Macedonia, instead referring to it as *Ta Skópia* after the capital – and you can't go anywhere in Greece these days without coming across officially placed stickers proclaiming that "MACEDONIA WAS, IS, AND ALWAYS WILL BE GREEK AND ONLY GREEK!"

The ongoing argument for legitimacy hinges mostly on whether the ancient Macedonian kings were pure-bred Hellenes (the Greek position), Hellenized barbarians (the neutral conclusion), or proto-Slavs (the Macedonian claim).

The pendulum swings back

In effect, the Macedonian problem led to Mitsotakis's political demise. In the early summer of 1993 his ambitious foreign minister, **Andonis Samaras**, disaffected with his leader, jumped on the bandwagon of resurgent Greek nationalism to set up his own party, **Politikí Ánixi (Political Spring)**. His platform, still right-wing, was largely based on action over Macedonia, and during the summer of 1993 more **Néa Dhimokratía** (ND) MPs broke ranks, making *Politikí Ánixi* a force to be reckoned with. When parliament was called upon in September to approve severe new budget proposals, it became clear that the government lacked sufficient support, and early elections were called for October 1993. Mitsotakis had also been plagued for nearly a year by accusations of phone-tapping, theft of antiquities to stock his large collection in Crete, and links with a nasty and complicated contracts scandal centred around the national cement company.

On October 11, Papandreou romped to election victory with 169 parliamentary deputies; in an exact reversal of the 1990 results, ND lost in 85 percent of the constituencies (including the entire east Aegean and Dodecanese), though the *Synaspismós* disappeared from the electoral map, replaced as the third party in parliament by Samaras' *Politikí Ánixi* and the unreconstructed Communists, now under Aleka Papariga, with nine deputies each. The youthful Miltiades Evert, ex-mayor of Athens, replaced Mitsotakis as head of *Néa Dhimokratía*, so that – along with ex-KKE head Florakis – two of the "dinosaurs" of post-junta politics had passed from the scene.

The morning after

And so, a frail-looking Papandreou, now well into his seventies, became prime minister for the third time. He soon realized that the honeymoon was going to be neither as sweet nor as long as it had been in the Eighties.

PASOK immediately fulfilled two of its pre-election promises by removing restrictions on the reporting of statements by terrorist groups, and de-privatizing the Athens city bus company. The new government also set about improving the health system, and began to set the wheels in motion for Mitsotakis to be tried for his alleged misdemeanours, though all charges were mysteriously dropped in January 1995, apparently by orders of Papandreou himself.

The root of popular dissatisfaction, of course, remained the economy, which was still in dire straits; PASOK could hardly claim to have won any diplomatic battles over Macedonia, despite a lot of tough posturing. The only concrete move was the imposition in October 1993 of a **trade embargo** by the Greeks, which landed them in

Islets: Nisídhes, Vrahonisídhes and Vráhi

The Dodecanese and to a lesser extent the east Aegean are dotted with scores of tiny, uninhabited **islets**, frequented only by fishermen and yacht passengers. They are, however, cherished and minutely classified by the Greeks themselves, despite a resounding lack of natural endowments. Twin islets **Ímia/Kardak** were recently the focus of a major international incident.

A **nisídha** (plural *nisídhes*) is defined as any islet of 4–16km², and might at some point in the past have supported a small permanent population, though now it does so only as part of a rather daring Greek government programme established in 1995 (see below). Waterless specks smaller than 4km² are further subdivided as **vrahonisídhes**, which have enough soil to support a thin covering of thorny vegetation, and **vráhi**, essentially gull roosts with no soil at all.

As far as the Greeks are concerned, the **sovereignty** of these islets is an open-and-shut case; they were ceded by Italy to Greece in 1947 as part of the same treaty that included the larger Dodecanese. Threats to *vrahonisídhes* are seen as merely the thin end of the wedge, with the Turks deemed intent on graduating to larger, inhabited islands unless firmy opposed. Memories of Turkey's 1974 intervention in Cyprus, where over one-third of that island was overrun, are still fresh in Greece, and regarded – along with several recent islet incidents – as incontrovertible proof that an inherently expansionist Turkey harbours designs on more of the Aegean.

For their part, the Turks claim that the Dodecanese were strictly speaking not Italy's to give away, as their seizure by the Italians in 1912 had never been acknowledged by treaty. Moreover, Turkey has never ratified the Geneva Convention of 1958, nor the more recent **Law of the Sea**, whereby a country can claim territorial waters of up to twelve nautical miles around its islands. Various Turkish pronouncements have made it clear that any attempt by Greece to do so, effectively turning the Aegean into a Greek lake, would be considered by Turkey an act of war. Fishing rights and (further north) access to oil deposits are at stake, adding an economic dimension to what is ostensibly a matter of national honour and the reputation of domestic politicians.

In July 1995, the Greek Defence Ministry announced that the **colonization** of numerous uninhabited islets across Greece was to be officially encouraged; applications from "responsible" persons (ie no hippies or dope fiends), both foreign and Greek, were invited, with promised provision of basic shelter, desalinated water, solar electricity and satellite telephones, as well as a long lease. Several of the islets fell within the limits of the Dodecanese, precariously poised between larger islands and the Anatolian mainland. Overseas Greek consulates and embassies were immediately deluged by eager calls from prospective drop-outs, to the extent that phones had to be put off the hook. As ever in the Balkans, there was an ulterior motive behind the Defense Ministry's altruism; by subsidizing resettlement of these long-neglected outposts, it hoped to emphasize their essential Greekness.

The first step in strengthening Greece's territorial claims was to plant Greek flags on these islets, which Greek navy patrol boats did during the latter half of 1995. This was bound sooner or later to provoke a Turkish reaction. In the event, an initial flare-up occurred on January 25, 1996, when a Turkish vessel ran aground in stormy weather on one of two islets, each less than 3km², poised between Kalólimnos and the Bodrum peninsula. The skipper refused assistance from a Greek coast guard boat, claiming that the islet was Turkish territory, despite the presence of a Greek flag (planted in this case by the mayor of Kálimnos) and its description as **Ímia** on international nautical charts. For the Turks, this pair of islets was and always had been **Kardak**, and two days later some Turkish journalists landed by helicopter and replaced the Greek flag with a Turkish one. On January 28, the Greek navy appeared, restoring the Greek colours and leaving a permanent guard.

By January 30, more than twenty heavily armed naval vessels from each side were manoeuvring around each other in the vicinity of the goat-inhabited *vrahonisídha*, and journalists the world over were scrambled for detailed maps – the Ímia/Kardak duo is simply too minute to show up on conventional atlases. Then a Greek helicopter apparently developed a fault and went down, with three airmen drowned; if it were actually spooked by Turkish aircraft, or even shot down, the fact was concealed so as not to further inflame public opinion. For days the Greek and Turkish media focused almost exclusively on the developing crisis; war fever gripped each country, and provocative statements were issued by both political leaderships. Turkey in particular had just emerged from an inconclusive general election, and the consensus even there was that caretaker Prime Minister Ciller was indulging in a Falklands-style diversionary ploy to rally national opinion behind her.

In the end, a shooting war was only averted by intensive, round-the-clock diplomatic pressure on both sides; as of January 31, both Greece and Turkey were required to remove their flags and commandos from the islets, and their fleets from the general area, pending mediation.

It was the worst such scare since a 1987 oil-prospecting dispute in the North Aegean, and probably will not be the last. Many outside observers still have difficulty believing the seriousness of the conflict, dismissing it as scarcely more than a teapot-tempest that escalated out of control. Unfortunately for the parties involved it remains a deadly serious issue, with long historical antecedents and manifold potential implications.

trouble with the European Court of Justice. By contrast, alone among NATO members, Greece was conspicuous for its open **support of Serbia** in the wars wracking the ex-Yugoslavia, ostentatiously breaking the embargo with supply trucks to Belgrade via Bulgaria.

Both the major parties received a good slap in the face at the **Euroelections** of June 1994, losing ground to the smaller parties. The major winners were Samaras, whose *Politikí Ánixi* almost doubled its share of the vote with two Euro-Seats, and the two left-wing parties, with the *Synaspismós* returning from the dead to take two seats like the KKE.

Nonetheless, in the municial and regional elections of autumn 1994, ND candidate Dhimitris Avramopoulos swept to victory in Athens, ahead of PASOK stalwart Theodhoros Pangalos, and the incumbent ND mayor of Thessaloniki retained office as well. For the first time ever, in a PASOK-sponsored reform, *nomárhi* (provincial governors) were directly elected, rather than appointed from Athens.

In March 1995, presidential elections were held in parliament to designate a successor to the 88-year-old Karamanlis. The winner, supported by *Politikí Ánixi* and PASOK, was Kostis Stefanopoulos, former head of the dissolved party **DIANA** (Democratic Renewal), like *Politikí Ánixi* a breakaway movement from ND. A former lawyer, untainted by scandal, he had been suggested by Samaras and welcomed by Papandreou in a deal that would allow PASOK to see out its four-year term without ructions.

The prime scandal for 1995, which continued in spasms throughout the year, had to do with the maximum-security **prison of Korydhallos**, home to Koskotas and the former junta figures. Two mass breakout attempts bracketed the discovery of an extensive drug-dealing ring controlled from inside; a call girl was detected in Koskotas's cell, and the head warden was arrested after large quantities of guns, ammunition and narcotics were found in his office. Meanwhile, former junta boss Ioannides got married to a visitor, though presumably without Koskotas-style conjugal rights.

In November 1995, Greece **lifted its embargo** on "Macedonia", opening its mutual borders to tourism and trade; in return for this, the Macedonians agreed to drop controversial clauses from their constitution and replace the offending "star" in their flag. Relations, in fact, were instantly almost normalized, with only The Name still moot; current favourites are "New Macedonia" or "Upper Macedonia".

However, the emerging critical issue was the 76-year-old Papandreou's continued stewardship of PASOK, and the country, as he clung obstinately to power despite obvious signs of dotage. Numerous senior members of PASOK became increasingly bold and vocal in their criticism, no longer fearing expulsion or the sack as in the past. Such personalities included the so-called "**Gang of Four**", soon-to-be multi-portfolio Minister Vasso Papandreou (no relation), future Foreign Minister Theodhoros Pangalos, then-Trade Minister Kostas Simitis, and ex-Minister Paraskevas Avyerinos.

Late in November 1995, Papandreou was stricken with severe lung and kidney infections, and rushed to intensive care at the Onassis Hospital. The country was essentially rudderless for two months, as there was no provision in the constitution for replacing an infirm prime minister. At last, in mid-January 1996, the conscious but groggy Papandreou was pressurized to sign a letter resigning as prime minister (though not, as yet, of PASOK); thus departed the last "dinosaur" of post-1974 politics. The "palace clique", consisting of Mimi Liani and entourage, were beaten off in the parliamentary replacement vote, in favour of the allegedly colourless but widely respected technocrat **Simitis**, who seems to be just what Greece needs after years of incompetent flamboyance.

General elections are due for autumn 1997; the goals of the two main parties are now virtually indistinguishable, with the main differences being methodology and, as ever, personalities. One of the many reasons for Mitsotakis' eventual failure was his lack of bedside manner, which consistently alienated those naturally predisposed to support him, not to mention the outraging of opponents. PASOK's inherent advantage lies in its ability to convince its labour union constituency of the need to occasionally swallow bitter pills. If Simitis does not last out term of office – already Papandreou's ex-head-of-staff, Tsohatzopoulos, and other old-guardists are sharpening their knives – most obviously by failing to be confirmed as head of PASOK at the summer 1996 party congress, the odds are on a prime ministerial contest between Vasso Papandreou and the increasingly popular ND mayor of Athens, Dhimitris Avramopoulos.

Greece now languishes in the EU's economic cellar, ranked below Portugal, though recent critical earmarks are vastly encouraging. The austerity programmes and a "hard drachma" programme have finally driven inflation down into single figures for the first time in decades. Increasingly amicable relations with its northern Balkan neighbours – Greece is the principal foreign investor in Bulgaria, for example – promise to generate jobs and drive down unemployment, currently just over nine percent.

Tourism, accounting for seven percent of GNP, was down twenty percent across the nation in 1995, leading the new government, with the "Gang of Four" in key positions, to promise renewed efforts to improve infrastructure, especially on the islands – Rhodes' fibre-optic phone system marks a first step. Long-promised yacht marinas and roads should finally be completed with EU assistance, while spas, casinos and golf courses are to be built or renovated. Cheap flight-only and backpacker tourism will be strongly discouraged in favour of special-interest, high-spending visitors such as walkers, divers, cavers, and so on.

Much of this, of course, depends on improvement of **relations with Turkey** (see islet box, above). Basic geographical realities dictate that the east Aegean and Dodecanese, the last territories incorporated into the Greek state, are those least securely clasped to the mother country. If push comes to shove – and any bets of military restraint are off in the wake of recent Balkan events – all of these islands are fundamentally indefensible; a Turkish bomb lobbed onto island airport runways every few hours will suffice to keep them from being resupplied and guarantee their capture by Turkey within a matter of days.

In Simitis, Turkey has a potential interlocutor to resolve Aegean problems; on taking office, he stated: "Greece's (recent) intransigent nationalism is an expression of the wretchedness that exists in our society. It is the root cause of the problems we have had with our Balkan neighbours and our difficult relations with Europe." A breath of fresh air in the often stale public Greek discourse, but he faces an uphill task: the opposition roundly pilloried Simitis for acknowedging US assistance in defusing the recent islet crisis, and the social climate in Greece still condones public attacks on Jews, Catholics, Muslims Turkish or otherwise, Jehovah's Witnesses, gays – in short, anyone who differs from the Hellenic ideal.

Wildlife

Dodecanese and east Aegean wildlife – in particular the flora – can prove an unexpected source of fascination. In spring, the colour, scent and variety of wildflowers, and the resulting wealth of insect life, are breathtaking. Islands cut off from continental landmasses have had many thousands of years to cultivate their own individual species. Overall, there are some two thousand species of flowering plants on the islands (over half of which exist on Sámos alone), many of them unique to Greece.

Some background

Around eight thousand years ago, Greece and her islands were thickly forested. Aleppo (*Pinus halepensis*) and Calabrian (*Pinus brutia*) pines grew in coastal regions, giving way to Cephallonian and silver fir or black pine up in the hills and lower mountains. But early civilizations changed all that, and most of Greece, like most of Europe, is an artificial mosaic of habitats created by forest clearance followed by agriculture in the form of crops or stock-grazing. As long ago as the fourth century BC, Plato was lamenting the felling of native forests on the hills around Athens. This was not all bad for wildlife, though: the scrubby hillsides created by forest clearing and subsequent grazing are one of the richest habitats of all.

This century, Greece has on the whole escaped the intensification of agriculture so obvious in Northern Europe. For the most part, crops are still grown in small fields without excessive use of pesticides and herbicides, while flocks of goats graze the hillsides in much the same way as they have done for the last few thousand years. On the minus side is damage from rapid urbanization and tourist development, generally carried out with little sympathy for the environment; worse still has been the rapidly accelerating deforestation (see box overleaf).

One peculiarly Greek bonus is that wildlife here probably has the longest recorded history of anywhere in the world. Aristotle was a keen naturalist, Theophrastus during the fourth century BC was one of the earliest botanists, and Dioscorides, a first-century AD physician, wrote a comprehensive book on the herbal uses of plants.

Flowers

What you will see of island **flora** depends on where and when you go. Plants cease flowering (or even living, in the case of annuals) when it is too hot and dry – the high summer in Greece plays the same role for plants as winter does in northern Europe. Perennials survive in coastal Greece either by producing leathery or grey, hairy leaves with a minimum surface area, or by dying back to giant tuberous rootstalks – both stragegies for preserving moisture.

The best time to go is in **spring**, which comes to the southern Dodecanese in late February or early March, with the east Aegean lagging behind by as much as a month. Late April or May, marked by the yellow flowers of broom (*Spartium junceum*) or gorse (*Calycotome villosa*), signals the onset of **summer**; once the worst heat is over by late September, there's another burst of activity on the part of **autumn** flowering species such as pink cyclamen and autumn crocus (*Colchicum* spp.). Mid- or late October will see the first rains, but **winter** flowers only get underway after Christmas, continuing into late February.

Seashore

The spectacular yellow horned poppy (*Glaucium flavum*) can be found growing on shingled banks, and sea stocks or Virginia stocks among rocks behind beaches. A small pink campion (*Silene colorata*) is often colourfully present before June.

Salt-tolerant tamarisk trees often fringe the sand, while further inland, wherever they find adequate fresh water, sprout clumps of Europe's largest grass, the giant calamus reed, which can attain almost four metres in height. Near the river-mouths and in the damp ravines of Lesvos grows – instead of the usual pink-flowered oleander – the yellow azalea (*Rhododendron luteum*), found nowhere else in Greece.

Between August and October, look for the enormous, fragrant, white flowers of the sea daffodil (*Pancratium maritimum*) at the edge of sand dunes. The sea squill (*Drimia maritima*) also flowers in early autumn, inland as well as in the coastal zone, with tall spikes of white flowers rising from huge bulbs.

Cultivated Land

As a rule, large plantations prove less rewarding than the small hay **meadows** that are often brilliant with annual "weeds" in late spring – blood-red corn poppies (*Papaver rhoeas*), several species of gladiolus, and daisies – forced into flowering early by the hot summers.

Fallow farmland is good for bulbous perennials, in particular, a gorgeous, multicoloured variety of anemone (*Anemone coronaria*) that blooms early in the year throughout most of the islands. The scarlet turban buttercup (*Ranunculus asiaticus*) on Rhodes and Sámos' sweet-smelling blue hyacinths (*zoumboúlia* in Greek), ancestor of the cultivated variety, also emerge during late February and March.

Appearing between March and July is the wild snapdragon (*Antirrhinum majus*), which loves chinks in low **rock walls**. Here too, from May to August, blaze forth the white-to-pinkish flowers of the spiny **caper**; the edible bit is the unopened flower bud, and on many islands the thorny shoots are also pickled and eaten whole.

Among exotics, the century plant (*Agave americana*), naturalized around the Mediterranean since the eighteenth century, is a familiar sight on the islands; the plant flowers once in its lifetime during mid-summer, after which the formidably spiky leaf-rosette withers away. It's commonly used as a "fence substitute", like another import, the yellow-flowered **prickly pear** (*Opuntia indica*), supposedly brought back by Columbus from the New World. Its scarlet fruit, ripening in September, tastes like watermelon but requires peeling and putting through a blender to get rid of spines and seeds respectively.

Hillsides

With their blend of shady and sunny conditions, **hillsides** provide a versatile habitat. **Shrubs** are varied; colourful yellow brooms flower in early summer, and bushy rockroses (*Cistus* spp.) exhibit masses of magenta or white flowers in spring, especially May. Scattered among the shrubs is the occasional Judas tree (*Cercis siliquastrum*), which flowers early in spring, making a blaze of pink against the green hillsides that stands out for miles. Beneath the shrubs grow **aromatic herbs** – sage, rosemary, thyme, oregano and lavender – often with spiny species of Euphorbia. These occur principally within the *frígana*, barren **limestone slopes** scattered with scrubby bushes. (The higher hillside environment of the *maquis*, with its junipers and other dense prickly scrub, is better for birds.)

Peer around below the shrubs and herbs, or at their margins, and you will find a wealth of orchids, anemones, grape hyacinths, irises and perhaps the delicate fritillary butterfly if you are lucky.

Orchids here are much smaller and altogether more dignified than the tropical varieties in florists' shops. On both Rhodes and Sámos there are nearly fifty species, mostly of the genera *Orchis* and *Ophrys*, blooming according to altitude from March until May. The delicate and unusual flowers of the *Ophrys* species – so-called bee orchids – imitate the shapes, markings and scents of insects in order to attract them for pollination.

Irises are beauties, too, appearing between February and June according to species and island. Among several varieties here, the small, blue *Gynandris sisyrinchium* only flowers in the afternoon; you can actually sit and watch them open around midday.

You can often find deserted, shady **terraces** full of cyclamen, either *Cyclamen persicum* (ancestor of the domestic variety) or *Cyclamen repandum*, both exhibiting white or pink blooms in early spring. Spectacular peonies, out in May, bloom on slopes above 400m on several islands. Those on Kárpathos are white subspecies of *Paeonia clusii*, while those of Sámos and Rhodes are more common, usually pink *Paeonia mascula*.

Forest fires

Since 1928, **fires** have reduced Greece's proportion of forested land from just under one-third to just under one-fifth, with the most rapid loss since 1974. On the larger islands of the east Aegean and Dodecanese, including Rhodes, Kárpathos, Sámos, Ikaría and Híos, huge infernos raged almost annually from 1981 until 1994. So far only Kós and Lésvos have escaped comprehensive damage.

A tiny fraction of these summer disasters occur naturally, through an unhappy coincidence of sunlight refracted through a glass shard and the highly volatile, resinous *maquis* shrubbery and pine which cover the middle altitudes of these islands. As for the other fires, **conspiracy theories** – ever popular in Greece – variously assign the blame to the CIA, KGB, Freemasons, Mossad, the PLO, Turks, Albanians, Bosnians, etc, but the stark truth is that the vast majority are the result of **arson** perpetrated by local islanders. Motives are simple and sordid: clearing land for grazing or building, touristic developers forcing stubborn farmers to sell up at depressed prices, or hampering tourism on a rival island or beach. There is always an upsurge prior to elections, the result of surreptitious promises by candidates to reclassify burnt forest land as suitable for development should they attain office. The **Orthodox Church** and the **Forest Service** own and administer vast tracts of land in a quasi-feudal system, pursuing an erratic method of taxation in addition to promulgating policies that enrage private owners and encourage firebugs.

The recurrence of blazes is often used as a justification by the Forest Service for the bulldozing of numerous dirt tracks through woods, presumably to allow fire engines easier access. Unfortunately this creates as many problems as it solves, since arsonists take advantage of the opportunity to drive their jerry-cans full of petrol to the scene of operations. Experience has shown that only Hercules transport planes, modified for dumping seawater on the flames, make a decisive difference in **fire control**, but these cannot fly at night. Accordingly the arsonists generally do their work just before dusk, on a windy day, so by the time morning arrives the fire is often way out of control. In recent years the authorities have taken to stationing at least two fire-extinguishing planes at major east Aegean and Dodecanese airports, but there aren't always enough to go around.

Ground surveillance can be woefully inadequate; thus far only Lésvos has 24-hour summertime watches maintained on strategic ridges, and only Rhodes has installed anything resembling a network of rural standpipes (conspicuous in and around Petaloúdhes).

The underlying problem is social: there's simply no consensus in Greece that woodlands have any intrinsic value, now that few trees are tapped for resin or used in boatbuilding, and goats or villas will win hands down in any confrontation. Only slowly is a connection being made between fire damage and subsequent winter flash floods or steadily dropping water tables, and only when tourist receipts begin to fall as a result of denuded scenery will there be belated conversion to "Green consciousness." The saddest element of the story is that most of the lost vegetation was a mature crop of Aleppo, Calabrian and (on Sámos) black pines, which will be replaced haphazardly if at all. In typical Mediterranean conditions, these trees grow so slowly that none of the readers of this book will live to see a mature forest on many islands.

Once the heat of the summer is over, **autumn bulbs** come into their own, with species of crocus and their relatives, the pink-to-purple colchicums and the yellow sternbergias, and finally the pink autumn *Cyclamen graecum* flowering from October until early December. Around the New Year, **heather** (*Erica manipuliflora*) provides a blaze of pink on slopes with acidic soil.

Birds

Greece has a large range of resident Mediterranean birds, and an additional bonus is the seasonal presence of **migratory species** that winter in East Africa but breed in northern Europe. Between January and mid-May they migrate up the Nile valley before moving across the eastern Mediterranean, to return in autumn in less concentrated flocks. Most birds navigate by the stars, so a thick mist or heavy cloud will force them to land; you can sometimes see spectacular "falls" of migrants.

Seasonal **salt marshes** and **coastal lagoons** on Kos, Sámos and Lésvos are excellent territories for birdwatching, especially during the spring and autumn migrations. A wide variety of herons and egrets mingles with smaller waders such as the avocet and the black-winged stilt with its ridiculously long, pink legs. Here, too, you'll find both European species of **pelican**, which breed in Greece. **Flamingoes** arrive in January, lingering until April; upwards of two hundred individuals can be counted at the Sámos marsh on a given winter's day.

On the **outskirts of towns** and in the **fields** there are some colourful residents. Small predatory birds such as woodchat shrikes, kestrels and red-footed falcons can be seen perched on telegraph wires, and lesser kestrels nest communally and noisily in many small towns and villages. Dramatically coloured hoopoes and bee-eaters, striking golden orioles, nightingales and the rare Rupell's warbler are sparsely represented in **woodland** and **olive groves**, especially on still-wooded mountain ranges of Kós, Rhodes and Sámos. The Sardinian warbler is prevalent on rough scrubby hillsides, the male with a glossy black cap and distinct red-rimmed eyes. Lésvos plays host to two species of **nuthatch** native to Asia Minor: Krüper's nuthatch in the pine forests around Ayiássos, and rock nuthatch on the barer slopes above Eressós.

Raptors are relatively rare in the islands, but the cliffs and islets west of Monólithos, on Rhodes, as well as the islet of Télendhos, are known to harbour Eleonora's falcons, especially during late spring and summer. Lésvos shelters a population of Lanner falcons, which feed on chukar partridges.

The monotonous "poo" sound of the diminutive Scops **owls** (*koukouváyia* in Greek), can often be heard around island villages at night. Their tone is similar to that of the **nightjar**, a sinister, rather dumpy bird, often caught squatting on the road by car headlights. By contrast, the little owl (*Athena noctua*), *giónis* in Greek, is active by day as well, favouring chimneys and corners of ruined houses; it has a strange repertoire of cries, chortles and a throaty hiss.

Mammals

The variety of Greek island **mammals** is fairly limited, owing to long isolation from the mainland and ruthless hunting. Most of the Dodecanese and east Aegean islands have the usual range of rodents such as rats, mice and rabbits; the local hedgehog has the distinction of a white underbelly. On the larger, more forested islands, particularly Sámos which is separated from Anatolia by the narrowest of straits, there are martens, weasels and even the odd jackal, but no foxes, badgers or squirrels, nor large predators, such as bears or wolves.

Dolphins and **porpoises** are a fairly common sight in the Dodecanese, often shadowing ferries to feed on fish stirred up by its wake. The extremely rare **Mediterranean monk seal** is still occasionally seen near Sámos (see box, p.258).

Reptiles and amphibians

Greece contains over forty indigenous species of **reptile**, half of the European total, thanks to its hot, rocky terrain. Many are wall **lizards**, of which most of the islands have their own subspecies: small with a brownish striped back, often with an orange or yellow belly. Watch a dry, sunny wall almost anywhere in the islands, and you're bound to see them.

On all of the southern Dodecanese, including Rhodes, you may see the *agama* or Rhodes dragon (*Agama stelio*). Growing up to 30cm, these look like miniature, spiny-backed dragons, their brown or grey skin patterned with pale diamonds.

In the bushes of the *maquis* and *frígana* you may see the Balkan green lizard, a brightly tinted animal up to half a metre long, most of which is tail; you can often spot it running on its hind legs, as if possessed, from one bush to another.

At night, **geckos** replace the lizards. These are small (less than 10cm long), with large, dark eyes and round, adhesive pads on their toes that enable them to walk upside down. Although the islanders have various disparaging beliefs about geckos (their Greek name translates as "polluter"), they help keep down mosquitoes and other biting insects. The chameleon is an increasingly rare sight on some of the eastern Aegean islands. It lives in bushes and low trees, and hunts by day; its colour is greenish but variable.

All three European **tortoises** can be found in Greece. They have suffered to varying extents from the pet trade, but you can still find them basking in the mid-morning between shrubs and rocks on sunny hillsides. They come in all sizes, from 5 to 30cm long depending on age. A good way to detect them is by ear; they make a constant rustle as they lumber around, and whenever you see one, look for more, since they seem to stick together. A closely related reptile is the **terrapin**, basically an aquatic freshwater tortoise. Again, both European species live in Greece, and they're virtually a guaranteed presence at river mouths on Límnos, Lésvos, Kós and Rhodes.

Greece has plenty of **snakes**, but (as in most habitats) they're shy and easily frightened.

Flora and fauna field guides

MEDITERRANEAN WILDLIFE

A C Campbell *The Hamlyn Guide to the Flora and Fauna of the Mediterranean* (Hamlyn/Country Life). Very useful, but out of print, so try to find a secondhand copy; also published as *The Larousse Guide to the Flora and Fauna of the Mediterranean* (Larousse).

FLOWERS

Helmut Baumann *Greek Wild Flowers and Plant Lore in Ancient Greece* (The Herbert Press, UK). Lots of interesting snippets about the age-old Greek relationship with plants.

Marjorie Blamey and Christopher Grey-Wilson *Mediterranean Wild Flowers* (HarperCollins, UK). Comprehensive field guide.

Paul and Jenne Davies, Anthony Huxley *The Wild Orchids of Britain and Europe* (Chatto & Windus/Hogarth Press, UK). A splendid book for orchid freaks, with details on where to look for them – including sites in Greece.

Pierre Delforge *Orchids of Britain and Europe* (HarperCollins, UK). More up to date than the preceding volume, but with some inaccuracies in translation.

Anthony Huxley and William Taylor *Flowers of Greece and the Aegean* (Chatto & Windus/Hogarth Press, UK). Best book for flower identification. It doesn't describe all the Greek flowers – no book does – but it's an excellent general guide with quality photographic illustrations.

Oleg Polunin and Anthony Huxley *Flowers of the Mediterranean* (Chatto & Windus/Hogarth Press, UK). Good, versatile fallback if Huxley and Taylor are unavailable.

PLANT CHECKLISTS

Kárpathos; *Kokkári (Sámos)*; *Sámos*; *Líndhos/Pefkos (Rhodes)*; and *Rhodes*, which includes birds, reptiles and butterflies. All of these small pamphlets, compiled by naturalist **Lance Chilton**, are available through Marengo Publications, 22 River View, Retford, Notts DN22 7UL (☎01777/705588); or BSBI Publications, Peterborough, UK. Contact them for current prices and information, as this series is slowly expanding.

BIRDS

Petersen, Mountfort and Hollom *Field Guide to the Birds of Britain and Europe* (Collins, UK/Stephen Green Press, US); **Heinzel, Fitter and Parslow** *Collins Guide to the Birds of Britain and Europe* (Collins, UK/Stephen Green Press, US). There are no specific reference books on Greek birds. These two European field guides have the best coverage, with the former, ageing but excellent, retaining an edge.

George Handrinos and T Akriotis *Birds of Greece* (A&C Black, UK). A comprehensive guide that includes island birdlife.

MAMMALS

Corbet and Ovenden *Collins Guide to the Mammals of Europe* (Collins, UK/Stephen Green Press, US). As good a guide as they come.

FISHES

Ioannis Batjakas & Alistair Economakis *Coastal Fishes of Greece* (Efstathiadhis, Athens); **George Sfikas** *Fishes of Greece* (Efstathiadhis, Athens). Neither is exhaustive or error-free, but a good start to identification.

INSECTS

Michael Chinery *Collins Guide to the Insects of Britain and Western Europe* (Collins, UK/Stephen Green Press, US). Although this doesn't include Greece, it gives good general information about the main insects you may see.

Lionel Higgins and Norman Riley *A Field Guide to the Butterflies of Britain and Europe* (Collins, UK/Stephen Green Press, US). A field guide that will sort out all the Greek butterflies for you, though it's a bit detailed for the casual naturalist.

REPTILES AND AMPHIBIANS

Jiri Cihar *Amphibians and Reptiles* (Conran Octopus, UK). Selective in coverage, but does include most endemic species of the Dodecanese and east Aegean.

Although the overwhelming majority are non-poisonous – assorted racers, grass snakes and the like – Greece does have a number of front-fanged venomous snakes, including the nose-horned viper, as poisonous as they come in Europe.

On those islands with permanent streams, you can't miss the **frogs** and **toads**, especially in spring. Greece has the green toad, with an obvious marbled green and grey back, as well as the common toad. Tree frogs (*Rana arborea*) are small, live in trees or shrubs, and call very noisily at night. These have a stripe down their flank and vary in colour from bright green to golden brown, depending on where they are sitting – they can change colour like a chameleon.

Insects

About a third of all insect species are **beetles**, ubiquitous in Greece. You might see one of the dung beetles rolling a ball of dung along a path like the mythological Sisyphus, or a rhinoceros-horned beetle digging a hole in a sand dune.

The **grasshopper** and **cricket** family are well represented, and most patches of grass will contain a few. Grasshoppers produce their chirping noise by rubbing a wing against a leg, while crickets do it by rubbing both wings together. Cicadas are not related to the locust or grasshopper – they're more of a large leafhopper. Their continuous whirring call is one of the characteristic sounds of the Mediterranean summer noontime, and is produced by the rapid vibration of two membranes called tymbals on either side of the body. If you look closely at bushes and small trees, you might be rewarded with a stick insect or a praying mantis, rarely seen because of their excellent camouflage.

The most prominent Greek insects are the **butterflies**. Any time from spring through most of the summer is good for spotting them, and there's usually a second flight for many species in the autumn. The three varieties of swallowtail are easily distinguished by their large size, yellow and black shading, and long spurs at the back of the hind wings. Cleopatras are brilliant yellow butterflies, related to the brimstone of northern Europe, but larger and more colourful. Look out for green hairstreaks – a small jewel of a butterfly attracted to the springtime flowers of the asphodel, a widespread plant of overgrazed pastures and hillsides. One final variety typical of the Dodecanese islands is the festoon, an unusual butterfly with yellow, red and black zigzags.

Music

Island folk music, like many Greek cultural traditions, is a mix of East and West. The older songs, invariably in Eastern-flavoured minor keys, have direct precedents in the forms and styles of both religious and secular Byzantine music, and also that of medieval Turkey and Iran; almost all native Greek instruments are descendants of those used thoughout the Islamic world. To this Middle Eastern base both Slavs and Italians have added their share, and as a result the repertoire of traditional and more modern Greek pieces is extraordinarily varied.

Unlike on Crete or the mainland, where you can often catch the best music in special clubs or *kéndra*, Aegean island performances tend to be spontaneous and open-air. The best forums for hearing regional music are the numerous summer festivals keyed to local saints' days (see "Festivals" in *Basics*), celebrated in a village *platía* or a rural monastery dedicated to the saint. Song material, not surprisingly in the case of the smaller islets, touches most commonly on exile, the perils of the sea and – in a society where long periods of separation and arranged marriages were the norm – thwarted love. And like many folk musics the world over, island music (*nisiótika* in Greek) relies heavily on pentatonic tuning.

The Dodecanese

Of all the island groups in Greece, the **Dodecanese** arguably have the most vital musical tradition, owing to their isolation from the mainland, mutual separation and (until 1943) the political and emotional charge associated with preserving customs in the face of Italian persecution. In particular, the southerly arc, consisting of Kássos, Kárpathos and Hálki, is still the most promising area for hearing live music. The main instrument here is the **lýra**, a three-stringed fiddle directly related to the Turkish *kemençe* of the Black Sea and Thrace. This is played not on the shoulder but balanced on the thigh, often with tiny bells attached to the bow, which the musician can jiggle for rhythmical accent. The three metal strings are tuned in fifths (G, D and A); the player improvises on the outer two, with the centre one merely a drone.

At Ólimbos, north Kárpathos (see box p.123), this instrument commonly accompanies *mandinádhes*, improvised satirical couplets about local personalities and incidents. Also occasionally heard are *paraloyés* (**epic ballads**), again dating back in content and form to the Byzantine era. Kássos is a rich repository for melodies and lyrics, which find favour even on neighbouring Kárpathos; many are based on the events of the 1824 Kassian holocaust.

Usually the *lýra* is backed up by at least one **laoúto**, derived from the Turkish/Arab oud but fitted with a long, fretted neck and four courses of double strings tuned in fifths. These are rarely used to their full potential – a *laoúto* solo per se is an uncommon treat – but a good player will find the harmonics of a virtuoso *lýra* piece, at the same time coaxing a pleasing, chime-like tone from his instrument.

At several places in the Dodecanese, particularly northern Kárpathos, a primitive **bagpipe**, the *askómandhra* or *tsamboúna*, joins the *lýra* and *laoúto*. It reached Greece from Asia Minor during late Roman times; Greek nationalists like to point to the presence of this (and other) instruments in Byzantine frescoes of the Nativity as "proof" that Greek music is free of Islamic influences, but such instruments have evolved simultaneously and independently in pastoral societies across Eurasia. During the colonels' dictatorship the playing of the bagpipe was banned on some of the more accessible islands, lest foreigners think the Greeks too primitive.

On most of the other Dodecanese, you'll find the *lýra* replaced by a more familiar-looking **violí**, essentially a western violin – an example of this is Sími, where just one violinist and no *lýra* players still perform. In some locales, music for **unaccompanied voices** exists: Arhángelos on

A selective discography

Almost every island described in this book is represented in the following discography; that said, coverage is thin and much has been lost by the failure to record worthy vernacular musicians. All the titles below are fairly easily obtainable in Greece, or by special order through the shops cited below.

An older, inexpensive series are the **"Songs of . . ."** releases done by the *Society for the Dissemination of National Music* (Greece). There are now more than thirty of these, each covering one geographical area or type of traditional music. All include notes in English and are easily available in Athens at the **Museum of Musical Instruments**, Dhioyénous 1–3, Pláka, or at record stores such as *Musiki Gonia*, *Metropolis*, *Xylouris* and *Tzina*, within a few hundred metres of each other on Panepistimíou at nos. 36, 39, 54 and 57 respectively.

Songs of Kassos and Karpathos (*SDNM 103*). The Kárpathos side is unremittingly poignant (or monotonous, depending on your tastes), enlivened by interesting passages on the *tsamboúna*. You'll still hear material like this at Ólimbos festivals. The Kássos side is more sweetly melodic, closer to Crete both musically and geographically.

Songs of Rhodes, Chalki and Symi (*SDNM 104*). The pieces from Sími are the most accessible, while those from Rhodes and Hálki show considerable Cretan influence. All material was recorded in the early 1970s; you're fairly unlikely to hear similar pieces live today, though Sími retains the instrumentation (*violí*, *sandoúri*) heard here.

Songs of Mytilene and Chios (*SDNM 110*), **Songs of Mytilene and Asia Minor** (*SDNM 125*). The Mytilene (Lésvos) sides are the highlight of each of these discs. Sublime instrumental and vocal pieces, again from the mid-1970s. Most selections are from the south of the island, particularly Ayiássos, where a tradition of live festival music was – and still is – stronger.

Songs of Ikaria & Samos (*SDNM 128)* Much older material, from the 1950s, only recently released. Even then it was obvious that indigenous styles here were dying out, as there is extensive reliance on "cover versions" of songs common to all the east Aegean and Anatolian refugee communities, and the music – mostly choral with string accompaniment – is executed by the SDNM "house band" of the time. The Ikarian side is the more distinctive, though marred by irritating voice-over narration.

Iy Tilos Zei keh Tragoudha (*PanVox X 33 SPY 16397*). 1994 studio recording, featuring male and female vocals backed by *violí*, *laoúto* and *sandoúri*. Mostly songs for various phases of weddings, though not really dance music.

Tragoudhia keh Skopi tis Kalymnou (*Syrtos 564*). Harsh but compelling, even haunting, songs reminiscent of Kálimnos itself. No longer part of the island's repertoire but revived in this 1993 production by native musician Manolis Karpathos, accompanied by *tsamboúna*, *laoúto* and *violí*.

Kastellorizo (*Syrtos 561*). Another Manolis Karpathios production; the studio recording highlights the material to good effect.

Musica Populare del Dodecaneso (*Albatros*). Italian release from the 1970s, still available in the UK. A variety of dances and songs from the Dodecanese, including some wonderful dances from Kós that have virtually disappeared.

Yioryios Konitopoulos, Irini Konitopoulou-Legaki *Athanata Nisiotika* (*Tzina/Aster 1020*). This 1978 warhorse, beloved of bus drivers, can still be found in Athens; Vol. 2 (*Tzina Aster 1023*) is not nearly as good and is best avoided. Although the Konitopoulos clan hails from Náxos in the Cyclades, they are popular throughout insular Greece.

Toh Konitopouleïko (ie Yioryios Konitopoulos on *violí*, brother Vangelis on *laoúto*, sister Angeliki and niece Stella doing vocals) *Thalassa keh Paradhosi* (*EMI 14C 064 71253*). A 1982 disc, easier to find than the preceding and slicker, but no less worthy for that: standard taverna or party fare throughout the islands.

Seryiani sta Nisia Mas (*MBI 10371/2*). Excellent two-volume CD compilation of various *nisiótika* artists and hits from the 1960s onwards. High point on Vol. 1 is arguably Emilia Hadzidhaki's rendition of "*Bratsera*", a song particular to Kálimnos.

*For record hunting in the UK, the best source is **Trehantiri**, 367 Green Lanes, London N4; (☎0181/802 6530), which also operates a worldwide mail-order service. In the USA, try (among others) **Down Home Music** on San Pablo Avenue (affiliated with Arhoolie/Polylyric Records) in El Cerrito, CA.*

Rhodes, generally conceded to be the musical capital of the island, is known for *kanákia* or wedding songs, based on Byzantine hymns and supposedly imperial palace music. Particular to Halki are *helidhonísmata* or **"swallow songs"**, chanted since Roman times in early March to welcome these birds, heralds of spring.

Kálimnos preserves a vibrant if melancholy musicality, heavily reliant on *tsamboúna* and *violí*, and with regional characteristics despite its modest size; for instance, melodies and rhythms from Árgos, Aryinónda and Skália supposedly differ from those of rest of island. A legend claims that these villagers are descendents of Argive stragglers from the Trojan war; the village name of Árgos, and the fact that their danceable *syrtos* exists only in one other, Peloponnesian Argolid village, are given as support of this hypothesis.

If you remember Nikos Kazantzakis's classic novel (or the movie), Zorba played a *sandoúri* (**hammer dulcimer**) for recreation. Today, accomplished players of this instrument, with its one hundred or so double strings, are few, and it's been relegated to a supporting role in *nisiotiká* (island songs); in actual fact it was hardly known on the east Aegean islands (or the Dodecanese) until well into this century, when Anatolian refugee musicians introduced it. The *sandoúri* is scarcely used on Kálimnos, as the local melodic intervals are unsuited to its chromatic abilities; by contrast, on neighbouring Léros and Lipsí it's one of the favourite instruments at festival times.

East Aegean Islands

There's more obvious Asia Minor and Constantinopolitan influence on the **east Aegean** islands, both in material and instrumentation. Largely because of the refugee background of its population, there is no longer an indigenous musical tradition on Sámos. Matters are slightly better on adjacent Ikaría, especially at summer festivals in the Ráhes villages, where the local goat-skins appear in the form of *tsamboúnes*. On Lésvos, *violí* (here too, as further south, having replaced the *lýra*), clarinet, lapdrum (*toumberléki*) or shoulder drum (*daoúli*) and sometimes brass instruments are encountered at festivals, an ensemble virtually identical to that used in northwest Anatolia both before and after 1923.

The keyed European **clarinet** – as opposed to simple oboe-like single-reed screechers – were unknown in Greece before 1830, and (depending on whom you believe) were introduced either by the gypsies or members of the first royal court. Backing in the past was often provided by an acoustic guitar (*kithára*), *laóuto* or *sandoúri*, though increasingly you'll be confronted (or affronted) by a rock-'n'-roll-type, bass-guitar-and-drum rhythm section.

The above account is based partly on the relevant chapters of *World Music: The Rough Guide* (Penguin), available at all good North American and UK bookshops and record retailers.

The islands in literature

Secrets of Sími

William Travis and his wife Caroline came to live on Sími during the mid-1960s when it was still well off the tourist route, much less home to an expatriate community. Having set aside a bit of money in the yacht charter business, Travis was able to stay for three years, putting his boating skills to use along an island coast tailor-made for small craft. *Bus Stop Symi*, originally published in 1970 by Rap & Whiting, and unfortunately long out of print, is the chronicle of their time there. This extract is reproduced with the kind permission of Watson, Little Ltd.

The German forces finally abandoned Symi in December of 1944. When orders for their withdrawal were received they contained the instruction that the considerable stocks of explosives and munitions held on the island were to be destroyed rather than shipped elsewhere. At that time the major portion of these stores were held in numerous warehouses scattered about the town and, lacking time perhaps to move the explosives up into the hills and wishing to destroy them in one operation, German working parties set about the task of consolidating the various caches into one central dump. The final site selected for the operation was an unfortunate one.

The physical and spiritual centre of Symi's township is the old acropolis, a rocky outcrop atop the hillock separating the Upper and Lower Towns. This natural eminence bears upon it a complete record of the islet's human history, for Neolithic, Pelasgian, Classical, Roman, Byzantine, Crusader, Frankish, Venetian, Turkish and Italian remains can be traced there, often tiered one upon another within its one-acre extent. In 1944 the acropolis was topped by one of the island's finest churches, the Church of the Ascension of the Virgin, whilst around the base of the low cliffs on which it was perched clustered a whole complex of houses, storerooms and buildings belonging to the wealthier merchants of the Upper Town. It was here that the retiring German troops decided to consolidate their munitions and destroy them. A regrettable necessity of war made infinitely more regrettable due to two grim factors. Firstly, the chosen method of destruction was by blowing up the whole dump and, secondly, and far more serious, the civilians living in and about the area were not consulted nor warned of the operation. In fact, some unknown officer had given precise instructions to the soldiers taking part that the whole scheme was to be carried out with the strictest military secrecy. Luckily for Symi, these orders were not obeyed.

Rudi – big, blond and Bavarian – Symi has no record of your surname, only of your religion which was Catholic, and your rank which was corporal. You, toiling day-long with your men, carrying ammunition boxes up the cobbled streets to their final destination beneath the walls of Our Lady of the Ascension, continually asked those of the villagers you met with and knew by sight: "Hey, Symiot – when is the celebration of the Ascent of the Virgin?" and when they replied, saying "August 15th of course, but why do you ask?" – you gave the cryptic reply: "Wrong, quite wrong. Ask me tomorrow and I'll tell you..."

And the next day you said the same and the day following as well. But by then your conundrum was well known, with people openly discussing the riddle, seeking to see within it some present application and, consequently, when on the fourth day you gave your version of the date of the Virgin's Ascension as ... "tonight at eight you will see Her rise. Tonight at eight, mark you!" – it did not take the townsfolk long to tumble to your meaning. All that day, as unseen as mice behind the wainscot, the people of the Upper Town moved bed and baggage and what valuables they could from door to door and balcony to balcony, down a long corridor of neighbourly hands, to relatives and friends in other areas. Old people were carried piggy-back and small children in baskets. Caged birds went too, and so did those few cats that had remained uneaten. By dusk all was quiet and all was deserted with no sign of life about the citadel other than those few German soldiers detailed to guard the hidden mine. At eight o'clock an observer on a distant campanile saw two blobs of yellow light moving down the hill away from the doomed area and at exactly ten past eight the Church of the Virgin *did* ascend in a sheet of flame and with a roar that shattered windows throughout the town, besides totally demolishing over 260 houses adjacent to the acropolis. Had not a Bavarian corporal muttered his riddle to those he passed, how many Symiots might have died in that explosion? Five hundred perhaps – maybe more. As it was, the only fatality was an octogenarian known as Maria who, when told of what was going on, said: "I was born in this house. I have knelt in this one church all my life. I shall die here in my house along with my church" – and did.

And Rudi, what of Rudi, I asked?

Did anyone in the town ever hear from him afterwards? Did he write to those he had saved or did anyone seek to contact him?

"Hah! Rudi – no, he never wrote," I was told. "And you know why not, Vassili? The Germans left here the following day on board a ship that had called to collect them. Within an hour of leaving it struck a mine or was torpedoed. Out of the four-hundred-odd people on board some seventeen were saved. But not Rudi..."

The Church of the Virgin of the Ascension went up and within hours Rudi – surname unrecorded, Bavarian, a Catholic, serving as a corporal in the German Army occupying Greece – went down.

Thus war's see-saw.

****

One morning, shopping in Yalou, I came across a unique scene. There, clustered around a long table in the little square known as Pallas Athene – on account of the plaster statue of that Britannia-like deity which surmounts the gable of a house overlooking it – was a strange mixture of Symiots. At one end sat the mayor, Dr Nikitiades, flanked by his secretary and the Town Clerk. At the other sprawled the curly-bearded, piratical figure of Papas Anastsius with, in turn, two of his acolytes. Plumb in the middle of the table stood an ornate silver candlestick and in it a standard yellow offertory candle. Between the two groups and standing, not sitting, were a line of Symiot shepherds – lanky, sun-blackened creatures, characterized by their beautiful and uniform soft boots and divergent crooks.

"What goes on?" I asked.

"It's the auction of the grazing on Nimos [the islet just north of Sími], Vassili. It happens every four years."

"But what happens?" I insisted.

"Wait and see," I was told.

After a mumbled prayer Papas Anastasius lit the taper and silence fell. For five minutes nothing happened till the mayor, out of the blue said "Twenty thousand..." – thus setting, so I was told in a whisper, the arbitrary minimum price acceptable by the community as rent for that particular auction. Again silence, till a puff of wind caused the candle-flame to gutter. "Twenty-two", "Twenty-four", "Twenty-eight..." – the shouts came tumbling one upon the other for, as I now learnt the winner of the auction was he whose bid was uttered last before the candle went out – whether blown out by wind or burnt out by time. The sudden breeze dropped, the flame steadied and the bidding lapsed. Another five minutes passed, with random bids made partly in jest and partly by way of testing out the opposition, and the grazing rights stood at an even thirty thousand. The bidders grew silent, with eyes on the candle, for the day was calm and further wind-eddies seemed unlikely. There remained but a quarter-inch of wax before the offers started up once more, and then the cries flew thick and fast across the table: "Thirty-five, thirty-seven, thirty-seven fifty, thirty-eight two..." – the stump dissolved into a pool of dark wax overflowing the holder and still the little flame lived on. "Forty-one, forty-one and a half, forty-two, forty-two and two, forty-two and four..." – but it was too late, the flame had gone out in a little puff of oily smoke and the bidder of forty-two thousand and two hundred drachma had won the right to graze five hundred sheep on Nimos islet for the next four years. Making a quick calculation in my head I said to my companion: "But surely nearly eighty-five drachma per head is expensive grazing, when sheep and goats can free-range here on Symi? And which poor shepherd can afford to put down six hundred pounds in hard cash for the privilege, anyway?"

"Ssh, Vassili – it's not just the grazing, you ignorant foreigner! He who has the right to graze his sheep on Nimos has the right to go there anytime, right? Without causing comment or arousing suspicion. And the far side of Nimos faces Anatolia and can't be seen from Yalou or Horio, right? What better place to use as a starting point for a little trip to Turkey, eh – or at which to unload ships coming back . . . Nimos is uninhabited, remember? Now do you understand why some people give the shepherds money with which to bid? And what does it matter? The community chest gains ten thousand drachma a year it would not otherwise see and, if it were not Nimos, there would be some other place used for this night-traffic across to Turkey . . ."

Crooked Captains

A diaspora Greek two generations removed from Kássos, bleakest of the Dodecanese, Elias Kulukundis visited his ancestral island for the first time in 1964. The result of a lengthy stay was *Journey to a Greek Island*, published by Cassell, London, in 1968, and now out of print. This extract is reprinted with the permission of Simon & Schuster. Often reading like non-fiction García Márquez, it is unsurpassed as an introductory exploration to local history, anthropology and genealogy, not just Kassian but Dodecanesian.

Like a number of other relatively barren Greek isles, Kássos has long made its living from the sea. At the time of the 1821 uprising, it possessed the fourth largest fleet after Ídhra, Spétses and Psará. Of these isles, only Kássos remained a maritime power after independence, and Kassiots are still disproportionately represented in the contemporary Greek shipping industry. In his discussion of the history of Kasiot seafaring, Kulukundis does not avoid the subject of piracy – occasionally indulged in by the islanders during the first half of the last century. What follows, however, details the other, less well-known practice of barratry.

It was customary at that time, as it is today, for the cargo owner to charter a captain's ship at a given rate. After the agreement had been reached, the captain would simply load the cargo on his ship and sail away with it, and unless the charterer posted a representative or supercargo to accompany the ship and protect his interests, he would have to trust the captain for the duration of the voyage. The voyages of sailing ships lasted several weeks, and during that time, anything might happen. The captain might encounter heavy weather and find himself in danger of foundering unless he lightened his ship by jettisoning all his extra masts and rigging and even a portion of the cargo if necessary. In that event, under the laws of general average, the captain would not be responsible for the loss of cargo, and it would have to be sustained solely by the charterer. This was where certain captains were cunning enough to see a special opportunity. A captain might not encounter heavy weather at all, only *claim* to have encountered it.

The coasts of the Aegean Islands and mainland Greece are full of tiny coves, secret places where a ship might put in unnoticed, under the cover of a moonless night. There, by prearrangement, a caique might come out to meet the ship, and as it drew alongside, the captain might strike a stealthy bargain with the caique's owner to *sell* him a portion of the cargo. After the agreement had been concluded, a portion of the cargo would be lowered into the caique. The captain would sail out onto the high seas again, then to the island of Zante where there were certain legal experts. They could doctor the log of the voyage to show that on such and such a day, under the stress of heavy weather, the captain had found it necessary to jettison his extra masts and spars and sails (items which might never have existed) as well as that portion of the cargo he had actually sold. At the conclusion of the voyage, the captain would enjoy a double profit: the rate of hire agreed upon with the charterer, plus the proceeds of the sale. Then, his winter's work done in a single voyage, he could return to his native island and roister in the café.

The practice was widespread in the Aegean after the [Greek] Revolution, taking the place of piracy of old. The island of Zante, which had probably begun as a natural haven for mariners after a storm, became a nest of log-doctorers. Gradually, it became so common for captains to put into Zante after the sale of cargo, that underwriters refused to pay a claim if the ship had stopped there for any reason. Meanwhile, the Greek Government, anxious to protect the reputation of its growing merchant marine, ran down offenders and imposed heavy penalties on them. And wherever Greek captains were suspected of barratry, the Greek Government posted a consul to report any illegal sales.

Barratry became very popular among certain Kasiots. It appealed to their naturally wily nature, as much for its own sake as for any profit it would yield. They would sail home to Kasos, anchor outside the Bucca [the port] and sell a portion of the cargo to the island merchants. Then, sending the ship on to Zante to its doctors, they would ascend victorious to the café.

But no Kassiot ever got rich on barratry, and the names of the barrators have dropped long ago from the shipping history of the island. After the captain had sold the cargo, he would be open to blackmail at the hands of his very accomplices; and often in the years ahead, he would have to pay out much more than he had made by the original transaction.

Sometime in the latter half of the nineteenth century, a Kasiot captain whom we can call Captain Nikos put into Salonika to find a cargo. It was a very slack season, and cargoes were difficult to find, so for lack of anything better he contracted with two Jewish rabbis to carry a cargo of flagstones at a very unprofitable rate. But the rabbis rubbed salt into his wounds.

"You're a Kasiot, aren't you?" they said.

Captain Nikos said he was.

"Well, in that case we shall have to post supercargoes to keep watch over our flagstones."

"Very well," said Captain Nikos, taking no offense at this discrimination. "Who will be your supercargoes?"

"We will," said the rabbis. "Both of us."

"You will?" said Captain Nikos, smiling. "Very well."

So the rabbis packed their belongings and prepared to sail with Captain Nikos to keep watch over their flagstones. And in the meantime, Captain Nikos was thinking: "Two supercargoes to watch over flagstones? What must they think of me? If I sold all their stones at twice their value, I still would not make enough to pay for my expenses. But very well. Let them come if they wish. I will see they have an exciting voyage."

In the meantime, an idea had grown on him. The rabbis had heard so much about the mischief of certain Kasiots, Captain Nikos thought he could not very well disappoint them. Since they distrusted him so openly, even with a cargo of flagstones, he would not be one to let them down. He would sell their cargo anyway, worthless as it was, under their very noses.

So Captain Nikos set sail from Salonika, already smirking over what he planned; and the two rabbis sailed with him. Standing stiffly on either side of the tiller in their black robes and beards and broad brimmed black hats, they watched Captain Nikos with eagle eyes. When the ship sailed out beyond the harbour, a strong wind came up. And although the rabbis did not realize it, Captain Nikos did what any seaman knows not to do. He steered the ship broadside to the wind, so that immediately it began to roll.

"What's that?" said the rabbis, taken by surprise.

"The wind," said Captain Nikos.

"Ah, the wind," said the rabbis solemnly, composing themselves once again on either side of Captain Nikos. But now the ship was rolling so fiercely they had trouble keeping their balance. Though neither of them said a word and did not even look at each other, very soon they were both pale as ghosts.

"Is this normal?" said one rabbi at last, in a voice weak with nausea and with fear.

"As normal as the wind," said Captain Nikos.

"But what will hapen?"

"I don't know. If you wish, you may go below where you can lie down and be more comfortable."

The rabbis looked at each other. For one longing moment they looked in the direction of their cabin. But at last, bravely, they decided against it.

"No, we must stay here to keep watch over our flagstones," they said.

"Very well," said Captain Nikos, raising his voice above the wind and water. "But if you must stand here, at least take hold of something. I'm afraid you may be thrown into the sea."

At that moment, appearing to be steering carefully in the face of danger, Captain Nikos turned the wheel violently one way and then the other, so that the ship plunged down towards the menacing white water, reprieving itself from catastrophe at the last moment, only to plunge down toward it again on the other side.

"But what is happening?" cried the rabbis. "Is this a storm?"

"Yes," said Captain Nikos, "a storm."

"Is it a bad one? Is it dangerous?"

"Any storm is a bad one, but this is the most dangerous storm I have ever seen."

"God of Moses. But what will happen? Will we drown?"

"We may," said Captain Nikos. "We are so heavy and the wind is so strong that at any moment we may go over."

"Go over? You mean into the sea?"

"Into the sea."

"God of Aaron, and is there nothing we can do?"

"Do? What should we do?"

"Is there nothing we can do to save ourselves?"

"Of course.

"What?"

"Pray. Pray to your God."

"Pray to our God? Is there nothing else?"

"Is that not enough?"

"God of Moses, is there nothing we can do to save ourselves? If we are so heavy, can't we lighten?"

"Lighten? How lighten?"

"If a ship is too heavy, they say the captain can throw some of the cargo overboard."

"Throw some of the cargo overboard?" said Captain Nikos. "You are asking me to throw some of the cargo overboard?"

"Why not?" cried the rabbis. "That would save us, wouldn't it? We would be lighter then, and we would be able to make it through this storm."

"Of course we would. We would be lighter in an instant, and the ship would right itself and be out of danger, and then there would be an end to this terrible sickness and dizziness and rolling first one way and then the other."

"Oh, dear God of Isaac, then let us lighten! God of Jacob, let us throw some of the cargo overboard."

"No," said Captain Nikos. "Upon my honour, as a captain and as a Kasiot, no."

"But why? Why in the name of God?"

"Because later, when we reached our destination, you would say we did not meet bad weather at all, that I didn't really throw the cargo overboard but sold it for my own profit. And as a Kasiot captain, I would rather drown than hear such accusations."

"Say you sold the cargo? Captain Nikos, put it out of your mind! We trust you completely!"

"Then why did you sail with me to watch over your cargo? That is the reason you find yourselves in this needless danger when you could be safe in your homes this very moment."

By now, the rabbis were close to tears.

"Oh why, Captain Nikos? We do not know why! We wish we had never sailed with you. But that is all forgotten. We promise you, on the bones of all the prophets, we shall never sail with you again. Only please, Captain Nikos, throw some of our flagstones overboard. You can trust us, Captain Nikos. We will sign a paper. We will do anything you say. Only please, Captain Nikos, before it is too late."

Captain Nikos deliberated for one unendurable moment.

"Very well," he said, "if you insist, I agree. But one of you must begin. That one." He pointed to one rabbi. "Let it be him. Let him cast the first stone."

"I will, I will," said the rabbi. "Only hurry, for the love of God, hurry before all is lost."

Captain Nikos directed his crew to open the cargo hatch and lift out one of the stones for the rabbi to throw overboard. As agreed, the rabbi awkwardly cast the first stone. Afterwards, at a signal from Captain Nikos, the seamen began to lift out a few of the stones, one by one, and throw them overboard. At that moment, Captain Nikos manipulated the wheel in such a way that a huge wave curled over the side and almost broke upon the rabbis.

"For the love of God," cried captain Nikos, "go below now, or the next wave will carry you away."

Without a word, the rabbis scurried below out of the menacing sea and wind. As soon as they disappeared, Captain Nikos ordered his men to stop what they were doing.

"What are you doing there, my lads?" he said. "Throwing stones into the sea? Have you lost your minds?"

Laughing, the crew stopped throwing stones into the sea, closed the hatch, and went about their business. After a discreet interval, Captain Nikos steered out of the wind, as even any landlubber knows he should. The ship righted itself, and the storm subsided into a placid Aegean afternoon.

The rabbis, by that time, were sound asleep. Delivered from the jaws of death and the terrible nausea which had menaced them far worse, they slept through the dinner hour and far into the night. And they were still asleep, near midnight, when Captain Nikos sailed into a deserted cove, and beckoning the owner of a caique to draw alongside, sold him the remaining flagstones. The next day, sailing toward their destination on an empty ship, the rabbis signed a paper Captain Nikos had prepared, attesting to the fact that the ship had met heavy weather a few miles out of Salonika, and at their insistence, the captain agreed to jettison the cargo. One of the rabbis, they admitted, had cast the first stone.

Captain Nikos' story became proverbial on Kasos. He was such a notorious barrator, he would sell flagstones for the sport of it, and he became the first Kasiot in history to get his supercargoes to doctor the log.

Ikarian Idiosyncracies

Joseph Georgirenes was Archbishop of the diocese of Samos from 1666 until 1671, when – weary of Turkish interference – he voluntarily

retired to the monastery of the Apocalypse on nearby Pátmos. Originally from Mílos, he had an involved outsider's view of his pastoral flock, if an occasionally jaundiced one. Following his residence on Pátmos, Georgirenes emigrated for unspecified reasons to London, where in 1677 he wrote *A Description of the Present State of Samos, Nicaria, Patmos, and Mount Athos*, which was translated into English by an unidentified acquaintance; its hundred-plus pages are packed with a wealth of detail concerning Ottoman rule, religious observance, agriculture and ethnography.

The most commendable thing of this Island [Ikaría] is their Air and Water, both so healthful, that the People are very long liv'd, it being an ordinary thing to see persons in it of an hundred years of Age, which is a great wonder, considering how hardily they live. There is not a Bed in the Island, the Ground is their Tick, and the cold Stone their Pillow, and the Cloaths they wear is all the Coverlet they use. They provide no more Apparel than what they wear all at once, when that is past wearing any longer, then think of a new Suit. Betwixt their ordinary times of Eating, there is not a piece of Bread to be found in the Isle. A little before Dinner, they take as much Corn as will serve that Meal, grind it with a Hand-Mill, bake it upon a flat Stone; when 'tis Bak'd, the Master of the Family divides it equally among the Family; but a Woman with child has two shares. If any Stranger comes in, every one parts with a Piece of his own share to accommodate the Stranger. Their Wine is always made with a third part Water, and so very weak and small. When they drink it, so much as is thought sufficient is put into one large Bowl, and so passes round. The Nicarians [Nicaria was the medieval name for Ikaría] are the only Islanders of all the Archipelago, that neither keep Wine to sell, nor lay it up in Wooden Vessels, but in long Jars, cover'd all over in the Ground. When they have a mind to Tap it, they make a Bung-hole in the top, and draw it out with Canes. Their Houses are so plain, that all the Furniture you can see is an Hand-Mill, besides this, there is nothing but bare Walls: That little they have besides is all hid under Ground; not so much for fear of the Corsairs (from whom their Poverty is a sure guard) as out of Custome. Nor are they all so poor, as not to be able to buy Beds, but custome has brought them into a contempt of Beds, as meerly superfluous; insomuch, that when they Travel into other Islands, they refuse the offer of a Bed. A Priest of Nicaria coming into Samos, was courteously entertain'd by those of his Order, and at Night was offer'd a Bed to lye in; he thank'd them, but refus'd, nor could by any importunity be prevail'd upon, but told them the Earth was his Mother, from whence he would not keep a distance; besides he was afraid of being Sick, if he should lye in a Bed; and therefore if they had a kindness for him, they must give him the liberty of sleeping after his own Country way.

When I went to visit them as Arch-Bishop, and ignorant of the custom of the Country, carry'd no Bed. At Night, where I first lodg'd, asking for a Chamber, they told me they had not other than that where I first came; then asking for a Bed, they told me it was not the Custom of the Country; then desiring to borrow some Bed Cloaths for Love or Money, all they brought me was one Smock made of course Dimity.

They have no great communication one with another, any farther than the publick times of Sacred Solemnities, or Civil Business doth cause them to come together. At other times they keep strictly within the narrow Sphere of their own affairs. Formal Visits, Treats, and Entertainments are things unknown. If any business do put them upon a Visit to their Neighbour, they come not close to his Door, but stand off at a great distance, and call aloud to him; If he make them answer, they discourse the Business they came about, standing off at the same distance; except they be earnestly invited to come in. And this way of discoursing at a distance they practise more in the Fields and Mountains; their Voices being so strong, that 'tis ordinary to talk at a Miles distance; sometimes at four or five, where the Valleys interpos'd between two hills, give advantage to the Voice. Sometimes they can discourse at that distance, that the carriage of the Sound through the Winding of the Valleys, shall require half a Quarter of an Hours time; and yet they make distinct, and proper Answers, both audible and intelligible, without the help of a Stentorophonical Trumpet.

Their Habit for the Men, is a Shirt, and over it a short cassock, down to the Knees, to which, in Winter they add only a short Vest, that reaches a little below the middle. Stockings they never wear. Their Shoes are only a piece of thin

Copper, bow'd to the shape of their Feet, and every one is his own Shoe-maker. The Women have nothing but one Smock, but so large, that they wrap it double, or treble down to the Girdle, but below the Girdle single. The Priests, for greater reverence in the Church, tye two Towels about their Legs, the one is their usual Bonnet, and the other their Girdle: so that they perfom sacred Offices ungirt, as well as uncover'd.

Of all the Isles of the Archipelago, this only admits of no mixture with Strangers in Marriage, nor admits any stranger to settle with them: They being, as they pretend, all descended of the Imperial Blood of the Porphyrogenneti, must not stain their noble Blood with inferiour Matches, or mixtures with *Choriats*, or Peasants, for so they term all the other islanders.

Porphyrogenneti, were those of the Blood Royal, in the Days of the Greek Emperours, so call'd, from their wearing of Purple, which was a Badge of Royalty, and allow'd only to Princes of the Blood; and not from an house call'd Porphyra, where the Empresses were wont to lie in. But Purple was throughout the East, the known Badge of Royalty. Hence came that unsanctify'd Wit, and learned'st Writer that ever oppos'd the Christian Religion with his Pen, to be call'd Porphyrius: For his true name in the Language of Syria, his native Country, was Malchus, or King; but the Greeks did paraphrase it Porphyrius, or Purple-robed; that being a Colour peculiar to Kings.

They have a great Happiness, by reason of their poverty, in not being molested by the Turks, who think it not worth their while to come among them, nor if they should, were they likely to enjoy any quiet, without keeping a stronger Guard than the Revenues of the Isle would maintain. Once they slew a Caddee [judge] sent by the Grand Signior [ie the Sultan], and being summon'd to Answer for their Crime, they by common consent own'd the Fact, but would name no particular Man. So that the Turkish Officers looking upon their beggarly Cloaths, thought there was neither gain nor glory in punishing such Miscreants, and than in Justice, they must punish all, or none, dismiss'd them untouch'd. From that time no Turk ever troubled them: For they take all courses imaginable to seem poor; and wheresoe'er they come abroad, they count it no shame to beg Alms: Yet they make a shift every year to levy three hundred Crowns for the Arch-Bishop. They are govern'd by a Proesti [council of village elders] of their own chusing, who also levys their Haratch or Tribute to the Grand Signior, and takes care to carry it to the Aga [Turkish local chieftain] of Scio. As for their Religion, it is the same with that of Samos; but their Priests are more ignorant.

Thus you have an account of a small Island, the Poorest, and yet the Happiest of the whole Aegean Sea. The Soil is Barren, but the Air is Healthful; their Wealth is but small, but their Liberty and Security is great. They are not molested withe the Tyrannous Insolence of a Turkish Officer, nor with the frightful Incursions of barbarous and merciless Pirates. Their Diet and Apparel is below the Rate of Beggars in other Countrys, and their Lodging is a thying of no more care, or cost, than that of the Beasts of the Field, yet their Bodies are strong and hardy, and the People generally long liv'd. They live with as little forecast, as if they expected not to survive a day, being contented to satisfy the present necessities of Nature. They do properly *in diem vivere*, or as we say, From Hand to Mouth. They have but little, yet they never Want. Their Ignorance is equal to their Poverty, and contributes much to their content. And how well they esteem of their own condition, their contempt of their Neighbouring Islands, and scorning to mix with them in Alliance by Marriage, is a manifest sign. Whence we may learn, that they approach the nearest to Contentedness in this Life; whose desires are contracted into the narrowest compass.

Books

Where separate editions exist in the UK and USA, publishers are detailed below in the form "British Publisher/American Publisher", unless the publisher is the same in both countries. Where books are published in one country only, this follows the publisher's name.

O/p signifies an out-of-print – but still highly recommended – book. University Press is abbreviated as UP.

Travel and general accounts

Howard Baker *Persephone's Cave* (University of Georgia Press, long o/p). Intimations of ancient worship on a reverential tour of Sámos, with good period detail from before the advent of tourism.

Joseph Braddock *Sappho's Island: A Paean for Lesbos* (Constable, o/p). Precious little on the modern island, but good background on ancient Mytilini and on the naive painter Theophilos.

Charmian Clift *Mermaid Singing* (Michael Joseph, o/p). Kalimnos as she found it in the 1950s.

Lawrence Durrell *Reflections on a Marine Venus* (Faber & Faber/Penguin). Durrell spent two post-World War II years as a press officer on Rhodes; this was the result, rich in period detail but purple in the prose as always, and faintly patronizing to the islanders.

John Ebdon *Ebdon's Iliad* (Unwin). Ever-popular chronicle of Rhodes, Kós and Kárpathos as they (and their package trade) were in the early 1980s. No claims to profundity, but fun for light reading.

Joseph Georgirenes *A Description of the Present State of Samos, Nicaria, Patmos and Mount Athos* (Noti Karavia, Athens; limited facsimile edition). An occasionally hilarious account of these spots as they were in the mid-seventeenth century, showing if nothing else that regional character was already well developed in medieval times. A choice morsel is excerpted on pp.375–76.

William Johnson *The Monk Seal Conspiracy* (London, Heretic Books; o/p). Greenpeace activists versus the islanders on Sámos of the late 1970s.

Elias Kulukundis *Journey to a Greek Island* (Cassell, o/p). More properly, a journey back through time and genealogy by a diaspora Greek two generations removed from Kassos, poorest of the Dodecanese. A passage is excerpted on pp.372–74.

Willard Manus *This Way to Paradise – Dancing on the Tables* (Lycabettus Press, Athens). An American expatriate's memoir of 35 years in Líndhos, Rhodes.

Nicholas G Pappas *Castellorizo: An Illustrated History of the Island and its Conquerors* (Halstead Press, New South Wales, Australia). The latest word, from a Sydney "Kassie" who has raised some eyebrows by asserting, among other things, that the islet never supported more than 10,000 permanent inhabitants.

William Travis *Bus Stop Symi* (Rapp & Whiting, o/p). The result of three years' residence there in the mid-Sixties; insightful, though Travis erroneously prophesied that the place would never see tourism. Some passages are reproduced on pp.370–72.

Classics, history and ethnography

The Classics

Many of the classics make good companions for a trip around Greece – especially the historians Thucydides and Herodotus. It is hard to beat Homer's *Odyssey*, either, for reading when you're battling with or resigning yourself to the vagaries of island ferries.

The following are all available in Penguin Classic paperback editions:

Herodotus *The Histories*
Homer *The Odyssey, The Iliad.*
Thucydides *History of the Peloponnesian War*
Xenophon *The History of My Times*

Ancient history and culture

Walter Burkert *Greek Religion* (Blackwell, Oxford, UK/Harvard UP, US, 1985 o/p). Ancient religion, that is; a thorough discussion of ancient rites, cults and deities in this translated German classic.

A R Burn *History of Greece* (Penguin). Probably the best general introduction to ancient Greece, though for fuller and more interesting analyses you'll do better with one or other of the titles following.

John Kenyon Davies *Democracy and Classical Greece* (Fontana/Harvard UP). Established and accessible account of the period and its political developments.

M I Finley *The World of Odysseus* (Penguin). Good on the interrelation of Mycenaean myth and fact.

Robin Lane Fox *Alexander the Great* (Penguin). An absorbing study, which mixes historical scholarship with imaginative psychological detail.

Oswyn Murray *Early Greece* (Fontana/Harvard UP). The Greek story from the Mycenaeans and Minoans through to the beginning of the Classical period.

F W Walbank *The Hellenistic World* (Fontana/Harvard UP). Greece under the sway of the Macedonian and Roman empires.

Byzantine and Medieval Greece

Nicholas Cheetham *Medieval Greece* (Yale UP, o/p in US). General survey of the period and its infinite convolutions in Greece, with Frankish, Catalan, Venetian, Byzantine and Ottoman struggles for power. Very little specifically on the islands of this guide, but useful for keeping tabs on the main players.

John Julius Norwich *Byzantium: the Early Centuries; Byzantium: the Apogee; Byzantium: the Decline* (all Penguin/Knopf). Perhaps the main surprise for first-time travellers to Greece is the fascination of Byzantine monuments; this recently completed trilogy provides a terrific narrative history of the empire.

Michael Psellus *Fourteen Byzantine Rulers* (Penguin). A fascinating contemporary source, detailing the stormy but brilliant period from 976 to 1078.

Steven Runciman *The Fall of Constantinople, 1453; The Great Church in Captivity* (both Cambridge UP); *Byzantine Style and Civilisations* (Penguin, o/p in US). Good narrative histories, with more of a slant towards art, culture and monuments in the latter two.

Timothy Callistos Ware *The Orthodox Church* (Penguin). Good introduction to what is effectively the established religion of Greece.

Modern Greece

Timothy Boatswain and Colin Nicolson *A Traveller's History of Greece* (Windrush Press/Interlink; Greek printing by Efstathiadis). Slightly dated (1990) but well-written overview of all periods Greek.

Winston Churchill *The Second World War, Vol. 5: Closing the Ring* (Penguin). Allied Aegean campaigns, with detailed coverage of battles on and around Rhodes, Léros, Sámos and Kós.

Richard Clogg *A Concise History of Greece* (Cambridge UP). A remarkably clear and well-illustrated account of Greece from the decline of Byzantium to 1991, stressing recent decades.

Douglas Dakin *The Unification of Greece, 1770–1923* (Ernest Benn/St Martin's Press, both o/p). Account of the foundation of the Greek state and the struggle to extend its boundaries.

H. A. Lidderdale, trans. and ed. *The Memoirs of General Makriyannis, 1797–1864* (Oxford UP, o/p). The "Peasant General", one of the few honest and self-sacrificing protagonists of the Greek uprising, remedied lifelong illiteracy at the age of 32 to set down this apologia of his conduct, in vivid demotic Greek. Heartbreaking in its portrayal of the schisms, linguistic and otherwise, that tore the country apart over the next century.

Michael Llewellyn Smith *Ionian Vision, Greece in Asia Minor, 1919–22* (Allen Lane/St Martin's Press, both o/p). Standard work on the Anatolian campaign and the confrontation between Greece and Turkey leading to the exchange of populations, with many of the refugees ending up on the larger East Aegean islands.

Mark Mazower *Inside Hitler's Greece: The Experience of Occupation 1941–44* (Yale UP). Rather choppily organized, and just a bit on the islands, but the standard of scholarship is high and the photos alone justify the price. Demonstrates how the complete demoralization of the country and incompetence of conventional politicians led to the rise of ELAS and the onset of civil war.

William McNeill *The Metamorphosis of Greece since World War II* (University of Chicago,

London/Chicago, o/p). Exactly as the title says, engagingly covered; worth the effort to find in second-hand shops.

Yiannis Roubatis *Tangled Webs: The US in Greece 1947–67* (Pella Publishing, US). Chronicles recording American involvement in Greece during the lead-up to the miltary coup.

C M Woodhouse *Modern Greece, A Short History* (Faber & Faber). Woodhouse was active in the Greek Resistance during World War II. Writing from a right-wing perspective, his history (from the foundation of Constantinople in 324 to the present), is briefer and a bit drier than Clogg's, but he is scrupulous with facts. *The Rise and Fall of the Greek Colonels* (Granada, o/p Watts), recounts the (horror) story of the dictatorship, while *The Struggle for Greece, 1941–49* (Hart-Davis, o/p/Beekman), is a masterly and by no means uncritical account of this crucial decade, explaining how Greece emerged without a Communist government.

Ethnography

Juliet Du Boulay *Portrait of a Greek Mountain Village* (Oxford UP). Specifically Ambéli on Évvia, and while falling outside the territory of this book, this classic is still applicable to most of Greece.

John Cuthbert Lawson *Modern Greek Folklore and Ancient Greek Religion: A Study in Survivals* (University Books, New York, o/p). This is to Greece what *The Golden Bough* is to the world at large. Worth scouring libraries and antiquarian dealers for.

Gail Holst *Road to Rembétika: Songs of Love, Sorrow and Hashish* (Denise Harvey, Greece, but available in the UK). The predominant Greek urban musical style of this century, evocatively traced by a Cornell University musicologist. Be sure to get the most recent printing, as the discography is regularly updated.

Clay Perry *Vanishing Greece* (Conran Octopus/ Abbeville Press). Well-captioned photos depict the threatened landscapes and way of life in rural Greece; includes good coverage of Ólimbos on Kárpathos and Volissós on Híos. Now out in paperback.

Archeology and art

John Beckwith *Early Christian and Byzantine Art* (Penguin/Yale UP). Illustrated study placing Byzantine art within a wider context.

John Boardman *Greek Art* (Thames & Hudson, UK). A very good concise introduction in the "World of Art" series.

Sinclair Hood *The Arts in Prehistoric Greece* (Penguin/Yale UP). Sound introduction to the subject.

Roger Ling *Classical Greece* (Phaidon, UK). Another useful and illustrated introduction.

Gisela Richter *A Handbook of Greek Art* (Phaidon/Da Capo). Exhaustive survey of the visual arts of ancient Greece.

Suzanne Slesin et al *Greek Style* (Thames & Hudson/Crown). Stunning and stylish interiors from various designer-owned island houses (including some on Rhodes).

R R R Smith *Hellenistic Sculpture* (Thames & Hudson, UK). Modern reappraisal of the art of Greece under Alexander and his successors.

Modern Greek fiction

Titles marked with a * are part of a highly recommended "**Modern Greek Writers**" series, currently numbering ten titles, issued by Kedros Publishers (Athens).

Maro Douka *Fool's Gold* (Kedros, Greece)* Describes an upper-class young woman's involvement, and subsequent disillusionment, with the clandestine resistance to the junta and her pompous male colleagues.

Eugenia Fakinou *The Seventh Garment* (Serpent's Tail, UK). The modern history of Greece – from the War of Independence to the colonels' junta – is told through the life stories of three generations of women. A rather more succesful experiment than **Fakinou**'s *Astradeni* (Kedros, Greece*), in which a young girl – whose slightly irritating narrative voice is adopted throughout - leaves the island of Sími, with all its traditional values, for Athens.

Stratis Haviaras *When the Tree Sings* (Picador/ Simon & Shuster, both o/p); *The Heroic Age* (Penguin, o/p). Two-part, faintly disguised autobiography about coming of age in Greece in the 1940s, by the poetry curator at Harvard library. Written in English because Haviaras felt his experiences too keenly to set them down in Greek.

Nikos Kazantzakis *Zorba the Greek; Christ Recrucified* (published in the US as *The Greek Passion*); *Report to Greco; Freedom or Death* (Captain Mihalis in the US); *The Fratricides* (all

Faber & Faber/Touchstone). The most accessible (and Greece-related) of the numerous novels by the Cretan master. Even with inadequate translation, their strength – especially that of *Report to Greco* – shines through.

Athena Dallas-Damis *Island of the Winds* (Karatzas, US; Efstathiadis, Athens, Greece). Rather breathy historical fiction set around the 1821–23 events on Híos, by a woman with roots on the island.

Stratis Myrivilis *Life in the Tomb* (Quartet/New England UP). A harrowing and unorthodox war memoir based on the author's experience on the Macedonian front during 1917–18, well translated by Peter Bien. Completing a kind of trilogy are two later novels, set on the north coast of Lésvos, Myrivilis's homeland: *The Mermaid Madonna* and *The Schoolmistress with the Golden Eyes* (Efstathiadis, Athens, Greece). Translations of these are not so good, and tend to be heavily abridged.

Dido Sotiriou *Farewell Anatolia* (Kedros, Greece)*. A classic since its appearance in Greece three decades ago (it is now in its 52nd printing), this is an epic chronicle of the traumatic end of Greek life in Asia Minor, from the 1912 Balkan War to the catastrophe of 1922. The narrator is a fictionalized version of the author's father; in the finale, he escapes across the narrow strait of Mycale to Sámos, as did many in those turbulent years.

Irini Spanidhou *God's Snake* (Picador/Penguin, o/p in UK). The story of a daughter trying to break free of the all-pervasive legacy of her father, a Greek army general.

Demetrios Vikelas *Loukas Laras* (Doric Publications, UK, o/p). Classic nineteenth-century novel set mainly on Híos.

Alki Zei *Achilles' Fiancée* (Kedros, Greece)*. A recent best seller exploring identity and values amid a maze of time shifts, from the German occupation to the civil war, exile in Tashkent and Paris, and a return to Greece. The author is of partly Samian descent.

Modern Greek poetry

With two Nobel laureates in recent years – George Seferis and Odysseus Elytis – modern Greece has an extraordinarily intense and dynamic poetic tradition. Translations of all of the following are excellent.

C P Cavafy *Collected Poems* (Chatto and Windus/Princeton UP). The complete works of perhaps the most accessible modern Greek poet, resident for most of his life in Alexandria.

Odysseus Elytis *The Axion Esti* (Anvil Press/Pittsburgh UP); *Selected Poems* (Anvil Press/Viking Penguin, o/p in US); *The Sovereign Sun* (Bloodaxe Books). The major works, in good English versions, of a poet with roots on Lesvos.

Yannis Ritsos *Exile and Return, Selected Poems 1967–1974* (Anvil Press/Ecco Press). A fine volume of Greece's foremost Leftist poet.

Modern Greek Poetry (Efstathiadis, Athens, Greece). Decent anthology of translations, predominantly of **Seferis** and **Elytis**.

George Seferis *Collected Poems, 1924–1955* (Anvil Press/Princeton UP, o/p in US). Virtually the complete works of the Nobel laureate, with Greek and English verses on facing pages.

Specific guides

Archeology

A R and Mary Burn *The Living Past of Greece: A Time Traveller's Tour of Historic and Prehistoric Places* (Herbert Press/HarperCollins). Unusual in extent, this covers sites from Minoan through to Byzantine and Frankish, with good clear plans and lively text – though only about a third of the book is devoted to the islands.

Evi Melas (ed) *Temples and Sanctuaries of Ancient Greece: A Companion Guide* (Thames & Hudson, o/p). Excellent collection of essays on the main sites, written by archeologists who have worked at them.

Alexander Paradissis *Fortresses and Castles of Greece* (Efstathiadis Group, Athens). As it says, in three extremely prolix volumes; widely available in good Greek bookshops. Volume III covers the islands of this book.

Island & regional guides

Lycabettus Press Guides (Athens, Greece). Although this series has not been updated in some years, the volumes on Pátmos and Kós in particular are still available, and well worth consulting.

Marc Dubin *Trekking in Greece* (Lonely Planet, UK/US). Includes the best day-hikes on Rhodes, Sími, Tílos, Níssiros, Sámos, Híos and Lésvos, plus extensive preparatory and background information. New version with an English publisher out in 1998.

Ellias Kollias *The Knights of Rhodes: The Palace & the City* (Ekdotiki Athinon, 1991). The last word on the Order's history and monuments, by the archeologist long in charge of Rhodes province.

Ferries and yachting

H M Denham *The Aegean: A Sea Guide* and *The Ionian Islands to the Anatolian Coast* (John Murray, UK; O/P). For many years, the standard cabin reference if you were out yachting. You want the second volume cited for the sake of its coverage for Kássos, Kárpathos and Rhodes.

Rod Heikell *Greek Waters Pilot.* (Imray, Laurie, Norrie & Wilson, UK only). Rather better than the preceding, which it has superseded.

Frewin Poffley *Greek Island Hopping* (Thomas Cook, UK). A user-friendly guide to the networks of Greek ferries and hydrofoils, with exhaustive timetables, good port-town plans and imaginative maps; updated regularly, and a useful supplement to this guide's "Travel Details" sections.

Food and drink

I Batjakas & A Economakis *Coastal Fishes of Greece* (Efstathiadis, Athens, Greece). A few omissions, but overall a serviceable guide to most of the fish you're likely to see snorkelling, at the market, or at table.

Andrew Dalby *Siren Feasts* (Routledge, US/UK). Subtitled *"A history of Food and Gastronomy in Greece"*, this analysis of classical and Byzantine texts demonstrates just how little Greek cuisine has changed in three millennia; also excellent on the introduction and etymology of common garden plants and herbs.

Miles Lambert-Gócs *The Wines of Greece* (Faber & Faber, UK/US). Comprehensive survey of the emerging, and improving, wines of Greece, with plenty of historical detail; unfortunately few of these wines will be found in typical tavernas.

Bookshops

The islands covered in this guide are without exception bereft of decent bookshops. If you're stopping over, however, **Athens** has a number of excellent ones, at which many of the recommendations above should be available; all are centrally located. Try: *Eleftheroudhakis*, Níkis 4; *Compendium*, Níkis 28; *Iy Folia tou Vivliou*, Panepistimíou 25; and *Pantelidhes*, Amerikís 11. In **London**, the *Hellenic Bookservice*, 91 Fortess Rd, Kentish Town, London NW5 1AG (☎0171/267 9499), and *Zeno's Greek Bookshop*, 6 Denmark St, WC2H 8LP (☎0171/836 2522), are knowledgeable and well-stocked specialist dealers in new, secondhand and out-of-print books on all aspects of Greece.

Language

So many Greeks have lived or worked abroad in America, Australia and, to a much lesser extent, Britain, that you will find someone who speaks English in the tiniest island village. Add to that the thousands attending language schools or working in the tourist industry – English is the lingua franca of most resorts, with German second – and it is easy to see how so many visitors come back having learnt only half a dozen restaurant words between them.

You can certainly get by this way, but it isn't very satisfying, and the willingness to say even a few words will upgrade your status from that of dumb *tourístas* to the honourable one of *ksénos*, a word that can mean foreigner, traveller and guest all rolled into one.

Learning Basic Greek

Greek is not an easy language for English-speakers, but it is a very beautiful one, and even a brief acquaintance will give you some idea of the debt owed to it by western European languages. On top of the usual difficulties of learning a new language, Greek presents the additional problem of an entirely separate **alphabet**. Despite initial appearances, this is fairly easily mastered – a skill that will help enormously if you are going to get around independently (see the alphabet box following, and the place-name transliteration tables after each island account). In addition, certain combinations of letters have unexpected results. This book's transliteration system should help you make intelligible noises, but you have to remember that the correct **stress** (marked throughout the book with an acute accent) is crucial to getting yourself understood.

Greek **grammar** is more complicated still: nouns are divided into three genders, all with

Language-learning Materials

TEACH-YOURSELF GREEK COURSES

Breakthrough Greece (Pan Macmillan; book and two cassettes). Excellent, basic teach-yourself course – completely outclasses the competition.

Greek Language and People (BBC Publications, UK; book and cassette available). More limited in scope but good for acquiring the essentials, and the confidence to try them.

Anne Farmakides *A Manual of Modern Greek* (Yale UP/McGill UP; 3vols). If you have the discipline and motivation, this is one of the best for learning proper, grammatical Greek; indeed, mastery of just the first volume will get you a long way.

PHRASEBOOKS

Greek, A Rough Guide Phrasebook (Rough Guides). For an up-to-date, accurate pocket phrase book not full of "plume de ma tante"-type expressions, look no further than Rough Guide's very own; English-to-Greek is sensibly phonetic, though Greek-to-English section, while transliterated, requires mastery of the Greek alphabet.

DICTIONARIES

The Oxford Dictionary of Modern Greek (Oxford University Press). A bit bulky but generally considered the best Greek—English, English—Greek dictionary.

Collins Pocket Greek Dictionary (HarperCollins). Very nearly as complete as the *Oxford* and probably better value for money.

Oxford Learner's Dictionary (Oxford University Press). If you're planning a prolonged stay, this pricey two-volume set is unbeatable for usage and vocabulary. There's also a more portable one-volume *Learner's Pocket Dictionary*.

different case endings in the singular and in the plural, and all adjectives and articles have to agree with these in gender, number and case. (All adjectives are arbitrarily cited in the neuter form in the following lists.) Verbs are even worse, with active verbs in several conjugations, passive

The Greek alphabet: transliteration

Set out below is the Greek alphabet, the system of transliteration used in this book, and a brief aid to pronunciation.

Greek	Transliteration	Pronounced
Α, α	a	a as in father
Β, β	v	v as in vet
Γ, γ	y/g	y as in yes, except before consonants and a, o or long i, when it's a throaty version of the g in gap
Δ, δ	dh	th as in then
Ε, ε	e	e as in get
Ζ, ζ	z	z sound
Η, η	i	i as in ski
Θ, θ	th	th as in theme
Ι, ι	i	i as in ski
Κ, κ	k	k sound
Λ, λ	l	l sound
Μ, μ	m	m sound
Ν, ν	n	n sound
Ξ, ξ	ks	ks sound
Ο, ο	o	o as in toad
Π, π	p	p sound
Ρ, ρ	r	r sound
Σ, σ, ς	s	s sound
Τ, τ	t	t sound
Υ, υ	i	indistinguishable from η
Φ, φ	f	f sound
Χ, χ	h/kh	harsh h sound, like ch in loch
Ψ, ψ	ps	ps as in lips
Ω, ω	o	o as in toad, indistinguishable from o

Combinations and dipthongs

ΑΙ, αι	e	e as in get
ΑΥ, αυ	av/af	av or af depending on following consonant
ΕΙ, ει	i	long i, exactly like η
ΕΥ, ευ	ev/ef	ev or ef, depending on following consonant
ΟΙ, οι	i	long i, identical again
ΟΥ, ου	ou	ou as in tourist
ΓΓ, γγ	ng	ng as in angie; always medial
ΓΚ, γκ	g/ng	g as in goat at the beginning of a word,; ng in the middle
ΜΠ, μπ	b	b at the beginning of a word; mb in the middle
ΝΤ, ντ	d/nd	d at the beginning of a word; nd in the middle
ΤΣ, τσ	ts	ts as in hits
ΤΖ, τξ	tz	j as in jam

Note on diaereses (umlauts)

The diaeresis or umlaut is used in Greek over one of two adjacent vowels to change the pronunciation that you would expect from the preceeding table; often it can function as the primary stress in this book (though Greek typesetters manage to fit in a simple acute accent between the two dots). In the word *kaïki* (caique), the presence of the umlaut changes the pronunciation from "cake-key" to "ki-ee-key", and additionally the middle 'i 'carries th eprimary stress. In the word païdhákia (lamb chops), the diaeresis again changes the sound of the first syllable from "pay" to "pah-ee", but in this case the primary stress is on the third syllable.

ones, and passive ones used actively(!). To begin with at least, the best thing is simply to say what you know the way you know it, and never mind the niceties. Even "Eat meat hungry" should get a result; if you worry about your mistakes, you'll never say anything.

Katharevoussa, Dhimotiki

Greek may seem complicated enough in itself, but problems are multiplied when you consider that for the last century there has been an ongoing dispute between two versions of the language: *katharévoussa* and *dhimotikí*.

When Greece first achieved independence in the nineteenth century, its people were almost universally illiterate, and the language they spoke – *dhimotikí*, "demotic" or "popular" Greek – had undergone enormous change since the days of the Byzantine Empire and Classical times. The vocabulary had assimilated countless borrowings from the languages of the various invaders and conquerors, namely the Turks, Venetians, Albanians and Slavs.

The finance and inspiration for the new Greek state, and its early leaders, came largely from the Greek **diaspora** – Orthodox families who had been living in the sophisticated cities of central and eastern Europe, or in Russia. With their European notions about the grandeur of Greece's past, and lofty conception of Hellenism, they set about obliterating the memory of subjugation to foreigners in every possible field. And what better way to start than by purging the language of its foreign accretions and reviving its Classical purity?

They accordingly devised what was in effect a new form of the language, **katharévoussa** (literally "cleansed" Greek). The complexities of Classical grammar and syntax were reinstated, and Classical words were dusted off and resuscitated. To the country's great detriment, *katharévoussa* became the language of the schools and the prestigious professions, government, business, the law, newspapers and academia. Everyone aspiring to membership in the elite strove to master it – even though there was no consensus on how many of the words should be pronounced.

The *katharévoussa/dhimotikí* debate has been a highly contentious issue through most of this century. Writers – from Sikelianos and Seferis to Kazantzakis and Ritsos – have all championed the demotic in their literature, as has the political Left in its rhetoric, while crackpot right-wing governments forcibly (re-)instated *katharévoussa* at every opportunity. Most recently, the colonels' junta of 1967–74 reversed a decision of the previous government to teach in *dhimotikí* in the schools, bringing back *katharévoussa*, even on sweet wrappers, as part of their ragbag of notions about racial purity and heroic ages.

Dhimotikí returned once more after the fall of the colonels and now seems here to stay. It is used in schools, on radio and TV, after a fashion by newspapers (with the exception of the extreme right-wing *Estia*) and in most official business. The only institutions that refuse to bring themselves up to date are the Church and the legal professions – so beware rental contracts.

This is not to suggest that there is now any less confusion. The Metaxas dictatorship of the 1930s changed scores of village names from Slavic to Classical forms, and these official place names still hold sway on most road signs and maps – even though the local people may use the *dhimotikí* form. Thus you may see "Plomárion" or "Innoússai" written on officially authorized maps or road signs, while everyone actually says Plomári or Inoússes.

Greek words and phrases

Essentials

Yes	*Néh*
Certainly	*Málista*
No	*Óhi*
Please	*Parakaló*
Okay, agreed	*Endáksi*
Thank you (very much)	*Efharistó (polí)*
I (don't) understand	*(Dhen) Katalavéno*
Excuse me, do you speak English?	*Parakaló, mípos miláteh angliká?*
Sorry/excuse me	*Signómi*
Today	*Símera*
Tomorrow	*Ávrio*
Yesterday	*Khthés*
Now	*Tóra*
Later	*Argótera*
Open	*Aniktó*
Closed	*Klistó*
Day	*Méra*
Night	*Níkhta*
In the morning	*Tóh proï*
In the afternoon	*Tóh apóyevma*
In the evening	*Tóh vrádhi*
Here	*Edhó*
There	*Ekí*
This one	*Aftó*
That one	*Ekíno*
Good	*Kaló*
Bad	*Kakó*
Big	*Megálo*
Small	*Mikró*
More	*Perisótero*
Less	*Ligótero*
A little	*Lígo*
A lot	*Polí*
Cheap	*Ftinó*
Expensive	*Akrivó*
Hot	*Zestó*
Cold	*Krío*
With	*Mazí*
Without	*Horís*
Quickly	*Grígora*
Slowly	*Sigá*
Mr/Mrs	*Kírios/Kiría*
Miss	*Dhespinís*

Other Needs

To eat/drink	*Trógo/Píno*
Bakery	*Foúrnos, psomádhiko*
Pharmacy	*Farmakío*
Post office	*Tahidhromío*
Stamp	*Gramatósima*
Petrol station	*Venzinádhiko*
Bank	*Trápeza*
Money	*Leftá/Hrímata*
Toilet	*Toualéta*
Police	*Astinomía*
Doctor	*Iatrós*
Hospital	*Nosokomío*

Requests and Questions

To ask a question, it's simplest to start with *parakaló*, then name the thing you want in an interrogative tone.

Where is the bakery?	*Parakaló, o foúrnos?*
Can you show me the road to . . . ?	*Parakaló, o dhrómos ya . . ?*
We'd like a room for two	*Parakaló, éna dhomátio ya dhío átoma?*
May I have a kilo of oranges?	*Parakaló, éna kiló portokália?*
Where?	*Poú?*
How?	*Pós?*
How many?	*Póssi* or *pósses?*
How much?	*Póso?*
When?	*Póteh?*
Why?	*Yatí?*
At what time . . . ?	*Tí óra . . . ?*
What is/Which is . . . ?	*Tí íneh/pió íneh..?*
How much (does it cost)?	*Póso káni?*
What time does it open?	*Tí óra aníyi?*
What time does it close?	*Tí óra klíni?*

Talking to People

Greek makes the distinction between the informal (*esí*) and formal (*esís*) second person, as French does with *tu* and *vous*. Young people, older people and country people nearly always use *esí* even with total strangers. In any event, no one will be too bothered if you get it wrong. By far the most common greeting, on meeting and parting, is *yá sou/yá sas* – literally "health to you".

Hello	*Khérete*
Good morning	*Kalí méra*
Good evening	*Kalí spéra*
Good night	*Kalí níkhta*
Goodbye	*Adío*
How are you?	*Tí kánis/Ti káneteh?*
I'm fine	*Kalá ímeh*
And you?	*Keh esís?*
What's your name?	*Pos se léneh?*
My name is . . .	*Meh léneh . . .*
Speak slower, please	*Parakaló, miláte pió sigá*
How do you say it in Greek?	*Pos léyeteh sta Eliniká?*

continues over

Talking to People (cont.)

I don't know	*Dhén ksére*
See you tomorrow	*Tha se dhó ávrio*
See you soon	*Kalí andámosi*
Let's go!	*Pámeh!*
Please help me	*Parakaló, na me voïthísteh*

Greek's Greek

There are numerous words and phrases which you will hear constantly, even if you rarely have the chance to use them. These are a few of the most common.

Éla!	Come (literally) but also Speak to me! You don't say! etc.
Orísteh?	What can I do for you?
Embrós! or *Léyeteh!*	Standard phone responses
Ti néa?	What's new?
Ti yíneteh?	What's going on (here)?
Étsi k'étsi	So-so
Pó-pó-pó!	Expression of dismay or concern, like French "O la la!"
Pedhí moú	My boy/girl, sonny, friend, etc.
Maláka(s)	Literally "wanker", but often used (don't try it!) as an informal address.
Sigá sigá	Take your time, slow down
Kaló taxídhi	Bon voyage
Ópa!	Whoops! Watch it!

On the Move

Aeroplane	*Aeropláno*
Bus	*Leoforío*
Car	*Aftokínito*
Motorbike, moped	*Mihanáki, papáki*
Taxi	*Taksí*
Ship	*Plío/Vapóri/Karávi*
Bicycle	*Podhílato*
Hitching	*Otostóp*
On foot	*Méh tá pódhia*
Trail	*Monopáti*
Bus station	*Praktorío leoforíon*
Bus stop	*Stássi*
Harbour	*Limáni*
What time does it leave?	*Tí óra févyi?*
What time does it	*Tí óra fltháni?*
arrive?	*Pósa hiliómetra?*
How many kilometres?	*Pósses óres?*
How many hours?	*Pou pas?*
Where are you going?	*Páo sto . . .*
I'm going to . . .	*Thélo ná katévo stó . . .*
I want to get off at . . .	*Ó dhrómos yía . . .*
The road to . . .	*Kondá*
Near	*Makriá*
Far	*Aristerá*
Left	*Dheksiá*
Right	*Katefthía*
Straight ahead	*Éna isitírio ya . . .*
A ticket to . . .	*Éna isitírio me*
A return ticket	*epistrofí*
Beach	*Paralía*
Cave	*Spiliá*
Centre (of town)	*Kéndro*
Church	*Eklissía*
Sea	*Thálassa*
Village	*Horió*

Accommodation

Hotel	*Ksenodhohío*
A room . . .	*Éna dhomátio . . .*
for one/two/three people	*yía éna/dhío/tría átoma*
for one/two/three nights	*yía mía/dhío/trís vradhiés*
with a double bed	*méh megálo kreváti*
with a shower	*méh doús*
Hot water	*Zestó neró*
Cold water	*Krío neró*
Can I see it?	*Boró ná tóh dho?*
Can we camp here?	*Boróume na váloumeh tín skiní edhó?*
Campsite	*Kámping/Kataskínosi*
Tent	*Skiní*
Youth hostel	*Ksenón neótitos*

The time and days of the week

Sunday	*Kiriakí*
Monday	*Dheftéra*
Tuesday	*Tríti*
Wednesday	*Tetárti*
Thursday	*Pémpti*
Friday	*Paraskeví*
Saturday	*Sávato*
What time is it?	*Tí óra ínheh?*
One/two/three o'clock	*Mía íy óra, dhío/trís íy óra*
Twenty to four	*Tésseres pará íkosi*
Five minutes past eight	*Októ kéh pénde*
Half past eleven	*Éndheka kéh misí*
In half an hour	*Séh misí óra*
In a quarter-hour	*S'éna tétarto*

Months and seasonal terms

January	*Yennári*
February	*Fleváris*
March	*Mártis*
April	*Aprílis*
May	*Maïos*

June	*Ioúnios*	12	*dhódheka*
July	*Ioúlios*	13	*dhekatrís*
August	*Avgoustos*	14	*dhekatésseres*
September	*Septémvris*	20	*íkosi*
October	*Októvris*	21	*íkosi éna*
November	*Noémvris*	30	*triánda*
December	*Dhekémvris*	40	*saránda*
Summer schedule	*Therinó dhromolóyio*	50	*penínda*
Winter schedule	*Himerinó dhromolóyio*	60	*eksínda*
		70	*evdhomínda*
Numbers		80	*ogdhónda*
1	*énos éna/mía*	90	*enenínda*
2	*dhío*	100	*ekató*
3	*trís/tría*	150	*ekatón penínda*
4	*tésseres/téssera*	200	*dhiakóssies/ia*
5	*pénde*	500	*pendakóssies/ia*
6	*éksi*	1000	*hílies/hília*
7	*eftá*	2000	*dhío hiliádhes*
8	*okhtó*	1,000,000	*éna ekatomírio*
9	*enyá*	first	*próto*
10	*dhéka*	second	*dhéftero*
11	*éndheka*	third	*tríto*

A glossary of words and terms

Ancient Architecture and History

ACROPOLIS Ancient, fortified hilltop.

AGORA Market and meeting place of an ancient Greek city.

AMPHORA Tall, narrow-necked jar for oil or wine.

APSE Polygonal or curved recess at the altar end of a church.

ARCHAIC PERIOD Late Iron Age period, from around 750 BC to the start of the Classical period in the fifth century BC.

ARCHITRAVE Horizontal masonry atop temple columns; same as entablature (cf).

ATRIUM Open, inner courtyard of a Roman house, as on Kós.

BASILICA Originally colonnaded, early Christian church adapted from Roman models, found at several sites in the Dodecanese and east Aegean.

BOULEUTERION Auditorium for meetings of an ancient town's deliberative council.

BYZANTINE EMPIRE Created by the division of the Roman Empire in 395 AD; this, the eastern half, was ruled from Constantinople (modern Istanbul). Sámos, Rhodes, Híos, Kós, and Lésvos were all important members of the Aegean theme or province.

CAPITAL The flared top, often ornamented, of a column.

CELLA Sacred room of a temple, housing the cult image.

CLASSICAL PERIOD Essentially from the end of the Persian Wars in the fifth century BC until the unification of Greece under Phillip II of Macedon (338 BC).

CORINTHIAN Decorative columns, festooned with acanthus florettes.

DORIAN Northern civilization that displaced and succeeded the Mycenaeans and Minoans through most of Greece around 1100 BC.

DORIC Simple, minimalist columns with little ornament, dating from the Dorian period.

DRUM Cylindrical or faceted vertical section, usually pierced by an even number of narrow windows, upholding a cupola.

ENTABLATURE The horizontal linking structure atop the columns of an ancient temple.

EPARHÍA Greek Orthodox diocese, also a subdivision of a modern province analagous to a county.

EXEDRA Display niche for statuary.

EXONARTHEX The outermost west vestibule of a church, when a true narthex is present.

FORUM Market and meeting place of a Roman-era city.

GEOMETRIC PERIOD Post-Mycenaean Iron Age era named for the style of its pottery; begins in the early eleventh century BC with the arrival of Dorian peoples. By the eighth century BC, with the development of representational styles, it becomes known as the Archaic period.

HELLENISTIC Pertains to the art and architecture of the last and most unified "Greek empire", created in the wake of Alexander the Great's Macedonian empire and finally collapsing with the fall of Corinth to the Romans in 146 BC.

HEROÖN Shrine or sanctuary, usually of a demi-god or mortal.

ICON Representation of a saint or holy personality painted on a board, the object of veneration and pilgrimage in the Orthodox Church.

IONIC Elaboration of the older Doric decorative order; Ionic temple columns are slimmer with deeper "fluted" edges, spiral-shaped capitals, and ornamental bases.

KOUROS Nude Archaic or Classical statue of an idealized young man, usually portrayed with one foot slightly forward of the other.

MACEDONIAN EMPIRE Empire created by Philip II in the mid-fourth century BC.

MEGARON Principal hall or throne room of a Mycenaean palace.

METOPE see **FRIEZE**

MINOAN Crete's great Bronze Age Civilization, which dominated the Aegean from about 2500 to 1400 BC.

NAOS The inner sanctum of an ancient temple; also, any Orthodox Christian shrine.

NARTHEX Western vestibule of a church, traditionally for catachumens and unbaptized;

typically frescoed with scenes of the Last Judgment.

NEOLITHIC Earliest era of settlement in Greece, characterized by the use of stone tools and weapons together with basic agriculture. Divided arbitrarily into Early (c 6000 BC), Middle (c 5000 BC), and Late (c 3000 BC).

ODEION Small amphitheatre, used for musical performances, minor dramatic productions, or councils.

PANDOKRÁTOR Literally "The Almighty"; generally refers to the stern portrayal of Christ in Majesty frescoed or in mosaic in the dome of many Byzantine churches.

PEDIMENT Triangular, sculpted gable below the roof of a temple; *aetoma* in Greek.

PROPYLAION Monumental, columned gateway of an ancient building; often used in the plural, propylaia.

PYLIÓNAS (ES) Ornate decorated doorways found in Rhodion villages.

STELE Upright stone slab or column, usually inscribed; an ancient tombstone.

STOA Colonnaded walkway in Classical-era marketplace.

TEMENOS Sacred precinct, often used to refer to the sanctuary itself.

THOLOS Conical or beehive-shaped building, especially a Bronze Age tomb.

Medieval and Modern Greek terms

AGORÁ The commercial "high street" of any village or town.

ÁNO Upper; common prefix element of village names.

ARHONDIKHÓ Elaborate mansions of the medieval upper classes, found for example in Hóra, Pátmos and Líndhos, Rhodes.

ASTIKÓ (Intra) city, municipal, local; said of phone calls and bus services.

ÁYIOS/AYÍA/ÁYII Saint or holy (m/f/plural). Common place name prefix (abbreviated Ag. or Ay.); often spelt AGIOS or AGHIOS.

DHIMARHÍO Town hall.

DHOMÁTIA Rooms for rent in purpose-built blocks or private houses.

FROÚRIO Medieval castle.

GARSONIÉRA/ES Studio villa, self-catering apartment/s.

HOKHLÁKI Mosaic of coloured pebbles, found in church or house courtyards in Rhodes and the southern Dodecanese.

HÓRA Main town of an island or region; literally it means "the place". An island hóra is often known by the same name as the island.

IERÓN Literally, "sacred" – the sanctuary between the altar screen and the apse of a church, reserved for priestly activities.

IKONOSTÁSIS Screen between the nave of a church and the ierón, supporting at least three icons.

IPERASTIKÓ Inter-city, long-distance – as in phone calls and bus services.

KAFENÍO Coffeehouse or café; in a small village the centre of communal life and probably serving as the bus stop, too.

KAÏKI (plural **KAÏKIA**) Caique, or medium-sized boat, traditionally wooden and used for transporting cargo rather than passengers; now refers mainly to island excursion boats.

KALDERÍMI Cobbled mule-tracks and footpaths.

KÁMBOS Fertile agricultural plateau, usually near a river mouth.

KÁSTRO Any fortified hill (or a castle), but most usually the oldest, highest, walled-in part of an island hóra.

KATHOLIKÓN Central church of a monastery.

KÁTO Lower; common prefix element of village names.

KENDRIKÍ PLATÍA Central square.

KIOUPÍ, KOUMÁRI Large Ali-Baba-style clay urns used for storing olive oil.

KSENÓNAS Inn run by a small municipality or a monastery

MELTÉMI North wind that blows across the Aegean in summer, starting softly from near the mainland and hitting the Dodecanese and certain of the east Aegean islands full on.

MONÍ Formal term for a monastery or convent.

NÉOS, NÉA, NÉO "New" - a common prefix to a town or village name.

NOMÓS Modern Greek province – there are more than fifty of them.

PALEÓS, PALEÁ, PALEÓ "Old" – again a common prefix in town and village names.

PANAYÍA Virgin Mary.

PANIYÍRI Festival or feast – the local celebration of a holy day.

PARALÍA Beach or seafront promenade.

PERÍPTERO Street kiosk.

PÍRGOS Tower-mansion found on Lésvos, Sámos or Híos.

PLATÍA Square, plaza.

SKÁLA The port of an inland island settlement, nowadays often larger and more important than its namesake, but always younger since built after the disappearance of piracy.

TAVERNA Restaurant; see "Eating and Drinking" in *Basics*, p.36, for details of the different types of specialist eating places.

TÉMBLON Wooden altar screen of an Orthodox church, usually ornately carved and painted and studded with icons; more or less interchangeable with the ikonostásis.

Acronyms and initials

DANE *Dhodhekanisiakí Anónimi Navtiliakí Etería* (Dodecanesian Shipping Company), which runs the big ferries between Rhodes, Kós, Kálimnos, Léros and Pátmos, bound for Crete, Pireás or Thessaloníki.

EA Greek Left *(Ellinikí Aristerá)*, formerly the Greek Euro-communist Party (KKE-*Esoterikoú*).

ELAS Popular Liberation Army, the main resistance group during World War II and the basis of the communist army in the civil war.

EK Fascist party (*Ethnikó Kómma*), consisting mostly of adherents to the imprisoned junta colonel, Papadopoulos.

ELTA The postal service.

EOT *Ellinikós Organismós Tourismoú*, the National Tourist Organisation.

KKE Communist Party, unreconstructed.

KTEL National syndicate of bus companies. The term is also used to refer to bus stations.

ND Conservative (*Néa Dhimokratía*) party.

NEL *Navtiliakí Etería Lésvou* (Lesvian Shipping Co), which runs most of the northeast Aegean ferries.

OTE Telephone company.

PASOK Socialist party (Pan-Hellenic Socialist Movement).

Index

L

M

direct orders from

Amsterdam	1-85828-086-9	£7.99	US$13.95	CAN$16.99
Andalucia	1-85828-094-X	8.99	14.95	18.99
Australia	1-85828-141-5	12.99	19.95	25.99
Bali	1-85828-134-2	8.99	14.95	19.99
Barcelona	1-85828-106-7	8.99	13.95	17.99
Berlin	1-85828-129-6	8.99	14.95	19.99
Brazil	1-85828-102-4	9.99	15.95	19.99
Britain	1-85828-126-1	8.99	14.95	19.99
Brittany & Normandy	1-85828-126-1	8.99	14.95	19.99
Bulgaria	1-85828-183-0	9.99	16.95	22.99
California	1-85828-090-7	9.99	14.95	19.99
Canada	1-85828-130-X	10.99	14.95	19.99
Corsica	1-85828-089-3	8.99	14.95	18.99
Costa Rica	1-85828-136-9	9.99	15.95	21.99
Crete	1-85828-132-6	8.99	14.95	18.99
Cyprus	1-85828-032-X	8.99	13.95	17.99
Czech & Slovak Republics	1-85828-121-0	9.99	16.95	22.99
Egypt	1-85828-075-3	10.99	17.95	21.99
Europe	1-85828-159-8	14.99	19.95	25.99
England	1-85828-160-1	10.99	17.95	23.99
First Time Europe	1-85828-210-1	7.99	9.95	12.99
Florida	1-85828-074-5	8.99	14.95	18.99
France	1-85828-124-5	10.99	16.95	21.99
Germany	1-85828-128-8	11.99	17.95	23.99
Goa	1-85828-156-3	8.99	14.95	19.99
Greece	1-85828-131-8	9.99	16.95	20.99
Greek Islands	1-85828-163-6	8.99	14.95	19.99
Guatemala	1-85828-045-1	9.99	14.95	19.99
Hawaii: Big Island	1-85828-158-X	8.99	12.95	16.99
Holland, Belgium & Luxembourg	1-85828-087-7	9.99	15.95	20.99
Hong Kong	1-85828-066-4	8.99	13.95	17.99
Hungary	1-85828-123-7	8.99	14.95	19.99
India	1-85828-104-0	13.99	22.95	28.99
Ireland	1-85828-095-8	9.99	16.95	20.99
Italy	1-85828-167-9	12.99	19.95	25.99
Kenya	1-85828-043-5	9.99	15.95	20.99
London	1-85828-117-2	8.99	12.95	16.99
Mallorca & Menorca	1-85828-165-2	8.99	14.95	19.99
Malaysia, Singapore & Brunei	1-85828-103-2	9.99	16.95	20.99
Mexico	1-85828-044-3	10.99	16.95	22.99
Morocco	1-85828-040-0	9.99	16.95	21.99
Moscow	1-85828-118-0	8.99	14.95	19.99
Nepal	1-85828-046-X	8.99	13.95	17.99

In the UK, Rough Guides are available from all good bookstores, but can be obtained from Penguin by contacting: Penguin Direct, Penguin Books Ltd, Bath Road, Harmondsworth, West Drayton, Middlesex UB7 0DA; or telephone the credit line on 0181-899 4036 (9am–5pm) and ask for Penguin Direct. Visa, Access and Amex accepted. Delivery will normally be within 14 working days. Penguin Direct ordering facilities are only available in the UK and the USA. The availability and published prices quoted are correct at the time of going to press but are subject to alteration without prior notice.

New York	1-85828-171-7	9.99	15.95	21.99
Pacific Northwest	1-85828-092-3	9.99	14.95	19.99
Paris	1-85828-125-3	7.99	13.95	16.99
Poland	1-85828-168-7	10.99	17.95	23.99
Portugal	1-85828-180-6	9.99	16.95	22.99
Prague	1-85828-122-9	8.99	14.95	19.99
Provence	1-85828-127-X	9.99	16.95	22.99
Pyrenees	1-85828-093-1	8.99	15.95	19.99
Romania	1-85828-097-4	9.99	15.95	21.99
San Francisco	1-85828-082-6	8.99	13.95	17.99
Scandinavia	1-85828-039-7	10.99	16.99	21.99
Scotland	1-85828-166-0	9.99	16.95	22.99
Sicily	1-85828-178-4	9.99	16.95	22.99
Singapore	1-85828-135-0	8.99	14.95	19.99
Spain	1-85828-081-8	9.99	16.95	20.99
St Petersburg	1-85828-133-4	8.99	14.95	19.99
Thailand	1-85828-140-7	10.99	17.95	24.99
Tunisia	1-85828-139-3	10.99	17.95	24.99
Turkey	1-85828-088-5	9.99	16.95	20.99
Tuscany & Umbria	1-85828-091-5	8.99	15.95	19.99
USA	1-85828-161-X	14.99	19.95	25.99
Venice	1-85828-170-9	8.99	14.95	19.99
Wales	1-85828-096-6	8.99	14.95	18.99
West Africa	1-85828-101-6	15.99	24.95	34.99
More Women Travel	1-85828-098-2	9.99	14.95	19.99
Zimbabwe & Botswana	1-85828-041-9	10.99	16.95	21.99

Phrasebooks

Czech	1-85828-148-2	3.50	5.00	7.00
French	1-85828-144-X	3.50	5.00	7.00
German	1-85828-146-6	3.50	5.00	7.00
Greek	1-85828-145-8	3.50	5.00	7.00
Italian	1-85828-143-1	3.50	5.00	7.00
Mexican	1-85828-176-8	3.50	5.00	7.00
Portuguese	1-85828-175-X	3.50	5.00	7.00
Polish	1-85828-174-1	3.50	5.00	7.00
Spanish	1-85828-147-4	3.50	5.00	7.00
Thai	1-85828-177-6	3.50	5.00	7.00
Turkish	1-85828-173-3	3.50	5.00	7.00
Vietnamese	1-85828-172-5	3.50	5.00	7.00

Reference

Classical Music	1-85828-113x	12.99	19.95	25.99
Internet	1-85828-198-9	5.00	8.00	10.00
World Music	1-85828-017-6	16.99	22.95	29.99
Jazz	1-85828-137-7	16.99	24.95	34.99

In the USA charge your order by Master Card or Visa (US$15.00 minimum order): call 1-800-253-6476; or send orders, with complete name, address and zip code, and list price, plus $2.00 shipping and handling per order to: Consumer Sales, Penguin USA, PO Box 999 – Dept #17109, Bergenfield, NJ 07621. No COD. Prepay foreign orders by international money order, a cheque drawn on a US bank, or US currency. No postage stamps are accepted. All orders are subject to stock availability at the time they are processed. Refunds will be made for books not available at that time. Please allow a minimum of four weeks for